THE GRAMMAR BOOK

AN ESL/EFL TEACHER'S COURSE

MARIANNE CELCE-MURCIA
University of California
Los Angeles

DIANE LARSEN-FREEMAN
School for International Training
Brattleboro, Vermont

HEINLE & HEINLE PUBLISHERS
A Division of Wadsworth, Inc.
Boston, Massachusetts 02116

Library of Congress Cataloging in Publication Data

Celce-Murcia, Marianne.
    The grammar book.

    Includes bibliographies and index.
        1. English language--Study and teaching--Foreign
speakers.   2. English language--Grammar--1950–
I. Larsen-Freeman, Diane.   II. Title.
PE1128.A2C39   1983   428'.007   83-2267

Cover design by Diana Esterly

ISBN 0-8384-2850-9

First printing: October 1983

Printed in the U.S.A.

9 10 11

To Caroline and Brent

Acknowledgments

Many people have helped us over the past six years as we have worked at bringing these materials first from notes we used for our lectures to reproduced class notes, and then from class notes to textbook form. Several colleagues (namely, Kathi Bailey, Pat Carrell, Sidney Greenbaum, Sharon Klein, Elite Olshtain, Bill Rutherford, Jackie Schachter, and Sandra Thompson) have read and commented on the linguistic and/or pedagogical aspects of parts of the manuscript. Without their valuable and generous feedback this text would be less accurate and less useful. However, we hasten to add that none of these colleagues would agree completely with all of our materials and that any inaccuracies and infelicities that remain are solely our responsibility.

We are also indebted to our many students and teaching assistants who, over the years, have worked with these materials in preliminary and partial form and whose comments and feedback have very positively shaped and influenced the final form of this text. It would be difficult to acknowledge them all, but let us at least offer thanks to Cherry Campbell, Lorraine Kumpf, Brina Peck, and Ann Snow, who as teaching assistants used this text in several prepublication forms and made many very valuable suggestions. Also, Cindy Burns and Janet Entersz are students who have made important contributions to the completion of this text.

We would also like to thank Joan Samara for her superb typing and retyping of the manuscript, Joan Yentes for her excellent proofreading, and Bella Anikst and Caroline Gallego for their invaluable help with indexing.

Finally, we would like to express our appreciation to our spouses, Daniel and Elliott. Without their encouragement and support, this book would never have been completed.

To the Teacher

We have included more material in this text than you can teach in a one-term course that deals with the structure of English for prospective ESL/EFL teachers. Our reason for including so much material is that knowledgeable ESL/EFL teachers need to be aware of and familiar with all the topics included in the book if they want to be able to teach all learners effectively irrespective of their level of English proficiency.

From our own experiences in piloting these materials, we feel that after covering Chapters 1 through 9, you can then fill out your one-term course by choosing other chapters that you feel are most likely to be of use to the students in your class. Perhaps if your students have some ESL/EFL teaching experience, they themselves can select the chapters they feel would be most helpful to them after the first nine chapters have been covered.

There are many ways in which you can encourage your students to go beyond the chapters you are able to cover in your course, i.e., to explore some of the other chapters in the text as well as some of the "Suggestions for Further Reading." One such means might be to assign each student a short paper on a small topic not covered in class (a different topic for each student); another might be to require of each student the development of a series of teaching suggestions on some point not covered in class (again, a different teaching point for each student or small group of students).

In any event, we have found it overly ambitious to try to cover the book in less than two terms. If you do not have this much time, what we have learned is that if we are able to cover two-thirds of the text with our students, they are sufficiently prepared to read and apply the remaining chapters as they need them without any further formal instruction from us.

Preface

We have written this book in the hope that it will enable prospective and practicing teachers of English as a second or foreign language to better understand the grammar of the language they have chosen to teach. We also hope that the book will provide them with ideas for effectively presenting grammatical points to students of English as a second or foreign language.[1]

Linguists have much to contribute to the ESL/EFL teaching profession in the way of insights into English grammar. Unfortunately, linguistic analyses are often difficult to read and understand if one has not had extensive training in linguistics. In this book we have attempted to interpret and synthesize the relevant major linguistic sources for each grammatical structure with which we deal. We want the teacher to receive the full benefit of linguists' contributions in a comprehensible form, and since topics in English grammar are virtually limitless, we focus on those structures that the teacher needs to know about most.

In order to decide which topics in English grammar to treat, we consulted a number of ESL/EFL teachers and also examined more than a dozen commonly used ESL/EFL grammar books. From this survey we were able to identify the most frequently occurring structures which ESL/EFL teachers have to deal with in their classes.

We have been eclectic in our theoretical treatment in that we have selected analyses from several different linguistic approaches. For example, we have relied upon transformational grammar to deal with basic sentence parsing. In our experience transformational grammar is also useful for arriving at a basic understanding of certain syntactic operations such as the formation of negative sentences and questions. However, when the topics focus more upon meaning than upon form—which verb tenses or prepositions to use, for instance—we have also drawn insights from traditional grammar and case grammar. Since it is commonplace these days to acknowledge that the acquisition of a language involves more than the acquisition of forms and meanings of structures—it involves learning how to use these structures within contexts—we have examined certain structures such as articles and the passive voice from a discourse perspective. We have outlined in what contexts the passive voice is preferred over the active voice, for example. In other areas we have drawn on insights derived from usage studies designed to determine in what discourse contexts native speakers prefer one form over another. Thus we have attempted to systematically present the most useful information available to the ESL/EFL teacher, our overriding concern being comprehensiveness rather than theoretical purity.

---

1. For the sake of brevity, we will refer hereafter to English as a second or foreign language as ESL/EFL.

The core part of each chapter is our presentation of a grammatical construction. Because we conceive of our book not only as a reference book, but also as a text for teacher-trainees, we have followed the initial presentation with:

Suggestions for classroom teaching of the points discussed, recognizing that teachers will have to adapt them according to their own personal approach to ESL/EFL teaching

Exercises and discussion questions of both a factual and a problem-solving nature—the latter to encourage pedagogical application of the grammar points

A list of references including ESL/EFL texts, reference grammars, and published linguistic research that provides further information regarding the analysis and teaching of the points covered

The intent of this sequence is to lead the reader systematically from an understanding of the structure itself to an ability to use this understanding in the ESL/EFL classroom. This entails not only accumulating knowledge about the grammar of English, but also developing skills in linguistic analysis. Thus we urge that anyone using this text do all the exercises at the end of each chapter, as we conceive of these sections as being an integral part of the book and not simply fulfilling a supplementary function. For student and teacher reference, we have included suggested answers to the chapter exercises in an appendix at the back of the book.

Finally, we would be happy to hear about additional teaching suggestions, useful references we have omitted, as well as facts about English that readers feel we have not treated adequately—or not treated at all. We all have much to learn about the nature of the English language. Let us share in the task.

M. C-M.
D. L-F.

Contents

Chapter

1

Introduction

This text is an English grammar course for teachers of English as a second or foreign language (ESL/EFL). In order to put the text into perspective, let us briefly review the skills or competencies you are ideally expected to have as a well-trained teacher of English to speakers of other languages.

First of all, you are expected to have a good grasp of language teaching methodology—to know enough about available approaches and the nature of the learning process so that you can decide how to teach some particular aspect of the English language or a particular skill to a given group of students.

Second, you should be familiar with available materials in order to select the most appropriate textbook for a class or, if desirable, be able to prepare original materials. In some cases you may have to adapt mandated existing ones that do not meet the needs of your students. You must be able to judge both the accuracy and the appropriateness of materials and to change and supplement them as needed.

A third requirement is that you provide a good linguistic model. You should ideally be a native or near-native speaker of English. In the past this requirement has sometimes been elevated to such a degree that it has been felt that this is the only qualification you need to teach English to speakers of other languages; however, anyone who has attempted to teach English with only this skill immediately realizes that being a native or near-native speaker is not a sufficient qualification for being a language instructor. If you are a nonnative speaker of English, you can provide an excellent role model for your students by demonstrating good and fluent control of the English language.

This brings us to a fourth requirement: as a teacher of English as a second or foreign language you must know your subject matter. You must have conscious knowledge of the rules of the English language: the sound system, the grammatical system, the lexical system, and the discourse structure. It is the grammatical system of English, that is to say, those aspects of English grammar most frequently taught in the ESL/EFL classroom, which we will be emphasizing in this book. We will also be considering the means by which you can convey grammatical knowledge to your students other than explicitly lecturing on the rules, a practice that has proved its ineffectiveness over and over again.

Teachers of English seem to have a variety of reactions to the subject matter traditionally referred to as English grammar. Some have an aversion to it and whenever possible avoid either studying it or teaching it. Some others may feel indifferent yet believe it is necessary, and thus do what they can to understand it and present it effectively to their students. There are still

1

other teachers who enjoy studying English grammar for its own sake and cheerfully accept the challenge of presenting it clearly and interestingly to their students.

Even if you feel a bit insecure about your ability to deal with English grammar, it is important to realize that virtually all specialists and teacher trainers agree that a good grasp of English grammar is a necessary qualification for optimal effectiveness as an ESL/EFL instructor. Grammar affects your students' performance in all four skills: listening, speaking, reading, and writing. Likewise, your ability to read and understand relevant research in areas such as language acquisition, contrastive analysis, error analysis, and discourse analysis often is dependent in part on your prior knowledge of English grammar.

Furthermore, in the typical language classroom your knowledge of grammar is probably put to the test more often than any other skill you may have. Your students ask for explanations when they don't understand something. When a student makes an error, you should be able to detect it, diagnose it, and follow up with an effective correction strategy if you feel this is necessary. In the heyday of audio-lingualism it was frequently said: "Don't ask questions; just repeat after me." This kind of answer is no longer acceptable. Conveying grammatical information accurately and concisely is an important part of your job. And the way in which you perform this task has an influence on your students' attitude and confidence.

Of course, if your assumptions about how people best learn languages mean that you practice a more inductive approach to teaching grammar, you may choose never to provide or have your students induce an explicit grammar rule. Nonetheless, the study of grammar is an indispensable part of your preparation as an ESL/EFL teacher, since you will need to draw upon this knowledge when you consider how to divide the English language into meaningful chunks and how to sequence the chunks in a way most likely to facilitate their acquisition. Even if you choose not to adopt a grammatical syllabus, designing instead a notional-functional,[1] topical, or situational syllabus, your conscious knowledge of English grammar will be of help in deciding how much of the language to cover in a single lesson. Regardless of your syllabus type or your teaching approach, a knowledge of English grammar will be a valuable resource for you as you work with your students on the form of the language they will be producing.

Given that the ESL/EFL teacher should know a good deal about English grammar, a related issue involves the selection of a model or framework for the study of English grammar. Several models are available: traditional, structural, transformational, tagmemic, systemic, etc. Based on our experience, the most useful sentence-level model for the ESL/EFL teacher is the transformational one, since it views human language as dynamic rather than static and is process-oriented rather than form-oriented. For example, in a static model of grammar such as the structural one, questions are analyzed and presented independent of statements:

	Statements
Subject	Predicate
Hal	is a teacher.
	is kind.
	teaches Spanish.
	likes tacos.

---

1. See Wilkins (1976) for an elaboration of the notional-functional syllabus—as opposed to the grammatical syllabus—as a basis for language teaching.

	Yes-no Questions	
type 1.		
Aux	Subj.	Pred. complement
Is	Hal	a teacher? kind?
type 2.		
Do	Subj.	Pred. complement
Does	Hal	teach Spanish? like tacos?

Likewise, affirmative statements are analyzed and presented independent of negative statements.

Affirmatives	
Subject	Predicate
Georgette	writes novels. rides a bicycle. can swim. is pretty.

Negatives			
type 1.			
Subj.	Aux	Not	Pred. complement
Georgette	can is	not not	swim. pretty.
type 2.			
Subj.	Do	Not	Pred. complement
Georgette	does	not	write novels. ride a bicycle.

Such structural analyses—while being rigorous from a formal point of view—do not encourage you or your students to understand and exploit the similarities and differences that exist among related sentence types. Two of the best-known structural linguists, Bloomfield (1933) and Fries (1940), believed in the need for scientific rigor in linguistic description. Because they felt that meaning in language was too messy to deal with in an objective manner, the structuralists focused their attention on describing the forms of the spoken language.

Traditional grammar, while less rigorous in its statement of rules than either structural grammar or transformational grammar, did attend to meaning and usage as well as form.

Preceding the structuralists and writing in a loose, discursive style, traditional grammarians such as Jespersen (1922–1942) and Poutsma (1914–1929) produced multivolume grammars of the English language in which generalizations about form and usage are presented in an expository fashion and are typically supported by abundant examples drawn from literary materials. The traditional grammars of English thus compiled have been criticized as being long-winded and archaic (owing to the use of outdated literary sources as example data); however, they still provide—in many respects—the most readable and accessible information about the English language. In fact, almost all linguists currently doing research on English syntax will at some point in their work seriously review what the traditional grammarians have had to say about a given topic because of the scope of their work and the value of their insights, however informally those insights may have been expressed.

Other examples and other models could be discussed. Suffice it for us to say that we agree with Chomsky (1965) and others that for certain English syntactic structures both structural and traditional analyses of English grammar miss valuable and interesting generalizations that can readily be captured in a transformational analysis[2] of the language.

Let us now briefly consider the transformational model and the type of analysis it provides. The four processes that transformational theory attributes to all human languages are (1) movement or permutation, (2) substitution or replacement, (3) deletion, and (4) addition. How are these processes manifested in English grammar? If we start with an English statement such as "Hal is a teacher," we can compare it with the related question "Is Hal a teacher?" and see that a movement transformation accounts for the relationship. If we substitute *He* for *Hal* in the above statement, another type of transformation (i.e., substitution) can account for the difference and for the semantic relationship. If we next answer the question, "Is he a teacher?" by saying, "Yes, he is," we see the effect of a deletion transformation. A deletion transformation has removed *a teacher* from our answer. Repeating the words *a teacher* is unnecessary, since they are understood from the context. Finally, consider the following statement-question pair:

Georgette write $\boxed{s}$ novels.   Do $\boxed{es}$ Georgette write novels?

As well as the movement of the present tense/third person singular inflection from the main verb to the front of the sentence, the auxiliary verb DO has been added via a transformation of addition to form a grammatically acceptable question.

The transformational model of grammar—which tries to incorporate both the rigor of structural grammar and the insights of traditional grammar—has several components that we will very briefly introduce here. First of all, there are the phrase structure rules, which generate the basic or underlying structure of the sentence. Lexical items are then inserted to complete the meaning or semantic representation of the sentence at this stage. Next, the transformational rules apply to change the basic structure into a surface structure representation. Finally, the rules of the morphological component and then the rules of either the phonological or the orthographical component apply, depending on whether one is referring to speech or writing, to give the surface structure a phonetic or orthographic realization. The model can be represented schematically as follows:

---

2. We wish to make it clear at the outset that when we apply (or criticize) transformational grammar, we are referring specifically to Chomsky's model, i.e., *Aspects of the Theory of Syntax* (1965), and not to the "generative semantics" model, which has been developed in the work of Lakoff, Ross, McCawley, and others.

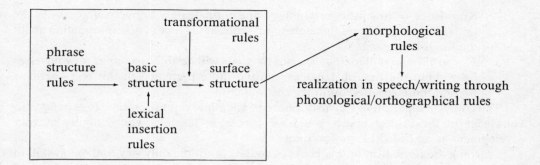

The portion of the above model enclosed in the rectangle will be our primary focus in this book whenever we present a transformational analysis.

Our presentation of transformational rules in this text is a departure from what you will find in books whose main purpose is to introduce students to transformational grammar. Our primary objective in this book is to convey to you facts and generalizations about the English language—not the transformational-generative model of grammar. However, we do feel that by working within a linguistic model, you will also be able to develop skill in linguistic analysis. Therefore, we give you some exposure to linguistic formalism, i.e., the phrase structure rules of transformational grammar. We present the phrase structure rules and as nonsymbolic an account of transformational operations as possible. We ask you to learn the names of the transformational rules and to be able to state and manipulate the change(s) a given rule produces in syntactic strings to which it applies (i.e., we expect active understanding of transformational operations); however, we do not expect you to read, understand, and use transformational rules in one of the usual symbolic notational systems, e.g.:

DO support

structural description: $X + \text{tense} + A + Y \longrightarrow$
$$1 \quad 2 \quad 3 \quad 4$$
structural change: $1 + 2 + \text{do} + 3 + 4$
condition(s): "A" is *not* one of the following:
    1. lexical verb
    2. auxiliary verb
    3. copula

For the reasons given above, we will not present rules in this form and refer those among you who desire such formalism to Chomsky (1965), Akmajian and Heny (1975), and Huddleston (1976), among others.

Doubtless even the limited formalism we do provide some of you will find excessive; others will question whether ESL/EFL teachers really benefit from it. Our rationale for including the formalism, which we feel will help readers develop skill in linguistic analysis, is three-fold:

1. Our book is not intended solely to be a compendium of facts about the English language. More facts than those we include here can be found in reference grammars. What we do hope is that you will gain not only a knowledge of the facts, but also an awareness of why the facts are the way they are. For this reason, we have intended this book to be a unified course.

2. Knowledge of linguistic terminology and formalism will give you access to the linguistics literature and therefore to a continuous source of new information about the English language.
3. As you develop skill in linguistic analysis, you will be able to uncover for yourselves facts about the English language beyond those presented in this text—perhaps beyond those reported on in the literature.

Thus, we feel that skill in linguistic analysis will allow you to continue to expand your knowledge of the subject matter you have chosen to teach as you continue in your development as an ESL/EFL professional.

Learning the formalism in this book, of course, is not the only way to develop skill in linguistic analysis—but it is one way. We give primary emphasis to the transformational model of grammar, since we feel it will provide you with valuable insights into many syntactic structures of English grammar such as question formation, negation, and relative clauses. We recognize, however, that you are often concerned with other areas such as article usage, prepositions, tenses, and modal auxiliaries. The latter areas are not particularly amenable to transformational analysis. For example, if we want to explain the similarities and differences between pairs of sentences such as the following, transformations become irrelevant:

He is *a* doctor.   You *should* eat dinner.
He is *the* doctor.   You *must* eat dinner.

In such cases we adopt a more expository approach. We present the underlying system of the grammatical area—always attempting to convey the semantic information and other important generalizations that you need.

In addition to a traditional expository treatment, we also make occasional use of some of the concepts of case grammar by adapting the analysis of Fillmore (1968). Very briefly, case grammar views the verb (or predicating element) as the core of the sentence. All the nouns (or noun phrases) in the sentence can then be related to the verb in terms of a specific semantic function (or case relationship). Consider the role of each noun in a sentence such as the following:

Herb | broke | the bottle with   his foot.
Noun 1   verb   Noun 2   Noun 3
          core

The verb core is *break*—which happens to be in the past tense—and the first noun *Herb* is the AGENT, the initiator of the event or action expressed in the sentence. The second noun is the THEME,[3] the most neutral noun in the sentence, i.e., the noun that has been changed, moved, created, etc., as a result of the action. The third noun is the INSTRUMENT, the object used to bring about the action or event. A number of other common case relationships are possible, and they are illustrated in the following sentences, each sentence introducing one or two new cases:

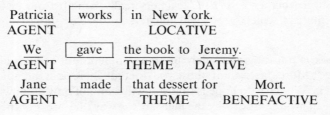

Patricia | works | in New York.
AGENT   LOCATIVE

We | gave | the book to Jeremy.
AGENT   THEME   DATIVE

Jane | made | that dessert for   Mort.
AGENT   THEME   BENEFACTIVE

---

3. The term *theme* is borrowed from Gruber (1965).

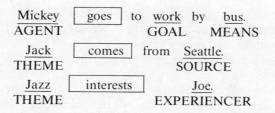

Note that many cases such as INSTRUMENTAL, LOCATIVE, and DATIVE tend to be preceded by prepositions in an English sentence. In case grammar, *subject* and *object* are surface slots or positions and any noun that is not functioning as the surface subject or object of the verb must be preceded by a preposition. The preposition in turn, gives clues as to the semantic function of the noun it precedes. Thus, case grammar is useful whenever we discuss the role and meaning of prepositions in English or those sentence structures that make systematic use of prepositions.

Thus the textbook will follow a transformational framework where useful but will switch to a more traditional expository format or to some other framework when necessary so that essential topics can be covered. Likewise, we frequently bring in facts about language typology (i.e., what goes on in other languages), about second language acquisition (i.e., typical or possible learner errors), and about discourse analysis (i.e., grammar beyond the sentence level) where such information is available to us and useful to you.

We do not expect you to bring a great deal of linguistic sophistication to this course. We do, however, assume that you know the basic parts of speech (noun, verb, adjective, adverb, pronoun, preposition, article, and auxiliary verb) and that you will be able to identify the basic sentential constituents (subject, predicate, direct and indirect objects). A few other terms which might prove useful to know are *affix, inflection, gender, number, case,* and *person*. If you are not familiar with these grammatical terms, we suggest that before you proceed any further, you consult a traditional reference grammar such as Frank's *Modern English* (1972) for definitions.

As you read this text, you will become increasingly aware of the fact that the "rules" of English grammar are often variable because of differences in register and dialect. English has a formal register which is used in expository writing and in formal speeches. English also has an informal register used in informal conversation and in informal writing, e.g., in letters to close friends. In appropriate contexts both registers are acceptable and are parts of Standard English. Unacceptable forms are either nonstandard, i.e., characteristic of a dialect that is different from Standard English, or ungrammatical forms that are not acceptable to any native speaker of English. Such ungrammatical forms are often produced by ESL/EFL learners.

The following diagram gives you some indication of these register differences and of the acceptability continuum in English.

Acceptable	*Formal Register—written, formal grammar* e.g.: There exist a number of alternatives that we should consider.
(Standard Dialect)	*Informal Register—spoken, colloquial grammar* e.g.: There's several ways of looking at this problem.
Unacceptable	*Nonstandard Dialects of English* e.g.: I didn't say nothing. *Ungrammatical (not English)* e.g.: I no say that.

As ESL/EFL teachers you must be prepared to recognize and teach both formal and informal register, as the context demands, and to be aware of the different types of unacceptability that you may be asked to deal with in the classroom.

In each of the following chapters other than the conclusion we have included teaching suggestions, some of which grew directly out of the grammatical analysis presented. You may, of course, have to adapt them to your own teaching style and situation. We have also provided exercises to enable you to check your understanding of the grammatical facts covered and your ability to apply this information to the classroom situation. For example, you will be asked to analyze mistakes of a certain kind frequently made by ESL/EFL learners and to suggest what you could do to help your students avoid these mistakes in the future. A final feature of each chapter is a list of references including ESL/EFL textbooks, reference grammars, and articles that will give you additional information and ideas concerning the topic of the chapter, if you wish to explore the topic further.

An understanding of the grammar points and teaching suggestions presented in this book together with practice performing the exercises should—from our experiences in using the materials with our students—equip you with the working knowledge of English grammar that our professional standards require.

References

Akmajian, A., and F. Heny (1975). *Introduction to the Principles of Transformational Syntax*. Cambridge, Mass.: MIT Press.

Bloomfield, L. (1933). *Language*. New York: Holt, Rinehart, and Winston.

Chomsky, N. (1965). *Aspects of the Theory of Syntax*. Cambridge, Mass.: MIT Press.

Fillmore, C. (1968). "The Case for Case," in E. Bach and R. Harms (eds.), *Universals in Linguistic Theory*. New York: Holt, Rinehart, and Winston.

Frank, M. (1972). *Modern English*. Englewood Cliffs, N.J.: Prentice-Hall.

Fries, C. C. (1940). *American English Grammar*. New York: Appleton Century Co.

Gruber, J. (1965). *Studies in Lexical Relations*. Unpublished MIT Ph.D. dissertation in Linguistics. Reproduced by the Indiana University Linguistics Club, January 1970.

Huddleston, R. (1976). *An Introduction to English Transformational Syntax*. London: Longman.

Jespersen, O. (1922–1942). *A Modern English Grammar on Historical Principles* (7 vols.). London: Allen and Unwin.

Poutsma, H. (1914–1929). *A Grammar of Late Modern English* (5 vols.). Groningen: P. Noordhoff.

Wilkins, D. A. (1976). *Notional Syllabuses*. London: Oxford University Press.

2

Word Order and Phrase Structure Rules—Part I

GRAMMATICAL DESCRIPTION

Word order in English and other languages

In English, word order within sentences is more rigid than it is in many other languages, or than it was in English 1,000 years ago. One reason for this is that English has lost most of its original Germanic system of inflections. This was a system of (1) suffixes on nouns and adjectives that reflected the gender, number, and case of every noun in a sentence and (2) suffixes on verbs that reflected the person and number of the subject noun. Without recourse to this full range of inflections to mark subjects (and objects of various kinds) English came to rely on a more fixed word order to distinguish subjects from objects. This rather fixed word order operates in conjunction with prepositions, which help to indicate the semantic functions of various objects.

The basic underlying word order in an English sentence is:

$$\underline{\text{Subject}} - \underline{\text{Verb}} - \text{Direct}\underline{\text{Object}}$$

Example: Joe   writes   poetry.

Thus we say that English is an S-V-O language like French, Spanish, and many other languages. However, a major difference between English and French, on the one hand, and Spanish, on the other, is that both English and French require that a subject noun appear in all sentences, whereas Spanish does not have this requirement for sentences with pronominal subjects, e.g.:

I speak English.   Je parle français.   (Yo) hablo español.

Actually, the preferred version of the Spanish example omits the first person subject pronoun *yo*. Spanish can delete pronominal subjects because it has a rich system of verb inflections which unambiguously indicate the person and number of the subject.

If you have only studied languages like English, Spanish, and French, you might assume that all languages follow the S-V-O word order pattern. In fact, several other languages such as Cantonese and colloquial Egyptian Arabic are also S-V-O. However, there are three major orders for these constituents in the languages of the world, and S-O-V and V-S-O are the two alternatives to S-V-O.[1] Some major languages that follow the subject-object-verb pattern as their basic ones are Japanese, Korean, and Persian. Some languages that use the verb-subject-object pattern as the basic order are Malayo-Polynesian languages such as Tagalog, the classical versions of Semitic languages such as Hebrew and Arabic, and Celtic languages like Welsh and Breton.

Thus what you, as an ESL/EFL teacher, should be cognizant of is that there may exist basic sentence-level organizational differences between your students' native language(s) and English. Such gross ordering differences within sentences tend to cause learning problems. They are a source of error mainly at the beginning level, but you should be aware of the existence of such differences at whatever level you are teaching.

Phrase structure rules

In this chapter and in Chapter 3, we will introduce the phrase structure rules of English. Through a series of such rules we will analyze in greater detail the basic structure of the English sentence. The rules are arranged in a hierarchy so that the first rule tells us what the largest unit, namely, the sentence, is comprised of. The next rule takes one of the constituents of the sentence and further breaks it down to reveal its composition. By the end of Chapter 3 we will have accounted for all the component parts of basic English sentences.

It is important for you to perform such an analysis in order to develop an understanding of the basic structural units of English. Your students often tend to commit errors of a fundamental nature because they have not yet gained an appreciation for which components of a sentence in English are obligatory and in what order both obligatory and optional constituents must appear.

Let us turn now to our first phrase structure rule:

1                                     $S \longrightarrow (SM)^n \ NUC$

The arrow means that the notion of S *sentence* is expanded (or rewritten) to include an optional sentence modifier SM—the parentheses indicate the optionality of this constituent—and an obligatory sentence nucleus NUC. For now we will limit the term *sentence modifier* to words like *perhaps, maybe, yes,* and *no.* These are sentential adverbs, i.e., adverbs that modify an entire sentence.[2] Later, other types of sentence modifiers such as the question marker Q and the negation morpheme *not* will also be introduced. This is why the rule has the superscript *n,* which allows us to generate any number of sentence modifiers.

A handy way of representing this rule more graphically is to draw a tree diagram. If we were to provide an example sentence (e.g., Perhaps John works here) to illustrate our first rule, we would construct a *tree* with two *branches.*

---

1. This three-way typology should not be interpreted too strictly. For many languages qualifications must be made regarding this typology to explain basic word order patterns. For example, German word order is mixed (SVO and SOV) and both Mandarin and Vietnamese appear to have word orders that are shifting from SVO to SOV. In addition, linguists have found a small number of languages that seem to follow other orders such as OSV.

2. We want the reader to realize that "sentence modifiers" consist of those lexical items and syntactic markers that influence the entire nucleus. Furthermore, one, two, three, or more such items (lexical and/or syntactic) may be present as SMs in any given sentence.

Perhaps John works here.

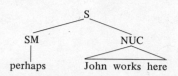

The triangle under NUC indicates that we have not yet completed our analysis of this constituent or these constituents. The second phrase structure rule expands (or rewrites) the nucleus:

2
$$\text{NUC} \longrightarrow \text{NP} \quad \text{AUX} \quad \text{VP} \quad (\text{Advl})^n$$

This rule indicates that the nucleus gets expanded to include a noun phrase NP, an auxiliary element AUX, a verb phrase VP, and an unlimited number of optional adverbials such as ones of time, position, manner, reason, and frequency. When we apply rules 1 and 2 to the same example sentence we used above, our tree diagram looks like this:

Perhaps John works here.

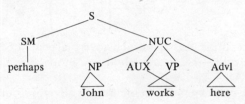

The noun phrase

The next phrase structure rule expands the noun phrase NP to include an obligatory head noun N, an optional determiner (det), and an optional plural inflection (pl); alternatively, NP may be expanded as a pronoun *pro*.

3
$$\text{NP} \longrightarrow \begin{Bmatrix} (\text{det}) \quad \text{N} \quad (\text{pl}) \\ \text{pro} \end{Bmatrix}$$

The braces to the right of the arrow indicate that either "(det) N (pl)" or "pro" must be chosen, but not both. When both a determiner and a plural marker are selected, they must agree in number. Thus, we have *this book* but not *these book*[3] or *this books*. Assuming that we wanted to generate a noun phrase with a definite article and a plural inflection, the tree for our slightly modified example sentence would grow as follows:

Perhaps the boys work here.

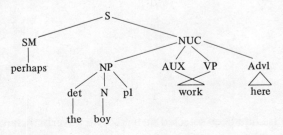

3. The asterisk preceding this example is used to indicate that what follows is ungrammatical. This convention will regularly be used throughout this text.

If the sentence were "Perhaps they work here," the NP slot would be filled by a pronoun:

Note that a pronoun, therefore, is not really a noun substitute, but rather replaces an entire noun phrase. We will discuss pronouns more fully in Chapter 10.

The internal structure of adverbials

We will now move temporarily forward in the rules to see what can happen to each optional adverbial of time, position, manner, etc., that was generated in rule 2. Rule 9 provides us with three syntactic possibilities for each sentence-final adverbial generated by rule 2:

9
$$\text{Advl} \longrightarrow \begin{Bmatrix} \text{Advl. Cl.} \\ \text{PP} \\ \text{Advl. P.} \end{Bmatrix}$$

Remember that the braces indicate that for each adverbial generated, one, but only one, of the three choices must be selected—i.e., an adverbial clause Advl. Cl., a prepositional phrase PP, or an adverbial phrase Advl. P.

An adverbial clause gets expanded to include an adverbial subordinator followed by a new sentence:

10   Advl. Cl. ⟶ Adv Sub S

This rule reintroduces S—an element already present in rule 1. To expand the new S, we would go back to rule 1 and begin the process all over again. In branching-tree form the base structure for a sentence with an adverbial clause looks like this:

Perhaps the boys left before their father found them.

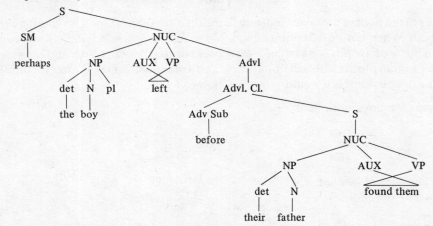

If a prepositional phrase had been selected instead of an adverbial clause, the following rule would apply:

11   PP ⟶ P NP

The prepositional phrase is expanded into a preposition P and a noun phrase NP. Since *noun phrase* has already been expanded in rule 3, we would again have to go back and apply our earlier rule for NP expansion in order to diagram the following sentence:

Perhaps the boys work in the city.

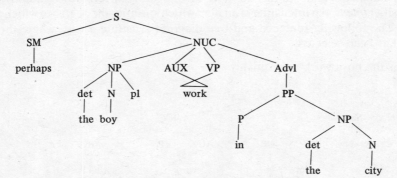

Note that prepositions are being used here to give nouns with temporal (time) or positional (place) meaning an adverbial function. As a general rule, nouns do not function on their own as adverbs in English. For example, we have the following sentences where the nouns *Monday* and *home* become adverbial with the help of the preceding prepositions:

> Max will stay here until Monday.   Mr. Green works at home.

However, in some sentences, such as the following, prepositions are optionally deletable (for further discussion, see Chapter 19):

> I've lived in New York (for) three years.   I'll get the wine (on) Thursday.

And in some sentences, for a variety of other reasons, prepositions simply do not occur before certain nouns that are used adverbially (for further discussion, see Chapter 19):

> Jack went *home*.   He will return *tomorrow*.

To preserve the integrity of our phrase structure rules and to show that the adverbials in all of the three above pairs of sentences are very similar in their semantic function, we use similar underlying representations for all of them, e.g.:

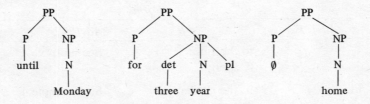

The first tree contains an obligatory preposition. The second tree contains an optional preposition, and we will ultimately capture this optionality with a special rule (see Chapter 19 for details). The third tree has an empty preposition node because nouns like *home* (when preceded by a directional verb), *tomorrow,* and *yesterday,* and noun phrases like *next year* and *last week* do not permit a preceding preposition in English even when they are functioning adverbially. Thus, the above representations allow us to show that prepositions help nouns to function as adverbs but that in some cases the preposition is not overtly expressed.

The other possible expansion of the adverbial is an adverbial phrase Advl. P., which is rewritten as follows:

12   Advl. P. ⟶ (intens)^n Adv

This means that an adverbial phrase contains an obligatory adverb *Adv* optionally preceded by an intensifier *intens*. An intensifier is an item which specifies the degree to which an adverb will apply. The following sentence and tree diagram illustrate a case where the optional intensifier has been selected:

Perhaps the boys work very quickly.

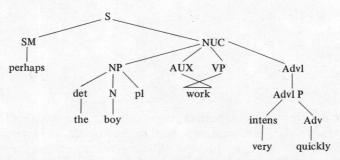

The superscript *n* after the optional intensifier allows for more than one intensifier to occur. Some intensifiers may be repeated (the linguistic term for such repetition is *reduplication*).

very, very quickly

Other series of intensifiers can consist of different lexical items.

really very quickly

In either case, the meaning of the intensifier is strengthened.

Before we close this discussion of the structure of adverbials, we should point out that some interesting patterns exist between the semantic function of an adverbial and its form or internal structure. As the matrix below demonstrates, most form-meaning combinations are possible. The empty boxes in the matrix indicate that an adverbial with this meaning does not take this form in English.

| | Form | | |
Meaning	Advl. P.	PP	Advl. Cl.[4]
direction		to the store ∅[6] there	See footnote 4
position	locally[5]	in the garden ∅[6] here	See footnote 4

4. There are other clauses that have an adverbial function of position or frequency such as "I know *where he lives*" or "Come *as often as you can*." However, the origin of such clauses is structurally different from those in the above matrix, and they are dealt with in Chapters 27 and 35, respectively.

5. Some single-word adverbs such as *locally* and *temporarily* do not normally take intensifiers. They are exceptions, and this fact would have to be specified in their lexical entries. Information about lexical entries is found in Chapter 5.

6. The ∅'s in the above diagram represent deleted prepositions. (See Chapter 19 for further details.)

Meaning	Form		
	Advl. P.	*PP*	*Advl. Cl.*[4]
manner	(very) quickly	with gusto	as you would like it
time	(quite) recently	at six o'clock ∅[6] next week	after he had seen the report
frequency[7]	(very) often (almost) always	∅[6] every Monday	See footnote 4
purpose		for the glory	so that he could stay
reason		because of[8] the weather	because we wanted to go there

Ordering of sentence-final adverbials

As has been shown earlier in rule 2, several adverbials can occur at the end of a sentence (the end of the nucleus in this grammar text). Often grammar texts suggest a fixed order that the adverbials should follow; however, there is some disagreement, since different grammars suggest different orders for the adverbials of manner, place (or position), and time:

Manner-Place-Time: Place-Manner-Time:
She ate quietly in her room last night.   He walked home quickly last night.

One problem with both of these orders is that they are not complete: adverbials of frequency, purpose, and reason, for example, have been omitted. Another problem is that the adverbial of place (or position) has served as a cover term for two distinct categories, namely, adverbials of direction, which occur with verbs of motion and tend to precede adverbials of manner:

He walked home quickly.   ?He walked quickly home.

and adverbials of position, which occur with nonmotional verbs and may either precede or follow adverbials of manner:

She ate $\begin{Bmatrix} \text{quietly in her room} \\ \text{in her room quietly} \end{Bmatrix}$

When they occur together, adverbials of direction tend to precede adverbials of position:

He ran around the track at the park.   ?He ran at the park around the track.

Furthermore, when adverbials of manner, direction, and position all occur together, the adverbials of direction and position tend to remain adjacent (i.e., the adverbial of manner must either precede or follow both the adverbial of direction and the one of position).

He ran $\begin{Bmatrix} \text{quickly around the track at the park} \\ \text{around the track at the park quickly} \\ \text{*around the track quickly at the park} \end{Bmatrix}$

There is general agreement that adverbials of time follow the types of adverbials we have already discussed (i.e., direction, manner, and position), but where do adverbials of frequency

---

7. Single-word adverbs of frequency (*often, occasionally, always,* etc.) are treated in Chapter 16.

8. Some common prepositions require a second supporting preposition. More details about this can be found in Chapter 19.

fit in? There are, in fact, two possible orders that adverbials of time and frequency[9] may exhibit with respect to each other:

$$\text{She eats lunch quickly} \begin{Bmatrix} \text{every day at noon} \\ \text{at noon every day} \end{Bmatrix}.$$

Adverbials of reason and purpose tend to follow all the others:

$$\text{She eats lunch quickly every day} \begin{Bmatrix} \text{because she likes to go back to the office and read} \\ \text{in order to have some time to read} \end{Bmatrix}.$$

However, when adverbials of reason and purpose both occur in the same sentence, the adverbial of purpose tends to precede the adverbial of reason:

> Jane went to San Diego in order to visit her uncle because she hadn't seen him for a long time.
> *Jane went to San Diego because she hadn't seen her uncle for a long time in order to visit him.

Given all the above observations concerning the ordering of adverbials, we concede that it might be possible to provide a rule that would summarize all the facts. However, such a rule would be awkward and also unrealistic, since it would be most unusual for any sentence to have more than two or three sentence-final adverbials. Therefore, we suggest that ESL/EFL students be exposed to a series of general ordering principles with the teacher using meaningful language contexts to present them over a period of time:

Re: adverbials of manner, direction, and position:
   1.   Direction tends to precede manner.
   2.   Manner and position have variable order with respect to each other.
   3.   Direction tends to precede position, and they tend to be adjacent.
Re: adverbials of time and frequency:
   1.   Time and frequency tend to follow direction, manner, and position.
   2.   Time and frequency have variable order with respect to each other.
Re: adverbials of purpose and reason:
   1.   Purpose and reason tend to follow all other adverbials.
   2.   Purpose precedes reason.

The ordering of sentence-final adverbials thus exhibits some variability, yet it is far from being a random order, since sequences such as the following are unacceptable:

> *Jane walked this morning to the shopping center.
> *Marcia fixes dinner every day quickly.
> *Harry goes jogging in order to stay fit in the morning.

Another reason for not formulating one comprehensive rule for the ordering of adverbs is that no order (or series of orders) will work all the time for all sentences and for all discourse contexts. This is because a number of other principles are at work that can influence the order of sentence-final adverbials:

1.   Shorter adverbials tend to occur before longer ones, irrespective of the general ordering principles given above:

---

9. Many grammars also consider adverbials of time and frequency as one and the same category, i.e., time. However, these adverbials answer different questions (When? How often?) and should be kept apart.

June arrived at 10 o'clock with her usual flair. (i.e., time before manner)

2. An adverbial that is the focus of the speaker's message may occur early regardless of the general order. Often special pauses and special intonation accompany such a marked ordering:

We left the party, because it was boring, well before midnight. (i.e., reason before time)

A related consideration is that when two or more adverbials of the same category occur in the same sentence, the most specific one tends to come first and the most general one last:

Josh was born at 2 a.m. on July 8th in 1947. (three time adverbials)
He was born in a small town in Wyoming. (two position adverbials)

Also, the adverbs of frequency we discuss here (e.g., *every day, once a week*) are different from the preverbal adverbs of frequency that we discuss in Chapter 16 (e.g., *sometimes, always*).

Conclusion

In this chapter we have deliberately presented only about half of the phrase structure rules that we will need for describing basic English sentences. The rules needed to expand the auxiliary and the verb phrase will be presented in the following chapter.

TEACHING SUGGESTIONS

As we said earlier, not only do ESL/EFL students have to learn all the parts of an English sentence, they also have to master the order in which these constituents appear. As an ESL/EFL teacher you would not want to present the phrase structure rules with the formalism used here; however, you certainly can make use of this information to point out to your students that a constituent has been omitted or rule of order violated.

1   One rule that you would probably want to teach in a lesson is the rule governing the usual order of sentence-final adverbials. The following is one way in which this might be accomplished (an idea suggested by Robin Abramson):

Step 1: The teacher makes a statement containing one or two adverbials about himself or herself and asks a question of a student that will elicit the same type of statement.

Example questions:
a. *Teacher:*   I drove to school today. How did *you* get here?
   Student: I took the bus (here).
b. *Teacher:*   I come to English class every day. How often do you come (to class)?
   Student: I come (to English class) every day.
c. *Teacher:*   I eat lunch in the cafeteria at noon every day. Where do you eat lunch?
d. *Teacher:*   Do you know why I come here at 8:00 every morning? I come here at 8:00 every morning because I want to teach English. Why do you come here?

Step 2: The teacher puts the following sentence on the blackboard:

	1	2	3	4	5

Aza comes <u>here</u> <u>promptly</u> <u>at 8:00</u> <u>every day</u> <u>because she wants to learn English.</u>

Step 3: The teacher tells students that each part she or he has underlined is called an adverbial. The teacher then asks students:

a. What does number 1 describe? ([to] where—direction)
b. What does number 2 describe? (how—manner)
c. What does number 3 describe? (when—time)
d. What does number 4 describe? (how often—frequency)
e. What does number 5 describe? (why—reason)

Step 4: The teacher divides the class into three groups. The teacher then passes out a handout. Each handout contains sentences with scrambled adverbials. Each group is to work on one set of sentences and correct any improper order of adverbials. Students may refer to the model on the blackboard. (If more than one order is acceptable, both orders should be given as answers.) For the purposes of this exercise, only postverbal ordering of the type illustrated in the example in Step 2 should be discussed. (Later in Chapter 29 we show that some adverbials occur sentence-initially for emphasis, e.g., Because of the bad weather we stayed at home.) An example set of sentences for the handout might be:

a. Mary studies daily there.
b. The prime minister visited three times last week the United Nations.
c. She ate lunch because she was hungry quickly in the cafeteria.

Step 5: When the groups are finished, students in each group give their answers, and the class or the teacher corrects where necessary.

2   Another grammatical point introduced in this chapter is the agreement required between certain determiners and the number of the noun that follows them. Thus, the sequences below on the left are acceptable while the sequences on the right are not:

this rod	*these rod
these rods	*this rods
that rod	*those rod
those rods	*that rods

The Cuisenaire rods of various lengths and colors, a tool used in the Silent Way approach (see Gattegno, 1976), provide an excellent device for teaching these agreement patterns once all the colors have been learned.

    Step 1: Teacher (holding the rods—one in one hand, two in the other):

This rod is yellow. These (rods) are red.

Students (holding the rods—practice using all colors until pattern is established):

This rod is blue. These (rods) are black.   This rod is white. These (rods) are orange.

Step 2: Teacher (holding one rod and having placed another rod of another color off at a distance):

This rod is light green. That $\begin{Bmatrix} \text{rod} \\ \text{one} \end{Bmatrix}$ is brown.

Students manipulate rods of various colors and practice the pattern until it is established.
    Step 3: Teacher (holding two rods of one color and having placed two others of another color off at a distance):

These rods are red. Those (rods) are yellow.

Students manipulate rods of various colors and practice the pattern until it is established.

Step 4: Teacher stands at a distance from the students to elicit the use of distinct demonstratives based on proximity. Teacher is holding one rod and one student is holding another.

Teacher: What color is this rod?
Student: It's yellow.
Teacher: What color is that rod?
Student: It's red.

Students manipulate rods and practice with each other until the pattern is established. The same thing can then be done for the plural (*Teacher:* What color are these rods? *Student:* They're black) followed by extended student practice in pairs or small groups.

Step 5: Students ask teacher questions while they and teacher hold rods of various quantities and colors.

Student: What color is this rod?
Teacher: It's dark green.
Student: What color are those rods?
Teacher: They're brown.

Step 6: Students manipulate rods and structures (number and distance) in any combination or sequence they wish and communicate with each other in pairs or small groups using these patterns. Teacher merely supervises at this stage.

EXERCISES

(Note: Since we feel it is more important for you to provide your students with good examples than with verbal definitions, we ask you to do exercises like the first one below throughout the text.)

Test your knowledge of the structures introduced

1. Provide an original example sentence illustrating each of the following concepts. Underline the pertinent word(s) in your example:

adverbial of reason	sentence modifier
adverbial of frequency	adverbial clause of time
adverbial of manner	intensifier
adverbial of direction	deletable preposition
adverbial of position	

2. Draw partially specified tree diagrams for the following sentences using the rules given in this chapter:

a. The girls talked after the teachers left.
b. Surely John exercises on Sunday.
c. The baby cried because she was hungry.
d. Fortunately his brothers work very quietly.
e. Perhaps Mary has been studying in the library.

Test your ability to apply what you know

3. The following sentences contain errors that are commonly made by ESL/EFL learners. How would you make the learners aware of these errors, and what exercises or activities would you provide to help the learners correct the errors or avoid them in the future?

a. *He took his brother yesterday to the store.

b. *Those woman are·striking for peace.

c. *John ran for shelter because was raining.

4. What are the similarities and differences in the structure of the time adverbials in these sentences?

a. We'll eat at 10 o'clock.

b. I've studied English for ten years./I've studied English ten years.

c. I'm going to Dallas next week.

5. A student asks you why it's O.K. to say "I went to school," "I went to church," "I went to work," etc. but not O.K. to say "I went to home." How will you answer this question?

BIBLIOGRAPHY

References

Gattegno, C. (1976). *The Common Sense of Teaching Foreign Languages.* New York: Educational Solutions, Inc.

Suggestions for further reading

Other versions of the phrase structure rules for English can be found in the following sources (the last two references are less formal than the first three):

Akmajian, A., and F. Heny (1975). *Introduction to the Principles of Transformational Syntax.* Cambridge, Mass.: MIT Press.

Culicover, P. (1976). *Syntax.* New York: Academic Press.

Keyser, S. J., and P. M. Postal (1976). *Beginning English Grammar.* New York: Harper and Row.

Liles, B. (1971). *An Introductory Transformational Grammar.* Englewood Cliffs, N.J.: Prentice-Hall.

Wardhaugh, R. (1972). *An Introduction to Linguistics.* New York: McGraw-Hill.

Some good suggestions for teaching the order of adverbials are found in:

Danielson, D., and R. Hayden (1973). *Using English: Your Second Language.* Englewood Cliffs, N.J.: Prentice-Hall, Chap. 13.

Hayden, R., D. Pilgrim, and A. Haggard (1956). *Mastering American English.* Englewood Cliffs, N.J.: Prentice-Hall, pp. 35–45.

3

Phrase Structure Rules—Part II

GRAMMATICAL DESCRIPTION

Review

In the preceding chapter the following phrase structure rules were presented and discussed:

1          $S \longrightarrow (SM)^n \text{ NUC}$

2          $\text{NUC} \longrightarrow \text{NP AUX VP } (Advl)^n$

3          $NP \longrightarrow \begin{Bmatrix} (\text{det}) \text{ N (pl)} \\ \text{pro} \end{Bmatrix}$

9          $Advl \rightarrow \begin{Bmatrix} \text{Advl. Cl.} \\ \text{PP} \\ \text{Advl. P.} \end{Bmatrix}$

10   Advl. Cl. $\longrightarrow$ Adv Sub   S

11   PP $\longrightarrow$ P   NP

12   Advl. P. $\longrightarrow (\text{intens})^n \text{ Adv}$

This chapter will supply the phrase structure rules we need in order to represent the English verb system adequately.

The structure of the English verb system

The verb system of English can be discussed in terms of its forms—the inflections and structures it makes use of—or it can be discussed in terms of how it expresses "real time" distinctions such as the past, the present, and the future. In this chapter we will investigate the forms of the verb system, and the meanings of the verb system will be dealt with in Chapter 6.

      The tense forms of any language are a selective rendering of the temporal distinctions one can logically make with reference to time in the real world. The system is selective because *tense,* in the structural sense, refers only to the inflections one can use with finite (i.e., inflectable) verbs to express past, present, or future time. Given this point of view, English has only two tense forms—past and present. If we exclude the verb BE for the moment, the past tense may be realized through either regular suffixation:

We walk | ed | to school. (*walk*)

or other irregular vowel and consonant changes:

We <u>saw</u> the principal.   (*see*)   We <u>bought</u> some books.   (*buy*)

The present tense is explicitly marked in the case of third person singular subject nouns:

He walk | s | to school.

or expressed implicitly with a lack of marking for all other subjects:

$$\left.\begin{array}{l}\text{I}\\\text{you}\\\text{they}\\\text{we}\end{array}\right\}\ \text{walk}\ \boxed{\emptyset}^{1}\ \text{to school.}$$

From a structural point of view, English has no grammatical future tense, since future time is expressed using auxiliary verbs or adverbs of time in combination with the present tense instead of a grammatical future tense (i.e., an inflected form of the verb).

The verb BE is more highly inflected than other verbs in English and can express the present through three forms: *am, is, are,* and the past through two forms: *was, were.* See Chapter 4 for details.

Every nonimperative English sentence must have either a modal auxiliary or grammatical tense—past or present. In addition, English has two structural aspectual markers[2]— the progressive aspect and the perfective aspect—that can be described in grammatical terms. The progressive aspect is marked by the presence of the auxiliary BE plus the present participle (-ING) suffixed to the verb. For example:

1.   I walk to school. (present tense, no aspect)

2.   I | am | walk | ing | to school. (present tense, progressive aspect)
         BE . . . ING

Likewise, the perfective aspect can be described in structural terms as the presence of the auxiliary HAVE plus the past participle (sometimes called the -EN form) of the verb. For example:

1.   I saw the principal. (past tense, no aspect)

2.   I | had | see | n | the principal. (past tense, perfective aspect)
        HAVE . . . EN

Phrase structure rules for the auxiliary

The English verb has many potential auxiliary elements that must be accounted for in the phrase structure rules. Consider the following sentences:

1.   John wrote a book.
2.   John should write a book.
3.   John has written a book.
4.   John is writing a book.
5.   John is going to write a book.
6.   Write a book!

---

1. The symbol ∅ represents zero. Applied in this case, it means no inflection.

2. Here we discuss aspect from the structural point of view. In Chapter 6, where we treat aspect semantically, HAVE . . . EN is no longer an aspect but is part of the tense system of English.

If we consider the auxiliary as everything but the subject *John* and the verb phrase *write a book,* we see that the auxiliary + the verb in each sentence consists of the following elements:

1. past tense + write = *wrote*
2. modal *should* + write = *should write*
3. pres tense + perfect HAVE ... EN + write = *has* writ*ten*
4. pres tense + progressive BE ... ING + write = *is* writ*ing*
5. pres tense + the periphrastic modal *be going to* + write = *is going to write*
6. imperative mood + write = *write*

Thus, as we previously mentioned, nonimperative English sentences obligatorily take grammatical tense or a modal. If some auxiliary verb other than a modal is present, it carries the tense. If no tense-bearing auxiliary verb is present, the main verb will carry the tense (e.g., sentence 1 above).

Four different optional auxiliary verbs may be present: a modal auxiliary[3] (e.g., *will, can, must, shall, may*), a periphrastic modal (e.g., *be going to, have to, be able to*),[3] the perfective aspect (HAVE plus the past participle), and the progressive aspect (BE plus the present participle).

Sometimes more than tense or a modal auxiliary occurs in the AUX of a single sentence. For example:

1. John had to be writing a book. (past tense, periphrastic modal, and progressive aspect)
2. John has been writing a book. (present tense, perfective and progressive aspects)
3. John should have written a book. (modal and perfective aspect)
4. John will have been writing a book. (modal, perfective and progressive aspects)
5. John will have to have written a book. (modal, periphrastic modal, and perfective aspect)
6. John had to have been writing a book. (past tense, periphrastic modal, perfective and progressive aspects)

The tree diagram for the example 6 sentence given above would be:

John had to have been writing a book.

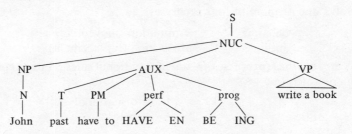

As we have just seen, whenever three or more auxiliary elements occur together, the perfective precedes the progressive and a periphrastic modal precedes either of the two aspects. A modal can precede a periphrastic modal and also either of the two aspects. (If two or more tense-bearing auxiliary verbs are present, the first of these auxiliary verbs will carry the tense.)

These relationships can be summed up in the following rule:

---

3. Modal auxiliaries and periphrastic modals are discussed further in Chapter 7.

4
$$AUX \rightarrow \left\{ \begin{Bmatrix} T \\ M \end{Bmatrix} \text{(PM) (perf) (prog)} \\ \text{IMPER} \right\}$$

Here the auxiliary is AUX. It is made up of tense (T) or a modal (M) followed by the other optional auxiliary elements: periphrastic modal (PM) and the perfective (perf) and progressive (prog) aspects. (IMPER stands for imperative, a tenseless verb form in English, which will be explained in detail in Chapter 11.)

We have already learned that grammatical tense in English is either past or present. This choice is stated in phrase structure rule 5.

5
$$T \rightarrow \begin{Bmatrix} \text{past} \\ \text{pres} \end{Bmatrix}$$

The perfective and progressive aspects are expanded into their auxiliary verbs and accompanying grammatical inflections in rules 6 and 7, respectively.

6   perf ⟶ HAVE ... EN

7   prog ⟶ BE ... ING

Notice that we are using the EN as a symbol for the past participle. Past participles in English are not always formed with an EN, as the following examples show:

Look the same as the past tense form	-en[4]	Vowel alternations
learned	written	sung
read	eaten	drunk
taught	seen	begun

ESL/EFL students will need ample practice using the various past participles in order for them to master the many forms.

Thus far the only rules we have applied are phrase structure rules. They generate the basic structure to which lexical items are added to complete the semantic representation of the sentence. In most cases various changes must be made on the output of the phrase structure rules in order to produce grammatical English surface structures. The kinds of changes that take place involve one or more of four processes:

deletion	permutation (movement)
addition	substitution (replacement)

The rules that carry out these processes are transformational rules. Thus our grammar has the following sequence of rules:

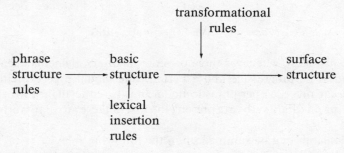

---

4. Even those verbs which add EN are often phonologically and/or orthographically irregular.

In order to have a basic structure like the one in the preceding tree diagram become a surface structure, we have to apply a special transformational rule called affix attachment. When this rule is applied, every dependent auxiliary inflection (i.e., tense, EN, ING) attaches to the immediately following lexical element to produce an inflected lexical item:[5]

John had to have been writing a book.

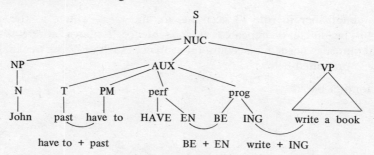

For example, in the above tree the affix attachment rule applies three times (3×) and then morphological rules apply to accomplish the following:

1. Past tense combines with *have to* to produce *had to*.
2. EN combines with BE to produce *been*.
3. ING combines with *write* to produce *writing*.

Phrase structure rules for the verb phrase

Leaving the auxiliary elements aside for the moment, we also know that English verb phrases can be complicated. Consider the following sentences:

1. John is a teacher.
2. Alice is very pretty./Alice is very, very pretty.
3. The students are here.

4. John studies.
5. John studies mathematics.
6. John put the books on the table.
7. John is fond of books.

A phrase structure rule that would allow us to account for all such structural possibilities follows:

$$8 \qquad VP \longrightarrow \left\{ \begin{array}{l} BE \left\{ \begin{array}{l} NP \\ AP \\ PP \end{array} \right\} \\ V \quad (NP) \quad (PP) \end{array} \right\}$$

(AP refers to an adjective phrase.)

Can you determine which part of the rule would be used to generate each of the above sentences? For example, the first three sentences could be accounted for by the following subrules contained within rule 8:

a.   VP ⟶ BE   NP
b.   VP ⟶ BE   AP
c.   VP ⟶ BE   PP (where P = ∅)

---

5. The plural marker of the noun phrase does not work this way; instead, it is attached from right to left (the boy___ pl).

See if you can figure out the others. The only element in rule 8 needing further expansion is the adjective phrase, which like the adverbial phrase, can be expanded into an optional intensifier and an obligatory adjective—but unlike the adverbial phrase, may also take an optional prepositional phrase.

13                                     $AP \longrightarrow (intens)^n$ Adj (PP)

The optional intensifier in rule 13 accounts for the *very*—which, as the superscript n indicates—can be single or repeated as in sentence 2 above, whereas the optional prepositional phrase is needed to account for sentences such as 7. The tree diagram for this last sentence is presented below:

John is fond of books.

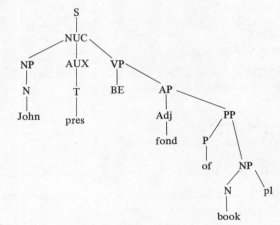

In order to derive the surface structure of this sentence, we need one other transformational rule—in addition to affix attachment—and that is the rule for subject-verb agreement that would give us the correct lexical form of the verb BE for this particular sentence. The transformational rules would apply as follows:

Output of base:[6] John pres BE fond of book pl
Affix attachment (2$\times$): John BE + pres fond of book + pl
Subject-verb agreement and morphological rules:[7] John is fond of books.

You'll recall that the attachment of the plural inflection (or affix) to the noun goes from right to left, whereas affix attachment for verbs goes left to right and moves over one constituent:

John pres BE, fond of book pl

In the last line of any derivation that we give in this text, we add all necessary conventions of the written language such as capitalization and punctuation so that the final output is an acceptable written sentence. We could have used a separate rule to explicitly capture these additions but decided not to, since the focus of this text is on grammar rather than speech or writing per se.

---

6. We refer to this as *output of base* because lexical items have already been added to the product of the phrase structure rules.

7. Morphological rules change *book* + pl into books. Subject-verb agreement, which we will discuss further in Chapter 4, combines with morphological rules to realize BE + pres as *is* in the environment of a third person singular subject.

PPs that are inside vs. outside the verb phrase

The structure of the verb phrase in a sentence like "John put the books on the table" is our next concern. The tree diagram of this sentence is given below:

John put the books on the table.

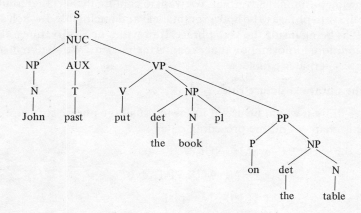

In a sentence like this one the verb phrase includes the prepositional phrase as an integral part, not as an optional modifier or specifier because the following sentence without the prepositional phrase is ungrammatical—i.e., the phrase is needed to structurally complete the verb and thus is part of the verb phrase (not an optional element of the nucleus).

*John put the books.

In other sentences, however, the prepositional phrase supplies supplementary rather than complementary information, and would be generated as an optional part of the nucleus rather than an obligatory part of the verb phrase. For example, the following sentences are grammatical with or without the PP in parentheses, thus requiring that the PP be generated in the nucleus rather than the verb phrase:

John washes the car (on Saturday).   Bill told Alice the news (with regret).
Mary jogs (through Central Park).

This notion of when a PP is either inside or outside the verb phrase (i.e., is part of either the verb phrase or the nucleus) is often difficult to determine. It is likely, in fact, that a continuum rather than a dichotomy exists here. For our current purposes, however, the most important thing to consider is grammaticality. In sentences like the following:

I handed a note to John.   I wrote a note to John.

we can say that *to John* is more closely associated with the verb *hand* in the first sentence than it is with the verb *write* in the second sentence, since

*I handed a note.

is ungrammatical, whereas the following sentence is not:

I wrote a note.

Thus we say that the PP is inside the verb phrase in *hand a note to John* but outside the verb phrase (branches directly off the NUC) in *write a note to John*.

Consider also the following pair, which shows us that grammaticality and meaning seem to interact in this decision-making process:

The child lay in the hammock.   *The child lay.

The verb *to lie* (much as the verb *to BE* would be in the same context) is somehow incomplete without a following positional adverbial. We want to capture the fact that a subject must *lie somewhere* for the verb phrase to be both grammatical and intelligible. In such a case we must analyze the PP as being inside the verb phrase. It provides necessary, integral information, not optional, additional information that expands the nucleus. We shall return to this issue again in several other later chapters.

Summary of the phrase structure rules

At this point we think it would be useful for us to list all the phrase structure rules we have discussed in this chapter and the preceding one:

1            $S \longrightarrow (SM)^n \ NUC$

2            $NUC \longrightarrow NP \ AUX \ VP \ (Advl)^n$

3            $NP \longrightarrow \begin{Bmatrix} (det) & N & (pl) \\ pro \end{Bmatrix}$

4            $AUX \longrightarrow \begin{Bmatrix} \begin{Bmatrix} T \\ M \end{Bmatrix} \ (PM) \ (perf) \ (prog) \\ IMPER \end{Bmatrix}$

5            $T \longrightarrow \begin{Bmatrix} past \\ pres \end{Bmatrix}$

6            $perf \longrightarrow HAVE \ldots EN$

7            $prog \longrightarrow BE \ldots ING$

8            $VP \longrightarrow \begin{Bmatrix} BE \begin{Bmatrix} NP \\ AP \\ PP \end{Bmatrix} \\ V \ (NP) \ (PP) \end{Bmatrix}$

9            $Advl \longrightarrow \begin{Bmatrix} Advl. \ Cl. \\ PP \\ Advl. \ P. \end{Bmatrix}$

10            $Advl. \ Cl. \longrightarrow Adv \ Sub \ S$

11            $PP \longrightarrow P \ NP$

12            $Advl. \ P. \longrightarrow (intens)^n \ Adv$

13            $AP \longrightarrow (intens)^n \ Adj \ (PP)$

Conclusion

This concludes our presentation of the basic phrase structure rules of our grammar. Additional rules will be added from time to time in subsequent chapters as necessary.

TEACHING SUGGESTIONS

1 The important thing to stress with the progressive and perfective aspects is that they are both formed with two constituents which are not next to each other in the surface structure.

progressive—a form of BE plus the present participle (ING) attached to the main verb
perfective—a form of HAVE followed by the past participle (EN)

A common error committed by ESL/EFL students is to omit one of the two necessary constituents when forming one of the aspects (i.e., the auxiliary verb or the inflection).

a. Perhaps one of the most natural ways to introduce the progressive is to let everyone in the class do whatever she or he wants to for a minute and then begin describing (this can also be a review of the verb BE) what they are doing.

Teacher:	I'm talking. What are you doing?
Student 1:	I'm reading.
Teacher:	What is Harold doing?
Student 2:	He's sleeping.
Teacher:	Ask Sasha and Margot what they're doing.
Student 3:	What are you doing?
Sasha and Margot:	We're talking.

(Students take over the teacher's role.)

b. The perfect of experience (i.e., "Have you ever . . . ?") is a good context for introducing the perfective aspect and contrasting it with the simple past.

Teacher:	Tell me something you want to do but have never done.
Student 1:	I want to visit Seattle.
Teacher:	José has never visited Seattle. Have you/Has anyone ever visited Seattle?
Student 2:	Yes, I went there last year.

Teacher continues to elicit things students have never done but would like to do; however, the students take over the drilling.

Student 3:	I have never played baseball. Have you ever played baseball?
Student 4:	No, I haven't.

2 Another problem arises when the ESL/EFL student has to learn to deal with all the irregular past tense and past participle forms. The regular past participle forms, like the regular past tense, cause no undue hardship. This is because both are formed with the addition of the *ed* inflectional affix for all persons and numbers:

I walked	we walked	I have walked	we have walked
you walked		you have walked	
he, she, it walked	they walked	he, she, it has walked	they have walked

However, there are many different irregular forms of past tense verbs and past participles. These will all have to be presented as separate vocabulary items—a few introduced from time to time in a 10-minute portion of a class hour.

A good way of organizing such a lesson is to introduce together those past tense verbs and past participles which conform to the same phonological pattern. For example:

Verbs that pattern like <u>blow</u>, <u>blew</u>, <u>blown</u>
                          pres   past   past participle

These can all be presented together. The following is one way this could be accomplished:

 a. Teacher writes the following paragraph on the blackboard and then reads it out loud.

> Yesterday the wind <u>blew</u> very hard. It had never <u>blown</u> that hard before. I <u>knew</u> when it first began that it would be bad for my garden. The plants that <u>grew</u> out in the open were hurt badly. Only a few which had already <u>grown</u> strong survived the wind storm. If I had only <u>known</u>, I would have planted them closer to my house.

 b. Teacher has students read the paragraph once out loud and discusses with class any new vocabulary. Teacher calls particular attention to the past tense and past participle forms of the underlined verbs:

blow	blew	blown
grow	grew	grown
know	knew	known

 c. Teacher gives students an exercise where students have to supply the correct form of a given infinitive verb for a number of sentences, e.g.:

(to grow)   I have never _____ tulips before.
(to throw)   After waiting a moment, the pitcher _____ the ball to the catcher.

3   Olson and Shalek (1981) suggest that game-type activities be used to practice past participles. One of their ideas is to use a tree with many branches as a visual prop for a verb conjugation game. Each tree branch has several pockets for cards, and on each branch the pocket closest to the trunk has been filled with a card that gives one example of the verb conjugation pattern that the branch represents. The class (or a group) is then given a stack of cards which must be put into the remaining pockets in the tree branches. Sample cards are as follows (note that all three verb forms should be visible even when the card is placed in the pocket):

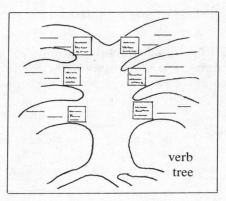

verb tree

blow	sing	buy
blew	sang	bought
blown	sung	bought
- - -	- -	- - -

keep	become
kept	became
kept	become
- -	- - -

4   With regard to verbs that take an obligatory adverb of direction or position, Valerie Sandoval suggests two exercises:

 a. Have students identify and complete any ungrammatical sentences, e.g.:

1. John put the books   3. The baby cried
2. Here are the flowers   4. The tired old woman lay

b. Have students complete sentences using visual aids such as the following:

THE BABY LAY...

ANN PUT THE FLOWERS...

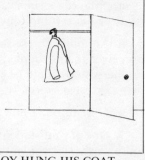

ROY HUNG HIS COAT...

EXERCISES

Test your knowledge of what has been presented

1. Provide an original example sentence illustrating each of the following concepts, and underline the pertinent word(s) in your examples:

periphrastic modal	imperative
modal auxiliary	adjective phrase
perfective aspect	PP inside the verb phrase
progressive aspect	PP outside the verb phrase

2. Draw tree diagrams for the following sentences:

a. Ian is going to be taking that class next quarter.
b. He has been jogging since noon.
c. Anne could have done her homework.
d. Jim might come tomorrow.
e. She has been very helpful.
f. We left the chairs in the hallway.
g. Maybe they are newcomers.
h. The meeting has to be at noon.
i. Sara is very fond of cats.

3. Apply the affix transformation to the following outputs of tree diagrams (and specify how many times it is applied in each case):

a. I pres have to BE ING go now.
b. John pres HAVE EN pass the test.
c. We pres HAVE EN BE ING swim all summer.

4. Are the PPs in the following sentences part of the verb phrase or part of the nucleus? Explain your answer.

a. I do the shopping on Saturdays.
b. The old man stepped off the curb.
c. Bob isn't at home.
d. Jane lives in Phoenix because of the weather.
e. They got in trouble.
f. We made that decision for several reasons.
g. A prowler was lurking in the bushes.

Test your ability to apply what you know

5. The following sentences contain errors that are commonly made by ESL/EFL learners. How would you make your students aware of these problems? What exercises would

you use to practice the correct pattern and prevent such errors from recurring?

a. *She can swims very fast.   c. *Bob will to come tomorrow.
b. *Jane is jump rope.   d. *The man been to Chicago twice.

6. Although phrase structure rules should not be presented to ESL/EFL students in the form given in this chapter, they do yield important insights into English structure. One of the insights which should be emphasized in grammar classes has to do with the composition of the progressive aspect. In light of the following errors, what should be emphasized?

a. *She running now.   b. *She is run now.

7. One of your students asks you why a certain grammar text claims that English has no future tense. This student feels that English *has* a future tense. How would you answer this question?

BIBLIOGRAPHY

References

Olson, C., and S. Shalek (1981). "Games and Activities Based on Grammatical Areas Which Are Problems for the Intermediate ESL Student." Unpublished manuscript, School for International Training, Brattleboro, Vt.

Suggestions for further reading

For the historically original form of phrase structure rules written within a transformational grammar of English, see:

Chomsky, N. (1957). *Syntactic Structures.* The Hague: Mouton.

For alternative versions of these phrase structure rules, see:

Akmajian, A., and F. Heny (1975). *Introduction to the Principles of Transformational Syntax.* Cambridge, Mass.: MIT Press.
Culicover, P. (1976). *Syntax.* New York: Academic Press.
Liles, B. (1971). *An Introductory Transformational Grammar.* Englewood Cliffs, N.J.: Prentice-Hall.
Wardhaugh, R. (1972). *Introduction to Linguistics.* New York: McGraw-Hill.

For useful lists of verbs with irregular past tense and past participles, see:

Clark, R., P. Moran, and A. Burrows (1981). *The ESL Miscellany.* Brattleboro, Vt.: Pro Lingua Associates.
Frank, M. (1972). *Modern English.* Englewood Cliffs, N.J.: Prentice-Hall, pp. 61–66.
Nadler, H., and L. Mavelli (1971). *American English, Grammatical Structure,* Book 3. Philadelphia, Pa.: The Center for Curriculum Development, Inc., pp. 71–76.

4

The Copula and Subject-Verb Agreement

GRAMMATICAL DESCRIPTION

Introduction

ESL/EFL learners are exposed to the forms of the copula (the verb BE) and the third person singular inflection almost immediately in their earliest English classes or in any English-speaking environment they happen to experience. The forms are superficially simple to understand, and yet they pose problems for learners at all levels. The copula poses the greatest problems at the initial stage. However, research on L2 morpheme acquisition (Dulay and Burt [1974], Bailey et al. [1974], Larsen-Freeman [1975]) has shown that the third person singular present tense form causes persistent problems for learners even at the more advanced stages of proficiency.

In this chapter we will take a close look at these problem areas. They will reemerge regularly in the following chapters; however, we felt that a detailed treatment at this stage would be wise, given the pervasiveness of the learning problems that these forms entail.

The copula BE

The functions of BE

Since BE functions as an auxiliary verb as well as the copula, we should first take a look at these distinct functions. Our rule for expanding the verb phrase was presented in the preceding chapter:

$$VP \longrightarrow \left\{ \begin{array}{l} BE \left\{ \begin{array}{l} NP \\ AP \\ PP \end{array} \right\} \\ V \ (NP) \ (PP) \end{array} \right\}$$

The BE referred to in this rule is the copula. It links nonverbal predicates (nouns, adjectives, and certain adverbs) with their subjects and serves as a carrier for tense and subject-verb agreement.

This function of BE is distinct from the use of BE in the progressive aspect, where BE combines with -ING to make the meaning of the verb more concrete and limited. This BE always occurs in conjunction with a main verb, and it is thus referred to as an auxiliary verb. The progressive aspect is only one of many auxiliary verb functions that BE has. It is also an auxiliary element in the passive voice (see Chapter 17) and in several periphrastic modals (see Chapter 7).

Why the copula is different from other verbs

The rule for expanding the verb phrase makes a clear distinction between the copula BE and all other verbs in English. There are at least four very good reasons for making such a distinction. First of all, the copula has more distinct forms with respect to person, number, and tense than any other verb in English. The traditional paradigm for the copula compared with that for a verb such as *walk* makes this clear:

	copula BE			
	Present tense		*Past tense*	
	sg.	*pl.*	*sg.*	*pl.*
1st person	I am	we are	I was	we were
2nd person	you are	you are	you were	you were
3rd person	he, she, it is	they are	he, she, it was	they were

	verb walk			
	Present tense		*Past tense*	
	sg.	*pl.*	*sg.*	*pl.*
1st person	I walk	we walk	I walked	we walked
2nd person	you walk	you walk	you walked	you walked
3rd person	he, she, it walks	they walk	he, she, it walked	they walked

A verb like *walk* has two present-tense forms and one past-tense form:

PRESENT: walks—third person singular
walk —all other persons and numbers
PAST: walked—all persons and numbers

The copula, on the other hand, has three distinct present-tense and two past-tense forms. Some of the forms are more restricted in their range than others, and this is represented in the following diagrams:

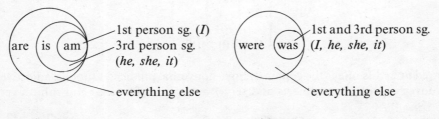

present tense   past tense

This multiplicity of forms explains why learners sometimes use the wrong form of the copula in their speech or writing:

*You is late.   *We was on time.

In fact, *is* and *was,* the most frequent present- and past-tense forms of the copula, tend to be overused by ESL/EFL learners and also by speakers of nonstandard English dialects.

Second, the copula is freely followed by adjectives (or adjective phrases), whereas other verbs are followed by noun phrases or prepositional phrases, but not by adjective phrases.

Verbs such as *seem, appear,* and *grow* may also be followed by adjectives; however, most transformational descriptions of English point out that sentences with this surface pattern are derived from an underlying infinitive which has been deleted (we discuss such constructions in Chapters 30 and 34):

Joseph seems (to be) sad.   The boy grew (to be) tall.
That argument appears (to be) weak.

The verb *become* might also be considered a counterexample to the generalization that adjectives do not follow verbs, but in fact it is not. Historically, the verb *become* is a lexicalization of the verb phrase "to come to be." For example:

Naomi became more optimistic.
(came to be)

Once the verb *become* established itself in English, other verbs of the same semantic class, i.e., change-of-state verbs, such as *turn* could also occur with adjectival complements by analogy:

Mel's hair turned gray.

Since the so-called exceptions to the rule which states that the copula takes adjectives but that other verbs do not can be explained either transformationally (*seem, appear, grow*) or historically and analogically (*become, turn*), we feel that the generalization holds and helps to explain why BE is different from other verbs.

Third, the syntactic behavior of the copula, which acts like an auxiliary verb with regard to question formation (see Chapter 9), negation (see Chapter 8), and other constructions, is different from that of other verbs like *walk,* which require the addition of a DO auxiliary.

Hal | is | an engineer.   Hal walk | s | to work.

| Is | Hal an engineer? | Does | Hal walk to work?

Hal | is | n't a teacher.   Hal | does | n't walk home.

Finally, the copula does not occur in all languages but all languages have verbs. Especially in the present tense, many languages have nothing equivalent to the copula; speakers of such languages simply express the literal equivalent of sentences like the three below, and this pattern readily transfers to English:

*Hal engineer.   *Hal in the next room.
*Hal tall.

This lack of universality of the copula is understandable if we consider that semantically it is not a necessary form; it is a syntactic marker in English, a linking element that carries tense and subject-verb agreement. In fact, children learning English as their mother tongue often omit the copula in their early speech as do many second language learners of all ages when they are learning English. Second language learners have been observed to omit the copula regardless of whether or not their native language has an equivalent form. All these phenomena are related to the fact that the copula is a marked form (i.e., it is not universal; it is somehow both idiosyncratic and redundant).

The copula as a learning problem

For all the above reasons the ESL/EFL teacher must be sensitive to the problems that his or her learners will have with the copula—especially if the learners are at the beginning level, since they may have a tendency to omit it. (For those students whose native language has no copula, this initial tendency will be even more pronounced.) The other problem, of course, involves use of the wrong form of BE. Sufficient opportunity for meaningful practice can overcome both these problems.

Subject-verb agreement

Third person singular present

For verbs other than BE, subject-verb number agreement (sometimes referred to as subject-verb concord) poses a problem only in the present tense, where third person singular forms are explicitly inflected while other forms are not.

	Number	
Person	*Singular*	*Plural*
1st	I speak French.	We speak French.
2nd	You speak French.	You speak French.
3rd	He/she/it (the parrot) speak $\boxed{s}$ French.	They speak French.

Some typical grammatical errors

Given such an asymmetric paradigm, the ESL/EFL learner tends to simplify and leave off altogether the third person singular inflection:

*He live in Seattle.   *She say she will come.

Occasionally, however, some learners will overgeneralize the inflection and apply it to uninflectable forms such as modal auxiliaries (see Chapter 7):

*Jack cans dance disco.

or use it in agreement with subjects of inappropriate person and/or number:

*$\left\{ \begin{array}{l} \text{I} \\ \text{They} \\ \text{You} \end{array} \right\}$ goes to Stanford.

Yet another reason why learners overuse this form is that they interpret the *-s* ending as a plural marker on the verb to be used in agreement with plural subjects:

*$\left\{ \begin{array}{l} \text{They} \\ \text{The boys} \end{array} \right\}$ goes to the movies often.

Finally, it has also been observed that Spanish speakers tend to initially overuse this inflection with the second person singular pronoun because a similar form is used in their language for this person:

Spanish: Tu habla ⌐s⌐ inglés.   English: *You speak ⌐s⌐ English.

Agreement errors may be phonological or perceptual rather than syntactic or morphological

ESL/EFL teachers should be aware of the fact that some learners of English fully understand the third person singular present ending and can produce it systematically when they write in English; however, they omit it frequently when they are speaking because the sound system of their native language tends not to permit final /s/ sounds in particular or final consonants in general. Speakers of French and a variety of other languages have been observed to do this.

Of course, other reasons for the slow and late acquisition of the third person singular inflection—even when there is no phonological interference from the learner's native language—might be its lack of perceptual saliency[1] and its low frequency of occurrence in native speaker speech (Larsen-Freeman, 1976). The form also tends to be omitted for these reasons.

Problems in subject-verb agreement

Since subject-verb agreement is a problem for learners at all levels and even puzzles native speakers at times, many reference grammars or style handbooks include a discussion of this topic. One of the most comprehensive treatments is in Crews (1980). He provides the reader with the preferred form as well as acceptable alternatives and covers more rules than most other sources. However, Crews tends to be more *prescriptive* than *descriptive* in his account; i.e., he tells the reader what to do rather than telling the reader what educated native speakers do. We try to be as descriptive as possible in our review of the rules of subject-verb agreement because we feel the ESL/EFL teacher must be aware of current usage as well as the traditional rules.

When we discuss the usage preferences of native speakers with respect to subject-verb agreement, we draw heavily on studies done by Van Shaik (1976) and Farhady (1977). They both surveyed the performance and preferences of large numbers of native speakers and pointed out a number of discrepancies between traditional rules and the elicited performance of native speakers.

Whereas some cases of subject-verb agreement are puzzling mainly to nonnative speakers, several cases cause difficulty for native and nonnative speakers alike. We will now review many of the problematic areas in subject-verb agreement along with the more predictable and obvious rules.

The general rule

In the most straightforward cases the subject-verb agreement rule tells us to use the third person singular inflection if the subject is a singular proper name, a singular common noun, a mass noun, or a third person singular pronoun. Elsewhere, i.e., for proper or common plural nouns, for first or second person singular pronouns, or for plural pronouns, no inflection is used in the present tense:

---

1. What is meant by the perceptual saliency of a form is whether or not it is easy for learners to hear. Because final consonants and consonant clusters tend to be more weakly articulated in English than initial consonants or clusters, this morpheme is in fact somewhat difficult to hear.

Third person singular inflection

John walk [s] to school.

The bus stop [s] here.

This water taste [s] funny.

She want [s] an apple.

No inflection

The Smiths walk to church.

These books contain good information.

$\begin{Bmatrix} \text{I} \\ \text{You} \end{Bmatrix}$ want an apple.

$\begin{Bmatrix} \text{We} \\ \text{You} \\ \text{They} \end{Bmatrix}$ want an apple.

These examples of the general rule are easy and cause little or no difficulty—at least not at the conceptual level. However, there are so many special or difficult cases concerning this rule that we will fill several pages with subrules and examples as we try to give you a complete picture of the problem.

Collective nouns (see Chapter 15) may take either a singular or plural inflection depending on the meaning.[2]

The Gang of Four has been discredited. (= the gang as a whole)
The Gang of Four have been discredited. (= the individual gang members)

Rules for persistently troublesome cases

1   *Some common and proper nouns ending in* -s—*including* -ics *nouns—are singular and take a singular inflection.*

No news is good news.   Physics is a difficult subject.
This series is very interesting. Wales is a lovely area to visit.

2   *Plural titles of books, plays, operas, films, etc., take the singular.*

Great Expectations was written by   *The Pirates of Penzance* is a lovely
   Dickens.   operetta.

3   *Nouns occurring in sets of two take the singular when the noun* pair *is present, but the plural when* pair *is absent—regardless of whether one pair or more is being referred to.*

A pair of trousers is on the sofa.   This pair of shoes needs new heels.
Todd's trousers are on the sofa.   These shoes need new heels.

4   A number of *takes the plural, but* the number of *takes the singular.*

A number of students have dropped that course.
The number of students in this school is 2,000.

5   *Fractions and percentages take the singular when they modify a mass noun and the plural when they modify a plural noun; either the singular or the plural may be used when they modify a collective noun.*

MASS: One-half of the toxic waste has escaped.
             Fifty percent of the toxic waste has escaped.

PLURAL: Two-thirds of the students are satisifed with the class.
             Sixty-six percent of the students are satisfied with the class.

---

2. In American English there still is a strong tendency to use the singular inflection with a collective noun subject. In British English plural inflections are more freely used:
   (Am. E.)   My family is on vacation.   (Br. E.)   My family are on holiday.

COLLECTIVE: One tenth of the population of Egypt $\left\{\begin{array}{l}\text{is Christian} \\ \text{are Christians}\end{array}\right\}$.

Ten percent of the population of Egypt $\left\{\begin{array}{l}\text{is Christian} \\ \text{are Christians}\end{array}\right\}$.

6 *Conflicting rules for* none *and problems with* all, each, *and* every.

Many traditional grammars state that when used as a subject, *none* is always singular regardless of what follows in a prepositional phrase. The argument for this rule is that *none* means *not one.* However, usage surveys give us a different picture. When *none* refers to a mass noun, the inflection is uncontroversially singular, but when it refers to a plural noun—human or nonhuman—usage seems to be more or less equally divided between the singular and plural inflection.

The percentages that we supply under the example sentences indicate the proportion of native speakers that favored each form in the survey cited.

MASS: None of the toxic waste has escaped.

PLURAL (Human):   None of those firemen _____ hearing the alarm
        enjoy—47%; *enjoys*—53%

go off. (Van Shaik, 1976)

PLURAL (Nonhuman):   None of the costumes he has tried _____ him.
        fit—50%; *fits*—50%

(Farhady, 1977)

Clearly, the traditional rule is inadequate. Additional research based on analysis of spoken and written English should be carried out to see if a more adequate rule of usage exists. In the meantime, ESL/EFL teachers must be aware of the fact that when *none* refers to a plural noun, either the singular or the plural inflection may be used, if current usage is any indication.

Although *none* is the most problematic quantifier with respect to subject-verb agreement, ESL/EFL learners also experience problems with the quantifiers *all, each,* and *every(one).*

The rules for subject-verb agreement with *all* are as follows: If the noun that *all* modifies is a mass noun subject, then subject-verb agreement is singular:

All (of) (the) water is polluted.

If *all* modifies a countable plural subject noun, subject-verb agreement is plural:

All (of) (the) students have arrived.

A problem arises, however, when *all* is used to quantify a collective noun subject (see Chapter 15). Theoretically, one should be able to use either singular or plural subject-verb agreement in such cases. We tested such an item with 40 native speakers of English, and the results seem to support this theoretical duality:

All of my family _____ present.
        is—55%; *are*—43%; no response—2%

Many style books, however, admonish us not to use the preposition *of* after the quantifier *all* in our writing. We thus administered a similar item, minus the *of,* to the same group of people a week later. The results were as follows:

All my family _____ present.
        is—68%; *are*—26%; used both—6%

Thus the presence or absence of the preposition *of* definitely seems to have an effect on subject-verb agreement, since in the item without *of* our consultants favored singular agreement to a noticeably greater degree.

When the subject quantifier is *each* or *every(one)*, the rules are more straightforward. When the quantified subject noun is singular, there is no problem: the subject-verb agreement is always singular, e.g.:

$$\left\{ \begin{array}{l} \text{Each} \\ \text{Every} \\ \text{Each and every} \end{array} \right\} \text{student has a textbook.}$$

However, when the quantified noun refers to a definite plural set, there can be problems for ESL students since the quantifiers are grammatically singular yet the set they are modifying is notionally plural, e.g.:

$$\text{Each of his examples} \left\{ \begin{array}{l} \text{was} \\ \text{were} \end{array} \right\} \text{out of context.}$$

$$\text{Every one of these athletes} \left\{ \begin{array}{l} \text{runs} \\ \text{run} \end{array} \right\} \text{the mile in four minutes.}$$

The traditional prescriptive rule maintains that singular subject-verb agreement applies in such cases because *each* and *every(one)* are functioning as grammatically singular subjects. In these cases native speaker preference closely mirrors the prescriptive rule, since the same 40 subjects that reported divided usage for *all* were in agreement (93% or greater) that the verbs in the above two sentences should be *was* and *runs*. Thus the prescriptive rule and current usage both support singular subject-verb agreement for subjects with *each* and *every(one)*. ESL/EFL students should thus be made aware of this rule and encouraged to follow it, especially in their writing.

7 *Confusion with* majority *and* minority.

Depending on which reference grammar one consults, the nouns *majority* and *minority* are variously described as singular, plural, or collective. Sometimes conflicting statements occur within one and the same grammar.[3]

The only truly satisfying description of these words that we found was in Fowler (1965: pp. 349–350, 366). Fowler maintains that *majority* and *minority* have three related but slightly different meanings:

1. An abstract or generic meaning that refers to superiority of numbers; the reference can be human or nonhuman, but the number is always singular, e.g.:

The great majority is helpless.

2. A specific meaning where one of two or more sets has a numerical plurality (*majority*) or numerical inferiority (*minority*); the examples make reference to political parties, and grammatically these cases are like collectives and can be either singular or plural, e.g.:

The majority was/were determined to press its/their victory.

---

3. Quirk et al. (1972), for example, put *majority* and *minority* under collectives on p. 190 and then on p. 366 cite the following as an example of a grammatically singular subject being perceived as notionally plural, i.e., being attracted to the plural: The majority of them are Moslems.

3. A specific meaning where most (*majority*) or less than half (*minority*) of an explicit set of persons is being referred to. Here the number agreement should always be plural, e.g.:

A majority of my friends advise it.

What we need is a definitive usage study that will confirm or modify Fowler's classification as appropriate.

The limited data we have from Van Shaik and Farhady support Fowler's first and third categories, respectively:

A majority of votes _____ needed to win. (Van Shaik, 1976)
is—81%; *are*—19%

The majority of Democrats _____ opposed to local blackouts of the Game of
are—80%; *is*—20%

the Week. (Farhady, 1977)

We need more complete, more definitive data before we can make a final statement; however, until then, Fowler's analysis seems the best one available.

8 *Plural unit words of distance, money, time, etc., take the singular.*

distance: 1,000 miles is a long distance.
money: 2 million dollars is a lot of money.
time: 5 years is a long time to spend on an M.A. thesis.

9 *Arithmetical operations take the singular.*

addition: One plus one $\left\{ \begin{matrix} \text{is} \\ \text{equals} \end{matrix} \right\}$ two.

subtraction: Four minus two $\left\{ \begin{matrix} \text{is} \\ \text{equals} \end{matrix} \right\}$ two.

multiplication: Two times two $\left\{ \begin{matrix} \text{is} \\ \text{equals} \end{matrix} \right\}$ four.

division: Ten divided by two $\left\{ \begin{matrix} \text{is} \\ \text{equals} \end{matrix} \right\}$ five.

The proximity principle

For the correlatives *either . . . or* and *neither . . . nor* traditional grammarians argue for the proximity rule; i.e., subject-verb agreement should occur with the noun nearest to the verb:

Either my sister or *my brothers are* going to do it.

Neither the books nor *the movie was* helpful.

Either my brothers or *my sister is* going to do it.

Neither the movie nor *the books were* helpful.

Do native speakers consistently follow the proximity principle? Not really, but they support it more strongly for *either . . . or* than they do for *neither . . . nor*.

Either your eyesight or your brakes _____ at fault. (Van Shaik, 1976)
was—31%; *were*—69%

Either the professor or her assistants _____ explain every lesson.
has to—33%; *have to*—67%

(Farhady, 1977)

Neither the students nor the teacher_____that textbook. (Van Shaik, 1976)

likes—49% *like*—51%

Apparently, *neither . . . nor* can easily be perceived as a negative conjunction, which would explain the slight preference for the plural form that Van Shaik's questionnaire elicited.

Personal pronouns pose special problems when used with the correlatives, where the rule of proximity would have us produce *either you or I am, neither you nor he is,* etc. In such cases, Farhady and Van Shaik found even less agreement with the proximity principle than they did when correlatives involved regular nouns:

Neither you nor he_____able to answer the question. (Farhady, 1977)

was—40%; *were*—60%

Neither you nor I _____trained for that job. (Van Shaik, 1976).

am—12%; *is*—15%; *are*—73%

The immediately preceding example is especially interesting because *are* is a gap-filling substitute for *am* in some other constructions (*I'm going, too, aren't I? Aren't I lucky?*). *Am* is apparently too limited a form for use in those correlatives where *I* is the second noun phrase constituent.

One other case where the proximity principle does in fact apply and where traditional grammar would not prescribe its use is in sentences beginning with *there* followed by conjoined noun phrases.[4]

Traditional rule: There are { a girl and two boys / two boys and a girl } in the room.

Proximity rule: There { is a girl and two boys / are two boys and a girl } in the room.

We have informally surveyed many native speakers, and a majority apply the proximity rule in such cases. So again we seem to have a situation where the actual usage preference of native speakers differs from the traditional prescription.

The principle of nonintervention

Many reference grammars make a point of emphasizing that a singular subject noun or pronoun should take a singular verb inflection; the speaker or writer should ignore all plural forms in intervening prepositional phrases and other expressions such as *together with, along with, as well as,* and *not others.*

When common or proper nouns are subjects, the nonintervention principle seems to be well supported:

The major cause of highway accidents in 1976_____drunk drivers.

was—93%; *were*—7%

   (Farhady, 1977)

Peter, along with his 3 brothers,_____to open a store. (Van Shaik, 1976)

plans—84%; *plan*—16%

The boy, not his parents,_____being punished. (Van Shaik, 1976)

is—88%; *are*—12%

However, when the subject followed by the prepositional phrase is *either* or *neither,* the

---

4. For a discussion of subject-verb agreement in *there* sentences with nonconjoined subjects, see Chapter 21.

nonintervention principle weakens and perhaps comes into direct conflict with the proximity principle.[5]

Neither of them _____ ready for marriage. (Van Shaik, 1976)
is—66%; are—34%

Neither of them _____ enough money to afford a car. (Farhady, 1977)
has—50%; have—50%

A problem with relative-clause antecedents

Subject-verb agreement is particularly problematic in certain types of relative clauses. In an example such as the following:

Marsha is one of those rare individuals who _____ finished the M.A. early.
have/has

traditional grammars maintain that the antecedent of *who* is *individuals* and thus *have* is the correct verb form. This antecedent rule conflicts with the nonintervention principle; also, it does not agree at all with the preferences of the native speakers that Van Shaik and Farhady surveyed:

Jack is one of those rare individuals who _____ decided on a definite career.
have—16%; has—84%

(Farhady, 1977)

He is one of the best students that _____ ever come to this school.
have—14%; has—86%

(Van Shaik, 1976)

In fact, of the five survey items Van Shaik and Farhady used, only one was a bit weaker than the two above with respect to contradicting the rule for this type of relative clause:

I am one of those who _____ equal rights. (Van Shaik, 1976)
favor—35%; favors—65%

However, even in this example, where the presence of the *I* subject and pronominal use of *those* appear to be mitigating factors, the rule is still contradicted by an almost 2:1 margin. Clearly, most native speakers are using *one* as the antecedent of *who* or *that,* and the rule should be rewritten to reflect actual usage more accurately.

The clausal subject rule

Traditional grammar tells us that when a clause functions as a subject, the subject-verb agreement is singular—regardless of any plural noun phrases that occur as part of the subject clause or the verb phrase, e.g.:

That the children want friends doesn't surprise me.
What they want is revolutions everywhere.

---

5. Van Shaik (1976) and Farhady (1977) only surveyed responses for *neither.* We suspected that similar problems might also arise with the usage of *either,* so we surveyed 43 consultants concerning the usage of *either* in a similar construction:

Either of the stories _____ going to be acceptable.
is—74%; are—24%; accepted both—2%

While there is also some weakening of the nonintervention principle in this item, it appears that *either* is perceived a bit more strongly as being singular than is *neither.* (See the description of correlative conjunctions in Chapter 23 for further discussion of this issue.)

We do not have survey information on this type of agreement; however, we suspect that the second type of subject clause cited above causes some difficulty—even among native speakers. This seems especially true when the verb is followed by a plural noun phrase.

Conclusion

In most English sentences subject-verb agreement is straightforward and noncontroversial. However, it is quite clear that there are a number of unresolved questions, too. In fact there may well be other problems that we have inadvertently omitted from this discussion. We do not claim to have exhausted the topic.

One of the reasons for the problems is that subject-verb agreement has both syntactic and semantic aspects. When a form is syntactically singular but semantically plural (or vice versa), there is a potential conflict. Another reason may be the existence of several different principles dealing with potentially conflicting aspects of subject-verb agreement. We have seen sentences where the proximity principle conflicts with the nonintervention principle and other sentences where the nonintervention principle conflicts with the antecedent principle. Where such conflicts occur, subject-verb agreement becomes problematic.

Our advice to ESL/EFL teachers is that they be aware of the major traditional rules and also of those instances where current usage seems to clearly deviate from the traditional prescription. Also, informal contexts will permit a greater range of acceptable forms than will formal contexts; thus teachers must be flexible about their correction standards.

In this grammar course our sentence derivations will indicate that subject-verb agreement has taken place only in those sentences where it explicitly applies to produce a special verb form. However, we want to emphasize that a subject-verb agreement check is needed only for sentences that have a tensed auxiliary. In actual fact, though, all verbs other than BE never require subject-verb agreement if past tense appears in the AUX or if the subject is plural.

Consider the following tree diagram and derivation for a sentence which requires subject-verb agreement.

Max is a lawyer.

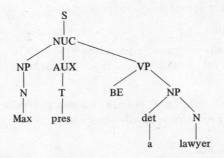

Output of base: Max pres BE a lawyer
Affix attachment: Max BE + pres a lawyer
Subject-verb agreement and morphological rules: Max is a lawyer.

In this example, even if you change the tense to past or if you change the subject (number, person), subject-verb agreement will still be required.

Now consider this second example:

Max knows a lawyer.

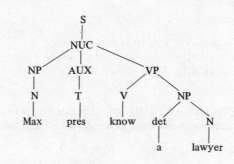

Output of base: Max pres know a lawyer
Affix attachment: Max know + pres a lawyer
Subject-verb agreement and morphological rules: Max knows a lawyer.

In this second example, if the AUX is changed to past tense or if the subject NP is changed to a plural form (e.g., *my brothers*), then there would be no subject-verb agreement applied and the form of the verb would not be affected in any way by the subject-verb agreement rule.

Of course, in those cases where there is no tense in the AUX (i.e., the AUX is a modal auxiliary or IMPER), there never is any subject-verb agreement, since subject-verb agreement is possible only in sentences that have a tensed auxiliary.

TEACHING SUGGESTIONS

1 The copula BE causes ESL/EFL students trouble because it is the most irregular verb in the English language. A lot of practice will have to be given to all its various forms:

present		*past*	
I *am*	we *are*	I *was*	we *were*
you *are*		you *were*	
he, she, it *is*	they *are*	he, she, it *was*	they *were*

a. One technique for practicing *am, are,* and *is* in context is to conduct a chain drill with your students' names:

Student 1:   I am Fatimah. Who are you?
Student 2:   I am José. You are Fatimah. Who are you?
Student 3:   I am Juan. You are José. She is Fatimah. Who are you?

b. Sometimes the plural forms can be practiced using nationalities when two or more students in an ESL/EFL class are from the same country.

Student 1 to 2:   We are Mexican. Are they Mexican?
Student 2:   No, they aren't.
  (To 3 and 4):   What are you?
Students 3 and 4:   We are Persian.

c. The present tense forms of BE should also be practiced with adjectives and prepositional phrases.

Teacher: I am (I'm) tired today. Are you tired?

Student 1:	Yes, I am.
Teacher:	Is he tired?
Class:	Yes, he is.

Student 1:	I am in class. Are you in class?
Student 2:	Yes, I am. Is Ali in class?
Student 1:	Yes, he is. Is Miriam in class?
Student 2:	Yes, she is.

d. To practice the past tense forms of BE, past time contexts must be created. The teacher can set the pattern and then have students practice with each other.

Teacher:	I was in class yesterday. Were you?
Student 1:	Yes, I was.
Teacher:	Were we in class yesterday?
Student 1:	Yes, we were.

(Student 1 takes over the role of teacher.)

Teacher:	Was Carlos late today?
Class:	Yes, he was.
Teacher:	Was Kin Lee late?
Class:	Yes, she was.
Teacher:	Were they late?
Class:	Yes, they were.

(A student then takes over the role of teacher.)

2   The problematic area with regular present tense verbs other than BE involves the third person singular form of the verb. Since the third person singular form of the verb is the only one inflected for person and number agreement, ESL/EFL students frequently omit the necessary *s* marker by simplifying or by overgeneralizing the basic pattern to third person singular. This seems to be a persistent problem, long after students are supplying other verb tense inflections on a regular basis.

I walk	we walk
you walk	
he, she, it walk*s*	they walk

Practice with the present tense should thus put a great deal of focus on the third person singular inflection and on the contrast with all other persons. The teacher can introduce a fictional character *Jack* and talk about what he *does* every day.

He get*s* up at 7 a.m.	He run*s* in the park at 5:00.
He eat*s* breakfast at 7:30.	He come*s* home at 6:00.
He goe*s* to work at 8:00.	etc.

Teacher:	What does Jack do at 7 a.m.?
Student:	He gets up.
Teacher:	When do you get up?
Student:	I get up at 8.
Teacher:	Ask Maria when she gets up and then tell us what you found out.
Student:	When do you get up, Maria?
Maria:	I get up at 6:30.
Student:	She gets up at 6:30.

etc.

EXERCISES

Test your knowledge of what has been presented

1. Provide an original example sentence illustrating each of the following concepts. Underline the pertinent word(s) in your example.

the copula function of BE	third person singular present inflection
an auxiliary function of BE	the proximity principle
collective noun subject	the nonintervention principle
mass noun subject	the clause principle

2. Draw tree diagrams and provide derivations for the following sentences:

a. I am very tired.

b. Jacques is from France.

c. Pedro works for the mayor.

d. We live in an apartment.

e. My parents were teachers.

f. Barbara was working in Rome last year.

3. When is the subject-verb agreement transformation applied? In other words, in what instances should your ESL/EFL students be aware that verbs must agree with subjects in person and number? Also, in what instances should subject-verb agreement *not* be applied?

4. Name and illustrate two cases where the traditional subject-verb agreement rule is *not* supported by current usage.

Test your ability to apply what you know

5. The following sentences contain errors that are commonly made by ESL/EFL learners. How would you make the learners aware of these problems? What exercises would you use to practice the correct pattern and prevent such errors from recurring?

a. *Is you from Mexico?

b. *Felix go to school every day.

c. *I tired.

d. *Nora wills read the book.

e. *They sings in a choir.

6. What will you say to an intermediate to advanced ESL/EFL student who complains to you that you correct mistakes in his compositions when he writes sentences like this one but that he hears native speakers say things like this all the time?

Either my roommates or my friend Bill are going to buy the refreshments.

7. How would you present the rules for fractions and percentages (see rule 5 above) to an intermediate-level high school ESL class? What contexts would you provide to help them have meaningful practice?

BIBLIOGRAPHY

References

Bailey, N., C. Madden, and S. Krashen (1974). "Is There a 'Natural Sequence' in Adult Second Language Learning?" *Language Learning* 24:2, 235–243.

Crews, F. (1980). *A Random House Handbook* (3d ed.). New York: Random House.

Dulay, H., and M. Burt (1974). "Natural Sequences in Child Second Language Acquisition." *Language Learning* 24:1, 37–53.

Farhady, H. (1977). "Subject-Verb Agreement in English: a Usage Study." Unpublished English 215 paper, UCLA.

Fowler, H. (1965). *A Dictionary of Modern English Usage* (2d ed., revised by Sir Ernest Gowers). Oxford: Clarendon Press.

Larsen-Freeman, D. (1975). "The Acquisition of Grammatical Morphemes by Adult ESL Students," *TESOL Quarterly* 9:4, 409–421.

Larsen-Freeman, D. (1976). "An Explanation for the Morpheme Acquisition Order of Second Language Learners." *Language Learning* 26:1, 125–134.

Quirk, R., et al. (1972). *A Grammar of Contemporary English,* London: Longman.

Van Shaik, J. D. (1976). "Subject-Verb Agreement in English: What the Books Say vs. Native Speaker Usage." Unpublished English 215 paper, UCLA.

Suggestions for further reading

Other reference grammars or handbooks on style or usage with useful descriptions of subject-verb agreement are:

House, H. C., and S. E. Harman (1950). *Descriptive English Grammar.* Englewood Cliffs, N.J.: Prentice-Hall.

Irmscher, W. F. (1972). *The Holt Guide to English.* New York: Holt, Rinehart, and Winston.

Quirk, R., and S. Greenbaum (1973). *A Concise Grammar of Contemporary English.* New York: Harcourt, Brace, Jovanovich.

Perrin, P. G., et al. (1962). *Handbook of Current English.* Glenview, Ill.: Scott, Foresman, & Co.

ESL texts with useful discussions and exercises for treating subject-verb agreement are:

Danielson, D., and R. Hayden (1973). *Using English: Your Second Language.* Englewood Cliffs, N.J.: Prentice-Hall.

Hayden, R., et al. (1956). *Mastering American English.* Englewood Cliffs, N.J.: Prentice-Hall.

Praninskas, J. (1975). *Rapid Review of English Grammar.* Englewood Cliffs, N.J.: Prentice-Hall.

For a text with a presentation of the BE copula and accompanying exercises, see:

Brinton, D., and R. Neuman (1982). *Getting Along: English Grammar and Writing* (Book 1). Englewood Cliffs, N.J.: Prentice-Hall, pp. 17–19.

5

The Lexicon

GRAMMATICAL DESCRIPTION

Introduction

In the model of transformational grammar we are sketching, most lexical items or words are inserted into the basic structure of a sentence before the application of transformational rules. This would be the function of the lexical insertion rules depicted in our diagram on page 5.[1] There are a few exceptions to this generalization such as lexical items with grammatical function that are inserted somewhat later by transformational rules (e.g., DO-support discussed in Chapter 8) or surface lexical items that replace other previously inserted lexical items and/or features through the application of transformational rules (e.g., Wh-replacement, which we will consider in Chapter 12).

All lexical items belong to a part of speech. That is to say, they are nouns, auxiliary verbs, verbs, adjectives, adverbs, determiners, intensifiers, or prepositions. The major parts of speech (e.g., nouns, verbs, adverbs, and adjectives) constitute *open* lexical categories—i.e., they are very large categories and can readily add new lexical items or discard old ones. The other parts of speech (e.g., determiners, intensifiers, prepositions, and auxiliary verbs) constitute *closed* lexical categories, since they contain far fewer items than the open ones and they do not readily add new items or discard old ones. They are often described as having a grammatical as well as a lexical function, which is quite true.

Types of lexical information

First of all, every lexical item in the language must be entered in the lexicon (which is a comprehensive list of all words and productive derivational affixes in the language) and represented on a number of levels, which include at least the following:

1. spelling (orthography)
2. phonetic representation (pronunciation and syllabification)
3. syntactic features and restrictions
4. semantic features and restrictions
5. morphological irregularity—only where needed

---

1. We will not discuss how these rules operate in this text but rather will confine our remarks to what ESL/EFL teachers should know about the lexicon.

Consider, for example, the word *child*. The lexical entry for this word would indicate its spelling *child* and its pronunciation, /čayld/. Syntactic features and restrictions would include the word's part of speech (i.e., noun) and the fact that it is a countable noun. Semantic information would include the concept *human* and also information indicating that the word is neutral regarding the male/female distinction. It would contrast the term *child* with similar terms for younger humans such as *infant* and *baby,* and it would also contrast the word with parallel items denoting older humans such as *adolescent* or *adult.* With respect to morphological irregularity the lexical entry would also note the fact that the noun *child* has an irregular and idiosyncratic plural, *children,* which is not generated by the usual rules for forming plurals in English.[2]

Speakers of English use this lexical information in various ways: orthographical information is used when we alphabetize things, phonological information is used when we make words rhyme, and syntactic information is used when we match determiners and nouns appropriately, e.g.:

this child	*these child	many children
these children	*this children	*much children

Semantic information is used when we accept a lexical item in certain constructions as meaningful:

The child slept two hours.

and reject it in others as nonsensical—at least in any literal sense:

*The child evaporated two hours ago.

In order to truly know how to use a word appropriately in English, then, a speaker would need to know more than simply the "meaning" of the word.

Productive processes of English word formation

In addition to fairly structured information such as we have given in the above examples, the lexicon also contains rules governing the three productive processes of English word formation: compounding, affixation, and incorporation.

Compounding

Compounding is a word-formation process that occurs in some languages but not in others. For example, the Germanic languages (this includes English) and the Chinese languages make rich use of compounding, but the Romance languages (e.g., French, Spanish, Italian, and Portuguese) make less frequent use of compounding and when they do employ this device, the rules are different. ESL/EFL students who speak a native language with little or no word compounding may have trouble understanding and using compound words.[3] Such students may paraphrase instead of using a compound (e.g., *the sheet for the bed* instead of *the bed sheet*) or reverse the order of elements in a compound (e.g., say "wine table" for "table wine"). Some of the most frequent English compounding patterns are:

Noun + Noun: milkman, baby blanket, raincoat, ...
Adj. + Noun: blackbird, greenhouse, cold cream, ...

---

2. The only way that nouns are morphologically irregular is with respect to plural formation. Only countable nouns, of course, can have such irregularity.

3. The written form of compound words is an additional complication. Some compounds are written as one word, some as two words, and some are hyphenated. Use your dictionary when in doubt.

Noun + Verb-er: baby sitter, can opener, screw driver, . . .
Adj/Adv + Noun-ed: bow-legged, near-sighted, dim-witted, . . .
Directional particle + Verb: overstate, underrate, outdo, . . .

There are many other compounding patterns. For additional patterns and lists of compound words in English, you should consult Marchand (1969) or Adams (1973).

Morphological affixation

There are two kinds of morphological affixes in English: inflectional and derivational. An inflectional affix carries grammatical meaning and changes the form of a word without changing its basic part of speech. An example of an inflectional affix would be the *ing* on the verb *watch* as in "I am watching television." *Watch* still serves as a verb after the *ing* has been affixed but the *ing* signals that the action is a currently ongoing one.

There are eight inflectional affixes in English:

progressive aspect (watch*ing*)   plural (book*s*)
third person singular present tense   possessive (John'*s*)
  (walk*s*)   comparative (clear*er*)
past tense (jump*ed*)   superlative (clear*est*)
past participle (eat*en*)

They all come at the end of a word and hence are called suffixes. The only inflectional affixes which are not suffixes are the irregular plural, past tense, and past participle forms (e.g., *men, took, swum*) which have internal inflectional vowel changes or no changes at all (e.g., *deer, put*).

We should also note that the pronunciation of some of the regular suffixes changes depending upon the phonological environment in which they occur. The *-ed* regular past suffix, for instance, is pronounced /əd/ after /t/ and /d/ as in *wanted* but is pronounced /d/ after all other voiced sounds (e.g., *played*) and /t/ after all other voiceless sounds (e.g., *walked*).

The regular plural, possessive, and third person singular present tense suffixes all pattern the same way:

	Plural	Possessive	Third person singular present tense
After /s/, /z/, /š/, /ž/, /č/, /ǰ/ the suffix is pronounced as /əz/	judges	Rose's	rushes
After all other voiced sounds, the suffix is pronounced as /z/	dogs	John's	runs
After all other voiceless sounds the suffix is pronounced as /s/	cats	Mark's	walks

The derivational affixes can change the meaning and sometimes the part of speech of the word stem. They can be prefixes (e.g., *un*bend) and suffixes (e.g., argu*ment*). A word can even have both (e.g., *un*think*able*). When one part of speech is changed to another, it is more likely to be through the addition of a suffix than a prefix.

Working with your ESL/EFL students on the meanings of some common prefixes (e.g., *anti-, bi-, ex-, inter-, pre-*) and common suffixes (e.g., *-able, -er, -ish, -less, -ness*) can help them to expand their productive and receptive vocabularies. It is also worthwhile spending some time on the common suffixes whose major function is to signal part of speech. -*Ous*, -*ly*, -*ary*, and -*ful*, which transform nouns into adjectives (fam*ous*, friend*ly*, custom*ary*, success*ful*), would be examples of these. Yorkey (1970) includes exercises which could aid you in this endeavor. You may also wish to consult Willis (1975) for a study indicating which affixes your students should master first.

A final point to be made is that when both a derivational and inflectional suffix are affixed to the same word, the inflectional suffix occurs last.

weaknesses   *weaksness

Incorporation

The third important lexical process is incorporation. This occurs when some element in the sentence becomes part of another element. In one kind of incorporation the underlying verb is very general and a noun object has become incorporated into the verb to show that something is being added (1), taken away (2), or used for doing something (3). For example:

1. He put butter on his bread. ⟶ He *buttered* his bread.
   He poured water over the plants. ⟶ He *watered* the plants.

2. She removed the dust from the furniture. ⟶ She *dusted* the furniture.
   She took the pits out of the olives. ⟶ She *pitted* the olives.

3. He cut the log with a saw. ⟶ He *sawed* the log.
   She gathered up the leaves with a rake. ⟶ She *raked* the leaves.

Another kind of incorporation, which is less structurally definable, also adds an affix to a noun which is incorporated and which then functions as an adjective. For example:

There are lots of clouds in the sky today. ⟶ It's *cloudy* today.
The wind is blowing a lot today. ⟶ It's *windy* today.

Note that all these incorporation patterns allow us to express ideas more economically, using fewer words. Different languages have different incorporation patterns. You should be aware of this fact. Both Nilsen (1971) and Celce-Murcia (1973) have done exploratory work on patterns of incorporation, a process which some other linguists describe as *conversion*.

Rules of meaning extension

There are also rules in the lexicon for specifying general processes of meaning extension. An example of one would be the rule which allows us to put an indefinite article before a noncount noun to indicate one subtype of that noun.

General term (uncountable)	Species specific term (countable)
fruit	a (kind of) fruit
gas	a (kind of) gas
salt	a (kind of) salt

Example: I like *fruit*. A *fruit* I am especially fond of is the apricot.

And although it has not been studied carefully, there would also be rules for regular metaphorical extension and usage:

Nature: literal	*Nature: personified*
the wind blew	the wind whispered
the brook rippled	the brook laughed
the saplings swayed	the saplings danced

Syntactically relevant lexical features

Since we are primarily concerned with grammar or syntax in this text, we will now focus on lexical features that are syntactically relevant.

Determiner-noun restrictions

Within noun phrases, determiner-noun restrictions are important since a few determiners co-occur only with uncountable nouns (e.g., *much* and *little*), other determiners co-occur only with singular countable nouns (e.g., *a, each*), and still others co-occur only with plural countable nouns (e.g., *these, all, many, few*). Note that some adjectives also co-occur only with plural nouns (e.g., *various, divergent*). There are, of course, also determiners that may occur with all nouns irrespective of countability or number (e.g., *my, the, his*). However, to ensure that only grammatical sequences are produced, the countability and number restrictions of all determiners and nouns must be explicitly stated in their lexical entries. Nouns have other features that influence syntactic behavior; for example, proper names referring to people (e.g., John, Mr. Jackson, Albert Einstein) do not co-occur with articles; however, common nouns referring to people, do (e.g., a man, the men, some men). More will be said about these matters in Chapter 14, which deals with article usage.

Verb-noun restrictions

The phrase structure rules of our grammar do not distinguish between verbs that take objects (i.e., transitive verbs) and verbs that do not take objects (i.e., intransitive verbs). This information is specified in the lexical entries of verbs. The lexical features (−transitive) for *occur* and (+transitive) for *bring* allow us to generate sentences such as the following:

The event occurred on November 9th.[4]   The man brought a gift.

and help us explain the unacceptability of sentences such as these:

*The event occurred the man.   *The man brought.

There are, of course, verbs that occur both transitively and intransitively with little or no change of meaning. These are the change-of-state verbs, where the direct object in the transitive sentence is the subject of the intransitive one.

John *opened* the door.	The door *opened*.
Inflation *increased* prices.	Prices *increased*.

These verbs would be marked (±transitive) in the lexicon.

There is also a special class of transitive verbs that permits surface deletion of a recoverable, understood object:

Bill smokes cigarettes.	Bill smokes.
Harry drinks liquor.	Harry drinks.

---

4. Note that if this sentence were "The event occurred November 9th," it would still be intransitive. "November 9th" is not the direct object of *occur* but the object of a deleted preposition "on."

Such verbs are, nonetheless, consistently transitive and would be marked as such in the lexicon with the added specification that a recoverable object often does not appear in the surface structure of a sentence containing such a verb. The recoverable object(s) must also be specified in the lexicon.

Some verbs require an adverbial of position or direction and are ungrammatical if the adverbial element is lacking:

The child lay in the hammock.	*The child lay.
I handed the note to John.	*I handed the note.

This information will also be indicated in the lexical entry of such verbs.

Adjective-PP restrictions

Adjectives that follow the verb BE, like verbs, are either transitive or intransitive; however, when an adjective takes an object, this object noun must be preceded by a preposition. Adjectives that can only function transitively like *to be fond of, to be related to* cannot occur without an object.

Intransitive adjectives	*Transitive adjectives*
Joe is handsome.	Sue is fond of sweets.
The book is green.[5]	*Sue is fond.
	John is related to Ralph.
	*John is related.

Again, like verbs, there are adjectives that can be used both transitively and intransitively without a change of meaning in the adjective itself; i.e., the object perhaps limits the scope of the adjective but does not change its meaning. For example:

Sally is nervous.	Sally is nervous about the examination.

All information about the transitivity or intransitivity of adjectives will be included in their lexical entries.

Co-occurrence restrictions involving prepositions

Frequently, a verb or a transitive adjective must be followed by a particular preposition (e.g., to rely *on* X; to discourage X *from* Y; to be cognizant *of* X) or a given noun phrase must be preceded by a particular preposition (e.g., *in* my opinion, *to* my mind, *from* my point of view). Such co-occurrence restrictions must also be made explicit in the lexicon.

Lexical collocation

Other information that should ideally be provided in a lexicon designed to serve ESL/EFL learners are collocations, i.e., those words that frequently co-occur in a predictable

---

5. Note that the intransitive adjective *green* can be used transitively in an idiomatic expression like *He's green with envy,* where "green" is being used figuratively. Separate lexical entries are needed in such cases. Also, many transitive adjectives with intransitive homophones represent a figurative or different meaning without constituting a fixed phrase such as *green with envy*. We are thinking about pairs such as

$$sick—sick\ about\ \begin{Bmatrix} the\ weather \\ the\ game \end{Bmatrix} \qquad mad—mad\ with\ \begin{Bmatrix} love \\ passion \end{Bmatrix}$$

In such cases separate lexical entries for the intransitive and the transitive adjective are also needed.

syntagmatic relationship.[6] In other words, if a particular noun such as *professor* occurs frequently as the subject of the verb *lecture* in English speech and writing, this fact should be noted because it would be difficult for a learner to use *professor* as a subject appropriately in a variety of contexts without also having knowledge of the verb *lecture*. Such collocational relationships also occur in patterns other than the subject-verb one and are often subtle and not at all obvious to the learner:

Adjective-Noun, e.g., *a tall building* rather than **a high building*
Adverb-Adjective, e.g., *statistically significant* rather than *?statistically important*
Verb-Direct Object, e.g., *ask* or *answer a question* rather than **say* or *tell a question.*

Seal (1981) has investigated in detail certain instances of the immediately preceding pattern. He used both a computer-based corpus analysis and elicitation tasks to identify the significant verb collocates of several nouns functioning as direct objects. The significant collocates were those verbs that co-occurred 10 percent of the time or more when a given noun was functioning as a direct object.

Certainly it would be useful for ESL/EFL learners to have access to the significant collocates of all the lexical items they are expected to acquire and use. Much additional research, however, will have to be carried out before such information will be readily available.

Semantic restrictions[7]

The information given in lexical entries also allows us to account for semantic well-formedness (or semantic incompatibility) in several types of constructions:

1. *subject-verb*
   The door opened.   **The door sneezed.*
   The idea developed.   **The idea laughed.*

2. *verb-object*
   He surprised me.   **He surprised the rock.*
   The noise annoyed us.   **They annoyed my curiosity.*

3. *adjective-noun*
   The pregnant mare   **The pregnant stallion*
                              *The intelligent building
   The intelligent $\left\{\begin{array}{l} \text{child} \\ \text{dog} \end{array}\right\}$

Common nouns are concrete or abstract, and concrete nouns are—in addition—living or nonliving, animate or inanimate, and human or nonhuman. Verbs, likewise, are often very specific concerning the kinds of subject or object nouns they can co-occur with. For example,

---

6. Syntagmatic relationships exist within the sentence: subject-verb, verb-object; determiner-noun; intensifier-adjective. In opposition to syntagmatic relationships, we have paradigmatic relationships, which exist across sentences: I *am* a student; You *are* a student; He *is* a student, etc.

7. These semantic restrictions are probably universal and thus are not something we have to teach second language learners; however, they still constitute information that is included in the lexical entry of an item and that is part of its meaning. Also, as we already mentioned above, semantic restrictions are often disregarded in figurative extensions of meaning. This is particularly true of certain types of fiction, e.g., children's stories, fables, allegories.

the verb *sneeze* requires an animate subject—and a higher-order animal at that. The verb *pray* is even more specific in that it requires a human subject. Verbs such as *surprise* and *annoy* require animate objects. An adjective like *pregnant* can only modify or describe a mature female animate noun, whereas an adjective like *intelligent* may co-occur with any higher-order animate noun. Furthermore, only living nouns (i.e., plants and animals) can literally *die,* and only concrete (as opposed to abstract) nouns can literally do things like *fall, break,* and *mildew.* All such semantic co-occurrence restrictions are captured in the lexicon.

Another fact to reiterate is that when words look and sound the same but have very different meanings and functions (e.g., *work* in "I have a lot of *work*" and "He can't *work* the machine") there must be a separate lexical entry for each distinct meaning and function.

Fillmore's approach to distinguishing verb meanings (see Fillmore, 1968) has applicability here. Beginning with the examples below, Fillmore proceeds to elaborate the semantic distinctions that must be captured in the lexical entries of the verbs *touch, strike,* and *break.*

1. Peter touched the window.   3.   Peter broke the window.
2. Peter struck the window.

Fillmore points out that *break* in (3) is different from *touch* in (1) and *strike* in (2) in that it has a related intransitive sentence that the other two verbs do not have:

4. The window broke.

In addition, the verb *break* seems to require that its theme (i.e., *window* in the above examples) be rigid, while *touch* and *strike* do not share this requirement. Consider these examples:

5. Peter touched the dog.   7.   Peter broke the dog.
6. Peter struck the dog.

In (5) and (6) the dog can be a living animal and the difference in meaning is one of relative intensity of impact; i.e., *striking* denotes a stronger impact than *touching.* In (7), however, the dog has to be an inanimate figure made of plaster, glass, etc.

Several other useful generalizations about these verbs were made by Fillmore, but these examples demonstrate that to understand a lexical item entails knowing precisely how it differs from other similar items.

Conclusion

The information the nonnative speaker of English must master regarding the lexicon is extensive. It is not sufficient simply to know many words and their general meanings. For each word the nonnative speaker must master a network of syntactic and semantic features and co-occurrence restrictions in order to use the word appropriately. Often insufficient attention is given to these problems in the ESL/EFL classroom.

TEACHING SUGGESTIONS

1   When teaching vocabulary, it's good not to just teach words but to teach clusters of information that will help students to use the words correctly.

For example, use *a/an* when introducing countable nouns (e.g., *a* theory), use *to* when introducing verbs (e.g., *to* arrive), show that verbs are transitive by adding an indefinite object like *something* (e.g., to propose *something*), and use *to be* when introducing adjectives (e.g., *to be* naïve). Also indicate those prepositions needed—where relevant (e.g., to be interested *in* something).

2 Low intermediate ESL/EFL students often confuse the related forms of a word associated with different parts of speech. If a new vocabulary item has related forms in other parts of speech, these words should also be introduced with example sentences that make the parts of speech easily distinguishable but that make the learner actively discriminate with the fill-in-the-blank process. For example:

<blockquote>
a theory   to theorize   to be theoretical
</blockquote>

John is very (1) _____ about everything. He has just developed a new (2) _____ . He (3) _____ that the less one works, the more one will succeed at certain tasks.

3 Intermediate to advanced ESL/EFL students often confuse related derivations with the same root and the same part of speech; e.g., the following are all adjectives:

various	discriminating	identifying	fortunate
varied	discriminatory	identifiable	fortuitous

Exercises that teach students to distinguish such forms provide contexts that call for one or the other, but not both, forms, e.g.:

<blockquote>
(discriminating, discriminatory)
</blockquote>

a. The black students complained because some of the school regulations were

_____ .

b. I knew that I could trust his judgment; he has _____ taste in such matters.

The students should understand why the words have the same root and part of speech (i.e., what the similarity in meaning is) yet why the words are different (i.e., what the crucial distinction is).

4 To encourage students to use productive affixes and word-formation processes that have been introduced to them, contextualized definition exercises such as the following can be useful:

a. A _____ is a machine that detects smoke in a home, school, or office building and sounds an alarm.

b. Someone who believes in and follows the ideas of Marx is called a _____ .

c. A person who employs others is an (1) _____ ; a person who is employed by someone else is an (2) _____ .

5 Exercises such as the following which encourage the learner to use the appropriate form of a stem are also useful. Whenever possible, it is better to use coherent texts rather than isolated sentences.

It was a (wind) (1) _____ day last Monday. I realized when I got up at 6 a.m. that it would be (not pleasant) (2) _____ to do my half hour of (jog) (3) _____ . However, I got into my sweat suit and (courage) (4) _____ trotted out the front door.

6   One area of lexical subclassification that causes tremendous problems for the ESL/EFL learner is the division of nouns into *mass* and *count*:

Mass	Making mass nouns countable	Count
furniture (*furnitures)	a piece of furniture	a table, a chair . . . tables, chairs
fruit (*fruits)	a piece of fruit	an apple, a pear . . . apples, pears
information (*informations)	a piece of information	a news bulletin, bulletins
chalk (*chalks)	a piece of chalk	
luggage (*luggages)	a piece of luggage	a suitcase, suitcases
clothing (*clothings)	a piece of clothing	a suit, a dress . . . suits, dresses
⋮	⋮	⋮

This list could be extended almost indefinitely. Most languages also utilize—at least semantically—concepts such as singular vs. plural and mass vs. count. The problem is that what is classified and perceived as a mass noun in English often functions as a countable noun in another language. For example, the equivalent of the English mass noun *furniture* is a plural count noun in French and Spanish. Likewise, the Japanese equivalent of the English mass noun *chalk* is perceived as a countable noun. Thus the French speaker says *furnitures* and the Japanese says *a chalk*—even though they have mastered number distinction and article usage. The only way to overcome this problem is to focus on the mass/count distinction at all levels with reference to both grammar and vocabulary.

The above chart offers a paradigm; however, drills such as the following are needed for practicing this distinction with intermediate-level students. For example:

Fill in the blanks with *luggage, a piece of luggage, a suitcase,* or *suitcases*:

John just bought the (1) _____ he will need for his trip to Europe. It's a very handsome set. That attaché case over there is (2) _____ belonging to John. I can't remember how many (3) _____ John will take with him for clothes and personal belongings. I think he's taking too much (4) _____ !

EXERCISES

Test your understanding of what has been presented

1. Provide an original sentence exemplifying each of the following concepts. Underline the pertinent word(s) in your example.

verb requiring an adverb of position	derivational affix
determiner requiring a mass noun	transitive adjective
incorporated noun	transitive verb
change-of-state verb	common noun
noun compound	irregular noun
inflectional affix	proper noun

2. What is the nature of the unacceptability in each of the following examples? Is it a semantic or syntactic problem?

a. *The burglar lurked.
b. *It fascinated the alarm clock.
c. *The cat fell asleep the kitten.
d. *I don't like these book.

Test your ability to apply what you know

3. If your students produce the following utterances, what errors have they made? How would you make them aware of these errors, and what exercises would you prepare to correct them?

a. *I got many *informations* from the book.
b. *He likes good wine and has *discriminatory* taste.
c. *In* my point of view, that's a bad idea.
d. *John is inconsiderate; he's not a *tact* person.
e. *We had to read *much* books for that course.
f. *When the ball *breaked* the window, the boys ran away.
g. *Americans use *crackerfires* on the 4th of July.
h. *Photography has *passionated* me since I was a child.
i. *Mr. Wilson was not aware *to* his daughter's problems.
j. *Mrs. Henderson was very *in*pleasant to me.

4. With regard to the singular/plural number distinction in English, how would you classify nouns like the following? If you feel they form a distinct group, explain why and indicate how this should be accounted for in the lexicon.

class	team	committee	herd
group	crew	regiment	flock

BIBLIOGRAPHY

References

Adams, V. (1973). *An Introduction to Modern English Word Formation.* London: Longman.
Celce-Murcia, M. (1973). "Incorporation: A Tool for Teaching Productive Vocabulary Patterns." *Workpapers in TESL,* UCLA, vol. 7.
Fillmore, C. J. (1968). "Lexical Entries for Verbs." *Foundations of Language* 4, 373–393.
Marchand, H. (1969). *Categories and Types of Present-Day English Word Formation* (2d ed.). Munich: C.H. Beck'sche Verlagsbuch.
Nilsen, D. (1971). "The Use of Case Grammar in Teaching EFL." *TESOL* 5:4, 293–302.
Seal, B. (1981). *In Search of Significant Collocations.* Unpublished M.A. thesis in TESL, UCLA.
Willis, M. (1975). *Affixation in English Word Formation and Applications for TESL.* Unpublished M.A. thesis in TESL, UCLA.
Yorkey, R. (1970). *Study Skills for Students of English as a Second Language.* New York: McGraw-Hill.

Suggestions for further reading

For some background reading on lexical theory, see these references:

Aronoff, M. (1976). *Word Formation in Generative Grammar.* Linguistic Inquiry Monograph 1. Cambridge, Mass.: MIT Press.
Gruber, J. (1965). *Studies in Lexical Relations.* Unpublished doctoral dissertation in linguistics, MIT. (Copies have been available off and on from the Indiana University Linguistics Club, Bloomington, Ind.)

For nontechnical references dealing with word derivation in English (lists and explanations are provided), see the books by Adams (1973) and Marchand (1969) cited in the above references.

For a list of verbs and adjectives followed by particular prepositions, consult:

Clark, R., P. Moran, and A. Burrows (1981). *The ESL Miscellany.* Brattleboro, Vt.: Pro Lingua Associates.

For exercises dealing with problematic lexical distinctions such as *make/do* and *say/tell,* see:

Brinton, D., and R. Neuman (1982). *Getting Along: English Grammar and Writing* (Book 2). Englewood Cliffs, N.J.: Prentice-Hall, pp. 55, 64–66, 172–173, 225–226.

For many examples of compounding patterns, see:

Bolinger, D. (1975). *Aspects of Language* (2d ed.). New York: Harcourt, Brace, Jovanovich, pp. 114–115.

For concrete suggestions and materials regarding the teaching of vocabulary and/or of affixes, see the following:

Barnard, H. (1971). *Advanced English Vocabulary* (several volumes have appeared since 1971). Rowley, Mass.: Newbury House.

Baudoin, E. M., E. S. Bober, M. A. Clarke, B. K. Dobson, and S. Silberstein (1977). *Reader's Choice.* Ann Arbor: University of Michigan Press.

Celce-Murcia, M., and F. Rosensweig (1979). "Teaching Vocabulary in the ESL Classroom," in Celce-Murcia and McIntosh (eds.), *Teaching English as a Second or Foreign Language.* Rowley, Mass.: Newbury House.

Frank, M. (1972). *Modern English: Exercises for Non-native Speakers* (Part I). Englewood Cliffs, N.J.: Prentice-Hall.

Martin, A. V., et al. (1977). *Guide to Language and Study Skills.* Englewood Cliffs, N.J.: Prentice-Hall.

McKay, S. (1980). "Teaching the Syntactic, Semantic and Pragmatic Dimensions of Verbs." *TESOL Quarterly* 14:1, 17–26.

Willis, M. (1975). Cited in the above references. See especially pp. 139–157, which deal with textbook evaluation and teaching suggestions.

Yorkey, R. (1970). See above references.

6

The Tense-Aspect System: Forms and Meanings

GRAMMATICAL DESCRIPTION

Introduction

In Chapter 3 a form-oriented, transformational account of tense and aspect in English was presented, and the following phrase structure rule was introduced:

$$\text{AUX} \longrightarrow \left\{ \begin{array}{l} \left\{ \begin{array}{l} \text{T} \\ \text{M} \end{array} \right\} \text{(PM) (perf) (prog)} \\ \text{IMPER} \end{array} \right\}$$

According to this rule the auxiliary of a nonimperative English sentence has either a modal auxiliary or a tense marker (which a later rule specifies as either *past* or *present*), and several optional components: periphrastic modals, perfective aspect, and progressive aspect. The expression "future tense" was viewed as a misnomer, since in English finite verb stems are not inflected to express future time in the way they are in other languages such as French. English was shown to have several nontense means of signaling future time (e.g., modal auxiliaries, periphrastic modals, and adverbs of time).

However, the language teacher must be concerned with meaning as well as form. The meaning of tenses entails a language-specific way of dealing with time and the relationship of events and interlocutors to time. Because tense systems are language-specific, it is not surprising that ESL/EFL learners have a great deal of difficulty mastering the English tense-aspect system. Thus it is important that you understand as much as possible about it.

Over the years English teachers and some traditional grammarians have blurred the formal distinctions between time, tense, and aspect. Instead they have tended to refer to the twelve traditional English "tenses," which we shall review here by citing the major uses (though by no means all uses) of each such "tense." We feel that this review is necessary because so many ESL/EFL teaching materials and many reference grammars, too, view the English tense system in this way. If you are working with beginning or low-intermediate-level students, you may choose to introduce your students to the sentence-level uses of these twelve tenses as they are listed below. Once your students appear comfortable with these, however, we recommend that you help your students to view tense usage from a higher, or discourse-level, perspective. One way to do this is to introduce the Bull framework, which we discuss below.

The uses of the twelve traditional "tenses"

In our discussion of the tenses that follows, it should be noted that tenses 1 through 8 are more frequent and important to the ESL/EFL learner than tenses 9 through 12. Furthermore, of these more important tenses, tenses 1, 2, 3, 5, and 7 can be viewed as the core system.

Of course, one of the major challenges in teaching students how to use the tenses of English is not so much having students learn the uses of each individual tense but getting students sensitized to the differences between and among the tenses. Helz (1979) can be consulted for a discussion of each tense and its uses vis-à-vis the other tenses with which it contrasts.

1. Simple present

a. Habitual actions in the present:

> He walks to school every day.

b. General timeless truths, e.g., physical laws or customs:

> Water freezes at 0° C.
> Mexicans take a "siesta" after their midday meal.

c. With BE and other stative verbs in the present tense (see under Stative Verbs below): Sensory perception (e.g., see, hear, taste, . . .)

> I see a large house on the corner.

Mental perception and emotions (e.g., know, doubt, love, hate)

> I know Mr. Jackson is a teacher.   Sally loves daisies.

Relationships (e.g., have, own, owe, belong to, . . .)

> He owes me a lot of money.   The car belongs to Bill.

d. In the subordinate clause with verbs in future time:

> After he finishes work, he'll do the errands.

e. In the subordinate clause of future conditional sentences:

> If she passes the bar exam, she'll be able to practice law.

f. Expresses future (when a scheduled event is involved; usually with future time adverbial):

> I have a meeting next Wednesday at that time.

g. Present event/action or speech act:

> Here comes the pitch; Jackson swings   I resign from the commission.
> and misses.

h. Conversational historical present[1] (used to refer to past events in narration):

> "So he stands up in the boat and waves his arms to catch our attention."

---

1. See Wolfson (1978) for a fuller description of the function of this use of the present tense form.

2. Present progressive (or continuous)

a. Event/action in progress:

> He is attending a meeting now.   He is walking to school now.

b. Temporary activity (action will end and therefore lacks the permanence of the simple present tense):

> I'm studying geology at the University   Phyllis is living with her parents.
> of Colorado.

c. Repetition or iteration in a series of similar ongoing actions:

> Henry is kicking the soccer ball around the backyard.

d. Express future (when event is planned; usually with future time adverbial):

> She's coming tomorrow.

e. Emotional comment on present habit (usually co-occurring with *always* or *forever*):

> He's always acting up at these affairs.   He's always delivering in a clutch situa-
> (disapproving)   tion. (approving)

3. Simple past

a. A definite single completed event/action in the past:

> I attended a meeting of that commit-   He walked to school yesterday.
> tee last week.

b. Habitual or repeated action/event in the past (suggests that some change in this habit/event has taken place):

> Sam walked his dog every day last   It snowed almost every weekend last
> year.   winter.

c. An event with duration that applied in the past with the implication that it no longer applies in the present:

> Prof. Nelson taught at Yale for 30 years.

d. With stative verbs in the past time (cf. items in c under simple present tense):

> He appeared to be a creative genius.   She loved daisies.
> I saw a large house on the corner.   He owed me a lot of money.
> I knew that John was a teacher.

e. Past conditional or imaginative events in the subordinate clause (to be discussed further in Chapter 25):

> If he took better care of himself, he   I wish you were here.
> wouldn't be absent so often.

4. Past progressive

a. An action in progress at a specific point of time in the past:

> He was walking to school at 8:30 this morning.

b. Past action (simultaneous with some other event):

Karen was washing her hair when the phone rang.

While Alec was traveling in Europe, his house was painted.

c. Repetition or iteration in some ongoing past action:

Jake was coughing all night long.

5. Simple future (here just with *will*)

a. An action to take place at some definite future time:

He will walk to school tomorrow.

b. A future habitual action or future state:

Joel will take the bus to work next year.   I'm sure everything will be fine.

c. A situation that may obtain in the present and will obtain in the future but with some future termination in sight:

Nora will live in Caracas until she finishes school.

d. Future conditionals (main clause):

If you go, you'll be sorry.

6. Future progressive

a. An action that will be in progress at a specific time in the near future:

He will be walking to school at 8 a.m. tomorrow.

b. Duration of some specific future action:

Mavis will be working on her thesis for the next ten years.

7. Present perfect

Often expresses how the speaker views himself relative to the event(s) he is talking about:[2]
a. A situation that began in the past and that continues into the present:

I have been a teacher since 1972.

b. A past experience with current relevance:

I have already seen that movie.

c. A very recently completed action:

Mort has just finished his homework.

d. An action that went on over time in the past and that is completed with the moment of speaking:

The value of the Johnsons' house has doubled in the last 4 years.

e. With verbs in subordinate clauses of time or condition:

She won't be satisfied until she has finished another chapter.

If you have done your homework, you can watch TV.

---

2. See Moy (1977) for a readable account of how use of the present perfect can relate to the speaker's point of view.

8. Present perfect progressive

a. A situation or habit that began in the past (recent or distant) and that continues up to the present:

> I have been living in Seattle for 7 years now.
> He has been walking to school for several years now.
> Burt has been going out with Alice.

b. The incompleteness of an action in progress:

> I have been reading a book.

(Compare with the completed meaning of "I have read a book.")

9. Past perfect

a. An action completed in the past prior to some other past event:[3]

> He had already walked to school before I could offer him a ride.

b. In the subordinate clause of past conditional or imaginative events:

> If Sally had studied harder, she would have passed the exam.

10. Past perfect progressive

a. An action or habit taking place over a period of time in the past prior to some other past event:

> He had been walking to school before his father bought him a bicycle.

> Carol had been working very hard, so her doctor told her to take a vacation.

b. A past action that is in progress gets interrupted by another past action:

> We had been planning to vacation in Pennsylvania but changed our minds when so much of it got badly flooded.

11. Future perfect

a. A future action that will be completed prior to a specific future time:

> I will have finished all this typing by 5 p.m.[4]

b. A state or action that will be completed in the future prior to some other future time or event (near or distant):

> He will have walked to school before you finish your breakfast.

> At the end of the summer the Blakes will have been married for 10 years.

---

3. Note that since a time word like *before* in this example already tells us the order of events, simple past tense may be used instead of the past perfect in this sentence without any loss of meaning:

> He already walked to school before I could offer him a ride.

4. Note that the same meaning can be expressed using the copula BE plus adjectives or participles without using a perfect tense, e.g.:

I'll be { ready / finished } by 5 p.m.   The typing will be { available / completed } by noon.

12. Future perfect progressive

a. Durative or habitual action that is taking place in the present and that will continue into the future up until or through a specific future time:

He will have been riding his bike to school for two years by the time he graduates in June.

On Christmas Eve our family will have been living in Chicago for 20 years.

From the semantic point of view the traditional approach to tense and aspect is superior to the structural or transformational approach, since a greater number of meaningful distinctions can be made using the traditional approach. However, this approach is also quite limited in that it views both tense and time as linear,

$$\longleftarrow \text{past} \underline{\quad} \text{present} \underline{\quad} \text{future} \longrightarrow$$

and tries to explain all the above "tenses" using time lines and a simple linear format. What happens is that we get an oversimplification in the representation of complex tenses such as the present perfect. We discuss an improvement over this approach on pages 67–69.

Interaction among the tenses

Another limitation of the traditional system is that it fails to capture the fact that certain tenses tend to occur together in discourse whereas others do not. Consider the following narrative, which is given from the point of view of present time:

I have a splitting headache that I've had for 2 hours. I think I am going to take a couple of aspirin tablets. (possible substitution: "I will (I'll)" for "I am going to")

Here we have the *present* tense in the first clause, the *present* perfect in the second clause, and *going to* with a *present* tense auxiliary in the final clause. Arbitrary changes in the tense sequence are not permissible, and if made, may produce an ungrammatical piece of discourse. Below we have a sequence of tenses describable as *present—past—future,* and this tense switching accounts for the narrative's ungrammaticality:

*I have a splitting headache that I had for two hours; I think I will take a couple of aspirin tablets.

(In the above version, the simple past form *had* is used where the present perfect *have had* is required.)

Similar observations can be made about samples of discourse written from the point of view of past time. Consider the following:

The little girl cried her heart out. She had lost her Teddy Bear and was convinced she wasn't ever going to find him. (possible substitution: "would never" for "wasn't ever going to")

The first clause is simple *past,* the second clause is the *past* perfect, and the third is the *going to* future but with a *past* tense auxiliary. Again, if we make arbitrary changes in the tenses used in the narrative, there will be negative consequences for the flow of the discourse:

The little girl cries her heart out. She lost her Teddy Bear and is convinced she won't ever find him.

This version of the narrative is comprehensible and not obviously ungrammatical, but it comes out sounding somewhat disjointed and awkward when compared with the original, since one does not normally jump from present tense to past tense to future tense within one and the same piece of discourse. Yet this is precisely what many nonnative speakers of English do when they speak and write in English. One reason for this may be that they have learned the English tense system bit by bit at the sentence level without ever learning how the bits interact in longer pieces of discourse.

The Bull framework

The best system that we have encountered for explaining the subtleties of the English tense-aspect system at the discourse level is the Bull framework. (We should mention at the outset, however, that it should be used only with intermediate and advanced-level students because of its complexity.) This framework was first developed by William Bull in 1960 for describing tense in Spanish, but it can be applied to any language. It posits four axes of orientation, or points of view, with respect to time: present, past, future, and hypothetical. We will not discuss Bull's hypothetical axis in this chapter because we treat conditional sentences in detail in Chapter 25. Therefore, we will apply Bull's system to English using three of his four axes of time: present, past, and future. Each axis has a neutral or basic form and two possible marked forms—one signaling a time *before* the basic time of that axis and the other signaling a time *after* the basic time of that axis. Based on this semantic framework each "tense" of any language can then be placed in the appropriate slot on the appropriate time axis. See the chart below for our interpretation of Bull's axes applied to English and their corresponding verb tense forms.

Axis of orientation	*A time* before *the basic axis time*	*Basic axis time corresponding to the moment of reference*	*A time* after *the basic axis time*
Future time	Before 5:00 he will have finished all the chores. (future perfect)	He {will / is going to} eat dinner at 5:00. (simple future)	After 5:00 he {will / is going to} watch TV. (no distinct form—use simple future)
Present time	He has played golf since 1960. (present perfect)	He plays golf. (simple present)[5]	He is going to play golf next Sunday. (future of the present)
Past time	Before playing golf he had finished all his chores. (past perfect)	He played golf on Saturday afternoon. (simple past)	After playing golf, he went out to dinner with his golf buddies. (no distinct form—use simple past)

This framework helps us understand quite explicitly why two of the preceding narratives were smoother or more grammatical than the other two: in the preferred samples of discourse the author stayed within one axis of orientation, i.e., present or past, and made "before" and

5. Some teachers contend that the present progressive—not the simple present—is the basic present tense form in English; however, the fact that all English verbs can take the simple present but that many verbs cannot take the present progressive would argue against this position. A discussion of verbs that do not take the present progressive is included in the section on Stative Verbs in this chapter.

"after" time references that were appropriate to that axis; the author did not jump from one axis to the other.

Although the present and past time axes are the two axes most frequently used in English, we should at this stage also provide discourse samples that illustrate the application of the Bull framework to the future axis, which is another point of view for the speaker/writer:

> *Future time axis:*
> John will travel to Europe this summer. Before doing that he will have completed his B.A. in Math. After he returns to the States,[6] he will begin graduate work in Management.

The Bull framework and the work of other linguists

Having been presented with the Bull framework, a teacher might wish to raise the question of whether the above analysis differs substantively from previous analyses of the English tense-aspect system, and if so, how. The Bull framework permits an analysis that is like traditional accounts such as Jespersen's (1924), in that meaning has priority over form and also that it retains much of the traditional terminology for the tenses. It is, however, considerably more complex than traditional accounts in that not just one but three parallel time lines (i.e., the three axes of orientation) must be used to illustrate and explicate the system. This permits the system to account for tense sequence in discourse as well as in individual sentences. The Bull framework is also more sophisticated and subtle than the usual structural or transformational account of the English tense-aspect system in that it uses the so-called perfective aspect as a tense marker of "a time before" in each of the various axes, with the result that the progressive is analyzed as the only true marker of aspect in the English tense-aspect system. There is more on this below under Aspect.

Modifications of the Bull framework at the discourse level

Before discussing the role of the progressive aspect in English, we should like to briefly mention the work of Chafe (1972), since it implies modifications that should be added to the Bull framework to make it more complete with regard to accounting for the sequence of tenses in discourse. Chafe (1972:48–49) provides the following piece of discourse and the accompanying tense analysis:

Discourse	*Tense*
a. I went to a concert last night.	a. past
b. They played Beethoven's Second.	b. past
c. You don't hear that very often.	c. generic
d. I enjoyed it.	d. past
e. Next Friday I'm going to another concert.	e. future[7]
f. They're playing something by Stravinsky.	f. future[7]

---

6. Notice how the present tense is used in the subordinate clause while the whole sentence expresses the future. This follows a general principle of historical linguistics which holds that historically older forms and orders are preserved longer in subordinate clauses than in independent clauses. Since Old English had only two tenses (present and past) and used the present tense to express future time, this principle seems to apply here.
   For further discussion of this tense subordination problem, see Tregidgo (1979).

7. "Future" is Chafe's term for these tenses. Using the Bull framework, we would call them "after present" tenses occurring in the present time axis. Note that using *will,* the true marker of the future, would sound less appropriate than "after present" forms in e and f.

Using this illustration, he makes several generalizations. First of all, when a *tense* or *time* has been established in a discourse, this tense must be maintained unless:

A "generic" tense (i.e., simple present in c) temporarily suspends the requirement to continue the use of the same tense. (See the way c suspends the past tense requirement followed in a, b, and d.)

or

A new explicit time marker is introduced into the discourse which terminates the old tense and replaces it with another. (See *next Friday* in e and the new tense used in e and f.)

We feel that by combining Chafe's observations with the Bull framework, the sequence of tenses in discourse can be more adequately described than it has been previously.[8]

Aspect

Whereas tense relates to the time when an activity or state occurs, aspect in a language comments upon some characteristic of the activity or state. For example, the ING of the progressive is the aspectual marker in English. Its basic semantic function is to indicate that an activity is in process, i.e., has some duration, and therefore is imperfective or incomplete. However, the semantic features of the verb also influence the meaning of the progressive in any given sentence.

When it is attached to verbs denoting punctual actions (e.g., snap your fingers, slap his face), the progressive aspect is used to signal an iterative process, i.e., repetition, as opposed to a single act, which the simple tense signals.

> He is kicking the ball. ⎫
> He kicks the ball.   ⎬ present time

This distinction holds regardless of the time of the action.

> He was kicking the ball. ⎫
> He kicked the ball.   ⎬ past time

Other meanings that the ING can signal are likewise dependent upon the nature of the verb to which it is attached.

With quasi verbs of state (genuine verbs of state will be discussed below), in the present tense, ING signals a temporary (or specific) as opposed to a permanent (or nonspecific) state of affairs:

> Bill's living with his parents.   Bill lives with his parents.

In the past tense, the effect of the aspectual marker is a bit more subtle, since Bill's living with his parents is no longer true in either sentence:

> Bill was living with his parents.   Bill lived with his parents.

However, in the first sentence, we still see the effect of the ING as giving us the sense that

---

8. You may find many instances where recourse to Bull's work and to Chafe's still does not explain all acceptable sequences of tense in English. Their work is just a good beginning. Much more still needs to be done.

Bill's residence with his parents took place over an extended period of time. Since we can then view the state as having duration, we can talk about other events that took place while he was residing with his parents.

> Bill was living with his parents when he had the accident.

The simple past tense treats the state as being completive and therefore does not readily allow us to discuss events that took place during Bill's residence.

> ?Bill lived with his parents when he had the accident.

With durative actions (e.g., water the lawn, cook dinner), the progressive aspect suggests a single ongoing occurrence or a temporary state of affairs rather than a regular or habitual occurrence such as the simple present signals.

> Josh is cooking dinner.   Josh cooks dinner.

In the past tense the distinction is again more subtle, but still we can see how the use of the ING allows us to view the event in progress and discuss something that is going on simultaneous with the dinner being cooked.

> Josh cooked dinner.   Josh was cooking dinner...
>
> Josh cooked dinner when his friends   Josh was cooking dinner when his
>   came by.   friends came by.

The use of the simple past in the above example indicates the actions were sequential, not simultaneous (i.e., his friends came by and then he cooked dinner).

ING may also, when combined with the perfective, signal noncompletion as opposed to completion of the action in question.

> I have been reading the book.   I had been reading the book. . . .
> I have read the book.   I had read the book.

Thus, what the ING conveys is somewhat dependent upon the verb to which it is attached but, in general, signals that the activity/event is in progress and therefore incomplete regardless of the tense it co-occurs with. The notion of the progressive aspect is a useful one for you to be aware of. By having your students understand the basic meaning of the ING, they can see how the progressive tenses which incorporate the ING aspect differ systematically from the simple tenses.

In Chapter 3, we noted that there are two aspectual forms in the language: the progressive and the perfective. Although some analyses of the English verb phrase system do treat the perfective as an aspectual marker, we will adhere to the Bull framework and propose that the so-called perfective aspect is really an integral part of the English tense system, since it involves "time." (Recall that all the perfect forms signal "a time before the basic time" in each of the axes of orientation that Bull posits.) Thus, although English has two aspectual forms, only one, the progressive, conveys true aspectual meaning.

In terms of teaching the tenses, the advantage of using the Bull system is that one can begin by teaching four tenses:

> simple future   simple past
> simple present   future of the present (*BE going to*)

For the first three of these, one simply adds one form to them, the perfective (HAVE . . . EN), to form the time *before* the basic time within each axis:

future perfect	past perfect
present perfect	

Then to each of the seven forms, one can add the progressive aspect (BE . . . ING) to express a more limited meaning:

future progressive	future perfect progressive
present progressive	present perfect progressive
past progressive	past perfect progressive
future-of-present progressive	

Thus from six forms, i.e., four tenses and two aspect markers, we have accounted for a total of 14 "tenses."

Stative verbs[9]

We noted earlier (footnote 5) that not all English verbs can occur with the progressive aspect. Those that normally do not are verbs of state—or stative verbs—which fall into the following main categories:

1. *Sensory perception*—e.g., *see, hear, feel, taste, smell*—when an immediate and literal sensory perception is being expressed without any suggestion of hallucination or impermanence.

(perceptual)

I see a tree behind the house.
*I am seeing a tree behind the house.

(conceptual)[10]

I'm looking at a tree behind the house.

2. *Mental perception*—e.g., *know, believe, doubt, understand, remember*—with no expression of change over time or of discrete successive states.

(perceptual)

Zeke knows the answer.
*Zeke is knowing the answer.

(conceptual)

Zeke is thinking about the answer.

Note that general stative verbs that can express either sensory or mental perception are *seem* and *appear*.

3. *Emotion*—e.g., *want, desire, love, hate, like, dislike*—without any added expression of change over time or of exceptionally strong feeling.

We desire an explanation.   *We are desiring an explanation.

---

9. We have not included verbs of internal sensation (e.g., *hurt, itch, feel, ache*) among the subclasses of verbs that do not take the progressive aspect, since this subclass seems to occur with or without the progressive with very little difference in meaning:

My back aches./My back is aching.

10. Note that for perceptual events (sensory or mental) the subject is an experiencer, not an agent, whereas for conceptual events (sensory or mental) the subject is an agent—hence the distinction we get between see/look at, hear/listen to, etc. Many verbs with more than one meaning also exhibit this semantic distinction, e.g.:

I'm thinking about his speech. (conceptual—subject is agent)   What did you think of his speech? (perceptual—subject is experiencer)

Conceptual events, therefore, can occur with the progressive aspect; perceptual events cannot.

4. *Measurement*—e.g., *weigh, cost, measure, equal*

This steak weighs 10 oz.   *This steak is weighing 10 oz.

5. *Relationship*—e.g., *have, own, contain, entail, belong*

Phil has a new car.   *Phil is having a new car.

The archetypal verb of state is, of course, the copula BE:

He is hot.   *He's being hot.

In addition to resisting the progressive, stative verbs also do not occur in the imperative in those cases where the subject of the verb does not control the action (i.e., cannot be the agent).

*See a tree!   *Have a brother!
*Know the answer!   *Be hot.

Stative and nonstative variants

The difficulty with this verb class and its subdivisions is that many stative verbs—even the copula BE—have nonstative counterparts that are active in meaning and that may occur with the progressive.

STATE (subject is not the agent)
The steak weighs 12 oz.
You are a fool.
I taste cinnamon in these rolls.

ACTION (subject is agent)
The butcher is weighing the steak.
You're being a fool.
John has been tasting wine for three years now. (i.e., his occupation)

Separate lexical entries are needed for each meaning. Note that two of the stative verbs have a lexically distinct action counterpart (e.g., *see/look at, hear/listen to*). All this means that we have to think in terms of stative "meanings" rather than stative "verbs" to correctly understand and explain restrictions on the use of the progressive aspect in English.

Additional facts

Although we have called attention to several of these before, there are a number of difficult points that your students will have to learn about the English tense-aspect system such as:
  1. The use of the simple present and the present progressive to express future time:

The plane leaves at 10 p.m.   I am visiting my aunt tomorrow.

  2. The unexpected use of the present progressive with a stative verb to make an emotional comment about some habitual action:

Herbert is *always* hearing noises!

(Compare with the more neutral sentence "Herbert hears noises.")
  3. The use of the periphrastic modal *used to* to explicitly signal past habit as opposed to a single event.[11] The implication is that the habit no longer obtains in the present:

---

11. *Used to* is a periphrastic form syntactically (see the next chapter); however, semantically we feel it is most useful to view it as a part of the tense-aspect system, since it is an explicitly marked form of the simple past when it is used to express past habit. The modal *would,* of course, can also be used to signal past habit, but it is less frequently used to express this meaning than *used to.* Also the two forms appear to differ in subtle ways, but no definitive empirical study has been carried out to verify this:

Old Mr. Jones used to sit there and read.   Old Mr. Jones would sit there and read.
Finally, note that *would* is not appropriate as a short answer.
Do you play tennis every day?   No, but I used to.   *No, but I would.

> He walked the dog.   He used to walk the dog.

However, such cases can be learned as special conventions, and the majority of forms and functions are coherently accounted for in the Bull framework presented in the chart, and in the aspectual uses of BE ... ING described above.

Adverbs of tense and time

A handful of English adverbs exhibit very important interactions with certain verb tenses, namely, *still, yet, soon, already, anymore,* and *just.* We would be remiss if we did not point out a few of their most important functions. Consider how they all could be used as different answers to the following question:

Has Chris finished her M.A. thesis?

1. Yes, she (has) *just* finished it.
2. No, she hasn't finished it *yet.*
3. No, but she'll finish it *soon.*
4. Yes, she (has) *already* filed it.
5. No, she's *still* working on it.
6. No, she's not working on it *anymore.*

In answer 1 *just* signals recent completion while in 2 and 3 *yet* and *soon* signal current noncompletion (future completion is uncertain in *yet* but implied in *soon*). In answer 4 *already* is used to signal a result that turned out better (i.e., earlier) than anticipated, whereas *still* in answer 5 signals a state of affairs that is somehow worse (i.e., later) than anticipated. Answer 6 indicates noncompletion, and one is led to believe the task has been abandoned.

Note that dialect differences often occur in such contexts. In informal American English the above question and responses 1, 2, and 4 often occur in the simple past rather than the present perfect. British English, on the other hand, is much more apt to conserve the use of the present perfect in such contexts.

Consider also the following situation. A parent may ask his or her child either X or Y:

X: Have you done your homework *already*?   Y: Have you done your homework *yet*?

The question with *already* shows that the parent has been made to believe the homework is done but is surprised because he or she did not expect completion that early. The question with *yet* may be neutral, or it may be used to signal that the parent does not expect the homework to be finished but wants to make the child feel it should be.

Note also that within the present time axis *just* and *soon* appear to be complementary past and future markers—signaling recent completion in the past and expected completion in the immediate future respectively, e.g.:

> Joe has *just* finished his assignment, and I'm going to finish mine *soon*.

A final point is that *anymore,* which negates the past, can be viewed as complementary to *still,*[12] which affirms the present, e.g.:

> Helen's *still* living in Omaha, but she doesn't go to school *anymore*.

The semantically incomplete connotations of *yet, anymore,* and *still* and the semantically complete (or about to be completed) nature of *just, soon,* and *already*—as well as the tenses these forms co-occur with most frequently—are facts about English that you should be prepared to convey to your students.

---

12. Although it affirms the present, *still* often implies a negative evaluation:

Is Harold still writing his thesis? (He shouldn't be; he should have finished it long ago.)

TEACHING SUGGESTIONS

The most important teaching consideration coming out of the preceding discussion is that all learning of the English tense-aspect system should take place in context; i.e., the ESL/EFL teacher must, first of all, establish the appropriate time framework and, second, provide contexts that allow for natural practice of the forms involved.

1   The use of activity charts is a recommended technique in ESL/EFL classes. Two large wall charts each of which depicts four to eight activities such as the following are needed. Each picture should include and clearly indicate the time of each activity.

John's Daily Activities

a. Chart I   Chart II
    6:30 a.m. — get up   12:15 p.m. — talk to Mary
    7:00   — fix breakfast   12:30   — eat lunch
    7:45   — go to school   2:30   — study in the library
    9:00   — attend Math class (a   4:30   — go to work
              lecture)

Depending on which tense you are presenting or reviewing, you can use certain key questions to establish the context and the appropriate time axis:

b. *Key questions for teaching the verb forms using the charts:*

1. Present: What does John do every day (at 7:00)?
2. Present progressive: It's 6:30. What is John doing now?
3. Past: What did John do yesterday?
4. Past progressive: What was John doing yesterday at 9:00?
5. Present perfect: It's noon. What has John already done? What hasn't he done yet? It's 6:35. What has John just done?
6. Past perfect: What had John already done by noon yesterday? What hadn't he done?
7. Future: What will John do tomorrow? What is John going to do tomorrow?
8. Future progressive: What will John be doing at 2:30 tomorrow?
9. Future perfect: What will John have done by 4:00 tomorrow?

c. In such cases an appropriate initial teaching sequence with low-proficiency students might be:

1. Teacher presents story about what John does every day, referring to the appropriate picture, and the students listen.
2. Teacher models, students repeat.
3. Teacher asks questions in sequence, students reply.
4. Teacher asks questions out of sequence, students reply.
5. Teacher gives a time cue: one student asks the question, another answers.
6. Chain drill initiated by teacher: I get up at 7 a.m. When do you get up? etc.
7. Indirect cueing by teacher: Olga, ask Elena what she does every day.
8. Based on the charts, students write up a narrative describing what John does every day (can be done in groups and corrected in class).
9. For homework each student writes up a similar narrative describing what he or she does every day.

d. More proficient students needing only a brief review will not require all these steps. This sequence can be modified by you to best suit the needs of your class. The charts can be used for both an initial presentation of one tense or a review of one or more tenses.

2 These charts, however, do have their limitations—especially if you are dealing with the more complicated perfective-progressive verb forms. To teach these more advanced forms, you can use an imaginary biography giving details of someone's past, present, and future life. This can be effectively presented in the form of a scroll. The scroll would normally appear as one long piece of paper that you could slowly unroll to create suspense; however, it is presented below as two segments due to limitations of space. You can use a large width of shelf paper for drawing the scroll and masking tape for attaching the scroll to the front classroom wall or blackboard.

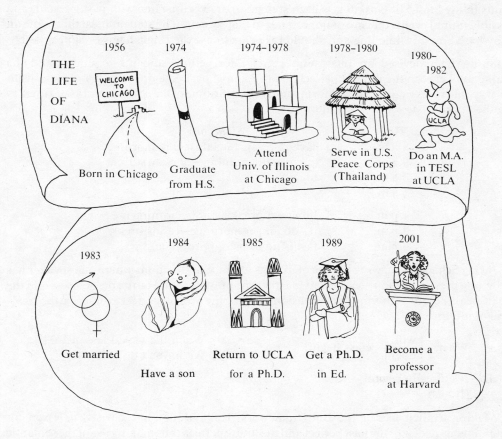

Some of the key questions used for teaching the more complex verb forms are:

  a. *Key questions for use of scroll*

  1. Present perfect progressive: It's 1970. (For) how long has Diana been living in Chicago?
  2. Past perfect progressive: In 1976, (for) how long had Diana been attending the University of Illinois?

3.   Future perfect progressive: In 1987, (for) how many years will Diana have been working on her Ph.D.?

b. Note that the scroll can be used to teach or review simpler tense forms as well. Again we make it a point to follow up such practice with questions relevant to the students in the class, e.g.:

How long have you been living in your dormitory?
How long had you been teaching in Brazil before you came here?
When you get your diploma, how long will you have been in college?

3 An autobiographical extension of the scroll exercise developed by Bill Gaskill can be used as the basis for a writing exercise in advanced ESL/EFL classes. Using the topic "Turning points in my life," Mr. Gaskill gets each student to draw a time line with past, present (and possibly future) events that are of importance to that student. The student must then write an essay based on this time line and should take care to use the English tenses appropriately.

4 Susan Ulm devised an interesting exercise for getting students to understand the distinction between the present perfect and the simple past. She provided her students with two ways of expressing the same information, varied the time of the context, and asked them to use the appropriate tense. For example:

Time	*Situation*
8 a.m.	I haven't eaten breakfast this morning
9 a.m.	(i.e., it's still morning—one can still eat
10 a.m.	breakfast)
11 a.m.	
1 p.m.	I didn't eat breakfast this morning (i.e.,
2 p.m.	it's no longer morning—eating break-
3 p.m.	fast is no longer appropriate).

5 Jackie Schachter suggests the use of dialogs to practice situations where one speaker has the wrong presupposition—expressed in either the present/future or the past tense—and the other speaker corrects this misapprehension by using the present perfect to describe the "real" state of affairs.

A: When $\begin{Bmatrix} \text{will} \\ \text{does} \end{Bmatrix}$ class begin?

B: It's already begun!
(It has)

A: When did we do lesson 16?
B: We haven't done it yet!

6 Making explicit use of the Bull framework, Kathi Bailey has devised a lesson for simultaneous review of the past perfect and the future perfect, thus making use of the semantic relationships and the adverbial markers they share, e.g.:

John will arrive at 9 p.m.
$\begin{Bmatrix} \text{By that time} \\ \text{Before then} \end{Bmatrix}$ I will have finished the book.

John arrived at 9 p.m.
$\begin{Bmatrix} \text{By that time} \\ \text{Before then} \end{Bmatrix}$ I had finished the book.

7 ESL/EFL teachers should give their intermediate and advanced students opportunities to write many texts (first short, then longer) such as the ones presented in the passages and dialogs provided on page 66 so that they develop the ability to utilize each of the three English time axes to their full extent. In pursuing such exercises, the teaching sequence should probably be the present axis, the past axis, and then the future axis. Also, tenses should be taught together with the adverbs that co-occur with them most naturally.

8 Eugene Parulis and Fiona Cook have suggested that the perfect of experience can be realistically practiced in a role-play simulating a job interview.

X: Have you ever $\begin{cases} \text{taken shorthand} \\ \text{done any computer programming} \\ \text{worked at night before} \\ \vdots \end{cases}$?

Y: $\begin{cases} \text{No, I haven't but I have} \ldots \\ \text{Yes, I have. I worked} \ldots \end{cases}$

EXERCISES

Test your understanding of what has been presented

1. Provide original example sentences (or texts) to illustrate the following terms. Underline the pertinent word(s) in your examples:

simple future	habitual past
present perfect	verb of state (stative meaning)
past time axis	durative action verb
progressive aspect	

2. Does the speaker of the following sentence still play tennis?

I used to play tennis.

3. Do the following sentences differ at all with regard to the ordering of events?

I had finished my homework before I played the piano.

I finished my homework before I played the piano.

4. The word *since* does not usually occur with the simple past tense. Why do you think this is so?

5. Compare and contrast the following pairs of sentences. Explain the ungrammaticality of the first sentence in a.

a. *John has been arriving all night. They have been arriving all night.
b. Did you go to Yankee Stadium? Have you gone to Yankee Stadium?
c. I have read the book.   I have been reading the book.

Test your ability to apply what you know

6. Why are the following sentences ungrammatical? If your students make these errors, how would you make them aware of the errors and what activities would you provide to help eradicate these errors?

a. *He has bought it last Saturday. c. *I can't go home until I'd cleared my
b. *The movie is costing $3.50.   desk.

7. ESL/EFL teachers frequently explain the "present progressive tense" by stating that it refers to events occurring now. After you have stated this rule, one of your students brings the following sentence to your attention. How would you respond to the student to account for this sentence?

I am leaving early tomorrow.

8. Certain time adverbials often occur with the present perfect tense. These are good signals to give to your ESL/EFL students. What are some of these signals?

9. ESL/EFL teachers often state that the present tense is used to refer to present time. Does the following sentence contradict this?

He reads *The New York Times* every Sunday.

10. ESL/EFL teachers often associate *now* with present progressive, but consider the following:

He goes to the store now.   Now you've done it!

What are the semantic notions that will make sense of these sentences? You don't have to give the technical terms. Think about under what conditions you might be able to say such sentences and then try to express the semantic notions.

11. Apart from the British and American dialect differences mentioned under Adverbs of Tense and Time, *just* and *already* can occur with the present perfect and/or the simple past. Is there a difference in meaning; i.e., would these sentences occur in different contexts?

a. Did you just hear the news about what happened in Dallas?

b. Have you just heard the news about what happened in Dallas?

BIBLIOGRAPHY

References

Bull, W. (1960). *Time, Tense, and the Verb: A Study in Theoretical and Applied Linguistics, with Particular Application to Spanish.* Berkeley and Los Angeles: The University of California Press.

Chafe, W. L. (1972). "Discourse Structure and Human Knowledge," in J. B. Carroll and R. O. Freedle (eds.), *Language Comprehension and the Acquisition of Knowledge.* Washington, D.C.: V. H. Winston and Sons, pp. 41-69.

Helz, W. (1979). "Of Time and Tense: An Analysis of the English Verb Tense System for the ESL Teacher." Unpublished Independent Professional Project, School for International Training, Brattleboro, Vt.

Jespersen, O. (1924). *The Philosophy of Grammar.* London: Allen and Unwin. (See especially Chaps. 19 and 20—both deal with time and tense.)

Moy, R. (1977). "Contextual Factors in the Use of the Present Perfect." *TESOL* 11:3, 303-310.

Tregidgo, P. S. (1979). "Tense Subordination." *English Language Teaching* 33:3, 191-196.

Wolfson, N. (1978). "A Feature of Performed Narrative: The Conversational Historical Present." *Language in Society* 7:2, 215-237.

Suggestions for further reading

For further discussion of the Bull framework espoused here, see Bull (1960) for the original Spanish framework or Tregidgo (1974) for a slightly different point of view.

Bull, W. (1960). (See above reference.)

Tregidgo, P. S. (1974). "English Tense Usage: A Bull's-Eye View." *English Language Teaching* 28:2, January.

For a form and function analysis of the English present perfect, see:

Feigenbaum, I. (1981). "The Use of the English Perfect." *Language Learning* 31:2, 393–408.

For a good survey of the theories that have been offered on the English perfect tenses, see McCoard (1978).

McCoard, R. W. (1978). *The English Perfect Tense Choice and Pragmatic Inferences.* Amsterdam: North Holland Publishing Co.

For a discussion of aspect, see:

Comrie, B. (1976). *Aspect: An Introduction to the Study of Verbal Aspect and Related Problems.* New York: Cambridge University Press.

For useful traditional descriptions of the English tense-aspect system, consult the following sources:

Allen, R. L. (1966). *The Verb System of Present-Day American English.* The Hague: Mouton.
Close, R. A. (1981). *English as a Foreign Language* (3d ed.). London: Allen and Unwin.
Frank, M. (1972). *Modern English.* Englewood Cliffs, N.J.: Prentice-Hall.
Jespersen, O. (1964). *Essentials of English Grammar.* University, Ala.: University of Alabama Press.
Palmer, F. R. (1968). *A Linguistic Study of the English Verb.* Coral Gables, Fla.: The University of Miami Press.
Quirk, R., and S. Greenbaum (1973). *A Concise Grammar of Contemporary English.* New York: Harcourt, Brace, Jovanovich.

For exercises and practical suggestions on how to teach the English tense-aspect system see:

Danielson, D., and R. Hayden (1973). *Using English: Your Second Language.* Englewood Cliffs, N.J.: Prentice-Hall.
Finocchiaro, M. (1974). *English as a Second Language from Theory to Practice.* New York: Regents Publishing.
Praninskas, J. (1957). *Rapid Review of English Grammar.* Englewood Cliffs, N.J.: Prentice-Hall.
Wohl, M. (1978). *Preparation for Writing: Grammar.* Rowley, Mass.: Newbury House.

7

Modal Auxiliaries and Periphrastic Modals

GRAMMATICAL DESCRIPTION

Introduction

In Chapter 6 all the components of our phrase structure rule for expanding the auxiliary in nonimperative sentences were discussed except for the modal auxiliary (M) and the periphrastic modal (PM):

$$\text{AUX} \longrightarrow \left\{ \begin{matrix} \left\{ \begin{matrix} \text{T} \\ \text{M} \end{matrix} \right\} \text{(PM) (perf) (prog)} \\ \text{IMPER} \end{matrix} \right\}$$

This chapter will complete our discussion of the constituents comprising the auxiliary in nonimperative sentences.

The form of English modals

Modal auxiliaries are one of the more difficult structures that you as an ESL/EFL teacher will have to deal with. One of the reasons for this is the form of modals. Your students, who have been told time and time again that third person singular present tense verbs in English require an *s* ending, will tend to incorrectly generalize this rule to modals. This generalization results in errors because modal auxiliaries (*can, will, shall, may*, etc.) are distinguished from other auxiliary verbs and from lexical verbs by their *lack* of tense with accompanying lack of subject-verb agreement:

Nontensed Modal		*Tensed Verb*	
I		I	
you		you	
she/he/it	can go	we	go
we		they	
they		she/he/it goes	

Another formal property of modals which causes your students some trouble is that modals precede a lexical verb without an intervening infinitive *to*. Your students will often err and use a *to* following modals:

*He can to go.

This may happen because they are following the rule in English which calls for an infinitive to precede the second verb in certain two-verb sequences:

He wants to go.   He plans to go.

An interlingual source of difficulty, of course, may be your students' native language. Not all languages have modal auxiliaries; in those which do not regular verbs or adverbs are used to perform the functions that modals have in English. A student coming from such a language background may feel the need to inflect modals as if they were main verbs.

In this grammar we describe modals as tenseless auxiliaries, which is what we believe they are in modern English. However, we would like to point out that historically modals have derived from main verbs that were either present or past tense in form:

Historically present-tense forms	*Historically past-tense forms*
can	could
will	would
may	might
shall	should
Ø[1]	must

On the basis of evidence such as the following, most transformational grammarians still claim, for example, that *can* is present tense and *could* the related past-tense form:

	Direct Speech	*In Backshifted, Formal Usage for Reported (i.e., Indirect) Speech*
John:	I *can* type.	John said that he *could* type.
Mary:	I *will* go.	Mary said that she *would* go.
Joe:	*Shall* I stay?[2]	Joe asked if he *should* stay.
Bill:	*May* I smoke?	Bill asked if he *might* smoke.

This is the main piece of evidence that grammarians cite to support the assignment of tense to modals. Since we shall demonstrate in Chapter 33, which deals with indirect speech, that such rules of tense shifting are often violated—especially with reference to modals—we feel that such evidence is very weak. Furthermore, there are numerous cases where so-called present tense modals refer to past time, e.g.:

Jim may have been late last night. (cf. Jim was late last night.)

---

1. Note that the modal *must*, which was the past tense of the verb *mōtan* in Old English, has taken on present meaning in current English. This explains in part why *must* has no related past tense counterpart and why the periphrastic modal *have to* expresses the past meaning of *must* (e.g., She must work today / She had to work yesterday), i.e., *must* is an historically past form which took on a present meaning after *mōtan* died out. Also, *have to*, which behaves like a periphrastic modal in many contexts, is not truly a periphrastic modal since it requires *do* support and may also take the perfective and progressive inflections.

2. Note that *should* can be viewed as the past tense of *shall* only if the speaker is asking for advice. When *shall* is used to express the future, *would* would have to function as the past tense of *shall*:

Joe: I shall see you later.   Joe said that he would see us later.

and many other examples where so-called past-tense modals refer to present or future time, e.g.:

(present)   That should be Sara.   (future)   You should see a doctor.

Thus there are no valid semantic reasons for maintaining the historical description. Also, the fact that the "present tense" modals would be the only present-tense auxiliaries that do not take the third person singular inflection, i.e., they are the sole exception to the subject-verb agreement rule, further supports our claim that modals are tenseless forms.

Modals and their periphrastic modal counterparts

Multiword forms ending in *to,* which function semantically much like true modals, are called periphrastic modals. For example:

Modal	*Periphrastic Modal*
can	be able to
will	be going to, be about to
must	have to, have got to
should, ought to[3]	be to,[4] be supposed to
would (=past habit)	used to
may	be allowed to

Notice that the periphrastic modals do not exhibit the same formal properties as the true modals in that the subject-verb agreement rule must be applied (except for *used to,* which is an inflected past tense) and all periphrastic modals require that a *to* infinitive precede the main verb:

$$\text{She} \left\{ \begin{array}{l} \textit{is}\ \text{able}\ \textit{to} \\ \textit{is}\ \text{going}\ \textit{to} \\ \textit{is}\ \text{allowed}\ \textit{to} \\ \textit{has}\ \text{got}\ \textit{to} \\ \vdots \end{array} \right\} \quad \text{go tomorrow.}$$

Other modal-like forms

In addition to the true modals and periphrastic modals there are some other modal-like forms in English such as *had better* (which signals advisability), *would rather* and *would prefer* (which signal preference), and *would like* (which signals desire), which should also be brought to your students' attention during a unit on modal auxiliaries. We will return to these later.

Sequences with more than one modal or periphrastic modal

One final point should be made regarding the formal properties of modals and periphrastic modals. Consider the following examples:

---

3. The form *ought to* is an intermediate form that can be classified as either a modal or a periphrastic modal. The *to* makes it look like a periphrastic modal, but it has no *be* or *have* auxiliary to carry tense, and the *ought* is historically a past-tense form. In the negative *ought* loses its *to* and functions as a true modal for many English speakers:

You oughtn't do that.   We ought not stay any longer.

4. Although we have indicated that *be to* is a periphrastic equivalent of *should* as in *What am I to do? be to* can also be a periphrastic equivalent of *will (I am to leave tomorrow)* and *must (You are to report tomorrow).*

*We can should study hard for the exam.

*I am able to must do the assignment.

I might be able to go to the game.

He will have to improve his English.

He is going to have to improve his English.

While further study is needed to determine what all the possible combinations are, we see from the first two examples that modal plus modal and periphrastic modal plus modal are not permissible sequences, whereas some combinations of modal plus periphrastic modal are possible. Our rule for AUX can explain the first four examples; however, the fifth example indicates that some combinations of two periphrastic modals also occur.[5] All this suggests that periphrastic modals behave syntactically more like main verbs than do modals, which are more clearly auxiliary verbs.

The meaning of modals

While all of the above formal properties may seem rather complicated, an additional problem in the teaching of modals arises when you attempt to convey to your ESL/EFL students the meaning of modals, periphrastic modals, and modal-like forms.

In traditional grammar books we often find large charts which attempt to summarize the form and meaning of modals. Such presentations, while useful and succinct, give a rather fragmented view of the modals, since they suggest that modals be learned and taught meaning by meaning and form by form. In our description of the modals (as we did in the case of tense and aspect) we want to give at least as much consideration to the semantic *system* as we do to the individual meanings and forms.

The best foundation for discussing the systematic meanings of modals is the "root" (we call it "social interactional") versus the "epistemic" (we use the term "logical probability") distinction discussed by Hofmann (1966). An example will be useful in making this distinction clear.

You *may* leave the room. (social interactional)

It *may* rain tomorrow. (logical probability)

Modals which have a social interactional function require that a person using them properly take into account the characteristics of the social situation. In our first example, the speaker is of sufficient authority to be able to grant permission to the listener. Furthermore, we can also infer that the context is likely a formal one, since the speaker chose to use *may* rather than *can* in his or her granting of permission. Knowing the social situation allowed the speaker to select the appropriate modal for this interaction. In the second sentence above, however, knowledge of the social situation would have little or no effect on the modal selected. What the speaker is intending to convey is the relatively low probability of precipitation. He or she would likely use *may* regardless of who his or her listener was or where the interaction took place.

As shown in the above examples with *may,* virtually all the modals have both social and logical functions. Students should be made aware of this and be given some guidance in working with the systems operating within each of these functions. We will now discuss these two areas in detail and follow with some other meanings of modals which do not conveniently fit into these two categories.

---

5. We could account for this in our AUX rule if we added a superscript to the periphrastic modal option indicating that sequences of two periphrastic modals are possible, i.e., $(PM)^2$.

Social interactional uses of modals

1. One major system in the social use of modals entails making requests. These can be requests of a general nature:

$$\left.\begin{array}{l} \text{Will} \\ \text{Would} \\ \text{Can} \\ \text{Could} \end{array}\right\}\ \text{you help me with this math problem?}[6]$$

or can be specific requests for permission:

$$\left.\begin{array}{l} \text{May} \\ \text{Might} \\ \text{Can} \\ \text{Could} \end{array}\right\}\ \text{I leave the room?}$$

Although historically both present and past forms of these modals can be used in making requests, only the historical present tense forms are likely to be used in responses to requests:

To general requests
$$\left\{\begin{array}{l} \text{Yes, I can. *Yes, I could.} \\ \text{Yes, I will. *Yes, I would} \end{array}\right.$$

To requests for permission
$$\left\{\begin{array}{l} \text{Yes, you may. *Yes, you might.} \\ \text{Yes, you can. *Yes, you could.} \end{array}\right.$$

The reason for this is that the historical past forms of modals are considered more polite and less presumptuous than the historical present forms, and therefore the person making the request will often use the historical past-tense forms to "soften" the request; however, the person being addressed is expected to respond directly and thus uses historical present forms—e.g.:

$$\left\{\begin{array}{l} \text{Yes, I can.} \\ \text{No, I can't.} \end{array}\right.$$

Also, the person responding to a request usually does not want to make the response sound conditional, which is a possible result if the historical past form of the modal is used:

Q: $\left\{\begin{array}{l} \text{Can} \\ \text{Could} \end{array}\right\}$ you help me with this math problem?

A: Yes, I could (if you would wait a few minutes while I finish this work).

Many ESL/EFL students, even at the advanced level, do not recognize that they are often perceived by native speakers of English as being abrupt and aggressive with their requests. If we could teach them to soften their requests by employing the historical past-tense forms of the modals, they might find their requests being better received, e.g.:

---

6. Note that periphrastic modals are not used to make requests—only to ask questions:

Will/Would you open the door? (possible request)   Are you going to open the door? (literal question only)

There is, however, a modal-like phrase which can be used to make a polite request:

Would you mind my playing the piano for a few minutes?

The interesting thing here is that DO may serve as an informal substitute for *would* but that *will* is an ungrammatical substitute.

Could (instead of can) I talk to you a minute?

Would (instead of will) you open the door?

There is a subtle difference between *can/could* and *will/would* in making requests such as that above which also should be pointed out. The former seems to imply: Is this possible . . . ? while the latter forms seem to query the willingness of the person being addressed. Further research is needed to show us in what contexts each set of forms is preferred and why.

When asking for permission, as in the above example, the use of *may* or *can* is significant. The greater the listener's degree of formal authority (as perceived by the speaker or asserted by the listener), the more likely the use of *may*. In the majority of situations, in America at least, there is a lack of defined formal authority, and *can* tends to be widely used.

2. The other major system in the social interactional use of modals involves the giving of advice. Notice that the systematicity lies in the fact that we can order the modals according to the speaker's degree of authority and/or conviction, or the urgency of the advice, e.g.:

You $\begin{Bmatrix} \text{might} \\ \text{could} \end{Bmatrix}$ see a doctor.
You should see a doctor.
You had better see a doctor.
You must see a doctor.
You will see a doctor!

Speaker's authority or urgency of the message increases, but not necessarily in equal increments.

From our experience, we have found introducing modals in this relative fashion to be far more enlightening to ESL/EFL students than it would be to introduce each form individually and to ascribe to each a distinctive meaning.

Logical probability uses of modals

The logical use of some of the same modals typically deals with an inference or prediction, e.g.:

Wilbur: Someone's at the door.
(inference) Gertrude: It may be Sydney.

You will see that we can establish a hierarchy for the logical use as we did for the social use. This time what increases is the degree of certainty regarding our inference:

Wilbur: Someone's knocking.
Gertrude: That $\begin{Bmatrix} \text{could} \\ \text{might} \end{Bmatrix}$ be Sydney.
That may be Sydney.
That should be Sydney.
That must be Sydney.
That will be Sydney.

Degree of certainty
(Again, degrees are not necessarily equi-distant)

Notice that adjectives and adverbs can often be used to paraphrase the logical use, but only rarely the social use, of a modal.

could, might — possibly, possible
may   — perhaps, quite possible(-ly)
should   — probably, probable
will   — certainly, certain

These are illustrated here according to the degree of probability regarding our prediction, e.g.:

Degree of Probability

It $\left\{\begin{array}{l}\text{could, might}\\ \text{may}\\ \text{should}\\ \text{will}\end{array}\right\}$ rain tomorrow.   It is $\left\{\begin{array}{l}\text{possible}\\ \text{quite possible}\\ \text{probable}\\ \text{certain}\end{array}\right\}$ that it will rain tomorrow.

Other uses of modals and modal-like forms

There are four other uses of modals and modal-like forms which do not function in either the social or logical uses described above. They are:

Ability—*can,*[7] *be able to:*
    I can speak Indonesian.
    Superman is able to leap tall buildings with a single bound.
Desire—*would like to:*
    Sarah would like to travel around the world.
Offer—*would* you *like* (frozen formula in questions expressing an invitation):
    Would you like anything to drink?
Preference—*would rather* (X than y), *would prefer to:*
    Brad would rather study languages than mathematics.
    George would prefer to go to school instead of working.

In some ways one could argue that *would like to* and *would prefer to* are really simply modal + verb + infinitive combinations. We suggest, however, teaching them with other modal forms, since otherwise ESL/EFL students do not always learn to treat them as frozen formulas and often err by saying things like:

*I will prefer to stay.   *Will you like some cake?

Additional facts

After presenting the general functions of English modals to your class such as the social vs. the logical distinction, you will have to discuss some of the more specific details of their usage. Although you would certainly not want to present them all in one lesson, the following are important facts about modals that you should be aware of in order to help your students use modals appropriately:

1. The negation of a modal and the negation of the corresponding periphrastic modal usually have parallel semantic effects:

I cannot do it. / I am not able to do it.   You should not lie. / You are not sup-
We will not do it. / We are not going to   posed (to) lie.
    do it.

---

7. It would perhaps be more accurate to say that *can* expresses "potential." Then for animate agent subjects potential means "ability":

Jack can swim./His dog Fido can fetch sticks.

and for inanimate subjects potential means "possibility," since here the subjects are themes, not agents. Also, the verb is often in the passive voice (see Chapter 17):

This business can be reorganized./The fence can be painted.

However, *you must not go* and *you don't have to go*[8] are clearly distinct—the former expressing the speaker's prohibition and the latter the listener's choice.

2. It is also essential to realize that there are important semantic differences that occur when the logical modals are negated. The two probability scales below will help illustrate this:

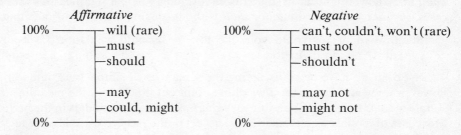

Affirmative		*Negative*	
100%	will (rare)	100%	can't, couldn't, won't (rare)
	must		must not
	should		shouldn't
	may		may not
	could, might		might not
0%		0%	

Use the test frame "That _____ be the solution" to check your intuition regarding these scales. The unusual features are as follows:

  a. While *can* is rarely used to express logical probability in affirmative sentences, it is used frequently in negative sentences.
  b. The logical probability of *can/could* in affirmative sentences is very low; however, in negative sentences, it is high, i.e., 100%!
  c. The negative element in *can't, couldn't,* and *shouldn't* may be contracted in statements reflecting logical probability; however, it is rarely contracted with *may* and *might* in such sentences, and in some dialects is not contracted with *must,* perhaps to avoid confusion with the negated situational modal *mustn't* (= prohibition).

3. There is generally a difference in the degree of formality between use of a modal and the corresponding periphrastic modal, the latter being more informal, especially when phonologically reduced. Often other words in the sentence also reflect this difference in degree of formality, e.g.:

The United States must conserve its resources.	We { have to (hafta) / have got to (gotta) } conserve our resources.
The exam will count 50% of your grade.	It's going to (gonna) count 50% of your grade.
You should tell your parents about this.	You ought to (oughtta) tell your folks about this.

However, the reverse seems true when we consider the case of *can/be able to.*

Can you do it?   Are you able to do it?

Here the periphrastic form seems more formal than the modal.

4. One modal that we failed to mention above which can be used for requests is *shall.* Since it is used so infrequently these days, we prefer to teach this form to our students mainly for reception, rather than production.[9] When it does occur, it will usually be found in requests

8. Note that another possible though less frequent equivalent for *You don't have to go* is *You needn't go. Need* is unusual in that it functions as a modal in negatives and occasionally in questions (*Need I wait for them?*) but always resembles a main verb in affirmative statements (*You need to go.*)

9. Certainly the old prescriptive rule—i.e., use *shall* with *I* and *we,* and *will* elsewhere—no longer holds true for American English.

for advice involving the first person, and even here *should* can substitute for *shall*:

Shall I call her or will you?   Shall we go to the Natural History Muse-
um today?

Shall does, however, occur in some frozen formulas where it signifies an invitation. In such cases, *should* cannot substitute for *shall* without causing a change of meaning:

Shall we dance? (Would you like to   Should we dance? (Is it advisable that
dance?), i.e., an invitation   we dance?), i.e., a question

5. So far we have been discussing the semantics of simple (i.e., unmodified) modals; however, we would be remiss if we didn't point out that not all the meanings attributed to simple modals have corresponding meanings with the same modals in the perfective aspect. Most uses of modals with the perfective aspect or the passive voice involve logical uses, not social ones, e.g.:

John must have been out of town for the   The Giants will be beaten by the Dodg-
4th of July. (inference)   ers. (prediction)

Notice also that the use of HAVE (. . . EN) plus the past participle indicates past as opposed to present inference, e.g.:

He must be a teacher. (at the present   He must have been a teacher. (at some
time)   previous time)

This is compatible with the semantic function of HAVE . . . EN described in the preceding chapter, i.e., within each time axis specified, HAVE . . . EN was used to signal a past time in relation to the basic time form of the axis.

In an article in the *TESOL Quarterly,* Bowen and McCreary deal at length with the semantics of the modal perfects. They underscore the importance of impressing our ESL/EFL students with the fact that not all meanings of the simple modals can be expressed with perfect modals. The following is a chart of the semantic notions expressed by modal perfects adapted from the Bowen and McCreary article (1977:289). It has been modified to fit the categories we have already discussed with regard to simple modals:[10]

Social Interactional:
Advisability/obligation
You *should have paid* him a better salary.
They *might have* at least *sent* her a get-well card.
They *could have* at least *paid* the postage.

Logical Probability:
Inference
She *can't have finished* the entire assignment yet.
He *must have been* here earlier today.
They *should have arrived* in London by now.
Possibility
Pierre *may have been* Belgian.

---

10. Bowen and McCreary (1977) do not point out that perfect forms of some periphrastic modals and modal-like forms also exist:

We were to have told them about that.   (Did you lock the door?)
You (had) better have!

He *might have seen* her already.
He *could have come* on the early train.
Who *can* that *have been*?
    Prediction
He *will have left* by the time we get there.
By then I *shall have collected* the last cent of what he owes.

6. Although not as frequent as modal + HAVE . . . EN there are some possibilities for modals to occur with the progressive aspect or with both the progressive aspect and a perfect verb tense. Again, the semantics are complicated and there are ambiguities, but the progressive seems to add concreteness and a sense of present time to such statements, e.g.:

I must go. (exhortation, vague time reference)
I must be going. (more concrete, present time reference, i.e., *now*!)

He could work. (a suggestion or a possibility)
He could be working. (a stronger suggestion or an inference with present time reference)
He could have been working. (an inference with past reference but also possible current relevance, e.g., "since 8 a.m.")

7. *Would, could,* and *should* followed by HAVE . . . EN usually, although not always, carry the implication that the action referred to was not accomplished. These three modals are an integral part of expressing unreal conditional statements in English. We will deal with these forms in some detail in Chapter 25 when we discuss conditionals, e.g.:

I would have been rich by now (if I had done X, but I didn't).
I could have gone swimming yesterday (but I didn't).
He should have waited before he jumped (but he didn't).

Conclusion

This then concludes our discussion of the modal auxiliaries in English. We freely admit that it is far from complete. We have omitted discussion of archaic or shifting modals such as *dare* and *need.* We have not gone into as many semantic subtleties as we would have liked to (e.g., similarities and differences between *should, ought to, be to,* and *be supposed to*). Many such uses of modals require further study. Earlier we said that this structure often causes many problems for the ESL/EFL student partly because its form differs from that of other auxiliary and lexical verbs, and partly because it is difficult to be explicit about the meaning. In the teaching suggestions which follow, we have shown some ways in which the systematicity of the modals we have discussed here could be revealed to your classes.

TEACHING SUGGESTIONS

1   Several of the social interactional modals form a continuum from "weak suggestion" to order, "command!" This pattern can be taught both formally and informally using thermometers as visual aids to show the degree of necessity involved. (Remember that the different forms do not necessarily have equal semantic distance between them.)

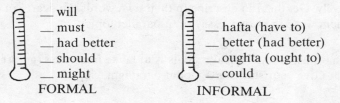

__ will
__ must
__ had better
__ should
__ might
FORMAL

__ hafta (have to)
__ better (had better)
__ oughta (ought to)
__ could
INFORMAL

Students would then be given hypothetical situations to respond to. They would have to decide whether (a) the situation is formal or informal, (b) which degree of strength is called for. (Note: If only one thermometer is used with, say, beginners, step a is not necessary.) For example:

$$\text{``What} \begin{Bmatrix} \text{do} \\ \text{will} \\ \text{would} \end{Bmatrix} \text{you say if} \dots \text{''}$$

a. You are a teacher who wants to let a certain student know that it is essential to come to class on time.

b. You want to tell a close friend who needs money for an emergency that one possibility is for him to sell his car.

c. A fellow professor is not being paid the proper salary, and you think it would help if he saw the Dean.

2   Other uses of the social interactional modals can be taught using dialogs, e.g.:

Teacher: Class, for tomorrow you will read Chapter 4 and do the exercises for that chapter.

Student X: (at the end of class) I can do all those exercises. They're too easy. Would you please give me another assignment?

Teacher: Do the first exercise anyway. But you may write an essay instead of doing the others.

Student X: Thank you. That's what I'll do.

3   One of the uses of the logical probability modals is to predict something such as the chance of rain tomorrow. Show your students what degree of prediction is expressed by each modal:

(possibly)	weak, outside chance:	It (could, might) rain tomorrow.
(perhaps)	stronger chance:	It may very well rain tomorrow.
$\begin{Bmatrix} \text{probably} \\ \text{likely} \end{Bmatrix}$	strong chance:	It probably will rain tomorrow.
(certainly)	certainty:	It will rain tomorrow.

a. For oral practice, have students express (using a modal) situations such as the following with the degree of prediction suggested by the context (or the teacher):

(1) There's a 30 percent chance of rain tomorrow.
(2) There's an 80 percent chance of rain later today.
(3) The probability of good weather this coming weekend.
(4) The probability of man's landing on Mars during the next 20 years.

b. For written practice, have students read a paragraph or essay using modals predictively. Get them to describe in their own words the degree of each prediction. Have them write their own essay on a parallel topic.

4   The other main use of the logical modals is to make inferences (guesses) about current states/situations. Give your students a modal paradigm, e.g.:

Someone's knocking at the door.

weak inference:	That could/might be Sydney.
stronger inference:	That may be Sydney.
strong inference:	That should be Sydney.
very strong inference:	That must be Sydney.
absolute certainty in making an inference (rare):	That will be Sydney.

a. For oral practice, have students react to situations (using a modal) such as the following:
   (1) Student X is not in class today.
   (2) Student Y is falling asleep/is thinking of something else.
   (3) The local football star has not been playing as well as usual.

b. For written practice, one might try translation from the students' native language into English or vice versa as a check on comprehension (i.e., reading) and production (i.e., writing).

5   In teaching the modal-like forms for preference (*would rather*) and desire (*would like to*), the following chart prepared by Lida Baker could be used as a model to explain the meanings of these auxiliaries. After going over the model, the teacher should try to elicit comparable sentences from students.

Example	Reality	Attitude
would rather	Present/Future	
I would rather eat an apple than a banana.	It hasn't happened yet.	apple—good banana—less good
I would rather not work next Monday.	It hasn't happened yet.	negative
	Past	
I would rather have seen the movie than read the book.	I read the book.	movie—good book—less good
I would rather not have read the book.	I read the book.	negative
would like to	Present/Future	
I would like to go to Acapulco.	It hasn't happened yet.	positive
I wouldn't like to have his job.	I don't have his job.	I'm glad I don't have his job.
	Past	
I would have liked to see John at the party.[11]	I didn't see him.	I'm sorry I didn't.
I wouldn't have liked to wait in that line for the tickets.[11]	I didn't wait in the line.	I'm glad I didn't.

---

11. Some native speakers feel these sentences are more acceptable if the perfective HAVE . . . EN is in the infinitive:

> I would like to have seen John at the party.
> I wouldn't like to have waited in that line for the tickets.

6   We have already indicated that *be going to* is a periphrastic modal corresponding to the true modal *will*. While the former can often be substituted for the latter, there are restricted situations where one or the other is the preferred form. Supply your students with contexts such as the following, which were taken from a paper by Stafford (1975), and ask them to choose (1) or (2). Then discuss their choices with them, and they should begin to become sensitive to the differences.

a. You are on a tour of Disneyland with your friends. As you step off one of the rides, you suddenly lose your balance and shout:

> (1) "Help, I will fall."   (2) "Help, I'm going to (gonna) fall."

Difference: *Going to* is the preferred form, since it is used with actions that are just about to happen.

b. An army officer is talking to a superior officer.

> "Well, sir, if our strategies continue to be successful, the war
> (1) is going to soon be over."   (2) will soon be over."

Difference: *Will* is probably the preferred form when a more formal register is called for.

c. A shy 17-year-old boy calls up a girl he's been admiring all year. He says,

> (1) "Will you meet me at the show this   (2) "Are you going to meet me at the
> Friday?"   show this Friday?"

Difference: *Will* is used for requests/invitations; *be going to* is inappropriate in such contexts.

EXERCISES

Test your understanding of what has been presented

1. Provide original example sentences that illustrate the following concepts. Underline the relevant word(s) in your examples.

periphrastic modal	a sequence with more than one modal or
social interactional use of a modal	periphrastic modal
logical probability use of a modal	polite form of a request
function of a perfect-form modal	

2. Account for the ambiguity of the following sentence:

> His mother says he may go.

3. Account for the semantic difference between the two sentences in each of the following pairs:

a. It must be nighttime.   It must have been nighttime.
b. Will you help me with this problem?   Would you help me with this problem?
c. I was able to go to the library last   I could have gone to the library last
   night.   night.
d. The ground is wet.   The ground is wet.
   It may have rained last night.   It must have rained last night.
e. You should do your homework.   You had better do your homework.

Test your ability to apply what you know

4. In terms of what is understood about the activity described, what do the three following sentences have in common?

a. They could have warned us.

b. They should have warned us.

c. They would have warned us.

5. Students of yours have made the following errors. In each case explain the nature of the error, and state what activities you would provide to correct it.

a. *Sally cans help you with your home-work.

b. *You will can go there.

c. *John must to speak Japanese.

d. *May you cash this check, please?

e. *We should study a lot for that class last term.

6. How do the presuppositions of the speaker differ in the following sentences?

a. Could you tell me how to get to the bus stop?

b. Would you tell me how to get to the bus stop?

7. Consider the verb forms *need* and *dare*:

a. I need to see him.

b. You needn't worry.

c. Do we dare think that?

d. Need I bring anything?

e. I dare you to do that.

Are they modals, periphrastic modals, regular lexical verbs, or a mixture of these forms?

8. We said earlier that modals with the perfective aspect often involve logical uses, not social ones. What happens to the social meaning of granting permission in the following example when the simple form of the modal is changed to perfect?

The principal said Joe may go.   The principal said Joe may have gone.

9. Sometimes when referring to ability in the past, one can use the periphrastic modal but not the true modal:

I was able to pick up the tickets last night.   *I could pick up the tickets last night.

At other times, both the periphrastic modal and the true modal are acceptable:

I could read at an early age.   I was able to read at an early age.

Furthermore, even the ungrammatical sentence above is acceptable when it is negated:

I couldn't pick up the tickets last night.

Can you think of a generalization that would account for the restriction with *could*?

BIBLIOGRAPHY

References

Bowen, J. D., and C. F. McCreary (1977). "Teaching the English Modal Perfects," *TESOL Quarterly* 11:3, 283–301.

Hofmann, T. R. (1966). "Past Tense Replacement and the Modal System," Computational Laboratory, Harvard University, NSF Report 17.

Stafford, C. (1975). "Expressing the Future: *Will* vs. *Going to*." Unpublished English 215 paper, UCLA, fall, 1975.

Suggestions for further reading

For good traditional descriptions of English modal auxiliaries, see:

Close, R. A. (1981). *English as a Foreign Language* (3d ed.). London: Allen and Unwin, pp. 110–131.
Ehrman, M. (1972). *The Meanings of the Modals in Present-Day American English.* The Hague: Mouton.
Frank, M. (1972). *Modern English.* Englewood Cliffs, N.J.: Prentice-Hall, pp. 96–105.
Leech, G. (1971). *Meaning and the English Verb.* London: Longman, pp. 69–98.

For a useful discussion of differences between *will* and *going to,* see:

Martin, M. (1978). "Future Shock: A Pedagogical Analysis of Will and Going To," in J. Schachter and C. H. Blatchford (eds.), *ON TESOL '78.* Washington, D.C.: TESOL.

For interesting accounts of English modals and for perspectives on the root (social)/ epistemic (logical) distinction that differ somewhat from the one presented here, see:

Cook, W. A. (1978). "Semantic Structure of the English Modals," *TESOL Quarterly* 12:1, 5–15.
Diver, W. (1964). "The Modal System of the English Verb," *Word* 20:3, 322–352.
Palmer, F. R. (1979). *Modality and the English Modals.* London: Longman.
Tregidgo, P. S. (1982). "Must and May: Demand and Permission," *Lingua* 56:75–92.

For good suggestions on the teaching of modal auxiliaries, consult:

Bowen, J. D., and C. F. McCreary (1977). See above reference for citation.
Brinton, D., and R. Neuman (1982). *Getting Along: English Grammar and Writing* (Book 2). Englewood Cliffs, N.J.: Prentice-Hall, pp. 114–115, 193, 228–230.
Danielson, D., and R. Hayden (1973). *Using English: Your Second Language.* Englewood Cliffs, N.J.: Prentice-Hall, Chap. 8, pp. 85–91.
Hayden, R., D. Pilgrim, and A. Haggard (1956). *Mastering American English.* Englewood Cliffs, N.J.: Prentice-Hall, pp. 110–115.
Praninskas, Jean (1975). *Rapid Review of English Grammar* (2d ed., Lesson 24). Englewood Cliffs, N.J.: Prentice-Hall, pp. 233ff.

8

Negation

GRAMMATICAL DESCRIPTION

Types of negation

Negation in English is a very broad topic. When syntactic negation applies to an entire sentence, it is expressed using the particle NOT, e.g.:

> John is *not* at home. (=It is not the case that John is at home.)

This is the type of negation we will be discussing in this chapter. Sentence-level negation can, however, also be expressed semantically by using *no,* a negative quantifier, to modify a noun or as the first element in an indefinite pronoun. (This type of sentence-level negation will be discussed later in this chapter and again in Chapter 15.) For example:

> *No* sailors are on the ship./*No*body is on the ship. (They all have shore leave.)

On the other hand, it is also possible for NOT to apply only to a phrase, e.g.:

> Michele has decided to not pay taxes this year. (As a protest, deliberate civil disobedience)

or it may apply to a word, in which case the negation is signaled by a negative prefix, e.g.:

> Harry is *un*coordinated. (He's the opposite of coordinated, i.e., clumsy.)

We can show that two of the above examples involve a type of sentence-level negation and that the other two do not by adding question tags[1] to each of the four example sentences:

SENTENTIAL: { John is not at home, *is he*?
{ No sailors are on the ship, *are they*?
PHRASAL: Michele has decided to not pay taxes this year, *hasn't she*?
LEXICAL: Harry is uncoordinated, *isn't he*?

As Klima (1964) points out in his comprehensive description of negation in English, the tags in the above sentences give us evidence that the first two sentences are syntactically negative while the other two are not, regardless of what negative particles or words they may contain.

---

1. Question tags will be discussed in detail in Chapter 13. All that we need to know now is that negation is normally reversed in a tag; i.e., if the statement is syntactically affirmative, the tag is negative and vice versa.

Problems for ESL/EFL students

Many of your ESL/EFL students will find syntactic negation problematic, especially if they are at the beginning level. The main reason is that different languages tend to place their negative particle in different positions in the sentence.

Spanish (preverbal)	Juan *no* habla inglés.
	(John) (speaks) (English)
German (postverbal)	Johann geht *nicht* zur Schule.
	(John) (goes) (to school)
English (postauxiliary)	John will *not* talk to Judy.

You may wish to consult Schumann (1979) for a discussion of the influences of the native language on the acquisition of English negation by ESL/EFL learners.

Also, many languages allow multiple negation in one sentence, which, if done in English, usually produces nonstandard sentences such as "I did*n't* say *no*thing to *no*body!"

A final problem involves the form of the negative particle. Some languages do not have distinct forms for expressing their equivalents of English NOT and *no*. Furthermore, English NOT is usually contracted in speech and in informal writing—few languages contract their negative particle—and this results in negative sentences that are harder for learners to hear and to read than these same sentences would be if the NOT were consistently produced as a separate, uncontracted word.

An analysis of negation in English

Keeping all these subtleties and problems in mind, let us now proceed with a discussion of English sentence-level negation formed with the particle NOT.

Consider, first of all, the following pairs of sentences:

1.	a. I can swim.	b. I cannot swim.
2.	a. Mr. Smith is a teacher.	b. Mr. Smith isn't a teacher.
3.	a. We have read that book.	b. We haven't read that book.
4.	a. Mary is going to give a party.	b. Mary isn't going to give a party.
5.	a. Joe has been studying in the library.	b. Joe has not been studying in the library.

It is clear that what distinguishes the *b* sentences from the *a* sentences is the presence of the negative particle NOT or its contracted and suffixed form -N'T.

To produce the basic structure of all these sentences, we generate NOT as a sentence modifier since the negation applies to the entire sentence—not just to the verb or the auxiliary elements. A schematic representation of this would be as follows:

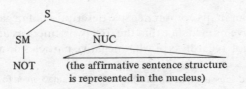

To be more precise, the basic structures for sentences 1b and 2b would be as follows:

I cannot swim.

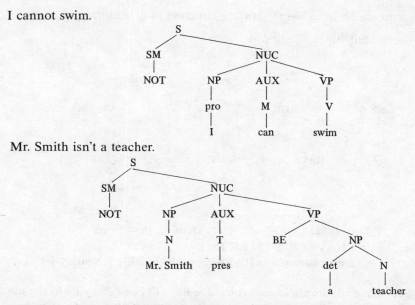

Mr. Smith isn't a teacher.

In order to capture the appropriate generalization about correct placement of the negative particle NOT in English sentences, let us return to a consideration of sentences 1 to 5. In examining these sentences, we can make several observations about negative formation in English:

a. From sentence 1b we see that if there is a modal auxiliary present in a sentence, the negative particle NOT is placed after the modal and before the main verb, in this case, *swim.*

b. An examination of sentence 2b tells us that if the copula BE is the main verb of the sentence, the negative particle follows the copula.

c. Likewise, NOT follows a HAVE auxiliary if it is present in a sentence such as 3b.

d. From sentence 4b, we learn that the NOT follows the first lexical element in a periphrastic modal.

e. Finally in sentence 5b we observe that the NOT follows the HAVE auxiliary verb even though a BE auxiliary verb is also present since HAVE is the first auxiliary verb.

NOT placement

What generalization can be drawn from all these observations? In English the negative particle is placed after the first auxiliary verb in a sentence. If there is no auxiliary verb, but there is a BE copula, then the NOT follows BE. As was pointed out earlier, English has a rule of postauxiliary negation. Many other languages, like Spanish, use a preverbal negation rule. Thus you will often find beginning-level ESL/EFL students producing sentences such as:

*He no(t) can go.

This generalization, which we will call our NOT-placement rule, will allow us to generate a near surface form for sentences 1b and 5b. Only affix attachment, subject-verb agreement, and morphological rules[2] are needed to produce grammatical surface structures.

---

2. Recall that morphological rules are those rather mechanical rules that tell us things like BE + EN ⟶ *been, man* + pl ⟶ *men,* etc. In other words, they take a near surface-level string of lexical items and grammatical markers and produce a grammatical surface structure.

Let us take sentence 5b from base to surface structure as an example.

Joe has not been studying in the library.

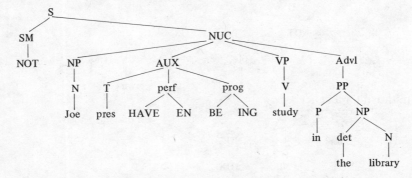

Output of base: NOT Joe pres HAVE EN BE ING study in the library

NOT placement: Joe pres HAVE NOT EN BE ING study in the library

Affix attachment (3× = 3 applications): Joe HAVE + pres NOT BE + EN study + ING in the library

Subject-verb agreement and morphological rules: Joe has not been studying in the library.

We will also need a rule which optionally[3] reduces NOT to -N'T and attaches it to the appropriate verb. This will account for the contracted form of NOT found in sentences 2b, 3b, and 4b. Many combinations of -N'T with an auxiliary verb are regular, but some are irregular:

Regular—disyllabic negatives
did + n't ——→ didn't
would + n't ——→ wouldn't
have + n't ——→ haven't
    etc.

Irregular orthographically and/or phonologically—monosyllabic negatives
will + n't ——→ won't ('l' is lost, vowel changes)
can + n't ——→ can't (one 'n' lost)
do + n't ——→ don't (vowel sound changes)
    etc.

With this NOT contraction rule we can now also produce sentences such as 2b and 3b. Let us go through the entire derivation of 3b as an example:

We haven't read that book.

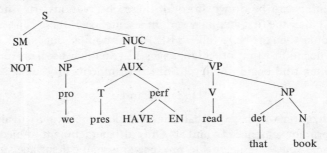

---

3. A transformation which must be applied to produce a grammatical sentence is "obligatory," while a transformation that may be applied to a grammatical sequence to produce a stylistic variation is "optional."

Output of base: NOT we pres HAVE EN read that book
NOT placement: we pres HAVE NOT EN read that book
NOT contraction: we pres HAVE + N'T EN read that book
Affix attachment (2✕): we HAVE + N'T + pres read + EN that book
Morphological rules:[4] We haven't read that book.

In addition to sentences such as 1b to 5b, there are a number of other negative sentence types that must be accounted for. Consider the following sentences:

6.   a. Jack speaks Spanish.   b. Jack doesn't speak Spanish.
7.   a. I wrote the letter.   b. I did not write the letter.
8.   a. We live in Chicago.   b. We don't live in Chicago.

The affirmative sentences in 6a through 8a are different from those in 1a through 5a in that neither an auxiliary verb nor the copula BE is present. The negative sentences in 6b through 8b are also different from the earlier examples because some form of the auxiliary DO has been introduced.

In order to account for these sentences, we must expand our generalization about English negation. What we have said before still holds, but now we note that if there is no auxiliary verb or BE verb present in the sentence, a new auxiliary verb, i.e., DO, is introduced to precede the negative particle and carry the tense marker in the sentence.

We will call the rule which adds DO to such a negative sentence DO support. Let us now go through the derivation of sentence 8b to observe the interaction of all the transformational rules discussed thus far in this and the preceding chapters.

We don't live in Chicago.

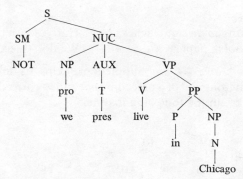

Output of base: NOT we pres live in Chicago
NOT placement: we pres NOT live in Chicago
DO support: we pres DO NOT live in Chicago
NOT contraction: we pres DO + N'T live in Chicago
Affix attachment (1✕): we DO + N'T + pres live in Chicago
Morphological rules: We don't live in Chicago.

These rules will allow us to derive any single-clause nonimperative sentence in English containing a syntactic-level occurrence of NOT or -N'T.

---

4. When subject-verb agreement does not apply (i.e., when there is no BE verb which carries tense and no third person singular subject and no present tense verb), the application of morphological rules will have to be listed as a step separate from subject-verb agreement.

On American vs. British preferences

Note that the preferred British alternative to a sentence like "I don't have a car" would be "I haven't a car." Another more colloquial British and American alternative is "I haven't got a car." Although American speakers do accept and sometimes even use sentences like "I haven't a car," it should be recognized that they are more typically British than American.

Some —→ *any* suppletion[5]

We have seen above that negation in English is different from negation in many other languages, i.e., it is postauxiliary rather than preverbal or postverbal. Another unusual feature of English negative sentences we referred to earlier is that there usually can be only one overt negative particle per sentence.[6] Many other languages (even some dialects of English) permit two or more negative particles in the same sentence, and students speaking such a language or dialect tend to produce nonstandard sentences like this one:

*I didn't buy no books.

The standard form for this sentence, of course, is

I didn't buy any books.

How do we account for the presence of *any* in negative sentences? First of all, we should recognize that the affirmative counterpart of the above sentence is

I bought some books.

If we examine the following pairs of sentences, we can see that where the determiner *some* occurs in affirmative sentences of various types, *any* functions as the determiner in the negative counterpart.

Affirmative	*Negative*
Harry wants *some* sandwiches.	Harry doesn't want *any* sandwiches.
We need *some* paper.	We don't need *any* paper.

A rule referred to as "*some* —→ *any* suppletion" helps us to capture the notion that *some* —→ *any* in the environment of a preceding *not* and to correctly derive sentences such as "I didn't buy any books" in the following manner:

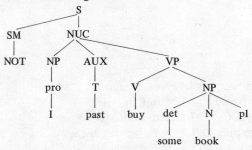

---

5. "Suppletion" is a term used to describe grammatically related forms that are not etymologically related (i.e., that do not have the same historical root). For example, *go* and *went* are suppletive forms—so are the inflected forms of the copula BE—so are *good* and *better*. Thus we also consider *some* and *any* to be suppletive forms.

6. It is of course possible to have a sentential negative (i.e., *not*) along with a phrasal or lexical negative in the same sentence, although such sentences are rare (e.g., You can*'t* just *not* turn in your homework. Milly is *not un*coordinated). Sentences like these function in discourse as markers of surprise or contradiction or understatement. They are rarely the initial sentence in a conversation or text; i.e., they are a reaction to something previously said or done or written.

Output of base: NOT I past buy some book pl
NOT placement: I past NOT buy some book pl
DO support: I past DO NOT buy some book pl
Some ⟶ *any* suppletion: I past DO NOT buy any book pl
NOT contraction: I past DO + N'T buy any book pl
Affix attachment (2×): I DO + N'T + past buy any book + pl
Morphological rules: I didn't buy any books.

Recall that a brief discussion of the kinds of nouns that may occur with the determiners *some* and *any* was presented in Chapter 5, which covered lexical features.

Emphatic negatives

Sentences with a *no* determiner in the verb phrase such as

We have had no rain since March.

or an indefinite pronoun beginning with *no-* in the verb phrase such as

I saw no one.

function semantically as emphatic counterparts of sentences we have already looked at in this chapter, i.e., sentences with NOT or -N'T and some form of *any* in the verb phrase. Thus the following sentences would be the nonemphatic counterparts of the two above sentences.

We haven't had any rain since March.   I didn't see anyone.

If it had already been established in the previous discourse that *rain* (or the lack of it) is the topic, the first sentence would be rendered as "We've had none since March." *None* is the negative pronoun form for *no* + noun (plural or mass).

When a count noun follows the *no* determiner, it may be either singular or plural, depending upon certain conditions. If the speaker is making a general claim about the absence of something, he or she will use a plural form.

There are no *books* required for the course.

Some ESL/EFL students have found this odd, since one wouldn't expect a plural form to be used to assert the absence of something; however, *books* is used here in a generic or general sense and therefore the plural is the appropriate form. We will have more to say about generic forms in our chapter on articles.

On the other hand, when a speaker is referring to a specific noun, he or she is likely to use a singular form for the count noun following *no*:

I can't give you the laundry because you have *no receipt.*

Sentences with *no* forms in the verb phrase, while semantically similar to sentences with NOT . . . *any,* have a different basic structure in that they have negative determiners lexically inserted into the base.[7] To illustrate this, here's how the tree would look for the first sentence in this section:

---

7. Remember, however, that use of either the determiner *no* or the sentence modifier NOT results in sentence-level negation.

We have had no rain since March.

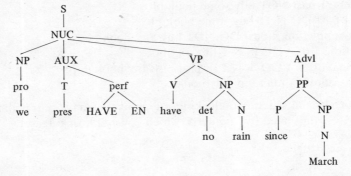

Although no definitive research has been done, we can see that the alternatives with *no* certainly have a different meaning and function from those with NOT or -N'T plus *any*. They are more emphatically negative and the negation seems to be focused on the following noun or on the negative indefinite pronoun itself rather than disbursed throughout the sentence. However, there is sufficient semantic similarity to merit this brief discussion of the *no* + noun pattern.

In addition to this pattern, we also draw your attention to the compound pronouns:

some-	*any-*	*no-*
someone/body	anyone/body	no one, nobody
something	anything	nothing
somewhere	anywhere	nowhere
etc.	etc.	etc.

They would be introduced into a sentence following the process discussed so far in this chapter. The compound pronouns in the first column would be found in affirmative sentences. If the sentence is negated with NOT, the pronouns in the first column would be lexically inserted into the base, but would be transformed into the pronouns of the second column[8] by the *some* ⟶ *any* suppletion rule. If the scope of the negation is more emphatic and focused, the pronouns in the third column will be lexically inserted into the base from the start.

Conclusion

This concludes our initial discussion of negation in English. We will return to this area when we examine many other topics such as questions, pronouns, quantifiers, and preverbal adverbs of frequency.

TEACHING SUGGESTIONS

1   One of the best ways of getting your beginning-level nonnative speakers of English to understand NOT placement and DO support is to use a flannel board with words and

---

8. It is, of course, also possible for the pronouns in the second column to be directly generated in the base. They are used independently of NOT to convey a general, selective meaning, which is parallel to the other meaning of the determiner *any*, e.g.:

Any fool can tell you that.   Joe would follow Linda *anywhere*.
Anyone can do that.

inflections on slips of paper or an overhead projector with words and inflectional endings on individual pieces of plastic that can be moved around. Thus you could present the class with a sentence like the following (let them listen and repeat):

You could then change ⬚SWIM⬚ to ⬚DIVE⬚, put a strip of paper or plastic with ⬚NOT⬚ above this second sentence and ask students to place it inside the sentence properly. Finally you would ask the student to read the negative sentence she or he had produced. (Note: If this is your students' first experience with negative sentences, you should complete several examples for them to observe and hear before asking them to do this.) After all the familiar sentence patterns with the verb BE and the auxiliary verbs have been practiced and understood, the teacher can introduce the DO-support problem beginning with plural subject sentences such as the following (have them listen and repeat):

Then ⬚CANDY⬚ is changed to ⬚HOMEWORK⬚ and ⬚DO⬚ and ⬚NOT⬚ are placed above the new sentence, and they are inserted before the verb in that order, with you pointing out that the ⬚DO⬚ is carrying the tense and showing number agreement with the subject. Have them do this with several other sentences.

The next step, of course, would be for you to deal with sentences such as this one:

⬚MARIA⬚ ⬚SPEAK⬚⬚S⬚ ⬚SPANISH⬚

After ⬚SPANISH⬚ has been changed to ⬚ENGLISH⬚, ⬚DO⬚ and ⬚NOT⬚ are again placed above the sentence and inserted before the verb in that order. Then the ⬚S⬚ on *speaks* is moved over to follow ⬚DO⬚ (i.e., to follow the *first* verb form in the sentence), at which point a newly introduced form, ⬚DOES⬚, can be substituted for the two strips ⬚DO⬚ and ⬚S⬚. This exercise will require more drill than the previous ones. After the rearrangement and substitution have been completed, your student(s) should say the sentence and practice several others like it.

2 To develop communicative ability in using negation, the students should have extensive opportunity to use the transformations appropriately and to discriminate the use of affirmative and negative forms.

a. To practice negation orally in the context of a process of elimination—a context that uses the full form *not*—Jacquelyn Schachter suggests the use of incomplete pictures that can be used to elicit a series of negative statements leading to a guess.

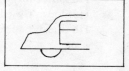

S1: It's not a house.
S2: It's not a tree.
S3: It's not a man.
S4: Maybe it's a car.

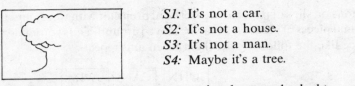

S1: It's not a car.
S2: It's not a house.
S3: It's not a man.
S4: Maybe it's a tree.

b. Later they can be given pictures of objects on exercise sheets and asked to complete reinforcing sentences in writing as follows:

What's this?
It _____ a house.

What's this?
It _____ a house.
It's a _____ .

What's this?
It _____ a tree.
It's a _____ .

What's this?
It _____ a tree.

Pictures with two or three objects of the same kind should also be used to elicit the plural, e.g., They are/are not houses.

c. The teacher can ask questions or make statements that will deliberately elicit a negative response (in this context, short responses and contraction of the *not* particle should be encouraged), e.g.:

T: Do you speak French, Juan?
J: No, I don't (speak French). I speak Spanish.

T: Honolulu is in Oregon.
S: No, it isn't (in Oregon). It's in Hawaii.

d. For practicing the use of *not* to express contrast have your students write up two lists that describe a friend or relative—an affirmative list and a negative list. These lists should bring out the main characteristics in the person. Your students can then make a brief oral presentation to the class based on these lists. Encourage them to use *but* to bring out the contrasts and to use *and* to bring out similarities. You may have to give them a model of what you expect them to do, e.g.:

"My brother Ali"

YES	NO
He is tall.	He is not fat at all.
He studies hard.	He doesn't waste time.
He speaks English.	He doesn't speak French.
etc.	etc.

"Let me tell you about my brother Ali. He is tall and not fat at all. He studies hard and doesn't waste time. He speaks English, but not French."

3   One way of getting students to practice the *some-any* suppletion rule in context is this role-playing situation:

A persistent host or hostess keeps offering food and drink to an unexpected guest, who has just finished eating dinner and is not at all hungry or thirsty—the host(ess) keeps offering, and the guest keeps refusing.

a: Would you like some
$$\left\{ \begin{array}{l} \text{nuts} \\ \text{cookies} \\ \text{tea} \\ \text{coffee} \\ \text{candy} \\ \text{grapes} \\ \vdots \end{array} \right\} \quad ?$$

b: No, $\left\{ \begin{array}{l} \text{thanks} \\ \text{thank you} \end{array} \right\}$, I don't want any _____ . $\left\{ \begin{array}{l} \text{I've just eaten.} \\ \text{I'm not hungry.} \\ \text{I'm not thirsty.} \end{array} \right\}$

EXERCISES

Test your understanding of what has been presented

1. Provide original sentences or pairs of sentences that illustrate the following concepts. Underline the pertinent word(s) in your examples.

NOT contraction	word-level negation
DO support	multiple negation
some → *any* suppletion	grammatical
sentence-level negation	ungrammatical

2. Give basic structures and complete derivations for the following sentences:

a. We might not be having that class today.
b. Alice doesn't know any jokes.
c. You haven't been around this neighborhood.
d. The boys did not break the window.
e. They have no children.
f. Meg is not about to listen to Philip.

Test your ability to apply what you know

3. If your students produce the following sentences, what errors have they made? How will you make them aware of the errors, and what exercises will you prepare to correct them?

a. *He no go to Harvard.
b. *I not understand that.
c. *She don't be the teacher.
d. *I didn't do nothing.

4. Starting with the few examples given in this chapter for regular (disyllabic) and irregular (monosyllabic) contracted NOT verb forms, complete the list and suggest a way of

teaching the irregular forms to your students.

5. Another optional contraction rule is AUX *contraction*. It accounts for the contraction of present tense forms of BE and present and past-tense forms of *will* and HAVE with the subject noun phrase, which is often a pronoun; e.g.: *I am* ⟶ *I'm; He is* ⟶ *he's*. List all the combinations that the AUX contraction rule would produce. Explain the ambiguity of *you'd* and *it's*. Why can we have either NOT *contraction* or AUX *contraction* in a negated sentence but not both? That is:

Jack isn't a teacher.   *Jack'sn't a teacher.
Jack's not a teacher.

6. Many relatively advanced ESL/EFL students systematically refuse to contract the negative particle in their speech and written work. How would you teach them the fact that contraction is expected (i.e., the norm) in informal speech and writing?

7. One of your students asks you why you have indicated that the following sentence in his composition is incorrect:

I have not studied no other foreign language besides English.

What would you say?

BIBLIOGRAPHY

References

Klima, E. (1964). "Negation in English," in Fodor and Katz (eds.), *The Structure of Language.* Englewood Cliffs, N.J.: Prentice-Hall, pp. 246–323.

Schumann, J. (1979). "The Acquisition of English Negation by Speakers of Spanish: A Review of the Literature," in R. Andersen (ed.), *The Acquisition and Use of Spanish and English as First and Second Languages.* Washington, D.C.: TESOL.

Suggestions for further reading

For the most comprehensive and thorough treatment of negation in English, see Klima (1964) cited above.

For other transformational accounts of negation in English (for comparison with the one presented in this chapter), refer to these sources:

Culicover, P. (1976). *Syntax.* New York: Academic Press, pp. 120ff.

Liles, B. (1971). *An Introductory Transformational Grammar.* Englewood Cliffs, N.J.: Prentice-Hall, pp. 43–50.

For an interesting nontransformational account of *any* and its relation to negation, see:

Bolinger, D. (1977). *Meaning and Form.* New York and London: Longman, Chaps. 2, 3.

For a useful traditional description of negation in English, consult the following source:

Jespersen, O. (1966). *Essentials of English Grammar.* University, Ala.: University of Alabama Press, Chap. 28.

For further pedagogical suggestions on teaching negation, consult these textbooks:

Hayden, R., D. Pilgrim, and A. Haggard (1956). *Mastering American English.* Englewood Cliffs, N.J.: Prentice-Hall, pp. 3–12.

McIntosh, L., T. Ramos, and R. Goulet (1970). *Advancing in English.* New York: American Book Co., pp. 4–7.

9

Yes-No Questions

GRAMMATICAL DESCRIPTION

Introduction

A question is referred to as a yes-no question when the person responding is expected to answer "yes" or "no" (e.g., "Are you feeling better?"), as opposed to the way one supplies information in answering a question such as "What is today's date?"

Problems for learners

Yes-no question formation in English is often difficult for beginning ESL/EFL students to master. One reason may be the way yes-no questions are formed in their native language. English forms yes-no questions by means of inversion—so do some other languages, such as German, but generally their inversion rule is simpler than the English one. Inversion is by no means a universal way of forming yes-no questions. Some languages use phrases or particles at the beginning or end of a sentence to signal that what follows or precedes is a yes-no question. Other languages signal yes-no questions with rising intonation.[1] Since the inversion rule that forms yes-no questions in English is a bit complicated, ESL/EFL learners often tend not to invert and to depend on intonation instead. Your job as the ESL/EFL teacher will be to give your students plenty of practice with the inversion rule when they use yes-no questions in English.

An analysis of yes-no questions

Consider the following yes-no questions:

1. Are the children playing in the yard?
2. Will John study linguistics?
3. Has Alice gone home?
4. Were you able to see George?

---

1. There are times when native speakers of English produce uninverted yes/no questions with rising intonation because of factors such as the speaker's presuppositions, emotional level, and whether or not a new topic is being introduced (see Vander Brook, Schlue, and Campbell, 1980). For example, if the speaker presupposes he or she will receive an affirmative answer from a listener, he or she may well say, "You saw the game last night?" However, it should be emphasized that inverted questions are the norm, i.e., the yes-no question form used by native speakers most of the time.

A reasonable explanation for the generation of these yes-no questions from basic structures would be some sort of movement rule (the transformation is called subject/auxiliary inversion) which would advance the auxiliary verb and tense marker to the first position in the question. However, without further qualification, such a rule does not work in all cases and could result in the generation of unacceptable question forms as well:

*Has been he practicing the piano?   *Were able to you see George?
*Could have been Mike home?

Thus if there is more than one lexical element in the auxiliary and the whole auxiliary is fronted, an ungrammatical question is generated. Yes-no questions in English have only one auxiliary element to the left of the subject NP. Furthermore, the auxiliary that is moved to sentence initial position is the auxiliary which occupies the first position in the sequence of auxiliaries in the base structure.
Thus,

*Has the family will be reunited?

is unacceptable since the HAVE of the perfect aspect would never precede a modal in an English sentence. [Recall the order of elements in AUX: $\begin{Bmatrix} T \\ M \end{Bmatrix}$ (PM) (perf) (prog)].

Next, consider the following sentences:

Are they your paintings?   Were they absent?
Is he your teacher?

From these examples we can see that when a sentence contains the copula BE as the main verb and no auxiliary verb, the BE gets fronted. Thus, whenever we use the term "subject/auxiliary inversion" we include the copula BE in this rule as well. Just as with all tensed auxiliary verbs, we note that the fronted BE verb does not appear in its infinitive form on the surface level and therefore must be accompanied by the tense marker when it moves.[2]

The Q marker which appears in the basic structure is a sentence marker which calls for the yes-no question transformation (i.e., subject/auxiliary inversion). It is the feature that distinguishes yes-no questions from statements.

Let's examine one example to see the subject/auxiliary inversion transformation in operation:

Sentence: Had Mark seen the letter?

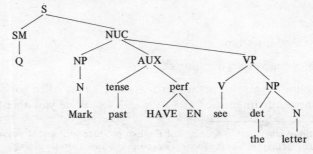

---

2. Note that in British English, the main verb *have* will also be fronted in the formation of yes-no questions as in: "Has he a car?" While such a form is not considered ungrammatical in American English, it is not common. There is also the colloquial alternative with *have got* (Has he got a car?) where *have* is functioning as an auxiliary in both British and American English.

Output of base: Q Mark past HAVE EN see the letter
Subject/auxiliary inversion: past HAVE Mark EN see the letter
Affix attachment (2X): HAVE + past Mark see + EN the letter
Morphological rules: Had Mark seen the letter?

In addition to the types of yes-no questions shown in the preceding examples, it is also possible to form a yes-no question in English without the presence of an auxiliary verb or the copula BE. Consider the following examples:

> Mary saw her friend.   John works hard.
> The boys go to school.

Obviously, if we were to front the main verb + tense marker in these sentences as we did with BE, ungrammatical questions—in current though not in historically earlier forms of English—would result:

> *Saw Mary her friend?   *Works John hard?
> *Go the boys to school?

When a main verb exists in a basic structure marked with a yes-no question marker and it is other than BE (or HAVE in certain British English sentences[3]), only the tense marker gets inverted. Since tense cannot stand alone in English, a tense carrier, the DO auxiliary, must be added by the DO-support transformation, which we encountered in the preceding chapter.

Such a transformation, you will recall, inserts DO following the tense marker when the tense marker is separated from an auxiliary verb or a main verb. The application of the subject/auxiliary transformation in sentences without an auxiliary verb or BE copula will result in application of the DO-support rule. For example:

Do they work here?

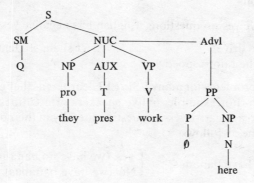

Output of base: Q they pres work here
Subject/auxiliary inversion: pres they work here (Tense is separated from a main or auxiliary
    verb to which it could attach.)
DO support: pres DO they work here
Affix attachment (1X): DO + pres they work here
Morphological rules: Do they work here?

---

3. See footnote 2 for an example.

Here is another example: Did John see the movie?

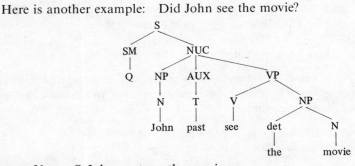

Output of base: Q John past see the movie
Subject/auxiliary inversion: past John see the movie
DO support: past DO John see the movie
Affix attachment (1✗): DO + past John see the movie
Morphological rules: Did John see the movie?

Notions such as basic structure, the subject/auxiliary inversion transformation, and tense carrier help us to gain insight into the process of question formation in English. We would not be doing a service to our ESL/EFL students, however, by using such terminology. What generalizations about yes-no questions can we make that would be useful for our students?

ESL/EFL students should be taught that in a yes-no question the auxiliary verb (the first one in a sentence) should appear initially and mark the tense of the question. If there is no auxiliary, the copula BE should be fronted and carry tense. If there is no auxiliary or BE verb to carry tense, DO must be introduced in initial position and combined with the tense to serve this function.

Negative yes-no questions

In addition to affirmative yes-no questions, English has negative yes-no questions such as:

Can't he drive?   Isn't she a student?
Hasn't the rain stopped yet?

There are semantic problems for many ESL/EFL learners as they encounter negative yes-no questions in English. For example, native speakers of a Chinese language or a West African language react to a negative yes-no question literally in their own language. In literal translation, this would be as follows:

Don't you have bananas? $\begin{cases} \text{Yes, (we have no bananas).} \\ \text{No, (we have bananas).} \end{cases}$

The native speaker of English, on the other hand, reacts to negative yes-no questions as if they were affirmative ones, with the only difference being one of presupposition, e.g.:[4]

Don't you have bananas? $\begin{cases} \text{Yes, (we do).} \\ \text{No, (we don't).} \end{cases}$

As an ESL/EFL teacher you should be aware of this fundamental semantic difference and you should find out whether your students react to negative yes-no questions the English way

---

4. Compare "Don't you have bananas?" with "Do you have bananas?" The former is used when the speaker thought the hearer would have bananas and then suddenly received information to the contrary, whereas the latter is used in situations without any expectations or in situations with positive expectations.

or the other way. If they react the other way, considerable practice will be needed to make the difference clear and to avoid the possibility of miscommunication.

A less common alternative form, which is formal but nonetheless acceptable, for the three yes-no questions cited above would be as follows:

> Can he not drive?   Is she not a student?
> Has the rain not stopped?

In contrast, the following questions are unacceptable in current English:

> *Can not he drive?   *Is not she a student?
> *Has not the rain stopped?

How then can we account for negative yes-no questions? Transformational grammar offers a solution to the problem of generating only the acceptable negative yes-no questions. By ordering our transformations properly we can both produce acceptable forms of the negative question and eliminate any possibility of producing the ungrammatical ones.

Example sentence: Is John not swimming?

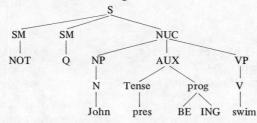

To produce a negative question in which negative contraction does not occur, the following order should be followed:

Output of base: NOT Q John pres BE ING swim
NOT placement: Q John pres BE NOT ING swim
Subject/auxiliary inversion: pres BE John NOT ING swim
Affix attachment (2✕): BE + pres John NOT swim + ING
Subject-verb agreement and morphological rules: Is John not swimming?

If we wanted to produce a negative question with a contracted negative from the same basic structure (i.e., "Isn't John swimming?"), the following order of transformations would be appropriate:

Output of base: NOT Q John pres BE ING swim
NOT placement: Q John pres BE NOT ING swim
NOT contraction: Q John pres BE + N'T ING swim
Subject/auxiliary inversion: pres BE + N'T John ING swim
Affix attachment (2✕): BE + N'T + pres John swim + ING
Subject-verb agreement and morphological rules: Isn't John swimming?

Next, consider the following negative question:

> Doesn't he live here?

In a question such as this we know that the DO-support transformation must operate, but how is it ordered with respect to the other transformations?

We have already learned that in a negative statement the NOT placement transformation must precede the DO-support transformation because it is the structural change which results from the NOT placement transformation which provides the motivation for applying the DO-support transformation.

Thus, the basic structure and first two transformations for the above negative question would look like this:

Doesn't he live here?

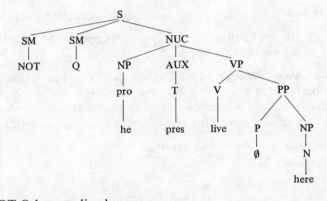

Output of base: NOT Q he pres live here
NOT placement: Q he pres NOT live here
DO support: Q he pres DO NOT live here

Moreover, we know the order of negative contraction and subject/auxiliary inversion transformation with respect to each other. NOT contraction must precede the subject/auxiliary inversion transformation in order to produce negative questions with contracted negatives. Thus,

NOT contraction: Q he pres DO + N'T live here

If we consider DO our first lexical auxiliary verb, it gets inverted (along with the tense and the contracted affix -N'T) by our subject/auxiliary inversion transformation.

Subject/auxiliary inversion: pres DO + N'T he live here

We finish the derivation by applying the affix attachment transformation and the subject-verb agreement transformation, respectively:

Affix attachment (1×): DO + N'T + pres he live here
Subject-verb agreement and morphological rules: Doesn't he live here?

What insight does this analysis give us with regard to the formation of negative yes-no questions in English?

In English negative questions, the negative may appear in both contracted and uncontracted forms. Only the contracted form may appear sentence-initially as part of an auxiliary verb, however. The uncontracted NOT will appear internal to the sentence preceding the remainder of the auxiliary or the VP.

In a usage study that argues against our analysis of negative yes-no questions, Kontra (1981) documents the occurrence in contemporary English of uncontracted negative questions such as the following:

a. Is not linguistics a branch of psychology?

In our analysis we have ruled out such questions and argue instead that *b* is the grammatical form:

b. Is linguistics not a branch of psychology?

We view the *a* type question as a very formal and rather archaic historical vestige, i.e., something reminiscent of Elizabethan literature or the King James version of the Bible, and thus we strongly feel that the *b* version is the preferred contemporary form. Evidence for our position comes from the fact that the *a* type question has a limited distribution; the subject of the *a* type question may never be a pronoun, whereas the *b* type question takes pronominal subjects freely:

a. *Is not it a branch of psychology?   b. Is it not a branch of psychology?

We do admit, however, that the older form may still occur occasionally in formal English writing—particularly so, perhaps, if the author has had heavy exposure to English literature or English versions of the Bible that were produced two or more centuries ago.

A final note on contracted negative yes-no questions concerns the lexical gap that occurs in the first person singular. We can say all of the following:

He/she/it isn't. ⟶ Isn't he/she/it?
You/they/we aren't. ⟶ Aren't you/they/we?

However, we cannot contract the verb BE and the NOT in *I am not* unless we use nonstandard *I ain't*. Thus we also have no grammatically related yes-no question form unless we also use nonstandard *ain't I?* This, of course, holds true for question tags as well as yes-no questions. What speakers of English often do in yes-no questions and question tags (but not in statements) is to substitute *are* for *am* and contract. Thus:

I am not. ⟶ Aren't I?

This illogical gap-filler arose because there were strong social and educational stigmas against the use of *ain't*. *Aren't I* is mainly a colloquialism, but it may puzzle your perceptive ESL/EFL students when they encounter it; so you should be prepared to explain why we sometimes say *aren't I* in yes-no questions and in tag questions.

Short answers to yes-no questions

It is unlikely that the response to a yes-no question will be in the form of a full sentence:

Is Ramón an engineering student?

Yes. $\begin{Bmatrix} \text{He is} \\ \text{He's} \end{Bmatrix}$ an engineering student.

No. He isn't an engineering student.

Although these answers are possible, such replies may give the listener the impression that the speaker is annoyed by the question. ESL/EFL teachers should be aware of the possible negativity expressed by a full-sentence answer to a yes-no question and not insist on their students answering questions with full sentences, as teachers are sometimes wont to do.

A more neutral form of reply to a yes-no question is the so-called "short answer."

Is Ramón an engineering student? $\begin{Bmatrix} \text{Yes, he is.} \\ \text{No, he isn't.} \end{Bmatrix}$

If the yes-no question begins with the copula BE, as in our example sentence, the short answer is formed with the same form of the BE verb that appeared in the question if there is a third person subject. Notice that BE is not contracted in an affirmative short answer.[5]

*Yes, he's.

If the reply is negative, the NOT is usually contracted with the BE, although an uncontracted NOT is also possible,

$$\text{No,} \quad \left\{ \begin{array}{l} \text{he's} \\ \text{he is} \end{array} \right\} \quad \text{not.}$$

if a more formal or emphatic answer is warranted. Of course, if the question asks about the second person,

Are you an engineering student?

the reply would require that a different form of BE be used,

$$\left\{ \begin{array}{l} \text{Yes, I am.} \\ \text{No, I'm not.} \end{array} \right\}$$

one that doesn't allow for contraction of BE with NOT (i.e., *amn't).

When the yes-no question begins with an auxiliary verb, and the sentence contains only one auxiliary verb, that auxiliary verb is used in the short answer.

With a modal:

Can he go? $\left\{ \begin{array}{l} \text{Yes, he can.} \\ \text{No, he can't.} \end{array} \right\}$

With HAVE ... EN:

Has he gone? $\left\{ \begin{array}{l} \text{Yes, he has.} \\ \text{No, he hasn't.} \end{array} \right\}$

With BE ... ING:

Is he going? $\left\{ \begin{array}{l} \text{Yes, he is.} \\ \text{No, he isn't.} \end{array} \right\}$

If the sentence contains more than one auxiliary verb, the short answer may also contain an auxiliary verb in addition to the one which begins the question, although if the second or third auxiliary verb is some form of BE, the speaker usually omits it.

With modal + HAVE ... EN:

Will he have gone? $\left\{ \begin{array}{l} \text{Yes, he will} \quad \left\{ \begin{array}{l} \text{have.} \\ \text{'ve.} \end{array} \right\} \\ \text{No, he won't} \quad \left\{ \begin{array}{l} \text{have.} \\ \text{'ve.} \end{array} \right\} \end{array} \right\}$

With modal + BE ... ING:

Will he be going? $\left\{ \begin{array}{l} \text{Yes, he will (be).} \\ \text{No, he won't (be).} \end{array} \right\}$

With modal + HAVE ... EN + BE ... ING:

Will he have been going...? $\left\{ \begin{array}{l} \text{Yes, he will} \quad \left\{ \begin{array}{l} \text{have} \\ \text{'ve} \end{array} \right\} \quad \text{(been).} \\ \text{No, he won't} \quad \left\{ \begin{array}{l} \text{have} \\ \text{'ve} \end{array} \right\} \quad \text{(been).} \end{array} \right\}$

---

5. Actually, no single auxiliary verb is contracted with the subject in an affirmative short answer.

*Yes, he'd.   *Yes, he'll.

With HAVE . . . EN + BE . . . ING:

Has he been going there often? $\left\{\begin{array}{l}\text{Yes, he has (been).}\\ \text{No, he hasn't (been).}\end{array}\right\}$

If there is no auxiliary verb or copula BE, DO is used in the short answer as it is in the question:

Does he go there often? $\left\{\begin{array}{l}\text{Yes, he does.}\\ \text{No, he doesn't.}\end{array}\right\}$

While these short-answer forms are worth teaching ESL/EFL students, one should bear in mind that even these forms do not occur frequently as responses to yes-no questions. In a discourse analysis of speech samples collected from a wide variety of contexts, Winn-Bell Olsen (1980) found that short forms were used rather infrequently by native English speakers—in fact, only 8 percent of the time—as answers to yes-no questions in her data (26/329 instances). She discovered that native speakers were much more likely to answer questions with a direct "yes" (or its colloquial variants, e.g., "yup," "yeah," "uh huh") or a direct "no" (or its variants, e.g., "nah," "nope," "uh uh"), each often followed by some sort of expansion. Indirect affirmations/denials or hedges (e.g., "Does it make you uncomfortable to talk about the problem?" "I guess maybe in a sense it does") accounted for a rather large percentage of the answers as well. Finally, a significant portion of the answers were formulaic expressions of confirmation or denial (e.g., "I doubt it"). Since 23 out of 26 occurrences of short-form answers in her data were found in conversations between strangers or in self-conscious speech, Winn-Bell Olsen hypothesizes that the more distant the relationship between speakers or the more uncomfortable the situation, the more frequently speakers tend to use short-form answers.

Some/any variation in yes-no questions

In yes-no questions there is subtle variation between *some* and *any* that cannot be explained using the *some/any* suppletion rule discussed in the preceding chapter. Consider questions like these:

1. Do you want $\left\{\begin{array}{l}\text{some}\\ \text{any}\end{array}\right\}$ coffee?   2. Do you have $\left\{\begin{array}{l}\text{some}\\ \text{any}\end{array}\right\}$ scratch paper?

A polite hostess making an offer for the first time would undoubtedly use *some* in her version of the first question. The same question with *any* is more informal, less directed, and may also be anticipating (or encouraging) a negative response—e.g.:

"I'm getting myself some coffee. $\left\{\begin{array}{l}\text{Do you}\\ \text{Does anyone}\end{array}\right\}$ want any?"

In the second question, however, *any* would probably occur as often as *some*. Here the speaker is making a request rather than an offer, and since *scratch paper* is a relatively low-value commodity, the speaker may feel justified in down-playing the request, in making it as casual as possible. The use of *some* in the second question could indicate that the speaker feels a sense of urgency or importance about obtaining the scratch paper.

Elliptical yes-no questions

At some point you will want to expose your intermediate- and advanced-level students to informal yes-no questions that occur without an overt initial auxiliary. Such questions are fairly frequent in informal conversations between native speakers and are different from uninverted yes-no questions.[6]

(Are) you going to the movies?   (Were) they supposed to finish the work
(Has) she been feeling better?   last night?
(Do) you know Fred Callaghan?

In such questions the auxiliary is optionally deletable because it is recoverable from other grammatical and lexical information in the question and from the discourse context. It would probably not be of high priority for your students to practice using such elliptical yes-no questions, but they should develop comprehension of this form and perhaps an ability to automatically supply the missing auxiliary.

In transformational terms we could account for this phenomenon with a rule of optional auxiliary deletion that could apply to certain yes-no questions, given certain conditions.

The periphrastic modals and yes-no questions

The periphrastic modals, unlike the modal auxiliaries, vary with regard to yes-no question formation. Most treat their first element as an auxiliary verb that can be inverted, but a few require DO support. The latter will have to be practiced separately.

Behave like Auxiliaries
(first element inverts)   *Require* Do *Support*
be going to ("Are you going to stay?")   used to ("Did you use to?"[7])
be able to   have to ("Do you have to?")
be to
be supposed to
had better
would rather
would like to
would prefer to

Conclusion

This ends our discussion of yes-no questions. Many of the things we have considered here, however, will come up again, particularly when we examine wh-questions in Chapter 12.

---

6. Uninverted yes-no questions may presuppose an affirmative answer (see statement intonation below) or they may express counterexpectation (i.e., surprise, disbelief), whereas elliptical yes-no questions are merely very informal variants of normal, inverted questions and convey no special presupposition or expectation. Note the difference in intonation, too:

UNINVERTED: You've been to Acapulco?   or   You've been to Aca/pul/co?
                (surprise intonation)   (statementlike intonation)

ELLIPTICAL: (You) been to Aca/pulco?
                (normal question intona-
                tion)

Here the difference between *you* and *you've* is very slight; native speakers attend mainly to the intonation differences to distinguish between uninverted and elliptical yes-no questions. See Vander Brook et al. (1980) for more details.

7. Some people write this question as "Did you used to?" However, "Did you use to?" is the preferred written form, since the past-tense inflection should be marked only in the *first* auxiliary element.

TEACHING SUGGESTIONS

1   As was suggested in Chapter 8 for negatives, the flannel board or overhead projector is also a useful device for teaching yes-no question formation. For sentences containing an auxiliary verb or BE, you can demonstrate fronting by substituting a question mark card for the period card and then moving the appropriate auxiliary verb card to sentence initial position. For example:

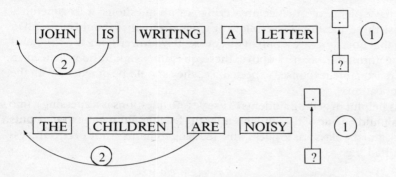

In order to form yes-no questions without an auxiliary verb or BE, you will need to insert a DO card in the front of the sentence after substituting a question mark card for the period card. For example:

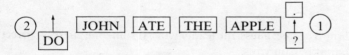

Next, you will explain to your students that the function of the DO is to "carry the tense" for the question. This can be demonstrated by replacing the DO card with *did* and the *ate* card with *eat* after substituting the ? for the . . Thus:

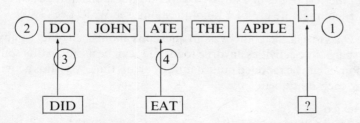

Cards could also be used to show that the DO carries the tense and person markings.

(1) Put these on flannel board.   JOHN EAT S APPLES .

(2) Substitute ? at the end of the sentence and introduce DO to front of sentence.

(3) Show that the S of *eats* gets moved to the initial DO by moving the S from its

position after EAT to a position following DO . Immediately replace DO S with a new card $\boxed{\text{DOES}}$ explaining that rewriting *do* plus third person singular

present as *does* is a convention we follow. After several examples have been done by the teacher, it is good to have student volunteers come up and practice forming questions by moving and substituting the cards. If you have the time, you could even prepare (or have students prepare) pieces of paper with the words, question marks, and morphemes for each student to manipulate at his or her desk.

2   Although students have plenty of practice answering yes-no questions, it is sometimes difficult to get them to ask these questions. The following types of activities should be useful in this regard. Remember that questions are a part of discourse. Beyond verifying the structural facts of yes-no question formation as in 1 above, these questions should be practiced in contexts with true and reasonable responses expected; i.e., they should be practiced with the expectation of communication.

a. One game that is helpful in getting students to use yes-no questions is a guessing game where the leader, who should be one of the students after the teacher has demonstrated, puts an object in a paper sack and the class has to guess what the sack contains—however, only yes-no questions are permitted, e.g.:

S1:	Is it hard?	*S4:*	Is it solid?
L:	No.	*L:*	No.
S2:	Is it round?	*S5:*	Is it a balloon?
L:	Yes.	*L:*	Yes.
S3:	Is it a ball?		
L:	No.		

If 20 questions are asked without a correct guess, the leader wins. If someone guesses correctly within the 20-question limit, that person wins.

b. Other yes-no question games that use the same approach and encourage generation of yes-no questions are "What's My Line?" (members of the class select unusual occupations for themselves (e.g., astronaut) and the rest of the class must ask yes-no questions and guess) and "Who am I?" (a member of the class pretends to be a well-known historical or contemporary figure (e.g., Napoleon) and the rest of the class must ask yes-no questions and guess).

For other games that encourage the use of yes-no questions, see W. R. Lee (1979).

3   Getting students in the class to ask each other yes-no questions about each other's native country, academic major, spare-time activities, favorite foods, etc., can be useful in that some practice with negative responses can be recycled quite naturally at this time. Also, this activity helps students get to know each other better, e.g.:

S1:   Are you from Mexico?
S2:   No, I'm not. I'm from Guatemala.

S3:   Do you study engineering?
S4:   Yes, I do.

S5:   Do you enjoy disco dancing?
S6:   No, I don't. I'm a lousy dancer.
        etc.

4   With beginning-level students who need a more controlled activity, a chain drill activity can be used to elicit a yes-no question followed by either an affirmative or a negative response.

T:	Are you a student?	T:	I'm a teacher.
S1:	Yes, I am.		Are you a teacher?
	Are you a student?	S1:	No, I'm a student.
S2:	Yes, I am.		Are you a teacher?
	Are you a student?	S2:	No, I'm a student.
	⋮		⋮

5 You can introduce a series of pictures that tell a story. First, get the class to tell the story (e.g., The man walked out the front door and tripped over his son's wagon. He scolded his son and told him to put the wagon in the garage. The boy did this. A while later the man went into the garage and tripped over his son's wagon again!).

After telling the story the class would review and expand on the story by asking only yes-no questions of each other, e.g.:

Did the man trip over the wagon?	Did he scold his son?
Did he hurt himself?	etc.
Was he angry?	

6 A problem-solving activity that your students can do in pairs to further reinforce the use of yes-no questions is dialog-completion exercises such as the following one in which missing yes-no questions must be supplied by each pair:

A: I come from Egypt. (1) _____ Mexico?
B: No, I'm from Ecuador.
A: (2) _____ Engineering?
B: Yes, I do. (3) _____ too?
A: No, I'm studying Physics.

After all the pairs have completed such an exercise, the completions can be compared and, where necessary, corrected. Often more than one alternative is possible.

7 Sometimes reciting verse or poetry can be a pleasant reinforcement of a grammatical structure. Several of Christina Rossetti's poems, for example, make repeated use of yes-no questions. They lend themselves to reading aloud in pairs or groups—one can ask the question, the other can answer it. If you feel your ESL/EFL students would enjoy such an activity, we recommend that you experiment with this type of reinforcement for yes-no questions.

EXERCISES

Test your understanding of what has been presented

1. Provide original example sentences that illustrate the following concepts. Underline the pertinent word(s) in your examples.

negative yes-no question
  with contraction (informal)
  without contraction (formal)
yes-no question with DO support
yes-no question without DO support
yes-no question with a periphrastic
    modal
  requiring DO support
  not requiring DO support

short-form answers
elliptical yes-no question
the semantics of responses to negative
    yes-no questions in English

2. Give the basic structure and complete derivation for the following sentences:

a. Did he write the letter?
b. Wasn't she in San Francisco yesterday?
c. Have you been living in New York?

d. Would her brother come to the party?
e. Has Mr. Jones not read the report?
f. Aren't we supposed to do the dishes?

3. What rules have been violated as the following questions were formed?

a. *Do she went?
b. *Could have he gone?

c. *Runs he fast?

4. What do the NOT placement transformation and the subject/auxiliary inversion transformation have in common?

Test your ability to apply what you know

5. If your students produce the following starred items, what errors have they made? How will you make them aware of the errors, and what exercises will you prepare to correct them?

a. *Saw you the hole?
b. *Did you threw the ball?
c. *Is not she intelligent?

d. Do you like ice cream?
   *Yes, I like.

6. You have ESL/EFL students who react to negative yes-no questions literally (e.g., "Yes, we have no bananas"). What will you do to show them the difference between their response system and the English response system to negative yes-no questions?

7. You have a student who never inverts his yes-no questions in English in speech and who indicates yes-no questions only with intonation. When you tell him that he should invert, he replies that he often hears native speakers use uninverted questions. What would you say to this student?

BIBLIOGRAPHY

References

Kontra, M. (1981). "On English Negative Interrogatives," in J. E. Copeland and P. W. Davis (eds.), *The Seventh LACUS Forum 1980*. Columbia, S.C.: Hornbeam Press.

Lee, W. R. (1979). *Language-Teaching Games and Contests* (2d ed.). London: Oxford University Press.

Vander Brook, S., K. Schlue, and C. Campbell (1980). "Discourse Analysis and Second Language Acquisition of Yes-No Questions," in D. Larsen-Freeman (ed.), *Discourse Analysis and Second Language Research*. Rowley, Mass.: Newbury House.

Winn-Bell Olsen, J. (1980). "In Search of Y/N S-AUX: A Study of Answers to Yes-No Questions in English." Paper presented at the 6th Annual Meeting of the Berkeley Linguistics Society, February.

Suggestions for further reading

For other transformational analyses of English yes-no questions, see:

Culicover, P. (1976). *Syntax*. New York: Academic Press.

Stockwell, R. P., P. Schachter, and B. H. Partee (1973). *The Major Syntactic Structures of English*. New York: Holt, Rinehart and Winston.

For a nontransformational account of English yes-no questions, see:

Bolinger, D. L. (1957). *Interrogative Structures of American English (The Direct Question)*. Publication 28 of the American Dialect Society, University, Ala.: University of Alabama Press.

For some good ideas for ways of getting your students to understand and practice yes-no questions, consult the following references:

Brinton, D., and R. Neuman (1982). *Getting Along: English Grammar and Writing* (Book 1). Englewood Cliffs, N.J.: Prentice-Hall, pp. 60–61, 65–66.

Danielson, D., and R. Hayden (1973). *Using English: Your Second Language*. Englewood Cliffs, N.J.: Prentice-Hall, pp. 1–12.

Dart, A. K. (1978). *ESL Grammar Workbook 1*. Englewood Cliffs, N.J.: Prentice-Hall, pp. 1, 3, 6, 42, 47, 53, 66–67.

10

Pronouns and Possessives

GRAMMATICAL DESCRIPTION

Introduction

In this chapter we examine the form and function of the personal and possessive pronouns as well as treating other common ways of expressing possession in English. We also present the form of the reflexive, indefinite, and demonstrative pronouns as well as some other forms that function much like the demonstratives.

Discussion of other pronouns in English—such as reciprocal and relative pronouns—will be reserved for later chapters.

Personal pronouns

The following are the subject and object forms of the personal pronouns in English:

	Subject		*Object*	
	singular	*plural*	*singular*	*plural*
1st person	I	we	me	us
2nd person	you	you	you	you
3rd person	she/he/it	they	her/him/it	them
	(one)[1]		(one)[1]	

Both subject and object forms are used to refer to noun phrases which have been previously mentioned or which can be inferred from the context. Subject pronouns, of course, function as subjects in sentences.

Amos felt sad. *He* wanted to go. (i.e., *Amos* wanted to go.)
Elizabeth dislikes Gordon. *He* always teases everyone. (i.e., *Gordon* always teases everyone.)

Object pronouns function as direct or indirect objects, or as objects of prepositions.

---

1. The personal pronoun *one* is a formal, general third person pronoun that neutralizes the gender distinction in *she/he* or *her/him*. Since it is formal, it is of lower frequency than the other personal pronouns.

Joan entered the room. Anthony gave *her* the message. (i.e., Anthony gave *Joan* the message.)

Have you heard from the Johnsons? This letter is from *them*. (i.e., This letter is from *the Johnsons*.)

In verbless or elliptical utterances the object pronoun sometimes replaces the subject form, which would be expected in a complete sentence or in a partially reduced sentence with a verb form.

Who received the letter?
- I received the letter.
- I did.
- Me.

In full sentences with the copula BE, personal pronouns used to take the subject form in formal English even in verb-phrase position.

It is I.   This is she.

This usage is now changing even in formal English, and in informal English, the object form of the pronoun is definitely preferred:

It's me.
This is her. (more likely in a sentence such as: *That's her.*)

The desire to use formal English and be "correct" has led some native speakers to use *I* even as a conjoined direct object or a conjoined object of a preposition.

?This concerns only you and I.   ?The article was written by Nancy and I.
?Between you and I, he's a fool.

These forms may soon become colloquially acceptable. They are occurring with ever-increasing frequency.

Subject and object pronoun forms usually do not cause undue learning hardship for ESL/EFL students, since the English pronominal system is far simpler than that of many other languages. There are a few problems ESL/EFL teachers should be aware of, however. Many non-English speakers have told us that they find the presence of only one second person pronoun form, i.e., *you,* disconcerting and too direct. There is no way to be either formal or intimate linguistically and no way to be explicitly singular or plural. Another source of initial confusion, due to the simplicity of the English pronoun system, might occur for students whose native language has inclusive and exclusive forms of the first person plural pronoun. Having two such forms is typical of languages of the Malayo-Polynesian family. Indonesian speakers, for example, use *kita* to mean *we* when the person addressed is included as in:

We should (all) go to the movies next Saturday.

whereas *kami* means *we* excluding the person addressed:

Are we late? (addressed to person who has been waiting)

Since inclusive and exclusive meanings are both contained in the English first person plural pronouns, students who distinguish these forms in their native languages should not have problems once they recognize that one form is used to express both meanings in English.

A more serious problem arises for students whose native language makes no gender distinction for third person singular pronouns. Such students understand the use of *he* or *she/him* or *her,* of course, but since they are not accustomed to observing the distinction in their mother tongue, they often use the English pronouns inappropriately. Mere rule explication will probably do little to aid in this area; however, contextualized practice in using the various third person pronouns should help heighten student awareness.

Also, ESL/EFL students will have to learn that certain inanimate objects are sometimes referred to with a feminine pronoun form, although the use of *it* is more common today. This has been true for ships, countries, cars, and until recently, hurricanes.

Of course, there is also the whole controversy regarding whether or not it is sexist (or discriminatory) to use the third person singular masculine form when one intends to include both the meaning of *he* and *she* as in:

When a person first arrives in a new country, he has many adjustments to make.

For now this controversy will have to be resolved by each individual. Even if you yourself don't find such references offensive, you might explain to your ESL/EFL students that some people do and that alternatives are possible:

When a person first arrives in a new country, he or she has many adjustments to make.
When people first arrive in a new country, they have many adjustments to make.

Possessive pronouns

Possessive pronoun forms fulfill two functions: they can serve as a possessive determiner before a noun phrase, or they can replace an NP inflected for possession. (In the former case they are called possessive adjectives in traditional grammars):

> This is Sheila's book. ──▶ This is *her* book. (possessive determiner)
> This book is Sheila's. ──▶ This book is *hers.* (possessive pronoun)

Depending on whether they precede an NP or stand alone as pronouns, two different forms exist in all cases but the third person singular masculine form:

	Determiner Function		*Pronominal Function*	
	singular	plural	singular	plural
1st person	my	our	mine	ours
2nd person	your	your	yours	yours
3rd person	her/his/its	their	hers/his/∅[2]	theirs
	one's		∅₂	

Although all languages have a way of signaling possession, they don't all regard the same things as possessable. In Spanish, for example, one refers to parts of the body using the definite article, whereas in English, we would use a possessive form.

> Compare: Spanish (literal translation):   I have broken the leg.
> English: I have broken my leg.

---

2. For all practical purposes, there are no possessive pronouns *its* and *one's.* The possessive determiners *its* and *one's* in the following sentences do not have pronominal counterparts.

> The cat is going to eat its dinner.   One should take care of one's health.
> *This dinner is its.   *Regarding health, one should take care of one's.

The acceptable version in the latter pair is more typically British than American. In American English we would more likely say "One should take care of his health" or—to avoid sexist language—"People should take care of their health."

Thus, one of the areas you may have to work on with your students is to help them become familiar with those semantic or lexical domains where the English possessive forms occur.

We should also mention two special syntactic constructions—one using the possessive determiner, the other using the possessive pronoun—which appear similar yet are slightly different in meaning:

Philip is one of our friends.   Philip is a friend of ours.

The first sentence means that we have an unspecified number of friends and that Philip is one of them. The second sentence makes no reference to our other friends but instead means that Philip is our friend and suggests that he may also be a friend of other people. Some reference grammars and ESL/EFL texts erroneously state or imply that such sentences are completely synonymous.

The possessive (in general)[3]

Form

In addition to the determiner and pronominal possessive forms, there are two other major ways of signaling possession in English:

1. The first is in writing by inflecting regular singular nouns and irregular plural nouns not ending in *s* with *'s*:

the baby's crib   the women's room

or by adding an apostrophe after the *s* ending of regular plural nouns and singular forms that already end in the sound *s*.

the boys' trip   Kansas' farmlands

The apostrophe added to regular plural nouns and singular nouns ending in *s* does nothing to alter the pronunciation of the word; however, the addition of the *'s* to singular and irregular plural nouns gets realized in speech as /s/ when it occurs after voiceless consonants, /z/ when it follows voiced consonants and vowels, and /əz/ after sibilants (i.e., /s/, /z/, /š/, /ž/, /č/, and /ǰ/), e.g.:

Mac's	/mæks/
Sam's	/sæmz/
Grace's	/greysəz/

2. Another way of signaling possession is by using the *of* possessive form where the possessor and thing possessed are inverted if one compares this order with that of the inflected *'s* form.

the man's name ⟶ the name of the man

From the above example, you might infer that the *'s* possessive and *of* possessive forms are interchangeable. This is not usually the case. Many ESL/EFL texts will tell the learner to use the *'s* form with human head nouns and the *of* form with nonhuman head nouns.[4] This rule accounts for examples such as:

---

3. In other grammatical descriptions, this form is sometimes called the genitive, since many other functions besides possession are signaled by it.

4. The head noun is syntactically and semantically the most important noun in a phrase or clause or construction that has two or more "nouns." (Here we are counting nouns or pronouns in determiner form as "nouns.") The other noun(s) are "modifier nouns."

Martine's *husband* (human head noun)
the end of the road (nonhuman head noun)

but not for

The dog's tail is wagging.

According to a study conducted by Khampang (1973) in which he tested native English speaker preference for the *'s* possessive versus the *of* form, the native speakers preferred the *'s* form whenever the head noun was animate. Moreover, the native speakers preferred the *'s* form even with inanimate head nouns when the noun could be viewed as performing an action, e.g.:

The train's arrival was delayed.

was preferred over

The arrival of the train was delayed.

To these fairly general applications of the *'s* possessive, we should add a few less common ones such as:

double possessives:	Hank's brother's car
nouns of special interest to human activity:	the game's history
	London's water supply
	(Quirk and Greenbaum, 1973:97)
natural phenomena:	the earth's gravity
	(Frank, 1972:15)

The *of* possessive, on the other hand, is preferred in all other instances, most commonly with lifeless things:

He stood at the foot of the bed.   *He stood at the bed's foot.

but, according to Khampang, the *of* possessive may be used even with human head nouns when the modifier noun is long:[5]

He's the son of the well-known politician.

was preferred over

He's the well-known politician's son.

or with long double possessives which, when short, normally take *'s* (e.g., Hank's brother's car):

What can I do for the husband of Dr. Smith's daughter?

was preferred over

---

5. Notice the reverse can also be true: that is, the *'s* possessive can be used with inanimate nouns, where it normally would not occur, in order to avoid an awkward sequence of two *of* phrases:

Many of the book's pages were torn.

was preferred over

Many of the pages of the book were torn.

Here the motivation for the preference appears to be stylistic or aesthetic rather than semantic.

What can I do for Dr. Smith's daughter's husband?

Likewise, if formality is the intent, the *of* possessive is preferred, whereas *'s* signals informality where both versions are possible:

Shakespeare's sonnets (informal)   the sonnets of Shakespeare (formal)

Thus, the fact that there are two possessive forms in English and that the rules for distinguishing their usage are not clear-cut may be one reason why ESL/EFL students often use possessive forms incorrectly. Another reason may be that the *'s* form occurs relatively infrequently in English compared with other inflectional morphemes such as the plural, the past tense, and the progressive; i.e., we know that when a morpheme is of low frequency in the input that learners receive, it is acquired later than the more frequently occurring morphemes are (Larsen-Freeman, 1976). Yet another reason may be interference from the student's native language. Regardless of the source of difficulty, two typical patterns of error are overgeneralization of the *of* form:

*The car of my friend is new.

and simplification where students omit the *'s* altogether and simply signal possession by juxtaposition of two NP's.

*My friend car is new.

One final observation which should be made about the *'s* possessive form is that like possessive pronouns, the noun which follows the inflected noun may be deleted if it can be inferred from context.

Where is your car?
It's being repaired so I borrowed *Ted's*. (i.e., Ted's car)

Function

It really is somewhat misleading to keep referring to the forms discussed in this chapter only as "possessives," since the same forms can express meanings other than the notion that something belongs to something or someone. In addition to showing possession, other major uses of the possessive forms[6] include:

1. Description:

    a debtor's prison = a prison for debtors

2. Amount/quantity:

    three dollars' worth of gasoline = an amount of gasoline worth three dollars
    one month's rent = the amount of rent for a month

3. Relationship/association:

    John's roommate = the person who rooms with John
    Manhattan's skyscrapers = the skyscrapers in Manhattan

4. Part/whole (the noun is a part of a larger noun):

    my brother's hand

---

6. There is some overlap among these meanings.

5.   Origin/agent:

   Shakespeare's tragedies = the tragic plays that Shakespeare wrote

Reflexive pronouns

The reflexive pronouns of English are the following forms:

	Singular	*Plural*
1st person	myself	ourselves
2nd person	yourself	yourselves
3rd person	herself, himself, itself	themselves

oneself

   Do you see anything unusual about the forms of the pronouns that precede the stem *self?* It should be apparent that the third person masculine singular reflexive pronoun *himself,* the third person plural reflexive pronoun *themselves,* and the neutral, formal third person *oneself* are formed differently from the others in that they contain the object form of the personal pronoun whereas the others contain the possessive determiner. This is a possible source of error for ESL/EFL students who imagine the paradigm to be regular and thus erroneously produce **hisself* and **theirselves,* which are forms that do in fact occur in some nonstandard dialects of English.

   We will discuss the main function of reflexive pronouns in the next chapter.

Indefinite pronouns

The so-called indefinite pronouns occur as compound forms:

	Some	*Any*	*No*	*Every*
-body	somebody	anybody	nobody	everybody
-one	someone	anyone	no one	everyone
-thing	something	anything	nothing	everything

Notice that they all are written as single words except for the phrase *no one. Body* and *one* mean "person" in general.[7] *Thing,* however, refers to an inanimate or abstract concept, or to an entity not definitely identifiable as a person (e.g., "Shhh! *Something* moved"). Whenever *one* can be used to mean the cardinal number instead, an indefinite pronoun or compound no longer results. In this case there is a two-word sequence with the number *one* receiving stress. Compare:

   Anyone could have gotten in free.
   Any one of us could have gotten in free; the other two would have had to pay.

---

   7. Bolinger (1977:14–15) aptly points out that *-one* and *-body* compounds do not occur in free variation. He suggests that *-one* signals nearness in both a spatial and psychological sense and that *-body* signals distance. Thus:

This present is for $\begin{Bmatrix} \text{someone} \\ \text{?somebody} \end{Bmatrix}$ very dear to me.

"Who should introduce the speaker?" I asked. "Oh, $\begin{Bmatrix} \text{anybody} \\ \text{?anyone} \end{Bmatrix}$," he replied disinterestedly.

All the compound indefinite pronouns require singular verbs. Nevertheless, the use of a plural pronoun such as *their* to refer back to the following singular compounds is acceptable in informal usage, e.g.:

$$\left\{\begin{array}{l} \text{Everyone} \\ \text{Everybody} \end{array}\right\} \quad \text{has} \quad \left\{\begin{array}{l} \text{his} \\ \text{their} \end{array}\right\} \quad \text{own way of doing things.}$$

Based on a conversational analysis she conducted, Nesbitt (1980:60) reports that the *everyone . . . their* combination actually occurred far more frequently than "the 'sexist' *his* form and the wordy *his or her* form." Presumably this same preference will carry over to the other indefinite pronouns and will result in their increasing acceptability in combination with plural pronouns:

?Somebody is driving without their lights.   ?Nobody had a good time, did they?
?Has anybody brought a watch with
   them?

Demonstrative pronouns

As we already indicated in the Teaching Suggestions section of Chapter 2, the demonstrative determiners of English vary along two dimensions: distance and number.

	Singular	*Plural*
Near	this	these
Far	that	those

When we first think of distance, we usually interpret this concept spatially. However, something can be close or distant in time as well. Thus we could say:

I liked this movie today better than that concert last night.

In an even more abstract sense we can use these terms to refer to a discourse sequence in which a new referent (i.e., *this*) is being compared with or distinguished from a previously established referent (i.e., *that*).

This point is not as clear as that one.

Germane to this chapter is the observation that the demonstrative determiners of English can also function as pronouns and represent an entire NP. Thus one could say:

Please fill these forms out.

or simply

Please fill these out.

if the context makes the noun "forms" clear.

Cardinal numbers also function this way:

He gave me three biscuits when I only wanted two.

as do the forms *some* and *any,* which we have already mentioned in previous chapters:

Do you want *some*? (The speaker is offering the listener cookies.)
No, I don't want *any.*

Another (one); the other (one); (the) other $\left\{ \begin{array}{l} (s) \\ (ones) \end{array} \right\}$

Another and *other* are often said to have a pronominal function similar to that of demonstratives, cardinal numbers, and quantifiers like *some* and *any*. Because it derives historically from *one + other, another* is singular and indefinite, e.g.:

> You've had only one cookie.   Would you like *another* (one[8])?

Other can function as a definite singular pronoun in combination with *the*, e.g.:

> You've only eaten one of the two cookies   Aren't you going to eat the *other* (one[8])?
> I gave you.

The plural form *others*—or the form *other* in combination with *ones*—can function as either an indefinite or a definite plural pronoun; in the second instance, it functions in combination with *the*, e.g.:

> These apples are sour. $\left\{ \begin{array}{l} \textit{Others} \\ \textit{Other ones} \end{array} \right\}$ I have bought at this store have been
>
> sweeter.

> The red apples are sweet. The $\left\{ \begin{array}{l} \textit{others} \\ \textit{other ones} \end{array} \right\}$ are sour.

In both the above examples, note that *others* or *other ones* refers to *other apples*.

We have now accounted for all uses of *other* except for cases where it functions as an indefinite or definite modifier rather than a pronoun:

> The patient is allergic to penicillin; *other*   Wilbur is shy. The *other* people are more
> medications will have to be consid-   outgoing.
> ered.

Actually, *another* and *other*, as well as the demonstratives and the cardinal numbers, are always functioning as modifiers in the underlying structure; however, they have often been discussed in the literature as "pronouns" because they may be used to refer back to a head noun. The head noun, of course, is always implied by ellipsis or substitution (i.e., *one/ones*) whenever *another, other*, a demonstrative, or a cardinal number occurs.

Conclusion

The English pronoun system is not as complicated as that of many other languages. Nevertheless, there is considerable detail for your students to master in learning the forms and uses of the pronoun system and of English possessives. Your job will require that you give your students continued exposure and meaningful practice to aid them in their acquisition of these structures.

---

8. In these examples the optional form *one* is a substitute expression for the noun *cookie*. The plural counterpart to this function of *one* is *ones*, e.g.:

> I don't like these cookies as much as the *ones* Sally baked.

For a more complete description of these and other noun substitutes in English, see Halliday and Hasan (1976).

TEACHING SUGGESTIONS

1 Cuisenaire rods can be very useful for introducing and practicing subject and object pronouns, since the rods can make the meaning clear.

Subject Pronouns
Give a green rod to Pheng.
What did Esteban do?
He gave a green rod to Pheng.

Give two blue rods to Paolo.
What did Antonella do?
She gave two blue rods to Paolo.

Object Pronouns
Give a green rod to her.
Give it to Antonella.

Give two blue rods to him.
Give them to Paolo.

Take the red rods from them.
Take them from Paolo and Antonella.

2 A good way for children to practice the possessive pronouns with parts of the body is to play "Simon Says" and to amplify the game with questions, e.g.:

T: Simon says, touch your head.
T: What did you (sg.) do?/What did you (pl.) do?
S1:   I touched my head./We touched our heads.
        or
T: What did he do?
S2:   He touched his head.
        etc.

3 A transformation drill may be useful for demonstrating and practicing the correspondence between possessive determiners and pronouns.

My book is blue. ⟶ Mine is blue.   Their car is orange. ⟶ Theirs is orange.

4 Penny Larson (1977) suggests preparing flash cards as an aid to teaching the *'s* possessive form. On each flash card (no smaller than 5 by 8 inches), paste a picture of a person and a picture of an item ("the Sears catalog is good for pictures of people and any discount catalogs are good for pictures of items"). Print a name on the card under the picture of the person. Use common American names or the names of your students. Be sure you have both singular and plural items and people. Then teach the new pattern by holding up a flash card and asking:

T: What's this?   *Students:* It's a book.
T: Who's this?   *Students:* It's John.
T: Whose book is this?   *Students:* It's John's book.
                                           or
                                           It's John's.

Go through the cards once with the teacher asking and the students answering. Then, ask the students to ask you the WHOSE question. When they are comfortable with the pattern, they can ask and answer each other. Pass out the cards, keeping a couple yourself so they can practice *this/that*.

5 Give your students a passage where the possessives have been replaced with a blank line and two NP's in parentheses. Have them write the correct form of the possessive on each line, explaining why they made the choices they did. For example:

Last Saturday I went shopping. It was (1) _____ (my friend/birthday) and I wanted to buy a gift. I drove (2) _____ (my father/car) to town. When I arrived, I realized the (3) _____ (center/shopping district) was already quite crowded. Etc.

EXERCISES

Test your understanding of what has been presented

1. Provide your own sentences to illustrate the following terms. Underline the word(s) illustrating the term:

subject pronoun	reflexive pronoun
object pronoun	indefinite pronoun
possessive pronoun	demonstrative pronoun
possessive determiner	's possessive
	of possessive

2. Explain the ungrammaticality or awkwardness of the following sentences:

a. ?[9]The room's walls are dirty.
b. *Him and she are going to Akron next weekend.
c. *This *Time* magazine is mines.
d. *There's no one here besides I.

Test your ability to apply what you know

3. If your students produce the following sentences, what errors have they made? How will you make them aware of the errors, and what exercises will you prepare to correct them?

a. *The house of my friend is on the corner.
b. *He kicked hisself for not remembering her name.
c. *This is Mary bicycle.
d. *Everybody from all the classes are going.

4. In second language morpheme acquisition studies it was found that the 's possessive form was supplied far less accurately in obligatory contexts by ESL/EFL students than many other morphemes (Dulay and Burt, 1974). We have already mentioned several reasons why the 's form causes problems for learners. Can you think of any other feature(s) of this structure which would account for its frequent misuse or omission?

5. In English there are constructions called noun adjuncts which consist of two nouns juxtaposed to create a noun compound. The one in attributive position functions much as an adjective would, e.g.:

jewelry store   table leg
stone wall

As Andersen (1979) points out, the Spanish construction for both the English 's possessive form and noun adjunct is the same, e.g.:

possessive—Milly's garden—el jardín de Milly
noun adjunct—a baseball player—un jugador de beisbol

Given these facts, what sort of problems would you anticipate a Spanish speaker having with

---

9. We use a question mark here and elsewhere to indicate marginal grammaticality (i.e., when native speakers do not seem to agree whether a given form is grammatical or ungrammatical).

English 's possessives? What two types of errors involving the possessive form in English would you expect these learners to commit?

6. We've already seen how the indefinite pronoun *one* can mean "everyone" in a general sense as in

> One never knows who real friends are until times like these.

What other pronoun (or pronouns) in English can also more informally mean "everyone in general"?

7. In this chapter we've mentioned the objection some people raise these days to using the third person singular masculine pronoun when people of both genders are being referred to. Many people reject the solution of using slash lines as in his/her or s/he because they feel it is stylistically awkward. Aside from creating a new neuter pronoun, which is a solution some have suggested, what are other acceptable ways of circumlocuting the usage of *he, his,* and *him* when these forms are used in a general sense?

8. One of your students heard a native speaker of English say "This prize was given to Edgar and I." Your student asks you if this sentence is O.K. What will you reply?

BIBLIOGRAPHY

References

Andersen, R. (1979). "The Relationship between First Language Transfer and Second Language Overgeneralization: Data from the English of Spanish Speakers," in R. Andersen (ed.), *The Acquisition and Use of Spanish and English as First and Second Languages.* Washington, D.C.: TESOL.

Bolinger, D. (1977). *Meaning and Form.* New York and London: Longman.

Dulay, H., and M. Burt (1974). "Natural Sequences in Child Second Language Acquisition," *Language Learning* 24:1, 37–54.

Frank, M. (1972). *Modern English: A Practical Reference Guide.* Englewood Cliffs, N.J.: Prentice-Hall.

Halliday, M., and R. Hasan (1976). *Cohesion in English.* London: Longman.

Khampang, Phon (1973). "A Study of the s-Genitive and the of-Genitive in English." Unpublished English 215 paper, UCLA, fall, 1973.

Larsen-Freeman, D. (1976). "An Explanation for the Morpheme Acquisition Order of Second Language Learners," *Language Learning* 26:1, 125–134.

Larson, P. (1977). "Teaching Possessives," *CATESOL Newsletter* 8:4.

Nesbitt, L. S. (1980). "Problems in Teaching Oral American English to ESL Students: A Conversation Analysis and ESL Textbook Review," *CATESOL Occasional Papers,* 6.

Quirk, R., and S. Greenbaum (1973). *A Concise Grammar of Contemporary English.* New York: Harcourt Brace Jovanovich.

Suggestions for further reading

For explanations and exercises of various pronoun sets and possessives, see:

Brinton, D., and R. Neuman (1982). *Getting Along: English Grammar and Writing* (Book 1). Englewood Cliffs, N.J.: Prentice-Hall, pp. 33–34, 97.

Hayden, R., D. Pilgrim, and A. Haggard (1956). *Mastering American English.* Englewood Cliffs, N.J.: Prentice-Hall, Chap. 18.

Krohn, R. (1971). *English Sentence Structure.* Ann Arbor: University of Michigan Press.

For extensive theoretical treatment of pronouns and possessives, consult:

Stockwell, R., P. Schachter, and B. Partee (1973). *The Major Syntactic Structures of English.* New York: Holt, Rinehart and Winston, Chaps. 4, 11.

For rules on possessive formation and exercises dealing with the indefinite pronouns, see:

Danielson, D., and R. Hayden (1973). *Using English: Your Second Language.* Englewood Cliffs, N.J.: Prentice-Hall, pp. 120–121, 128–129.

Rutherford, W. E. (1977). *Modern English* (2d ed., vol. 2). New York: Harcourt Brace Jovanovich, pp. 45–71.

11

A Closer Look at Transformations—
Imperatives and Reflexives

GRAMMATICAL DESCRIPTION

Review and further discussion of transformations

In Chapter 1, the four basic types of transformational operations (i.e., movement, addition, deletion, and substitution) were briefly introduced and example English sentences were provided to illustrate them. In Chapter 3, we first encountered two specific transformational operations, i.e., affix attachment and subject-verb agreement. In Chapters 8 and 9, a number of additional transformational rules were introduced:

Major	*Minor*
NOT Placement	*Some* ⟶ *any* Suppletion
NOT Contraction	Optional Auxiliary Deletion
DO Support	
Subject/Auxiliary Inversion	

At this point, we will explore the notion "transformation" in greater detail.

As we have seen in Chapters 2 and 3, the function of the phrase structure rules is to generate the basic structure of a sentence. Although the analysis that the phrase structure rules provide is useful in understanding English structure, people obviously do not speak in basic structures. Rules which operate on the underlying base structures and which eventually change them into acceptable, grammatical English sentences (i.e., surface structures) are known as transformations.

Such rules are a useful component of our grammar if we want to explain how synonymous sentences, those that have the same meaning but different forms, can be derived from the same basic structure. For example, the following sentences are recognizable as sharing the same meaning and yet having surface structures which are not identical:

Synonymy

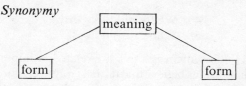

Mr. Wilson, who is a psychology professor, is on leave.

Mr. Wilson, a psychology professor, is on leave.

Here an optional rule deleting the relative pronoun *who* and the copula BE accounts for the synonymy.

On the other hand, transformational rules also explain how ambiguous sentences can result when two different basic structures are realized by the same surface structure as in the following example:

Ambiguity

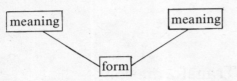

Sue likes Peter more than Robert.

The two meanings here, of course, are:

1. Sue likes Peter more than (she likes) Robert.

2. Sue likes Peter more than Robert (likes Peter).

In this case two different optional deletion rules—indicated by the parentheses in the above paraphrases—have operated on two different strings and have produced the same surface form, thus resulting in ambiguity.

As previously stated, in terms of their function, transformations fall into four types of operations. The examples which follow (and which supplement those provided in Chapter 1) deal mainly with the manipulation of surface structure elements but do serve to further illustrate these four processes.

Addition:

He can swim, can't he?   He swims, doesn't he?

(DO is added to carry the tense and number in the second tag question.)

Deletion:

John is taller than Mary *is.* ──▸John is taller than Mary.

Substitution:

John doesn't play the harmonica but Mary *plays the harmonica.* ──▸John doesn't play the harmonica but Mary *does.*

Movement:

She *put on* her new clothes. ──▸She *put* her new clothes *on.*

The phrase structure rules which we examined in Chapters 2 and 3 generate basic structures underlying a sentence such as:

1. Sally drove home.

They do *not* directly produce sentences such as:

2. Did Sally drive home?
3. Sally didn't drive home.

4. Where did Sally drive?
5. Who drove home?

Most speakers of English intuitively feel that sentences 2 to 5 are related in important ways to sentence 1, and transformational grammarians believe that the best way to capture the intuitions that English speakers have about these syntactic relationships is through transformations. Thus sentence 2 can be related to 1 by virtue of the transformations of subject/auxiliary inversion and DO support, which form a type of yes-no question, as was shown in Chapter 9. Likewise, 3 can be related to 1 by assuming that the transformations of NOT placement, DO support, and NOT contraction have applied to the same underlying elements to produce a negative rather than affirmative statement. This was demonstrated in Chapter 8. The transformations needed to describe sentences 4 and 5 above will be discussed in the next chapter. In the remainder of this chapter and in many of the chapters which follow, we will be exploring the operation of other transformational rules. We do not go into detail on the mechanics of the rules, since we feel that what an ESL/EFL teacher needs most is an understanding of how the rules work rather than an ability to read or restate the symbolic form of the rule. To be specific, in this chapter, we will look at sentences with reflexive pronouns and at imperatives, since these sentence types are often used to demonstrate the need for transformations or to show how other English structures operate.

The reflexive transformation

In the preceding chapter we discussed the form of the reflexive pronouns. In this chapter we will discuss their derivation. The reflexive transformation operates on any basic structure string containing two noun phrases—NPs—in the same sentence (i.e., S) that are identical in reference. It adds "+ pro" and "+ reflexive" features to the rightmost of two such NPs and selects the appropriate lexical item as a replacement for this NP.

The following is a basic structure requiring the application of the reflexive transformation:

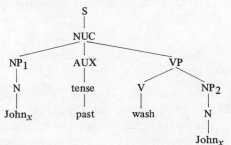

(The subscript x means that both NPs are identical in reference as well as form.)

Output of base: John$_x$ past wash John$_x$
Reflexive: John past wash himself
Affix attachment (1✕): John wash + past himself
Morphological rules: John washed himself.

It is important to note that if there is another sentence embedded in the main sentence, the reflexive rule will operate only when the two identical NPs occur in the same sentence (i.e., where the nucleus of S is defined by the phrase structure rules as $NUC \longrightarrow NP\ AUX\ VP\ (Advl)^n$). Without such a condition on reflexivization, an incorrect complex sentence such as the following could be generated:

*(I know ((that you dislike myself))).
  S1   NP   S2

Here *I* and *myself* are not part of the same underlying sentence. S2 is embedded in S1.

However, grammatical sentences such as the following must still be permitted by the rules since *the man* and *himself* are part of the same sentence (S1), a sentence which has been interrupted momentarily by an embedded sentence (S2).

(The man   ((who was slicing the salami))   cut himself.)
S1   Adj   S2

In English, reflexive pronouns tend to occur as obligatory objects of certain verbs that we refer to as *reflexive verbs,* e.g.:

to behave oneself   to pride oneself on something

(cf. Bill behaved $\begin{Bmatrix} \text{*him} \\ \text{*Mary} \\ \text{himself} \end{Bmatrix}$.)   (cf. Ann prided $\begin{Bmatrix} \text{*Susan} \\ \text{herself} \\ \text{*her} \end{Bmatrix}$ on her

achievement.)

Note that the indefinite reflexive pronoun, *oneself,* is used when reflexive verbs are cited in infinitive form. Sentences with *oneself* such as "One should behave oneself," are possible but relatively rare.

Most frequently, however, reflexive pronouns are used with verbs that could just as well take nonreflexive objects (nouns or pronouns):

John shaved himself.   Mary gave herself a bath.

John shaved $\begin{Bmatrix} \text{Bill} \\ \text{him} \end{Bmatrix}$ Mary gave $\begin{Bmatrix} \text{her baby} \\ \text{her} \end{Bmatrix}$ a bath.

Sometimes (though not always) the reflexive pronoun occurring with either type of verb may be deleted:

Bill should behave.   *Mary gave a bath (i.e., meaning "Mary
John shaved.   gave herself a bath").[1]
*Ann prided on her achievement.

The exact conditions that either allow or disallow such a deletion are not completely clear; however, it appears that the reflexive pronoun must be the direct object as well as be the last noun phrase constituent in the verb phrase for deletion to be possible.

Also, notice that reflexive pronouns may be introduced by other transformations in other types of sentences, e.g.:

John himself is to blame for this mess.

Rules accounting for other uses of reflexives such as this emphatic use will be introduced in Chapter 29.

Imperatives

If we examine commands such as

Go away.   Be quiet.

we are struck by the fact that there is no overt subject noun phrase. Such sentences would seem to be in violation of one of our phrase structure rules, which indicates that every English

---

1. But note that *Mary bathed herself/Mary bathed* do qualify as another synonymous pair similar to *John shaved himself/John shaved.*

sentence must have both a subject (i.e., NP) and a predicate (i.e., AUX VP (Advl)^n):

$$\text{NUC} \longrightarrow \text{NP AUX VP (Advl)}^n$$

We could modify our phrase structure rules to account for imperatives by putting parentheses around the subject NP, thus signifying optionality. However, we have independent syntactic evidence to suggest that the underlying or basic structure for an imperative sentence does indeed contain a subject NP, specifically a second person pronoun.

One source of evidence comes from the operation of the reflexive transformation, which we have just considered. Remember we said that the reflexive transformation would work only when the two underlying NPs were identical in reference. Notice the form of the reflexive when it occurs in an imperative.

Wash yourself!   Wash yourselves!

If basic structure subjects other than second person singular or plural were possible in imperative sentences, the following imperatives would also be acceptable; however, they are not:

*Wash myself!   *Wash itself!

*Wash himself!   *Wash ourselves!

*Wash herself!   *Wash themselves!

Furthermore, it is possible to produce an imperative and still retain the second-person subject; however, this type of sentence occurs less frequently than the subjectless imperative and occurs in different discourse contexts:[2]

You wash yourself! (singular subject)   You wash yourselves! (plural subject)

Thus we have reason to believe that a singular or plural *you* subject NP underlies all imperatives other than those representing special subtypes to be discussed later.

Our phrase structure rule for the auxiliary constituent of an English sentence, i.e.:

$$\text{AUX} \longrightarrow \left\{ \begin{array}{l} \left\{ \begin{array}{l} T \\ M \end{array} \right\} \text{PM (perf) (prog)} \\ \text{IMPER} \end{array} \right\}$$

draws a sharp distinction between imperative and nonimperative sentences and claims that imperative sentences are "tenseless." The strongest evidence in favor of this analysis are those imperatives formed with the copula BE:

You be quiet!   Be on time!

If these sentences had a "present tense" instead of an IMPER auxiliary in their underlying structure, what form of BE would we expect the subject-verb agreement rule to produce?

*You are quiet!   *Are on time!

Since such imperatives are ungrammatical and do not occur, we can assume that imperatives do not contain a tensed auxiliary and that the affix attachment rule joins IMPER to the

---

2. The *you* imperative is often retained when one is giving instructions to children and wants to be explicit (e.g., "Billy, you come here"). It is also used along with appropriate gestures to avoid ambiguity when addressing a large group—not necessarily of children (e.g., "Mr. Holmes, you sit over there"). When addressing an individual adult, a retained *you* generally signals an emphatic, unfavorable meaning (e.g., "You shut up!"). Because of the function and meaning of this imperative form, the polite form *please* does not occur with this type of imperative (e.g., *Please, you come here*).

following verb or copula to produce the bare infinitive by suppressing subject-verb agreement[3] For example, the basic structure for the imperative "(You) leave the room" would be as follows:

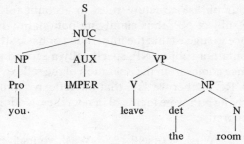

The subsequent derivation includes one obligatory transformation (affix attachment) and one optional transformation (*You*-subject deletion):

Output of base: you IMPER leave the room
You deletion (optional): IMPER leave the room
Affix attachment (1×): leave + IMPER the room
Morphological rules: Leave the room.

Without the optional *you* deletion, the surface structure is: You leave the room.

The transformationalists' account of imperatives is thus in agreement with that of the traditional grammarians such as Jespersen (1966), who suggested that all imperatives have an understood *you*. However, by using transformational rules, we can make Jespersen's intuition explicit and give syntactic arguments in support of it.

Negative imperatives

Negative imperatives are somewhat more complicated than their affirmative counterparts. They are also different from nonimperative negatives.

Three types of negative imperatives occur, but they all derive from a common basic structure. Consider these examples:

1. a. Don't you be late!
    b. Don't be late!
    c. Do not be late!
    d. *Do $\begin{Bmatrix} \text{not you} \\ \text{you not} \end{Bmatrix}$ be late!

2. a. Don't you run!
    b. Don't run!
    c. Do not run!
    d. *Do $\begin{Bmatrix} \text{not you} \\ \text{you not} \end{Bmatrix}$ run!

An examination of both these sets of sentences reveals that the rule of NOT placement operates differently in imperatives than in nonimperative sentences—i.e., even when the

---

3. Some transformational analyses of the imperative (e.g., Liles, 1971) have suggested that the underlying structure of all imperatives contains *will* because *will* often occurs in imperative tags, e.g., *Come in, won't you?* The output of the base for *Be quiet* in such an analysis would be *You will BE quiet.* There are, however, two arguments against such an analysis: (1) *(you) be quiet* and *you will be quiet* have different meanings. Traditional grammars refer to the latter as a peremptory future, not an imperative; (2) if one puts *will* in the underlying form of an imperative, the modal must be deleted; this, in turn, makes it virtually impossible to account for negative imperatives, which require a DO auxiliary, in any principled way. We therefore feel that it makes better sense to describe the *will* tags on imperatives as unsystematic, conventionalized forms similar to the use of *shall we* tags with *Let's* imperatives, e.g., *Let's go see a movie, shall we?* Such tags are discussed in Chapter 13 along with the more predictable tag forms.

copula BE is the main verb, the negative particle precedes all constituents in the verb phrase. The DO-support rule must apply in all negative imperatives because the IMPER auxiliary cannot combine with the particle NOT. It must attach to a verb or an auxiliary verb, and the auxiliary DO is added to fill this void. Furthermore, in 1a and 2a the positions of the subject *you* and the *don't* auxiliary occur in an unexpected order: their positions are reversed. The rule that accounts for this special process is subject/auxiliary inversion. It applies to reverse the order of *you* and imperative *don't* whenever the subject NP *you* is retained because DO followed by -N'T or NOT must come first in a negative imperative.

The basic structure for all three sentences in 1 is as follows:

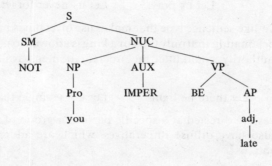

In order to derive 1a "Don't you be late!" the following rules would apply:

Output of base: NOT you IMPER BE late
NOT placement: you IMPER NOT BE late
DO support: you IMPER DO NOT BE late
NOT contraction: you IMPER DO + N'T BE late
Subject/auxiliary inversion: IMPER DO + N'T you BE late
Affix attachment (1✕): DO + N'T + IMPER you BE late
Morphological rules: Don't you be late.

The related negative imperative without a surface *you* subject—e.g., 1b "Don't be late!"—is derived as follows:

Output of base: NOT you IMPER BE late
NOT placement: you IMPER NOT BE late
DO support: you IMPER DO NOT BE late
NOT contraction: you IMPER DO + N'T BE late
You deletion: IMPER DO + N'T BE late
Affix attachment (1✕): DO + N'T + IMPER BE late
Morphological rules: Don't be late.

The related imperative with an uncontracted NOT particle (e.g., 1c "Do not be late!") would share the above set of rules except that the optional rule for NOT contraction would be omitted. Note that if the NOT is uncontracted, the *you* subject must be deleted.

*Do not you be late.

Note that a semantically-related negative imperative is produced if we use *never* in initial position, e.g., *Never do that again!* (cf. *Don't you ever . . .*)

Other sentence types similar to imperatives

In addition to the above imperatives some grammarians describe an inclusive imperative, i.e., an imperative that includes the speaker with the addressee(s):

Let's go to the movies.   Let's not stay here any longer.

In these sentences the speaker is taking the initiative. In an informal context with a contracted *us,* this type of utterance is a suggestion. In a formal context with an uncontracted *us* it's a signal for the group to follow the speaker's instructions or to agree with the judgment the speaker expresses.

Let us pray.   Let us never forget that.

Another imperative-like sentence type that makes use of *let* but is not inclusive (contains no *us*) is the kind of proclamation that only God or a king is allowed to make; i.e., the mere fact that such a power or authority would utter the proclamation ensures that what is said will occur:

Let there be light!   Let not a single male infant be spared!

Normal imperatives are directed at a specific person or group of persons; however, in colloquial usage we also have diffuse imperatives, which are addressed at anyone and everyone who is present:

Somebody open the door. (somebody = one of you here)
Don't anybody move! (not + anybody = none of you here)

Note that such diffuse imperatives would be inappropriate if two people were conversing. A speaker alone, however, who is addressing an imaginary or wished-for audience can also use a diffuse imperative (e.g., "Somebody help me!"). Note that diffuse imperatives are different from more specific imperatives that begin with the name of the person being addressed:

John, come here!

In such cases a *you* can also occur, given an appropriate context:

John, you come here!

However, this cannot be done with diffuse imperatives because their subjects are indefinite third person pronouns, not the definite second person pronoun.

*Somebody you open the door!

The function of imperatives

The usual explanation for when it is appropriate to use imperatives is that they are used when there is a power differential between speaker and listener which favors the speaker and gives the speaker the authority to command the listener to do something. For example, a sergeant can command a private to do something. Ervin-Tripp (1982), however, prefers the generalization that imperatives are used when "cooperation is assumed." This is a more general principle which explains not only cases of power differential, but also observations such as the following:

1. "Equals" who are well known to each other use imperatives when working on a joint task (i.e., there is no difference in power between them, but cooperation is assumed).

For example, politeness conventions can be suspended in requests and invitations as well as orders in such cases:

> Close the door.   Have a cookie.
> Give me a light.

2. "Equals" who presume they have rights over something use imperatives.

Ervin-Tripp noted that even young children are sensitive to this second condition. If one child is playing with another child's toy, the owner of the toy demands, "Give me back my toy." If the child is not the owner and has no right to the toy, however, he or she is more likely to make the request less forceful, e.g., "Can I play with that toy?"

This same principle or set of assumptions might also explain why imperatives are used where there is an urgency to the message:

> Stop!
> Look out!   (cooperation is assumed)

or where there is some strong emotion such as anger involved:

> Hey, buddy! Watch where you're going!

(The speaker feels his or her rights have been infringed upon.)

In other situations, it is more likely that a speaker would use a mitigated or softer version of an imperative:

> *Please* shut the door.[4]   Shut the door, *would you (please)*?

or use a directive of an entirely different form to accomplish the same task:

> Would }
> Could } you please shut the door?   I'd appreciate your shutting the door.
>   Etc.
> I wonder if you would shut the door.

Thus ESL/EFL students need to be aware of the limitations in using imperatives so their messages are not misconstrued as being rude. They need to know when it is appropriate to use an imperative and with whom.

TEACHING SUGGESTIONS

1   The third person reflexive pronoun can be effectively presented, elicited, and practiced through the use of pictures depicting reflexive activities such as:

a. a girl looking at herself in the mirror.   d. children dressing themselves.
b. a boy washing himself.   e. a cat cleaning itself.
c. a man shaving himself.

2   To elicit the first and second person reflexive pronoun forms, the classroom situation can be used. The teacher can mime activities like washing himself or herself and ask "What am I doing?" to elicit "You're washing yourself." Similarly the teacher can give a student a mirror,

---

4. In contrast to polite imperatives with *please*, imperatives with *just* often convey a threat or a challenge, e.g., *Just (you) wait and see!* Unlike *please*—see footnote 2—such imperatives with *just* freely occur with an overt *you* subject. However, not all imperatives with *just* convey negative messages since they can express gentle advice as well as threats, e.g., *Just be patient; everything will work out.*

ask him to look in the mirror, whereupon the teacher will say "Who(m) do you see?" to elicit "I see myself" from the student. This response can then be the basis of a follow-up question directed at another student, "Who does he see?" to elicit "He sees himself." etc.

3   James Asher (1977) has developed a methodology for teaching a second language which he calls "Total Physical Response." Within this approach, the second language learner carries out commands issued solely in the target language by the teacher. By gradually building up a syntactic and lexical repertoire, the learner is increasingly able to respond appropriately. We find the idea of having students act out commands effective as a first step in teaching imperatives, as it reinforces the syntactic pattern with action by the student. Thus, "Bring me the red pencil" could be uttered very early in a course if the contextual cues were sufficient. Ultimately a whole sequence of actions could be performed as Asher suggests, giving ample listening and receptive practice for the imperative form.

4   For practice with both affirmative and negative imperatives the class can play a version of "Simon Says," where the students have to do whatever is stated unless the negative is present (note that the pace must be quick), e.g.:

> *T:*   Simon says, "Stand up."
> *T:*   Simon says, "Turn around."
> *T:*   Simon says, "Don't sit down."

Anyone who sits down is eliminated from the game, which continues until the class has one or two winners.

This type of game can give students practice in forming negative imperatives. After students become more proficient in forming negatives, allow students to volunteer to lead the game.

5   To practice the productive use of imperatives the teacher can lead students through an exercise in which some "operation" is performed. The following are the steps suggested by Pat Moran:

a. The teacher models a chain of commands and accompanying actions which perform "an operation." For example, an operation might be to write and mail a letter. The steps would be to pick up a pen, write a letter, sign the letter, fold the letter, address the envelope, put the letter into the envelope, seal the envelope, put a stamp on the envelope, and mail the letter.

b. The teacher repeats the operation once again, pantomiming the steps and giving the commands.

c. The students then "perform" the operation in response to commands from the teacher.

d. The students give the directions to the teacher.

e. The students give the directions to each other.

EXERCISES

Test your understanding of what has been presented

1. Provide original example sentences or pairs of sentences that illustrate the following concepts. Underline the relevant word(s) in your examples:

synonymous sentences	reflexive verb
ambiguous sentence	deletable reflexive pronoun
imperative:	inclusive imperative
affirmative	diffuse imperative
negative	

2. Give tree diagrams and complete derivations for the following sentences:

a. Be quiet.

b. He dressed himself every morning.

c. Come here.

d. Mary looked at herself in the mirror.

e. Don't you forget her birthday.

3. Why are the following sentences ungrammatical?

a. *I hurt herself.

b. *She go away.

c. *Leaves the room!

d. *He feels that Mary likes himself.

Test your ability to apply what you know

4. The following sentences contain errors that are sometimes made by ESL/EFL students. How would you make your students aware of these errors if they made them, and what remedial exercises would you provide to help them avoid such errors in the future?

a. *They hurt theirselves.

b. *I hurt me.

c. *Not to sit on that chair!

5. A special condition on negative imperatives mentioned in this chapter is that the basic structure subject NP (*you*) must be deleted if the NOT particle remains uncontracted. Thus whereas "Don't you be late!" is an acceptable negative imperative, neither *Do you not be late! nor *Do not you be late! is grammatical. Many relatively advanced ESL/EFL students systematically refuse to contract the negative particle in their speech. Can you foresee any problems in practicing negative imperatives with such students? How would you convey the fact that the contraction is absolutely necessary in negative imperatives that retain the *you* subject?

BIBLIOGRAPHY

References

Asher, J. (1977). *Learning Another Language through Actions: The Complete Teacher's Guidebook.* Los Gatos, Calif.: Sky Oak Productions.

Ervin-Tripp, S. (1982). "Ask and It Shall Be Given to You: Children's Requests." Paper presented at the 33rd Annual Georgetown University Roundtable on Languages and Linguistics.

Jespersen, O. (1966). *Essentials of English Grammar.* University, Ala.: University of Alabama Press.

Liles, B. (1971). *An Introductory Transformational Grammar.* Englewood Cliffs, N.J.: Prentice-Hall.

Suggestions for further reading

For a good summary and evaluation of all the various linguistic analyses that have been proposed to account for imperative sentences, see this source:

Stockwell, R., P. Schachter, and B. Partee (1973). *The Major Syntactic Structures of English.* New York: Holt, Rinehart and Winston, pp. 633–670.

For other transformational analyses of imperatives, see:

Akmajian, A., and F. Heny (1975). *An Introduction to the Principles of Transformational Syntax.* Cambridge, Mass.: MIT Press.

Culicover, P. (1976). *Syntax.* New York: Academic Press.

For detailed information on Asher's imperative-based Total Physical Response methodology, consult the source cited above in the references (Asher, 1977).

For useful traditional descriptions on the usages of reflexive pronouns, see:

Jespersen, O. (1966). *Essentials of English Grammar.* University, Ala.: University of Alabama Press, pp. 111–112.

Praninskas, J. (1975). *Rapid Review of English Grammar* (2d ed.). Englewood Cliffs, N.J.: Prentice-Hall, p. 78.

Quirk, R., and S. Greenbaum (1973). *A Concise Grammar of Contemporary English.* New York: Harcourt Brace Jovanovich (see index for several page references).

For some additional ideas for teaching the reflexive pronouns, see these references:

Frank, M. (1972). *Modern English Exercises for Non-Native Speakers,* Part I: Parts of Speech. Englewood Cliffs, N.J.: Prentice-Hall, pp. 24–25.

Rutherford, W. E. (1977). *Modern English* (2d ed., vol. 2). New York: Harcourt Brace Jovanovich, pp. 32–34.

For additional ideas on using "operations" to practice imperatives, see:

Nelson, G., and T. Winters (1980). *ESL Operations: Techniques for Learning while Doing.* Rowley, Mass.: Newbury House.

For classroom games that provide for practice of imperatives, see:

Lee, W. R. (1979). *Language-Teaching Games and Contests* (2d ed.). London: Oxford University Press.

12

Wh-Questions

GRAMMATICAL DESCRIPTION

Introduction

Wh-questions (e.g., Who wrote this letter? What's your name? Where are you going?) are a complex topic because of the variety of wh-question types in English and because some of them are definitely harder to learn than others. For instance, consider the three example questions at the beginning of this paragraph. The first two are fairly easy to master; the third one is more difficult, and ESL/EFL learners trying to produce this sentence will often say *Where you are going?* In this chapter we hope to help you understand why this happens. We would also like to emphasize that the ability to form and use wh-questions is a very important skill for ESL/EFL learners to acquire. Such questions are used for social interaction (What's your name? What are you doing after class?), for getting directions (Where is Campbell Hall? Which way is the library?), for eliciting information or explanations (What time is it? Why did you heat the test tube?), and for eliciting vocabulary (What's this? What do you call this tool?). In short, it is hard to imagine anyone making progress in learning and using oral English without a good grasp of wh-question formation.

In some traditional grammars, yes-no questions are called "general" questions because the whole proposition is being questioned. The same traditional grammars refer to wh-questions as "specific" questions, since a specific constituent or constituents in the underlying sentence are being questioned—i.e., the speaker/writer is asking the listener/reader to fill an information gap in a given sentence. This is why wh-questions are also sometimes referred to as "information" questions.

Consider the following sentences:

Did someone walk the dog?   Who walked the dog?

Notice that while the yes-no question presupposes nothing and only asks if someone walked the dog, the wh-question presupposes that someone did, in fact, walk the dog and asks that this person be identified.

Types of wh-questions

This brings us to the issue of how many different kinds of wh-questions there are in English, i.e., how many constituents can function as the information gap in a wh-question? There are at least nine different types that you should be aware of:

1.   Subject NP: *What* happened? *Who* left?
2.   Object NP: *Who(m)* did you see? *What* did you do?
3.   Object of a preposition: *Who(m)* did you talk to?/To *whom* did you talk?
4.   Adverbials of time, place, manner, reason, and means:

When did you leave?   *Why* is he laughing?
Where did you go?   *How* did he get to the party? (by bus)
How did she dance? (gracefully)

5.   Demonstrative determiners:

What ⎫
Which ⎭ book do you want?

6.   Possessive determiners: *Whose* book is that?
7.   Quantity determiners: *How many* cars does she have? *How much* wine did he drink?
8.   Intensifier: *How* smart is she? *How* fast can he run?
9.   Adjective phrase (state, condition): *How* are you?

The rules needed for deriving these kinds of wh-questions will be presented in this chapter. The first thing to realize, however, is that there is a fundamental and important difference between wh-questions that focus on the subject NP or the determiner of the subject NP and wh-questions that focus on some element in the predicate, which includes everything in the nucleus of the sentence but the subject [i.e., AUX VP (Advl)^n].

Consider the following examples and, in each case, compare the wh-question with the underlying statement, which is given in parentheses.

I	II
Something in the subject NP is being questioned	Something in the predicate is being questioned[1]

a.   Who left? (someone left)
b.   Whose book is on the table? (some-.
      one's book is on the table)

a.   What did you read? (you read some-
      thing)
b.   Where did Sam go? (Sam went some-
      where)

These examples indicate that when something in the subject NP is being questioned, the structure of the wh-question matches the structure of the underlying statement. The only change needed is the substitution of the appropriate wh-word (i.e., *who* for *someone* in Ia and *whose* for *someone's* in Ib). This substitution is, in fact, accomplished by the application of a transformational rule referred to as "wh-replacement," which we will discuss shortly.

Let us return now to the wh-questions where something in the predicate is being questioned. When we compare these questions with their underlying statements, we can see that a number of changes have taken place:

---

1. As Quirk and Greenbaum point out (1973:198), there is no wh-word in English that directly questions the verb; however, the predicate as a whole can be questioned with focus on the verb by using *what* as the direct object of the general action verb *do,* e.g.:

      X: What are you doing?   *Y:*   I'm thinking.

1. The appropriate wh-word has been substituted for the constituent being questioned.
2. The wh-word has moved to the front of the question.
3. The first auxiliary verb and the subject noun phrase have been inverted—just as in yes-no questions.
4. DO support has occurred where no auxiliary verb or copula BE is present—just as in yes-no questions.

So instead of the one additional transformational rule that we needed to derive *Who left?* four major rules will be needed to derive *What did you read?* and two of these rules are common to both yes-no and wh-questions.

Wh-questions that focus on the subject

Let us first examine a sample tree diagram and derivation for a wh-question that focuses on the subject NP.

Who broke the window?

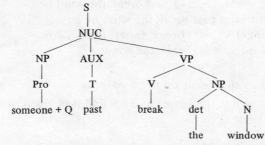

The feature + Q attached to the subject NP distinguishes this question from its more general yes-no counterpart—"Did someone break the window?" Other than this added specificity in the scope of the Q marker, the basic structure of a wh-question is similar to the basic structure of a yes-no question.

One of the transformational rules needed to derive the above sentence is "wh-replacement," which is a special lexical substitution rule consisting of many possible instances.

Wh-replacement
a. someone + Q⟶*who(m)*
b. something + Q⟶*what*
c. $\left\{\begin{array}{l} \text{in} \\ \text{at} \\ \emptyset \\ \text{on} \end{array}\right\}$ some $\left\{\begin{array}{l} \text{where} \\ \text{place} \end{array}\right\}$ + Q⟶*where* (i.e., advl location + Q⟶*where*)
d. $\left\{\begin{array}{l} \text{during} \\ \emptyset \\ \text{at} \end{array}\right\}$ sometime + Q⟶*when* (i.e., advl time + Q⟶*when*)
e. in some manner + Q⟶*how* (i.e., advl manner + Q⟶*how*)[2]
f. for some reason + Q⟶*why* (i.e., advl reason + Q⟶*why*)[3]
g. by some means + Q⟶*how* (i.e., advl means + Q⟶*how*)
h. someone's + Q⟶*whose*

---

2. Note that an adverb of manner can be either an adverbial phrase (e.g., *(very) gracefully*) or a prepositional phrase (e.g., *with grace*).

3. Note that even though adverbial wh-questions of reason are analyzed as deriving from a prepositional phrase in the base, an adverbial of reason could just as well be in the form of a clause (because . . .).

i. some + Q ——→ *what, which*
    $\left\{ \begin{array}{l} + \text{ det} \\ + \text{ demon} \end{array} \right\}$

j. so + Q ——→ *how* (e.g., *how* long, *how* quickly)
    [+ intens]

k. so $\left\{ \begin{array}{l} \text{much} \\ \text{many} \end{array} \right\}$ + Q ——→ *how* $\left\{ \begin{array}{l} \text{much} \\ \text{many} \end{array} \right\}$ (e.g., *how* many books, *how* much money)
    [+ det]

l. somehow + Q ——→ *how*
    [+ adj]

If we take the output of the basic structure represented above and apply the following three rules, the derivation would be as follows:

Output of base: someone + Q past break the window
Wh-replacement: who past break the window
Affix attachment (1✕): who break + past the window
Morphological rules: Who broke the window?

Wh-questions that focus on the predicate

Let us now turn to the basic structure and derivation of a wh-question that focuses on something in the predicate.

What did George say?

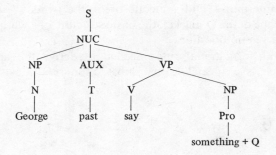

As with the previous question, the first rule to apply is wh-replacement:

Output of base: George past say something + Q
Wh-replacement: George past say what

In English there is a general condition on wh-questions which tells us that the wh-word must be moved to initial position—if it is not already in that position. (Many other languages also share this condition with English.) Thus the next rule we apply to the derivation is wh-fronting.

Wh-fronting: What George past say

Another general condition on English wh-questions requires that we invert the subject and the first auxiliary if we have moved a wh-word to initial position. Recall that the first tensed auxiliary verb, if there is one, also moves with the tense. Thus our next rule is subject/auxiliary inversion[4] (this is not a widely spread rule for wh-questions, and most other languages do not have such a condition):

Subject/auxiliary inversion: what past George say

Since there was no auxiliary verb present, the tense marker has been stranded without a verb to attach itself to, thus requiring the addition of DO:

DO support: what past DO George say

Now only the following rules are needed to derive this question:

Affix attachment (1×): what DO + past George say
Morphological rules: What did George say?

The wh-fronting rule mentioned above is a transformational rule that has some special cases and exceptions. If a determiner or intensifier is marked + Q, the constituent it modifies must be moved to the front of the string along with the determiner or intensifier; i.e., this condition is obligatory, e.g.:

Which book do you want?	(*Which do you want book?)
Whose car do you like best?	(*Whose do you like best car?)
How full is the building?	(*How is the building full?)—not grammatical with the same meaning as the other question

If the object of a preposition is marked with + Q, the preposition may either be left behind or be moved up to the front of the string along with the NP; i.e., this condition is optional,[5] although it must be noted that the first alternative below is formal, while the second is informal and is becoming more frequent in speech, e.g.:

For whom did you buy that?   Who did you buy that for?

Also, we occasionally encounter a wh-question where the question word is the object of a preposition within another prepositional phrase:

By virtue of what authority are you doing that?

In such a case, the entire prepositional complex must be fronted; there is no way the preposition *of* or the words *by virtue of* can be left behind when wh-fronting takes place.

---

4. Wh-fronting and the Q marker in the SM of yes-no questions are not the only causes of subject/auxiliary inversion in English. The fronting of certain negative and exclamatory constituents will also cause subject/auxiliary inversion to take place (e.g., Never have I seen such a sight. Such an idiot is my cousin marrying!).

5. There is a frozen formula with *what . . . for* that is an exception to this rule: in questions such as "What did you do that for?" the preposition may not be moved forward; it must remain at the end (cf. *"For what did you do that?"). This is perhaps so because *what . . . for* is informal and leaving the preposition at the end is characteristic of informal register. Likewise, we can also think of at least one case where the preposition *must* move forward with the wh-word and may not be at the end, e.g.:

Since when have you been living here? (*When have you been living here since?)

The explanation for this may be that *since* is not a true preposition but an adverbial subordinator that also functions as a preposition.

Wh-questions with the copula BE

Before concluding our analysis of major wh-question types, let us consider this example:

What is that object?

Some of you may think at first that the subject NP is being questioned and that only wh-replacement is needed. However, you should ask yourself what the underlying statement is (i.e., whether the question more closely resembles statement *a* or *b*):

a. That object is a stethoscope.   b. A stethoscope is that object.

In the sentence you have chosen, which noun phrase gets changed to a wh-form? Does it move to the front of the sentence, or is it already in initial position? You should have chosen statement *a*. Since in *What is that object?* the predicate noun and not the subject noun is being questioned, the correct basic structure for this question is:

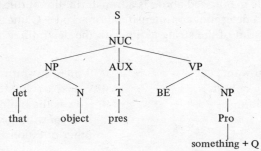

The transformational rules needed to derive this wh-question are:

Output of base: that object pres BE something + Q
Wh-replacement: that object pres BE what
Wh-fronting: what that object pres BE
Subject/auxiliary inversion: what pres BE that object
Affix attachment (1×): what BE + pres that object
Subject-verb agreement and morphological rules: What is that object?

In other words, one must always fully and accurately reconstruct the underlying statement when analyzing the meaning and derivation of a wh-question. Wh-questions with the copula BE are particularly troublesome to analyze. Fortunately, they are not that difficult for ESL/EFL students to master. The mistake that beginners sometimes make is omitting the copula:

*What your name?

Uninverted wh-questions

It should perhaps also be mentioned that wh-fronting and subject/auxiliary inversion may be suppressed in certain wh-questions that express surprise or disbelief (e.g., He did *what*? You went *where*?) or when more than one constituent in a sentence is marked + Q (e.g., *Who* said *what* to *whom*?). Kathi Bailey (personal communication) has also brought to our attention the fact that physics teachers often use uninverted wh-questions as a pedagogical technique (i.e., as a teaching or testing device) to elicit answers from their students, e.g.:

This is what? (teacher is pointing to a piece of lab equipment)
So, 2 × 2 + y equals what?

These utterances are not truly functioning as wh-questions, since the teacher already knows the answer and hopes that the students know the answer, too. The uninverted wh-word is almost always *what* in a physics class, for example. However, in another subject matter such as history, teachers will also use *when* and *where* in such uninverted questions:

The war ended when?   That battle took place where?

Negative wh-questions

Like negative yes-no questions, negative wh-questions that question something in the predicate also have two different surface forms depending on whether NOT contraction has taken place. For example, the two following negative wh-questions share the same basic structure:[6]

Why did you not do the work? (formal)   Why didn't you do the work? (informal)

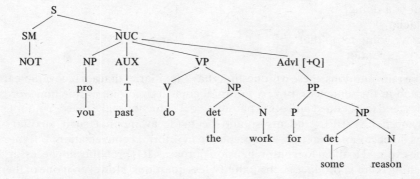

The derivation is as follows if we want to produce the uncontracted or formal version of this sentence.

Output of base: NOT you past do the work *for some reason* + Q
NOT placement: you past NOT do the work *for some reason* + Q
DO support: you past DO NOT do the work *for some reason* + Q
Wh-replacement: you past DO NOT do the work why
Wh-fronting: why you past DO NOT do the work
Subject/auxiliary inversion: why past DO you NOT do the work
Affix attachment (1×): why DO + past you NOT do the work
Morphological rules: Why did you not do the work?

In order to derive the contracted or informal version of the negative question, the NOT-contraction rule would have to apply at some point after DO support and before subject/auxiliary inversion in the above derivation, i.e., probably just after DO support as in the following derivation:

Output of base: NOT you past do the work *for some reason* + Q
NOT placement: you past NOT do the work *for some reason* + Q
DO support: you past DO NOT do the work *for some reason* + Q
NOT contraction: you past DO + N'T do the work *for some reason* + Q

---

6. Note, however, that the discourse function of these two questions can be very different. The informal contracted version often expresses a negative evaluation implicitly or explicitly (e.g., Why didn't you do the work? (You should have!)). The more formal uncontracted version is not likely to be used this way; i.e., it's both more formal and more neutral.

Wh-replacement: you past DO + N'T do the work why
Wh-fronting: why you past DO + N'T do the work
Subject/auxiliary inversion: why past DO + N'T you do the work
Affix attachment (1×): why DO + N'T + past you do the work
Morphological rules: Why didn't you do the work?

Ellipsis in wh-questions

Just as was true of yes-no questions, it is also possible to encounter wh-questions that focus on the predicate and have a deleted auxiliary. This is especially true of informal conversations where you may expect to find native speakers producing wh-questions such as these:

Question	*Deleted Auxiliary*
Where you been hiding?	(have)
What you doing?	(are)
(whatcha)	
How we going to do that?	(are)
(gonna)	

Like the yes-no questions, these wh-questions have auxiliaries that are recoverable from other information in the sentences. In very informal contexts, redundant function words such as auxiliaries tend to be elided and other phonological reductions take place. Your intermediate and advanced ESL/EFL students should be made aware that such auxiliary-less wh-questions do occur and that they are acceptable in informal conversation; i.e., your students should be exposed to them for comprehension purposes. It is probably not necessary to spend time teaching them to produce such auxiliary-less questions. However, if one of them should produce such a question, it should not be considered a grammatical error; i.e., you should judge whether the context was informal enough to warrant such usage and if the pronunciation was acceptable.

TEACHING SUGGESTIONS

1   When working with beginning students, it is advisable to do some early work with subject NP focus in wh-questions so that they can become familiar with some common wh-words without worrying about subject/auxiliary inversion at the same time, e.g.:

Who is writing on the board?   What happened?

One way of doing this is to ask everyone in the room to keep doing something different from the others. The teacher can then establish the pattern with the present progressive:

T:	Who is opening the windows?	*T:*	Who is combing her hair?
S1:	Ramon (is).	*S1:*	Michele (is).

Then the students can take over the activity:

S1:	Who is drawing pictures?	*S2:*	Who is sleeping?
S2:	Ali (is).	*S3:*	Yen-Mai (is).
			etc.

2   The easiest and most frequent wh-questions involving subject/auxiliary inversion contain the copula BE, so they should be among the first wh-questions practiced with beginners, e.g.:

What's this?   Where is John?

How are you?

To facilitate practice of the first of these patterns, the teacher can bring in a bag (or several duplicate bags) of kitchen utensils and gadgets (beginning-level students will not have full control of this vocabulary) and the students will work as a class—if it's a small class—or in groups until everyone has learned all of the vocabulary thoroughly using questions and responses like these to elicit vocabulary from each other.

{ What's this/that (in English)?   { (It's) a _____ .

{ What's this/that again?   { I think it's a _____ .

                                          { I don't know.

The teacher will supply vocabulary only if no one else knows the word; e.g.:

S1:   What's this?   *S5:*   What's this?

S2:   A can opener.   *S2:*   I don't know.

S3:   What's this?   *S3:*   I don't know.

S4:   I think it's a funnel.   *T:*   It's a spatula.

S1:   What's this again?

S2:   A can opener!

3   The biggest problem for beginning students—and often intermediate students too—is forming a wh-question that requires subject/auxiliary inversion with a main verb other than the copula BE.

Nancy Reed (personal communication) has developed a useful strategy for relating information the students have already learned about subject/auxiliary inversion in yes-no questions to the generation of wh-questions. Using charts or a flannel board or the overhead projector to provide visual as well as aural reinforcement, she asks students yes-no questions and then follows up each yes-no question immediately with a more specific wh-question structurally related to the yes-no question, e.g.:

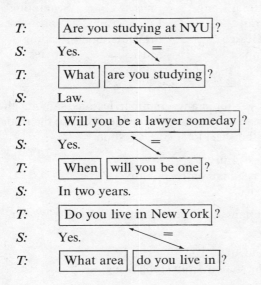

T: | Are you studying at NYU | ?

S: Yes.   =

T: | What | are you studying | ?

S: Law.

T: | Will you be a lawyer someday | ?

S: Yes.   =

T: | When | will you be one | ?

S: In two years.

T: | Do you live in New York | ?

S: Yes.   =

T: | What area | do you live in | ?

S: Greenwich Village.

T: Did you take the English placement test ?

S: Yes.

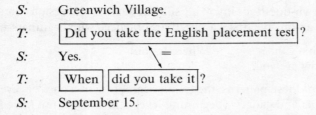

T: When did you take it ?

S: September 15.

Using these paradigms, Mrs. Reed then cues a student to ask another student a yes-no question, which he or she then follows up with another appropriate wh-question that the teacher can cue if necessary, e.g.:

T: Juan, ask Ming-Lee if she is increasing her English vocabulary.

J: Are you increasing your English vocabulary ?

M-L: Yes.

T: Ask her *how* she's doing it.

J: How are you doing it ?

M-L: By reading.

Eventually, the students are able to carry on such dialogs without cues, and they get a lot of practice using wh-questions that require subject/auxiliary inversion and, where needed, DO support. The relationship between yes-no questions and these types of wh-questions has been made explicit. And the recurrence of common question formation errors such as *What you are doing?* can thus be reduced.

4   In a language class it is good if all the students know each other's names and something about each other's backgrounds. A good way of handling this is a class information sheet; everyone receives a copy of it and is told to memorize it:

Student	*Native Language*	*Native Country*	*Major Field*	*Hobby*
Joe Chin	Cantonese	Hong Kong	Physics	Swimming
Mansoor Ghafari	Persian	Iran	Engineering	Sports—soccer
Nina Rojas	Spanish	Mexico	Pre-Nursing	Reading
Eiko Watanabe	Japanese	Japan	Music	Movies
⋮	⋮	⋮	⋮	⋮

This information can subsequently be used for many grammar lessons—among them, practice with wh-questions. As a cue the teacher mentions the name of one of the students along with an information category from the sheet to elicit a question.

> Cue: Nina—native country.
> Q response: What is Nina's native country?
> Short answer: Mexico.

Alternatively, the teacher could cue a specific language, country, etc., and then say "student" to elicit *who* questions.

> Cue: Hong Kong—student
> Q response: Who is the student from Hong Kong?
> Short answer: Joe.

This way the students learn about each other—not everyone will recall everything correctly from the class sheet—and practice wh-questions, too. If the students are preuniversity or if they are homogeneous, which is typical of EFL classes, other relevant background information can be incorporated such as the number of siblings or favorite TV program or movie star.

5   As your students are mastering the formation of wh-questions, it is also imperative to provide them with communicative practice. One approach, particularly for a new class, is to have students pair up and interview each other. On sheets of paper the students should be given the noun headings (as used in forms and applications) for the information they must elicit from their partners using wh-questions:

Information Needed	Wh-question	Answer
Name		
Nationality		
Local address		
Academic major		

After doing the exercises orally, they should record their wh-questions and their partner's responses. The various questions asked to elicit each piece of information can be compared to check for accuracy and to show that there are often several ways of asking the same question. Questions to come out of the procedure would include:

> What's your name?
> Where do you come from?/What's your nationality?
> Where do you live now?/What's your address?
> What are you studying?/What's your major?

Later each student can "introduce" his or her partner to the class.

6   Songs and games can also be used to reinforce and practice wh-questions. Useful songs for this purpose would be "Where Have All the Flowers Gone?" "What Shall We Do with the Drunken Sailor?" and others. For descriptions of games that involve interrogation or interviewing (both tasks require wh-questions), see Lee (1979) or Gasser and Waldman (1979).

EXERCISES

Test your understanding of what has been presented

1. Provide an original example sentence for each of the following concepts. Underline the relevant word(s) in your examples.

> wh-question focusing on the subject
> wh-question focusing on a preposition object (Give both versions.)
> wh-question focusing on a determiner:

       possessive
       demonstrative
       quantity
    uninverted wh-question
    negative wh-question
       contracted
       uncontracted
    wh-question with ellipsis of the auxiliary

2. Give tree diagrams and complete derivations for the following wh-questions:

a. How is your father today?
b. Who should we invite to the party?
c. Whose book is on the table?
d. How long is the table?
e. What didn't you understand?
f. Where does your brother study physics?

3. Why are the following sentences ungrammatical?

      *Which did he buy car?   *Whose did he steal handbag?

Test your ability to apply what you know

4. If your students produce the following sentences, what errors have they made? How will you make them aware of the errors, and what exercises will you prepare to correct the errors?

a. *Where you are going?
b. *What you want?
c. *To whom did he say that to?
d. *Where Benny?

5. It has been suggested that *why, what . . . for,* and *how come* are wh-words that all may be used to ask the same question.

      Why did he say that?   How come he said that?
      What did he say that for?

What are some differences in structure, meaning, and register between these expressions? Cite cases where they cannot be used to paraphrase each other.

6. The following wh-questions have been written on the blackboard of an ESL/EFL classroom. (The object of the lesson is to review wh-questions in the simple past.)

a. What did you do yesterday?
b. Where did you go?
c. What happened?
d. Who went with you?
e. When did you get home?

One of the students asks the teacher why three of the questions have a *did* auxiliary while the other two do not. If you were the teacher, how would you answer this student's question?

BIBLIOGRAPHY

References

Gasser, M., and E. Waldman (1979). "Using Songs and Games in the ESL Classroom," in M. Celce-Murcia and L. McIntosh (eds.), *Teaching English as a Second or Foreign Language.* Rowley, Mass.: Newbury House, pp. 49–62.

Lee, W. R. (1979). *Language-Teaching Games and Contests* (2d ed.). London: Oxford University Press.

Quirk, R., and S. Greenbaum (1973). *A Concise Grammar of Contemporary English.* New York: Harcourt Brace Jovanovich.

Suggestions for further reading

For other transformational analyses of wh-questions, see:

Akmajian, A., and F. Heny (1975). *An Introduction to the Principles of Transformational Syntax.* Cambridge, Mass.: MIT Press.
Culicover, P. (1976). *Syntax.* New York: Academic Press.
Stockwell, R. P., P. Schachter, and B. H. Partee (1973). *The Major Syntactic Structures of English.* New York: Holt, Rinehart and Winston.

For a useful nontransformational description of wh-questions, consult the following source:

Bolinger, D. (1957). *Interrogative Structures of American English (The Direct Question).* Publication 28 of the American Dialect Society. University, Ala.: University of Alabama Press.

For good suggestions on how to teach wh-questions, see the following textbooks:

Brinton, D., and R. Neuman (1982). *Getting Along: English Grammar and Writing* (Book 1). Englewood Cliffs, N.J.: Prentice-Hall, pp. 132–134, 204–206, 242–243, 262–264.
Danielson, D., and R. Hayden (1973). *Using English: Your Second Language.* Englewood Cliffs, N.J.: Prentice-Hall, pp. 13–23.
Rutherford, W. E. (1975). *Modern English* (2d ed., vol. 1). New York: Harcourt Brace Jovanovich, pp. 21–38.

The following article provides the ESL/EFL teacher with a critique of how wh-questions are taught in most textbooks and how books providing teaching techniques for teachers inadequately treat this area. The author follows up his criticisms with several constructive suggestions on how to better teach wh-questions:

Abbott, G. (1980). "Teaching the Learner to Ask for Information," *TESOL Quarterly* 14:1, 5–16.

13

Other Question Types

GRAMMATICAL DESCRIPTION

Introduction

In Chapters 9 and 12 we discussed yes-no questions and wh-questions, respectively. These are the basic question types in English. However, there are other question types and other ways of asking questions that the ESL/EFL teacher must be aware of. The first such type we will consider is the tag question, or the conversational question, as it is sometimes called.

Tag questions

A tag question is a short question which is appended to a statement when the speaker seeks confirmation of his or her statement.

John will go, won't he?   John won't go, will he?

Notice that question tags have both an affirmative and a negative form depending on the speaker's expectation. If the speaker expects a negative response from the listener, he or she will employ a negative statement with an affirmative question tag. On the other hand, if the speaker expects an affirmative response from the listener, he or she will use an affirmative statement with a negative question tag.

Why tag questions are problematic

Most other languages have something equivalent to the English question tag; however, this equivalent is often a frozen form that involves no syntactic complications; for example, French has *n'est-ce pas?* and German has *nicht wahr?* Native speakers of such languages sometimes latch on to a highly frequent tag form such as *isn't it?;* they overgeneralize this form and use it for all cases, which produces ungrammatical utterances like these:

*You're coming today, isn't it? *They were in New York last week, isn't it?

In some languages the tag formation convention merely consists of adding the equivalent for *no* or *yes* with rising intonation to a statement. Translated literally into English, this

160

convention produces utterances like the following, which are not uncommon among ESL/EFL learners:

?Mr. Johnson is a teacher, no?[1]   *We don't have homework today, yes?

While tags such as those in the two sentences cited above may serve a communicative function, they are expressed in unidiomatic—if not downright ungrammatical—English. Given the syntactic complexity of question tags, your task as an ESL/EFL teacher is a challenging one, i.e., getting your students to produce fluently tags that are both grammatically accurate and situationally appropriate.

Intonation in tag questions

Several grammars (e.g., Quirk and Greenbaum, 1973; Leech and Svartvik, 1975) provide descriptions of the two intonation patterns that occur with tag questions—the first pattern is generally acknowledged as being by far the more frequent one:

rising-falling: Marge has a car, doesn't she?

Marge doesn't have a car, does she?

rising: Marge has a car, doesn't she?

Marge doesn't have a car, does she?

Huang (1980) provides the best explanation that we have found for these two intonation patterns. He feels that the speaker's intonation indicates how strong his or her presupposition is that the original statement—affirmative or negative—will be confirmed by the listener. If the speaker uses rising-falling intonation, the presupposition is strong. If he or she uses rising intonation, the presupposition is weak and makes the tag similar to a neutral yes-no question.

A syntactic analysis of tag questions

Now consider the following sentences:

John has gone, hasn't he?
John hasn't gone, has he?

You are the teacher, aren't you?
You aren't the teacher, are you?

Paul will go to Europe, won't he?
Paul won't go to Europe, will he?

The secretary typed the letter, didn't she?
The secretary didn't type the letter, did she?

If we analyze these examples, we note that in forming a question tag, we must do the following:

1. Copy the subject, any tense marker, and the first auxiliary verb or BE copula after the main sentence. If there is no auxiliary verb or copula BE, DO must be added.
2. Make the tag negative if the sentence is affirmative, and make the tag affirmative if the sentence is negative.[2]

---

1. Native speakers do occasionally use *no*—but never *yes*—as a tag in limited, informal contexts. If *no* is the only tag or the most frequent tag a nonnative speaker uses, it probably means that he or she has not mastered the syntax of tag questions.

2. A negative preverbal adverb such as *never* (see Chapter 16) may appear in the first part of a tag question and have the same effect as *not:* They never say anything, do they?

3.   Pronominalize the subject (if it is not already a pronoun).
4.   Invert the order of the subject and the auxiliary in the tag.

If we consider the following examples, we can observe certain parallels between tags and yes-no questions:

John isn't going, *is he?*   John is going, *isn't he?*
Is John going? Is he going?   *Isn't John going? Isn't he going?*

In the tags the pronominalized subject and the auxiliary verb are in precisely the same slots they would fill in a yes-no question. Second, the negative element in the tag question must be contracted with the auxiliary if it precedes the subject NP, just as it must when it precedes the subject NP in a yes-no question.

*John is going, *is not he?*   John is going, *is he not?*
*Is not John going? *Is not he going?*   *Is John not going? Is he not going?*

The above example (i.e., John is going, is he not?) is a formal version of a tag question in which the uncontracted negative appears in the tag, but once again, the order of the elements is identical with that of yes-no questions. (In the remainder of this chapter, however, we will not look at such formal tags since tags are typical of informal, colloquial English and occur only rarely in formal contexts.)

Since tag questions seem to be syntactically comparable to yes-no questions in many ways, we can make use of several of our previous transformational rules to generate them.

A "TAG" sentence modifier (SM) is what indicates that the tag question transformation will take place. This transformational rule actually performs three operations:

1.   Copy the subject, any tense, and—if present—the first lexical auxiliary or the copula BE.[3]
2.   Pronominalize the subject (if it is not already a personal pronoun or an impersonal *it* or *there*). (See Chapter 21 for further discussion of *it* and *there*.)
3.   Move the Q marker to a position between the statement and the tag.

Operation 3 is necessary because we want the subject/auxiliary inversion rule to apply to the tag, not the statement.

Most tag questions contain a NOT (or -N'T) in either the statement or the tag. However, not all utterances with question tags necessarily contain a negative marker, and some may even contain two:

Phil's taking the issue to court, is he?
I can't, can't I? (in response to a statement such as "You can't sing an aria from *Aida!*")

In order to account for all four possibilities, NOT is generated as a sentence modifier in the base of most tag questions according to the number needed (i.e., one, two, or no occurrences of NOT). Since the position and scope of NOT is a semantic problem, we have added two features, one of which must accompany each instance of NOT that occurs in the base of a tag question:

[+NUC]   [+TAG]

Our typical tag questions will have a NOT marked as either [+TAG] or [+NUC], e.g.:

---

3. If no lexical auxiliary or copula BE is present, DO would have to be added immediately to such a string via the DO-support rule to support the tense marker.

John has gone, hasn't he? [+TAG]   John hasn't gone, has he? [+NUC]

In such tags the decision as to where the NOT placement rule should put the NOT is semantically motivated. If the speaker's assumption is negative, the NOT is placed in the nucleus. If the speaker's assumption is affirmative, the NOT is placed in the tag. A tag question such as the following will occur without a NOT in the underlying structure, e.g.:

Phil's taking the issue to court, is he?

A tag question such as the following one will occur with two NOTs in the underlying structure (i.e., one for the nucleus and one for the tag), e.g.:

I can't sing that aria, can't I?[4]

Consider this sentence and the following tree diagram and derivation:

John won't go, will he?

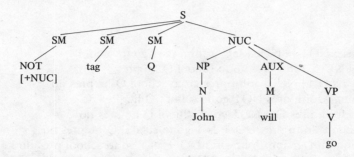

Output of base: NOT [+NUC] Tag Q John will go
Tag: NOT [+NUC] John will go Q he will
NOT placement: John will NOT go Q he will
NOT contraction: John will + N'T go Q he will
Subject/auxiliary inversion: John will + N'T go will he
Morphological rules: John won't go, will he?

The above basic structure with minor modifications (i.e., [+TAG] in the feature below the NOT) will generate the following statement with tag:

John will go, won't he?

Output of base: NOT [+TAG] Tag Q John will go
Tag: NOT [+TAG] John will go Q he will
NOT placement: John will go Q he will NOT
NOT contraction: John will go Q he will + N'T
Subject/auxiliary inversion: John will go will + N'T he
Morphological rules: John will go, won't he?

Just as with yes-no questions, and wh-questions, DO support is necessary when a question tag is adjoined to a sentence containing no auxiliary verb or copula BE:

John goes to school, doesn't he?   John doesn't go to school, does he?

---

4. The output of the base for this sentence would be: Output of base: NOT [+NUC] NOT [+TAG] TAG Q I can sing that aria.

In the second sentence above, the DO-support transformation would have to apply twice, once in the main sentence and once in the tag. The tree and derivation are given below to illustrate this.

John doesn't go to school, does he?

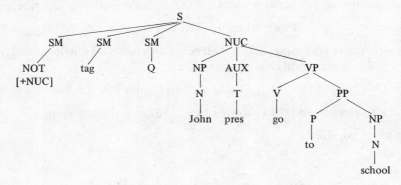

Output of base: NOT [+NUC] tag Q John pres go to school
Tag: NOT [+NUC] John pres go to school Q he pres
DO support: NOT [+NUC] John pres go to school Q he pres do
NOT placement: John pres NOT go to school Q he pres do
DO support: John pres DO NOT go to school Q he pres do
NOT contraction: John pres DO + N'T go to school Q he pres do
Subject/auxiliary inversion: John pres DO + N'T go to school pres do he
Affix attachment (2×): John DO + N'T + pres go to school do + pres he
Subject-verb agreement and morphological rules: John doesn't go to school, does he?

Marked tag questions

The preceding derivations have dealt with normal, "unmarked"[5] tag questions, where the tag is negative if the nucleus is affirmative and vice versa. The semantic motivation for these differences in NOT placement has been explained. We have also mentioned the existence of less frequently occurring "marked"[5] tags, where the NOT is either omitted or occurs twice:

So you're a student, are you?   Oh, I can't, can't I?

In the first type of marked tag, the absence of NOT signals some emotion on the part of the speaker.[6] Intonation is crucial. If positive, it shows the speaker is friendly, interested; if

---

5. The terms "unmarked" and "marked" have long been used in psycholinguistics as follows:

> unmarked—usual, typical, frequent linguistic forms
> marked—unusual, atypical, rare linguistic forms

Thus we refer to tag questions with the usual reversal of negation in the statement and tag as unmarked, whereas tag questions with no negation or with two negatives are considered marked. In Brown's (1981) study of the tags occurring in a large corpus, 95 percent of the tags were unmarked.

6. We have been told that the affirmative statement followed by an affirmative tag is used more frequently in British than in American English, and that the meaning can be merely verification rather than expressing some emotion—e.g.:

> That's your new house, is it?   The party's next Wednesday, is it?

Such dialect differences could be the cause of subtle misunderstandings when Britishers and Americans converse.

negative, this expresses the speaker's disbelief or sarcasm. In the second type, which occurs very rarely, the speaker is challenging something negative that someone else has just said.

Idiosyncratic and unsystematic tags

One further note should be made here with regard to question tags. This has to do with certain idiosyncratic forms such as:

Let's go, shall we?	I am going, aren't I?
We ought to go, shouldn't we?	Open the door, won't you?[7]

These tags are idiosyncratic in that there is no rule-based way of predicting the form of the tag given the form of the statement.

There are also numerous unsystematic lexical-type tags that are used in informal conversation:

You aren't going, right?	You are going, OK?
You aren't going, huh?	

(Note that such tags always occur with rising intonation.)

Additionally, there are a few full-question confirmers that occasionally occur in conversation:

That's a nice painting. $\begin{Bmatrix} \text{Do} \\ \text{Don't} \end{Bmatrix}$ you agree?

That isn't a very nice painting. $\begin{Bmatrix} \text{Don't} \\ \text{Do} \end{Bmatrix}$ you agree?

Semantically, it seems that such lexical tags and full-question confirmers can function as requests for confirmation just as regular question tags do. We do not have syntactic rules to predict their form, however, and therefore regard them as syntactically exceptional, though not necessarily semantically unusual, cases.

The discourse function of tag questions

In her study of the tag questions that occurred in a large corpus of spoken and written American English, Brown (1981) found empirical evidence for the claim that tags are primarily an informal, conversational device. She also found that tags have five major functions and several minor ones. Of the major functions that Brown noted, the first three seem to be related in that the speaker is checking information, whereas the last two are also related because the speaker is expressing feelings or opinions:

1. *Checking an inference* (43 cases): So that proves malice, doesn't it?
2. *Seeking agreement* (43 cases): They keep coming back, don't they?
3. *Inviting confirmation* (36 cases): Science is your favorite subject, isn't it?
4. *Expressing doubt* (27 cases): They can't get that big, can they?
5. *Expressing opinion* (21 cases): But that makes a mockery of belief, doesn't it?

For these major functions there were more than 20 occurrences of each type that Brown identified in her corpus. For the following minor functions, however, she found only five or fewer occurrences:

---

7. Notice that tags are sometimes added to imperatives to soften them or to make them more like requests or invitations (e.g., Come in, won't you?).

Keeping the conversation going (5 cases)
Expressing interest (5 cases)
Expressing humor or sarcasm (5 cases)

Beginning a conversation (3 cases)
Making a polite request (3 cases)
Expressing surprise (3 cases)

Responses to tag questions

Another finding that Brown made which is of interest to ESL/EFL teachers is that tags are different from other questions in that they do not necessarily have to be answered. In fact 29 percent of the tags in her corpus were not answered; i.e., the speaker just continued without leaving any time for a response from the listener(s). For the remaining cases where responses to tags did occur (i.e., 71 percent), they functioned as follows:

affirmative agreement, 17.5 percent
negative agreement, 7.5 percent
agreement statement, 6 percent
disagreement statement, 2.5 percent
agreement with modification, 22.5 percent

disagreement with modification, 10 percent
contradiction of inference, 5 percent

Furthermore, Brown pointed out that the traditional *Yes, he is* or *No, they can't* responses to tags that get presented in most ESL/EFL texts are very rare. In fact they occurred only 5 percent of the time in her corpus.

In contrast to what occurred with tag questions, Brown noted that the few full-question confirmers that did occur in her corpus (e.g., That's a nice picture. *Don't you agree?*) all elicited responses. In other words, if the speaker used a full-question confirmer rather than a tag, he or she always waited for and received a response from the listener.

Alternative questions

Another question type that we must consider is the alternative question. In an alternative question, the speaker offers the listener a choice of answers.

Will you go to Stanford or Berkeley?

Although these questions appear to take the form of yes-no questions, it would be obviously inappropriate to answer with a "yes" or "no." Yet that is exactly what many ESL/EFL learners do. In many other languages, such a question does not take a form similar to a yes-no question; it would take the form of a wh-question followed by the choices in tag form: Where will you go to school—Stanford or Berkeley? This latter option is, of course, also possible in English, and other alternative questions of this form occur:

What would you like—coffee, tea, or milk?

Where do you live—in Manhattan or the Bronx?

It would be difficult to write rules to generate all possible alternative questions, since the elements which are deleted are variable and may be deleted before or after the "or."

Will you go to Stanford or (will you go to) Berkeley?
Are you coming or aren't you (coming)?

Is it this or isn't it (this)?
Did you (leave early) or did your cousin leave early?

From these fully expanded alternative questions, we note that in English alternative questions result when two or more yes-no questions are structurally conjoined in a single utterance with *or* functioning as the conjunction. There is an important semantic difference between simple yes-no questions and such conjoined alternative questions. Yes-no questions are used in situations where the speaker wants to know whether the answer to the question is "yes" or "no." Alternative questions are used in situations where the speaker wants to force the listener to make a choice between two or more alternatives.

Notice also that there are differences among alternative questions depending on the degree of deletion or lack of deletion:

Did you buy it or not?   Did you buy it or didn't you buy it?
Did you buy it or didn't you?   Did you buy it or did you not buy it?

However, since intonation is as important as syntax in determining the meaning of alternative questions, we must await the results of a thorough discourse analysis that includes both parameters before we can draw any conclusions.

Potential ambiguity: yes-no questions and alternative questions

Another point we should make is that sometimes questions which on the surface appear to be alternative questions are really not alternative questions at all, but simple yes-no questions with conjoined objects. The following question is ambiguous with regard to this distinction:

Would you like coffee or tea?

Fortunately, this sentence is ambiguous only in writing. In speech the distinction would be clear, because the intonation patterns for the two possible questions are completely different.

Would you like coffee or tea?   Yes, { I'm thirsty / coffee, please }

Would you like coffee or tea?   Coffee, thank you.

Here, the first question is an offer in the form of a yes-no question with a conjoined object (coffee or tea) and it takes rising intonation. A "yes" or "no" is required here as part of the answer. The second question is a genuine alternative question with characteristic rising plus rising-falling intonation. A "yes" or "no" answer to this question would be inappropriate.

Finally, we will briefly mention some other forms which look like questions but which do not really function as questions.

Exclamatory "questions"

An exclamatory question is not a real question, although it may appear to be one, because the string has undergone subject/auxiliary inversion.

Isn't that grand!

This has the form of a yes-no question, but it's not really a question, since it has the force and intonation of an exclamation.

Rhetorical questions

Another surface structure which appears in question form is the rhetorical question. It is not a question in the usual sense, since it requires no response from the listener. A rhetorical question is different from a regular question in that the speaker uses it as a stylistic device to make an assertion or point.

Just because you've failed the first test, is that any reason to give up?

The speaker's message here is "Surely, no—that is no reason to give up." Sometimes the speaker actually answers the question as part of a monolog. Sometimes he or she does not and allows the answer to stand by implication. In either case, the speaker is not asking the listener for information or for a "yes" or "no" response.

TEACHING SUGGESTIONS

1   Tag questions are typical of conversation; so one good way to practice them is in dialogs, leaving blanks for tags that your students can supply, e.g.:

> *Hal:*   (It's a) nice day today, (1) _____ ?
> *Sara:*   It sure is. Say, you look good. You're losing weight, (2) _____ ?
> *Hal:*   I'm trying hard. What are you taking this quarter?
> *Sara:*   Economics and math.
> *Hal:*   Those are hard classes, (3) _____ ?

In practicing such dialogs, it would be wise to keep in mind some of the form-frequency data Brown (1981) included in her study. Tag questions are overwhelmingly present tense, and they occur most often with the copula BE or with DO-support verbs. Most subjects are third person singular or second person, and 75 percent of all tag questions have an affirmative statement with a negative tag.

2   The dialog practice should be done first with systematic tags such as those in 1. Later, the same type of practice can be applied to idiosyncratic tags.

> *Madge:*   Hi Joe. Come in, (1) _____ ? (won't you)
> *Joe:*   Thanks. I'm on time (2) _____ ? (aren't I) I thought I was on time, but the clock in the lobby says 7:45.
> *Madge:*   Don't worry. That clock is always fast. I ought to take a wrap, (3) _____ ? (shouldn't I)
> *Joe:*   Yes, it's quite cool outside. Let's go to the theater now, (4) _____ ? (shall we)

3   A good way to introduce alternative questions in a slightly controlled context is to use the *would rather* construction and to have your students practice food choices using pictures of food items that you have brought in. Each student would then come forward and choose two items and then address an appropriately contextualized question to a classmate:

> *Mariko:*   José, would you rather have a hot dog or a hamburger for lunch?
> *José:*   (I'd rather have) a hamburger.
>
> *José:*   Mei-wing, would you rather have a banana or ice cream for dessert?
> *Mei-wing:* (I'd rather have) a banana.

4   You can encourage practice of alternative questions and their proper intonation by pairing up students and asking them to use alternative questions to elicit information from each other. Each pair member has to ask the other an appropriate alternative question. The questions are then presented to the class for evaluation, e.g.:

> *X:*   Do you study early in the morning or at night?
> *Y:*   I study at night.

Y: Would you rather go to the movies or watch TV?

X: I'd rather go to the movies.

5   After explaining what rhetorical questions are and providing a number of examples, ask your intermediate or advanced ESL/EFL students to find and bring to class one example of a rhetorical question from a newspaper editorial, a published speech, a textbook, or an essay. Get the class to decide why the speaker or writer used a rhetorical question. Elicit the implied answer for any rhetorical question that the speaker or writer does not answer himself or herself.

EXERCISES

Test your understanding of what has been presented

1. Provide original example sentences that illustrate the following terms. Underline the pertinent word(s) in your examples.

tag question	a yes-no question that looks like an
idiosyncratic	alternative question
marked	alternative question
unmarked	rhetorical question

2. Give tree diagrams and complete derivations for the following sentences with tag questions:

a. Jerry isn't president, is he?

b. The Smiths go to every concert, don't they?

3. Why are the following sentences ungrammatical?

a. *John wants to go, didn't he?

b. *Is it going to rain or where is it raining?

c. *He left, did not he?

d. *Susan never laughs, doesn't she?

4. What would the complete form of these utterances be?

a. Is Janet blue-eyed or not?

b. Looking forward to vacation, aren't you?

c. Was it Bill or was it Bob who wrote this letter?

Test your ability to apply what you know

5. If your students produce the following sentences, what errors have they made? How will you make them aware of their errors, and what exercises will you prepare to help your students correct these errors?

a. *We're going, isn't it?

b. *This is nice music, yes?

c. *Native speaker:*   Would you like coffee or tea?

   ESL/EFL student: Yes.

6. Under what circumstances would an English speaker utter (2) in the following pairs rather than (1)?

a. 1. It is going to rain, isn't it?   2. It isn't going to rain, is it?
b. 1. Do you want to go or not?   2. Do you want to go or do you not want
                                                                     to go?

c. 1. You did, didn't you?   2. You did, did you?

BIBLIOGRAPHY

References

Brown, C. (1981). "What Discourse Analysis Reveals about Tag Questions." Paper presented at the Annual TESOL Conference, Detroit, March 6.

Huang, J. (1980). "Negative Yes/No Questions in English: Forms and Meanings." Unpublished English 215 paper, UCLA.

Leech, G., and J. Svartvik (1975). *A Communicative Grammar of English.* London: Longman.

Quirk, R., and S. Greenbaum (1973). *A Concise Grammar of Contemporary English.* New York: Harcourt Brace Jovanovich.

Suggestions for further reading

For other transformational accounts of tag questions, see the following sources:

Akmajian, A., and F. Heny (1975). *An Introduction to the Principles of Transformational Syntax.* Cambridge, Mass.: MIT Press.

Culicover, P. (1976). *Syntax.* New York: Academic Press.

For a survey of transformational and other analyses of tag and alternative questions done prior to the early seventies, see:

Stockwell, R. P., P. Schachter, and B. H. Partee (1973). *The Major Syntactic Structures of English.* New York: Holt, Rinehart and Winston.

For some good teaching suggestions for tag questions, consult the following:

Danielson, D., and R. Hayden (1973). *Using English: Your Second Language.* Englewood Cliffs, N.J.: Prentice-Hall, Chap. 3.

Rutherford, W. E. (1975). *Modern English* (2d ed., vol. 2). New York: Harcourt Brace Jovanovich, pp. 71–75.

For a teaching suggestion regarding the teaching of intonation in alternative questions, see this source:

Bowen, J. D. (1975). *Patterns of English Pronunciation.* Rowley, Mass.: Newbury House, pp. 189–190.

14

The Article System

GRAMMATICAL DESCRIPTION

Introduction

In a survey of the teaching problems of ESL teachers working in the Los Angeles area (Covitt, 1976), the teachers reported that article usage was their number one teaching problem. If we take a quick look at the languages of the world, this survey result is not surprising. Oriental languages, most Slavic languages, and most African languages, for example, do not have articles. On the other hand, languages which *do* have articles or article-like morphemes (e.g., French, Spanish, Persian, and the Semitic languages) often use these morphemes in ways that differ from the English article system. For example, many of these article-using languages mark the generic use of an abstract noun with their equivalent of the definite article. Thus, instead of saying *Beauty is truth* as the English poet Keats did, the literal equivalent of this sentence in one of these languages would be *The beauty is the truth*. Also, some of these languages can indicate definiteness or indefiniteness with a suffix or morpheme *following* the noun as opposed to the consistent prenominal position that articles have in English. Several Scandinavian languages and Persian, for example, make use of such a postnominal marker.

The picture we have been painting thus far with regard to articles is one of dissimilarity and idiosyncracy among languages. There are in fact a few universals regarding the definiteness of nouns and other morphemes that we should mention here. In all languages, proper nouns, personal pronouns, and possessive determiners are definite.

You may be wondering at this point how languages without articles can signal definiteness or indefiniteness. The most common means is word order; i.e., the noun in topic position is definite, whereas a noun in comment position tends to be indefinite.[1] Thompson (1978) gives us an explanation for the evolution of the English article system: she says that languages like English that use word order to signal grammatical relations such as subject and object tend to develop articles since new and old information cannot be consistently

---

1. In many languages discourse-based relationships such as "topic" (i.e., old information that most likely has been an item of discussion in the discourse) and "comment" (i.e., new information relevant to the topic) determine word order rather than grammatical relations such as "subject" and "object" as is the case in English. Because of their discourse function, topics tend to be definite, whereas comments tend to contain indefinite nouns.

signaled through word order the way it is in topic-comment languages. Thus it is the definite and indefinite articles in languages like English that help us to identify new and old information: old information tends to be definite, while new information tends to be indefinite.

The historical development of articles in English is similar to that of most other languages which have developed an article system: the definite article is derived from the demonstrative signaling distance (i.e., *that*) while the indefinite article is derived from the numeral *one*. The latter derivation, for example, helps explain why the form of the indefinite article occurring before a word with an initial vowel sound is *an*; i.e., the *n* in *an* and *one* are historically related.

Structural facts about articles

Both structural and transformational grammarians have been largely unsuccessful with regard to explicating article usage. One reason for this is that neither school of analysis goes beyond the sentence level, and in article usage—to a great extent—we depend on the discourse context to determine what is definite and what is indefinite. What we can extract from the work of these grammarians, however, is some useful information about the classification of nouns. We know that all English nouns should be classified as either common nouns (e.g., a boy, a country, a planet) or proper nouns (e.g., Bob Robertson, Denmark, Saturn). In addition, all common nouns must be further classified as mass (e.g., water, clothing, luggage) or count (a beverage, a shirt, a suitcase) because only count nouns can have singular and/or plural forms:

Mass	*Count*
*two waters; *a water	two beverages; a beverage
*two clothings; *a clothing	two shirts; a shirt
*two luggages; *a luggage	two suitcases; a suitcase

Furthermore, this mass/count distinction will be shown to account for systematic differences in article usage.

Even though both the proper/common and the count/mass distinction seem to overlap in certain cases, these distinctions are useful and necessary for mastery of the English article system, which—from a structural or transformational point of view—we can summarize as follows:

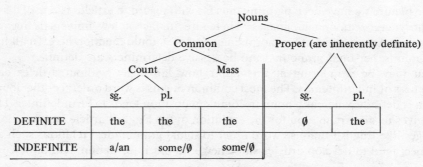

	Count sg.	Count pl.	Mass	Proper sg.	Proper pl.
DEFINITE	the	the	the	∅	the
INDEFINITE	a/an	some/∅	some/∅		

The mass-count distinction

As we mentioned above, a very important factor in correct article usage is the lexical classification of English nouns into mass vs. count. This distinction becomes problematic for many ESL/EFL learners, since although most languages make use of it, what is countable and what is mass varies from language to language. For example, *information* and *furniture* are mass nouns in English but countable nouns in French and Spanish, and *chalk* is a mass noun in English but a countable noun in Japanese.

Some English nouns are essentially mass (e.g., *bacon*) while others are essentially count (e.g., *a boy*). Examine the following paradigms:

MASS (a to e are ungrammatical)
a. *The bacon (a singular unit) is lying next to another one.
b. *A bacon fell onto my plate.
c. *The bacons got cold.
d. *Some bacons were in the cupboard.
e. *Bacons are for eating.
f. The bacon was too salty.
g. Some bacon was found in the cupboard.
h. Bacon is naturally salty.

COUNT (f to h are ungrammatical)
a. The boy played in the street.
b. A boy played in the street.
c. The boys played in the street.
d. Some boys played in the street.
e. Boys are made of snails and puppy-dog tails.
f. *The boy (uncountable amount) was not enough for the scout troop.
g. *Some boy made up the scout troop.
h. *Boy is made of snails and puppy-dog tails.

These paradigms are useful and help clarify the difference between mass nouns and count nouns—especially archetypical mass nouns such as *bacon* and archetypical count nouns such as *boy*. The paradigms and the terms "mass noun" and "count noun," however, suggest a strict dichotomy where there very likely is a continuum of sorts. Allan (1980), for example, applies a series of syntactic "tests" to demonstrate that the noun "car" is more countable than the noun "cattle," which has no singular form, and that the noun "mankind," which has a collective meaning, is less of a mass noun than the noun "equipment." Allan, in fact, argues for eight discrete levels of countability rather than the two we use here. However, despite our basic agreement with Allan's analysis, for pedagogical reasons, we will continue to view nouns as being either basically countable (i.e., singular, plural, collective; common, proper) or basically mass.

As an extension of our simplified two-feature analysis, we shall discuss some mass-to-count shifts[2] that commonly occur in English. There are, for example, some abstract mass nouns that can be made more concrete by treating them as countables (e.g., *life*) without a substantial difference in meaning. The rule here is that such a noun, when used with an article, denotes "an instance of" the mass noun in question, and it functions as a countable

---

2. We only elaborate on mass-to-count shifts here. The opposite shift (count ⟶ mass) is, of course, also possible:

an egg ⟶ You've got egg on your tie.

However, we emphasize mass-to-count shifts because these are more frequent than the reverse—perhaps because the countable common noun is the dominant or prototypical "noun" in English, i.e., the type of noun that attracts or assimilates other types most readily.

noun. Other nouns in this category are *beauty, truth, crime, law, education,* etc. With their dual mass-count function they can be used in every slot in the paradigm:

MASS———→COUNT

count
{
a. The life of the old man was forfeited.
b. A life is not proper payment for that.
c. The lives lost in the war were wasted.
d. Some lives were saved.
e. Lives are always lost in war.
}

mass
{
f. The life in the old man was fading fast.
g. Some life could be detected in the old man.
h. Life can be difficult at times.
}

Other regular shifts from mass to count involving concrete nouns are those where the count noun denotes "a kind/type of" as in:

MASS———→COUNT		
cheese	a cheese	cheeses
wine	a wine	wines
rice	a rice	rices
tea	a tea	teas

or a "unit/serving of" as in:

MASS———→COUNT		
coffee	a coffee	3 coffees
aspirin	an aspirin	2 aspirins
pastry	a pastry	several pastries
chocolate	a chocolate	some chocolates

Of course, there are also many idiosyncratic meaning relationships involving mass and count nouns that must be learned independent of any such regular semantic patterns; these are cases where there is no predictable mass —→ count shift, e.g.:

Mass	*Count—Singular*	*Count—Plural*
air (the atmosphere)	an air (melody)	airs (mannerisms)
glass (the silicate-based substance)	a glass (water tumbler)	glasses (spectacles)
iron (the metal)	an iron (for pressing clothes)	irons (golf clubs)
⋮	⋮	⋮

Special problems with proper nouns

Proper nouns, which include personal names, geographical names, and some other minor categories, also pose a few special problems. They are always definite, yet with the exception of a few instances (e.g., The Hague), they do not take the definite article in the singular unless the speaker is being extremely emphatic, e.g., *the* Mrs. Reagan (to distinguish President Reagan's wife from all other women with the same name). Plural proper names always take the definite article: the Johnsons, the Azores, etc., and are semantically collective.[3] When proper nouns

---

3. This notion of semantic collectivity can also help explain why proper names such as *the Soviet Union* and *the United Kingdom* take the definite article without an explicit plural, i.e., *union* and *kingdom* are collective nouns.

are used in common noun patterns, they are no longer functioning as proper nouns—i.e., they have become common nouns by virtue of an understood common head noun (the man called George ⟶ the George). For example, all the following sentences contain proper nouns that are being used as common nouns:

The George that called yesterday called again.

Some Ernests can surely be found in this crowd.

A John spoke to me all night long at the party.

Nine Marys were on the list.

Marvins are boring.

Another common source of proper names being used as common nouns are trade names. Thus we have:

Kleenex (a trade name) ⟶ a kleenex (= a paper tissue)
Xerox (a trade name) ⟶ a xerox of something (= a photocopy)

Geographical names prefer the article-less proper noun form; in fact with the passing of time or a change of events, unique common forms of geographical names with the article *the* seem to move toward the use of no article. We have evidence of this tendency from two sources. First of all, a change in status from colonial territory to independent statehood or nationhood can cause the loss of a definite article and other accompanying inflections, e.g.:

Unique Common Noun	*Proper Noun*
the Sudan	⟶ Sudan
the Cameroons	⟶ Cameroon

Second, as descriptive designations for singular entities gradually become familiar to us, i.e., places we are personally familiar with or hear mentioned frequently, the definite article in the original name tends to drop off, and this results in a proper noun,[4] e.g.:

Unique Common Noun	*Proper Noun*
the green park	⟶ Green Park
the Regent's park	⟶ Regent's Park
the river road	⟶ River Road
the Brookfield zoo	⟶ Brookfield Zoo

In such cases, two alternatives sometimes exist side by side (the earth—earth); one can view a geographical name such as *earth* as a unique common noun (i.e., with *the*) or as a proper name (without *the*).

Indeed a majority of geographical names function as proper nouns and occur without the article, as is shown in the following semantically based listing adapted from Hewson (1972):

continent: Asia, South America, Africa, . . .
country: Canada, France, Nigeria, . . .
county: Los Angeles County, Cook County, . . .
city: New York, London, Tokyo, . . . (exception: The Hague)
mountain: Mount Whitney, Mount Aetna, . . .
lake: Lake Michigan, Lake Baikal, . . . (exception: the Great Salt Lake)
island: Catalina Island, Staten Island, . . .
point: Point Dume, Point Mugu, . . .
bay: San Francisco Bay, Tampa Bay, . . .

---

4. Historically, this has happened quite often in English.

cape: Cape Cod, Cape Canaveral, . . .
park: Yosemite National Park, Douglas Park, . . .
street, road, avenue, boulevard, etc.: Yale Street, Wilshire Boulevard, . . .
square: Trafalgar Square, Union Square, . . .

As was previously stated, plural and collective proper names take the definite article, and geographical names have the following plural or collective subcategories:

countries (if viewed as unions, federations): the U.S.A., the United Kingdom, the USSR, . . .
lakes (if they form a set): the Great Lakes, the Finger Lakes, . . .
mountain ranges: the Rocky Mountains ⟶ the Rockies, the Andes, the Alps, . . .
islands (if viewed as a group): the Canary Islands ⟶ the Canaries, the Azores, the Bahamas, . . .

However, there are also a number of singular geographical names which function as unique common nouns (as opposed to true proper nouns) and which take the definite article. Consider the following list:[5]

regions:[6] the Caucasus, the Crimea, the Roussillon, . . .
deserts: the Sahara (desert), the Mojave (desert), . . .
peninsulas: the Monterey Peninsula, the Iberian Peninsula, . . .
oceans and seas: the Pacific (Ocean), the Mediterranean (Sea), . . .
gulfs: the Gulf of Mexico, the Persian Gulf, . . .
rivers: the Mississippi (River), the Amazon (River), . . .
canals: the Erie Canal, the Suez Canal, the Panama Canal, . . .

Some of these names, according to Hewson (1972), seem to be large and hard-to-define bodies of water (e.g., oceans, seas, and gulfs—as opposed to lakes). Still others represent flowing water or strips of water used for navigation or irrigation (e.g., rivers and canals). The remaining categories are land masses or areas that are hard to define:

regions—as opposed to countries or cities (Where exactly does one region begin or end?)
deserts—as opposed to arable land (Where exactly does the desert end and the arable land begin?)
peninsulas—as opposed to islands or continents (Where exactly does the peninsula end and the mainland begin?)

While Hewson's generalization is useful, it is not perfect, since one might well wonder why oceans, seas, gulfs, and peninsulas—which are unique common names—are harder to define than bays, points, and capes—which are proper names. Perhaps size is a factor here. In any case, something such as Hewson's observation seems preferable to memorization of lists, which is the current alternative ESL/EFL teachers have for dealing with geographical names.

Article usage

Whereas the above information is a summary of what structural, transformational, and semantic analyses offer, it still doesn't begin to tell us enough about usage. It doesn't tell us, for

---

5. Note the deletions of the head noun that are possible in many of these unique common nouns taking *the* and which we have indicated in parentheses.
6. Regions seem to be divided between those that take the article (see above) and those that do not, e.g., Appalachia, Alsace, Siberia.

example, when a common noun is definite or indefinite. For this aspect of article usage we have to consider the discourse context (i.e., how familiar the speaker/writer is (and thinks the listener/reader is) with the noun(s) being mentioned). Brown (1973) gives us a good way of visualizing the interaction of speaker and listener with regard to the article usage of nongeneric common nouns in English:

		Speaker (Writer) ⟶	
		specific referent	nonspecific referent
L i s t e n e r (Reader)	specific referent	definite: Can I have the car?	indefinite: There's a spy hiding in your cellar. I heard you once wrote an article on X.
	nonspecific referent	indefinite: I saw a funny-looking dog today.	indefinite: I don't have a car. I need a new belt.

Thus, as Brown's matrix indicates, the definite article is used properly only when the noun discussed has a specific referent (from the speaker's point of view) for both the speaker/writer and the listener/reader.

Definite article usage

Elaborating on his matrix, Brown (1973) suggests eight circumstances under which a noun may have specific reference for the speaker and the hearer alike (i.e., where an utterance would go into the upper left quadrant of the matrix):

1. *unique for all:* the moon, the earth, the sun
2. *unique for a given setting:* the blackboard, the ceiling, the floor
3. *unique for a given social group:* the car, the dog, the baby, the President
4. *unique by pointing, nodding, etc.:* the book, the chair
5. *unique because of characteristics that get attention:* the explosion, the streaker
6. *unique by entailment:* in talking about a house: the windows, the garden, the kitchen
7. *unique by definition:* the house with a view, the girl who speaks Basque
8. *unique by prior utterance:* I saw a funny-looking dog today. The dog . . .

To Brown's eight categories, we would add two more:

9. *unique by a specified order or rank in a set:* the last sentence on the page; the fastest runner in the heat
10. *unique by anticipation:* We found the hubcap of a car that must be very expensive.

Two of Brown's categories and one of ours correspond closely to concepts long used in traditional grammar. For example, category 8, *unique by prior utterance,* is traditionally referred to as *anaphora.* In other words, when a definite article plus a noun—or a pronoun, which is also a definite form—refers back to a noun previously mentioned in the discourse, we call this anaphoric reference. Category 4, *unique by pointing, nodding, etc.,* is traditionally referred to as *deixis,* which means that the physical context rather than the verbal context is making the noun in question definite. Thus when the pronouns *I* and *you* are used to refer to the speaker and the hearer, respectively, we speak of deictic reference. Finally, category 10, *unique by anticipation,* is called *cataphora* in traditional grammar. In such a case, the definite article points forward in the discourse in anticipation of subsequent specific information that would justify the use of a definite form; this phenomenon is also called cataphoric reference.[7]

Indefinite article usage

Brown's matrix shows us that the indefinite article is used to perform a number of discourse functions:

1. To introduce a noun to the listener that is specific for the speaker but not the listener, e.g.:

    > I saw a funny-looking dog today. (i.e., lower left quadrant of the matrix)

2. To show that the noun does not have a specific referent for either the speaker or the listener, e.g.:

    > I need a new belt. (lower right quadrant of the matrix)

3. To refer to a noun that is nonspecific for the speaker but which is assumed to be specific for the listener; i.e., the speaker guesses, or pretends to guess, e.g.:

    > *FBI man to homeowner:* Don't be coy. We know there's ⎫
    > *a spy* hiding in your cellar.   ⎬ i.e., the upper right
    > *Barbara Walters to King Hussein:* I understand you've   ⎬ quadrant of the
    > made *a proposal* to the Israelis concerning the West   ⎬ matrix
    > Bank.   ⎭

Potential ambiguity of the indefinite article

Note that the indefinite article—especially in object position—may be ambiguous as to whether it modifies a noun that is specific or nonspecific for the speaker. A later reference in the discourse to such an indefinite noun can help disambiguate.

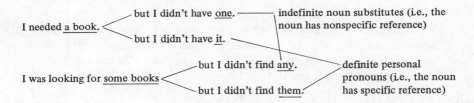

As the above examples show, only nonspecific, indefinite *some* undergoes *some* ⟶ *any* suppletion in negative sentences.

The indefinite article with predicate nominals

Neither the structural classification nor Brown's matrix includes mention of predicate nominals, i.e., nouns that typically follow the verb BE and that identify or classify the subject noun.

> This is a pencil.   John is a teacher.

---

7. There is, of course, a certain amount of overlap in the 10 categories listed above with respect to the traditional three (anaphora, cataphora, and deixis) in that 6 and 8 can be considered subcategories of anaphora while 2, 3, 4, and 5 all seem to have elements of deixis. Furthermore, 7, 9, and 10 can be considered examples of cataphora.

All the indefinite noun phrases in the structural classification or Brown's matrix can be made plural and can be preceded by *some*[8] (some funny-looking dogs, some belts, some spies); however, the *a/an* that modifies a predicate noun never takes *some* in the plural:

These are pencils.   John and Bill are teachers.
*These are some pencils.   *John and Bill are some teachers.

Thus there are some features of article usage peculiar to predicate nominals that the ESL/EFL teacher must be aware of, and there are also typical errors; e.g., the indefinite article is often omitted by learners before a singular predicate noun:

*This is pencil.

Indefinite vs. generic noun phrases

Christophersen (1939) observes that there is a contrast between the use of *sŏme* versus no article in sentences such as the following where there is an object noun rather than a predicate nominal:

I need sŏme chairs.   I need chairs.

The noun phrase *sŏme chairs* in the first sentence is quantitative but indefinite.[9] The noun phrase in the second sentence is qualitative, i.e., what Christophersen calls "parti-generic." No quantity—indefinite or definite—is being expressed.[10]

This distinction provides us with a useful transition to our last major topic in this chapter, generic usage of articles. Christophersen (1939) carefully distinguishes between toto-generic, parti-generic, and indefinite noun phrases as follows:

toto-generic: Chairs are useful pieces of furniture.
parti-generic: I need chairs.
indefinite, nongeneric: I need sŏme chairs.

Note that the quantifier *all* can be used to distinguish toto-generic from parti-generic since it is possible to more or less paraphrase a toto-generic statement but not a parti-generic statement by adding *all:*

toto-generic: All chairs are useful pieces of furniture.
parti-generic: *I need all chairs.

Again, this is because toto-generics are implicitly quantitative while parti-generics are qualitative. Toto-generic usage is what we will consider in the next section under the more general term "generic."

Generic usage

The use of articles and other inflections to convey generic meanings is a matter that is not very well treated in reference grammars and ESL/EFL textbooks. Quirk and Greenbaum (1973), for example, cite the following examples and state that all four patterns express generic meaning—the implication being that they all share the same meaning:

---

8. This *some* is very weakly stressed and is different from the quantifier *some* (Some men smoke—others don't) and demonstrative *some* (That was *some* party!), both of which are stressed. This *some* is transcribed as /sŏm/.

9. Note that it could be either specific or nonspecific.

10. Note that singular nouns cannot mark this distinction (I need a chair. *I need chair).

1. The German }
2. A German } is a good musician.
3. The Germans }
4. Germans } are good musicians.

Preliminary research by Stern (1977) indicates that these four patterns have very different distributions and that a great deal depends on whether generic statements are being made about humans, animals, plants, complex inventions/devices, or simple inanimate objects. Let us look at each of the above patterns more closely.

The pattern |The _____ (sg.)| , illustrated by sentence 1 above, represents formal usage. It
         (noun)

can be used to describe generically classes of humans, animals, organs of the body, plants, and complex inventions/devices. It is *not* appropriate as a generic pattern for simple inanimate objects:

*The book fills leisure time for many people.

In such an environment, however, either pattern 2 or 4 would be appropriate.

A book fills }
Books fill } leisure time for many people.

Pattern 1 predominates in informative or technical writing on animals, plants, musical instruments, and complex inventions or devices. Words like *class, symbol, representative, image,* and *stereotype* also tend to occur in sentences using this pattern.

The pattern |The _____ (pl.)| , illustrated by sentence 3 above, is the most limited
         (noun)

pattern of the four. It usually is used only to express generic facts about a human group that is of a religious, political, national, social, or occupational/professional nature.[11] Group affiliation is critical. This was not the case in pattern 1, where science-based class membership rather than group affiliation was the criterion. Thus the following are *not* acceptable generic statements.

*The tigers are ferocious beasts. }
*The roses need water. } (These sentences are acceptable as spe-
*The pianos are splendid instruments. } cific but not as generic statements.)

However, any of the three other patterns would produce acceptable generic statements for these examples. Some grammarians would claim that pattern 3 is not really generic (i.e., it's for plural proper names that express a collective meaning). Nevertheless, since this form is often used in formal writing in the social sciences instead of pattern 1, it should be discussed and considered along with the other patterns.

The pattern |_____ (pl.)| , illustrated by sentence 4 above, is a slightly less formal
         (noun)

counterpart to the first pattern discussed. Certainly in speech it occurs more frequently than pattern 1. In fact, it can be used in all the semantic environments where pattern 1 occurs; and, in addition, it can be used to make generic statements about simple inanimate objects:

---

11. Only rarely do plants or animals attain this type of necessary collective affiliation; e.g., *The redwoods* must be preserved forever. Save *the whales.*

Books fill leisure time for many people.

It is more concrete and frequent than pattern 1; i.e., it generalizes via pluralization rather than abstraction. It is important because it can be used in all contexts and because it ranges from semiformal to informal in register.

The other pattern | a/an + _____ (sg.) | , illustrated by sentence 2 above, is the most
                   | (noun) |

concrete and colloquial way of expressing a generality. It is used most appropriately when the context is specific:

> *Mrs. X (to Mrs. Y):* I don't know about you, but I think *a husband* should help out with the housework.

> *Background:* Joe gave Alice a puppy.
> *Alice* (on the phone with a veterinarian): Does *a puppy* need a rabies shot?

It can be used to express informal generalities for all semantic contexts; however, it cannot be used when collectivity or group cohesiveness is being expressed.

All of the above examples deal with countable nouns being used generically. Mass nouns, of course, can also be used generically, and when they are, no article is present.

> Water is essential for life.   Rice is a staple food.
> Man is mortal.[12]

This adds a fifth pattern to our inventory: | _____ |
                                                | (mass noun) |

Topic-specific generic usages

Names of diseases

The names of physical ailments and diseases constitute an area of generic noun usage that often causes learning problems because of the variety of article patterns and singular or plural forms they take; i.e., they run the whole gamut of generic noun patterns.

Pattern 1	*Pattern 2*	*Pattern 3*	or	*Pattern 4*	*Pattern 5*
the + noun	*a/an + noun*[13]	*the + noun + pl.*		*noun + pl.*	*mass noun*
the flu	a cold	(the) bends			influenza
the gout	a hernia	(the) mumps			pneumonia
the plague	a headache	(the) measles			malaria
:	an earache	(the) chickenpox			cancer
:	a backache	(x = ks)			:
	:	:			:

In addition to the variation created by the option of using either pattern 3 or 4 for certain diseases, the same disease sometimes has two different names occurring in two different patterns (e.g., the flu/influenza).

---

12. Here *man* refers to mankind in general and is not a countable man.
13. In British English all of the *-ache* compounds in this pattern except *headache* can also occur without the indefinite article, e.g., Joe has earache; however, there is considerable variation from region to region. The interested reader should consult Swan (1980) for a good discussion of British usage in this area.

Therefore, the name of a disease and its article usage pattern should be mastered as a unit if ESL/EFL students are to avoid making recurring errors when they refer to diseases.

Names of body parts

Whereas the names of diseases seem to use the full range of generic patterns available in English, only two patterns seem to be used for generic references to organs or parts of the body:

Pattern 1	*Pattern 3*
the + noun	*the + noun + pl.*
(for singular body parts)	(for plural or paired body parts)
the heart	the ears
the liver	the eyes
the stomach	the lungs
the bladder	the kidneys
etc.	the teeth (irregular plural)
	etc.

These patterns are used in both technical and nontechnical writing of a medical or health-related nature when generic reference is being made to parts of the body.

Abstract nouns and generic usage

In some preliminary research Bergsnev (1976) has shown that abstract nouns derived from verbs and adjectives often have both a mass and a count form for expressing a generality in English, e.g.:

Dependence on drugs is increasing.   A dependence on drugs is increasing.

Increase in input produces dramatic   An increase in input produces dramatic
changes in output.   changes in (the) output.

Some other abstract nouns that have this dual mass/count function in generic statements are:

acceleration	depression	priority
achievement	emphasis	retardation
deceleration	equilibrium	strain
decrease	expenditure	success
demand	growth	

Hard and fast rules of usage are not available; however, some guidelines are possible. The more concrete and informal the context, the better the countable form with the indefinite article sounds, e.g.:

Bill, don't you know that doctors say weight gain can put $\left\{ \begin{array}{l} \text{a strain} \\ \text{?strain} \end{array} \right\}$ on your heart?

On the other hand, the more abstract and formal the context, the better the version without the article sounds, e.g.:

Demographic change often causes $\left\{ \begin{array}{l} \text{dispersion} \\ \text{?a dispersion} \end{array} \right\}$

Some problematic uses of the definite article

From what we have already said in this chapter, we know that use of the definite article can be predicted in those cases where a noun referent is specific for the speaker and the listener owing to unique reference, prior mention, etc. It can also be explained if the noun is being used generically. In this section we want to mention briefly two uses of the definite article which do not appear to fit either of these categories very neatly.

Mechanical inventions and devices

Consider the following examples:

We listened to the news on *the radio*.[14]   Alice took *the train* to Boston.
I talked to Burt on *the phone*.

In such cases the hearer does not know the specific radio, phone, or train that is being referred to (sometimes even the speaker does not know); however, it is clear that a specific radio, phone, or train had to be involved. We would expect an indefinite article here, yet the definite article is being used in a way that seems to approach generic usage. However, this is quite different from the main generic usage of pattern 1 (e.g., *The elephant* is the world's largest land mammal). Perhaps this usage is closer to the diseases we have just mentioned, since when we say

John has the flu.

we mean that John has a case of the flu. Likewise, when we say

Alice took the train to Boston.

we mean that Alice took one specific instance of the noun class **TRAIN** to Boston.

Locations associated with activities

Examples such as the following are also problematic in a similar way:

I'm going to
{
  the store.
  the doctor/the doctor's (office).
  the bank.
  the park.
  the movies (British: the cinema).
  the beach.
  ⋮
}

Again, the hearer does not need to know the specific store, office, or bank involved. For communication, such specificity does not seem to be essential; so why is the definite article used instead of the indefinite article or no article? Perhaps we are again approaching generic usage here, for when we say

I'm going to the store.

we actually mean that we are going to the store that we typically or habitually go to for shopping.

Closely related to the above examples are those few cases where no article is used:

I'm going to
{
  school.
  church.
  ⋮
}

---

14. With regard to this pattern note that *television* is treated differently in British and American English. In British usage we see a program *on the television* (the telly, the tube) but in American usage we see it *on television*.

In such sentences we are focusing on the activity (i.e., studying/learning; worshiping/praying) rather than the location. Focus on the location would require the use of an article:

I'm going to a/the school.   I'm going to a/the church.

We recognize that our explanation for these usages is tentative; however, such expressions do occur frequently, and at some point every ESL/EFL teacher must find a way to present (and explain) these somewhat different usages of the definite article to his or her students.

Concluding remarks

Much more, of course, needs to be said about article usage in English. We hope that this chapter provides a foundation. We will discuss article usage again from time to time when it overlaps with other grammatical topics. For example, in the following chapter on quantifiers, we discuss the difference between pairs such as these where the presence of an indefinite article changes the meaning:

few/a few   little/a little

Then later in Chapter 21 we observe that most sentences with an expletive *there* in subject position contain noun phrases with indefinite determiners after the copula BE:

There's *a snake* in the bathtub!   There's *another problem* we should discuss now.

We also mention articles again when we discuss the superlative degree in Chapter 36, since the definite article typically co-occurs with this construction:[15]

Tom is *the* tallest one in the class.   We have *the* oldest car on the block.

In other words, article usage can't be compartmentalized. Articles are everywhere in English, and as an ESL/EFL teacher, you must be prepared to cope with the varied learning problems that your students will have related to the use of articles.

TEACHING SUGGESTIONS

1   a. Use the indefinite article to teach identification—first to distinguish *a* and *an,* and then the singular form vs. the article-less plural.

This is a/an _____ . (sg.)
This is a _____ . (sg.)/These are _____ s. (pl.)

Suggestions were made in Chapter 2 for teaching the distance concept (i.e., this/that; these/those) inherent in these constructions using cuisenaire rods and Silent Way methodology.

b. To stress normal indefinite noun usage—as opposed to predicate noun usage—have your students practice describing their possessions using *a/an* for singular nouns and *some* for mass or plural nouns.

I have a _____ . What do you have?   I have some _____ . What do you have?

---

15. These two superlative examples allow us to point out that *the* has two pronunciations in unstressed position in English: /ðɪ/ before vowels (*the oldest*) and /ðə/ before consonants (*the tallest*). *The* can also be pronounced /ðiy/ when it is stressed.

2   To practice the difference between mass vs. count use semantically similar items where the mass noun is a cover term and the count noun a specific item, e.g.:

T:	clothing
S1:	We need more clothing for this relief parcel.
S2:	Here's a blouse.
S3:	And here are two jackets.
T:	luggage
S1:	Would you like to buy some luggage?
S2:	Yes, I need two new suitcases.
S3:	And I need a garment bag.

Other mass categories you can use are: food, information, advice, transportation, etc.

3   The recounting of unsuccessful searches or attempts is a good context for practicing *some* —→ *any* suppletion for nouns with nonspecific reference. This involves plural and mass nouns only:

> I was looking for *some* history books. . . . I didn't find *any* (books).
> I wanted *some* water. . . . Nobody had *any* (water).

4   Geographical names: planets, countries, islands, etc. Help your students contrast the usage of nouns from the first group (those plural or collective geographical names that take *the*) with those in the second (singular proper nouns that take no article).

Group 1	Group 2
the Great Lakes	Ø Lake Michigan
the USA	Ø Holland
the Philippines	Ø Puerto Rico
the Soviet Union	Ø Russia
the Rockies	Ø Mount Whitney

5   Let your students practice common variants of equivalents and near-equivalents—one with the article, the other without the article:

Ø English	the English language
Ø Spanish	the Spanish language
Ø UCLA	The University of California at Los Angeles
Ø America	The United States of America
Ø Britain	The United Kingdom
Ø Europe	The Old World

6   Make your students aware of distinct but competing college and university name patterns that should not be mixed, e.g.:

Indiana University	never:
Oxford University	*The Stanford University
	*The Moscow University
The University of Illinois	*The London University
The University of Essex	exception:
	The Ohio State University

7 Give your students practice in expressing generic concepts appropriate to different registers:

cue: elephant/   { gigantic
huge

a. Formal—*The elephant* is gigantic/a gigantic animal.
b. Less formal—*Elephants* are huge/gigantic.
c. Colloquial—*An elephant* is huge.

8 Give them practice in MASS ⟶ COUNT category shifting:

(generic)   (specific)

tea ⟶ a tea/teas
Tea is a healthy beverage.   This is a nice tea. Try it.
                                 Sri Lanka (Ceylon) produces many teas.

9 Test your students' proficiency using the following types of exercises:

a. Translation from the native language into English—especially cases where the two systems differ with respect to the use of articles, e.g.:

French: La vie est belle.
English: ØLife is beautiful.
           *The life is beautiful.

b. Cloze (i.e., fill-in-the-blanks exercises)

(1) _____ Tale of (2) _____ Peter Rabbit

Once upon (3) _____ time there were (4) _____ four little rabbits, and their names were (5) _____ Flopsy, (6) _____ Mopsy, (7) _____ Cottontail, and (8) _____ Peter. They lived with their Mother in (9) _____ sand-bank, underneath (10) _____ roots of (11) _____ very big fir-tree.

10 Cloze dialogs such as the following can be used for both teaching and testing purposes (developed by Linda Chan-Rapp—based on Brown's matrix):

Instructions: Fill in the blanks with *the* or *a/an*.

Situation a
Student: How did I do on (1) _____ test?
Teacher: Well, actually you didn't do very well. Don't you have (2) _____ tutor?
Student: Yes. Mary's been tutoring me for two weeks now. It's been difficult to meet though, because I don't have (3) _____ car. Mary does have (4) _____ small Toyota, but it breaks down a lot and isn't reliable.

Situation b
Son: Hey, Dad, can I have (1) _____ car Friday night? I want to take Sally to (2) _____ school dance.
Dad: Well, that depends. Don't you have (3) _____ paper to write?
Son: Yeah, but it's almost done, and, besides (4) _____ friend told me Miss Fittich postponed it to next Friday.
Dad: Well, okay. But be back by 12:30.
Son: Thanks, Dad. Er . . . by the way, could I go buy (5) _____ new shirt for (6) _____ dance?

EXERCISES

Test your understanding of what has been presented

1. Provide your own sentences to illustrate the following terms. Underline the word(s) illustrating the term:

proper noun	predicate noun
proper name	generic usage with
geographical name	definite article
mass noun	indefinite article
abstract noun	parti-generic
indefinite noun	
specific	
nonspecific	

2. Explain the ungrammaticality of the following sentences:

a. *She has a coffee on her dress.
b. *They served us plenty of drinking waters.
c. *I have examination in French today.

Test your ability to apply what you know

3. If your students produce the following sentences, what errors have they made? How will you make them aware of these errors, and what exercises will you prepare to correct the errors?

a. *My brother is student.
b. *He is an European.
c. *I enjoy writing the poetry. It's my hobby.

4. In what way can the following sentence be ambiguous?

John is interested in buying a car.

5. The speaker of English can refer to the members of a national or ethnic group in various ways:

The German is hard-working.   Germans are hard-working.
The Germans are hard-working.

Can you detect any differences in these three patterns? Can you use all three patterns for all nationalities (i.e., are there any nationalities without an overt plural form)?

BIBLIOGRAPHY

References

Allan, K. (1980). "Nouns and Countability," *Language* 56:3, 541–567.
Bergsnev, L. (1976). "Variations in Article Usage with Abstract Nouns." Unpublished English 215 paper, UCLA, fall, 1976.
Brown, R. (1973). *A First Language*. Cambridge, Mass.: Harvard University Press.
Christophersen, P. (1939). *The Articles: A Study of Their Theory and Use in English*. Copenhagen: Einar Muhksgaard.
Covitt, R. (1976). "Some Problematic Grammar Areas for ESL Teachers." M.A. thesis in TESL, UCLA.

Hewson, J. (1972). *Article and Noun in English.* The Hague: Mouton.

Quirk, R., and S. Greenbaum (1973). *A Concise Grammar of Contemporary English.* New York: Harcourt Brace Jovanovich.

Stern, S. (1977). "Generic Use of Articles in English." Unpublished English 215 paper, UCLA, fall, 1977.

Swan, M. (1980). *Practical English Usage.* London: Oxford University Press.

Thompson, S. (1978). "Modern English from a Typological Point of View: Some Implications of the Function of Word Order," *Linguistische Berichte* 54:19–35.

Suggestions for further reading

For a valuable traditional account of article usage, see Christophersen (1939), cited above.

For a survey of transformational contributions to our understanding of article usage, see the chapter on Determiners in:

Stockwell, R., P. Schachter, and B. Partee (1973). *The Major Syntactic Structures of English.* New York: Holt, Rinehart and Winston.

For philosophical/semantic treatments of article usage in English, see the Hewson (1972) reference cited above and the following:

Vendler, Z. (1967). *Linguistics in Philosophy.* Ithaca, N.Y.: Cornell University Press.

For an interesting treatment of definiteness in English with reference to discourse considerations, see:

Chafe, W. (1972). "Discourse Structure and Human Knowledge," in J. B. Carroll and R. O. Freedle (eds.), *Language Comprehension and the Acquisition of Knowledge.* Washington, D.C.: V. H. Winston and Sons.

For a useful account of English article usage addressed to EFL teachers/ learners, see this source:

Close, R. A. (1981). *English as a Foreign Language* (3d ed.). London: Allen and Unwin.

For suggestions regarding the teaching of English article usage, see the following:

Brinton, D., and R. Neuman (1982). *Getting Along: English Grammar and Writing* (Book 1, pp. 179–180; Book 2, pp. 195–196). Englewood Cliffs, N.J.: Prentice-Hall.

Danielson, D., and R. Hayden (1973). *Using English: Your Second Language.* Englewood Cliffs, N.J.: Prentice-Hall, Chaps. 10, 11.

McIntosh, L., T. Ramos, and R. Goulet (1970). *Advancing in English.* New York: American Book Co., pp. 96–122.

Martin, A. V., et al. (1977). *Guide to Language and Study Skills.* Englewood Cliffs, N.J.: Prentice-Hall, pp. 7–20.

Wohl, M. (1978). *Preparation for Writing: Grammar.* Rowley, Mass.: Newbury House.

15

Measure Words, Collective Nouns, and Quantifiers

GRAMMATICAL DESCRIPTION

Introduction

Articles are only a part of the whole determiner system in English. In addition to using articles to signal whether nouns are definite or indefinite and generic or nongeneric, the English language has a variety of other resources for counting, measuring, and collecting. In some cases such resources help us make mass nouns countable; in other cases there are resources to help us measure the quantity of plural nouns or mass nouns; for yet other situations there are additional resources such as collective nouns that help us group plural count nouns into meaningful sets. We have decided to discuss all these topics in one chapter, since we view measuring, collecting, and counting (or quantifying) as related phenomena.

Measure words

Although not nearly as complicated as the noun classifier systems found in some other languages, English does have a number of general measure words (or unit words) such as the following, which must be learned by ESL/EFL students. These measure words are used to make mass nouns countable or more precisely quantifiable (e.g., a *slice* of bread, a *pinch* of salt) or to impose quantity on a set of count nouns too large to conveniently count individually (e.g., a *bowl* of peanuts, a *box* of apples), e.g.:

Container-based Measure Words
a *can* of _____
a *bottle* of _____
a *jar* of _____
a *carton* of _____

Portion-based Measure Words
a *slice* of _____
a *piece* of _____
a *bit* of _____
a *pinch* of _____

Note that the most general of these "general" measure words can also be used with abstract mass nouns, e.g., a *piece* of advice, a *bit* of good news.

In addition, English has a number of measure words for culturally-based specific quantities which should also be presented to ESL/EFL students. For example:

a *quart* of milk	a *bushel* of corn
a *teaspoon(ful)* of salt	a *peck* of strawberries
a *pound* of butter	a *yard* of fabric

Some plural count nouns without a singular form are viewed strictly as pairs, i.e., something having two equal parts, and the measure word *pair*[1] is used with these nouns, e.g.:

a *pair* of ⎰ trousers ⎱   *a ⎰ trouser ⎱
         ⎨ scissors ⎬   ⎨ scissor ⎬
         ⎩ tongs   ⎭   ⎩ tong   ⎭

Finally, there are some idiomatic measure words that are used to quantify certain mass or plural nouns—especially those referring to vegetables and other food items. These measure words characterize the units in which these food items typically exist, e.g.:

Vegetables   *Others*

a *head* of ⎰ *lettuce* ⎱   a *loaf* of bread
          ⎨ *cabbage* ⎬   a *hand* of bananas
          ⎩   ⎭   a *bunch* of grapes
a *stalk* of *celery*
an *ear* of *corn*
a *clove* of *garlic*

Most measure expressions in English follow the same basic syntactic pattern:

a/an ... one ⎫
two   ⎬   + measure word + of + Noun   ⎰ mass   ⎱
three   ⎬   (measure word is sg. or pl. depending on the ⎨ plural ⎬
  ·   ⎭   preceding number)[2]   ⎩   ⎭

A few exceptions to this syntactic pattern do exist, however. For example, ESL/EFL students sometimes overgeneralize this pattern when using a word like "dozen" and erroneously produce: *a dozen of eggs* or *two dozens of eggs*. In fact, they use this syntactic pattern with other noun-based cardinal numbers as well, erroneously producing:

*a ⎰ thousand ⎱ of people...   *two ⎰ thousands ⎱ of people...
  ⎨ hundred ⎬   ⎨ hundreds ⎬
  ⎩   ⎭   ⎩   ⎭

In other words, when you have a specific noun-based numerical word such as *dozen, hundred, thousand* with an indefinite plural head noun like *people* as in the above examples, the use of *of* is ungrammatical. Also, such numerical words remain in the singular even when numbers greater than *one* modify them, e.g.:

two dozen eggs   five thousand spectators

However, the use of *of* is necessary in the following two situations:

---

1. The measure word *pair* also occurs with other nouns that occur mainly, though not exclusively, as pairs (e.g., a pair of shoes, a pair of earrings); however, these nouns may also occur in the singular (an old shoe, a jade earring, etc.).

2. Certain measure words are variable as to whether or not they take a plural ending after a plural determiner. A few never take the plural marker, e.g., ten (head/*heads) of cattle. Note that the measure word *head* used with *lettuce* or *cabbage* is different from the one used with *cattle* in that it usually is pluralized [e.g., two *head(s)* of cabbage/lettuce]; however, the singular form sometimes occurs here too.

1. A plural numerical word is used with general rather than specific number reference to convey the general sense of a large number:

hosts of angels	hundreds of people
lots of cars	dozens of exercises

2. A specific number is used as a unit word preceding a definite plural noun (or pronoun):

a hundred of the old people   two hundred of them

We conclude our discussion of measure words by pointing out that specific quantity measure words are used in other syntactic contexts than the one we have presented above. They also occur frequently, for example, in verb phrase position after the copula BE, the verb HAVE, and stative verbs of measure such as *weigh, equal, contain, hold,* and *stand,* e.g.:

Joe weighs 200 pounds.   This jar has a capacity of two quarts.

In this usage the measure phrase is often followed by an adjective, e.g.:

Brent is four years old.   This table is six feet long.

If this type of measure-phrase construction is used as a prenominal modifier without *of,* the plural inflection of the measure word is lost, e.g.:

Joe is a 200-pound athlete. (*a 200-pounds athlete)
Brent is a four-year-old boy. (*a 4-years-old boy)

Collective nouns

There is a parallel between collective nouns and measure words in that for collective phrases such as

a team of hockey players   a group of children

the collective nouns *team* and *group* impose a structure on the indefinite plural nouns *hockey players* and *children* just as the measure word *piece* imposes countability on mass nouns such as *furniture* and *bread.* Also, just as the measure words for vegetables were idiomatic in phrases like *a head of cabbage* and *a clove of garlic,* collective nouns are used idiomatically to describe a variety of animal groups,[3] e.g.:

a school of fish, a pride of lions, a swarm of bees

Collective noun subjects may take either singular or plural subject-verb agreement. Although singular subject-verb agreement is preferred in American English, there is some dialectic variation here, since in British English plural subject-verb agreement occurs much more frequently:

American: The government has not been responding to the will of the people.
British: The government have not been responding to the will of the people.

In both dialects, however, speakers or writers reveal their view as to whether a given collective noun should be interpreted as a whole unit or as the individual members or components

---

3. There used to be many more of these idiomatic collectives for animals in older forms of English (e.g., a *gaggle* of geese, a *brace* of partridges), but most of them have become archaic if not obsolete. English currently prefers more general collectives for animals (e.g., *herd, flock*).

which make up the unit. They do this by choosing a pronoun (or other anaphoric item) that refers back to the collective noun. The singular or plural number of the pronoun (or the other anaphoric item) provides the clue. An example from Celce (1970) elucidates this point:

I saw the mob; it was on the verge of riot-   I saw the mob; they were on the verge of
ing.   rioting.

In the first sentence, of course, the speaker is conceiving of "the mob" as a whole group; in the second sentence, the speaker is thinking more in terms of the individuals that make up the group. The fact that the speaker has this choice is a test for whether or not a given noun is collective; i.e., collective nouns, by definition, have a potential duality of number.

This duality of number is, of course, also observable in other anaphoric forms such as reflexive pronouns, possessive determiners, and relative pronouns, e.g.:

$$\text{The committee blamed } \left\{ \begin{array}{l} \text{itself} \\ \text{themselves} \end{array} \right\}.$$

$$\text{The committee blamed } \left\{ \begin{array}{l} \text{its} \\ \text{their} \end{array} \right\} \text{chairman.}$$

$$\text{The committee } \left\{ \begin{array}{l} \text{which was} \\ \text{who were} \end{array} \right\} \text{annoyed at the chairman....}$$

Celce points out that there are three main types of collective nouns as exemplified in the following lists:

I Common Collectives	II Unique Collectives	III Generic Collectives
(a/the) class	the Vatican	the clergy
(a/the) team	the Kremlin	the bourgeoisie
(a/the) crew	(the) Congress	the intelligentsia
(a/the) government	(the) Parliament	the aristocracy
.	.	.

Each of these lists contains collective nouns which in a given context can either be singular or plural in number, depending upon the particular view of the noun that the speaker or writer wishes to convey.

Quantifiers

It is not easy for ESL/EFL students to learn how to use the numberlike quantifiers, which are another type of prenominal modifier. These quantifiers are words or phrases which indicate the amount, number, or proportion of the noun which follows. They are particularly troublesome because ESL/EFL students need to master the distinction between the positive or negative connotations associated with them, the restrictions on their syntactic distribution, and the rules of usage for each quantifier.

Positive and negative connotations of quantifiers

The following two continua—while not exhaustive—do reveal that a certain systematicity exists among the numberlike quantifiers as to which of them connote a positive meaning and which a negative sense. The diagonal lines connect items or sets of items that logically contradict each other. The dotted line between *none/no* and *all* indicates an opposition, i.e., the extreme negative item and the extreme positive item, respectively. The dotted line and arrow going from *not all* to *some,* etc., indicates an inverse implicational relationship [e.g., if it is true that not all my pens are yellow, this is the same as saying that (at least) some of them are not yellow].

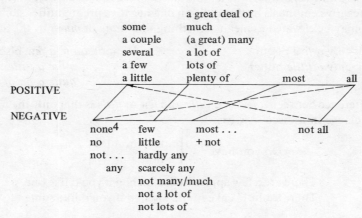

As we have stated, the solid diagonal lines indicate the quantifiers that express a minimal contradiction with respect to each other. Thus:

A: There were *some* musicians at the party.
B: That's not true. There were *no* musicians!

A: Jason must have *a lot of* friends.
B: You're wrong. He has very *few.*

A: *All* the dancers wore red shirts.
B: No, *not all.* Some wore yellow shirts.

It is, of course, possible to use more than the minimum logical contradiction if the facts warrant a stronger response.

A: *All* Republicans are anti-environment.
B: That's not true. *Most* of the Republicans I know are *not* anti-environment.

The negative meaning is made explicit in many of the negative counterparts of the positive quantifiers. The negative connotation of these, therefore, should be obvious to ESL/EFL students. This is not always the case, however, with quantifiers such as the following: *scarcely/hardly any* (vs. *many/much*) and *few/little* (vs. *a few/a little*). The following examples make explicit the connotations implied by the latter group:

He took *a few* (= some, several) biscuits with the result that *few* (= not many) were left for the rest of us.

He then took *a little* (=some) butter, with the result that *little* (=not much) was left for the rest of us.

As our continua show, the quantifiers in these pairs do not directly contradict each other but rather convey different meanings. Notice that another way to capture the negative

---

4. The quantifiers *no* and *none* seem to be in complementary distribution. *No* is used only with indefinite head nouns; *none* is used with definite head nouns and as a pronoun:

No rain fell in the Sahel last year.   Has there been any rain this year? *None* thus
None of the people there could escape the   far.
  drought.

connotation in the second quantifier in each of the above examples would be to paraphrase *few* as *not many* and *little* as *not much.* Note also that the first quantifier in each example may be given a negative emphasis by the addition of a negative prequantifier such as *only, just,* or *but,* or they may be elevated to mean something like *many* or *much* by the addition of *quite.*

He took *only a few* biscuits.   He took *quite a few* biscuits.
He took *only a little* butter.

He took $\left\{ \begin{array}{l} \textit{quite a little} \\ \textit{quite a bit of} \end{array} \right\}$ butter.

Another difference between *a few* or *a little* and *few* or *little* is that only the former can occur in the first clause in a discourse, e.g.:

Do you have $\left\{ \begin{array}{l} \text{a few minutes} \\ \text{a little time} \end{array} \right\}$?

There are a few apples in the kitchen if you'd like one.
There's a little cake in the kitchen if you'd like some.

Few and *little,* however, generally require more context, because a negative or contradictory tone must be established before these quantifiers can be used, e.g.:

Harold was lonely and desperate; he had few friends and little money.

Many ESL/EFL students omit the indefinite article when they use *a few* or *a little.* While the result is not necessarily an ungrammatical sentence, the listener or reader is likely to be confused by the use of an implicitly negative quantifier where a positive one seems to be required by the discourse:

?I have few good friends back home. They write to me often.

Details such as the above are subtle; however, they are understood and used by all native speakers of English and will therefore have to be taught and practiced in the ESL/EFL classroom.

The syntax of numberlike quantifiers

For correct determiner-noun number agreement all of the above quantifiers—and others like them—must be classified as to whether they occur with count nouns only, mass nouns only, or with both:

Count (Plural)	Mass	Both Plural and Mass
a couple of	a little	(not) a lot of
several	little	(not) lots of
a few	(not) much	some
few	a great deal of	plenty of
(not) many	:	most (. . . not)
:		(not) all
		no/none
		hardly any
		scarcely any
		:

When determiner-noun agreement is not observed, ungrammatical sentences occur:

*Why do Americans have so much cars?

There is often a great deal more involved than determiner-noun number agreement in the syntactic behavior of quantifiers. We will illustrate some of this syntactic complexity using *much, many, a lot of,* and *lots of* as examples.

As the above classification shows us, *much* is used before mass nouns and *many* is used with plural count nouns. In some cases, these quantifiers can be used to determine whether the meaning of the noun they modify is count or mass. The following pairs illustrate this point:

We didn't order much coffee. (not a large quantity of coffee beans or ground coffee)	They don't have much company. (visitors)
	They don't have many companies. (business firms)
We didn't order many coffees. (a small number of cups of brewed coffee)	

(Of course, the plural ending of the noun also indicates that the plural form must be a count noun, while the use of *much* with the unmarked noun indicates that it is a mass noun—not a singular count noun.)

Also, when *much* and *many* are used as pronouns, the verb form associated with each reflects the difference: i.e., *many* requires a plural verb, whereas *much* agrees with a singular verb.

Many are called every year.   There isn't much to be learned.

Syntactically, *lots* and *a lot of* are distinct from *much* and *many*. First, the verb must agree with the number of the object of the preposition (i.e., *of*) rather than with *a lot* or *lots*. In addition, *a lot of* and *lots of* occur freely with both count and mass nouns.

A lot of people were there.   A lot of time was wasted.
Lots of people were there.   Lots of time was wasted.

Second, the use of the preposition *of* distinguishes *much* or *many* from *a lot* or *lots*. *Much* and *many* are followed by *of* only when the nouns that they quantify are definite (i.e., identified):

Before a definite noun: *Many of Betty's friends* go on picnics.
    They don't spend *much of their time* studying.

Before an indefinite noun: *Many people* go on picnics in the summer.
    They don't spend *much time* studying.

In contrast, *lots of*[5] and *a lot of* are always used with *of* unless they are functioning as nouns or pronouns:

He ate
{
    a lot at the picnic.
    a lot of sandwiches at the picnic.
    a lot of the sandwiches I made at the picnic.
    *a lot sandwiches at the picnic.

He ate
{
    lots at the picnic.
    lots of sandwiches at the picnic.
    lots of the sandwiches I made at the picnic.
    *lots sandwiches at the picnic.

---

5. Some English speakers feel that *lots of* is a slightly stronger quantifier than *a lot of* (i.e., that it signifies a greater amount). The fact that *lots of* can be reduplicated (*lots and lots and lots . . . of*), while *a lot of* cannot, seems to support this intuition.

The agreement of *many* and *much* with *count* and *mass* nouns, respectively, also occurs in negatives (*not many, not much*) and questions (*how many/how much*) as well as statements. This particular distinction is a problem for many ESL/EFL learners who speak languages that have one word for English *many* and *much*. The tendency in such cases is to overuse *much*:

*John has much friends. *How much books do you have?

The usage of numberlike quantifiers

Returning to our set of four quantifiers once again, we feel that explaining the usage of these words is even more complicated than explaining the syntax. The usual rule of thumb given in ESL/EFL texts is:

Use *many* or *a lot of* (*lots of*) in affirmative statements and *many* or *much* in questions and
  negative contexts:

This rule is often followed by examples:

Jake has many friends.   */?Jake has much money.
Jake has a lot of money.

Does Jake have $\begin{Bmatrix} \text{many friends} \\ \text{much money} \end{Bmatrix}$?   Jake doesn't have $\begin{Bmatrix} \text{many friends} \\ \text{much money} \end{Bmatrix}$

We will show how this information is incomplete (and perhaps misleading) below.

Likewise, some grammarians have attempted to explain this usage problem by saying that *a lot of* and *lots of* are found in informal language whereas *much* and *many* are reserved for more formal language. Even if this were true (certainly *a lot of* is used by modern writers for serious prose), ESL/EFL students would need more guidance than this in choosing the correct quantifier for a given context.

Fortunately, Neuman (1975) conducted a usage survey in which she attempted to define more rigorously the contexts in which each of these various quantifiers would be most appropriate. Although she cautions that her study is preliminary, she does report the following distinctions:

1. Unmodified *much* (i.e., without a preceding intensifier such as *very*) is used in positive assertions but only in very formal written contexts.

For example, if you are writing a letter to the person that you hope will be your future employer, you might write:

I have been working for ten years with the RAND Corporation and I have accumulated
  much experience with computers.

But even in this example, Neuman reports that although *much* was preferred by native speakers over *a lot of* or *lots of,* another quantifier, *a great deal of,* was preferred over *much.*

Except for very formal written language, *a lot of* is preferred over unmodified *much* in positive assertions. For example, in the following pair of sentences, the first was preferred by native speakers over the second, which is at best marginal.

Boy, do I have a lot of homework tonight! ?Boy, do I have much homework tonight!

2. In informal language, *a lot of* or *lots of* is preferred in positive assertions, whereas *many* or *much* is preferred after *not,* e.g.:

I used to find *lots of* time to read *a lot of* good novels, but now I don't have *much* free time, so I don't read *many* books.

3. Neuman reports that *many,* like *much,* is affected by the formal/informal distinction, with native speakers preferring *many* over *a lot of* in formal language, e.g.:

Today, more people are raising children alone, and *many* women are discovering that the act of being the sole parent can be devastating.

4. Neuman also mentions that *many* is used to indicate a more limited, countable quantity, whereas *a lot of* tends to indicate an exceptional amount or quantity which is further from the norm. For example, *a lot of* or *lots of* is preferred over *many* in such a context:

Every day she has a new dress. She could wear a new outfit every day for weeks.

She has $\begin{Bmatrix} a\ lot\ of \\ lots\ of \end{Bmatrix}$ dresses.

The inverse is true for negative contexts, where *not many* indicates a smaller, more negative quantity than *not a lot of*:

Jane doesn't have many friends. (few)
Jane doesn't have a lot of friends. (some but not many)

Neuman's study did not examine larger pieces of discourse. When we did this informally, it became clear that unmodified *much* and *many* cannot readily be used in short responses to yes-no and wh-questions, whereas most of the other quantifiers in the same category may be used in such responses:

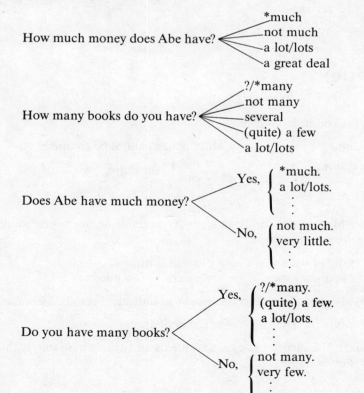

How much money does Abe have?
— *much
— not much
— a lot/lots
— a great deal

How many books do you have?
— ?/*many
— not many
— several
— (quite) a few
— a lot/lots

Does Abe have much money?
Yes, { *much.
        a lot/lots.
        ⋮ }
No, { not much.
       very little.
       ⋮ }

Do you have many books?
Yes, { ?/*many.
        (quite) a few.
        a lot/lots.
        ⋮ }
No, { not many.
       very few.
       ⋮ }

Behre (1967) did a frequency and usage study on *much, many, a lot of, lots of,* and related quantifiers as they occurred in the writings of Agatha Christie. Much of what he found corroborates Neuman's survey. Behre, for example, found that the following register differences occurred:

Strongly colloquial: *lots of, plenty of*
Both colloquial and formal: *much, many, a lot of*

Formal: *a* $\begin{Bmatrix} good \\ great \end{Bmatrix}$ *deal of, a* $\begin{Bmatrix} good \\ great \end{Bmatrix}$ *many*

Also, while *a lot of* and *lots of* were twice as frequent overall as *a good/great deal of,* the latter quantifiers did increase in frequency when the text involved narration and description—as opposed to when the text contained dialog and conversation, where *a lot of* and *lots of* were overwhelmingly preferred (Behre, 1967:44).

Thus, as with so many other grammar points we have discussed, what at first appears to be a rather straightforward distinction is revealed, after some careful examination, to be far more complicated in terms of actual usage than initial observation indicated.

Conclusion

Many ESL/EFL texts do not do justice to measure words or collective nouns and say little about quantifiers beyond contrasting the use of *much/many* and the meanings of *a few/few* and *a little/little.* The quantifier-collector system of English is definitely more complicated than such textbooks would suggest and deserves more attention in the ESL/EFL classroom than it is receiving at present. Further usage studies (along the lines of the ones carried out by Neuman and Behre) would be very helpful.

TEACHING SUGGESTIONS

1 *Measure Words*
   a. Begin by reviewing the count/mass distinction.

Count nouns can be counted: Mass nouns cannot be counted:

$\begin{Bmatrix} a \\ one \end{Bmatrix}$ chair, two chairs, three chairs,   * $\begin{Bmatrix} a \\ one \end{Bmatrix}$ furniture, *two furnitures,
⋮   ⋮

   b. Introduce quantifiers. Mass nouns can be made into countable nouns by preceding the mass noun with a measure word:

a bottle of wine   a piece of furniture
two bottles of wine   two pieces of furniture

Similar measure words can also be used with count nouns to indicate a certain amount:

a box of pencils   a bushel of apples

   c. Practice measure words. Use pictures as cues to students and ask them to supply the appropriate measure word. For example:

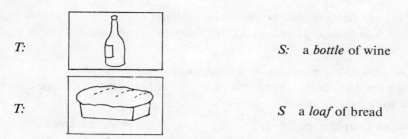

T: *S:*   a *bottle* of wine

T: *S*   a *loaf* of bread

d. Game—"What did you buy at the supermarket?" A student starts the game by saying:

"I went to the supermarket and I bought . . ." completing the sentence with a measure word expression and a noun beginning with the letter A, for example, "a bag of apples."

The second student must repeat the sentence and add to it with a measure word and a noun beginning with the letter B, for example, "I went to the supermarket and I bought a bag of *a*pples and a bunch of *b*ananas."

The third student might add: "I went to the supermarket and I bought a bag of *a*pples, a bunch of *b*ananas, and a box of *c*ookies."

Game continues until all students have had a chance or until all 26 letters of the alphabet have been used.

2 *Numberlike Quantifiers*

a. Introduce quantifiers that are like indefinite numbers:

Show count/mass distinction
many
a few
few } only with plural countable noun
a couple of
several
much
a little } only with mass noun
little

Show your class the positive and negative continua from this chapter and explain the affirmative and negative connotations using contextualized examples, e.g.:

Roy: Gosh, Ed. You look really worried. Do you have *a lot of* problems on your mind?
Ed: *Few* problems, Roy, but the ones I have are big ones.

b. Give students paraphrase exercises such as the following, where the teacher supplies a sentence with a quantifier and asks students to paraphrase the sentence using another quantifier.

(1) *T:*   There was *little* money left after the shopping spree.
    S: There wasn't *much* money left after the shopping spree.
(2) *T:*   *Most* of the items were bought during the first hour of the spree.
    S: *More than half* of the items were bought during the first hour of the spree.
(3) *T:*   However, *a few* items were purchased later.
    S: However, *some* items were purchased later.

c. Discuss syntactic and semantic restrictions on the use of certain quantifiers. Help students induce rules from dialogs. Here is an example adapted from Neuman (1975) in which *much* and *a lot of* are contrasted:

John: I have a lot of homework to do tonight. Do you have much?
Carol: Yes, I have a lot tonight, but I won't have much tomorrow night. We have an exam tomorrow morning.

d. Have students complete modified cloze passages in which quantifiers have been omitted, e.g.:

(1) _____ the tennis courts were being used when we arrived on Saturday. We were fortunate to get the last one. There sure were (2) _____ people there. (3) _____ looked really professional, however. Etc.

3   Collective Nouns

a. Have your students do some fill-in exercises to practice the use of collective nouns that co-occur with certain head nouns referring to animals, e.g.:

Fill in the blanks with *flock, herd, pride, swarm,* as appropriate:

(1) The rancher had a large _____ of cows to feed.
(2) The shepherd was watching over his _____ of sheep.
(3) When I went to Lion Country Safari, I saw a _____ of lions.
(4) The farmer was attacked by a _____ of bees.

b. Your more advanced students can practice paraphrasing statements in order to achieve a more precise (and often more formal) restatement by using collective nouns where appropriate, e.g.:

All (of) the members of the committee were in favor of tabling the motion.

rewrite: The entire committee was in favor of tabling the motion.

The victory would have been impossible without the cooperation of all (of) the members of the team.

rewrite: The victory would have been impossible without the cooperation of the whole team.

c. Nancy Marwin suggests the following courtroom exercise for practicing collective nouns in context. The teacher first divides the class into small groups and then distributes a handout with the essential material for a story-writing exercise:

The setting is a courtroom where a gang of thieves, all members of the same family (the Braysons), are on trial. Outside a crowd has gathered: a group of reporters, a crew of cameramen, etc. Inside are the other participants: a team of lawyers, the judge, and the jury. A committee of government employees are also present as observers.

The groups of students are then instructed to begin writing a story using this material, including the collective nouns, and focusing on both units and individuals where appropriate. They are told to be careful to use correct number agreement based on meaning when they refer back to collective nouns using personal, reflexive, and relative pronouns.

EXERCISES

Test your understanding of what has been presented

1. Provide original example sentences that illustrate the following terms. Underline the pertinent word(s) in your examples.

measure word (unit word)	quantifier for mass nouns only
general	quantifier for count and mass nouns
specific quantity	negative connotation quantifier
idiomatic	collective noun
numberlike quantifier	singular reference
quantifier for count nouns only	plural reference

2. Account for the ungrammaticality or the semantic problem in each of the following sentences:

a. *There are chalk on the blackboard tray.
b. *There were a lot people at the garage sale.
c. *Although he had few close friends, he was very lonely.

3. Explain the difference in meaning between the following pairs of sentences:

a. (1) Many of the people in this town voted for Reagan in 1980.
   (2) Many people voted for Reagan in 1980.
b. (1) The class didn't quiet down; it was in a boisterous mood.
   (2) The class didn't quiet down; they were in a boisterous mood.
c. (1) He doesn't have a lot of ambition.
   (2) He doesn't have much ambition.
d. (1) Thanks a lot.
   (2) Thanks lots.

Test your ability to apply what you know

4. The following sentences contain errors that are sometimes made by ESL/EFL students. Account for the ungrammaticality or awkwardness, and explain how you would make your students aware of such errors. What remedial exercises would you provide?

a. *I still have much problem with this language.
b. *With eight millions of people New York City used to have the largest population of any city in the world.
c. ?He eats much food every day.
d. *He said he was hungry, so I made him a big sandwich with three breads.
e. *I don't understand two-words verbs.

5. In addition to the three categories of collective nouns described in this chapter, there are also a number of adjectivally derived nouns in English that may be considered as generic collectives. Nouns like "the meek," "the dead," "the rich," when they have human reference, resemble generic collective nouns in a number of ways: they are always preceded by "the," they are not overtly singular or plural, and they may refer to a whole group in general terms rather than to a particular or unique group. One problem with calling them collective nouns is

that they do not exhibit the potential duality of number when one uses pronouns and the like to refer back to them. Explain.

6. One of your best students has acquired the rule that accounts for why the measure word is plural in a, whereas it is singular in b because of its prenominal modifier function:

a. This house is fifty *years* old.   b. It's a fifty-*year*-old house.

This student looked at the newspaper on Sunday and found the following headline, "Greece: a Centuries-old Framework for Contemporary Living" (*Los Angeles Times,* cover of *Home* magazine, Mar. 14, 1982). She asks you why the headline uses the form *centuries* instead of *century* because she recognizes that the measure word is being used as a prenominal modifier. What would you say?

BIBLIOGRAPHY

References

Behre, F. (1967). *Studies in Agatha Christie's Writings: The Behaviour of a good (great) deal, a lot, lots, much, plenty, many, a good (great) many.* Gothenburg Studies in English. Göteborg: Elanders Boktryckeri Aktiebolag.
Celce, M. (1970). "The Duality of Collective Nouns," *English Language Teaching* 24:2.
Neuman, R. (1975). "Much Confusion." Unpublished English 215 paper, UCLA, fall, 1975.

Suggestions for further reading

For a semantic treatment of English quantifiers, see:

Hogg, R. M. (1977). *English Quantifier Systems.* Amsterdam: North Holland Publishing Co.

For a more traditional treatment of English quantifiers directed toward the EFL teacher/student, see:

Close, R. A. (1981). *English as a Foreign Language* (3d ed.). London: Allen and Unwin, Chap. 4.

For a unified transformational treatment of article and quantifier usage, see:

Stockwell, R., P. Schachter, and B. Partee (1973). *The Major Syntactic Structures of English.* New York: Holt, Rinehart and Winston, Chap. 3.

For exercises dealing with quantifiers that you might want to use with your students, see:

Danielson, D., and R. Hayden (1973). *Using English: Your Second Language.* Englewood Cliffs, N.J.: Prentice-Hall, Chap. 10.
McIntosh, L., T. Ramos, and R. Goulet (1970). *Advancing in English.* American Book Co., pp. 105–113.
Rutherford, W. E. (1975). *Modern English* (2d ed., vol. 1). New York: Harcourt Brace Jovanovich, pp. 132–146.

For a description of collective nouns, see:

Celce, M. (1970). See above references for citation.

16

Preverbal Adverbs of Frequency[1]

GRAMMATICAL DESCRIPTION

Introduction

In Chapter 2 we mentioned the adverbials of frequency that usually occur at the end of a sentence. Some of these adverbials express a specific and others a general sense of frequency:

> Bob does his laundry *once a week.* ⎫
> I brush my teeth *every day.* ⎬ specific frequency

> Helen does the dishes *once in a while.* ⎫
> You should write your parents *every now and then.* ⎬ general frequency

If we want to be more precise, we can refer to such adverbials as "adverbials of specific or general frequency."[2] Although these adverbials tend to occur at the end of the sentence (i.e., the activity is in focus), they may also occur initially if the adverbial of frequency is in focus:

> *Once a week* Bob does his laundry.
> *Every now and then* you should write your parents.

In contrast to these adverbials of specific or general frequency, English also has a class of preverbal adverbs[3] of frequency that tend to occur most naturally in the middle of a sentence.[4]

---

1. We are very grateful to George Bedell for his comments on an earlier version of this chapter, which helped us make major improvements in this version.

2. We have not provided phrase structure descriptions for many general and specific adverbials of frequency such as *once a week, once in a while, every now and then,* etc., because their analysis is simply too complicated to be worth doing. *Once a week,* for example, would have an underlying structure corresponding roughly to

$$\text{``} \left\{ \begin{array}{c} \emptyset \\ on \end{array} \right\} \text{ one time } \left\{ \begin{array}{c} during \\ in \end{array} \right\} \left\{ \begin{array}{c} every \\ each \end{array} \right\} \text{ week''}$$

Such a string would require a series of lexicalizations and syntactic reductions before we finally arrived at *once a week.*

3. We have borrowed the term "preverbal adverb" from Klima (1964).

4. Note that whereas adverbials of specific or general frequency tend to be phrases (with exceptions such as *weekly, yearly, daily, hourly*), preverbal adverbs of frequency tend to be single words, although they may take intensifiers and thereby form adverbial phrases (e.g., *very often, almost always*). Sometimes both types of adverbs of frequency occur in statements of habitual action, e.g., *I usually do my laundry once a week.* When this happens, the preverbal adverb is modifying the specific adverbial of frequency; in other words, preverbal adverbs of frequency modify the entire sentence—they do for the sentence what quantifiers do for the noun phrase—whereas general or specific adverbials of frequency modify the activity expressed in the verb phrase.

Josh *never* writes his parents.   Bill has *often* forgotten to make his bed.
Mary is *always* late for class.
I can *usually* do my shopping on Satur-
    day.

As we shall see later, the preferred position for such adverbs of frequency is complicated but predictable. Because of the complexity, however, misplacement of these forms is a common problem for ESL/EFL learners—and even some native speakers—who produce ill-formed sentences such as the following:

*Always Mary is coming late to class.   *Bill has forgotten often to make his bed.

In this chapter we will discuss the semantic system and the syntactic rules that govern the use of preverbal adverbs of frequency. We will also point out some similarities and differences between preverbal adverbs of frequency and related adverbials or quantifiers.

The semantics of preverbal adverbs of frequency

Resemblance to quantification

Similar to the quantifiers described in the preceding chapter, preverbal adverbs of frequency fall along either the positive or the negative continuum of a scale on which *always* constitutes the positive extreme and *never* the negative one. Again, there are several pairs of positive and negative terms that logically contradict each other. (See the diagonal lines in the diagram.) Because of the semantic similarities between quantifiers and preverbal adverbs of frequency, a semantically related quantifier is indicated in parentheses at each point in the diagram.

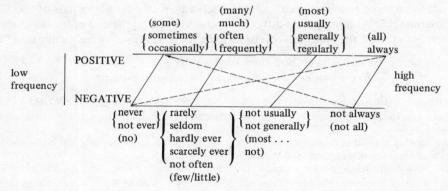

Note: The dotted line between *never* and *always* signals an opposition. The dotted line and arrow going from "not always" to "sometimes/occasionally" signals an inverse implication (e.g., If Jack is not always on time, this is the same as saying that Jack is sometimes not on time or that Jack is sometimes late).

Note that many sentences with preverbal adverbs can in fact be paraphrased with sentence-final adverbials containing semantically related quantifiers:

John *always* gets up at 7 a.m.   John gets up at 7 a.m. *all the time.*
Bob *sometimes* reads the paper.   Bob reads the paper *some of the time.*
Students *often* drink beer.   Students drink beer *on many occasions.*

Likewise, the wh-question of frequency "How often?" has its quantifier-based counterpart in "How many times?"

How often have you gone to Boston?   How many times have you gone to Boston?

Negative preverbal adverbs

As Klima (1964) has pointed out, we can verify the negative or affirmative nature of preverbal adverbs by observing their behavior in unmarked tags, since an affirmative preverbal adverb co-occurs with a negative tag and vice versa.

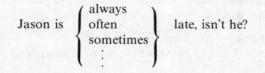

Jason is { always / often / sometimes / ⋮ } late, isn't he?

(i.e., these are affirmative preverbal adverbs)

Mavis { never / seldom / scarcely ever / ⋮ } goes out, does she?

(i.e., these are negative preverbal adverbs)

In those cases where lexically negative preverbal adverbs occur as single lexical items, a phrasal counterpart is also available:

We have *never* gone to Seattle. (lexical)   Burt *seldom* watches TV. (lexical)
We *haven't ever* gone to Seattle. (phrasal)   Burt *doesn't often* watch TV. (phrasal)

There will be further discussion of the interaction of negation and preverbal adverbs in a later section of the chapter, under Interaction with NOT.

Minimum logical contradictions

The solid diagonal lines on the above continua signal those preverbal adverbs that express a minimum logical contradiction with respect to each other, e.g.:

A: Bill *sometimes* does the dishes.   *A:* It's *often* hot in Seattle.
B: No, that's not true. He *never* does the   *B:* No, you're wrong. It's *seldom* hot
dishes.   there.

Note also that the preverbal adverbs expressing the highest frequencies (i.e., *usually,* etc., and *always*) have only phrasal negative counterparts; that is, there is no single lexical item that expresses the minimal logical contradiction on the negative side for *usually* or *always*:

A: We *usually* follow the rules.   *A:* Peter is *always* on time.
B: We do *not usually* make any excep-   *B:* No, Peter is *not always* on time. He's
tions.   sometimes late.

As we pointed out in the last chapter with respect to quantifiers, it is also possible to contradict a preverbal adverb of frequency with a stronger form than the minimal contradiction if circumstances warrant such a response, e.g.:

A: Peter is *always* on time.   *B:* No, that's wrong. He's *hardly ever* on
time.

Interaction with tense and aspect

Praninskas (1975) points out that since preverbal adverbs of frequency are used to express approximately how many times a habitual action or condition is repeated, they are typically not used with the progressive aspect. Instead, the simple present tense, the present perfect tense, and the simple past tense (in its habitual sense) tend to co-occur with these adverbs:

Professor Johnson is always busy.   Joe often studied until midnight.
I have never visited Japan.

In fact, we would add that all adverbials of frequency—not just the preverbal adverbs—tend to co-occur with tenses that are used to express habitual action:

Horace goes to the movies once a week.
Alberta drank champagne every now and then.

While we agree with Praninskas's generalization, we would, however, point out that the progressive aspect may co-occur with preverbal adverbs of frequency when the speaker's message carries emotional overtones:

Orville is always hearing noises. (i.e., he hallucinates)

Compare this with the less emotional, more objective sentence:

Orville always hears noises. (i.e., he has a keen sense of hearing)

The preverbal adverb of highest frequency, i.e., *always,* also closely resembles certain adverbs that express iteration or duration, although *always* is less emphatic than *continually* or *constantly*:

Sydney is $\left\{ \begin{array}{l} \text{always} \\ \text{continually} \\ \text{constantly} \end{array} \right\}$ grouchy.   Martha $\left\{ \begin{array}{l} \text{always} \\ \text{continually} \\ \text{constantly} \end{array} \right\}$ loses things.

(durative: a continuing state of affairs)   (iterative: a series of events)

The scope of preverbal adverbs

Perhaps the most important semantic generalization to make about preverbal adverbs is that in any given sentence, they modify the entire sentence in which they occur. The following paraphrases make this clear:

Barry frequently drives faster than the speed limit. (It is frequently the case that Barry drives faster than the speed limit.)
Cynthia never smiles at strangers. (It is never the case that Cynthia smiles at strangers.)

The syntactic analysis of preverbal adverbs that we provide below will make this generalization explicit.

A syntactic analysis of preverbal adverbs of frequency

It has been established that a preverbal adverb of frequency—much like the negative particle NOT operating at the syntactic level (see Chapter 8)—modifies the entire sentence in which it occurs; the phrase structure rules, therefore, should generate it as a sentence modifier in the base structure:

Gerald seldom does the shopping.

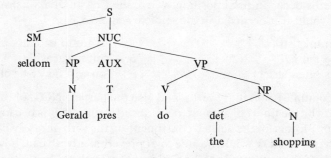

The derivation of sentences with preverbal adverbs

In order to derive the above sentence, we need a transformational rule of preverbal adverb placement that would move *seldom* between the subject NP *Gerald* and the present tense auxiliary. The derivation can then proceed as follows:

Output of base: seldom Gerald pres do the shopping
Preverbal adverb placement: Gerald seldom pres do the shopping
Affix attachment (1✕): Gerald seldom do + pres the shopping
Subject-verb agreement and morphological rules: Gerald seldom does the shopping.

This rule of preverbal adverb placement accounts for all sentences without an auxiliary verb such as the above example. It thus also accounts for imperatives:

Never be rude.

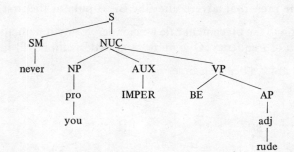

Output of base: never you IMPER BE rude
Preverbal adverb placement: you never IMPER BE rude
You deletion: never IMPER BE rude
Affix attachment (1✕): never BE + IMPER rude
Morphological rules: Never be rude.

In addition, this placement rule operates in all cases where there is an auxiliary verb or copula BE which carries emphatic or contrastive stress; i.e., the preverbal adverb always precedes a stressed auxiliary or copula, e.g.:

You never *are* ready on time!   Jim never *did* talk to Raymond![5]
I never *have* met the president!

---

5. Note that in this example the auxiliary verb DO has been added via DO support to carry the emphatic stress as well as the tense. For further discussion of this function of DO, see Chapter 29.

This placement rule also accounts for reduced sentences where the copula BE or one or more auxiliary verbs occur in final position, where the first auxiliary cannot take reduced stress the way it would if it occurred in a complete sentence, e.g.:

A: Is Mr. Franks strict?	*A:* I want to be class president.
B: Yes, he often is.	*B:* You never will (be).
(cf. Yes, he is often strict.)	(cf. You will never be class president.)

Thus unlike the copula BE, auxiliary verbs, and also the particle NOT, preverbal adverbs of frequency may not be the final constituent in a reduced clause. This is because these adverbs may not serve as pro-forms for the deleted constituents in the verb phrase, whereas the copula BE, an auxiliary verb, or NOT would be able to. A preverbal adverb can, however, substitute for the entire nucleus in a truncated or elliptical response such as "Yes, often" (i.e., preverbal adverbs are pro-clauses rather than pro-verbs).

The preverbal adverb placement rule, however, is more complicated than the above examples suggest, since sentences such as the following constituted the most frequently occurring pattern when we examined preverbal adverbs in natural discourse; they must also be derived, and they cannot be accounted for by the above version of the placement rule:

Mary is always late for class.	Bill has often forgotten to make his bed.
I can usually do my shopping on Satur-day.	Mickey has always been on time.

The preverbal adverb placement rule must therefore be expanded to include the following contexts:

> When the nucleus has a BE copula or one or more auxiliary verbs with reduced stress, place the preverbal adverb after the BE copula or the first auxiliary verb.

With this addition to the placement rule we can derive any statement containing a one-word preverbal adverb of frequency. One more sample derivation will help illustrate this.

Mickey has always been on time.

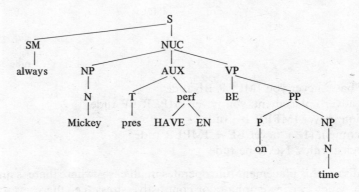

Output of base: always Mickey pres HAVE EN BE on time
Preverbal adverb placement: Mickey pres HAVE always EN BE on time
Affix attachment (2✕): Mickey HAVE + pres always BE + EN on time
Subject-verb agreement and morphological rules: Mickey has always been on time.

Interaction with NOT

The semantically negative preverbal adverbs of frequency (e.g., *never, seldom*) may not co-occur with the negative particle NOT if the NOT derives from the sentence modifier:

*Jim is not never on time.   *Betsy doesn't seldom do her homework.

They do occasionally occur with the NOT expressing phrasal negation (see Chapter 8):

Sandra is seldom able to not eat chocolates.

and they occur freely with lexical negation (see Chapter 8):

Mrs. Beck has never been unkind.

(Recall that both phrasal and lexical negation are different from syntactic negation.)

The semantically positive preverbal adverbs of frequency, on the other hand, occur not only in affirmative statements but also in negative statements in combination with NOT (or -N'T), as the following examples illustrate:

1. a. Florida often $\left\{ \begin{array}{l} \text{isn't} \\ \text{is not} \end{array} \right\}$ cold in winter.

    b. Florida is often not cold in winter.

    c. Florida $\left\{ \begin{array}{l} \text{isn't} \\ \text{is not} \end{array} \right\}$ often cold in winter.

2. a. Professor Potter usually $\left\{ \begin{array}{l} \text{hasn't} \\ \text{has not} \end{array} \right\}$ attended faculty meetings.

    b. Professor Potter has usually not attended faculty meetings.

    c. Professor Potter $\left\{ \begin{array}{l} \text{hasn't} \\ \text{has not} \end{array} \right\}$ usually attended faculty meetings.

3. a. New Mexico sometimes $\left\{ \begin{array}{l} \text{isn't} \\ \text{is not} \end{array} \right\}$ cold in winter.

    b. New Mexico is sometimes not cold in winter.

    c. *New Mexico $\left\{ \begin{array}{l} \text{isn't} \\ \text{is not} \end{array} \right\}$ sometimes cold in winter.

4. a. Peter often $\left\{ \begin{array}{l} \text{doesn't} \\ \text{does not} \end{array} \right\}$ do his homework.

    b. *Peter (does) often not do his homework.

    c. Peter $\left\{ \begin{array}{l} \text{doesn't} \\ \text{does not} \end{array} \right\}$ often do his homework.

5. a. ?Mort always $\left\{ \begin{array}{l} \text{doesn't} \\ \text{does not} \end{array} \right\}$ do his homework.[6]

    b. *Mort (does) always not do his homework.

    c. Mort $\left\{ \begin{array}{l} \text{doesn't} \\ \text{does not} \end{array} \right\}$ always do his homework.

These five sets of examples offer a seemingly bewildering array of word order options in sentences where a preverbal adverb of frequency and NOT co-occur. The confusion can be

---

6. Even if 5a is acceptable (not all of the native speakers we consulted would accept it), it certainly means something different from 5c—i.e., the former would mean that Mort never does his homework; the latter would mean that Mort sometimes doesn't do his homework.

partly alleviated, however, if we recognize that the occurrences of NOT in sentences 1c, 2c, 4c, and 5c modify only the preverbal adverbs—not the entire sentences. In such cases, NOT is functioning as part of a negative phrasal preverbal adverb (i.e., *not often, not usually, not always*). In fact, the reason why 3c is unacceptable is that the sequence *not sometimes* does not exist as a negative phrasal preverbal adverb. (*Not sometimes* is also the only one of these four phrases which cannot function as a response to a question.)

Once we stipulate that negative phrasal preverbal adverbs beginning with *not* follow the same placement rules as NOT itself, the derivation of either the simple or contracted version of sentences 1c, 2c, 4c, or 5c is quite simple:

Mort doesn't always do his homework.

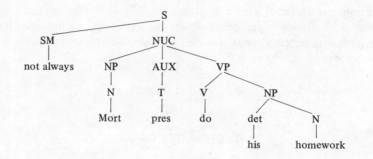

Output of base: not always Mort pres do his homework
Negative preverbal phrasal adverb placement (i.e., like NOT placement): Mort pres not
    always do his homework
DO support: Mort pres DO not always do his homework
NOT contraction: Mort pres DO + N'T always do his homework
Affix attachment (1×): Mort DO + N'T + pres always do his homework
Subject-verb agreement and morphological rules: Mort doesn't always do his homework.

However, even with this analysis for the phrasal negative forms, we still have to account for the grammatical and ungrammatical *a* and *b* sentences cited above. In the sentences in sets 1, 2, and 3—where either the copula BE or an auxiliary verb is present—we have two possible word orders:

1.   The preverbal adverb of frequency precedes the auxiliary verb or BE copula and the NOT follows the auxiliary verb or BE copula, e.g.:

1a. Florida often $\begin{Bmatrix} \text{isn't} \\ \text{is not} \end{Bmatrix}$ cold in winter.

2.   The preverbal adverb and NOT (in that order) follow the auxiliary verb or BE copula, e.g.:

1b. Florida is often not cold in winter.

We suspect that a subtle semantic distinction is being expressed here; namely, that the preverbal adverb is being emphasized in 1a and that the NOT is being emphasized in 1b; however, verification of this hypothesis demands a complete study at the discourse level. For the present, we will give each word order variant the same basic structure in which the adverb and NOT are both generated independently as sentence modifiers:

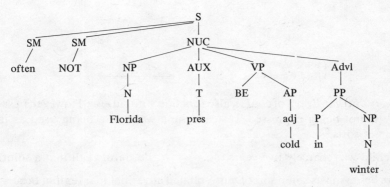

It is possible to provide a transformational analysis to explain the differences in word orders 1 and 2.[7] We will not, however, use up space here to give full sample derivations, since the main thing to remember is that two orders are possible when the copula BE or an auxiliary verb occurs in the nucleus, and the NOT follows the preverbal adverb, e.g.:

Professor Potter usually $\left\{ \begin{array}{l} \text{hasn't} \\ \text{has not} \end{array} \right\}$ attended faculty meetings.

Professor Potter has usually not attended faculty meetings.

but that only one word order is possible when neither of these elements is present, and the NOT follows the preverbal adverb, e.g.:

Mort always $\left\{ \begin{array}{l} \text{doesn't} \\ \text{does not} \end{array} \right\}$ do his homework.

*Mort does always not do his homework.

Statements and questions with *ever*

The particle *ever*[8] interacts with preverbal adverbs of frequency in a number of ways. First of all, it is used to complete *scarcely* and *hardly* when they function as preverbal adverbs of frequency:

Joan has $\left\{ \begin{array}{l} \text{scarcely} \\ \text{hardly} \end{array} \right\}$ ever gone to bed after midnight.

*Joan has $\left\{ \begin{array}{l} \text{scarcely} \\ \text{hardly} \end{array} \right\}$ gone to bed after midnight.

In such cases, *scarcely ever* or *hardly ever* would be generated as phrasal preverbal adverbs in the base and follow the same rules of preverbal adverb placement discussed above.

---

7. In word order 1 the NOT is placed first following the usual rules. Then the adverb, which is placed second, must be placed such that it precedes the auxiliary (i.e., it must follow the first part of the preverbal adverb placement rule because the copula BE or the first auxiliary verb carries some stress by virtue of the adjacent NOT. This is particularly true if the BE or auxiliary verb has contracted with NOT). This rule ordering accounts for 1a, 2a, 3a, and 4a—and even 5a for those speakers who find this sentence acceptable. In word order 2 the adverb is placed first, and it is placed according to the two subrules for preverbal adverb placement on pages 207 and 208. Then the NOT is placed after the adverb. However, the restriction on the use of this word order is that BE or a lexical auxiliary must be present in the nucleus in order for this option to be grammatical. This is why 4b and 5b are ungrammatical; i.e., the auxiliary DO would not be present in the nucleus of these sentences prior to the placement of the adverb.

8. *Ever* is not listed on the semantic continua for preverbal adverbs of frequency (see p. 204) because it is midway between the positive and negative lexical items. It occurs mainly in questions or in negatives as a part of phrasal combinations with *not, hardly,* or *scarcely*.

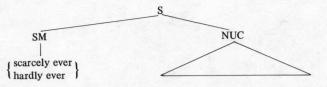

Scarcely and *hardly* do, of course, also function without *ever*. However, in such sentences, frequency is not being expressed. Instead, these words are being used as intensifiers or quantifiers of sorts:[9]

The child was scarcely five years old.   I'd hardly call that a solution!

or they are behaving as some sort of tense-related adverbial marker that occurs with the past perfect tense:

Joan had $\left\{ \begin{array}{c} \text{hardly} \\ \text{scarcely} \end{array} \right\}$ gone to bed when the phone rang.

Another phrasal use of *ever* occurs in the phrase *not ever,* which functions as a negative phrasal preverbal adverb—much as *not often* and *not always* have already been shown to do.

Jason won't ever propose to Hazel.

Compare with:

Florida isn't often cold in winter.
Professor Potter hasn't always attended faculty meetings.

In such a case, *not ever* would be generated as a phrasal sentence modifier in the base and, like other negative phrasal preverbal adverbs, would be placed in the nucleus following the rules for NOT placement:

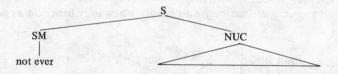

There is, of course, a lexical counterpart to *not ever;* namely, *never:*

Jason won't ever propose to Hazel.   Jason will never propose to Hazel.

Klima (1964) suggests that these variants are equivalent. However, to be fully certain of this, we need further research since Bolinger (1977) and others have long maintained—with good justification—that a difference in form signals a difference in meaning or discourse function. Perhaps the version with *never* is more emphatic.

The most important syntactic function of *ever* is its role in yes-no questions of frequency. Here two sentence modifiers—the *ever* and the Q marker—when used together, signal this common type of yes-no question.

---

9. Quirk and Greenbaum (1973) refer to *scarcely* and *hardly* as "minimizers," which is a good way to characterize them semantically in such contexts.

Have you ever been to Acapulco?

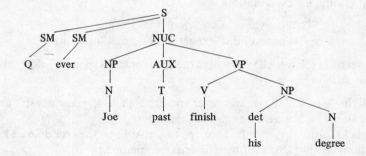

Ever—even though not explicitly negative—follows the same rules of placement as NOT:

Output of base: Q ever you pres HAVE EN BE to Acapulco
Ever placement: Q you pres HAVE ever EN BE to Acapulco
Subject/auxiliary inversion: pres HAVE you ever EN BE to Acapulco
Affix attachment (2×): HAVE + pres you ever BE + EN to Acapulco
Morphological rules: Have you ever been to Acapulco?

Consider the following derivation where no copula BE or auxiliary verb is present. Here, in particular, we can see that *ever* follows the same rules of placement as does NOT:

Did Joe ever finish his degree?

Output of base: Q ever Joe past finish his degree
Ever placement: Q Joe past ever finish his degree
DO support: Q Joe past DO ever finish his degree
Subject/auxiliary inversion: past DO Joe ever finish his degree
Affix attachment (1×): DO + past Joe ever finish his degree
Morphological rules: Did Joe ever finish his degree?

The phrasal form *not ever* also interacts with the question marker to form negative yes-no questions of frequency:

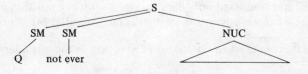

Since phrasal *not ever*—like *not often, not always,* etc.—also follows the same rules as NOT placement, the derivation of such questions poses no problem. The only unusual thing to note here is that NOT contraction and the subsequent fronting of -N'T with the auxiliary seems to be almost obligatory since sentences 1b and 2b below are rare and very formal. 1c and 2c are ungrammatical.

1. a. Doesn't your brother ever go to church?
   b. Does your brother not ever go to church?
   c. *Does not your brother ever go to church?
2. a. Aren't you ever going to study Spanish?
   b. Are you not ever going to study Spanish?
   c. *Are not you ever going to study Spanish?

Here we have been deriving yes-no questions with *ever* as the preverbal adverb. We should add that the positive preverbal adverbs also occur in yes-no questions. When they do, they follow the same pattern of derivation as we have used for *ever:*

$$\text{Does Mark} \left\{ \begin{matrix} \text{ever} \\ \text{sometimes} \\ \text{often} \\ \text{usually} \\ \text{always} \end{matrix} \right\} \text{sing in the shower?}$$

Some other uses of *ever* that we should note in passing are the following:

1. In structures that look like wh-questions, the use of *ever* after the wh-word makes the question, in reality, an exclamation:

> Whoever told you that!
> Wherever did you get such a ridiculous outfit!

2. In adverbial relative clauses where the speaker lacks specific information but assumes some sort of indefinite reality:

Goodnight, Mrs. Calabash, wherever you are.[10] (The speaker doesn't know where Mrs. Calabash is, but assumes she is somewhere.)
Give this to John, whenever he happens to arrive. (The speaker doesn't know when John will arrive, but assumes he will arrive sometime.)

3. In nominal relative clauses parallel to the immediately preceding adverbial relative clauses:

> Whoever told you that doesn't know what he's talking about.
> Whatever he says is nonsense.

4. In words and phrases like *evermore, forever, ever after,* and *ever and ever, ever* has the meaning of *always;* i.e., only in these somewhat formulaic or archaic expressions does *ever* convey a given sense of frequency, i.e., *always.*

Preverbal adverbs in sentence-initial and sentence-final position

Thus far we have discussed only the basic mid-sentence position of preverbal adverbs of frequency. Some of these adverbs may also occur initially. Most important among those

---

10. This was the famous oft-repeated closing line of the late comedian, Jimmy Durante.

occurring initially are the negative adverbs of zero or low frequency, which cause subject/auxiliary inversion to accompany their movement to initial position:[11]

$$
\text{We have} \left\{
\begin{array}{l}
\text{never} \\
\text{seldom} \\
\text{rarely} \\
\text{scarcely ever} \\
\text{hardly ever}
\end{array}
\right\} \text{seen such a sight!}
$$

$$
\left.
\begin{array}{l}
\text{Never} \\
\text{Seldom} \\
\text{Rarely} \\
\text{Scarcely ever} \\
\text{Hardly ever}
\end{array}
\right\} \text{have we seen such a sight!}
$$

Not all sentences containing *never, rarely,* etc., may undergo this change of word order. The speaker or writer typically must be expressing an exclamation of sorts; if not, the change in word order is strange or unacceptable.

John has never washed his socks.   ?Never has John washed his socks.

We refer to the transformation involved in the acceptable derivations cited above as "negative constituent fronting" and note that the subsequent need for subject/auxiliary inversion has a precedent in the wh-fronting rule that we introduced in Chapter 12. Positive preverbal adverbs may also occur sentence initially—but they do not cause subject/auxiliary inversion:

$$
\left.
\begin{array}{l}
?/\text{*Always}^{12} \\
\text{Sometimes} \\
\text{Occasionally} \\
\text{Frequently} \\
?\text{Often}^{13} \\
\text{Usually} \\
\text{Generally}
\end{array}
\right\} \text{Sara walks her dog after dinner.}
$$

The adverb fronting rule which will be introduced and discussed in Chapter 29 will account for the syntax of such sentences. A more important question is: Why do many—though not all—preverbal adverbs sometimes occur in initial position; i.e., what does their initial position signal? Close (1981) suggests that logical contradiction is a likely environment for a sentence-initial preverbal adverb:

A: Peter is always on time.
B: No, Peter isn't always on time. *Sometimes* he's late.

---

11. Negative preverbal adverbs are not the only negative forms that cause subject/auxiliary inversion when fronted. Most, if not all, negative constituents have this effect in English:

Not since Hiroshima has mankind seen such devastation.

12. *Always* and its paraphrases (e.g., *all the time*) are very rare in initial position. Many native speakers feel that such sentences are ungrammatical.

13. Some speakers of English will accept *frequently* but not *often* as a sentence-initial preverbal adverb, and almost everyone we consulted feels more comfortable with *frequently* than with *often* in this position. The only explanation we can offer is that the longer -*ly* adverbs seem more acceptable in initial position than the shorter adverbs. *Sometimes,* of course, would be an exception to this generalization.

There probably are other contexts that encourage sentence-initial use of preverbal adverbs. Further research would help answer this question more fully.

There are also some prepositional phrases semantically similar to the preverbal adverbs *generally* and *usually* that typically occur in initial position:

As a rule
In general } Sara walks her dog after dinner.

However, the longer phrasal preverbal adverbs (positive or negative) do not readily move to initial position:

?Almost always Sara walks her dog after dinner.
?Not usually does Sara walk her dog after dinner.
?Not always does Sara walk her dog after dinner.

Thus the set of preverbal adverbs that may occur in initial position is more restricted than the set which occurs sentence medially.

Even more restricted is the set of preverbal adverbs that may occur in final position:

William does the dishes {
sometimes
occasionally
often
frequently
?usually
?rarely
?seldom
*never
*always
}.

The explanation for this patterning appears to be semantic in that the preverbal adverbs corresponding to the *some* and *much/many* ranges on the positive semantic continuum are the ones that occur most readily in final position:

(some)	(much/many)
sometimes	often
occasionally	frequently

(see p. 204 for the two complete continua)

The main thing to remember is that *all* preverbal adverbs of frequency occur in the specified medial position, whereas only a subset occurs sentence initially and an even smaller subset sentence finally. Furthermore, medial position is by far the most frequent, while these adverbs occur in initial position only about 10 percent of the time and in final position less than 5 percent of the time.

Some discourse considerations

Many reference grammars and ESL/EFL textbooks state that *How often* begins a wh-question that asks about frequency. What they usually do not point out is that such questions tend to elicit responses containing specific (or general) adverbials of frequency rather than preverbal adverbs of frequency. In fact, a response with a preverbal adverb could be considered vague, evasive, or even rude:

A: How often do you go to the movies?   B: { I go about once a week.
                                              ?I go (fairly) often.

A: How often do you study in the li-   B: { I study there every night.
    brary?   ?I always study there.

The above questions begin with "How often do you . . .", and they are asking about the frequency of current habitual activities. There are other questions beginning with "How often . . ." that involve the perfect of experience; a specific or general frequency is expected in the response. Again, most preverbal adverbs are inappropriate, and *always* is impossible.

A: How often have you been to Acapulco?

        ⎧ Three times.
        | Many times.
B: ⎨ ?Seldom.
        | ?Frequently.
        ⎩ *Always.

Yes-no questions with *ever*—like the above "How often. . . ?" questions—may ask about either specific experiences or the frequency of habitual actions:

        Specific experience: Have you ever been to Acapulco?
        Frequency: Do you ever study in the library?

Yes-no questions with *ever* that ask about specific experiences tend to elicit specific responses—i.e., again, responses with a preverbal adverb of frequency are too vague:

A: Have you ever been to Acapulco?
        ⎧ Yes, for one week back in 1971.
B: ⎨   ⎧ sometimes ⎫
        ⎩ ?Yes, I ⎨ usually   ⎬ go there.
                          ⎩   ⎭

On the other hand, yes-no questions with *ever* that ask about the frequency of habitual actions readily elicit responses with a preverbal adverb of frequency, and they are the only questions with *ever* that can do this:

A: Do you ever study in the library?

        ⎧ always   ⎫
        | usually |
        | often |
B: I ⎨ sometimes ⎬ do.
        | rarely |
        ⎩ never   ⎭

Thus preverbal adverbs are not normally elicited by wh-questions and can be naturally elicited by only one type of yes-no question (i.e., questions about the frequency of habitual actions). This observation has ramifications for our teaching suggestions, since we want our students to practice using preverbal adverbs in contexts that are as natural as possible.

TEACHING SUGGESTIONS

General note to the teacher: Not all preverbal adverbs occur with equal frequency in discourse. We examined about 23,000 words of transcribed conversation (American, 14,000 words; British, 9,000 words). Altogether there were 79 occurrences of preverbal adverbs distributed as follows:

never—32	ever (in questions)—9	usually—2
always—19	occasionally—3	generally—1
sometimes—13		

The only thing that surprised us about this count was the fact that *often* did not occur even once in the approximately 23,000 words. It would be interesting to have comparable data from a written corpus to see what, if any, register differences there are.

1   Ask students—based on their personal experience—to qualify statements that the teacher provides by selecting the appropriate preverbal adverb of frequency from a list and then placing the adverb correctly in the sentence:

(list of adverbs: *always   often   sometimes   seldom   never*)
T: Juan is late for class.   *S2:*   Juan is never late for class.
S1:   Never.

2   Students can ask each other yes-no questions with *ever* that ask about current habitual actions. Where appropriate, these questions should be answered with a preverbal adverb of frequency.

S1:   Do you ever play tennis?   *S2:*   Do you ever shop on Fifth Avenue?
S2:   Sometimes.   *S3:*   Never.

3   Have students paraphrase a quantifier or specific adverbial of frequency with the appropriate preverbal adverb of frequency.

T: Betty gets up at 7 a.m. every day.   *T:*   Phil has been to London many
S1:   Betty always gets up at 7 a.m.   times.
                                                S2:   Phil has often been to London.

4   Students should have a chance to logically contradict and correct statements using preverbal adverbs. The teacher should make statements that deserve to be contradicted and corrected; i.e., the students know the facts are different.

T: Joe always walks to school.   *T:*   Mr. Smith often drinks coffee.
S1:   No, that's not true.   *S2:*   No, that's not true.
        Joe doesn't always walk to school.   He rarely drinks coffee.
        Sometimes he drives.   He usually drinks tea.

5   Have students interview each other in pairs to discover some of their partner's habits. They should find out something that the other one (a) *never does,* (b) *seldom does,* (c) *sometimes does,* (d) *often does,* (e) *usually does,* and (f) *always does.* Then these newly discovered facts should be organized into a short composition or speech and presented to the class as a personality sketch of a class member. For example:

Mohamed is a very interesting person. He always goes jogging in the morning, and he usually does push-ups and sit-ups too to stay in shape. Also, he often plays soccer after school. Because he is so athletic and careful about his health, he never smokes and seldom drinks. Sometimes his studies interfere with his sports, and he doesn't like that.

6 Have students work in groups to describe events that surround some notable event such as an earthquake, an election, the Olympics, or the World Cup. Ask them to use preverbal adverbs of frequency to describe these related events. For example:

> an earthquake
> Some animals always know when an earthquake is going to occur.
> People sometimes panic during an earthquake.
> Homes and buildings are often damaged by an earthquake.

7 Sharon Voss suggests that the teacher prepare large flashcards—each with a preverbal adverb of frequency. When each student has a flashcard, the class members must first arrange themselves into a positive group and a negative group. Then, within each of the two groups, they should order themselves from high to low frequency according to the meanings of the preverbal adverbs of frequency on their flashcards. Each student then says an original sentence using his or her preverbal adverb of frequency and, if necessary, receives comments and corrections from peers. The teacher should also get the students to discuss the appropriateness of the sentences containing the preverbal adverbs (e.g., Would an alternative sound better?).

EXERCISES

Test your understanding of what has been presented

1. Provide original sentences that illustrate the following terms or rules. Underline the pertinent word(s) in your examples.

specific or general adverbial of frequency
preverbal adverb of frequency
    positive
    negative
phrasal preverbal adverb of frequency
    positive
    negative
negative constituent fronting (with preverbal adverb)

2. Provide tree diagrams and derivations for the following sentences:

a. Mr. Nelson rarely waters his lawn.
b. I have often overslept.
c. Jim is not always correct.
d. Have you ever tasted papaya?

3. Why are the following sentences or dialogs ungrammatical?

a. *Is not he ever going to finish his degree?
b. *Marvin does often not dance.
c. *A:* Are you ever late to class?
    B: *I am never.

Test your ability to apply what you know

4. If your students produce sentences like these, what error(s) have they made? How will you make them aware of the errors, and what activities will you provide to correct these errors?

   a. *José can play sometimes handball after work.
   b. *Rarely we can eat outside in the garden.
   c. *I have not never told a lie.

5. What is the difference in meaning, if any, between the sentences in each of the following pairs?

   a. Alice uses dental floss.   c. Who could think that?
      Alice always uses dental floss.   Whoever could think that!
   b. Florence hasn't ever studied Latin.
      Florence has never studied Latin.

6. What, if anything, is inappropriate with the responses to these two questions? What is the explanation for any problem you detect?

   a. *A:* How often do you go to the beach?   b. *A:* Have you ever been to Europe?
      B: Usually.   *B:* Sometimes.

7. A student asks you if there is any difference between these two sentences, and if so, when he should use one form rather than the other.

   a. I have always told the truth.   b. I always *have* told the truth.

What will you say?

BIBLIOGRAPHY

References

Bolinger, D. (1977). *Meaning and Form.* New York and London: Longman.
Close, R. A. (1981). *English as a Foreign Language* (3d ed.). London: Allen and Unwin.
Klima, E. (1964). "Negation in English," in J. Fodor and J. Katz (eds.), *The Structure of Language.* Englewood Cliffs, N.J.: Prentice-Hall, pp. 246–323.
Praninskas, J. (1975). *Rapid Review of English Grammar.* Englewood Cliffs, N.J.: Prentice-Hall.
Quirk, R., and S. Greenbaum (1973). *A Concise Grammar of Contemporary English.* New York: Harcourt Brace Jovanovich.

Suggestions for further reading

For brief but useful discussions of preverbal adverbs of frequency, consult the following sources:

Close, R. A. (1981). *English as a Foreign Language* (3d ed.). London: Allen and Unwin, pp. 173–175.
Leech, G., and J. Svartvik (1975). *A Communicative Grammar of English.* London: Longman, pp. 81–82.
Quirk, R., and S. Greenbaum (1973). *A Concise Grammar of Contemporary English.* New York: Harcourt Brace Jovanovich, pp. 233–236.

For some suggestions on how to teach preverbal adverbs of frequency, see the following textbooks:

McIntosh, L., T. Ramos, and R. Goulet (1970). *Advancing in English.* New York: American Book Co., pp. 9–10.
Praninskas, J. (1975). *Rapid Review of English Grammar.* Englewood Cliffs, N.J.: Prentice-Hall, pp. 52–53, 64.

17

The Passive Voice

GRAMMATICAL DESCRIPTION

Introduction

The English passive (e.g., The sandwich was eaten by the child, Oranges are grown in California) is a problem for non-English speakers, mainly with regard to usage. Even though ESL/EFL students can easily learn to form the passive, they have problems learning when to use it. There are several reasons for this. A few languages don't even have a passive voice. Most languages, however, have a passive that is more limited than the English one. Such languages will use word order, impersonal constructions, or other devices to express the equivalent of an English passive sentence. Only a few languages have a more generalized passive than English. For example, Kinyarwanda, a Bantu language, can make even a locative phrase the subject of the passive, as in *On the bus was eaten a sandwich by John,* which would not be acceptable in English. Although it has a more limited passive than English, Japanese, too, sometimes makes use of the passive where English does not. The shifting of focus off the subject in Japanese is seen to be a less direct, more polite way of making a statement or asking a question. For most English learners, however, the passive will occur more frequently in English than in their native language and there will be a wider variety of passive sentence types in English than in their own language.

A review and an analysis of the passive

To better understand the English passive, we should return to some of the notions presented in the early chapters of this text. At that time we noted that English is a "subject-verb-object" language and that common alternatives to the S-V-O order are S-O-V and V-S-O. We also briefly introduced case grammar, which views every noun phrase in a sentence as exhibiting a semantic function in relation to the verb. Some of these functions were agent, theme, location, and instrument. All the structures that we have described so far view the S-V-O order as being basic for the active voice. Thus, if we have a verb *to sketch* in the past tense, an agent *John,* and a theme *the picture,* we would produce the statement *John sketched the picture,* and we can diagram the basic structure of this statement as follows:

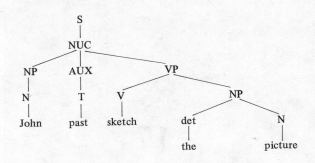

The English sentence has two focus positions—subject, the main focus position; and object, the secondary focus position. The active voice gives agents primary focus and themes secondary focus. Another way of explaining this is to say that in an active English sentence with a transitive verb we expect the agent to be the subject and the theme to be the object. However, there are occasions when the discourse context constrains us to make the theme (rather than the agent) the subject of a transitive verb, i.e., to give the theme primary focus. The result is a sentence in the passive voice, e.g., *The picture was sketched by John.* Note that the S-V-O word order is still being followed more or less, but that the auxiliary has been expanded to include BE . . . EN[1] to mark the passive voice and the preposition *by* precedes the demoted agent. We can diagram the basic structure of the above passive sentence as follows:

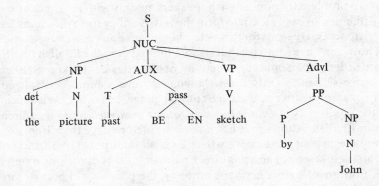

In comparison with the active voice the agent has become relatively unimportant in the passive. We can demonstrate this by producing other passive sentences that are similar to the one above but which do not overtly express an agent, e.g.:

The picture was sketched in fifteen minutes.

The picture was sketched during class today.

Most grammarians agree that such sentences imply an agent but that explicit identification of the agent is either unnecessary or impossible (i.e., the speaker cannot identify the agent). The tree diagram for one of these agentless passive sentences follows:

---

1. The past participle and the passive participle are the same verb form, i.e., EN; however, the past participle derives from a HAVE auxiliary while the passive participle derives from a BE auxiliary. Both auxiliary elements may occur in the same sentence, e.g., Computers have been manufactured in Japan for many years now.

The picture was sketched in fifteen minutes.

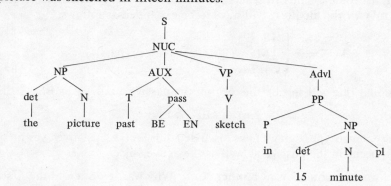

Active and passive sentences

Compare the following sets of sentences:

Active	*Passive*
I drew Mary's portrait.	Mary's portrait was drawn by me.
The child ate the sandwich.	The sandwich was eaten by the child.
The choir practiced the song.	The song was practiced by the choir.

Consider the syntactic relationships between these two sets of sentences. What structural differences can you detect between the active and passive sentences? You should have noticed the following:

1. Addition of BE ... EN (i.e., the auxiliary verb BE plus the passive participle) in the passive sentences.
2. Inversion of the nouns signifying the agent and the theme with respect to subject and object position in the sentence.
3. Although pronominal agents are fairly rare in the passive, when they do occur, the case of the pronoun changes from subject to object (or vice versa if the theme is a pronoun), e.g., the change from *I drew* ... to ... *was drawn by me.*
4. Insertion of the preposition *by* before the demoted agent in the passive version.

Where does BE ... EN get added in relation to all the other elements in the AUX? Let us consider the structure of the auxiliary element in a few grammatical passive sentences:

> They may have been seen by the night watchman.
> (AUX = M HAVE ... EN BE ... EN)
> These data have been being computerized for two years now.
> (AUX = pres HAVE ... EN BE ... ING BE ... EN)

and also in some ungrammatical passive sentences:

> *They may be had seen by the night watchman.
> (AUX = M BE ... EN HAVE ... EN)
> *These data were being had computerized for two years now.
> (AUX = past BE ... ING BE ... EN HAVE ... EN)

From these examples we know that the BE ... EN is added immediately following all other auxiliary elements occurring in the underlying structure since no other ordering will be grammatically acceptable. Thus, in order to account for passive as well as active sentences in English, our rule for the auxiliary will have to be expanded as follows:

$$\text{AUX} \longrightarrow \left\{ \begin{matrix} \left\{ \begin{matrix} T \\ M \end{matrix} \right\} \text{ (PM) (perf) (prog) (pass)} \\ \text{IMPER} \end{matrix} \right\}$$

and an additional rule will specify the form of the passive auxiliary as BE ... EN:

$$\text{pass} \longrightarrow \text{BE ... EN}$$

All the major sentence types that we have discussed thus far (i.e., negatives, yes-no questions, wh-questions) occur in the passive as well as the active voice:

> This letter was not written by my brother.   Why was it written in the first place?
> Was it written by your sister?

As these examples show, the BE in the passive BE ... EN operates like the BE of the progressive or the BE functioning as a copula in the formation of negatives (re: NOT placement) and questions (re: subject/auxiliary inversion).

Semantic and lexical differences

An issue of importance to ESL/EFL teachers concerns the semantic differences that exist between the active and the passive voice. First of all, passive and active sentences may sometimes differ in meaning—especially when they contain numerals or quantifiers—e.g., as Chomsky (1965) and Lakoff (1968) have pointed out, the active and passive sentences in the following two pairs are not completely synonymous.

> Everyone in the room speaks two languages. (i.e., any two lan-   ⎫
>   guages per person)   ⎬   Chomsky (1965)
> Two languages are spoken by everyone in the room. (i.e., two   ⎪
>   specific languages that everybody speaks)   ⎭

> Few people read many books. (i.e., There are few people in this   ⎫
>   world who read lots of books.)   ⎬   Lakoff (1968)
> Many books are read by few people. (i.e., There are many books   ⎪
>   that are read by very few people.)   ⎭

Second, there are active voice sentences with surface structure objects that do not have a passive equivalent since the verbs are not truly transitive, e.g.:

> Mike has a car.   Roger weighs 200 pounds.
> *A car is had by Mike.   *200 pounds was weighed by Roger.

Likewise, there are passive sentences in English that have no active voice variant, e.g.:

> Mehdi was born in Tehran.   It is rumored that he will get the job.
> *Someone bore Mehdi in Tehran.[2]   *Someone rumors that he will get the job.

---

2. There is, of course, an active verb *to bear* as in "Joan bore three children," which is historically and semantically related to the passive *to be born*. However, there is no direct syntactic link between these verbs today, since we can't readily transform the active verb into the passive or vice versa. Thus two separate lexical entries are required.

This means that in the lexicon all English verbs must be marked as to whether they are compatible with the active voice, the passive voice, or with both. Some system such as the following could be used to describe verbs for this purpose:

± passive	− passive	+ passive
sketch	be	be born
draw	have	be rumored
eat	weigh (one meaning)	:
sing	:	
:		

As we have seen, it is not often the case that the so-called passive and active forms of a sentence are mere variants that focus on the agent in the active and the theme in the passive. With certain verbs and in certain situations either the active or the passive voice must be used exclusively. It is because of this that we have analyzed the active and the passive voice as different basic structures rather than deriving the passive from the active voice.

Agentless passives

The ESL/EFL teacher must also be very aware of the fact that the majority of passive sentences that occur in speech and writing (i.e., around 85 percent) do not have an explicit agent. For example:

Grapes are grown in the valley.   The papers have been destroyed.

Such sentences occur when the agent is understood, e.g., "farmers" in the first sentence above, or perhaps unknown, as in the second one.

In a usage study of the English passive Shintani (1979) suggests that we teach our ESL/EFL students when and why to retain the agent in those approximately 15 percent of passive sentences that have explicit agents—rather than trying to give them rules for omitting the agent in those 85 percent of passives that are agentless. She examined a large number of agents that were overtly expressed in passive sentences occurring in written and spoken discourse, and she concluded that almost all these agents could be explained by one of the following generalizations:

1. The agent is a proper name designating an artist, inventor, discoverer, innovator, etc., who is too important to omit in the context, e.g.:

    The Mona Lisa was painted by *da Vinci*.

2. The agent is an indefinite noun phrase, i.e., new information, and is retained to provide the listener or reader with the new information, e.g.:

    While Jill was walking down the street, her purse was snatched by *a young man*.

3. The agent is an inanimate noun phrase which is retained because it is unexpected; i.e., we expect agents to be animate, and almost all omitted agents get reconstructed as animate nouns, e.g.:

    All the lights and appliances in the Albertson household are switched on and off daily by $\left\{ \begin{array}{l} an \\ this \end{array} \right\}$ *electrical device.*

One of Shintani's recommendations is that the agentless passive, which is the norm, should be emphasized much more than it now is in EFL/ESL teaching materials.

Different kinds of passives

The ESL/EFL teacher should realize that there are four formally distinct kinds of passive sentences in English:

Simple passives with BE . . . EN
Mary was hit by John.   Grapes are grown in that valley.

Simple passives with GET . . . EN
Barry got invited to the party.   John got hurt in the accident.

Complex passives with BE . . . EN
It is rumored that he will get the job.   John is thought to be intelligent, etc.
That he will get the job has been decided.

Complex passives with HAVE . . . NP . . . EN[3]
Hal had his car stolen last weekend.
Alice had her purse snatched while shopping downtown.

The complex passives will be treated in Chapter 34 when we take up aspects of complementation. At this point, however, let us consider a few of the differences between the simple BE passive and the simple GET passive in Modern English. Look at the following pairs of sentences. What differences do you perceive?

John was hurt in the accident.   He was invited to the party.
John got hurt in the accident.   He got invited to the party.

The answer was known to all of us.
*The answer got known to all of us.

In the first pair the BE passive is formal or neutral whereas the GET passive is colloquial and perhaps also suggests the emotional involvement of the speaker. In the second pair we see that the GET passive is more limited than the BE passive in that it can only be used with verbs denoting actions and processes, not states. This, of course, characterizes the fundamental difference between the two, i.e., GET emphasizes process while BE reports a state.

He got angered when he realized he was being manipulated. (His anger was roused over a
     period of time.)
He was angered when he realized he was being manipulated. (His anger was an
     immediate reaction to his realization.)

A further difference is suggested by the third pair above, which is that the GET passive may indicate some involvement on the part of the grammatical (i.e., surface) subject in bringing about the result. The BE passive is neutral in this regard. A further difference between the BE passive and the GET passive is that the GET passive takes an agent even more rarely than the BE passive. Some grammarians (especially British ones) maintain that the GET passive *never* takes an agent. We feel that this claim is too strong, since we have found that sentences like *Keith got struck by lightning* are acceptable to both the American and British English speakers that we have surveyed.

---

3. The complex HAVE passive is often ambiguous with the causative HAVE construction that is further discussed in Chapter 34.

Mary had her purse snatched. ⟨ passive   (The purse snatching happened to Mary. It was
                                              beyond her control.)
                              causative (Mary arranged for someone to snatch her purse.)

The GET passive is fairly frequent in colloquial English, yet it is hardly ever mentioned or taught in ESL/EFL texts; therefore, the ESL/EFL teacher needs to be particularly sensitive to this construction and to present it to his or her students as appropriate. Also, note that for the GET passive the final auxiliary element introduced by the passive rule would be GET . . . EN rather than BE . . . EN. To account for this we have to expand our rule for rewriting the passive as follows:

$$\text{pass} \longrightarrow \left\{ \begin{array}{l} \text{BE} \ldots \text{EN} \\ \text{GET} \ldots \text{EN} \end{array} \right\}$$

One important structural difference between the BE and the GET passive is that GET does not function as a true auxiliary in questions and negatives the way BE does. As a result of this, DO must function as an auxiliary for GET in questions and negatives (e.g., *Did* John *get* arrested? No, and he *did*n't *get* hurt either).

The interaction of the passive voice with modals and perfect tenses

As we pointed out in the discussion of the passive auxiliary (BE . . . EN), many other auxiliary elements can precede the passive marker. In fact, modal auxiliaries frequently co-occur with the passive voice in at least three distinct uses:

1. *Possibility/ability—Can* and *could* are used with the passive to express possibility or ability in the present and past, respectively. For example:

> present time: The star can be seen from the balcony.
> (= now)
> past time: The star could be seen from the balcony.
> (= a specific past time)

2. *Logical (predictive/deductive) use*—The logical modals discussed in Chapter 7 can be used with the passive voice to express present deductions or future predictions; when these deductions or predictions refer to past time, HAVE . . . EN must also be used. For example:

> present time: Mr. Johnson $\left\{ \begin{array}{l} \text{must} \\ \text{should} \\ \text{might} \\ \vdots \end{array} \right\}$ be elected mayor.
> (= before the election)

> past time: Mr. Johnson $\left\{ \begin{array}{l} \text{must} \\ \text{should} \\ \text{might} \\ \vdots \end{array} \right\}$ have been elected mayor.
> (= after the election)

3. *Making suggestions*—In order to express a suggestion the conditional modals (see Chapter 25) are used; also, HAVE . . . EN is used to express hindsight, i.e., suggestions about things that were unfulfilled in the past. For example:

> future time: More hospitals $\left\{ \begin{array}{l} \text{could} \\ \text{should} \end{array} \right\}$ be built.
> (= could be fulfilled in the future)

> past time: More hospitals $\left\{ \begin{array}{l} \text{could} \\ \text{should} \end{array} \right\}$ have been built.
> (= was not fulfilled in the past)

Studies are needed to determine which modals in which of their specific usages co-occur most often with the passive as opposed to the active voice. Also, it is important to note that the meaning of the modals in some so-called active-passive counterparts do not seem truly equivalent, e.g.:

People say that Dan is a fool.   =   It is said that Dan is a fool.

People may say that Dan is a fool.   ≠   It may be said that Dan is a fool.

When to use the passive

Pioneering studies by Huddleston (1971), Shintani (1979), and others provide us with some guidelines concerning when to use the passive. Raw frequency data, for example, indicate that the English passive is by far most frequent in scientific writing and that it is least frequent in conversation. Other discourse types can be placed along the frequency continuum:

The following guidelines, which were culled from many sources as well as from our own observations, may be of use in the absence of a complete and definitive usage study:

The passive is often used:

1. When the agent is redundant, i.e., easy to supply, and therefore not expressed.

Oranges are grown in California.

2. When the writer wants to emphasize the receiver or result of the action.

Six people were killed by the tornado.

3. When the writer wants to make a statement sound objective without revealing the source of information. (Although this sentence is more complicated than the other passives discussed here, we are retaining it to complete our usage guidelines.)

It is assumed/believed that he will announce his candidacy soon.

4. When the writer wants to be tactful or evasive by not mentioning the agent or when he or she cannot or will not identify the agent:

Margaret was given some bad advice about selecting courses.
Based on the total figure, it appears that an error was made in the budget.

5. When the writer wishes to retain the same grammatical subject in successive clauses, even though the function of the noun phrase changes from agent to theme.

George Foreman beat Joe Frazier, but he was beaten by Muhammad Ali.

6. When the passive is more appropriate than the active (usually in complex sentences):

(ACTIVE): Actual sample from the written work of a UCLA graduate student who is a native speaker of English and who had been told by high school and college composition teachers to avoid using the passive:

> The results of this second language learning experiment tend to confirm the hypothesis as Bogen, Paivio, Cohen and Witkin suggest that students learn in distinctively different ways.

> (PASSIVE): The professor's suggested change:

> The results of this second language learning experiment tend to confirm the hypothesis that students learn in distinctively different ways as was suggested by Bogen, Paivio, Cohen and Witkin.

In this context the passive is more appropriate than the active, since the hypothesis, which is the theme and also the NP of primary importance, can be fully stated before the writer mentions the source authors (i.e., agents), who are of secondary importance here.

7. When the theme is given information and the agent is new information.

> What a lovely scarf!   Thank you. It was given to me by Pam.

Stative passives

Most of the guidelines above describe usages of the passive that express actions or processes:

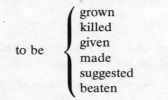

$$
\text{to be} \begin{cases} \text{grown} \\ \text{killed} \\ \text{given} \\ \text{made} \\ \text{suggested} \\ \text{beaten} \end{cases}
$$

A significant number of passive sentences in English, however, are stative passives; i.e., they function more like predicate adjectives than like passive verbs. This distinction will become clearer if we consider the following pair of sentences:

> The wells are located near the edge of the reserve.   The wells were located by two engineers.

Even though the verb *locate* appears in both sentences, two different meanings are being expressed. The first sentence is a stative passive without an agent and without an active voice counterpart; it gives the reader or listener the location of the wells. Note also that the present tense is used. This is typical though not universal for stative passives. The second sentence, however, does have an agent (i.e., the engineers), and it tells us that the engineers discovered the location of the wells; also, an active voice counterpart is possible. Some linguists maintain that stative passives are really adjectives, not true passives. Whatever analysis is used, you should be aware of the fact that some sentences that look like normal passives are in fact stative passives that have no agent and no active voice counterpart.

Change-of-state verbs

It is possible that an ESL/EFL student will ask you how to distinguish an active or passive sentence from the following kinds of agentless sentences that are possible with change-of-state verbs such as *open, close, change, burst, increase,* and *decrease.*

Sentences with Agents		Agentless Sentences
Active (overt agent)	Passive (implied or overt agent)	(change-of-state verbs)
John's brother burst the red balloon.	The red balloon was burst (by John's brother).	The red balloon burst.
Mike opened the door.	The door was opened (by Mike).	The door opened.
Sue's behavior last night changed Bill's opinion of her.	Bill's opinion of Sue was changed (by her behavior last night).	Bill's opinion of Sue changed.

What difference is there in meaning, if any, between the passive sentences and the agentless change-of-state sentences? When would you use the agentless sentence rather than the active or the passive sentence with an explicit or implied agent?

There are several situations in which agentless "change-of-state" sentences are preferred to either active sentences or passive sentences with or without expressed agents.

1. When the focus is on the change of state and the agent is irrelevant or very secondary:

The store opens at 9 a.m.

2. When the writer or speaker's objective is to create an aura of mystery or suspense—i.e., things seem to be happening without the intervention of an agent:

We were sitting quietly in front of the fire when suddenly *the door opened.*

3. When the subject is something so fragile or unstable (e.g., a balloon, a bubble, a cobweb) that it can break, change, dissolve, etc., without any apparent intervention on the part of any agent:

Left hanging on the fence, *the red balloon* suddenly burst and scared all of us.

4. When it is natural to expect change to occur (i.e., physical, social, or psychological "laws" seem to be involved):

Mrs. Smith's opinion of Ronald Reagan changed.

5. When there are so many possible causes for a change of state that it would be misleading to imply a single agent:

Prices increased.

Conclusion

We need to know more about the passive voice; in particular we need more information about when and why it is used. Many of the observations made in this chapter, however, give us a firmer basis for teaching the passive than do the typical exercises in ESL/EFL textbooks which merely exhort the learner to transform active sentences into passives (e.g., John ate the hot dog. ⟶ The hot dog was eaten by John). We believe that extensive or exclusive use of such exercises suggests to the learner that active and passive sentences are equivalent; thus such practices are misleading. Furthermore, the overwhelming number of passive sentences that occur in connected oral or written discourse do not even express an agent; also, the reasons for using the passive voice are different from those for using the active voice.

TEACHING SUGGESTIONS

1 The ESL/EFL teacher should at a fairly early stage introduce the passive as a change of focus from the active voice, e.g., after the students have mastered the simple past with transitive verbs and have had some experience with past participles—perhaps with the present perfect tense. This is done best with "agent-result" constructions. Use large flashcards that use pictures or words to cue the agent and the result. After giving an example to explain that the active voice puts focus on the agent whereas the passive puts focus on the result, present drills that make use of flashcards in the following manner:

> Facts—discoverer: Columbus
>   place: America
> *T:* (Puts the Columbus card to the left of the America card and tells the students to make a sentence focusing on *Columbus*)
> *Ss:* Columbus discovered America.
> *T:* (Puts the America card to the left of the Columbus card and tells the students to make a sentence focusing on *America*)
> *Ss:* America was discovered by Columbus.

Other items to pair up in this manner (use agents and results of interest to your students):

Agent	*Result*
Leonardo da Vinci	The Mona Lisa
Beethoven	The Moonlight Sonata
Shakespeare	Romeo and Juliet
Alexander Graham Bell	The telephone, etc.

Note that the passive participle of irregular verbs (e.g., *written*) may have to be drilled as a separate point.

2 To practice the more colloquial GET passive with action verbs, combine English practice with role playing and initiate a series of appropriate skits. First explain the GET construction using an example.

Imagine a series of cartoon pictures | a | b | c | d |

a. John sees a pretty girl.
b. John goes over and talks to the girl.

c. The pretty girl's husband arrives.
d. The husband punches John in the nose.

What did the husband do?
He punched John in the nose.

What happened to John?
He got punched in the nose.

If the students have understood the example, the teacher might then elicit a series of actions and utterances as follows:

> *T:* S1, do something stupid.
> *S1:* (falls off his chair)
> *T:* S2, say something insulting to S1.
> *S2:* "S1, you're really stupid."

T: What did S2 do?
S3:   He insulted S1. He said something insulting to S1.
T: What happened to S1?
S3:   He got insulted.

Then initiate other skits in this manner:

Sa, get yourself invited to a party.
Sb, get yourself scolded/reprimanded.
Sc, get yourself complimented (i.e., fish for a compliment).

3   Because the passive voice is used much more in written than in spoken English, many exercises on the passive voice should involve the use of a written text to complete orally or in writing. The following models for written exercises are taken from Slager (1973):

a. Present tense—no overt agent is expressed:

German is spoken in Switzerland. French and Italian are also spoken there. English is spoken in Canada. In some parts of the country, however, French is spoken, too. . . .

(Continue with discussion of Belgium, Yugoslavia, various republics of the Soviet Union, Cyprus, etc. Also do this with places where crops are grown—e.g., corn is grown in the Midwest, potatoes are grown in Idaho and Maine, lettuce is grown in California.)

b. Present tense—agent obligatory:

Some people are bothered by smoke. Others are bothered by noise, I. . . .

c. Simple past—agent omitted because it is unknown or unimportant:

Construction of these UN buildings was begun in 1950. The Secretariat was completed in 1951. The other buildings were completed in 1952, etc.

d. Modal passive—talk about city planning in your town:

New hospitals must be built. More parking spaces must be provided. The airport must be expanded, etc.

e. Perfective passive—use passage as a model for writing on a similar topic:

An old section of the city has recently been restored. Many changes have been made. Many of the old houses have been repaired. New businesses have been started. One old building has been converted into a theater, and many cultural activities have been developed. Education has not been neglected. New elementary and secondary schools have been built, and a new college has recently been opened. Now this old section of the city is no longer a slum. It has been changed into an exciting place to live and work.

4   Ask your students to look for five examples of the passive in their textbooks, in the newspaper, in advertising, etc. Refer them to the seven usage rules we have given for using the passive. Ask them to decide which usage rule seems to apply, e.g.:

Text: In 17 tests Brand X was judged better than Brand Y.

Usage explanation: Passive sounds objective but is used to be evasive (i.e., usage principle 4); we would want to know how many judges were used for each test and what percentage of the judges used in the 17 tests felt this way.

5   To encourage early use of the agentless passive, Jackie Schachter suggests using carefully selected imperatives, which also do not overtly mention the agent:

T (to S1): Tear up this letter.	*T (to S2):* What happened to the letter?
S1: (tears up the letter)	*S2:* It was torn up.

Since it is possible for S2 to answer *What happened to the letter?* with *Max tore it up,* a pattern will have to be established to show that the theme (in this case *the letter*) should be the subject of the response and that actions and consequences are being discussed without any overt mention of the agent. Other imperatives that could be used to practice this pattern are:

Correct this sentence. (A sentence with an obvious error is on the board.)
Take this chair out of the room.
Bring the chair back into the room.
Pass out these exercises. (The exercises could be four or five imperative sentences that
    should be changed into passive voice descriptions of what happened.)
Collect the exercises.

6   A simple experiment or cooking procedure involving several steps can also be used as a vehicle to practice the agentless passive. The experiment or procedure should be done in front of the class, with one or more volunteers following the teacher's instructions. Another student can write the steps on the board. For example, the procedure for making ice cream with an old-fashioned crank-style ice cream maker could be demonstrated. You will need a mixing bowl, a spoon, an ice cream maker, a small plastic spoon for each student, and all the fresh ingredients.

These steps get written on the board:
1. Break two eggs into the bowl.
2. Add one cup sugar and two teaspoons vanilla.
3. Blend the eggs, sugar, and vanilla together.
4. Add three cups of light cream.
5. Stir the egg mixture and the cream together.
6. Put the mixture into the ice cream maker.
7. Cover the maker and turn the handle.
8. Turn until the ice cream is so hard that the handle won't turn anymore.

After the class has had a chance to sample the fresh ice cream, ask them to write up a description of what happened using the agentless passive, e.g.:

How the Ice Cream Was Made
This is how ice cream was made in our class today. First two eggs were broken into the bowl. Then one cup of sugar and two teaspoons of vanilla were added and everything was blended together. After this, three cups of light cream were added and the mixture was stirred well. . . .

7   Thom Hudson has integrated writing practice in using the passive with a communication-oriented "survey" assignment. First, his students conduct a survey using only native speakers of English as their subjects. They have to gather some bio-data (e.g., sex, nationality, age, occupation, area of residence) and then ask a question (e.g., What is your favorite TV program?). When they tabulate and then write up their findings, the passive voice would very naturally occur with high frequency. Models such as the following can be provided:

TV Favorites: A Survey of 50 Americans
Fifty Americans in Chicago were asked by the author to identify their favorite TV programs during the week of May 12, 1981. "M.A.S.H." was mentioned most frequently (19 subjects), then "The Love Boat" (9 subjects), and the third choice was "Sixty Minutes"

(6 subjects). No other program was mentioned more than three times.

"M.A.S.H." was selected by men more often than women (12 men; 7 women) while women preferred "The Love Boat" (8 women; 1 man). Etc.

EXERCISES

Test your understanding of what has been presented

1. Provide original example sentences that illustrate the following terms. Underline the pertinent word(s) in your examples.

> active voice
> a passive with agent
> a verb that is never passive
> a verb that is always passive
> the agentless change-of-state verb construction
> the agentless passive
> the GET passive
> the stative passive

2. Give tree diagrams and derivations for the following sentences:

a. The report is being studied by the committee.
b. John was arrested yesterday.
c. The parcel should not have been delivered to the hospital.
d. Was the play written by O'Neill?
e. The work isn't going to be completed on time.

3. Why are the following sentences ungrammatical?

a. *Horace will be had tested on his Spanish proficiency.
b. *Two liters were contained by the bottle.

4. Are the following sentences normal or stative passives? Why?

a. The book was edited prior to publication.
b. We are quite satisfied with these arrangements.
c. Mr. Burke is seated at the end of the first row.
d. Swahili is spoken in East Africa.

Test your ability to apply what you know

5. If your students produce the following sentences, what errors have they made? How will you make them aware of the errors, and what exercises will you prepare for your students to correct them?

a. *I born in Tehran in 1950.
b. *The song was sang several times by the choir.
c. *I was died by my mother. (What the learner intended to say was: My mother died and it affected me greatly.)
d. *Korea has been cut down its birthrate from 3 percent to 2 percent.

6. It has been suggested that sentences with the BE passive and the GET passive are quite

distinct syntactically and semantically. Can you give at least one reason other than those suggested in the text for distinguishing these constructions?

7. One of your students asks you if there is any difference between the GET passive and the BE passive of the verb *to marry*. What would you tell her?

BIBLIOGRAPHY

References

Chomsky, N. (1965). *Aspects of the Theory of Syntax.* Cambridge, Mass.: MIT Press.

Huddleston, R. (1971). *The Sentence in Written English.* London: Cambridge University Press.

Lakoff, G. (1968). "Repartee: Negation, Conjunctions, and Quantifiers." Unpublished paper, Harvard University.

Shintani, M. (1979). "The Frequency and Usage of the English Passive." Unpublished Ph.D. dissertation in Applied Linguistics, UCLA.

Slager, W. (1973). "Creating Contexts for Language Practice," *TESOL Quarterly* 7, 1.

Suggestions for further reading

Interesting descriptions of the passive are available in:

Jespersen, O. (1964). *Essentials of English Grammar.* University, Ala.: University of Alabama Press, Chap. 12, pp. 120–123.

Lyons, J. (1969). *Theoretical Linguistics.* London: Cambridge University Press, pp. 371–388 deal with voice.

Svartvik, J. (1966). *On Voice in the English Verb.* The Hague: Mouton.

The journal *English Language Teaching* has useful articles on the passive voice in the following five issues: 17:2, January 1963; 18:2, January 1964; 20:2, January 1966; 21:3, May 1967; 27:2, February 1973.

Some good suggestions for teaching the passive are found in:

Brinton, D., and R. Neuman (1982). *Getting Along: English Grammar and Writing* (Book 2). Englewood Cliffs, N.J.: Prentice-Hall, pp. 291–293.

Danielson, D., and R. Hayden (1973). *Using English: Your Second Language.* Englewood Cliffs, N.J.: Prentice-Hall, pp. 58–59, 64.

Martin, A. V. (1977). *Guide to Language and Study Skills for College Students of ESL.* Englewood Cliffs, N.J.: Prentice-Hall, pp. 58–67.

Praninskas, J. (1975). *Rapid Review of English Grammar.* Englewood Cliffs, N.J.: Prentice-Hall, pp. 304–307.

Rutherford, W. E. (1975). *Modern English* (2d ed., vol. I). New York: Harcourt Brace Jovanovich, pp. 309–311, 315–316.

For a good exercise for teaching the GET passive, see:

Davis, P. (1977). *English Structure in Focus.* Rowley, Mass.: Newbury House.

18

Sentences with Indirect Objects

GRAMMATICAL DESCRIPTION

Introduction

Traditional grammars define an indirect object as a second noun object (the first being the direct object) that tells us *to whom* or *for whom* the action expressed in the verb is being carried out. To these two types of noun objects we will also add those that tell us *of whom* the action expressed in the verb is being requested. (Admittedly, there are far fewer indirect objects of this third form in English than there are of the first two.)

Joe gave *a book* to *Sally*.   Joe asked *a question* of *Sally*.
      direct   indirect   direct   indirect
      object   object   object   object

Joe made *a bookcase* for *Sally*.
      direct   indirect
      object   object

Notice that another form of these sentences is also possible:

      Joe gave Sally a book.   Joe asked Sally a question.
      Joe made Sally a bookcase.

We will discuss the derivation of sentences of this type below.

Since sentences with indirect objects contain two NP objects, it is often possible for an active sentence to have two related passive sentences, depending upon which noun phrase functions as the subject of the passive. We will be discussing this possibility further.

      Active: Joe gave a book to Sally.
      Passive: The book was given to Sally (by Joe).
                 Sally was given the book (by Joe).

The discourse context, of course, determines which noun phrase should be the subject of the passive sentence.

Problems for ESL/EFL students

Why do sentences with indirect objects sometimes cause problems for ESL/EFL students? First of all, students must be able to sort out whether a given verb takes an indirect object preceded by a *to, for,* or *of.* Then they must learn the conditions that English places on indirect object movement. Those especially who come from languages that allow the indirect object to occur freely next to the verb (e.g., French and Spanish) may produce ungrammatical sentences such as "*John opened me the door" instead of "John opened the door for me." Many students will be confused by the fact that verbs with similar meanings do not all allow the indirect object to occur next to the verb. Thus by analogy with

> He told me the answer.

students will incorrectly produce

> *He said me the answer.

Finally, some languages resist making the indirect object the subject of a passive sentence. For example, the literal translation of "Sally was given the book (by Joe)" would be ungrammatical in German. (In German the direct object or accusative case can become the nominative subject of the passive; however, the dative case cannot.) Students coming from such language backgrounds will need ample practice in forming English passive sentences where underlying indirect objects function as subjects.

The meaning of verb-indirect object combinations

Jacobson (1966) arranges the verbs which take indirect objects[1] into three semantic groups: "dative"[2] verbs such as *give,* "benefactive" verbs such as *make,* and "eliciting" verbs such as *ask.* Each group of verbs can be associated with the type of prepositional phrase that follows it. The ESL/EFL student would learn, then, that he or she must select *to* + NP in the case of the dative verbs (give, say, sell, explain, etc.), *for* + NP in the case of the benefactive verbs (make, buy, cook, prepare, etc.), and *of* + NP in the case of the "eliciting" verbs (ask, request, etc.). The "dative" verbs comprise the largest category, the "eliciting" verbs the smallest. Of course, students must learn to take into account the meaning of the verb as it is used in sentences, because some verbs will occur in more than one category depending on how they are used; however, in such cases two different meanings of the verb are involved, e.g.:

> I'll get this to him. (dative) = "deliver"
> I'll get this for him. (benefactive) = "take, obtain"

We should also note that there are a few verbs that only take indirect objects without a preceding preposition. In this case, the indirect objects always occur directly after the verbs in question, e.g.:

> The deal cost me a fortune.

This sentence presumably means something such as the following, and one might say that the underlying preposition appears in other contexts:

> The cost of the deal to me was a fortune.

---

1. Jacobson, however, does not refer to them as verbs which take indirect objects; rather, he considers them verbs which take direct objects plus complements.

2. "Dative" is the term used by Fillmore (1968) for such indirect objects, while Jacobson refers to them as "directional." You may want to consider following Jacobson's terminology for pedagogical purposes.

Another verb in this category is *charge:*

> The repairman charged me twenty-five dollars. (cf. He charged twenty-five dollars to my account.)

One final point to consider is that sentences with prepositional objects preceded by *for* such as the following may be ambiguous:

> John bought the book for me.

There are two possible interpretations of this sentence:

Proxy: John bought it for me (i.e., he acted on my behalf) because I didn't have time to buy it myself.

Benefactive: John bought it for me because my birthday was coming up and he wanted to give me a gift.

However, if the indirect object occurs directly after the verb in the above sentence (i.e., John bought me the book), only the benefactive interpretation is possible.

The structure of sentences with indirect objects

The verbs that take indirect objects in English share certain similarities and differences. One important difference is that for some of these verbs, the indirect object is indispensable to the meaning and the structure of the sentence, e.g.:

> *Joe gave a book.[3]
>
> (Joe gave $\left\{ \begin{array}{l} \text{a book to Mel} \\ \text{Mel a book} \end{array} \right\}$.)
>
> *Morgan handed the letter.
>
> (Morgan handed $\left\{ \begin{array}{l} \text{the letter to Peter} \\ \text{Peter the letter} \end{array} \right\}$.)

In other instances the meaning of the entire sentence, not just the verb, must be considered, since the indirect object may not be structurally required, but the sentence will have a different meaning depending on whether or not the indirect object is present, e.g.:

> Mr. Jensen found $\left\{ \begin{array}{l} \text{a job for me} \\ \text{me a job} \end{array} \right\}$. $\neq$ Mr. Jensen found a job. (i.e., for himself)

There are also many cases where the indirect object is not structurally essential but where it is strongly implied and thus seems to be present semantically. In addition, the meaning of these sentences does not change markedly if the indirect object is not overtly expressed, e.g.:

> Sam sold the car. (i.e., to someone)
> Barbara asked a question. (i.e., of someone)

In all the above examples, we can say that the indirect object is closely associated with the meaning of the sentence as a whole and the verb phrase in particular. However, in contrast to these cases, there are also instances where the indirect object is optional both structurally and semantically. In such a case we would have a complete sentence without the indirect object. If

---

3. Here we interpret *give* as the specific transfer of something from one person to another—not as the general *give,* which means "to donate." In this latter general sense, of course, no explicit indirect object is required. These two meanings of *give* would have separate lexical entries.

the indirect object is not explicitly stated, it is not even strongly implied. The two following sentences, for example, have optional indirect objects that seem much less closely related to the rest of the sentence than the other cases we have discussed above:

Bob made a bookcase (for Sally).   The teller cashed the check (for me).

As a related matter, we must also consider the role of the direct object in sentences that contain both a direct and an indirect object. First, there are cases where the direct object cannot be deleted whether or not the preposition preceding the indirect object is present, e.g.:

Peter handed the book to Alice.   *Peter handed Alice.
*Peter handed to Alice.

In such a case, both the direct and indirect object are interdependent, indispensable elements in the sentence. Second, in some cases, the direct object can be deleted, but only if the preposition preceding the indirect object is also deleted, e.g.:

We paid the money to Harry.   *We paid to Harry.
We paid Harry.

In such cases, the indirect object seems even more closely linked with and essential to the meaning of the sentence than does the direct object.

Finally, there are other cases where the direct object can be deleted, but the preposition preceding the indirect object must be retained. If the preposition is not retained, the meaning of the sentence changes, e.g.:

Sara cooks dinner for us.
Sara cooks for us.   ≠ Sara cooks us.

In such instances the direct object is the most important noun phrase in the predicate and the indirect object is not as closely linked to the meaning of the verb as it was in the two preceding cases.

Thus we have seen a number of cases in which the indirect object is essential to and/or very closely related to the rest of the verb phrase. We can capture this association in such cases by making the indirect object a part of the verb phrase in the underlying structure, as we have done in the following example:

I handed the note to him.

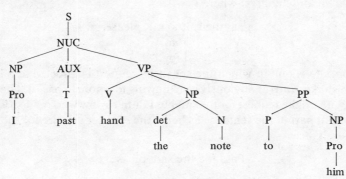

On the other hand, when the indirect object is not needed to complete the sentence structurally or it is not implied semantically, we propose that the indirect object be part of the NUC of the sentence rather than part of the verb phrase:

The teller cashed the check for me.

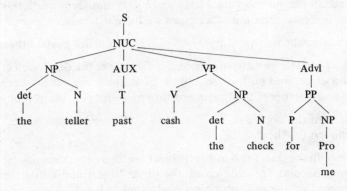

Indirect object movement

We have already given several examples in this chapter of the movement of the indirect object to a position directly following the verb. In this section we will discuss the function of indirect object movement—how the transformation operates and the conditions on its operation.

Function

Erteschik-Shir (1979) has proposed a discourse principle, which is useful for understanding the function of indirect object movement. It is the concept of dominance. Basically, a dominant constituent in a sentence is the one that a speaker has chosen to highlight, to call to his or her listener's attention. It is this constituent in a sentence which will probably be the topic of further conversation if there is to be any. Furthermore, in the string:

$$\text{V} \quad \text{NP}_1 \quad \left\{ \begin{array}{c} \text{to} \\ \text{for} \\ \text{of} \end{array} \right\} \text{NP}_2,$$

NP_2 (i.e., the indirect object) is the dominant noun phrase. If the speaker wanted to give prominence to NP_1 (the direct object) instead, indirect object movement would be applied and NP_2 and NP_1 would switch places, allowing NP_1 to be the dominant noun phrase.

To illustrate, the only context where

Pass the salt to me, please.

$$\text{V} \quad \text{NP}_1 \quad \left\{ \begin{array}{c} \text{to} \\ \text{for} \end{array} \right\} \text{NP}_2$$

would be appropriate is one in which the speaker's request is directed to a listener who is (1) holding a salt shaker and (2) obviously not knowing to whom to pass it. The listener might then reply, "Oh, I heard the request for the salt but I didn't know who made it." Most contexts define the important part of the sentence as being the speaker's desire for salt and therefore one more frequently hears:

Pass me the salt, please.

or—since the speaker is generally the indirect object by implication—simply:

Pass the salt, please.

If the person who complies with this request says anything at all, he or she would be likely to comment upon the direct object, or the salt, not upon the one who initiated the request, i.e., "Sure. Here it is."[4]

The indirect object movement transformation

Indirect object movement, then, is an optional transformation applied if the verb in question permits such movement and if the speaker chooses to make the direct object dominant. For example:

Joe gave Sally a book.

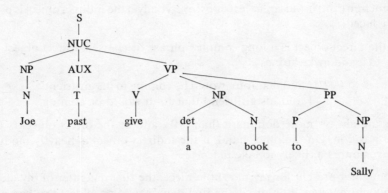

Output of base: Joe past give a book to Sally
Indirect object movement: Joe past give Sally a book
Affix attachment (1✕): Joe give + past Sally a book
Morphological rules: Joe gave Sally a book.

The Indirect Object Movement transformation, then, deletes the preposition before the indirect object and has the indirect object exchange places with the direct object. This holds true whether the indirect object is generated as part of the VP or as part of the NUC.

Conditions on indirect object movement

Erteschik-Shir's notion of dominance helps us understand why certain conditions are placed on indirect object movement:

1. For many, though not all dialects of English, the rule does not apply if the direct object is a pronoun and the indirect object is a noun.

We sent it to John.   *We sent John it.[5]

On the other hand, when the indirect object is a pronoun and the direct object is a noun (especially a nonspecific one), the rule is likely to be applied.

We sent him a package.

These observations can be explained by noting that pronouns are, as a rule, less dominant than nouns. Since pronouns usually have an anaphoric referent or a referent in the immediate physical environment, it is unlikely that a speaker would want to direct attention to them—

4. Of course, "dominance" can also be achieved by phonological means (i.e., stress) just as it can through syntax. For example, contrary to Erteschik-Shir's syntactic principle, one could say:

Pass *the sált* to me. (i.e., not the pépper!)   Pass *me* the salt. (i.e., not Róger!)

5. Sentences of this form are much more acceptable in British than American English.

their meaning is already clear from the context. This is not to say that an indirect object which is a pronoun would never occupy the dominant position, but when this does occur, a different interpretation would be necessary, e.g., a contrastive one.

We sent a package to him. (not her)

All other noun-pronoun combinations of direct and indirect objects are syntactically possible, although the intentions of the speaker will dictate the order.

We sent John the book.
We sent him ('im) it. (acceptable to most everybody if the indirect object is phonologically reduced)

2. If the direct object is a long complex phrase or clause, indirect object movement is necessary to avoid awkwardness:

?/*I told that John would be coming to his girlfriend.
I told his girlfriend that John would be coming.

Sentences are always more dominant than NPs, and so the direct object is moved to the dominant position. On the other hand, if the indirect object is heavily modified, indirect object movement is unlikely to take place.

I bought a present for my new little niece, the first daughter of my eldest brother.
?/*I bought my new little niece, the first daughter of my eldest brother, a present.

The speaker who elaborates either the direct or indirect object has already given it dominance. Such objects, therefore, are either moved to the dominant position (cf. the case of the direct object) or remain in the dominant position (cf. the case of the indirect object).

3. The main verb must belong to the class of verbs permitting the indirect object movement rule. Verbs like *give, send, ask, sell, pay, tell, hand, lend, show, offer,* and *teach* all readily accept this rule; however, *explain* and *open,* for example, do not.

Explain the answer to me.   Open the door for me.
*Explain me the answer.   *Open me the door.

All verbs that take indirect objects would have to be marked in the lexicon according to whether or not they can (or must) undergo indirect object movement. In general, monosyllabic verbs of Germanic origin allow indirect object movement; polysyllabic verbs and verbs of Romance origin do not allow indirect object movement.

± *indirect* *object movement*	− *indirect* *object movement*	+ *indirect* *object movement*
give	open	cost
send	explain	charge
lend	describe	bill
teach	say	:
tell	mention	
:	:	

We should note here that some of those verbs which do not allow indirect object movement to take place, do, in fact, still allow the indirect object to precede the direct object, especially if the latter is elaborated (e.g., is several phrases long or is a clause). In such a case, however, the indirect object always retains its preposition so we know that some rule other than indirect object movement has taken place.

> They mentioned the new restaurant on Putney Road to me.
> *They mentioned me the new restaurant on Putney Road.
> They mentioned to me the new restaurant on Putney Road.

4. Lakoff (1969) notes that in conjoined sentences there are also constraints on indirect object movement. If the verb is deleted in the second sentence, either both sentences must undergo indirect object movement, or neither may.

I gave John a book, and Bill a bicycle.	*I gave John a book, and a bicycle to Bill.
I gave a book to John, and a bicycle to Bill.	*I gave a book to John, and Bill a bicycle.

If the verb is retained in both parts, this constraint does not hold.

I gave a book to John, and gave Bill a bicycle.	I gave John a book, and gave a bicycle to Bill.

Sentences with indirect objects in the passive voice

We have already noted that English has more passive voice alternatives for sentences with indirect objects than some other languages do. This is especially true for sentences with indirect objects after dative and eliciting verbs; sentences with benefactive indirect objects are more likely to have only one possible passive voice subject, i.e., the direct object:

$$\text{This dress was made} \begin{cases} \text{for Mary (by Alice).} \\ \text{by Alice for Mary.} \end{cases}$$
*Mary was made this dress by Alice.[6]

The different versions that are possible involve (1) whether the agent will be expressed or not and (2) if the agent is expressed, whether the benefactive precedes or follows the agent. The benefactive, however, must be expressed; otherwise, we have another sentence with no indirect object at all (i.e., *The dress was made by Alice*). The discourse context would determine which version is most appropriate. The basic structure of such a sentence can be represented as follows, with the agent being considered optional (i.e., it would be omitted if it did not appear in the surface structure):

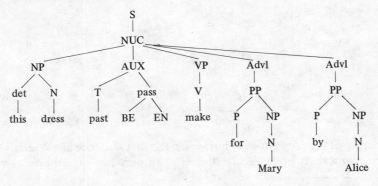

---

6. Several native speakers of British English have indicated to us that this sentence is acceptable in their dialect. For most speakers of American English, this is not the case.

Passive sentences with dative or eliciting verbs exhibit a wider range of possibilities, since these indirect objects (as well as the direct objects) can become the subject of a passive sentence:

ELICITING   The favor was asked of Paul (by Helen).
            Paul was asked the favor (by Helen).

DATICE   The book was given $\begin{cases} \text{to John (by Alice).}^7 \\ \text{by Alice to John.}^8 \end{cases}$

            John was given the book (by Alice).

The passive sentence selected depends on the discourse topic. In the dative example if the book is under discussion, the first alternative is appropriate; if John is the topic, the second version is used. The agent, *Alice,* is expressed only if it is an important or new piece of information; i.e., the agent is omitted if everyone knows that Alice gave John the book, or if no one knows who gave John the book, or if it doesn't matter who gave John the book.

Tree diagrams of these two sentences follow; again, the agent should be considered optional (i.e., it will appear in the tree diagram only if it occurs in the surface structure):

The book was given to John (by Alice).

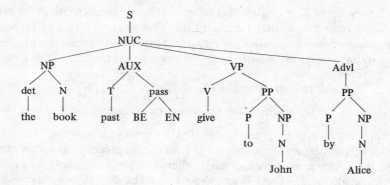

John was given the book (by Alice).

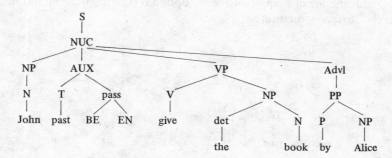

The ordering of the prepositional phrases in the first sentence again seems to depend on the discourse context. It appears that the most important—or dominant—piece of new

---

7. In some dialects of English—especially British—*The book was given John (by Alice)* is another acceptable version of this sentence. In American English retention of the preposition *to* is preferred.

8. Native speakers are divided regarding the acceptability of this sentence; however, it becomes more acceptable to all judges as the NP in the indirect object becomes longer or more complex: e.g., The book was given by Alice to John's father, who appreciated it very much.

information would come last. Thus, if the agent is more important than the receiver, we say

The book was given to John by Alice.

However, if the receiver is more important than the agent, we choose

The book was given by Alice to John.

In both cases, the noun in the first prepositional phrase is less strongly stressed than the noun in the second when these sentences are spoken.

We have emphasized that with certain verbs either the direct object or the indirect object can become the subject of a passive sentence. When the indirect object is part of the NUC and not the VP, however, a passive sentence with an indirect object as subject seems somehow less acceptable.

Alice mailed the letter to John.   ?John was mailed the letter by Alice.

Thus, we really have a continuum of acceptability with regard to indirect objects that are subjects of passive sentences. If the indirect object is part of the verb phrase, it is likely to be acceptable as the subject of a passive sentence. If the indirect object is part of the nucleus, such a passive subject seems less acceptable.

Another double object sentence type

The object complement construction is another type of sentence with a double object that you should not confuse with sentences containing indirect objects, e.g.:

Harold called Joe an idiot.   We christened our boat "the Bullfrog."
The Johnsons named their daughter
  Naomi.

Unlike the indirect object construction, this construction, which provides an epithet or name for the direct object, has no expanded form with a preposition. Some sentences, which look like object complements but which can be expanded to infinitives, should be considered infinitive complements that have undergone "to be" deletion:

We considered Joe an idiot.   We considered Joe to be an idiot.

Conclusion

As we have seen many times before, the more closely we examine a structure, the more complicated it seems to become. As usual, more research is needed; e.g., is there a principle to help us determine which verbs allow indirect object movement and which do not?

In the meantime, it would seem sensible for you to concentrate your efforts on teaching whether verbs take dative, benefactive, or eliciting indirect objects and which verbs do not allow indirect object movement. It will also be helpful if you can give your students some understanding of the discourse principle of dominance.

TEACHING SUGGESTIONS

1 To develop your students' sense of when indirect object movement is appropriate or inappropriate, group them in pairs to manipulate and discuss sentences with words written on cards or strips such as the following (asking them to decide whether or not the *to* can be deleted and what any subsequent word order changes would be):

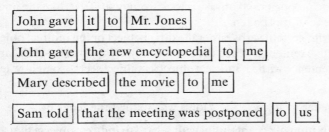

This exercise can also be done very effectively with the entire class by using an overhead projector and strips of transparency for the words or groups of words.

2   Sketch pictures or clip pictures from magazines that naturally elicit indirect objects, e.g.:

Jill   Nancy

Teacher: What is Jill doing?

Student: She's giving { Nancy (some) flowers.
                            { (some) flowers to Nancy.

(Either word order would be an appropriate response.) With more advanced students, the teacher should continue:

Teacher: (removes card from view) Do you think Nancy is happy?
Student: Yes.
Teacher: Why?
Student: Because Jill gave her flowers! (The word order with *to* would be less appropriate.)

3   To help students develop a sense of using the *to* preposition in those contexts where the indirect object is emphasized in a response, try a drill like this:

  a. *S1:*   Would you lend me your car?
     S2:   I can't. I've already promised to lend it to Harvey.
  b. *S3:*   Would you lend me your textbook?
     S4:   I can't. I've already promised to lend it to Judy.

4   Using verbs like *buy* and *make,* you can elicit addition of a benefactive *for-phrase* in the following manner:

a. *Teacher:*   John bought some candy.
   S1:   Who did he buy it for?
   Teacher: Himself.
   S1:   Oh, he bought it for himself!

b. *S2:*   Sarah made a dress.
   S3:   Who did she make it for?
   S2:   Me.
   S3:   Oh, she made it for you!

5   To practice the use of direct objects as passive subjects, students can give things—that the teacher provides—to each other with an appropriate follow-up question (Who was the _____ given to?):

a. *T:*   Paolo, give the candy to Maria.
   S1:   Who was the candy given to?
   S2:   It was given to Maria.

b. *T:*   Said, give the ruler to Roberto.
   S3:   Who was the ruler given to?
   S4:   It was given to Roberto.

Etc.

6   To practice the use of indirect objects as passive subjects, use consumer gripes as a context. One student can role-play the consumer affairs officer and the others can state their complaints.

a. *S1:*   What's your $\begin{Bmatrix} \text{complaint} \\ \text{problem} \\ \text{gripe} \end{Bmatrix}$?
   S2:   I was sold a bad car by AZ Used Cars.

b. *S1:*   What's your _____ ?
   S3:   I was sold a defective TV set by Jones Appliances.

c. *S1:*   What's your _____ ?
   S4:   I was sold a fake diamond by Bijou Jewelers.
   Etc.

EXERCISES

Test your understanding of what has been presented

1. Provide original example sentences to illustrate the following terms. Underline the pertinent word(s) in your examples.

direct object	dominance
eliciting indirect object	indirect object movement
benefactive indirect object	benefactive-*for*
directional indirect object	proxy-*for*
passive with indirect object as subject	object complement

2. Give tree diagrams and derivations for the following sentences:

a. I handed Sue the note.
b. He was offered a job by the supervisor.
c. The information was given to him yesterday.
d. We bought Horace a watch.
e. Did Martha ask George a question?

3. Why are the following sentences ungrammatical (or at best awkward):

a. *John hasn't sent his brother it.
b. *Mary bought for me the book.
c. *Roger asked a question to Phyllis.

4. List all the active and passive sentences—with and without indirect object movement—that would be related to the following information.

a. verb: send (past tense); agent: mother; direct object: the parcel; directional indirect object: Bob.
b. verb: bring (past tense); agent: Bill; direct object: some flowers; benefactive indirect object: Agnes.

Test your ability to apply what you know

5. If your students produce the following sentences, what errors have they made? How will you make them aware of the errors, and what exercises will you prepare to correct the errors?

a. *Explain me that rule again, please.
b. *Are you going to give to me an answer?
c. *Why didn't you open him the door?
d. *We didn't know so we asked to Harry.
e. *Please excuse me my poor English.

6. Bruce Fraser (personal communication) has suggested that the indirect object movement rule for verbs taking the preposition *to* is based on phonological considerations and will apply *only* if the verb is:

a. monosyllabic
b. bisyllabic with stress on the initial syllable, e.g.:

Tell John the answer.
Offer us something else.
?Whisper Ann the answer.

*Explain John the answer.
*Communicate Ann the answer.

Can you think of any exceptions to this rule? What about verbs that take the prepositions *for* and *of*?

7. ESL/EFL students sometimes have difficulty in distinguishing pairs such as the following—especially when they are listening. Think of ways that would help students learn what to watch for to clearly distinguish such sentences.

Mary was giving a sweater to John.   Mary was given a sweater by John.

8. One of your students asks you what kind of a verb *beg* is (dative? benefactive? eliciting?) and whether or not it can take an indirect object. How will you respond?

BIBLIOGRAPHY

References

Erteschik-Shir, N. (1979). "Discourse Constraints on Dative Movement," in T. Givon (ed.), *Syntax and Semantics,* vol. 12: *Discourse and Syntax.* New York: Academic Press.

Jacobson, R. (1966). "The Role of Deep Structures in Language Teaching," *Language Learning* 16:3-4, 153-160.

Lakoff, R. (1969). "Manual for Teachers of English as a Foreign Language." Unpublished manuscript.

Suggestions for further reading

For excellent discussions of the interaction of the passive voice and indirect object movement, see:

Fillmore, C. J. (1965). *Indirect Object Constructions in English and the Ordering of Transformations.* The Hague: Mouton.

Fillmore, C. J. (1968). "The Case for Case," in E. Bach and R. Harms (eds.), *Universals in Linguistic Theory.* New York: Holt, Rinehart and Winston.

For good traditional discussions of indirect objects, see:

Frank, M. (1972). *Modern English.* Englewood Cliffs, N.J.: Prentice-Hall, pp. 200-203.

Jespersen, O. (1964). *Essentials of English Grammar.* University, Ala.: University of Alabama Press, pp. 113-116.

For good lists and patterns for verbs taking indirect objects, see:

Praninskas, J. (1975). *Rapid Review of English Grammar.* Englewood Cliffs, N.J.: Prentice-Hall, pp. 200-203.

For some examples of exercises for teaching indirect objects, see:

Brinton, D., and R. Neuman (1982). *Getting Along: English Grammar and Writing* (Book 2). Englewood Cliffs, N.J.: Prentice-Hall, p. 138.

Danielson, D., and R. Hayden (1973). *Using English: Your Second Language.* Englewood Cliffs, N.J.: Prentice-Hall, pp. 56-58, 63.

Praninskas, J. (1975). *Rapid Review of English Grammar.* Englewood Cliffs, N.J.: Prentice-Hall, pp. 206-207.

Rutherford, W. E. (1975). *Modern English* (2d ed., vol. I). New York: Harcourt Brace Jovanovich, pp. 175-177.

19

Prepositions

GRAMMATICAL DESCRIPTION

Introduction: why prepositions are problematic

When ESL/EFL teachers are surveyed regarding their teaching problems (as in Covitt, 1976), prepositions emerge as a serious problem and are mentioned almost as frequently as articles; i.e., the teachers—as a group—feel that prepositions are the second most difficult aspect of the English language for their students.

Many factors support this perception of difficulty. First of all, information that is signaled by a preposition in English is often signaled by an inflection on a noun or an article in a highly inflected language like German, Latin, or Russian. Second, some languages like Japanese have *post*positions instead of *pre*positions; i.e., the structure that corresponds to a prepositional phrase is ordered so that the postposition follows the noun phrase instead of preceding it (PP——▸NP P). Furthermore, when compared with other languages that have prepositions, the number of prepositions in English tends to be greater. For example, Spanish has one preposition *en* that serves as the equivalent of three prepositions in English: *in, on,* and *at.* Another problem is the fact that prepositions often do not translate or match up well between related languages. Thus some of our ESL/EFL students have to cope with anomalies such as the following (which are also a problem when English speakers try to learn other languages):

English *to* = German *zu*   English *at* = German *an* (or *in* or *bei*)
          (but)   John is *at* home. = Johann ist *zu* Hause.

English *to* = French *à*   English *for* = French *pour*
          (but)   a glass *for* cognac = un verre *à* cognac

Such examples help point out that there are some highly unpredictable and language-specific usages of prepositions; however, we will not be focusing on cross-linguistic problems in this chapter, since we want to emphasize the systematic nature of certain prepositional usages in English. Also, we will not be concerned with those multiword prepositions consisting of more than two elements (e.g., *in lieu of, with regard to, as opposed to*). Likewise, the verb + particle combinations that form phrasal verbs (e.g., *Turn on* the light) will not be discussed here but in the following chapter; and the comparative prepositions (i.e., *than, like, as*) will be treated in Chapters 35 and 36 rather than here.

In this chapter we concern ourselves with the systematic uses of some of the more frequent English prepositions and with some of the more obvious teaching and learning problems that they entail. We have already dealt with specific prepositions in Chapters 10, 17, and 18, i.e., the *of* marking certain possessives, the *by* marking the agent in the passive, and the three prepositions used to mark dominant indirect objects (i.e., *to, for,* and *of*). In this chapter we will give a more comprehensive overview of English prepositions and their functions.

A closer look at the structure of prepositional phrases

Before discussing the semantic functions of prepositions, let us review the basic structure of prepositional phrases and consider some of the important variations that occur. The basic rule is PP——▸P NP; i.e., a prepositional phrase is a preposition plus a noun phrase.

Deletion of prepositions

From an earlier discussion (see Chapter 2) we already know that in some cases the preposition is deleted. Sometimes this deletion is optional, as in the following cases:

1. When the preposition *for* expresses a span of time:

> We have lived here (for) twelve years.
> (For) how long have you owned this house?

2. When the preposition *on* is used before days of the week (when the day is used alone or when the day of the week modifies another temporal noun such as *morning, afternoon, night*):

He went surfing (on) Saturday.   I bought these shoes (on) Friday night.

3. In responses to questions that would cue temporal use of *in, at, on,* or *for*:

How long have you lived here?   (For) two years.
When do you wake up?   (At) 7 a.m.

In other environments such as the following, the preposition must be deleted:

1. When the temporal noun phrase contains an ordinal or deictic proximate demonstrative determiner like *last, next, this,* or *these* or the head noun contains *before, after, next,* or *last* or *this* as part of its meaning (e.g., *yesterday, tomorrow, today*):

$$\text{I was busy (*on) } \left\{ \begin{array}{l} \text{last Friday} \\ \text{the day before yesterday} \end{array} \right\}.$$

$$\text{We will be in San Diego (*on) } \left\{ \begin{array}{l} \text{this Sunday} \\ \text{next Sunday} \end{array} \right\}.$$

$$\text{I'm going there } \left\{ \begin{array}{l} \text{(*on) tonight} \\ \text{(*for) next week} \end{array} \right\}.$$

2. When the temporal noun phrase contains a quantifier like *every* or *all*:

She goes to church (*on) every Sunday.   We stayed in Reno (*for) all week.

3. When a locative noun such as *home, downtown,* or *uptown* is used with a verb of motion or direction:[1]

> We went (*to) home.   We ran (*to) home.

---

1. Note that the concept of motion or direction is important, since *home* may take the preposition *at* with a stative verb:

> Ted stayed at home.   Is Jackie at home?

4. When the pro-adverbs *here* and *there* are used after the verb:[2]

We go (*to) there often.   Phyllis $\left\{\begin{array}{l}\text{comes}\\\text{is}\end{array}\right\}$ (*to) here every day.

Thus we can say that one variation of our rules should allow for the absence of the preposition, perhaps via a zero-preposition possibility:

$$PP \longrightarrow P\ NP$$
$$P \longrightarrow \left\{\begin{array}{l}P\\ \emptyset\end{array}\right\}$$

Another structural variation comes from the fact that several common and frequent prepositions require or permit a second supporting preposition in contexts involving cause or direction. We refer to them as double prepositions even though one can argue that the first element is an adverb:

out of   because of
off of   away from

(Note that *into* and *onto* historically were double prepositions but now are written as one word and can be considered single prepositions.) The double prepositions can be accounted for if we allow our basic rule for prepositional phrases to be expanded as follows to describe this additional structural possibility PP⟶P PP, e.g.:

out of the house

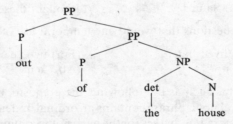

This means our revised and expanded rules for generating all these types of prepositional phrases in English might look like this:

$$PP \longrightarrow P \left\{\begin{array}{l}NP\\ PP\end{array}\right\}$$
$$P \longrightarrow \left\{\begin{array}{l}P\\ \emptyset\end{array}\right\}$$

For the sake of simplicity, however, we will continue with the rule PP⟶P NP unless the added complexity is necessary.

Lexical idiosyncracies of prepositions

Incorporation

An issue related to the deletion of prepositions was raised by Gruber (1965) when he pointed out that certain prepositions are sometimes incorporated into verbs and are

---

2. Occasionally deictic *there* or *here* is preceded by a preposition such as *in, out, over, under* to make it more specific adverbially:

We went in there.   Why did Phyllis come over here?

superficially lost in the process of relexification. The result is a shorter sentence and a verb that conveys more information, e.g.:

John *went across* the street.	Mr. Smith *walks past* our house at 8 a.m.
John *crossed* the street.	Mr. Smith *passes* our house at 8 a.m.

Co-occurrence with verbs and adjectives

Many English verbs and adjectives occur with one and only one preposition. Such a preposition must be entered in the lexical entry of the verb or adjective concerned, and it must be learned as an integral part of the verb or adjective even though these are still combinations of V + PP or adj + PP from the structural point of view.

Verb + prep.	*Adj. + prep.*
to rely on	to be afraid of
to detract from	to be interested in
to consist of	to be common to
to substitute for	to be composed of
to part with	to be susceptible to
⋮	⋮

Sometimes the same verb with two different prepositions will have significantly different meanings, e.g.:

provide for: You should provide for your old age now. (make provisions for)
provide with: The Red Cross provided us with blankets. (gave blankets to us)

However, sometimes two different prepositions can be used with the same verb with little or no change of meaning, e.g.:

Joe competes $\begin{Bmatrix} \text{with} \\ \text{against} \end{Bmatrix}$ his older brother too much.

Unfortunately, not enough attention has been paid to this problem in the ESL/EFL context. However, references such as Crowell (1960) should be of considerable help to ESL/EFL teachers and students who recognize this as a problem area and want to do something about it.

Prepositions that co-occur

Certain prepositions should be taught together as nonadjacent co-occurring constituents since they so often both occur in the same sentence (spoken and written discourse). We are thinking particularly in terms of the following four sets:

1. from . . . to (distance range, time range, or range of degree)
2. from . . . until/till (time range only)
3. out of . . . into (change of enclosure or state)
4. off (of) . . . on (to) (change of location with verbs like *take* and *put*)

Lexical compounding

The prepositions *out, over,* and to a certain extent *under,* have formed numerous verb compounds, some of which are frequent and common vocabulary items in English.

out + *V*	*over* + *V*	*under* + *V*	
outdo	overdo	underestimate ⎫	similar meanings
outrun	overrate	underrate ⎭	
outlast	overeat	underline ⎫	similar meanings
outgrow	overcome	underscore ⎭	
⋮	⋮	⋮	

Frequency

The nine most frequent prepositions in English are (in alphabetical order):

at, by, for, from, in, of, on, to, with

However, this grouping is somewhat misleading, because each form has multiple meanings and functions. Thus, each of these frequent prepositions must be studied in detail to isolate a small but optimal number of meaningful functions that it performs in English.

Functions of the preposition *at*

Hudson (1979) demonstrates one way that the functions of these frequent prepositions can be studied using *at* as the target preposition. She reviewed linguistic studies and the lexical entries for *at* in several unabridged dictionaries. By collapsing categories and synthesizing definitions, Hudson (1979:25–26) came up with seven functions or meanings for *at* that she felt were optimally general but detailed enough to make all the important distinctions:

1. Used to locate an object in space:

    The paper is lying at my feet.   She was writing at my desk.

2. Used to locate an object in time:

    He was here at one o'clock.   Everyone shook hands at the ratification of the treaty.

3. Used to indicate a state, condition, or engagement in a particular activity:

    I'm never at ease when taking a test.   The children are at play on the porch.

4. Used to indicate a cause or a source of an action or a state:[3]

    She wept at the bad news.   I'm upset at his handling of the situation.

5. Used to indicate direction toward a goal or objective:

    He shot at me.   That man over there is winking at us.

6. Used to express skill (or lack of it) in relation to a particular activity or occupation:

    He's slow at computing math problems.   She's a whiz at poker.

7. Used to indicate relative amount, degree, rate, value, ordinal relationship or position on a scale:

    He retired at 65.   I bought it at a bargain price.

---

3. Based on her experimental work, Hudson later recommended changing the label of category 4 to this: "Used to express a reaction to someone or something."

Given 305 common so-called idioms using *at* that Hudson had drawn from several sources, 20 native speakers of English were asked to sort these idioms into one of nine categories—i.e., the seven categories given above and these two as well:

8. Does not mean the same as or fit any of the categories.
9. I do not understand or use this expression.

216 out of the 305 items using *at* were put into the same category by the 20 subjects at the $p < .005$ level of significance.

Then, in a reverse of this procedure, Hudson took the seven lists of significant items identified by her 20 subjects and she asked 10 other subjects if they could describe the function of *at* for each of the seven lists. With the exception of the definition for category 4, which caused problems, good approximations of the other six definitions were reconstructed 80 percent of the time or more, and thus six of Hudson's seven functions were verified.

Further studies along these lines or studies that would examine the functions of a preposition in phrases drawn from actual discourse (written and spoken) would be very valuable, since what we also need to know is which of the above functions of *at* are most frequent and useful in English speech and writing. If we had such information, we could decide with more confidence which meanings of *at* (or any other preposition) our students should be exposed to initially and be encouraged to master first.

Semantic case functions

Fillmore (1968) describes many uses of prepositions as being caselike in nature (i.e., relationships among people and/or objects, not relationships dealing with space, time, degree, or manner, etc.). We have borrowed his cases and have added a few others that we feel are useful. (Note that a preposition may signal more than one case and that only highly frequent prepositions signal cases.) We do not claim that this list is an exhaustive one for English cases:

1. by (agentive)—It was done *by John.*
2. by (means)—We went there *by bus.*[4]
3. for (benefactive)—I bought the gift *for Mary.* (I bought Mary the gift.)
4. for (proxy)—He manages the store *for Mr. Smith.*
5. from (ablative, source)—Joe bought the car *from Bill.*
6. of (eliciting)—He asked a favor *of us.* (He asked us a favor.)
7. of (separation)—He robbed us *of our jewelry.* They cleared the field *of trash.*
8. to (dative)—I gave the book *to John.* (I gave John the book.)
9. to (direction, goal)—We drove *to Boston.*
10. with (instrument)—He broke the window *with a rock.*
11. with (comitative)—I went to town *with Jack.*
12. with (joining)—We presented him *with a gift.* The storm covered the mountain *with snow.*

In some types of sentences the order of cases is significant with respect to the prepositions that occur:

Unmarked Order: *Craig* planted *beans in his yard.* (=somewhere in his yard)
                   Agt   Theme   Loc

---

4. Note that *on foot* and *on horseback* are exceptions to *by bus, by car, by taxi, by train, by plane,* etc. Also, there are other prepositions such as *through* which also express means, e.g.:

She has accomplished a great deal through hard work. (i.e., by working hard)

Marked Order: *Craig* planted *his yard with beans.* (=all over his yard)
               Agt   Loc   Theme

Here the noun functioning as theme, i.e., *beans,* normally does not take a preposition; however, it does take *with* when a marked order of cases occurs. Likewise, the locative *in his yard* takes the preposition *in* when the normal order of cases is followed but does not when the marked order occurs. The following pair is another example of this phenomenon:

Unmarked Order: *Meg* took *the groceries out of the bag.* (=one by one, no rush implied)
               Agt   Theme   Loc
Marked Order: *Meg* emptied *the bag of groceries.* (=quickly, all at once)
               Agt   Loc   Theme

The verb may remain the same, e.g., *plant,* or it may change, e.g., *take out/empty;* the underlying cases of the nouns remain the same. However, the meaning of the sentence changes slightly. In each of the marked orders the action emphasizes the completeness of the theme with regard to the location—*with* signals that the theme completely covers the location and *of* separates the theme completely from the location. Thus, the ordering of these prepositional case functions must be taught to ESL/EFL students along with appropriate verbs and sentence types.

Reviewing semantically related case functions together

Frequently two or more case functions can usefully be reviewed in sets. Four examples of this technique follow:

1. Dative, benefactive, and eliciting—all may take indirect object movement:

        I gave the book to John. ⟶ I gave John the book.
        I bought the house for Mary. ⟶ I bought Mary the house.
        I asked a question of Alice. ⟶ I asked Alice a question.

2. Dative and ablative (there are often two related verbs of transfer: one dative and the other ablative; this is discussed at greater length in Gruber (1965)):

to (dative) *from* (ablative)

sell/buy	Native Germanic vocabulary (two forms)
give/take	Sam sold the car to Mary.
lend/borrow	Mary bought the car from Sam.
talk, write/hear	
rent/rent	French origin vocabulary (one form)
lease/lease	Mr. Bains leased the apartment to us.
	We leased the apartment from Mr. Bains.

3. Joining *with* and separating *of:*

        The cashier filled my bag *with groceries.*
        When I got home, I emptied the bag *of groceries.*

        verbs of joining (*with*): fill, cover, shower, anoint, etc.
        verbs of separating (*of*): empty, rob, strip, clear, etc.

4. Agentive and instrumental passives:

        The window was broken *by Jack.*   It was broken *with a rock.*
                     Agt   Inst

Other meanings of prepositions

In addition to case functions, other common meanings of prepositions relate in a variety of ways to the concepts of space, time, and degree. In order to illustrate this process, we have selected 20 common prepositions which exhibit space, time, degree, and other usages. Often the same semantic distinction is apparent in all three domains, e.g.:

> at = a specific point
> space: Meet me at 224 Park Avenue.
> time: Be there at 1 p.m.
> degree: Water boils at 100°C.

The following list—which classifies the meanings of 20 prepositions in terms of space, time, and degree—is not exhaustive. Also, you might find that you can fill in some of the blank spaces in our chart.

Prep.	Space	Time	Degree	Other (includes idiomatic usages)
at	*point/intersect:* meet at the corner	We met at 1:00.	Water freezes at 0°C.	
	target: Look at John./ Throw the stone at the wall.			He works at keeping in shape.
	general area: Meet me at the theater.	It rains at night there.		She's good at dancing.
about	*all around:* He ran about the yard.	*approx:* about 1:00	*approx:* about $1 about 70 degrees	*concerning:* a book about mathematics
above	*higher than:* above the picture (on the wall)		above $5 above freezing above average	above suspicion above reproach
against	*contact:* to lean against the wall	*conflict:* to work against the clock	*conflict:* two against four	*internal:* against one's will *external:* against all odds
around	*state:* The fence is around the house. *action:* The children run around the yard.	*approx:* around 1:00	*approx:* around $2 around 4 miles	
before	*in front of:* before the mast He stood before us.	*earlier than:* before 1960 before the accident		
below	*lower than:* below the surface		below zero below average	
between	*at an intermediate point in relation to two entities:* between the house and the street	between 1 and 2 o'clock	between 100 and 110 lbs.	between you and me
by	*nearness:* chair by the desk	*no later than:* by 5 p.m.	*reduplication* (gradual increase): little by little; inch by inch *degree of failure:* miss the target by a mile; miss the train by 3 minutes	*without help:* do by oneself

Prep.	Space	Time	Degree	Other (includes idiomatic usages)
for	*goal:* set out for Alaska *distance:* for 7 miles	*duration:* for 7 years	*exchange:* buy for $4	*reason:* California is famous for its wines. *goal/purpose:* fish for trout
from	*a starting point:* We traveled from N.Y. to L.A. *origin:* man from New York	work from 9 to 5	from 60 to 80 degrees from 5 to 7 dollars	*source:* paper is made from wood *cause:* wet from the rain
in	*enclosure:* The man is in the room.	*in a period:* WW II ended in 1945. *future appt.:* Come in 10 minutes.		*currency:* Pay me in dollars. *language:* Write, say it in English.
of	*names of geog. loc. or institutions:* the city of N.Y. the state of Texas the Univ. of Calif.	*before:* a quarter of ten	*fraction, portion:* one of the boys	*posses./assoc.:* a friend of mine *source:* a table made of wood
on	*contact:* on the wall *along:* on the Po; I live on this street.	*day, date:* on Sunday on Nov. 9th		*communication:* on the radio; on TV/the telly *concerning:* a book on magic; a lecture on modern art
over	*state of being above* (with or without contact): carry a sweater over his shoulder; the roof over our heads *action above:* jump over the fence	*spanning time:* over the weekend	*more than:* over an hour over $2 over 0°C	*communication:* over the radio, TV
through	*penetrate:* through the window; through the forest	*duration:* through the years		*endurance:* through thick and thin
to	*direction:* go to the movies	*until:* work from 9 to 5 *before:* a quarter to eleven	He is wise to that extent./He is wise to such an extent that …	*accompany:* dance to the music
toward(s)	*in the direction of:* walk toward the wall	toward morning	the temperature moved steadily toward 0°C	toward a lasting peace
under	*below* (state): be under the house *below* (action): crawl under the house	*less than:* in under an hour	under $1 under 10 men under 70 degrees	*condition:* under duress (stress)
with	*alongside, near:* even with the wall	*together:* He grew wiser with the years. He rises with the chickens.	*equal standing or ability:* rank with the best; run with the fastest	*in regard to:* pleased with the gift *manner:* spoke with ease

The above list is only a partial systematization of prepositions and their noncase meanings. An unabridged dictionary will provide you with many other definitions for each preposition listed above.

An example of a tighter systematization for a more limited set of prepositions is Quirk and Greenbaum's matrix for prepositions of position and direction (1973:146), which we have modified and simplified as follows:

	Positive Direction	*Position*	*Negative Direction*
point	to	at	(away) from
	———→X	⟨X	X——→
line or surface	on (to)	on	off (of)
area or volume	in (to)	in	out of

Such visual symbols, when used to reinforce semantic concepts, can be very effective in teaching prepositions.

Frequent sources of error

There are several groups of prepositions that are frequently confused by learners. The ESL/EFL teacher must be aware of these and be ready to provide learning activities that will help distinguish them.

1. Spatial meanings of *in, on, at:*

   John is standing on the sidewalk. (two-dimensional)

   John is in the house. (three-dimensional)

   John is at the corner. (one-dimensional: point/intersection)

   John is at the door/window. (in the general area)

2. Temporal meanings of *in, on, at:*

   It happened in 1960. (for months, seasons, years, and periods of the day—includes *the morning, evening, afternoon*)

   It happened on Dec. 10. (for dates and days of the week)

   It happened at 9:15. (for times of the day—includes *noon, midnight, night, dawn, dusk, sunrise,* and *sunset*)

3. Source meanings of *from* and *(out) of:*

   Paper is made from wood. (source not visibly obvious)

   This table is made (out) of wood. (source visibly obvious)

4. Use of *by, with, at* and some idiosyncratic prepositions following the passive participle:

   Regular: John was hit by Jack. (regular passive with agent expressed)

The hill was covered with flowers. (verb of joining without an agent, i.e., a stative passive)

I was surprised at the news. (like emotive adjectives—e.g., Joe was mad at us.)

Idiosyncratic: He was interested in my research.

5. Temporal use of *in/within* (note the contrast):

Come back in 30 minutes. (30 minutes from now)   Come back within 30 minutes. (between now and 30 minutes from now)

6. *Since/for* to express spans of time:

I have lived here since 1960. (refers to beginning of span)   I have lived here for 16 years. (refers to duration of span)

Variation in the use of prepositions

There are many cases where more than one preposition is acceptable in a given context. The ESL/EFL teacher (and ultimately the learner) must be aware of these cases. In the initial stages the more frequently used preposition or the usage prevalent in the area where the student is studying should be presented and practiced. Later the variation(s) can be introduced and emphasized receptively rather than productively.

1. spatial proximity: a house (by/near) the lake
2. time/degree approximation: happened (around/about) 10 o'clock; costs (around/about) $100
3. telling time: a quarter (to/of) ten
4. telling time: a quarter (after/past) ten
5. location along something linear: the towns (on/along) the Rhine
6. in time period: It happened (in/during) 1964.
7. temporal termination: work from 9 (to/until) 5.
8. location lower than something: (below/beneath/under) the stairs
9. location higher than something: (above/over) the table

Prepositional phrases that function like clauses

Some prepositional phrases can be best paraphrased by relating them to clauses:

1. *with:* The man with a red jacket/The man who has a red jacket
2. *without:* There are many married couples without children/who have no children.
3. *of:* He is a man of courage/a man who has courage.
4. *because of:* We stayed home because of the weather./We stayed home because the weather was (?bad).
5. *for:* He'll do anything for money./He'll do anything (in order) to get money./He'll do anything so that he gets money.
6. *by:* I enjoy { novels by Tolstoy/novels that are written by Tolstoy.
                    { paintings by Degas/paintings that are done by Degas.
7. *with:* I went to town with John./John went to town, and I accompanied him.

Conclusion

It may be more obvious now that you've read the chapter why prepositions cause such difficulty for ESL/EFL students. Nonetheless, there is some systematicity in the use of English prepositions which we have tried to show you in this chapter. Calling attention to it will doubtless lighten the burden for your students as they strive to master the use of English prepositions. Keep in mind that the problems learners have with prepositions are of three types:

1. Using the wrong preposition, e.g.:

    *My grandfather picked the name *on* me. (for)

2. Omitting a required preposition, e.g.:

    *I served the Army until 1964. (in)

3. Using a superfluous preposition, e.g.:

    *I studied (in) Biology for three years.

TEACHING SUGGESTIONS

Preliminaries:

Not all prepositional meanings are equally important for all subject matter. Do a survey to see which ones your students need most. Teach the most concrete meaning of a preposition first— usually the spatial meaning (if there is one) or a case function.

1   Use visual symbols whenever possible such as the Quirk and Greenbaum matrix symbols presented earlier—or symbols such as the following:

The circle is around the dot.
The dot is inside the circle.

The triangle is above the circle.

The square is below the circle.

The circle is between the triangle and the square.

2   Teach using contrasts in context using real objects or pictures: locative *in* vs. *on; through* vs. *on,* etc., e.g.:

The coin is in the box.

The coin is on the box.

He walked on the grass (i.e., a lawn).

He walked $\begin{Bmatrix} in \\ through \end{Bmatrix}$ the tall grass (i.e., in a field).

3 Teach and test prepositions using a modified cloze technique.

      I met John (1) _____ the corner of Fifth Avenue and 48th Street (2) _____ 9:30. He had come (3) _____ foot, whereas I had come (4) _____ subway. We both wanted to buy books (5) _____ New York. One bookstore had news of a sale painted (6) _____ the front window. We decided to go (7) _____ that bookstore.

4 Teach a whole set of related prepositions simultaneously (e.g., prepositions of direction) using a situational, game approach. This was first suggested to us by Nancy Chin.

Material: a large chart or map with the following objects and locations represented in a line or circle:

school	parking lot	bridge
street	supermarket	corner
lamppost	street	home
mailbox		

The relationship of the person's movement with respect to these objects is marked with arrows.

      When John gets *out of* school, he goes *across* the street, *under* the lamppost, *past* the mailbox, *through* the parking lot, *into* the supermarket, *out of* the supermarket, *along* the next street, *over* the bridge, *around* the corner, and then he's *(at)* home.

(Practice with first person and third person plural too.)

5 Have students practice the specific-to-general or general-to-specific sequences typically signaled by *at-on-in* in English for addresses and dates:

——————— AT ——— ON ——————————————— IN ———————

Most   Most
specific   general

a. I live at 825 Westwood Blvd.—most specific
    I live on Westwood Blvd.[5]
    I live in Westwood.
    I live in Los Angeles.   } progressively more general
    I live in California.
    I live in the United States.

b. Our daughter was born at 6:30 a.m.—most specific
    Our daughter was born on (a) Friday.
    Our daughter was born on October 27, (1972).
    Our daughter was born in the morning.
    Our daughter was born in October.   } progressively more general
    Our daughter was born in 1972.
    Our daughter was born in the '70s.

---

5. In British usage *in Westwood Blvd.* is also possible.

EXERCISES

Test your understanding of what has been presented

1. Provide an original sentence that illustrates each of the following terms. Underline the relevant word(s) in your examples.

instrumental case
"means" case
ablative case
double preposition
deletable preposition
   optional
   obligatory

preposition co-occurring with an adjective
preposition variation (i.e., synonyms)
co-occurring nonadjacent prepositions

2. Explain the ungrammaticality of the following sentences:

a. *You can rely John.
b. *In case someone phones, I'll be back by 15 minutes.
c. *He is interested by good books.

Test your ability to apply what you know

3. If your students produce the following sentences, what errors have they made? How will you make them aware of the errors, and what exercises will you prepare to correct the errors?

a. *John lives on 120 Main Street.
b. *I have lived here since two years.
c. *We discussed about the weather.
d. *We have some problems in our English.

4. How would you make an ESL/EFL student aware that the prepositions in the following sentences are ungrammatical? How would you get him or her to not use the preposition?

*After my evening class I went to home.
*I approached to the apartment quietly so as not to disturb my roommate.

5. How would you make an ESL/EFL student aware that the prepositions in the following sentences are optionally deletable and that the sentence sounds more colloquial without the preposition?

(For) how long have you been a teacher?   I'm going to the beach (on) Sunday.

6. Describe two prepositions other than the 20 listed in the large chart in this chapter that have multiple senses (space, time, degree, other) and do not express case functions.

BIBLIOGRAPHY

References

Covitt, R. (1976). "Some Problematic Grammar Areas for ESL Teachers." M.A. thesis in TESL, UCLA.
Crowell, T. L. (1960). *A Glossary of Phrases with Prepositions.* Englewood Cliffs, N.J.: Prentice-Hall.

Fillmore, C. J. (1968). "The Case for Case," in E. Bach and R. Harms (eds.), *Universals in Linguistic Theory.*
New York: Holt, Rinehart and Winston.

Gruber, J. (1965). "Studies in Lexical Relations." Ph.D. dissertation in Linguistics, MIT. (Has been duplicated
by the Indiana University Linguistics Club, Bloomington, Ind.)

Hudson, J. K. (1979). "Towards a Systematization of the Idiom List: A Sample Method with *AT.*" M.A. thesis in
TESL, UCLA.

Quirk, R., and S. Greenbaum (1973). *A Concise Grammar of Contemporary English.* New York: Harcourt Brace
Jovanovich.

Suggestions for further reading

For reference grammars with a good discussion of prepositions, see these texts:

Close, R. A. (1981). *English as a Foreign Language* (3d ed.). London: Allen and Unwin.

Frank, M. (1972). *Modern English—A Practical Reference Guide.* Englewood Cliffs, N.J.: Prentice-Hall.

Quirk, R., and S. Greenbaum (1973). Cited in above references.

For exercise books dealing primarily with prepositions, see the following:

Heaton, J. B. (1965). *Prepositions and Adverbial Particles.* London: Longmans, Green & Co.

Hill, L. A. (1968). *Prepositions and Adverbial Particles.* London: Oxford University Press.

Pittman, G. A. (1966). *Activating the Use of Prepositions.* London: Longmans, Green & Co.

For general textbooks that contain some good exercises for teaching prepositions, consult
the following:

Hayden, R., D. Pilgrim, and A. Haggard (1956). *Mastering American English.* Englewood Cliffs, N.J.: Prentice-
Hall.

Millington-Ward, John (1965). *Peculiarities in English Grammar.* London: Longman.

Wishon, G. E., and J. M. Burks (1968). *Let's Write English* (Book 1). New York: American Book Co.

20

Phrasal Verbs

GRAMMATICAL DESCRIPTION

Introduction

Traditional grammarians define a phrasal verb as a verb followed by a particle (variously described as a preposition, an adverb, or some combination of the two), e.g.:

I *got up* at 6 a.m. (*arose*) He *put off* the meeting. (*postponed*)
I will *look into* that. (*investigate*)

From the verb paraphrases given in the parentheses, you can see that the verb and particle seem to function like a single verb in each of these sentences. In this chapter we will view these particles as being similar to though not identical to prepositions,[1] and we will call them particles, i.e., a new part of speech distinct from adverbs or prepositions.

Why phrasal verbs are a problem

There are very few non-Germanic[2] languages that have phrasal verbs. Thus most ESL/EFL students will find such verbs strange and difficult. Yet they are such an important part of colloquial English that no one can speak or understand conversational or informal English easily without a knowledge of phrasal verbs. Some nonnative speakers have a tendency to overuse single lexical items in informal contexts where a phrasal verb would be much more appropriate, e.g.:

Question: Do you need an ashtray?
a. Answer: Yes, I want to *extinguish* my cigarette.
b. Answer: Yes, I want to *put out* my cigarette.

Response *a* sounds pedantic and awkward to native speakers since the single lexical item is formal and the context is informal. The phrasal verb equivalent given in *b* would thus be much more appropriate.

---

1. Many of the most frequent prepositions do not function as particles in phrasal verbs: *at, for, from,* and *with* never do, and *to* does only rarely (e.g., *come to* = regain consciousness).
2. The Germanic languages include English, German, Dutch, and the Scandinavian languages.

Certain particles such as *up, down, on, off,* and *back* can readily form phrasal verbs by combining with common verbs such as *be, come, go, do, make,* and *give.* Phrasal verbs are a highly productive lexical category in English; however, we have no way of knowing in advance exactly which verb will join with which particle to form a new phrasal verb. Furthermore, there is also a certain unpredictability as to what the meaning of a new phrasal verb will be since so many of them are used idiomatically.

A final learning problem involves the optional or obligatory separation of the verb and the particle depending on a number of factors, e.g.:

> Turn out the lights. }
> Turn the lights out. } Separation optional (direct object is not a pronoun)
>
> Turn them out. }
> *Turn out them. } Separation necessary (direct object is a pronoun)

We will be discussing this in greater detail below.

Lexical features of phrasal verbs

Like verbs consisting of a single word, phrasal verbs are transitive or intransitive:

Transitive phrasal verbs

> Harold *turned on* the radio.   Bibi *came across* a new recipe for fudge.
> I *called off* the meeting.

Others: do over (repeat), look over (examine), fill out (complete), find out (discover), etc.

Like regular transitive verbs, there are also some transitive phrasal verbs that on the surface sometimes appear to be intransitive:[3]

> Jacob got off at 42nd Street.

However, in sentences such as this one, some object NP such as *bus, trolley,* or *train* is implied even though it is not overtly expressed. In all such cases, the phrasal verb is consistently transitive, but it allows the object NP to be omitted when the information in the object is not important or is understood from the context.

Intransitive phrasal verbs

My car *broke down.*   Why don't you *come in*?
The boys were *playing around* in the yard.

Others: come back (return), come over (visit), come to (regain consciousness), pass out (faint), etc.

Of course, just as some regular change-of-state verbs (e.g., *open, close, increase, decrease*) may be both transitive and intransitive, there are some phrasal verbs that can have this dual function too, e.g.:

An arsonist *burned down* the hotel. (tran-   The hotel *burned down.* (intransitive)
    sitive)

---

3. Sometimes a transitive phrasal verb can be used intransitively with another meaning, e.g.:

Harold *turned on* to punk rock. (was strongly   Bibi really *came across* well. (made a good
    attracted by)   impression)

It is best to consider such homophonous items as two different phrasal verbs with two separate lexical entries.

Phrasal verbs that require prepositions

Like verbs and adjectives, many phrasal verbs always take a specific preposition. Examples of this type of phrasal verb plus preposition construction are:

put up with	get along with	cut down on	close in on
look in on	check up on	catch up with	make away with
look down on	check out of	stand up for	break up with
get away with	go in for	keep up with	drop in on
get down to	come up with	end up with	etc.
get back to	give in to	pick up on	

In these expressions the phrasal verb and preposition must be learned as a unit. Furthermore, in such cases, there is no separation (i.e., there cannot be a noun phrase between the verb and the particle or the particle and the preposition):[4]

$$\text{Gordon gets away with } \left\{ \begin{array}{l} \text{murder} \\ \text{it} \end{array} \right\} \text{ all the time.}$$

$$\text{*Gordon gets } \left\{ \begin{array}{l} \text{murder} \\ \text{it} \end{array} \right\} \text{ away with all the time.}$$

$$\text{*Gordon gets away } \left\{ \begin{array}{l} \text{murder} \\ \text{it} \end{array} \right\} \text{ with all the time.}$$

The only thing that can be added to such a string is an adverb (or adverbial phrase) between the particle and the preposition:

I haven't kept up fully with the work.
Mort has cut down almost completely on his smoking.

Thus far we have been discussing characteristics that phrasal verbs share with regular verbs; however, there is one syntactic distinction peculiar to phrasal verbs, which is that it is important to determine whether the particle of the phrasal verb is separable or inseparable. If the particle is separable, separation is obligatory when the direct object is a pronoun. If the particle is inseparable, there is no separation of the verb and particle under any circumstances.

Separable phrasal verbs

Bill threw away the ball.	*Bill threw away it.
Bill threw the ball away.	Bill threw it away.
He looked up the information.	*He looked up it.
He looked the information up.	He looked it up.

Others: take up (discuss), leave out (omit), pass out (distribute), give up (surrender), etc.

---

4. Although the overwhelming majority of phrasal verbs taking prepositions are of the intransitive, inseparable type we discuss here, we would be remiss in not pointing out that there are a few idiomatic transitive phrasal verbs that may take prepositions. In these cases a direct object intervenes between the verb and the particle, e.g.:

$$\text{She put } \left\{ \begin{array}{l} \text{it} \\ \text{the disguise} \end{array} \right\} \text{ over on him. (= She deceived/fooled him.)}$$

$$\text{I'll make } \left\{ \begin{array}{l} \text{it} \\ \text{the favor} \end{array} \right\} \text{ up to you. (= I'll return the favor/good deed.)}$$

Inseparable phrasal verbs

I came across an interesting article.	I came across it (last night).
*I came an interesting article across.	*I came it across (last night).
John ran into an old friend.	John ran into him.
*John ran an old friend into.	*John ran him into.

Others: get over (recover), go over (review), look into (investigate), etc.

To our knowledge there is no general rule or principle that would help us determine a priori which phrasal verbs are separable and which are inseparable. Thus, the question of separability or inseparability becomes one of the many lexical features that must be specified for phrasal verbs.

The largest, most productive category of phrasal verbs are the transitive separable ones where the particle may be separated from its verb if the direct object is a noun and must be separated from its verb if the direct object is a pronoun. However, as we have shown above, there are also a number of important inseparable phrasal verbs which should not be ignored in the ESL/EFL classroom.

Phrasal verbs that are always separated

There are a few separable phrasal verbs that seem to occur only with the verb and particle separated, e.g.:

$$\text{How can I get} \quad \left\{ \begin{array}{l} \text{the message} \\ \text{it} \end{array} \right\} \quad \text{through to him?}$$

*How can I get through the message to him?

$$\text{We'll see} \quad \left\{ \begin{array}{l} \text{this ordeal} \\ \text{it} \end{array} \right\} \quad \text{through together.}$$

*We'll see through this ordeal together.

The reason for the obligatory separation is presumably to avoid the ambiguity with the inseparable phrasal verbs that have the same form but a different meaning:

get through the lesson (finish)
see through his disguise (not be deceived by)

Such phrasal verbs are a small subcategory of separable phrasal verbs. Their lexical entries would have to indicate that particle movement is obligatory.

Lexical entries for phrasal verbs

In addition to specifying the verb, the particle, and the meaning of a phrasal verb, we have seen that the lexical entry of a phrasal verb must contain a great deal of syntactic information that answers questions such as the following:

1. Is the phrasal verb transitive or intransitive or both (i.e., change-of-state)? If transitive, can the object be omitted given sufficient context?
2. Is the particle separable or inseparable; if separable, is separation obligatory even without a pronoun object?
3. Does the phrasal verb take a preposition? If so, which preposition?

Distinguishing phrasal verbs from verb-plus-preposition sequences

One of the tests that can be used to distinguish a phrasal verb from a verb-plus-preposition sequence is movement of the particle or preposition in question to the front of a wh-question. If the movement transformation is acceptable, the form in question is probably a preposition.

For example, *look at* is a verb-plus-preposition combination:

Sara looked at the picture.   wh-question: At what did Sara look?

Although such a wh-question is often formal and may sound stilted, the preposition can be separated from its verb. A particle, on the other hand, cannot be separated from its verb in the same way. Consider the following example in which *make up* is a separable phrasal verb:

Phillip made $\begin{Bmatrix} \text{up the incident} \\ \text{it up} \end{Bmatrix}$.   wh-question: *Up what did Phillip make?

Another test for distinguishing the two forms is to see if the preposition or particle can be fronted in a relative clause (see Chapters 26 and 27). Such fronting is possible in verb-plus-preposition combinations:

The picture at which Sara looked reminded her of her childhood home.

Again, a rather formal structure results, but at least it is grammatical. This is not the case when the particle of a separable phrasal verb is fronted in a relative clause:

*The incident up which Phillip made was not true.[5]

A final test involves placing an adverb between the verb and the preposition or particle. With a verb-plus-preposition sequence the intervention of an adverbial is possible:

Sara looked quickly at the picture.

However, with a separable phrasal verb such intervention produces an ungrammatical sentence:

*Phillip made quickly up the incident.

A potential problem with this test is that there is some disagreement as to whether or not inseparable phrasal verbs permit an adverb between the verb and the particle. Many English speakers will not accept sentences such as the following, but some speakers will:

?He got quickly over his cold.
?I came suddenly across an interesting article.

At the very least, the above examples with inseparable particles are less acceptable than those with verb-plus-preposition combinations, and they are not as convincingly ungrammatical to all native speakers as are examples with phrasal verbs that have separable particles.

Thus, the two most reliable tests for distinguishing between phrasal verbs and verbs plus prepositions involve fronting of the particle or preposition in wh-questions and fronting of the same element in a relative clause.

Another thing we should mention is that some grammarians do not distinguish between verb-plus-preposition sequences and inseparable phrasal verbs; however, we feel that this is a mistake, since the two most reliable tests we have for identifying phrasal verbs, i.e., (1) unacceptable fronting in wh-questions and (2) unacceptable fronting in relative clauses, clearly identify the inseparable verb + particle combinations listed above as phrasal verbs in

---

5. This test recalls the famous example attributed to Winston Churchill, who replied to the critic who had admonished him not to end a sentence with a preposition by saying, "This is nonsense up with which I will not put." In this example, the phrasal verb with an obligatory preposition is "put up with." Since the preposition *with*—but not the particle *up*—may be separated from the verb in a relative clause, two grammatical paraphrases are available for Churchill's deliberately ungrammatical utterance:

This is nonsense which I will not put up with.   This is nonsense with which I will not put up.

spite of the fact that the particle does not separate from the verb and follow the direct object, e.g.:

What did you come across? This is the book which I just came across.
*Across what did you come? *This is the book across which I just came.
Who(m) did you run into? John is an old friend that I ran into yesterday.
*Into whom did you run?[6] *John is the old friend into whom I ran yesterday.

Verb + preposition combinations can, of course, undergo these fronting operations easily:

Bill is looking for his brother.   His brother is the one for whom Bill is
For whom is Bill looking?   looking.

A syntactic analysis of phrasal verbs

The analysis that we have been suggesting for phrasal verbs requires some minor changes in our phrase structure rules. In order to introduce particles (Prt) as a new part of speech, we need a new grammatical category that will allow us to generate phrasal verbs as well as regular verbs. To accomplish this the category "phrasal verb" (PV) is introduced as an alternative to "verb" (V) in the rule for expanding the verb phrase:

$$VP \longrightarrow \left\{ \begin{array}{l} BE \left\{ \begin{array}{l} NP \\ AP \\ PP \end{array} \right\} \\ \left\{ \begin{array}{l} V \\ PV \end{array} \right\} \; (NP) \; (PP) \end{array} \right\}$$

The new PV category is then expanded with an additional phrase structure rule as follows:

$$PV \longrightarrow V \; Prt$$

Thus the basic structure of a sentence such as *John turned off the light* would be:

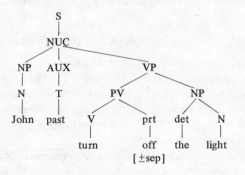

One application of the affix attachment rule followed by morphological rules would account for the derivation of this sentence; however, we know that the particle can also be separated from the verb (i.e., *John turned the light off*). How would this second sentence be derived using the same basic structure shown above? In order to derive the second sentence, we need a

---

6. This sentence is acceptable only if the meaning changes from "meet by chance"—which is the phrasal verb—to "physical contact/collision"—which is the homophonous verb-plus-preposition sequence.

transformational rule for particle movement. The following conditions apply to this rule:

1. The rule is optional if:
    a. The phrasal verb is transitive and has an overt direct object.
    b. The particle is separable and the object NP is not a pronoun.
2. The rule is obligatory if:
    a. The particle is separable and the object NP is a personal pronoun.
    b. The phrasal verb is marked for obligatory particle separation, e.g., *get . . . through* and *see . . . through.*
3. The rule does *not* apply if:
    a. The phrasal verb is intransitive.
    b. The particle is inseparable.

Given this particle movement rule, we can now derive *John turned the light off* from the above basic structure.

Output of base: John past turn off the light
Particle movement: John past turn the light off
Affix attachment (1✕): John turn + past the light off
Morphological rules: John turned the light off.

A similar tree diagram and derivation would be used to account for *John turned it off.* The pronoun *it* would simply replace the noun phrase *the light* as the object NP in the tree diagram.

What would the basic structure of a sentence with a phrasal verb plus a preposition look like? For example:

Aloysius looks down on your brother.

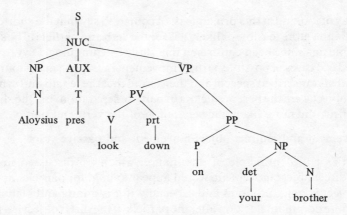

In this case the particle is inseparable because the phrasal verb is followed by an obligatory prepositional phrase. The rules of affix attachment and subject-verb agreement plus appropriate morphological rules will account for this sentence.

When verb and particle tend to be separated and vice versa

Since there are many cases where the verb and particle of a phrasal verb can be either together or separated, this makes many advanced ESL/EFL students ask when they should say *George turned off the light* as opposed to *George turned the light off.* Bolinger (1971) hypothesizes that the verb and particle are split when the information in the object noun phrase is old information, i.e., has already been mentioned or established as part of the discourse, and that this old information is often pronominalized:

$$\text{George turned} \quad \left\{ \begin{array}{l} \text{the light} \\ \text{it} \end{array} \right\} \quad \text{off.}$$

The other side of Bolinger's hypothesis is that the verb and particle are not split when the object contains new information:

George turned off the light.

This hypothesis is interesting; however, Ulm (1975) has carried out studies in an attempt to empirically verify Bolinger's hypothesis, and the results were not very successful. It appears that there are many interacting factors that limit Bolinger's hypothesis such as those separable verbs that always occur split; and—as Ulm discovered—the many theoretically separable verbs which in actual usage are seldom split unless the object is pronominal. We feel, however, that the following principle, which did come out of Ulm's work, is currently a useful usage principle to present to ESL/EFL students:

Principle: If the direct object is long (phonologically multisyllabic and/or grammatically complex), the particle should occur next to the verb.

Example: ?The President called the Under Secretary of the Interior up.
The President called up the Under Secretary of the Interior.
*/?When are we going to take the agenda item we postponed last Wednesday up?
When are we going to take up the agenda item we postponed last Wednesday?

The other way of looking at this principle is, of course, to say that the shorter and simpler the direct object is, the more feasible or likely it is for the verb and particle to be split. In fact, Ulm's usage principle has since been confirmed in a study by Cumming, Dwyer, and Snow (1982); they analyzed 650 cases of possible particle movement in English using four different corpora that consisted of transcribed speech, and they found that the length and syntactic complexity of the direct object were the best predictors of particle separation; i.e., the shorter and simpler the direct object, the more likely the separation of the verb and particle.

Particle movement and indirect object movement and passive voice

Erteschik-Shir's (1979) principle of dominance, which we discussed in Chapter 18 with respect to indirect object movement, would appear to hold for particle movement as well. If the direct object is not a pronoun and especially if it is a long and elaborate NP, it would occupy the more dominant position after the particle. If the direct object is a pronoun, it would likely be nondominant and would therefore naturally occur before the particle. Erteschik-Shir (1979) also discusses sentences where both particle movement and indirect object movement can apply. Consider the following sentence:

John paid back his loan to the bank.

If the particle movement transformation applied to this sentence, we would get:

John paid his loan back to the bank.

Here, as in the first sentence, the indirect object would be interpreted as being dominant. The particle movement transformation actually reinforces the dominance by separating the direct object from the indirect object, and thus the second sentence seems preferable to the first to most native speakers.

If, on the other hand, both indirect object movement and particle movement were applied to the same sentence, we would derive a sentence where the direct object was given dominance:

> John paid the bank back his loan.

This sounds more acceptable than the following sentence, where lack of particle movement makes the indirect object appear more dominant, thus detracting from the dominance of the direct object. It would also be in conflict with the fact that indirect movement had applied to decrease the dominance of the indirect object:

> ?John paid back the bank his loan.

Note that after movement the indirect object can occupy a position between the verb and the particle just as the particle movement transformation allows the direct object to do. If both transformations were applied, first the indirect object movement transformation and then the particle movement transformation—but this time the particle moved around both the direct and the indirect object—then we would get:

> John paid the bank his loan back.

where "his loan" is still more dominant than "the bank." However, in this sentence "his loan" is less dominant than it is in "John paid the bank back his loan."

Phrasal verbs, of course, can also occur in the passive as well as the active voice, e.g.:

> Active: Jack threw the ball away.
> Passive: The ball was thrown away (by Jack).

Note that the particle does not move in cases where the optional agent is retained, e.g.:

> *The ball was thrown by Jack away.

The situation is somewhat different, however, if we have sentences with both a direct object and an indirect object. In many of these cases, we have two possible passive sentences, e.g.:

> The bank was paid back the loan (by   The loan was paid back (to the bank)
> John).   (by John).

If the indirect object is the subject of the passive, the direct object can be made less dominant by particle movement, e.g.:

> The bank was paid the loan back (by John).

As we have already demonstrated, the particle does not move around the agent. This is true even if the direct object can be deleted, e.g.:

> *The bank was paid (the loan) by John back.

However, in those cases where the direct object is the subject of a passive sentence, no particle movement is possible, e.g.:

> *The loan was paid to the bank back (by   *The loan was paid (to the bank) by John
> John).   back.

Semantic distinctions

Fraser (1976) and others have pointed out that phrasal verbs exhibit interesting semantic differences. Fraser, for example, divides them into three groups.

Literal phrasal verbs

Literal phrasal verbs are those items where the particle retains its literal adverbial meaning as the *up* does in the following example:

$$\text{I hung} \quad \left\{ \begin{array}{l} \text{up the pictures} \\ \text{the pictures up} \end{array} \right\} \quad \text{on the wall.}$$

Some other examples of literal phrasal verbs are: *sit down, dish out, hand out,* and *take down.* These phrasal verbs are among the easiest for nonnative speakers to understand and acquire.

Completive phrasal verbs

Completive phrasal verbs are those where the particle indicates completed action. The particles *up, out, off,* and *down* all seem to be used this way; however, *up* is the one most frequently used in this function.

$$\text{I tore} \quad \left\{ \begin{array}{l} \text{up the piece of paper} \\ \text{the piece of paper up} \end{array} \right\} .$$

Some other completive phrasal verbs are: *mix up, wind up, wear out, fade out, burn down, run down, cut off, turn off,* etc.

Figurative phrasal verbs

Phrasal verbs are considered "figurative" when there is no systematic way of semantically associating the verb and the particle. This is true of the following example:

$$\text{She looked} \quad \left\{ \begin{array}{l} \text{up the information} \\ \text{the information up} \end{array} \right\} .$$

Some other figurative phrasal verbs are *turn up* (arrive, appear), *catch on* (understand), *give in* (surrender), *look over* (review), etc. Such phrasal verbs are the most difficult ones for ESL/EFL students to master.

Fraser also points out that in literal and completive uses of phrasal verbs, the particle may often be deleted without affecting the acceptability of the sentence, whereas in figurative uses the result is usually an unacceptable sentence:

Literal:
I hung the picture up on the wall.   I hung the picture on the wall.

Completive:
I tore up the piece of paper.   I tore the piece of paper.

Figurative:
She looked up the information.   *She looked the information.

When one tries to classify a large number of phrasal verbs according to Fraser's criteria, problems can emerge. For example, is *write up* completive or figurative? Is *throw out* figurative or literal or both—depending on the context? Problem cases aside, we still feel that such a semantic taxonomy is a valuable starting point for both analytical and pedagogical purposes.

Concluding remarks

In order to teach phrasal verbs more effectively, we need to know which ones occur most frequently and in what contexts. There are teaching materials that deal with phrasal verbs, but the items have been selected subjectively and intuitively. A more scientific basis for selection and presentation is needed. Also, a more extended examination of separable phrasal verbs occurring spontaneously in spoken and written discourse might uncover better guidelines for when the verb and particle should be split and when they should remain adjacent.

TEACHING SUGGESTIONS

1   Use dialog drills or short narratives centered around a common theme, e.g., *clothes* (put on, take off, wear out, try on, pick out):

John:	This shirt is all worn out. What can I wear?
Mother:	Try this shirt on. It's new.
John:	O.K. I'll put it on, but if it doesn't match my jacket, I'll have to take it off and pick out something else.

or *telephone* (call up someone, pick up the receiver, hang up the receiver):

I decided to call up Judy. I picked up the receiver, dialed her number, and waited. No one answered, so I hung up.

Keep repeating these with a Stevick-type Cummings device, which means that a question in the dialog is presented along with a number of alternative answers or rejoinders. Alternative forms of the question itself could be presented, e.g.:

John:	This shirt is all worn out. What should I do?
Mother:	Take it off and try on this one.
	Etc.

2   In paragraphs or passages unified by a theme have students substitute phrasal verbs for more lexically complex vocabulary items, e.g.:

When you finish a picnic, there are several things you should remember to do. Be sure to (1) _____ the picnic area you have been using, to (2) _____ the fire
        (neatly rearrange)   (extinguish)
before you (3) _____ all your belongings and (4) _____ .
        (gather and arrange in vehicle)   (depart in vehicle)

[Possible answers: (1) clean up, straighten up, or tidy up; (2) put out; (3) pack up; (4) drive off]

3   Develop an early sense of separable vs. inseparable phrasal verbs in students. Cindy Stafford uses a special notation and flashcards as learning aids.

inseparable	separable
come + across	put . . . away

Use short object noun phrases or pronoun objects in simple sentences and ask the students to split where possible or necessary, e.g.:

1. Look at this book. I _____ in the library.
   (it, came across)
2. Take this wrench and (a) _____ in the toolroom. Then (b) _____
   (it, put away)   (the hammer, put away)
   too.

4 Develop a feeling for the particle movement rule:

a. When it can apply and when it must apply:
   I put the dishes away. ←——→ I put away the dishes.
   I put them away. ←—— *I put away them.

b. When it's better not to move the particle:
   *I put the dishes we used for the picnic we had last week away. ——→ I put away the dishes we used for the picnic we had last week.

5 Writing: Danielson and Hayden (1973:167–168) group phrasal verbs into situations. Using these, get students to write informal dialogs, narratives, or letters using some or all of the phrasal verbs belonging to a given list (i.e., a semantically related list as in 1 above).

6 Susan Ulm (1975) suggests that you teach a unit on phrasal verbs with the same particle fulfilling the same function, e.g., *up* to signal completion with the following phrasal verbs of "total consumption": eat up, drink up, buy up, burn up, use up, etc.

7 If appropriate, expose your students to the use of phrasal verbs and similar types of lexical items in highly colloquial, slang expressions. Present some of these phrasal verbs in a way that facilitates understanding, e.g., the generally positive meaning of the preposition *on* and the generally negative meaning of the preposition *off* in expressions such as the following:

on	*off*
turn (someone) on	turn (someone) off
"arouse interest, attraction"	"repulsion, uninteresting"
be on to something	be off the track
"have the right start, the right idea"	"have the wrong approach, to be irrelevant"
right on!	
"that's good, I agree"	buzz off!
	"go away"

Using these phrasal verbs in narrative dialogs to bring out the meanings in context is helpful.

OFF—Whenever we have interesting discussions in class, Marvin asks questions that are really off the track. He turns me off. If I were the teacher, I'd tell him to buzz off because we'd have a better class without him.

ON—*Jim:*   I think I'm on to something. Do you like Flo?
Harry: Yeah. She really turns me on.
Jim: I'll try to fix you up with her.
Harry: Right on!

8 Judy Banks suggests using magazine ads—the pictures and the scripts—to teach phrasal verbs. Here are some examples of the type of materials she has used:

Picture	Script	Meaning of PV	Extension and Practice
a. a stack of six packs of low-tar brand cigarettes with NOW on the bottom	How does NOW stack up? At the bottom. The lowest in tar of all brands.	How does X rate? What's your opinion of X?	How does that new $\left\{\begin{array}{l}\text{movie}\\\text{restaurant}\\\text{teacher}\end{array}\right\}$ stack up?
b. sketch of an overweight person (backside)	Leave your fat behind. The Body Wrap from X Body Salon.	Get rid of X.	Leave your $\left\{\begin{array}{l}\text{worries}\\\text{cares}\\\text{problems}\end{array}\right\}$ behind.

EXERCISES

Test your understanding of what has been presented

1. Provide original example sentences to illustrate the following terms. Underline the pertinent word(s) in your examples.

verb plus preposition
separable phrasal verb
inseparable phrasal verb
intransitive phrasal verb
transitive phrasal verb
phrasal verb plus preposition
literal phrasal verb

completive phrasal verb
figurative phrasal verb
particle movement
   in the active voice
   in a passive sentence with an indirect
     object as subject

2. Give tree diagrams and derivations for the following sentences:

a. John warmed the soup up.
b. The man walked up the street.
c. The child ate it up.

d. I came across that book in the library.
e. Anne puts up with murder.   ·

3. Explain why the following sentences are ungrammatical or at best highly awkward.

a. *We called our neighbors on.
b. *I looked the report that John wrote in Dallas last week over.

c. *The lawyer ran his client into.
d. *I gave back him the money.

Test your ability to apply what you know

4. If your students produce the following sentences, what errors have they made? How will you make them aware of the errors, and what exercises will you prepare to correct the errors?

a. *The boys put away them.
b. *Will you place on the light?

c. *After two hours the candle had burned off.

5. Some textbooks teach phrasal verbs in groups according to the head verb so that a verb is presented along with all the particles it can take:

get up (arise)	I get up at 6:30 every day.
get in (arrive)	When did he get in?
get out (leave)	I told them to get out.
get over (recover from)	I finally got over the flu last week.
get back (return)	When did you get back?
get away (manage to leave)	How did they get away?

What do you think of this teaching strategy?

6. What are some arguments both for and against treating verb-plus-preposition sequences and phrasal verbs as the same structure (or the same kind of lexical item)?

BIBLIOGRAPHY

References

Bolinger, D. (1971). *The Phrasal Verb in English.* Cambridge, Mass.: Harvard University Press.
Cumming, S., J. Dwyer, and M. A. Snow (1982). "Figuring Particle Movement Out or Figuring Out Particle Movement." Unpublished Linguistics 253 paper, UCLA, winter, 1982.
Danielson, D., and R. Hayden (1973). *Using English: Your Second Language.* Englewood Cliffs, N.J.: Prentice-Hall.
Erteschik-Shir, N. (1979). "Discourse Constraints on Dative Movement," in T. Givón (ed.), *Syntax and Semantics,* vol. 12: *Discourse and Syntax.* New York: Academic Press.
Fraser, J. B. (1976). *The Verb-Particle Combination in English.* New York: Academic Press.
Ulm, S. C. (1975). *The Separation Phenomenon in English Phrasal Verbs.* Unpublished M.A. thesis in TESL, UCLA.

Suggestions for further reading

For reference grammars with a good description of phrasal verbs, see:

Frank, M. (1972). *Modern English—A Practical Reference Guide.* Englewood Cliffs, N.J.: Prentice-Hall.
Quirk, R., et al. (1972). *A Grammar of Contemporary English.* London and New York: Seminar Press (Secs. 12.19–28).

For an interesting syntactic analysis of phrasal verbs that analyzes the particle as a preposition, see the following:

Emonds, Joseph (1973). "Evidence That Indirect Object Movement Is a Structure Preserving Transformation," in M. Gross et al. (eds.). *The Formal Analysis of Languages.* The Hague: Mouton.

For a description of phrasal verbs and related constructions from the perspective of stratificational grammar, see:

Makkai, A. (1972). *Idiom Structure in English.* The Hague: Mouton.

For a reference dealing exclusively with the explanation and practice of phrasal verbs, see:

Hook, J. N. (1980). *Two-Word Verbs in English.* New York: Harcourt Brace Jovanovich.

Those references that contain exercises and information on phrasal verbs as well as prepositions are:

Crowell, T. L. (1960). *A Glossary of Phrases with Prepositions.* Englewood Cliffs, N.J.: Prentice-Hall.

Heaton, J. B. (1965). *Prepositions and Adverbial Particles.* London: Longmans, Green & Co.

Hill, L. A. (1968). *Prepositions and Adverbial Particles.* London: Oxford University Press.

For ESL/EFL textbooks with good exercises for teaching phrasal verbs, see:

Danielson, D., and R. Hayden (1973). *Using English: Your Second Language.* Englewood Cliffs, N.J.: Prentice-Hall.

Hayden, R., D. Pilgrim, and A. Haggard (1956). *Mastering American English.* Englewood Cliffs, N.J.: Prentice-Hall.

21

Simple Sentences with Nonreferential *it* or *there* Subjects

GRAMMATICAL DESCRIPTION

Introduction

In this chapter we have decided to treat together sentences with nonreferential *it* and *there* subjects. One reason for this decision is that both of these nonreferential words function syntactically as subjects in English; i.e., their behavior in yes-no questions and tag questions indicates that they undergo subject/auxiliary inversion:

> *It's* a nice day. *Is it* a nice day?
> *It's* a nice day, *isn't it*?
> *There's* a book on the table. *Is there* a book on the table?
> *There's* a book on the table, *isn't there*?

Although the *it* and *there* subjects in these sentences express no referential meaning, we know that in other contexts, these same words can indeed have a referential function:

> Where's *the book*? *It's* on the table. (*It* refers to *the book*.)
> Let's go out *in the garden*. It's cooler *there*. (*There* refers to *in the garden*.)

In this chapter we are concerned only with the nonreferential uses of *it* and *there* when they occur in subject position in simple sentences.

Thompson (1978) and others have suggested several reasons for the existence of such nonreferential subjects in English. In the case of nonreferential *it,* one reason is that every nonelliptical English sentence other than an imperative requires a surface subject. Languages like Spanish and Italian do not have this requirement, with the result that speakers of such languages—when speaking English—may produce ungrammatical sentences such as the following:

> *Is raining.   *Is 10 o'clock.

If translated literally into Spanish or Italian, these sentences would be perfectly acceptable.

One motivation for using nonreferential *there* is the general tendency English speakers have to introduce indefinite nouns (i.e., new information) in the verb phrase rather than in subject position, which is typically reserved for old information (i.e., definite nouns). Use of nonreferential *there* allows the speaker/writer to postpone the logical subject if it introduces new information. For example, when taken in isolation, sentence *a* sounds better than sentence *b* to most speakers of English because of this preference in spoken discourse.

a. There's a book on the table.   b. A book is on the table.

The presence of both nonreferential *it* and *there* subjects in English is a potential source of confusion to those ESL/EFL learners whose languages have no such subjects—or to those whose languages have only one such subject, the functions of which may overlap with the functions of English *it* and *there*. This state of affairs sometimes results in ESL/EFL learners producing errors such as the following:

> *There is very nice in Korea.
> *It's a picture on the wall.[1] (meaning: There's a picture on the wall.)

Any similarities that these two nonreferential subjects share are far outweighed by many obvious differences: *it* and *there* occur in different contexts and have different functions. This must be made clear to your intermediate-level ESL/EFL students if they are confusing these two forms. At the beginning level, however, it is best to introduce the forms separately in rich, complete contexts that will make the function of each word and the types of sentences in which it occurs very clear to your beginners.

Nonreferential *it*

We shall now examine three different analyses that have been proposed to account for sentences beginning with nonreferential *it*, which is associated mainly with statements of weather, time, and distance.

The incorporation analysis

Sentences such as the following, for example, are concerned with events involving precipitation:

> It is raining.   It is snowing.

We generally think of *rain* and *snow* as nouns, i.e., as the products of precipitation, yet in the above sentences they are functioning as verbs. To explain such sentences we appeal here to the linguistic notion of *incorporation* where a key word replaces a more general term in the same sentence and is then used in a new grammatical function. The incorporated word typically undergoes little or no change in form. Celce-Murcia (1973), for example, analyzes the general or universal verb in the above sentences as being very much like the verb *fall*. The underlying subject noun, which gets incorporated into the verb, is *rain* or *snow*, or another noun referring to a form of precipitation. Consider this sequence:

1. Rain is falling. (the most universal form of the sentence)
2. *Is raining. (incorporation takes place)
3. It is raining. (required surface subject is added for English)

We assume that 1 represents the most universal form of the sentence and that 2 is another form which represents the incorporation of the logical subject into the verb. The English surface structure is 3, which contains the filler subject *it*. For English, this final step is necessary because, as stated previously, every nonimperative English sentence must have a surface

---

1. Such sentences are also produced in the Black English dialect, which has nonreferential *it* subjects but no nonreferential *there* subjects.

subject regardless of whether the subject refers to anything or not. The interesting thing about the three alternatives cited above is that although 3 represents the usual way of expressing the notion of "rain in progress" in present-day English, the pattern represented in 1 closely reflects the Japanese idiom for expressing the same notion, and 2 represents a structure which is grammatical for Spanish or Italian and which was grammatical for Old English,[2] but which is no longer acceptable in Modern English.

In addition to describing events involving precipitation, statements with filler *it* also describe other general weather conditions:

It's sunny.   It's windy.

It's cloudy.   Etc.

It's foggy.

Building on the analysis presented above for verbs of precipitation, Gail Lee (personal communication) suggests that the logical or universal subject of such sentences is the noun that has been incorporated into the derived adjective; this adjective then takes on the form *NOUN + y,* and the meaning of the *-y* affix is "pervasiveness." Lee suggests the following progression:

1. Sun(light) is pervasive. (the most universal form of the sentence)
2. *Is sunny. (*sun + y*)[3] (incorporation and affixation take place)
3. It is sunny. (required surface subject is added for English)

Lee has further pointed out to us that the Cantonese way of expressing these descriptions of weather would translate into English (literally) as:

Sun
Clouds } is/are plentiful.
Fog

Lee's Cantonese data support such an incorporation-based analysis for sentences involving *-y* adjectives; however, we also have plenty of English sentences with filler *it* which describe the weather and which do not contain a *-y*-type predicate adjective and are thus less amenable to an analysis based on incorporation:

It's { hot. warm. cold. cool. fair. }

The noun paraphrase analysis

Thus the incorporation analysis has its limitations. Nonetheless, what we can associate with all three types of sentences discussed above is "the weather." (One might be tempted to

---

2. Old English had two alternative structures (regneþ/hit regneþ) for expressing the present-day sentence "It is raining."

3. Note that this stage involves both the incorporation of the subject noun into the adjective and the addition of the affix *-y* to the noun base to signal adjectival rather than nominal function as well as the meaning of pervasiveness.

say that in all of the above sentences, the *it* replaces some underlying noun such as *the weather*.) Consider, for example, exchanges such as the following:

Question	*Possible Answers*
What's the weather like?	It's raining.
What's it like out(side)?	It's cloudy.
	It's cold.

However, sentences with filler *it* may also describe a more specific aspect of the weather; namely, the temperature.

Question

What's the temperature outside?

How $\left\{ \begin{array}{l} \text{hot} \\ \text{warm} \\ \text{cold} \end{array} \right\}$ is it outside?

Possible Answers

The temperature is $\left\{ \begin{array}{l} 75°. \\ 40°. \\ \vdots \end{array} \right.$

It's $\left\{ \begin{array}{l} 75°. \\ 40°. \\ \vdots \end{array} \right.$

Therefore, an interpretation of filler *it* as *the weather* would be too narrow, since the *it* would have to replace the underlying noun *the temperature* in these latest examples.

The arguments of those who caution against giving nonreferential *it* a narrow interpretation become even stronger when we examine sentences dealing with a variety of time expressions such as the following:

Statement	*Associated Question(s)*	
It's Wednesday.	What day is it?	(These typically contain *it*.)
It's six o'clock.	What time is it?	
It's February 24th.	What's the date?	
It was 1880.	What was the year? What year was it? ?What year is it?	
	(These typically prefer the form without *it*.)	

In these cases we would have to say that the *it* subject is paraphrasing four different nouns:

TODAY is Wednesday.   THE DATE is February 24th.
THE TIME is six o'clock.   THE YEAR was 1880.

The problem, of course, is that too many related yet different meanings are being associated with *it*. Furthermore, this problem grows if we also add expressions of distance which represent another dimension of filler *it*.

How far is it to Fresno?	It's 200 miles to Fresno.
(What's the distance to Fresno?)	(The distance to Fresno is 200 miles.)

The environmental analysis

One solution to this problem—and probably the best one available—would be to follow Chafe (1970) and Bolinger (1977), both of whom refer to such usages of *it* as "ambient" *it*, which they claim is a syntactically necessary but lexically vague item. The meaning of ambient *it* derives from the rest of the sentence, which makes it clear to the listener/reader whether *time, distance, weather,* or *temperature* is being discussed. Expressing a view similar to that of Chafe and Bolinger, Thompson (1978) labels such usages of *it* as "environmental," and along with expressions of weather, time, and distance, she would include sentences of a more general environmental nature such as the following:

It gets a little rowdy on the ninth floor.   It's never crowded at the Pontiac Hotel.

This Chafe/Bolinger/Thompson analysis is somewhat different from most traditional and transformational accounts of filler *it,* which have labeled this form as a semantically meaningless item with an exclusively syntactic function, i.e., filling the required subject slot in a nonimperative sentence.

Note that we do not have an ambient or environmental *it* when the *it* in the sentence refers to someone specific in the physical context:

(Setting: Someone knocks at the door of a room.)
Question: Who is it?   Answer: It's me.

Here the *it* (in both the question and the answer) refers to "the one knocking at the door" and not to weather, temperature, time, etc. In fact we want to make the point that filler *it* can never be interpreted as a person or persons.

Summary of the functions of filler *it*

Filler *it* (alternatively, ambient *it*—or environmental *it*) occurs in a number of simple statements and questions in English dealing with weather, temperature, time, distance, and other environmental features. Use of this *it* allows such a question or answer to be shorter and less redundant than it would be if lexical subject nouns such as *time* and *weather* were used instead. Note, however, that the nouns implied by filler *it* are sometimes used explicitly to make a statement or question more formal and precise:

The time is (now) 10 o'clock.
The weather today is/will be fair and cool.

Other functions of filler *it* in complex sentences will be discussed in Chapters 30 and 34, which deal with complementation.

Sentences with nonreferential *there*

Syntactically and semantically, sentences with nonreferential *there* seem to fall into three major categories:

1. *Locative*
    There are several books on the table.   There used to be a tree behind the garage.

2. *Existential*
    a. *Unmodified*
       There is a $\begin{Bmatrix} \text{God} \\ \text{Santa Claus} \end{Bmatrix}$.
    b. *Modified*
       (1) *Prenominal adjective*
           There are mitigating circumstances.

(2) *Postnominal adjective*
There are two cars available.[4]
(3) *Postnominal adjectival PP*
There are two apartments for rent.[4]

3. *State of Event*
   a. *Noncompletive* (present participle)

There are several documents missing.

There was a man running around the track.

   b. *Completive* (passive participle)

There have been three people killed.

There were 10 houses destroyed (by the tornado).

The meaning of nonreferential *there*

Nonreferential *there* contrasts in meaning both with referential *there* and with its own absence. For the former contrast, consider the following where the first occurrence of *there* illustrates the nonreferential function, and the second occurrence illustrates adverbial *there*, which is referential.[5]

Have you ever been to New York?
There are many skyscrapers *there*.
 (1)   (2)
(*there* 2 refers to *in New York*)

Note that the nonreferential *there* 1 is pronounced with much less stress than the adverbial *there* 2. Also, while the latter never functions as a subject, it may occur sentence initially with accompanying subject-verb inversion:

There goes your father.

According to Bolinger (1977) the meaning or function of nonreferential *there* can best be explained by contrasting it with its absence:[6]

1.   An old barn is behind the poplars.
2.   There is an old barn behind the poplars.

---

4. Some may argue that such postnominal adjectival constructions derive from nonreferential *there* sentences with reduced relative clauses, e.g., *two cars that are available, several apartments that are for rent.* (Relative clauses are discussed in Chapters 26 and 27.) An important difference between the sentences cited here and sentences with full relative clauses, however, is that the former have a grammatical counterpart without *there,* whereas the latter do not, cf.

Two cars are available.   Two apartments are for rent.

*Two cars $\left\{ \begin{array}{l} \text{are that are available} \\ \text{that are available are} \end{array} \right\}$.   *Two apartments $\left\{ \begin{array}{l} \text{are that are for rent} \\ \text{that are for rent are} \end{array} \right\}$.

5. Bolinger (1977) and others argue that both of these functions of *there* are extensions of the same original form; however, given the needs of the ESL/EFL learner, we feel it is best to maintain the distinction clearly.

6. This view differs from the analyses of many traditional and transformational grammarians who consider *there* a meaningless structural element. See, for example, Stockwell, Schachter, and Partee (1973), where *there* is derived transformationally.

The difference here is one of discourse context: the first sentence is one piece of visual information in a longer background narrative; the second one is part of an oral description that utilizes a spatial organization. Compare these texts:

1a. The dilapidated farm does not appear to be inhabited. Some tall poplars shade the decaying house. An old barn is behind the poplars.
2a. Keep driving down this road, and you'll see a dilapidated farm. There are some tall poplars next to the house and (there's) an old barn behind the poplars.

The first text, which is unlikely to be spoken dialog, establishes a visual set, and the reader or listener expects that something is about to happen. The second text is likely to be speech or reported speech. It engages the listener more directly and evokes less impact or expectation. For these reasons, the first sentence sounds a bit odd if it is recalled or used as part of an oral testimony, while the second one sounds perfectly natural if used this way:

1b. ?To the best of my recollection, an old barn is behind the poplars.
2b. To the best of my recollection, there is an old barn behind the poplars.

Thus the meaning of nonreferential *there* is that it is a signal to the listener that he or she is about to be made aware of the location or existence of something.[7] No such explicit signal occurs in a sentence such as 1 above, which presupposes existence and describes the visual details.

Given that *there* does have a definable discourse function (i.e., a sentence with *there* functions differently from a counterpart sentence without *there*), we should not be surprised or disturbed by the fact that some *there* sentences do not have a grammatical counterpart without *there*:[8]

> There is a Santa Claus.
> *A Santa Claus is.
>
> There's another possibility that we haven't mentioned.
> *Another possibility is that we haven't mentioned.

Presumably, the use of *there* in these sentences has a discourse function as well. Following the general discourse principle that given information appears earlier in a sentence and new information appears later, the use of *there* allows postponing the introduction of the new information until sentence-final position (Rutherford, 1982).

Subject-verb agreement with nonreferential *there*

In terms of subject-verb agreement, nonreferential *there* is much more problematic than filler *it*, which always functions as a singular subject whether a singular or plural noun follows the verb:

> It's a nice day.   It's 400 miles to San Francisco.

In contrast to filler *it*, which is a true surface subject in all respects, nonreferential *there* is— among other things—a signal that the logical subject has been postponed. Thus in formal

---

7. Bolinger (1977) claims that asserting the location of something or asserting the existence of something are opposite sides of the same coin—i.e., if you locate something, it exists; if something exists, it is located somewhere.

8. This is, of course, a problem for all those who add *there* transformationally to preexisting structures in order to derive *there* sentences.

usage, subject-verb agreement is determined by the noun phrase following the verb, i.e., by the logical subject of the sentence:

There is a book on the table.   There are two books on the table.

Many reference grammars and most ESL/EFL textbooks present only this rule to the learner; however, what frequently occurs in the speech—as opposed to the writing—of even educated native speakers is a curious phenomenon whereby nonreferential *there* is perceived as a singular subject, and the logical subject is ignored for subject-verb agreement purposes. The following sentences, for example, were noted by Hudson (1975) during a brief period of data collection. They occurred in the classroom speech of UCLA professors and graduate students, who were all native speakers of either British or American English:

It helps them realize that there's dialects in English too.	There's a lot of differences among languages.
There's too many factions in Spain.	

The majority of such utterances occurred with the contracted form *there's*.[9] These English speakers could have used the plural contracted form *there're*; however, this alternative occurs only rarely with plural logical subjects—perhaps because of the awkwardness of articulating two consecutive weak syllables with final 'r' sounds. A more extensive follow-up study by Celce-Murcia and Hudson (1981), which examined transcribed spoken discourse, confirmed that *there's* predominates in informal speech even with plural logical subjects.

ESL/EFL students should be taught *there is* vs. *there are* since the distinction is still expected in formal—especially written—usage; however, they should also realize that, when speaking, native speakers of English often use *there's* with plural subjects.[10] It is certainly unrealistic for ESL/EFL teachers to expect their students to maintain this agreement rule in their speech when many native speakers ignore it. A better strategy might be to get ESL/EFL students to consistently say *there's* instead of *there is* because the contraction definitely makes the lack of agreement more acceptable:

There's too many factions in Spain.   ?There is too many factions in Spain.

A related issue, which was discussed in Chapter 4, is that the proximity principle tends to apply when conjoined noun phrase subjects follow *there*, with the result that the verb BE agrees with the number of the nearest conjunct rather than with the number of both noun phrases combined. This tendency occurs even in writing:

There are two boys and a girl in the room. (First conjunct is plural.)
There is a girl and two boys in the room. ⎫
?There are a girl and two boys in the room. ⎬ (First conjunct is singular.)

Verbs other than BE with nonreferential *there*

Even though BE is by far the most frequent verb following nonreferential *there*, it is by no means the only one. We have identified at least three semantically distinguishable classes of

---

9. In this regard note that locative (i.e., referential) *there, here,* and interrogative *where* sometimes exhibit the same subject-verb behavior in informal speech (i.e., *there're, here're,* and *where're* tend not to occur):

There's the two people I was talking about.   Here's the two books I promised you.
Where's the earrings you wore last time?

10. This is an obvious case of language change in progress. The written language, which maintains the old forms, is more conservative than the spoken language, which shows us where the language is heading.

intransitive verbs other than BE that occur in this context:

1. *Verbs of existence or position:* exist, live, dwell, stand, lie, remain, etc.

   Example: There exist several alternatives.
   At the edge of the forest there lived an old man.

2. *Verbs of motion or direction:* come, go, walk, run, fly, approach, etc.

   Example: There came three suspicious-looking men down the street.
   Along the river there walked an old woman.

3. *Event verbs that describe something happening, developing, or materializing:* develop, arise, appear, emerge, ensue, happen, occur, etc.

   Example: There arose a conflict.
   There ensued a dispute.

We have not given complete verb lists for the three classes. We feel that this would be next to impossible, since the English language contains many additional verbs in all three classes. In the absence of definitive frequency-based data, the best that ESL/EFL teachers can do is to convey to their more advanced students a feeling for the types of verbs other than BE that the students are likely to encounter following nonreferential *there*.

The definiteness or indefiniteness of the subject noun

In a number of reference grammars and in most transformational descriptions of English, it is stated that only indefinite subjects may co-occur with nonreferential *there*.[11] As a matter of fact, all the example sentences we have presented thus far in our chapter agree with this condition. This is presumably because new information is typically introduced with an indefinite determiner. Bolinger (1977) and Rando and Napoli (1978), however, have pointed out the existence of sentences such as the following:

1. There's the strangest man standing over there.
2. There will soon appear the definitive edition of "Hamlet."
3. There never was that problem in Miami.

The occurrence of *the* in 1 above is merely an odd prosodic fact of English for those superlative adjectives that require *-est* rather than *most.* In 1 the *-est* form is being used to mean a *very strange,* not *the strangest.* For those superlative adjectives that require *most,* either a definite or indefinite article may be used virtually interchangeably when this type of nonsuperlative meaning is being expressed:

$$\text{There's } \left\{ \begin{array}{c} a \\ the \end{array} \right\} \text{ most unusual man standing over there.}$$

The logical subjects in the other two sentences listed above have a definite determiner because they occur in environments that typically call for definite forms (recall our discussion of the functions of the definite article in Chapter 14):

Regarding 2: *uniqueness*—There can be only one "definitive" edition of any work.

---

11. Note that singular proper nouns, which normally take no article, take an indefinite article when co-occurring with nonreferential *there* (e.g., There is a Santa Claus). The same proper nouns with the verb *exist* and without nonreferential *there* would not have to have an article (e.g., Santa Claus exists).

Regarding 3: *anaphora* (*That problem* refers to something previously mentioned—e.g., friends have been discussing the problem of people freezing to death during winter in the colder parts of the United States because of the lack/cost of heating oil.)

Rando and Napoli (1978) also discuss at length the co-occurrence of nonreferential *there* and definite subjects in conversations such as the following, in which they claim *there* introduces a list:

Q: What's there to do at UCLA?
A: Well, there's the Sculpture Gardens, the Art Gallery, and a good coffee shop.
Q: Damn! Who knows about this?
A: There's you, me, and George. That's all.

In other words, the existence of a list is being asserted by the nonreferential *there* in these conversations. The noun phrases that follow the verb BE are members of the list.[12] The first conversation above supports Rando and Napoli's claim that either definite or indefinite determiners may co-occur with nouns on a list introduced by *there* and that the choice of the determiner depends on the context and the uniqueness or nonuniqueness of the noun(s) referred to. The second conversation above shows us that in such a list, personal pronouns occur only in their object form (subject forms such as *he, she, I,* do not occur). It also serves to point out that proper names on such a list occur without an article—in contrast to the nonlisting existential *there* sentences such as "There is a Santa Claus," which we discussed earlier.

Summary remarks on nonreferential *there*

We have seen that the scope and complexity of sentences with nonreferential *there* subjects is far greater than what most reference grammars or ESL/EFL texts would lead us to believe. We now need usage and frequency data to help us order our priorities for teaching ESL/EFL. We know we would want to deal with locative sentences and the subject-verb agreement dilemma at an early stage. But when should we introduce the various existential and state-of-event *there* sentences, which also occur in English? When do we teach the discourse function of *there*— i.e., when to use it and when to leave it out? When do we teach the verbs other than BE that can co-occur with nonreferential *there*? And when do we teach the "list" function of *there* and the related problem of article choice for the noun phrases that are members of the list? We do not have enough information at present to offer sound answers to these questions. Research that will help us answer these questions is now needed.

TEACHING SUGGESTIONS

1   Find pictures of scenes with rain, sleet, hail, or snow. Ask your class "What's happening?" to elicit:

It's raining.   It's snowing.

Discuss the semantically vague notion of *it* in such sentences (i.e., "weather"), but emphasize its important syntactic function (i.e., all English sentences require a surface subject).

---

12. Note that the list may consist of only one member (Well, there's George). Also, in a more explicit logical form, one might state the list formula as follows: There exists a list (w) such that it has as its member(s) x, (y, z, . . .).

2 Cue your students to ask each other questions requiring the filler subject *it*. Try not to use filler *it* in your question cue.

> *T:* Juana, ask Kim to tell you what kind of weather we have outside today.
> *J:* What's it like outside (today)?
> *K:* It's sunny.
>
> *T:* Lee, ask Maria for the time.
> *L:* What time is it?
> *M:* It's 10:30.

3 Use a current monthly calendar (poster size or a transparency on an overhead projector) to elicit and practice information about days, dates, etc. Again, try not to use filler *it* in your cue.

> *T:* Today's date.
> *S1:* What's the date?
> *S2:* It's the 10th of January.
>
> *T:* Yesterday—what day of the week?
> *S1:* What day was it yesterday?
> *S2:* (It was) Tuesday.

4 Show your students pictures of locations—insides of rooms, stores, shops, churches, museums, etc. Get them to identify what the picture represents and to introduce the things they see in the picture, e.g.:

> That's a picture of a toy store.
> There are lots of toys on the shelves.
> There are two sales clerks behind the counter.
>
> There are several shoppers in the store.
> There's a small dog in the corner.
> There's a rocking horse near the window.

5 Shaw and Taylor (1978) suggest that the teacher begin a chain drill based on signs of the zodiac (the information about signs and dates must be available if needed):

> *T:* Are you (an) Aries?
> *S1:* No.
> *T:* What are you?
> *S1:* Capricorn.
> *S2:* Are you _____?
>   (any sign)
>
> *S3:* No.
> *S2:* What are you?
> *S3:* Libra.

As the chain drill proceeds, the teacher keeps track of the results on the board:

> Capricorn ♂ ♂
> Libra ♀ ♀ ♂
> Aries ♀ ♂ ♀
> Gemini ♀ ♀
>
> Cancer ♂ ♂
> Taurus ♂ ♀ ♂
> etc.

When the sign and sex of everyone in the class has been recorded, the students should generate all the possible *there* sentences based on the teacher's chart:

> There are two Capricorns in the class.
> There are two male Libras in the class.
>
> There is one female Libra in the class.
> etc.

6 Alternatively, use the class information sheet (see p. 156) and get the students to describe the geographic composition of the class:

> There are (there's) two students from Japan in the class.
> There's one student from Russia in the class.
>   etc.

7 Have the students play a game to practice the existential use of *there*. Write on slips of paper a mixture of unusual real place names and fictional place names such as:

Xanadu, Passamaquoddy, Shangri-la, Ouagadougou

Post a large world map on the wall and divide the students into two teams. One student from team A will pick a slip of paper and proceed as follows:

Greta: Carlos, is there such a place as _____ ?
Carlos: Yes, (there is.)
Greta: Where is it?
Carlos: (gives location)

If Carlos is right (i.e., the place exists and he can give the location), his team gets a point. If not, Greta's team gets the point. The teams alternate selecting slips of paper.

8 In order to help students practice using *there* in an appropriate context, teachers can follow a suggestion by Stevick (1982). In this activity, one student is asked to describe a place that has a special significance for him or her. As the student describes the scene, he or she places cuisenaire rods on a table to indicate the location of things in the scene. Each statement by the student is repeated by the teacher. If the student makes a grammatical error while describing the scene, the teacher does not engage in overt error correction but rather repeats the student's statement using the correct form. For example:

Student: I am thinking of a place in my hometown. It is the plaza in the middle of the town. In the center of the plaza there is a big fountain. (The student places a rod down to mark the fountain.)
Teacher: I see. There's a big fountain in the center of the plaza.
Student: Yes, and there are bench around the fountain. (The student places rods around the first rod to represent the benches.)
Teacher: There are benches around the fountain.
　　　　　etc.

When the student has finished describing the scene, the teacher can repeat the entire description using the rods to recall the various aspects of the scene. At this point another student can be called upon to describe the scene. After this, the students can form small groups, with each group having rods and the task of reconstructing and describing the scene.

9 Kathi Bailey suggests that composing a letter or an audio tape to send home after moving to a new place provides a good context for integrating the use of nonreferential *it* and *there*— especially if the composing is done on a rainy day. If students are at a low level of proficiency, this exercise might work better as a cloze passage, i.e., a letter with all the *it's* and *there's* omitted, e.g.:

Dear Mom and Dad (or Whoever),
　　　It's raining (again) today, so I'll take time to write some letters. It's been raining for (three) days. There hasn't been any sun to speak of since (Friday).
My (dorm room/apartment) is okay.
　　．
　　．
　　．
(description of room using *there*—or referential *it* for contrast)
　　．
　　．
　　．

There are some nice people $\left\{\begin{array}{l}\text{on this floor}\\ \text{in this building}\end{array}\right\}$ but I haven't gotten to know many of them yet.

    etc.

EXERCISES

Test your understanding of what has been presented

1. Provide original example sentences that illustrate the following terms or concepts. Underline the pertinent word(s) in your examples.

filler *it* (also referred to as "ambient" or
   "environmental" *it*)
referential *it*
referential *there*

nonreferential *there*
locative
existential
there introducing a list

2. What are some verbs other than BE that occur with nonreferential *there*? Find some that weren't mentioned in the chapter. Can the semantic classification provided in the chapter account for them?

3. Why are the following sentences ungrammatical?

a. *There is Santa Claus.

b. *It are four o'clock.

c. (Who's going?) *There's I.

Test your ability to apply what you know

4. If your students produce the following sentences, what errors have they made? How will you make them aware of the errors, and what exercises will you prepare to correct such errors?

a. *There is sunny today.

b. *Is raining.

5. One of your ESL/EFL students comes to you and says, "I heard an American student say: At 4 p.m., there's usually a lot of empty rooms at school." The ESL/EFL student asks you why the native speaker—a graduate student—used incorrect subject-verb agreement. How will you answer?

6. What's the difference in meaning, if any, between:

a. A ball was in the street.
   There was a ball in the street.

b. The time is nine o'clock.
   It is nine o'clock.

BIBLIOGRAPHY

References

Bolinger, D. (1977). *Meaning and Form.* London and New York: Longman.

Celce-Murcia, M. (1973). "Incorporation: A Tool for Teaching Productive Vocabulary Patterns." *Workpapers in TESL,* vol. 7, June 1973, UCLA English Department.

Celce-Murcia, M., and J. K. Hudson (1981). "What 'there' Is to Subject-Verb Agreement." Paper presented at the annual TESOL Conference, Detroit. Mar. 5, 1981.

Chafe, W. (1970). *Meaning and the Structure of Language.* Chicago: University of Chicago Press.

Hudson, J. (1975). "A Pilot Study of *There's/There're* Usage in Colloquial English." Unpublished English 215 paper, UCLA.

Rando, E., and D. J. Napoli (1978). "Definites in *There*-Sentences," *Language* 54:2, 300–313.

Rutherford, W. (1982). "Functions of Grammar in a Language Teaching Syllabus." *Language Learning and Communication* 1, 1:21–37.

Shaw, P., and J. B. Taylor (1978). "Non-Pictorial Visual Aids," in S. Holden (ed.), *Visual Aids for Classroom Interaction.* London: Modern English Publications, pp. 15–19.

Stevick, E. (1982). *Teaching and Learning Languages.* New York: Cambridge University Press.

Stockwell, R. P., P. Schachter, and B. H. Partee (1973). *The Major Syntactic Structures of English.* New York: Holt, Rinehart and Winston.

Thompson, S. A. (1978). "Modern English from a Typological Point of View: Some Implications of the Function of Word Order," *Linguistische Berichte* 54, 19–35.

Suggestions for further reading

For general accounts of nonreferential *there* see the following:

Frank, M. (1972). *Modern English.* Englewood Cliffs, N.J.: Prentice-Hall.

Quirk, R., and S. Greenbaum (1973). *A Concise Grammar of Contemporary English.* New York: Harcourt Brace Jovanovich, pp. 418–421.

For transformational accounts of nonreferential *there* see these sources:

Culicover, P. W. (1976). *Syntax.* New York: Academic Press.

Stockwell, R. P., P. Schachter, and B. H. Partee (1973). *The Major Syntactic Structures of English.* New York: Holt, Rinehart and Winston.

For two useful accounts of the meaning and function of nonreferential *there,* see:

Bolinger, D. (1977). *Meaning and Form.* London and New York: Longman.

Breivik, L. E. (1981). "On the Interpretation of Existential *There*," *Language* 57:1, 1–25.[13]

For a corpus-based study of English sentences with *there,* see:

Erdmann, P. (1976). *There Sentences in English.* Munich: Tuduv-Verlagsgesellschaft.

For useful information on the meaning and the intonation contours of list and nonlist *there* sentences, see:

Rando, E., and D. J. Napoli (1978). "Definites in *There*-Sentences," *Language* 54:2, 300–313.

For descriptions of filler *it* in simple sentences, see the following:

Bolinger, D. (1977). *Meaning and Form.* London and New York: Longman.

Celce-Murcia, M. (1973). "Incorporation: A Tool for Teaching Productive Vocabulary Patterns." *Workpapers in TESL,* vol. 7, UCLA English Department, ESL Section.

The following textbooks contain useful suggestions for teaching nonreferential *there*:

Danielson, D., and R. Hayden (1973). *Using English: Your Second Language.* Englewood Cliffs, N.J.: Prentice-Hall.

Praninskas, J. (1975). *Rapid Review of English Grammar.* Englewood Cliffs, N.J.: Prentice-Hall.

The following textbook offers helpful suggestions for teaching filler *it* in simple sentences:

Chapman, J. (1978). *Adult English Three,* Unit 2. Englewood Cliffs, N.J.: Prentice-Hall.

---

13. Breivik's article came to our attention after we had written and revised this chapter. We were delighted to see that his analysis is fully compatible with ours.

These texts have useful exercises for teaching/testing the *it/there* distinction:

Brinton, D., and R. Neuman (1982). *Getting Along: English Grammar and Writing* (Book 2). Englewood Cliffs, N.J.: Prentice-Hall, pp. 196–197, 202–204.

Doty, G., and J. Ross (1973). *Language and Life in the U.S.A.* (3d ed., vol. 1). New York: Harper & Row, p. 411.

22

An Introduction to Conjunction

GRAMMATICAL DESCRIPTION

Introduction

In all of the previous chapters we have dealt with structures that have had only one nonsubordinate (or independent) sentence in the base. In fact the only rule that we have encountered for generating subordinate sentences within our current set of phrase structure rules has been the adverbial clause expansion rule:

$$\text{Advl. Cl.} \longrightarrow \text{Adv Sub S}$$

In this chapter we will deal with some surface structure sentences which are composed of two or more nonsubordinate (or independent) sentences in the base. In order to accommodate sentences of this type, we will have to add a new rule to our list of phrase structure rules:

$$\text{S} \longrightarrow \text{Conj} + \text{S}^{2+n}$$

This rule allows us to rewrite S as a conjunction followed by two or more sentences.

We should note here at the outset of this chapter that our analysis of conjoined sentences is an adaptation and simplification of the one presented in Stockwell, Schachter, and Partee (1973).

Four types of coordinating conjunctions

A rule such as the above one will allow us to generate basic structures such as the following:

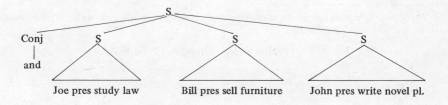

The conjunction movement transformation copies the initial (i.e., leftmost) conjunction so that it occurs between each conjoined S in the base and then erases the original conjunction:

Output of base: and Joe pres study law Bill pres sell furniture John pres write novel pl.
Conjunction movement: Joe pres study law and Bill pres sell furniture and John pres write novel pl.

An additional transformation, i.e., nonfinal conjunction deletion, optionally allows us to replace each nonfinal conjunction with a comma.[1]

Nonfinal conjunction deletion: Joe pres study law, Bill pres sell furniture and John pres write novel pl.

After undergoing affix attachment, subject-verb agreement, and morphological rules, this string of conjoined sentences will surface as:

Joe studies law, Bill sells furniture and John writes novels.

This example represents the simplest type of conjoined structure, since each sentence is unique (i.e., there is no repetition of information), and there is no need for any substitution, deletion, or addition.

Another type of syntactically conjoined structure follows. It is derived from a base which contains two sentences with a semantic contrast or conflict:

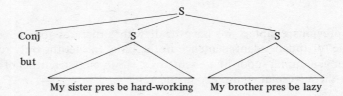

In this case, the semantic information would call for the conjunction *but* to be inserted in the base; however, the derivational process would be almost the same as it was for the earlier example with *and,* i.e., conjunction movement, affix attachment, subject-verb agreement, and morphological rules, resulting in "My sister is hard-working, but my brother is lazy."

A further type of syntactically conjoined structure results from a base in which the truth of only one of two or more alternatives is presupposed.

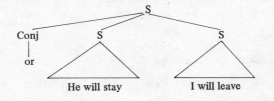

---

1. An orthographic convention further allows optional addition of a comma before the conjunction that signals the last sentence in the series, e.g.:

Joe studies law, Bill sells furniture, and John writes novels.

In this case, where the truth of only one of the underlying sentences (but not both or all of them) is assumed to be true, the conjunction *or* is used. After applying conjunction movement, no further transformations are needed, and we get the surface structure string:

He will stay or I will leave.

To conclude this section of the chapter, we will discuss one final type of coordinating conjunction, one which is more complicated than the others we've discussed so far. This conjoined structure is derived from a base which contains two negative sentences, both of which are true. Given an underlying structure with such a meaning, *nor* is the conjunction that gets inserted into the base. (Assume that NOT placement—or its equivalent—and any related transformations such as DO support or NOT contraction have already taken place in the constituent sentences.)

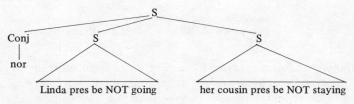

After the appropriate transformations we would get:

Linda is not going, nor is her cousin staying.

You will see from this example sentence why we said that conjoined sentences with *nor* were more complicated than the others we have considered. First of all, after the *nor* gets relocated through conjunction movement, it "absorbs" the negative particle NOT in the second sentence, leaving the second sentence without an overt negative. Second, subject/ auxiliary inversion must take place in the second sentence in order to generate a grammatical surface structure. This holds true even when the auxiliary verb is a DO which has been previously inserted—following the placement of NOT—to carry the tense marker. Another example is diagramed and derived below. (Assume that NOT placement and DO support have taken place in the constituent sentences):

Joy does not swim nor does Sally skate.

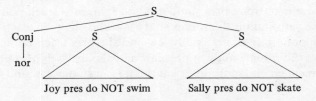

Derived output: nor Joy pres do NOT swim Sally pres do NOT skate
Conjunction movement: Joy pres do NOT swim nor Sally pres do NOT skate
NOT absorption: Joy pres do NOT swim nor Sally pres do skate
Subject/auxiliary inversion (in S2): Joy pres do NOT swim nor pres do Sally skate
Affix attachment (2X): Joy do + pres NOT swim nor do + pres Sally skate
Subject-verb agreement and morphological rules: Joy does not swim nor does Sally skate.

Conjoined sentences with identical information

Conjoined sentences that are more typical than any of the above examples contain some identical information in the underlying sentences since we don't usually conjoin sentences that have nothing in common. In many such cases we can substitute a pro-form[2] and retain all the major constituents present in the base.

In the following tree, the subject NPs of both of the underlying sentences contain identical information (i.e., *Joan*):

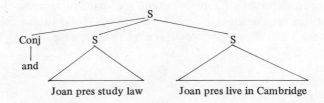

With the conjunction movement transformation, a pro-form substitution (in this case, the pronoun substitution of *she* for *Joan*), affix attachment, subject-verb agreement, and morphological rules we will derive the surface sentence:

Joan studies law and she lives in Cambridge.

If the structure remains essentially the same except that the lexical information is different, i.e., the structures are parallel,[3] then *too* is optionally added to emphasize this parallelism:

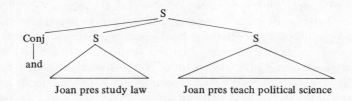

Output of base: and Joan pres study law Joan pres teach political science
Conjunction movement: Joan pres study law and Joan pres teach political science
Pro-noun phrase substitution: Joan pres study law and she pres teach political science
Too addition (optional): Joan pres study law and she pres teach political science too
Affix attachment (2✕): Joan study + pres law and she teach + pres political science too
Subject-verb agreement and morphological rules: Joan studies law and she teaches political science too.

When entire verb phrases are identical but subjects are not, a pro-verb may be substituted for the repeated verb phrase. In such a case, *too* must be added to complete the sentence (i.e., *too* addition is no longer optional):

---

2. A pro-form is a substitute form which refers to an identical constituent in either the sentence or the discourse. There can be pronouns (i.e., pro-noun phrases), pro-verbs, pro-adverbs, etc.

3. Structures are parallel if they have the same sequence of syntactic constituents and semantically similar lexical items, e.g., study law/teach political science; go in/come out; buy a car/lease an apartment.

Joe studies law and Bill does too.   *Joe studies law and Bill does.

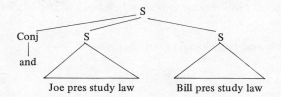

The derivation of this sentence would proceed as follows:

Output of base: and Joe pres study law Bill pres study law
Conjunction movement: Joe pres study law and Bill pres study law
Pro-verb phrase substitution (optional): Joe pres study law and Bill pres DO
Too addition (obligatory): Joe pres study law and Bill pres DO too
Affix attachment (2✕): Joe study + pres law and Bill DO + pres too
Subject-verb agreement and morphological rules: Joe studies law and Bill does too.

In this case since no other auxiliary verb is present, the pro-verb DO is added, and it carries the same tense marking as the verb that it replaced.

If an auxiliary verb or copula BE were present, there would be no need for an external pro-verb to be added. The auxiliary verb or the BE would function as the pro-verb, and the repeated verb phrase would simply be deleted, e.g.:

Martha can play the piano and Sheila   Mr. Jones is a carpenter and Mr. Wilson
can too.   is too.

If more than one auxiliary verb is present, it is generally only the first one in the string which is retained to function as the pro-verb. Sometimes, however, a second auxiliary verb may also optionally follow the first. When this occurs, the same rules obtain that we have already outlined in Chapter 9 under Responses to Yes-No Questions.

Steve has been working very hard and Debbie has (been) too.

One other possible variation for conjoined sentences with identical elements in the verb phrase is considerably more complex in terms of the number of rules needed for derivation.

Joe studies law and so does Bill.

For this sentence to be derived we will first have to move the conjunction, substitute a pro-verb, and add *too*.

Output of base: and Joe pres study law Bill pres study law
Conjunction movement: Joe pres study law and Bill pres study law
Pro-verb phrase substitution: Joe pres study law and Bill pres DO
Too addition: Joe pres study law and Bill pres DO too

In addition, we will have to apply the following rules:

Too ⟶ *so* suppletion: Joe pres study law and Bill pres DO so
So fronting: Joe pres study law and so Bill pres DO
Subject/auxiliary inversion: Joe pres study law and so pres DO Bill

Then, we would have to apply affix attachment, subject-verb agreement, and morphological rules to complete the derivation.

Conjoined sentences with identical negative elements

A set of rules similar to those above applies when both of the conjoined sentences contain NOT.

Joe doesn't work and Bill doesn't (work) either.

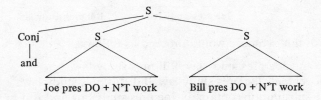

Conj — and

Joe pres DO + N'T work   Bill pres DO + N'T work

(For simplicity of presentation, we assume that NOT placement, DO support, and NOT contraction have all taken place in the constituent sentences.)

The only change needed in such a derivation is the addition of *either* instead of the *too* that was added when both sentences were affirmative:

Derived output: and Joe pres DO + N'T work Bill pres DO + N'T work
Conjunction movement: Joe pres DO + NT work and Bill pres DO + N'T work
Pro-verb phrase substitution:[4] Joe pres DO + N'T work and Bill pres DO + N'T
Either addition: Joe pres DO + N'T work and Bill pres DO + N'T either
Affix attachment (2✕): Joe DO + N'T + pres work and Bill DO + N'T + pres either
Subject-verb agreement and morphological rules: Joe doesn't work and Bill doesn't either.

We also want to be able to derive the other more complicated version of this sentence, i.e., Joe doesn't work and neither does Bill. To do this, we step back to the "*either* addition" rule in the above derivation, and we then add the following steps:

NOT incorporation: Joe pres DO + N'T work and Bill pres DO neither

This rule takes a preceding NOT or -N'T and incorporates it into *either,* thus forming *neither.* A rule of negative constituent fronting then moves *neither* to the beginning of the second sentence.

Negative constituent fronting: Joe pres DO + N'T work and neither Bill pres DO

At this stage subject/auxiliary inversion would have to apply, as it always does in English when a negative constituent is fronted.[5]

Subject/auxiliary inversion: Joe pres DO + N'T work and neither pres DO Bill

The rules of affix attachment, subject-verb agreement, and the morphological rules then produce:

Joe doesn't work and neither does Bill.

---

4. Note that we have the choice here of pro-ing the verb phrase (i.e., Joe doesn't work and Bill doesn't either) or skipping this step and leaving both sentences intact (i.e., Joe doesn't work and Bill doesn't work either).

5. Recall that this also occurs when negative preverbal adverbs are fronted (see Chapter 16):

I have never seen such a sight. ──→ Never have I seen such a sight!

Differences between *I do too/I don't either* and *so do I/neither do I*

In many English grammar textbooks, the affirmative expressions *I do too* and *so do I* and the negative expressions *I don't either* and *neither do I* are presented as synonymous forms which can be freely substituted one for the other.

	Uninverted	Inverted
affirmative	I do too	so do I
negative	I don't either	neither do I

However, despite the fact that we derive these forms from the same affirmative or negative underlying structures, they are not always interchangeable and thus not truly synonymous.

First of all, notice, as we said earlier, that *too* can be added to signal a repetition of some element in an affirmative verb phrase, and *either* can be added to signal some common element in the second of two negative verb phrases.

> I play first base and he does too.
> I don't play first base and he doesn't either.

In such cases, where the function is one of agreement with what was mentioned earlier, the inverted forms seem to be suitable substitutes:

> I play first base and so does he.   I don't play first base and neither does he.

However, the uninverted forms can also be used to add additional information to the second sentence in a conjoined pair where both sentences relate to the same semantic field, but where the verb phrases—and sometimes even the subjects—have no lexical information in common.

Identical Subjects
I play first base and I pitch too.
I don't play first base and I don't pitch either.

Nonidentical Subjects[6]

Speaking of baseball, $\left\{ \begin{array}{l} \text{I play first base and my sister pitches too} \\ \text{I don't play first base and my sister doesn't pitch either} \end{array} \right\}$.

In such cases, the inverted forms are not grammatical.

> *I play first base and so pitch(es) $\left\{ \begin{array}{l} \text{I} \\ \text{my sister.} \end{array} \right\}$.
>
> *I don't play first base and neither pitch(es) $\left\{ \begin{array}{l} \text{I} \\ \text{my sister} \end{array} \right\}$.

A second difference worth pointing out is that when these forms are used as rejoinders, only the uninverted forms may be shortened and used without an auxiliary verb. Also, when these forms are shortened, any subject pronoun involved must be changed to an object form.

a. I like softball.
b. Me too! (*I too!) (*So me!)

a. I don't like softball.
b. Me (n)either! (*I (n)either!) (*Neither me!)

---

6. Not all native speakers will accept such sentences as grammatical; however, we have evidence from discourse analysis (Celce-Murcia, 1980) that such sentences occur with reasonable frequency in informal conversation.

Shayne (1975) was successful in isolating a third context where the uninverted forms were strongly preferred over the inverted forms. This is where the "tag" is preceded by a logical connector such as *because, since, although,* or *in spite of the fact,* e.g.:

Macy's offers a lot of good buys, although
a. so does Gimbel's.
strongly preferred⟶b. Gimbel's does too.
c. no preference

We have seen several contexts above where the uninverted forms were necessary or were preferred over the inverted forms. The opposite also occurs. In a usage study, Celce-Murcia (1980) showed that native speakers preferred the inverted forms over the uninverted forms in those cases where an insult was intended. (The numbers in parentheses refer to the number of respondents preferring a given form.) For example:

You're a rotten egg and _____ .

(74) a. so is your father.   (8) c. no preference
(31) b. your father is too.

The uninverted forms are more frequent and versatile overall than the inverted forms; however, there are important discourse differences, and it is thus an unjustified simplification to treat the two affirmative (and two negative) forms as mere paraphrases of each other.

Conjoined sentences with identical major constituents

In the examples cited thus far, a pro-form often substituted for repeated constituents in conjoined sentences. When the major constituents (noun phrases, verb phrases, or adjective phrases) are identical, however, we can also delete the repeated constituent. Such a deletion necessitates a restructuring of the base, which in turn results in a single clause at the surface structure level.

For example, two sentences with identical subject NPs would be conjoined in this manner:

Joe studies music and lives in Manhattan.

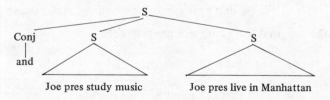

If we apply conjunction movement, delete the identical constituents, and then restructure, we have the following *intermediate* (i.e., *not underlying*) structure:

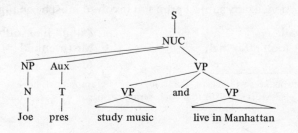

The further application of affix attachment, subject-verb agreement, and morphological rules yields: Joe studies music and lives in Manhattan. The entire derivation is given below:

Output of base: and Joe pres study music Joe pres live in Manhattan
Conjunction movement: Joe pres study music and Joe pres live in Manhattan
Identical constituent deletion: Joe pres study music and Ø Ø live in Manhattan
Restructuring: Joe pres study music and live in Manhattan (output string doesn't change but internal structure does—see above intermediate structure)
Affix attachment (2✕):[7] Joe study + pres music and live + pres in Manhattan
Subject-verb agreement and morphological rules: Joe studies music and lives in Manhattan.

Consider another such example that restructures sentences with identical verb phrases:

Joe and Marge study music.

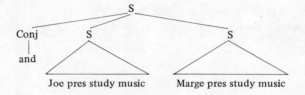

Conjunction movement, identical constituent deletion, and restructuring produce the following intermediate structure:

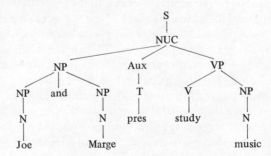

If we now apply affix attachment, subject-verb agreement, and morphological rules, the result is: Joe and Marge study music. The complete derivation can be represented as follows:

Output of base: and Joe pres study music Marge pres study music
Conjunction movement: Joe pres study music and Marge pres study music
Identical constituent deletion: Joe pres study music and Marge Ø Ø Ø
Restructuring: Joe and Marge pres study music
Affix attachment (1✕):[8] Joe and Marge study + pres music
Morphological rules: Joe and Marge study music.

In addition to the two major deletion-and-restructuring patterns we have illustrated above (i.e., those with identical subjects and verb phrases), there are also cases where the only

---

7. Note that in this derivation the one present tense auxiliary in the derived structure attaches to the first element in both of the conjoined verb phrases (i.e., it applies twice).

8. Note that the affix attachment in this example is different from that in the preceding one. In the previous case there were two conjoined verb phrases; so the rule had to apply twice. In this example there is only one verb phrase after the restructuring; so the affix attachment rule applies only once.

identical information is the verb or the copula BE. If the structures are otherwise fully parallel, deletion without restructuring is also possible, e.g.:

Mary ate an apple and Joe Ø a banana.   Mike is a lawyer and Ken Ø a teacher.

In such cases deletion is possible because the context (i.e., the parallel structure) allows the listener or reader to unambiguously supply the correct auxiliary and verb.

Conclusion

Before we end this chapter, we would like to point out that the two ways for avoiding repetition of identical constituents that we have discussed, i.e., pro-ing (or substitution) and deletion, are similar processes. In both cases, the speaker or writer's goal is to avoid repetition of identical information. The major difference is that substitution is less radical than deletion. If we substitute a pro-form for the identical information, the underlying structure remains intact; however, if we delete a major constituent, restructuring is necessary, and the result is only one surface sentence where there were originally two or more sentences in the underlying structure.

TEACHING SUGGESTIONS

1   A sentence-combining exercise would seem the most suitable activity for introducing and practicing the conjoining of two or more sentences. In the presentation stage, the students can be asked to supply sentences following the teacher's cues. For example, the teacher might say, "Can anyone give me two sentences telling us things you like to do?" A student might respond, "I like to cross-country ski," "I like to play tennis." The teacher might then see if anyone has any notions of how these sentences might be combined. If not, the teacher may show the class. Once the rules for conjoining have been established, the teacher may then introduce a picture as a stimulus and solicit both affirmative and negative statements from the class which describe the picture. When a number of statements have been collected, the students can be invited to combine the sentences using the new rules. Follow-up work with students divided into small groups, each group having its own picture, would be desirable for giving all students ample practice with conjoining sentences.

2   Shaw and Taylor (1978) have suggested that nonpictorial visual aids can be very useful stimuli for encouraging use of conjoined sentences in communicative exchanges among class members. For example, a baseball box score clipped from the previous day's newspaper could provide an opportunity for relevant practice. The statistics presented could allow for conjoined sentences such as:

> The Boston Red Sox scored eight runs, but they didn't win the game.
> Fred Lynn hit a single, a double, and a home run.
> The Red Sox didn't make an error, nor did the Yankees.

3   Shared information about the background of the students in the class can be used as a source for practicing sentences with *too* or *so*, which express agreement:

> Maria speaks Spanish and $\left\{ \begin{array}{l} \text{Pablo does too} \\ \text{so does Pablo} \end{array} \right\}$.

Isamu comes from Japan and $\left\{ \begin{array}{l} \text{Minoru does too} \\ \text{so does Minoru} \end{array} \right\}$.

4 To elicit conjoined negative sentences that make use of *either* or *neither*, the teacher can have his or her students prepare a list of four or five things that they do not like about the city they are living in. For example, if the students lived in Chicago, two of the lists might look like this:

Ali
1. I don't like the cold weather.
2. I don't like the snow and ice.
3. I don't like gray skies.
4. I don't like the food.

Shu-min
1. I don't like the food.
2. I don't like the cold weather.
3. I don't like the traffic.
4. I don't like the subway.

After the students have prepared their individual lists, they should be placed into pairs or small groups to see how many appropriate sentences they can say or write, e.g.:

Ali: I don't like the cold weather, and $\left\{ \begin{array}{l} \text{Shu-min doesn't either} \\ \text{neither does Shu-min} \end{array} \right\}$.

Shu-min: I don't like the food, and $\left\{ \begin{array}{l} \text{Ali doesn't either} \\ \text{neither does Ali} \end{array} \right\}$.

EXERCISES

Test your understanding of what has been presented

1. Give an example sentence to illustrate each of the following terms. Underline the pertinent word(s) in your examples.

        pro-form   optional *too* addition
        coordinating conjunction   parallel structure
        obligatory *too* addition

2. Give an example sentence or pairs of sentences illustrating application of each of the following rules:

        NOT incorporation   restructuring
        NOT absorption   pro-verb phrase substitution

3. Give the tree diagrams and transformations which apply to the following sentences:

a. Jim got the job, and he likes it.
b. Jill has a car and Jack does too.
c. I have read Tolstoy and Pushkin.

d. Alice doesn't swim, and Judy doesn't either.
e. Fuad and Sven study at Harvard.

4. Why are the following sentences ungrammatical?

a. *Sarah said she would go there, but she did.
b. *Doris doesn't sew nor doesn't Lee.

c. *Mike plays the guitar and so Kathi does.

Test your ability to apply what you know

5. If your students produce the following sentences, what errors have they made? How will you make your students aware of the errors, and what activities will you provide to correct such errors?

a. *I don't have a car and he doesn't too. c. *A:* I like to play baseball.
b. *Bill can play tennis and John can.   *B:* *I too!

6. ESL/EFL texts often present all the following constructions simultaneously in one lesson. Are there any reasons for teaching one version in each pair several lessons prior to teaching the other?

I speak English and $\begin{Bmatrix} \text{he does too} \\ \text{so does he} \end{Bmatrix}$. I don't smoke and $\begin{Bmatrix} \text{he doesn't either} \\ \text{neither does he} \end{Bmatrix}$.

7. In the second footnote to this chapter it was mentioned that in addition to pronouns and pro-verbs, there are also pro-adverbs. These can be substitute forms for adverbs of time and place such as:

I was in Syracuse last summer and he was *there then* too.

Can you think of any other pro-adverbs?

BIBLIOGRAPHY

References

Celce-Murcia, M. (1980). "A Discourse Analysis of 'I do too,' 'so do I,' and Similar Substitute Expressions, in J. Povey (ed.), *Language Policy and Language Teaching: Essays in Honor of Clifford Prator.* Los Angeles: English Language Services.

Shaw, P., and J. B. Taylor (1978). "Non-Pictorial Visual Aids," in S. Holden (ed.), *Visual Aids for Classroom Interaction.* London: Modern English Publications, Ltd.

Shayne, J. (1975). "I do too" versus "so do I." Unpublished English 215 paper, UCLA, fall, 1975.

Stockwell, R. P., P. Schachter, and B. H. Partee (1973). *The Major Syntactic Structures of English.* New York: Holt, Rinehart and Winston.

Suggestions for further reading

For elaboration of the semantic implications of joining sentences with *and, or,* and *but,* see:

Quirk, R., and S. Greenbaum (1973). *A Concise Grammar of Contemporary English.* New York: Harcourt Brace Jovanovich, pp. 257–259.

For a transformational analysis of conjunction, see:

Stockwell, R. P., P. Schachter, and B. H. Partee (1973). *The Major Syntactic Structures of English.* New York: Holt, Rinehart and Winston, Chap. 6.

For examples of sentence-combining exercises and exercises in the use of conjunctions, see:

Brinton, D., and R. Neuman (1982). *Getting Along: English Grammar and Writing* (Book 1). Englewood Cliffs, N.J.: Prentice-Hall, pp. 90–91, 97–98.

Hayden, R., D. Pilgrim, and A. Haggard (1956). *Mastering American English.* Englewood Cliffs, N.J.: Prentice-Hall, pp. 55–58.

In Book 2 of the Brinton and Neuman reference, there is also an exercise on *too* and *either* (pp. 149–150).

For more types of nonpictorial visual aids which can be used as stimuli for conjoined sentence production, see the article by Shaw and Taylor (1978) in the above references.

23

More on Conjoined Sentences

GRAMMATICAL DESCRIPTION

Introduction

In the preceding chapter we saw that coordinating conjunction occurred when two or more sentences were generated as one along with a coordinating conjunction, namely, *and, but, or,* or *nor.* Under certain circumstances, when two sentences are thus coordinated, the conjuncts (or conjoined elements) may be preceded by a correlative conjunction. Thus there are sequences such as the following, which we must also account for:[1]

both Conjunct$_1$ *and* Conjunct$_2$
either Conjunct$_1$ *or* Conjunct$_2$
neither Conjunct$_1$ *nor* Conjunct$_2$

In fact there is clearly a semantic similarity between the *too/either* tags discussed in the preceding chapter and two of the correlative conjunctions that we will cover in this chapter; however, such a semantic similarity is possible only when the underlying sentences have identical verb phrases and nonidentical subject NPs.

John likes baseball and $\left\{ \begin{array}{l} \text{Harry does too} \\ \text{so does Harry} \end{array} \right\}$.

Both John and Harry like baseball.

Pat doesn't like baseball and $\left\{ \begin{array}{l} \text{Sue doesn't either} \\ \text{neither does Sue} \end{array} \right\}$.

Neither Pat nor Sue likes baseball.

The syntactic rules for these semantically similar constructions, however, are quite different, and the rules for deriving correlatives will be covered in this chapter.

While many of the languages your students speak natively contain correlative conjunctions, it is often the case that the correlative conjunction and the sentential conjunction are identical in form, e.g., the *ni . . . ni* combination in Spanish, or the *ou . . . ou* combination in French. Since in English the correlative and the related conjunction are always lexically distinct, this can be an initial source of error or confusion for many ESL/EFL students.

---

1. In some grammars, *but* is also referred to as a member of the correlative set, i.e., *not (only) . . . but (also)*; however, it is often not syntactically parallel to the three other sets and will not be treated here.

Correlative conjunction

When a correlative is used in a surface structure sentence, it emphasizes the coordinate status of the two constituents. The second sentence in the following pair, for instance, intensifies the coordination between the two subject NP constituents:

Joan and Ellen study law.   Both Joan and Ellen study law.

Description

In the above example, a rule called "correlative addition" has been optionally applied to add the first member of the correlative pair before the conjoined constituents. This gives us the second sentence as an emphatic variant of the first. There is also another rule, "correlative movement," that allows us to produce a paraphrase of the second sentence above by moving the correlative conjunction to a position preceding the restructured verb phrase:

Joan and Ellen both study law.[2]

When it is the two VPs which are conjoined, we can have a sentence with correlative addition such as:

Joan studies both law and business.

Also, the correlative movement rule could again optionally apply to move the correlative conjunction to a position following the two conjuncts:

Joan studies law and business both.[3]

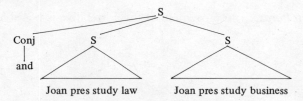

Output of base: and Joan pres study law Joan pres study business
Conjunction movement: Joan pres study law and Joan pres study business
Identical constituent deletion: Joan pres study law and Ø Ø Ø business
Restructuring: Joan pres study law and business
Correlative addition: Joan pres study both law and business

---

2. If the copula BE or an auxiliary verb precedes the verb phrase in such a sentence, two different correlative movements are possible:

Copula BE
Both Joan and Ellen are law students.
1.   Joan and Ellen both are law students.   2.   Joan and Ellen are both law students.

Auxiliary Verb
Both Joan and Ellen will study law.
1.   Joan and Ellen both will study law.   2.   Joan and Ellen will both study law.

Whatever subtle differences there are between the initial position of the correlative and the two possible positions after correlative movement must await description based on a usage study and discourse analysis. If we said anything at this point, we would only be speculating.

3. Not all native speakers are completely comfortable with this type of correlative movement in the verb phrase; however, it does occur, and we see no need to treat it differently from the correlative movement that occurs with subject noun phrases.

Correlative movement (optional):[4] Joan pres study law and business both
Affix attachment (1×): Joan study + pres law and business both
Subject-verb agreement and morphological rules: Joan studies law and business both.

Like the *both . . . and* combination, the addition of *either* to two sentences conjoined by *or* results in an emphatic version of the conjoined sentence. Unlike the *both . . . and* pair, however, *either . . . or* can conjoin full sentences as well as phrases.

Full Sentences	*Phrases*
Dave will get the job or Peter will get the job.	Dave or Peter will get the job.
	Either Dave or Peter will get the job.
Either Dave will get the job or Peter will (get it).	

Notice that with *either . . . or,* correlative movement can occur only when identical subjects—rather than identical verb phrases—are being conjoined and when at least one auxiliary verb or the copula BE is present.

*Identical Verb Phrases (*no correlative movement)
Either Dave or Peter will get the job.   *Dave or Peter either will get the job.

Identical Subject Noun Phrases (optional correlative movement if there is an auxiliary verb or the copula BE)

You either can go or stay.	Jack either is crazy or fearless.
You can either go or stay.	Jack is either crazy or fearless.

Identical Verb Phrases (no movement of the correlative is possible)

Full Sentences

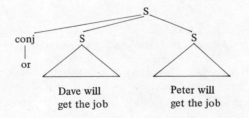

Output of base: or Dave will get the job Peter will get the job
Conjunction movement: Dave will get the job or Peter will get the job
Pro-noun phrase substitution: Dave will get the job or Peter will get it
Correlative addition: Either Dave will get the job or Peter will get it.
(An additional surface deletion here would produce: Either Dave will get the job or Peter will.)

Phrases

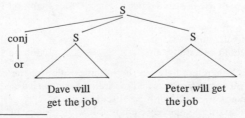

---

4. If this optional rule does not apply, the final result of the derivation is: Joan studies both law and business.

Output of base: or Dave will get the job Peter will get the job
Conjunction movement: Dave will get the job or Peter will get the job
Identical constituent deletion: Dave will get the job or Peter Ø Ø Ø Ø
Restructuring: Dave or Peter will get the job
Correlative addition: Either Dave or Peter will get the job.

Identical Subjects (correlative movement is possible)

Full Sentences

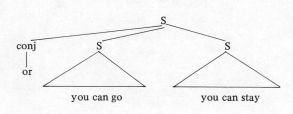

Output of base: or you can go you can stay
Conjunction movement: you can go or you can stay
Correlative addition: either you can go or you can stay
Correlative movement (optional): (a) You either can go or you can stay; (b) You can either go
or you can stay.

Phrases

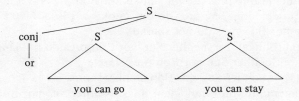

Output of base: or you can go you can stay
Conjunction movement: you can go or you can stay
Identical constituent deletion: you can go or Ø Ø stay
Restructuring: you can go or stay
Correlative addition:[5] you either can go or stay
Correlative movement (optional): You can either go or stay.

The final type of correlative structure to be considered here signals two negative alternatives, both of which are assumed to be true. In such cases, *nor* is the conjunction used and *neither* is its correlative partner. Once restructuring takes place—unlike the other pairs—the correlative conjunction must be added; i.e., it is obligatory rather than optional:

Neither Sue nor Bob smokes.   *Sue nor Bob smokes.

---

5. As a general rule, "correlative addition" places the correlative directly before the two parallel conjoined constituents; however, when the conjoined constituents are verb phrases with a copula BE or verb phrases preceded by an auxiliary verb, the correlative is first added before the BE or the auxiliary verb. It can then be optionally moved to a position following the BE or the auxiliary verb if desired.

Also unlike the other two correlatives, correlative movement cannot take place with either subject noun phrases or verb phrases:

*Sue nor Bob neither smokes.   *Sue smokes nor drinks neither.

Here the conjunction *nor* absorbs the NOT or -N'T in the restructured sentence. However, in this case the restructuring and the addition of *neither* also forces the absorption of the DO auxiliary because it is not needed for subject/auxiliary inversion as was the case in Chapter 22. Note that the occurrence of restructuring and the presence of *neither* would not absorb an auxiliary verb that is generated as part of the underlying structure (e.g., Neither Ted nor Bob can speak Spanish).

Identical Verb Phrases

Neither Sue nor Bob smokes.

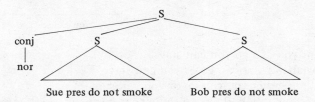

(Assume NOT placement and DO insertion have already occurred in the underlying sentences.)

Derived output: nor Sue pres do not smoke Bob pres do not smoke
Conjunction movement: Sue pres do not smoke nor Bob pres do not smoke
Identical constituent deletion: Sue pres do not smoke nor Bob Ø Ø Ø Ø
Restructuring: Sue nor Bob pres do not smoke
Correlative addition (obligatory): neither Sue nor Bob pres do not smoke
NOT/DO absorption: neither Sue nor Bob pres smoke
Affix attachment (1✗): neither Sue nor Bob smoke + pres
Subject-verb agreement and morphological rules: Neither Sue nor Bob smokes.

Identical Subjects

Sue neither smokes nor drinks.

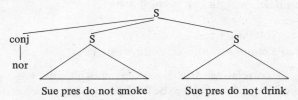

(Assume NOT placement and DO insertion have already taken place in the underlying sentences.)

Derived output: nor Sue pres do not smoke Sue pres do not drink
Conjunction movement: Sue pres do not smoke nor Sue pres do not drink
Identical constituent deletion: Sue pres do not smoke nor Ø Ø Ø Ø drink
Restructuring: Sue pres do not smoke nor drink
Correlative addition: Sue neither pres do not smoke nor drink (obligatory)

NOT/DO absorption: Sue neither pres smoke nor drink
Affix attachment (2×):[6] Sue neither smoke + pres nor drink + pres
Subject-verb agreement and morphological rules: Sue neither smokes nor drinks.

With regard to the *neither . . . nor* pair we should also note that a colloquial variant in some American English dialects involves using the conjunction *or* in place of *nor* after *neither.*

Formal	*Colloquial*
Neither Sue nor Bob smokes.	Neither Sue or Bob smokes.
Sue neither smokes nor drinks.	Sue neither smokes or drinks.

Summary of correlative conjunction

We summarize our observations with regard to the syntactic similarities and differences among the correlative conjunctions by asking three key questions and then providing the answers to these questions for each of the three correlative conjunctions.

	both . . . and	*either . . . or*	*neither . . . nor*
1. Is correlative addition optional?	Yes	Yes	No (It must occur after restructuring.)
2. Can it only conjoin phrases (i.e., not clauses)?	Yes	No—joins clauses too	Yes
3. As an additional option, is it possible to move the correlative?	Yes	Only with identical subject NPs and a copula BE or auxiliary verb	No

Subject/verb agreement for subject phrases with *either . . . or* and *neither . . . nor*

The prescriptive rule for subject-verb agreement for the last two correlative pairs we have considered here is one involving the principle of proximity: when two subjects are joined by *either . . . or* or *neither . . . nor,* the verb agrees with the nearest subject. However, in a published usage study, Tsai (1980) discovered that native speakers do not always abide by the proximity principle. While all 50 native speakers he consulted always chose a plural verb when both subjects were plural, they were not nearly as consistent when one or both of the subjects were singular. For example, 14 of the 50 respondents (28 percent) chose *is* over *are* to fill the blank in the following sentence:

Either the teacher or the students _____ correct.

The deviance from the proximity principle was even more marked for the *neither . . . nor* combination where a number as high as twenty of the native speakers (40 percent) selected the verb form *go,* which signals plurality, over its corresponding singular form *goes* in the following sentence frame:

Neither the students nor the teacher _____ to school on Sundays.

The same number chose *are* over *am* in the next sentence:

Neither John nor I _____ happy.

---

6. Note that when the tense element of the auxiliary—in this case, *pres*—precedes a conjoined verb phrase, the tense affix attaches to both of the verbs in the conjunction because it is modifying both of them.

Tsai interprets this finding as evidence that many native speakers tend to treat *neither... nor* much like *and* with regard to subject-verb concord.

Thus we see that while the conventional proximity principle was still favored by the majority of Tsai's respondents, there also appeared to be considerable discrepancy among his native-speaking consultants with regard to the form of the verb which follows correlatives. While ESL/EFL teachers would be perfectly correct in presenting the proximity principle to their students, they should also be aware that these students may be exposed to input from native speakers who regularly do not adhere to the principle.

Sentences with *respectively*

Few languages other than English have a word equivalent to *respectively*. By using this word, we take a sentence like this:

> Sam received an A and Harry received a B.

and transform it into:

> Sam and Harry received an A and a B, respectively.

The rule we will need in addition to the ones we've already used which will help us with this transformation is an optional rule referred to as *respectively* addition. *Respectively* is added to a sentence containing at least two restructured pairs of constituents. We refer to this process as multiple restructuring. The role of *respectively* is to disambiguate by indicating which constituent goes with which. For example, if we did not have the *respectively* in the above sentence, another possible interpretation would be that both Sam and Harry received two grades, namely, an A and a B. In the above sentence with *respectively,* the two restructured constituents are *Sam and Harry* and *an A and a B.*

The basic structure for this sentence is as follows:

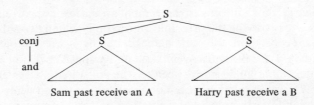

To derive the surface structure, the following transformations would apply:

Conjunction movement: Sam past receive an A and Harry past receive a B
Identical constituent deletion: Sam past receive an A and Harry Ø Ø a B
Multiple restructuring (2×):[7] Sam and Harry past receive an A and a B
Respectively addition: Sam and Harry past receive an A and a B respectively
Affix attachment (1×): Sam and Harry receive + past an A and a B respectively
Morphological rules: Sam and Harry received an A and a B, respectively.

Note that for this sentence, we can optionally move *respectively* to a position after the first pair of conjoined constituents. We refer to this rule as *respectively* movement:

> Sam and Harry, respectively, received an A and a B.

---

7. When multiple restructuring occurs, the conjunction *and* also multiplies and occurs between each pair of restructured constituents.

Notice also that the pairs of conjoined constituents in a sentence with *respectively* can consist of constituents other than NPs; i.e., prepositional phrases and entire verb phrases may also undergo multiple restructuring:

> Sam and Harry live in Boston and in Hartford, respectively.
> Sam and Harry sailed on the lake and kayaked upriver, respectively.

Reciprocal pronouns

Just as the equivalent of *respectively* is rare in other languages, so many other languages also do not have the lexically explicit reciprocal pronouns that English has (i.e., *each other* and *one another*). Sometimes reflexive forms are used in other languages to express the same semantic notion that reciprocal pronouns signal in English. For example, the following Spanish sentence—when considered in isolation—could be translated into English in either of two ways:

Los actores se maquillaron antes de salir al escenario.

The actors made each other up before going on stage.

The actors made themselves up before going on stage.

What is the semantic notion signaled by the use of reciprocal pronouns? Consider the following sentence:

> John and Bill admire each other.

What this sentence really means, of course, is that John admires Bill and—simultaneously— that Bill admires John. This analysis tells us that underlying this surface structure there must be two basic sentences which have become conjoined. Furthermore, the resulting conjoined sentence contains two pairs of constituents which must be ordered so that we know which goes with which. These conditions led Stockwell, Schachter, and Partee (1973) to suggest that multiple restructuring be considered an intermediate step in deriving a surface structure containing the reciprocal pronoun *each other*.

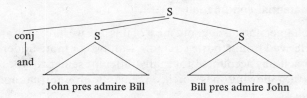

Conjunction movement: John pres admire Bill and Bill pres admire John
Identical constituent deletion: John pres admire Bill and Bill Ø Ø John
Multiple restructuring: John and Bill pres admire Bill and John

The condition for reciprocal pronoun substitution has been met by this intermediate string. This condition is that the second pair of conjoined elements be the reverse (or mirror image) of the first pair.[8] When this is the case, the reciprocal pronouns replace the second pair

---

8. Note that use of a reciprocal pronoun is incompatible with correlative conjunction (or vice versa), since correlatives are used where two pieces of information are parallel and reciprocal pronouns are used where two pieces of information are reversed.

of restructured constituents. Thus our derivation would proceed as follows:

Reciprocal pronoun substitution: John and Bill pres admire each other
Affix attachment (1×): John and Bill admire + pres each other
Morphological rules: John and Bill admire each other.

In some sentences the state or action is inherently reciprocal.

Sylvia's and Jane's views are similar to   Stu and Marsha kissed each other.
each other.

In order to avoid semantic redundancy in such cases, we can apply a late optional rule of reciprocal pronoun deletion, which produces:

Sylvia's and Jane's views are similar.   Stu and Marsha kissed.

The usual rule given to explain the distinction between the reciprocal pronouns (i.e., *each other* and *one another*) is that *each other* is used when there are two NPs involved whereas *one another* is the appropriate form to use when there are more than two NPs. While it may be the case that *each other* is preferred when there are two NPs:

?Sandy and Gail promised one another they would get together again.

it does not appear to be strictly a matter of the number involved when more than two NPs are being considered. Both of the following sentences, for example, seem acceptable and may in fact have different meanings:

At their annual reunion the family members shared with $\left\{\begin{array}{l}\text{one another}\\\text{each other}\end{array}\right\}$ the news
of the past year.

Certainly it would be useful to have a contemporary, empirical study on the use of *each other* versus *one another* so that the prescriptive rule of two versus more than two can be supported or revised.

Phrasal versus sentential conjunction

In the preceding chapter and throughout most of this one we have assumed that all conjoined constituents are derived from a basic structure with two or more underlying sentences, and indeed this approach has accounted for many different sentence types. However, there are sentences such as the following ones which, on semantic grounds, cannot be derived from two underlying sentences:

Gary and Sheila are a happy couple.
*Gary is a happy couple and Sheila is a happy couple.

The preacher joined Ann and Rick in Holy Matrimony.
*The preacher joined Ann in Holy Matrimony and the preacher joined Rick in Holy Matrimony.

Note also the inappropriateness of using the *both . . . and* correlative construction, which was permissible in the case of conjoined underlying sentences that shared information such as identical subjects.

*Both Gary and Sheila are a happy couple.

In the examples given above, it should be apparent that two noun phrases rather than two sentences are conjoined in the underlying structure. We can account for this by adding an alternative to our phrase structure rule for expanding the NP:

$$NP \longrightarrow \left\{ \begin{array}{l} (det) \ N \ (pl) \\ conj + NP^n \end{array} \right\}$$

With this revised rule the underlying structure and derivation of "Gary and Sheila are a happy couple" can be represented as follows:

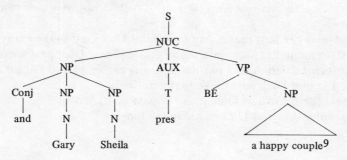

Output of base: and Gary Sheila pres BE a happy couple
Conjunction movement: Gary and Sheila pres BE a happy couple
Affix attachment (1×): Gary and Sheila BE + pres a happy couple
Subject-verb agreement and morphological rules: Gary and Sheila are a happy couple.

This new source also allows us to account for potentially ambiguous sentences such as the following:

Liz and Dick made many movies.

If the interpretation is that they made the movies together, phrasal conjunction would be the underlying source:

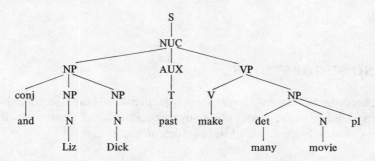

Output of base: and Liz Dick past make many movie pl
Conjunction movement: Liz and Dick past make many movie pl
Affix attachment (2×): Liz and Dick make + past many movie + pl
Morphological rules: Liz and Dick made many movies.

---

9. We have not analyzed the internal structure of this noun phrase, since we have not yet discussed the derivation of adjectives in prenominal position. This topic will come up in Chapter 28.

If, however, the interpretation of the ambiguous sentence is that each star made movies independent of the other, sentential conjunction would be called for.

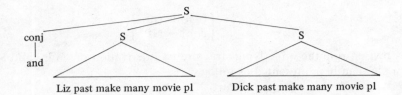

Output of base: and Liz past make many movie pl Dick past make many movie pl
Conjunction movement: Liz past make many movie pl and Dick past make many movie pl
Identical constituent deletion: Liz past make many movie pl and Dick Ø Ø Ø Ø Ø
Restructuring: Liz and Dick past make many movie pl
Affix attachment (2×): Liz and Dick make + past many movie + pl
Morphological rules: Liz and Dick made many movies.

Summary

In this chapter we identified two sources for conjoined NPs in the surface structure:

1. From conjoined sentences via deletion and restructuring
2. From conjoined NPs in the underlying structure

We analyzed sentences with correlative conjunctions, sentences with *respectively,* and sentences with reciprocal pronouns as instances where there are two underlying sentences in the basic structure. However, we noted that some conjoined constituents could not be derived from two underlying structures and thus introduced the concept of phrasal conjunction— with an accompanying phrase structure rule—to account for such cases. Furthermore, because English has two different sources for conjoined constituents, there are some sentences with conjoined constituents that are ambiguous.

TEACHING SUGGESTIONS

1 A possible context for having your students practice the use of *respectively* is to ask them to compare two friends, e.g., Doug and Marty, by writing conjoined sentences with *respectively*. The teacher can supply them with brief profiles on each:

Doug	*Marty*
lives in Phoenix	lives in Santa Barbara
15 years old	16 years old
has straight black hair	has curly blonde hair
likes sports cars	likes dune buggies
wants to be a jet pilot	wants to be a surfer

Of course, it would have to be made apparent to your students that *respectively* does not occur very frequently, even in written discourse, and that comparing the two friends using *respectively* is contrived just for practice.

2   As a way of introducing students to the syntactic and semantic elements inherent in the use of the reciprocal pronoun *each other,* Marie Bedell suggests the following procedure. (The sentences should be written on the board after they have been produced orally):

Teacher: (introduces a sentence) I saw Albert.
(Teacher asks a student to reverse the action.)
Student 1:   Albert saw me.
(Teacher asks another student to combine the two sentences.)
Student 2:   I saw Albert and Albert saw me.

Teacher explains that whenever we have two sentences that are the reverse of each other, we can avoid the repetition by conjoining the subjects and using *each other* as a substitute for the objects, e.g.:

Albert and I saw each other.

The teacher then provides several other sentences which the students can (a) reverse, (b) combine, and (c) paraphrase with *each other,* e.g.:

Phil hit George.   Sally likes Sam.

3   Sports commentators make frequent use of reciprocal pronouns during their broadcasts.

"The Boston Celtics have faced the New York Knicks many times before but never have they played each other with the fervor we've seen tonight."

If you are in a situation where your students can listen to English language sports broadcasts, have them collect examples of reciprocal pronouns used in such contexts.

In an EFL (or ESL) situation, supply your students with a nonpictorial visual aid (Shaw and Taylor, 1978) such as a summary of the results of the last two decades of World Cup Soccer championships. Have them generate sentences with reciprocal pronouns based on the information they've been given, e.g.:

Brazil and Italy have never played each other in a championship game.
Uruguay and England have faced each other twice recently.

4   To help your students see the difference between the reflexive and reciprocal pronouns—if this is a problem—visual reinforcement is useful:

themselves   *each other*

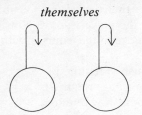

Then have your students apply these concepts to situations which they must paraphrase using either a reflexive or a reciprocal pronoun as appropriate, e.g.:

John cut himself and Bob cut himself.
(John and Bob cut themselves.)
Mary gave a present to Jill and Jill gave a present to Mary.

(Mary and Jill gave $\left\{ \begin{array}{l} \text{presents to each other} \\ \text{each other presents} \end{array} \right\}$.)

5   Gretchen Lettieri and Ian Green have created the following dialog for the purpose of reinforcing the conjunction *and* and introducing the correlative pair *both . . . and* to their students:

> *Setting: Coffee Shop*
> *Waiter:* Would you like our soup and salad special?
> *Customer 1:* What's the soup today?
> *Waiter:* Leek or potato.
> *Customer 2:* What kind of sandwiches do you have?
> *Waiter:* Ham and cheese, peanut butter and jelly, cream cheese and olives, BLT, hot dogs and hamburgers.
> *Customer 1:* What's a BLT?
> *Waiter:* Bacon, lettuce, and tomato.
> *Customer 1:* I'll have a hot dog [hesitates] *and* I'll have a hamburger.
> *Waiter:* You want a hamburger?
> *Customer 1:* I want both a hot dog and a hamburger.
> *Customer 2:* I'll have a hamburger and french fries.
> *Waiter:* Do you want lettuce on your hamburger . . . or do you want tomato?
> *Customer 2:* I want both lettuce and tomato.
> *Waiter:* And to drink?
> *Customer 2:* Both my friend and I would like coffee.

Following some work with the dialog, menus are distributed to the students, who form groups of three (a waiter and two customers) to practice *both . . . and* in ordering a meal.

6   As a remedial exercise for students having trouble with the subject-verb agreement rules for correlative pairs, Zeinab El-Naggar suggests the following:

After reviewing the rules for subject-verb agreement for *both . . . and, either . . . or,* and *neither . . . nor,* provide students situations where sentences containing these correlative combinations could readily be constructed, e.g.:

> SITUATION: The school football team is always losing.
> STUDENTS PRODUCE: Either the coach or the players are responsible.
> Either the players or the coach is responsible.
> Both the players and the coach are responsible.
> Neither the players nor the coach is responsible.
> Neither the coach nor the players are responsible.
> SITUATION: A student is discussing required courses with his or her academic advisor.
> STUDENTS PRODUCE: Either French or Spanish is required.
> Both French and Spanish are required.
> Neither French nor Spanish is required.

A written exercise sheet would then be distributed to conclude the remedial lesson, e.g.:

Supply the missing verbs in the following sentences. Use present tense.
1.   Either the doctor or the nurse _____ the Mercedes.
2.   Both Egypt and Morocco _____ in Africa.

EXERCISES

Test your understanding of what has been presented

1. Provide original example sentences or pairs of sentences that illustrate the following. Underline the pertinent word(s) in your examples.

correlative conjunction	correlative movement
phrasal conjunction	*respectively* addition
sentential conjunction	reciprocal pronoun deletion
reciprocal pronoun	multiple restructuring

2. Give the tree diagrams and the rules which would apply in order to derive the following sentences:

a. Robin and Batman are a duo.
b. John and Bill kissed Ann and Alice, respectively.
c. Ken and Doug hate each other.
d. Either Morris or Hansen could give the lecture.
e. John and Bill both speak Italian.
f. Neither you nor I should do that job.

3. Give the tree diagrams for each of the following sentences, paying attention to whether they involve sentential conjunction, phrasal conjunction, or are ambiguous. If they are ambiguous, give the two possible tree diagrams.

a. Gail and Tom have a car.
b. Burt and Joe passed the exam.
c. Smith and Jones are partners.

4. Why are the following sentences ungrammatical (or at best awkward or redundant)?

a. *Joe sang a duet and Harry sang a duet.
b. ?Mary hit Linda and Linda hit Mary, respectively.
c. ?Yale Street and Harvard Street are parallel to each other.
d. *Both I speak English and Spanish.

Test your ability to apply what you know

5. If your students produce the following sentences, what errors have they made? How will you make them aware of the errors and what exercises will you prepare to correct the errors?

a. *Bill and Jim respectively got law degrees.
b. *Planes arrive at noon and 3 p.m., respectively.
c. *Nor John nor Bill will win the election.
d. *Either Helen or Judy are going to host the party.

6. You have some students in your ESL/EFL class who consistently use reflexive pronouns where English requires reciprocal pronouns (e.g., *John and Mary were dancing with themselves all night long). What would you do in terms of explanations and exercises to help them overcome this type of error?

7. How does the use of the adjective *respective* differ from the use of the adverb *respectively*? What degree of similarity is there in meaning and use?

8. One of your ESL/EFL students says he heard a native speaker say:

John neither works or studies.

He asks you whether it is not the case that *neither* must always be followed by *nor.* What will your answer be?

BIBLIOGRAPHY

References

Shaw, P., and J. B. Taylor (1978). "Non-pictorial Visual Aids," in S. Holden (ed.), *Visual Aids for Classroom Interaction.* London: Modern English Publications, Ltd.

Stockwell, R. P., P. Schachter, and B. H. Partee (1973). *The Major Syntactic Structures of English.* New York: Holt, Rinehart and Winston, Chap. 6.

Tsai, P. (1980). "Neither Jane nor I are happy?" (An empirical study of subject-verb concord and its pedagogical implications.) *English Teaching Forum,* vol. 18, no. 1, January, pp. 19–24.

Suggestions for further reading

For theoretical treatments of sentential versus phrasal conjunction, consult:

Gleitman, L. R. (1969). "Coordinating Conjunctions in English," in D. Reibel and S. Schane (eds.), *Modern Studies in English.* Englewood Cliffs, N.J.: Prentice-Hall.

Lakoff, G., and S. Peters (1969). "Phrasal Conjunction and Symmetric Predicates," in D. Reibel and S. Schane (eds.), *Modern Studies in English.* Englewood Cliffs, N.J.: Prentice-Hall.

For a theoretical account of correlative addition and correlative movement, see:

Stockwell, Schachter, and Partee (1973) in the above references.

For a theoretical and empirical account of symmetric predicates, which typically imply reciprocal actions or states, see:

Sher, A. (1975). "Symmetric Predicates: A Theoretical and Empirical Study." Unpublished M.A. in TESL thesis, UCLA.

For some practical suggestions regarding the teaching of correlatives, see:

Danielson, D., and R. M. Hayden (1973). *Using English: Your Second Language.* Englewood Cliffs, N.J.: Prentice-Hall, pp. 124–125.

Rutherford, W. E. (1975). *Modern English* (2d ed., vol I). New York: Harcourt Brace Jovanovich, pp. 112–113.

Wohl, M. (1978). *Preparation for Writing: Grammar.* Rowley, Mass.: Newbury House, pp. 44–49.

For some suggestions on how to teach reciprocal pronouns, see:

Rutherford, W. E. (1977). *Modern English* (2d ed., vol II). New York: Harcourt Brace Jovanovich, Unit 16.

24

Logical Connectors

GRAMMATICAL DESCRIPTION

Introduction

With the exception of our discussion of conjoined sentences, we have restricted our examination thus far to the structural components of single sentences. In this chapter we will look beyond surface structures which comprise single sentences, and consider logical connectors—words or phrases whose function it is to show some logical relationship between two or more basic sentences or—in some cases—between a basic sentence and a noun phrase. Conjunctions and correlatives, as we have seen, have as much a syntactic as a semantic function and serve to coordinate clauses within a surface structure sentence; logical connectors have primarily a semantic, cohesive function, which holds within or between surface structure sentences (Halliday and Hasan, 1976:244).

Although using logical connectors properly is essential in the production of good writing, it is also important for ESL/EFL students to be able to recognize their function while reading and listening, and it is also important for the students to control the more common ones while speaking. Tomiyama (1980) found that native speakers were less able to correct ESL learners' global errors related to the use of connectors than their "local"[1] errors such as problems with article usage. The explanation for this given by Tomiyama is that the connector errors so distorted the intended message that the native speakers were unable to reconstruct the clausal relationship the author/speaker had attempted to convey.

Producing logical connectors is often more challenging than might at first be apparent. In addition to the usual semantic and syntactic knowledge students must possess in order to use logical connectors appropriately, they must also have a sensitivity to register. Having a sensitivity to register means that students must know, for example, if they are introducing an "effect clause," when to use a formal connector such as *in consequence,* and when the situation calls for a more informal connector such as *so.* One of the things that marks speakers as nonnative is their producing a logical connector of an inappropriate register. In any kind of informal situation, a native speaker of English would be surprised to hear somebody say *notwithstanding the fact that* to express the notion of concession. A connector such as *even though* would be much more likely.

---

1. The terms "local" and "global" errors come from the work of Burt and Kiparsky (1974).

Although logical connectors are probably best presented to a class group by group spread out over an entire term, we will treat them together here to facilitate classification and discussion.

A functional classification of logical connectors

Typically, logical connectors are presented according to the function they fulfill. The following, although not an exhaustive list, is an enumeration of the most common functions which logical connectors can express. We have chosen to follow Secord's hierarchy (1978) of functional categories, which in turn draws heavily from Halliday and Hasan (1976). We present an abbreviated version of her hierarchy below. No claim is made that within each group, all logical connectors are completely synonymous, since each may convey a different aspect of the category's meaning. However, we feel it is the similarities which should be drawn upon initially when presenting logical connectors to ESL/EFL students.

Like Secord, who basically followed Halliday and Hasan, the four broad headings under which we classify all the connectors are the following:

1.   Additive (used to signal addition, introduction, to show similarity, etc.)
2.   Adversative (used to signal conflict, contradiction, concession, etc.)
3.   Causal (used to signal cause/effect and reason/result, etc.)
4.   Sequential (used to signal a chronological or logical sequence)

We shall now proceed in greater detail with the classification.

Additive
1.   *Addition*
      a. Simple:

additionally	in addition (TO THIS)
also	furthermore
moreover	further
not to mention THIS[2]	and[3]
	too[4]
	either (negative)[5]

---

2. Following the convention of Halliday and Hasan (1976), THIS is a symbol we use to indicate that a referential item must follow a logical connector. In some cases the referential item for the logical connector is either implicit or can be stated explicitly. If this option exists for a particular logical connector, we will indicate the optionality of the reference word by using parentheses. Notice that sometimes when a reference word is optional, if it is made explicit, it must be preceded by a preposition, e.g., *in addition* (*to* THIS). In such cases the preposition is included with the THIS in parentheses.

3. We have viewed *and* before as a sentential and phrasal conjunction. Here we refer to it as a logical connector, since it can convey the meaning of "in addition."

4. We have also encountered this word before in Chapter 22 with reference to conjoined sentences. At that time we mentioned that *too* is used within a sentence to signal the addition of a repeated constituent in an affirmative verb phrase:

Marlene slaloms well and Burt does too.

But notice semantically *too* implies "in addition" and therefore rightfully should be considered a logical connector in this category. Furthermore, as it can in conjoined sentences, *too* can also be found in simple sentences where it does not signal the repetition of a constituent but rather functions in the discourse to mark an additional comment with the same theme as that of an earlier sentence:

A: For relaxation we play hearts and pinochle.   B: Do you enjoy bridge too?

5. Some logical connectors occur in a negative context or impose a negative meaning on the phrase or clause being connected to the text. In such cases, we have added the word "negative" in parentheses after the connector to signal this fact.

b. Emphatic:
   besides (THIS)   as well (AS THIS)

   not only THIS but . . . $\left\{ \begin{array}{l} \text{also} \\ \text{as well} \end{array} \right.$ what is more

c. Intensifying:
   in fact   actually
   as a matter of fact   indeed
   to tell (you) the truth   let alone (negative)
   to say nothing of (negative)   much less (negative)

d. Alternative:
   or   nor (negative)
   alternatively   on the other hand

2. *Exemplification*
  a. To exemplify a representative member:
     such as   as
     for example   like
     for instance
  b. To exemplify the most important member:
     especially   in particular
     particularly   notably
  c. To introduce an ordinary group member:
     including
  d. To introduce a specific example which comes in a separate sentence from the
    preceding general statement:
     for one thing   by way of example
     as an illustration   to illustrate

3. *Reference*
  To introduce a topic:
        speaking about THIS
        as for THIS
        considering THIS
        concerning THIS
        regarding THIS
        on the subject/topic of THIS

        with/in $\left\{ \begin{array}{l} \text{respect} \\ \text{regard} \\ \text{reference} \end{array} \right\}$ to $\left\{ \begin{array}{l} \text{THIS} \\ \text{the fact that} \end{array} \right.$

4. *Similarity*
     similarly   in a like manner
     likewise   by the same token
     in the same way   equally

5. *Identification*
  To identify a constituent for which the reader/listener has already been prepared:
     that is (to say)   specifically
     namely

6. *Clarification*
    To clarify or rephrase a preceding item:

    that is (to say)   in other words
    I mean   (to) put (it) another way

Adversative

1. *Conflict/Contrast*[6] (Two ideas incompatible or in contrast)

    but[7]   while
    however   whereas
    in contrast   conversely
    by way of contrast   on the other hand
    (and) yet   though (in sentence-final position)
    when in fact[8]

2. *Concession* (Reservation without invalidating the truth of the main clause)

    but   on the other hand[9]
    even so   despite THIS
    however   in spite of THIS
    (and) still   regardless (of THIS)
    (and) yet   notwithstanding (THIS)
    nevertheless   be that as it may
    nonetheless   granted (THIS)
    although   admittedly
    though   albeit
    even though

3. *Dismissal*
    a. Alternative circumstances (Quirk et al., 1972):

        either way   in either case
        whichever happens   in either event

    b. Universal circumstances—two or more possibilities (Quirk et al., 1972):

        whatever happens   in any case/event
        all the same   at any rate

4. *Replacement*
    a. To rectify a preceding item:

        (or) at least   (or) rather

    b. To substitute a positive statement for a negative one or to substitute an actual
        outcome for a prior expectation:

        instead

---

6. In some studies conflict and contrast are treated separately. We do not feel the criteria for distinguishing them are sufficiently clear-cut at this time to justify two separate categories.

7. Note that *but* (also dealt with in the preceding chapters on conjoined sentences) occurs as a logical connector primarily in oral language and is usually unaccented.

8. *When in fact* conveys the special meaning of simultaneously discrediting the validity of the first clause while affirming the truth of the second.

9. Some logical connectors belong to more than one category or subcategory. They are used in different ways by native speakers depending upon the context and the speaker's intentions. To illustrate, consider the following sentences in which the logical connector serves a different function:

The polls have indicated that inflation is the biggest problem facing the nation.
On the other hand, one could argue that the energy crisis is more detrimental to the economy. (contrast)
On the other hand, the energy crisis is also a major problem. (concession)

Causal

1. *Cause/Reason*

being that	due to (the fact that)
seeing that	in view of (the fact that)
since	owing to (the fact that)
as	for the (simple) reason that
inasmuch as	for
forasmuch as	in that
because (of the fact that)	

2. *Effect/Result*

so that	consequently
so	as a consequence
so much (so) that	thus
for this reason	hence
as a result (of THIS)	in consequence
because (of THIS)	accordingly
therefore	

3. *Purpose*

so	in the hope that
so { as to / that	for the purpose of
	to the end that
in order { that / to	for fear that (negative)
	for fear (negative)
with this in mind	lest (negative)
with this intention	

4. *Condition*

   a. To introduce the condition:

if	granted (that)
in case	granting (that)
provided that	as/so long as
providing that	even if
on (the) condition that	only if
in the event that	unless (negative)
given that	

   b. To introduce the consequence:

then	under those circumstances
if so	if not (negative)
in that case	otherwise (negative)
that being the case	

Sequential

1. *Chronological and Logical*

   a. Numerical:

   (chronological and logical)

in the (first) place	initially . . .; secondly . . .
first . . .; second . . .	

b. Beginning:
   (chronological)   (chronological and logical)
   at first   to start with
                                      to begin with
                                      for a start
                                      first of all
                                      initially

c. Continuation:
   (chronological)   (chronological and logical)
   previously   next
   after THIS   then
   afterwards
   eventually
   subsequently
   before THIS

d. Conclusion:
   (chronological)   (logical)
   finally   at last
   eventually   last but not least
   at last   as a final point
   in the end   lastly
                                        to conclude (with)

2. *Digression*
   by the way   incidentally   to change the subject

3. *Resumption*
   anyhow   to get back to the point
   anyway   to return to the subject
   at any rate   to resume

4. *Summation*
a. General:
   in conclusion   in summary
   to sum up   in sum
   to summarize

b. Review of main idea or purpose:
   as I have said   as has been mentioned/noted
   as was previously stated

c. Combination of effect/result and summary:
   then   consequently
   given (all) these points   thus
   therefore   hence
   so

d. Summary of points:
   on the whole   all in all
   altogether   overall
   in all

e. Condensation:

to make a long story short   in short
to put it briefly   to be brief
briefly   in a word

The syntax of logical connectors

The first time a new logical connector is presented to a class, it should be shown in a meaningful discourse context and also in the position in which it typically occurs in a sentence. In some cases the placement of a logical connector is restricted; i.e., it either occurs only in initial position in a clause, only clause medially, or only clause finally.

These three major positions and their variations can be represented schematically as follows:

Clause Initial
Before clause 1: Connector + clause 1 + clause 2
Before clause 2: Clause 1 + connector + clause 2[10]
Clause Medial
Clause 1 + part of clause 2 + connector + rest of clause 2
Clause Final
Clause 1 + clause 2 + connector

Sometimes a particular logical connector can occur in all three major positions. Of course, when a logical connector can occur in all three positions, one would expect that there would be a difference in meaning depending on its location and that free variation is not permissible. Salera (1978), in a study of logical connector mobility, hypothesized that the adversatives *however, nevertheless,* and *instead* would occur:

1. Clause initially if the situation calls for an emphatic, contrary-to-expectation expression.

The fire swept down Mandeville Canyon. We were forced to evacuate, convinced we would return to find ashes.

predicted as the preferred choice ──→a. Instead, we found our home completely untouched.
b. We found, instead, our home completely untouched.
c. other _____
d. Comment:

10. In the discussion which follows, we further distinguish two types of sentences where the connector precedes the second clause: those in which there is sentence-final punctuation after clause 1, e.g.:

Atlanta boasts an ideal geographic location. In addition, it enjoys a relatively mild climate.

and those in which the connector does not begin a new sentence, e.g.:

Atlanta boasts an ideal geographic location, and it enjoys a relatively mild climate.

We make this distinction because it is often the case that ESL/EFL learners err and use certain logical connectors to begin new sentences, when prescriptively at least, the connectors in question should not be used in this manner, e.g.:

We were tired. *So we went home.

2. Clause medially if the situation calls for a strong contrastive relationship (but one that is not emphatically counter to expectation) or one that expresses a reservation about the previous clause.

> Jack is a magazine columnist who is concerned that people aren't using words correctly. He notices that words sometimes mean different things to different people. This condition, he believes, could be corrected if people would use their dictionaries more often.

predicted as the preferred choice ——→ a. He knows, however, that they won't.
                                                     b. He knows that they won't, however.
                                                     c. other _____
                                                     d. Comment:

3. Clause finally if the situation calls for a contrastive comment or afterthought that is not as important as what went on before.

> Miriam has been running for over a year. Two months ago she went into training for a 15 kilometer race by running the hilly perimeter of UCLA. The week before the test, she knew she was ready—she was running smooth and easy. When she got to the race, she found the course more hilly than she had expected.

                                                     a. She nevertheless ran a good race.
predicted as the preferred choice ——→ b. She ran a good race nevertheless.
                                                     c. other _____
                                                     d. Comment:

In general, the results of Salera's study revealed a confirmation of the hypotheses, although agreement among native speakers with regard to the preferred sentence position of the logical connectors was by no means unanimous. More usage studies dealing with the mobility of these adversative connectors, not to mention the other categories of connectors, would be helpful.

In our discussion of the following categories, we illustrate the placement of logical connectors in the three locations.

Additive
Clause Initial
Before clause 1:

$\left. \begin{array}{l} \text{In addition to} \\ \text{Besides} \end{array} \right\}$ Atlanta boasting an ideal geographic location, it enjoys a relatively mild climate.

Before clause 2:
Sentence initial:
Atlanta boasts an ideal geographic location.

$\left\{ \begin{array}{l} \text{Also} \\ \text{In addition} \\ \text{Furthermore} \\ \text{Additionally} \\ \text{Moreover} \end{array} \right\}$, it enjoys a relatively mild climate.

Sentence internal:

Atlanta boasts an ideal geographic location, $\left\{ \begin{array}{l} \text{and} \\ \text{not to mention that} \end{array} \right\}$ it enjoys a relatively mild climate.

Clause Medial

Atlanta boasts an ideal geographic location.

It $\begin{Bmatrix} \text{also} \\ \text{moreover} \\ \text{furthermore} \end{Bmatrix}$ enjoys a relatively mild climate.

Clause Final

Atlanta boasts an ideal geographic location. It enjoys a relatively mild climate

$\begin{Bmatrix} \text{too} \\ \text{also} \\ \text{in addition} \\ \text{as well} \end{Bmatrix}$.

Contrast/Conflict

Clause Initial

Before clause 1:

$\begin{Bmatrix} \text{While} \\ \text{Whereas} \end{Bmatrix}$ most of our students have an easier time understanding English than

producing it, that was not Abdullah's problem.

Before clause 2:

Sentence initial:

Most students have an easier time understanding English than producing it.

$\begin{Bmatrix} \text{However} \\ \text{On the other hand} \end{Bmatrix}$, that was not Abdullah's problem.

Sentence internal:

Most of our students have an easier time understanding English than producing it,

$\begin{Bmatrix} \text{but} \\ \text{and yet} \end{Bmatrix}$ that was not Abdullah's problem.

Clause Medial

Most of our students have an easier time understanding English than producing it;

that was not, $\begin{Bmatrix} \text{however} \\ \text{on the other hand} \end{Bmatrix}$, Abdullah's problem.

Clause Final

Most of our students have an easier time understanding English than producing it.

That was not Abdullah's problem, $\begin{Bmatrix} \text{on the other hand} \\ \text{however} \end{Bmatrix}$.

Exemplification

Clause Initial

Before clause 2:

Intensive language instructional programs require a great deal of time.

$\begin{Bmatrix} \text{For example} \\ \text{For instance} \\ \text{As an example} \end{Bmatrix}$, students at the University of Michigan's English Language

Institute attend English classes four hours daily.

Clause Medial

Intensive language instruction programs require a great deal of time. Students at the

University of Michigan's English Language Institute, $\begin{Bmatrix} \text{for example} \\ \text{for instance} \end{Bmatrix}$, attend

English classes four hours daily.

Connector following example:

Intensive language instructional programs, the University of Michigan's

$$\left.\begin{array}{l}\text{for example} \\ \text{for instance} \\ \text{as an example} \\ \text{in particular}\end{array}\right\}, \text{ require a great deal of time.}$$

Clause Final

Intensive language instructional programs require a great deal of time. The students at the University of Michigan's English Language Institute attend English classes

four hours daily, $\left\{\begin{array}{l}\text{for example} \\ \text{for instance}\end{array}\right\}$.

Cause and Effect/Reason and Result

Precedes effect/result:

Clause Initial

Before clause 2:

Sentence initial:

Mavis hasn't taken good care of herself. $\left\{\begin{array}{l}\text{For this reason} \\ \text{Because of this} \\ \text{As a result}\end{array}\right\}$, she caught

a cold.

Sentence internal:

Mavis hasn't taken good care of herself; $\left\{\begin{array}{l}\text{so} \\ \text{therefore} \\ \text{consequently} \\ \text{thus}\end{array}\right\}$, she caught

a cold.

Clause Medial

Mavis hasn't taken good care of herself; she $\left\{\begin{array}{l}\text{therefore} \\ \text{thus}\end{array}\right\}$ caught a cold.

Clause Final

Mavis hasn't taken good care of herself. She caught a cold $\left\{\begin{array}{l}\text{as a result} \\ \text{for this reason}\end{array}\right\}$.

Precedes cause/reason:

Clause Initial

Before clause 1:

$\left.\begin{array}{l}\text{Due to the fact that} \\ \text{Because} \\ \text{Since}\end{array}\right\}$ Mavis hasn't taken good care of herself, she caught a cold.

Before clause 2 (also results in a change of clause order):

Sentence internal:

Mavis caught a cold $\left\{\begin{array}{l}\text{due to the fact that} \\ \text{since} \\ \text{because}\end{array}\right\}$ she hasn't taken good care of

herself.

Concession
   Clause Initial
      Before clause 1:
         Though
         Although
         Even though   } Claude went on a strict diet, he continued to gain weight.
         While
         In spite of the fact
         Despite the fact
      Before clause 2:
         Sentence internal (clauses are switched):

Claude continued to gain weight { even though / in spite of the fact that / despite the fact that / regardless of the fact that } he went on a strict diet.

   Clause Final

Claude went on a strict diet. He continued to gain weight { in spite of this / despite this / regardless / though }

We have not included all the logical connectors or all the possible permutations in the examples we have provided. What we have attempted to do is to illustrate the various positions that logical connectors can occupy and to reinforce our contention that an ESL/EFL teacher should not introduce logical connectors divorced from their semantic and syntactic contexts.

Clause ordering

As we have seen in two instances above, there are times when the clause order may vary—when

Connector + clause 1 + clause 2

varies with

Clause 2 + connector + clause 1.

In our examples this pattern held for the adversative logical connectors:

Even though Claude went on a strict diet, he continued to gain weight.
Claude continued to gain weight even though he went on a strict diet.

and for the causal logical connectors:

Because Mavis hasn't taken good care of herself, she caught a cold.
Mavis caught a cold because she hasn't taken good care of herself.

The question we want to pose is what the meaning difference is between the two clausal orderings. Secord (1977) conducted a usage study in which she found support for the following hypotheses with regard to the concessive logical connectors:

1. When the concessive clause is first, it reflects a counter-to-expectation which follows from the previous context or the speaker's presuppositions about the listener's viewpoint. It

serves to either discredit the previous context or indicate that the main clause which follows will not be in perfect agreement with that context or what the speaker believes the listener's opinion is, e.g.:

Although Hal's obnoxious, you have to admit he's a very intelligent guy.

2. When the concessive clause comes second, the main clause basically continues the train of thought from the previous context. The function of the concessive clause here is an admission, a yielding, a reservation, or an acknowledgment of some point related to the main point, e.g.:

Star Wars was still drawing crowds a year after its release, though in smaller numbers.

Thus, to account for such order variations and others which may exist, one should look to the discourse context in order to understand why speakers sequence the clauses joined by a logical connector in the order they do.

Reductions

Thus far we have discussed logical connectors which can precede clauses, occur medially within clauses, and follow full clauses. However, it is also the case that the clauses can be reduced in a number of ways and still be accompanied by logical connectors.

We illustrate some of these reductions using concessive logical connectors as an example:

1. Clauses lacking a surface subject and the verb BE:
   Though
   Although $\left.\right\}$ duly elected, he failed to assume office.
   Even though

2. Subjectless gerunds preceding or following the main clause:
   In spite of
   Despite $\left.\right\}$ being duly elected, he failed to assume office.
   Regardless of

   He failed to assume office $\left\{\begin{array}{l}\text{in spite of} \\ \text{despite} \\ \text{regardless of}\end{array}\right\}$ being duly elected.

Your students should thus be made aware that two (or more) full clauses are not always necessary when logical relationships are expressed.

Conclusion

We began this chapter by pointing out that an understanding of logical connectors would be of enormous help to ESL/EFL students in improving their reading, writing, speaking, and listening skills. Indeed, as Hunt (1965) has shown for native speakers of English and Larsen-Freeman and Strom (1977) and Larsen-Freeman (1978) have claimed for ESL learners, an English speaker/writer's ability to use logical connectors to subordinate one clause to another is a fair measure of the learner's overall "syntactic maturity" (Hunt's term). Thus, by helping our students understand the meanings of logical connectors and by encouraging them to develop a sensitivity to both the register and the syntactic variations that occur in the use of these expressions, we can encourage our students to grow in all four skills.

TEACHING SUGGESTIONS

1   Example Lesson Plan

The following is Maureen Secord's (1978:75–77) suggested method of presentation for logical connectors. Cause and effect logical connectors have been chosen to illustrate the general approach.

a. The teacher asks if any student(s) did not eat breakfast (lunch). When one responds, the teacher then asks if she or he is hungry. The teacher then writes on the board:

Ed didn't eat breakfast. He is very hungry.

b. The teacher elicits from students which clause expresses the reason and which is the result and labels each accordingly. The teacher puts a list of different logical connectors on the board to show which can precede the result clause and which can precede the reason clause.

(1) To introduce result (or effect)
  (a) As the second of two clauses:

Ed didn't eat breakfast; { so / therefore, / consequently, / thus, } he is very hungry.
  (reason)   (result)

  (b) As the second of two sentences:

Ed didn't eat breakfast. { For this reason / Because of this / As a result / As a consequence } , he is very hungry.

(2) To introduce reason (or cause)
  (a) As the second of two clauses:

Ed is very hungry { because / in that / due to the fact that } he didn't eat breakfast.

  (b) As the first of two clauses:

Being that / Because of the fact that / Since } Ed didn't eat breakfast, he is very hungry.

The teacher points out that while the result/effect clause or sentence introduced by a logical connector can only follow the reason/cause, the reason clause introduced by a logical connector can either precede or follow the result.

c. Using pictures, the teacher suggests (or elicits when possible) statements about the subjects, then asks why this statement is so. For example, one picture could be a woman wearing a beautiful dress. The teacher then asks: "This lady just bought a new dress. Why?" "She is going to a dance" or any other logical response would then be combined with the original statement with *since* or *because*. The teacher could then ask another student to rephrase this into a complex sentence with *so, therefore,* or *consequently.* If errors or confusion arise, the teacher could write each clause on the board and have students label the reason/cause and the result/effect clauses.

d. A more communicative class drill could be conducted wherein each student asks the next a "why" question with a verb phrase supplied by the teacher and another student could restate it with the opposite focus.

T: save money
S1:   Charles, why are you saving money?
S2:   I'm saving money because I am going to buy a car.
S3:   Charles is going to buy a car so he is saving money.

2   Once a particular group of logical connectors has been presented, an exercise of the following sort should be given to reinforce appropriate usage.

The most common drill, the combining of two sentences into one with a logical connector, has many variations: in unrelated sentences, in contextualized groups of sentences, in a paragraph containing unconnected sentences, and in dialogs. The following illustrates one such type:

How does this paragraph sound to you? How could you improve it by rewriting it with appropriate logical connectors?

Mrs. Andrews went downtown this morning. She had some errands to do. She took a bus. Her husband needed the car. Mrs. Andrews went to the bank first. She wanted to cash a check. It was early. The bank was not crowded. She wanted to look at some sweaters. She went to Bullock's. The streets were still wet. It had rained that morning. She walked very carefully. The streets were slippery. Her favorite soap opera began at noon. She hurried home. (Supplied by Maureen Secord)

3   Another common exercise involves sentence completion. For example:

Complete the following with a phrase or sentence which makes sense considering the semantics of the logical connector:

a. Betty is pretty besides _____ .
b. He gets ten hours of sleep each night, yet _____ .
c. There was no reason to stay any longer, so _____ .
d. Mr. Smith smokes too much; furthermore, _____ .
e. He forgot to mail the invitations to his party. As a consequence, _____ .

4   A way to make students sensitive to register differences would be to have them substitute a logical connector of one register with one from another. For instance, change each of the following example sentences with their logical connectors of formal register to a sentence containing a more informal logical connector:

a. He hadn't done his homework; consequently, the teacher was angry.
b. In spite of the fact that defeat was inevitable, the players continued to try their best to win the game.
c. Susan is very talented; moreover, she is personable.

5   A good transformation exercise to practice syntax would be one which would require students to move a logical connector from a sentence-initial position to a sentence-internal position and make the corresponding changes. Look at each example sentence; then using the logical connector provided in the parentheses, rewrite the example sentence. You might have to make some changes in the word order and syntax to produce an acceptable English sentence.

a. Besides having to worry about his own children, Mr. Clark has to worry about his neighbor's child. (as well as)
b. Because he hadn't prepared for the test, he performed very poorly. (thus)

6   Tom Gorman and Marjorie Walsleben offer us an additional way to get our students to practice using logical connectors. In an exercise type which they call a "completion exercise" (really a modified cloze passage), students are presented with a passage in which all the logical connectors have been deleted. At the end of the passage there is a word list containing all the logical connectors necessary to fill in all the blanks. The students are instructed to select the appropriate logical connector from the word list and insert it in the passage in its proper position. The following is a portion of an exercise from their classroom materials:

> (1) _____ , we may observe that animal communication systems are closed, (2) _____ human languages are open-ended. (3) _____ bees communicate, they will only be able to exchange variants of the same message—in what direction the nectar is and how far away. Apes cannot communicate freely about anything for which they do not have a specific signal, and (4) _____ in those cases the possibilities are extremely restricted. People (5) _____ , can talk about anything they can observe or imagine. (6) _____ , what they can say on any topic is almost unlimited. . . .

> *Word list*
> a. on the other hand
> b. whereas
> c. as long as
> d. finally
> e. even
> f. moreover

Such an exercise could also be used without supplying the word list if the students are sufficiently advanced.

EXERCISES

Test your understanding of what has been presented

1. Provide original example sentences that illustrate the following concepts. Underline the pertinent word(s) in your examples.

negative logical connector
formal register of a logical connector
referential word
concession

clause-initial vs. clause-medial vs. clause-final position for connectors
clause order variations

2. Account for the ungrammaticality of the following sentences:

a. David was working hard in the garden. *While George was napping in the hammock.
b. If you try hard, you will succeed. *Consequently Bill followed this advice and failed the test.
c. We took extra care to prepare for the storm. *In spite of it was devastating.
d. The general surrendered at last. *He never gave up in spirit although.

Test your ability to apply what you know

3. The following sentences contain errors that were made by ESL/EFL students. Account for the ungrammaticality, and explain how you would make your students aware of such errors. What remedial exercises would you provide?

a. *Although he gets up early, but he's always late to work.
b. *Most of our students work very hard. Even so, not Mohammad.

    c. *Because of I know it's hard to go to medical school, I am trying my best to make a good GPA.

    d. *I have visited many places as Marineland.

4. What type of difference, if any, exists between the sentences in the following pairs:

    a. (1) Due to the fact that she hasn't taken good care of herself, she caught a cold.
        (2) Due to the fact that she caught a cold, she hasn't taken good care of herself.

    b. (1) Even though he worked hard, he never got ahead.
        (2) In spite of his having worked hard, he never got ahead.

    c. (1) Because there has been very little rain lately, California is experiencing a severe drought.
        (2) As a consequence of having little rain lately, California is experiencing a severe drought.

5. What do both of the following groups of three sentences have in common?

    a. (1) In short, job opportunities for everyone is a right, not a privilege.
        (2) To sum up, job opportunities for everyone is a right, not a privilege.
        (3) In conclusion, job opportunities for everyone is a right, not a privilege.

    b. (1) Furthermore, one must consider the economic impact as well.
        (2) Moreover, one must consider the economic impact as well.
        (3) In addition, one must consider the economic impact as well.

BIBLIOGRAPHY

References

Burt, M. K., and C. Kiparsky (1974).."Global and Local Mistakes," in J. Schumann and N. Stenson (eds.), *New Frontiers in Second Language Learning.* Rowley, Mass.: Newbury House.

Halliday, M. A. K., and R. Hasan (1976). *Cohesion in English.* London: Longman.

Hunt, K. (1965). *Grammatical Structures Written at Three Grade Levels.* NCTE Research Report 3. Champaign, Ill.: National Council of Teachers of English.

Larsen-Freeman, D. (1978). "An ESL Index of Development," *TESOL Quarterly* 12, 4:439–448.

Larsen-Freeman, D., and V. Strom (1977). "The Construction of a Second Language Acquisition Index of Development," *Language Learning* 27, 1:123–134.

Quirk, R., et al. (1972). *A Grammar of Contemporary English.* New York: Seminar Press.

Salera, C. (1978). "The Mobility of Certain Logical Connectors." Unpublished English 215 paper, UCLA, fall, 1978.

Secord, M. (1977). "Contrastive and Concessive Relationships in English." Unpublished English 215 paper, UCLA, fall, 1977.

Secord, M. (1978). "A Categorization of Transitional Expressions in English." Unpublished M.A. thesis in TESL, UCLA.

Tomiyama, M. (1980). "Grammatical Errors and Communication Breakdown," *TESOL Quarterly* 14, 2:71–79.

Suggestions for further reading

For more detailed characterizations of the semantics of logical connectors, see the following:

Arapoff, Nancy (1968). "The Semantic Role of Sentence Connectors in Extra-Sentence Logical Relationships," *TESOL Quarterly* 2:4, 243–252.

Greenbaum, S. (1969). *Studies in English Adverbial Usage.* Coral Gables, Fla.: University of Miami Press.

Halliday, M., and R. Hasan (1976). See above references.

For exercises on the teaching of logical connectors:

Yorkey, Richard C. (1970). *Study Skills for Students of English as a Second Language.* New York: McGraw-Hill.

For suggestions on writing assignments which necessitate the use of logical connectors, see:

Arapoff-Cramer, Nancy (1974). "Toward a Hierarchial Sequencing of Writing Situations," in R. Crymes and W. Norris (eds.), *On TESOL '74.* Washington, D.C.: TESOL.

Lawrence, Mary (1972). *Writing as a Thinking Process.* Ann Arbor: University of Michigan Press.

25

Conditional Sentences

GRAMMATICAL DESCRIPTION

Introduction

In a survey of the most serious teaching problems encountered by ESL teachers in the Los Angeles area, Covitt (1976) found that conditional sentences ranked fifth.[1] This is not difficult to understand. Conditional sentences consist of two clauses and are therefore more complex syntactically than many other structures. Moreover, the semantics of all the various types of conditional clauses are subtle and hard to understand even for native speakers. Good comprehensive descriptions are not readily available. Furthermore, ESL/EFL students need a good grasp of the English tense system as well as the modal auxiliaries before they can cope with the full range of conditional sentences in English.

In addition to the general problems noted above, we must point out that ESL/EFL textbooks and reference grammars often provide somewhat oversimplified information. For example, numerous texts introduce and practice only three conditional structures (the labels used to describe these structures vary):

1. *Future Conditional:* If I have the money, I will take a vacation.
2. *Present Conditional:* If I had the money, I would take a vacation.
3. *Past Conditional:* If I had had the money, I would have taken a vacation.

Several reference grammars refer to the first sentence as a "real" or "possible" conditional as opposed to the second and third sentences, which refer to the "unreal/hypothetical" present and past, respectively.

Another problem is that ESL/EFL students, who have learned to associate past tense with past time, often find it hard to believe that sentences like the second one above refer to present and not past time. They become confused because they hear and read many types of conditional sentences which are not included in the three structures usually taught. In fact

---

1. The five most serious problems were ranked as follows:

articles	verbals (infinitives, gerunds, participles)
prepositions	conditionals
phrasal verbs	

one of the problems with such descriptions is that they do not treat the most frequent (and also the simplest) conditional sentence type in English:[2]

> If you boil water, it vaporizes.
> If Bobby goes swimming, he catches a cold.

In this chapter we provide a description of conditional sentences that should help the ESL/EFL teacher better understand this problematic topic.

A semantic overview of conditional sentences

English conditional sentences express three different kinds of semantic relationships: factual conditional relationships, future (or predictive) conditional relationships, and imaginative conditional relationships. We will discuss each of these types in turn.

Factual conditional sentences

Factual conditional sentences are of high frequency in everyday English, and yet they are overlooked altogether in many ESL/EFL textbooks. Factual conditionals include four types: generic, habitual, implicit inference, and explicit inference.

Generic factual conditionals express relationships that are true and unchanging, e.g.:

If oil is mixed with water, it floats.   If you boil water, it vaporizes.

Because of their unchanging truth value, these conditionals normally take a simple present tense in both clauses. They are especially frequent in scientific writing, since the sciences are often concerned with such absolute relationships.

Habitual factual conditionals resemble generic factuals in that they also express a relationship that is not bounded in time; however, the relationship is based on habit instead of physical law. Habitual factuals express either past or present relationships that are typically or habitually true, e.g.:

present: If I wash the dishes, Sally dries   *past:* If Nancy said, "Jump!" Bob
    them.   jumped.

This type of conditional sentence is frequent in conversation. Both clauses usually have the same tense: simple present in both clauses if the habitual relationship refers to extended present time; simple past in both clauses if the sentence refers to a past habit.

Note that for both generic and habitual conditionals it is possible to substitute *when* or *whenever* for *if* and still express more or less the same idea:

> When(ever) you boil water, it vaporizes.
> When(ever) I wash the dishes, Sally dries them.

Factual conditionals that express an implicit inference are different from generic or habitual factuals in that they express inferences about specific time-bound relationships. As such, they make use of a much wider range of tense and aspect markers and they also occur with certain modal auxiliaries. Schachter (1971:70) provides some examples of what we refer to as implicit inference conditionals:

If it's raining out there, my car is getting wet.
If smog can be licked in L.A., it can be licked anywhere.

---

2. Hwang (1979) demonstrates that ESL/EFL students cannot produce or interpret these simple, present tense conditionals as well as they can future conditionals.

If the radicals haven't made the government more responsive, they have wasted their
    time.
If there was a happy man in the world that night, it was John Tunney.

To these we add a few more examples of our own:

If you'll bring some wine, I'll bring some   If it's Tuesday, it's Sam's birthday.
    beer and potato chips.

Implicit inference conditionals, like their habitual counterparts, are conversational in
flavor, and like generic and habitual factuals, implicit inference factuals tend to maintain the
same tense and aspect or the same modal in both clauses—even though they make use of a
much wider range of tenses and auxiliary verbs. However, implicit inference factuals differ
from the other two types in that *when* or *whenever* cannot substitute for *if* without changing the
meaning and often making the sentence ungrammatical or awkward:

*When(ever) it's raining out there, my   ?When(ever) smog can be licked in L.A.,
    car is getting wet.   it can be licked anywhere.
    Etc.

The ungrammaticality or awkwardness here is due to the fact that this type of conditional is
expressing an inference rather than a generic or habitual relationship.
    The final type of factual condition, the explicit inference conditional, is the only case
where there is no strict parallelism of tense, aspect, or modal in both clauses. This is because
the condition (i.e., the *if* clause) is used as the basis for making an explicit inference; the result
clause thus contains an inferential modal—typically *must* or *should*:

If someone's at the door, it must be Peter.
If anyone has the answer, it should be Rod.

Explicit inferential factuals are similar to implicit inference factuals in that both refer to
specific time-bound events or states in the *if* clause. Also, both involve making inferences;
however, only the explicit inference factual overtly marks the inference process with an
inferential modal. Both can sometimes be used to describe the same relationship:

implicit inference: If it's raining out there, my car is getting wet.
explicit inference: If it's raining out there, my car must be getting wet.

Explicit inference conditionals, however, are more limited in range, since they cannot occur
with the same variety of tense and modal combinations that implicit inferences do;
nonetheless, examples like the above pair demonstrate the underlying similarity of these two
types of conditionals. Like implicit inference conditionals, explicit inference conditionals can
refer to past as well as present time. Recall (Chapter 7) that past inference after *must* or *should*
is expressed by HAVE . . . EN:

past implicit inference: If he was there, he saw the painting.
past explicit inference: If he was there, he must have seen the painting.

Future (or predictive) conditional sentences

Many other authors have discussed "future conditionals." For example:

If it rains, I'll stay home.

Such sentences express future plans or contingencies.

The normal pattern for this type of conditional is simple present tense in the *if* clause and some explicit indication of future time (e.g., *will* or *be going to*) in the result clause.

If you finish your vegetables, I'm going to (gonna) buy you an ice cream cone.
If Steve comes to class, he will get the answers to the quiz.

This is the only type of future conditional most ESL/EFL texts mention. However, sometimes the future outcome expressed in the result clause is not sufficiently certain to warrant use of *will* or *be going to,* in which case a weaker modal of prediction such as *may* or *should* can be used:

If you finish your vegetables, I may buy   If Steve comes to class, he should get the
    you an ice cream cone.   answers to the quiz.

Thus, the prediction scale that we outlined for modals in Chapter 7 also applies to the result clauses of future conditional sentences:

will, be going to	*certain (strong result)*
should	probable
may	possible (stronger)
might	possible (weak)

(progressively weakened result from *will* to *might*)

There is also a way to weaken the condition expressed in the *if* clause of a future conditional sentence by using the modal *should* or the verb *happen*—or both of them together.

If it $\left\{\begin{array}{l}\text{should} \\ \text{happens to} \\ \text{should happen to}\end{array}\right\}$ rain, I'll stay home.

Therefore, we feel that it is an incomplete treatment of the future conditional to present only one form to students (e.g., If it rains, I'll stay home)—especially if the students are at the intermediate or advanced level in their study of English, since they will be encountering the "weakened" versions of this construction in the speech and writing of native speakers.

Imaginative conditional sentences

The imaginative conditional sentences are perhaps the most problematic of the three main types in our description.[3] There are two subtypes of imaginative conditionals—hypotheticals and counterfactuals. Hypothetical conditionals express unlikely yet possible events or states in the *if* clause:

If Joe had the time, he would go to Mexico.

The *if* clause is not strongly negated here. There is an outside chance that Joe has (or will have) the time. Counterfactual conditionals, on the other hand, express impossible events or states in the *if* clause:

If Napoleon were alive today, he would be fighting the Soviets.

The *if* clause is strongly negated (i.e., Napoleon is not alive today nor will he be alive in the future).

---

3. We are indebted to Schachter (1971) both for the term "imaginative" and also for much of the following description and terminology.

In hypothetical conditionals the negative quality of the *if* clause can be even further weakened so that the possibility of the result occurring becomes stronger:

If Joe $\left\{ \begin{array}{l} \text{should have} \\ \text{happened to have} \\ \text{should happen to have} \end{array} \right\}$ the time, he would go to Mexico.[4]

This cannot happen in a counterfactual conditional where *should* occurs, since the *if* clause is strongly negated and the condition remains impossible:

*If Napoleon $\left\{ \begin{array}{l} \text{should be} \\ \text{should happen to be} \end{array} \right\}$ alive today, he would be fighting the Soviets.

Hypothetical conditionals can refer to the future as well as the present:

present: If Joe had the time, he would go to Mexico.
future: If Joe were to have the time, he would go to Mexico.

Counterfactual conditionals refer to the present or the past:

present: If Napoleon were alive today, he would be fighting the Soviets.
past: If Napoleon had been alive in 1940, he would have been fighting the Germans.

The problem with imaginative conditionals arises in the tenses used.[5] The past tense refers to the present time and the past perfect tense refers to past time. Furthermore, we have a vestige of the Old English subjunctive mood[6] in the use of *were* with singular first and third person subjects where *was* is the expected form:[7]

If Napoleon were here, he would be angry.

If I were the President, I would make some changes.

Even rarer in current English than the use of *were* to express the subjunctive mood in imaginative conditionals is the occasional use (now slightly archaic) of subjunctive BE, e.g.:

If it be wrong to have said this, I humbly apologize.

Sometimes the difference between using a future conditional and a hypothetical conditional is a matter of speaker choice:

future: If it rains, I will stay home.
hypothetical: If it $\left\{ \begin{array}{l} \text{were to} \\ \text{should} \end{array} \right\}$ rain, I would stay home.

The choice reflects the degree of confidence in the speaker's mind concerning the fulfillment

---

4. In colloquial American English, such an *if* clause sometimes contains a *would:*

If Joe would have the time, he would go to Mexico.

This results in a double "would" construction, which many prescriptive usage manuals rule out as unacceptable in formal English.

5. Hwang (1979) demonstrates that ESL/EFL students confuse hypothetical and counterfactual conditionals and cannot interpret them properly even when they are able to select the correct form on a multiple-choice test item. Many students interpret hypotheticals as if they were counterfactuals—thus ignoring a subtle but important semantic distinction in English.

6. See Harsh (1968) for a comprehensive description of the subjunctive in English.

7. In colloquial English *was* in fact often occurs in imaginative conditionals in lieu of *were* in such sentences.

of the condition: the future conditional expresses a greater degree of confidence that the condition is a real possibility than does the hypothetical conditional.

Summary

We realize that the above taxonomy of conditional sentences, while more comprehensive than most other descriptions available, still will not account for every possible conditional sentence in English. However, we feel that it provides a sufficiently rich set of distinctions to present to ESL/EFL students, since the most frequently occurring types have been included. Our description is summarized in the following diagram:

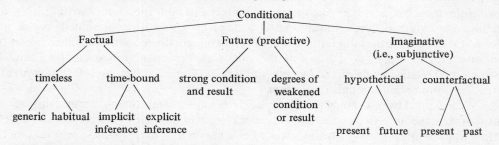

The most frequent conditional structures

Hill (1960) has claimed that English conditional sentences may contain 324 (i.e., 18 × 18) distinct tense-modal sequences; however, Hwang (1979) analyzed a corpus of English speech (63,746 words) and writing (357,249 words) representing diverse discourse types, and she found that seven—out of a total of about the 70 patterns that occurred—accounted for two-thirds of the conditional sentences in her corpora. Furthermore, she found that these seven patterns—with minor ranking differences—were most frequent in both the spoken and the written corpus.

The following table reproduces the most important frequency data reported by Hwang (p. 63):

	Structure	Speech (266 conditionals)	Ranking	Writing (948 conditionals)	Ranking
A:	If + pres., pres.	51 (19.2%)	1	156 (16.5%)	1
B:	If + pres., will/be going to	29 (10.9%)	2	118 (12.5%)	2
C:	If + past, {would, might, could}	27 (10.2%)	3	95 (10%)	4
D:	If + pres., {should, must, can, may}	24 (9%)	4	114 (12.1%)	3
E:	If + {were, were to}, {would, could, might}	23 (8.6%)	5	57 (6%)	6
F:	If + had + EN, {would, could, might} have + EN	10 (3.8%)	6	31 (3.3%)	7
G:	If + pres., {would, could, might}	7 (2.6%)	7	58 (6.1%)	5

Note: This chart accounts for only those conditional sentences in Hwang's corpora that followed the most frequent syntactic patterns; i.e., 171 of the total 266 conditional sentences in the spoken corpus and 629 of the total 948 conditional sentences in the written corpus.

Although Hwang identified 45 additional structures for the spoken corpus and 57 more for the written one, these all occurred with frequencies lower than 2 percent except for the eighth ranking structure in the written corpus, which occurred 21 times (i.e., 2.2 percent):

$$\text{Structure H:} \quad \text{If + past,} \begin{Bmatrix} \text{would} \\ \text{could} \\ \text{might} \end{Bmatrix} \text{have + EN}^{8}$$

While it is impossible to compare Hwang's structures with our taxonomy in any exact way, the above table does show us that present tense factual conditionals (i.e., structure A) are by far the most frequent type of conditional sentence in both speech and writing. They are followed by the classic future conditional (structure B), which is also represented in weakened form at the bottom of the table (structure G). Present imaginative conditionals are represented in structures C and E,[9] and past counterfactuals are represented in structures F and H. Structure D seems to be a mixed bag including both inferential factuals (*must, should*) and weakened future conditionals (*can, may*).

We feel that Hwang's study indirectly validates our semantic taxonomy, and this assures us that we have indeed accounted for the most frequent conditional structures in English. More importantly, however, Hwang's study helps to establish more realistic priorities for the ESL/EFL teacher. Present tense factual conditionals should be taught first and introduced early followed by future conditionals. Imaginative conditionals should be taught at a later time after the students have learned enough about perfect tenses and modals to provide the proper foundation.

A syntactic analysis of conditional sentences

It has been suggested—by linguists familiar with symbolic logic—that conditional sentences derive from a special type of coordinating conjunction:

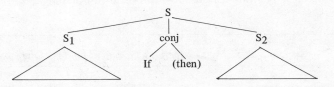

A subsequent rule would move the *if* to initial position, and the rest of the derivation would be straightforward. Although this puts the *if* clause in initial position, where it occurs most frequently,[10] there are some serious problems with this analysis. The true syntactic coordinating conjunctions such as *and, but,* and *or* that we analyzed in Chapters 22 and 23

---

8. Note that this structure can be a simplification of structure F

$$(\text{If + had + EN,} \begin{Bmatrix} \text{would} \\ \text{could} \\ \text{might} \end{Bmatrix} \text{have + EN})$$

in that the simple past replaces the past perfect in the *if* clause.

9. Structure E contains *were to* as well as *were,* which means that future hypotheticals are included here, too.

10. According to Ronkin (1976), *if* clauses preceded result clauses 72 percent of the time in the corpus she analyzed. The written discourse had a slightly higher percentage of initial *if* clauses (77 percent) than did the spoken discourse (69 percent).

can only join together sentences of the same type. In other words, statements are conjoined with statements, imperatives with imperatives, yes-no questions with yes-no questions, etc. For example:

Roger is a teacher and he lives in Santa Monica.

*Roger is a teacher and are you a teacher?

Come early, but don't tell anyone.

*Come early, but you are a teacher.

Are you a teacher or (are you) a student?

*Are you a teacher or go to school?

Conditional sentences appear to be a type of subordinate rather than coordinate conjunction, since clauses of different types can readily occur together:

If you are free, come to dinner Sunday.

If Henry comes, will you be angry?

If Sheila is happy, why is she crying?

Any syntactic analysis of conditionals must be compatible with these facts.

We agree with Quirk and Greenbaum (1973:323) that conditional sentences express the dependence of one set of circumstances (i.e., the result clause) on another (i.e., the *if* clause). Furthermore, in most cases, two clause orderings are possible.

If I go, George will go.

George will go if I go.

If Dracula returns, we will scream.

We will scream if Dracula returns.

In either order, the *if* clause sets up the condition and the main clause gives the result or outcome. We will therefore treat the *if* clause as an adverbial clause of condition. By so doing, we can generate conditional sentences using our existing system of phrase structure rules and transformations, e.g.:

George will go if I go.

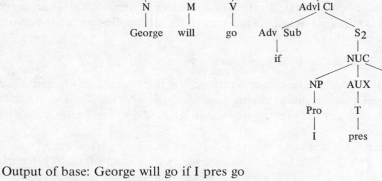

Output of base: George will go if I pres go
Affix attachment (1×): George will go if I go + pres
Morphological rules: George will go if I go.

The above underlying structure can also account for "If I go, George will go" provided that a rule of adverbial fronting (see Chapter 29) applies prior to affix attachment. Usually, the adverbial fronting rule is optional; however, there are cases where it appears to be virtually obligatory. We discuss these below under Ordering of Clauses.

Only one additional rule—"*then* insertion"—is needed to account for the appearance of *then* in conditional sentences such as the following:

If you went to the play, then you did not do your homework.

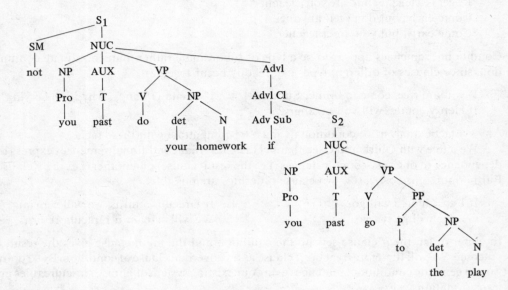

Output of base: not you past do your homework if you past go to the play
Adverbial fronting: if you past go to the play, not you past do your homework
Then insertion: if you past go to the play, then not you past do your homework
NOT placement: if you past go to the play, then you past not do your homework
DO support: if you past go to the play, then you past do not do your homework
Affix attachment (2✕): If you go + past to the play, then you do + past not do your homework
Morphological rules: If you went to the play, then you did not do your homework.

Note that *then* insertion is an optional rule that may be applied only after adverbial fronting of the conditional clause has taken place; i.e., the rule is not normally applied when the *if* clause follows the main clause:

?Then you did not do your homework if you went to the play.

The use of *then* in a conditional sentence overtly marks the fact that the result clause is a deduction which has been drawn from the circumstances expressed in the *if* clause. It would be helpful to have an empirically based study that would tell us more specifically when and where optional *then* occurs.

We do not include rules concerning tense-modal sequencing as part of our syntactic analysis of conditional sentences. We feel that such sequences are determined by semantic rather than syntactic constraints. In fact Hwang (1979:74), after doing a frequency and form analysis of conditional sentences, concludes that in addition to general rules of tense sequence (e.g., If pres, pres; If past, past, etc.), only two statements can be made about ungrammatical forms in conditional sentences: (1) logical uses of *might* do not occur in *if* clauses; (2) subjunctive *were* and *were to* do not occur in result clauses.

Other syntactic details

Subject/auxiliary inversion in conditionals

In conditionals with fronted *if* clauses containing certain auxiliary verbs such as *had* or *should,* it is possible to delete the initial *if*; however, when such a deletion takes place, subject/auxiliary inversion must follow:

> If I had known that, I wouldn't have said anything.
> Had I known that, I wouldn't have said anything.
> If the guests should arrive early, no one will be here to greet them.
> Should the guests arrive early, no one will be here to greet them.

Conditional clause pro-forms

As Halliday and Hasan (1976) have pointed out, there are certain pro-forms that can be used to replace the entire conditional clause following *if*: *so* is used if the clause is affirmative, *not* if the clause is negative. For example:

> Would you like to make a class presentation?   { If so, volunteer.
>   If not, you don't have to.

Ordering of clauses

We shall now discuss briefly the ordering of the clauses within a conditional sentence. It appears that the normally optional adverbial fronting transformation is sometimes virtually obligatory. Ronkin (1976) did a study of clause ordering and found that the *if* clause almost always precedes the result clause in three cases:

1. *Sarcastic speech*
   If he's intelligent, then I'm Albert   If you had half a brain, you'd be danger-
      Einstein.   ous.

2. *Tautologisms* ("repetition of the same word or phrase, or of the same idea or statement in other words"—*Oxford English Dictionary*)
   > If Harry is at the door, then Harry is at the door.

   Such tautologisms are more likely to be found in speech than in writing.

3. *Strong deductions*
   > A: Joyce went there last night.
   > B: Well, if Joyce went there, she saw what happened.

In the third context, speaker B is not making Joyce's seeing what happened conditional on her going there, for her going there is stated as a fact. "*If* does not mean on condition that, but on the assumption that . . . on the understanding that . . . given that. . . . It implies that on the basis of a stated fact a deduction is about to be made" (George [1968] quoted in Ronkin). Related to this third category, recall that *then* occurs only when the *if* clause has already been fronted; the addition of *then* before the result clause makes the deductive meaning even more explicit.

Although Ronkin investigated other linguistic environments, these were the only three types which usually resulted in unacceptable sentences when the clauses were reversed. Since the categories she was able to identify account for only a small percentage of sentence-initial *if* clauses, much work still remains to be done in describing the rules for clause ordering in conditional sentences.

Related forms

Hope and *wish*

The verb *hope* is similar to future (predictive) conditionals in that the same clauses that follow *hope* can also be either the *if* clause or the result clause of a future conditional. For example:

I hope (that) $\begin{Bmatrix} \text{John finishes his work} \\ \text{John will come} \end{Bmatrix}$.   If John finishes his work, he will come.

Both of these sentences imply that it is possible that John will finish his work and that he will come.

The verb *wish,* on the other hand, is similar to counterfactual conditionals in that the same clauses that follow *wish* can also be either the *if* clause or the result clause of a counterfactual conditional:

I wish (that) $\begin{Bmatrix} \text{John had finished his work} \\ \text{John could have come} \end{Bmatrix}$.

If John had finished his work, he could have come.

In both sentences we know that John didn't finish his work and that he didn't come. Also, the subjunctive forms that can occur in imaginative *if* clauses also occur after *wish:*

I wish I were a millionaire.   If I were a millionaire, . . .

Related to the verb *wish,* there is also the more formal and slightly archaic expression *would that,* which can be used in exclamatory imaginative conditionals to express wishes:

Would that I had a Rolls Royce!   Would that I could fly!
(I wish I had a Rolls Royce!)   (I wish I could fly!)

Only if and *unless*

Compare the following sets of sentences:

I will stay home if it rains.
I will stay home only if it rains.[11]

Don't apply for the job if you don't have an M.A.
Don't apply for the job unless you have an M.A.

Both *only if* and *unless* mark conditions that are exclusive; i.e., there is no other condition that will bring about the stated result. *If* and *if . . . not,* on the other hand, express weaker or more neutral conditions in that they do not exclude the possibility that other conditions might also bring about the same result. Thus we have the following semantic relationships expressed by conditional adverbial subordinators in English:

	Affirmative	*Negative*
open (unmarked) conditions	if	if . . . not
exclusive (marked) conditions	only if (sometimes: *if and only if*)	unless (= except if)

---

11. Note that when the *only if* clause is fronted, this forces subject/auxiliary inversion in the main clause:

Only if it rains, $\begin{Bmatrix} \text{will I stay home} \\ \text{*I will stay home} \end{Bmatrix}$.

We believe that this occurs because of the negative implication that *only if* conveys as part of its exclusive meaning; i.e., no other condition will bring about the result.

Most reference grammars and ESL/EFL textbooks equate *unless* with *if . . . not.* This is misleading, as Whitaker (1970) and Quirk and Greenbaum (1973) have pointed out, since there are cases where such a substitution produces an ungrammatical sentence:

> If it hadn't been for Zeke's daring rescue, we wouldn't be here.
> *Unless it had been for Zeke's daring rescue, we wouldn't be here.

Also, there are other contexts where substitution results in a change of meaning:[12]

> I couldn't have made it on time unless I'd had an executive jet.
> I couldn't have made it on time if I hadn't had an executive jet.

It is possible to interpret the first sentence as meaning that the speaker didn't have an executive jet and that he didn't arrive on time. The second sentence, however, means that he did have such a jet and thus did arrive on time.[13] Even in less complicated contexts, there always seems to be a difference between *unless* and *if . . . not:*

> If I can't go, I'll call you.
> (= I think I'll be able to go so I probably won't call you.)
>
> Unless I can go, I'll call you.
> (= I don't think I'll be able to go, so I'll probably call you.)

Thus we conclude that ESL/EFL teachers should refrain from teaching *unless* as the equivalent of *if . . . not.* In fact the only reasonable paraphrase relationship involving the above four subordinators exists between *only if* with an affirmative result and *unless* with a negative one:

Apply for the job only if you have an M.A.	Don't apply for the job unless you have an M.A.

Even though and even if

Consider the following examples:

You should visit Athens even though it is expensive.	You should visit Athens even if it is expensive.

In the first sentence the speaker knows that Athens is expensive but advises that the addressee visit it despite the cost. In the second sentence the speaker doesn't know definitely whether or not Athens is expensive—there is a possibility that Athens is expensive—but in any event, the advice is to visit it.

Thus *even though* expresses a concession. It is an emphatic form of *although. Even if* is conditional—in this case an explicit inference conditional—and it is an emphatic counterpart to *if.*

As the following example demonstrates, *even if* can also function emphatically in hypothetical conditionals:

I wouldn't marry you if you were the last person on earth!	I wouldn't marry you even if you were the last person on earth!

---

12. Such conditional sentences highlight another problem for ESL/EFL students. Hwang (1979) shows that they have severe problems interpreting conditionals with one or two negatives—so this must be an area to which the teacher gives special attention.

13. Both the ungrammatical example with *unless* and the difference in meaning in the executive jet examples can be explained by the fact that *unless* is incompatible with a counterfactual interpretation. *Unless* can be used hypothetically but not counterfactually.

Note that the *even if* clause can readily be fronted but that the *if* clause is strange if fronted in this type of exclamatory conditional:

?If you were the last person on earth, I wouldn't marry you!	Even if you were the last person on earth, I wouldn't marry you!

Thus it appears that we have isolated a context in which the *if* clause may not be fronted. (Recall the three contexts we discussed above under Ordering of Clauses where the *if* clause had to be fronted.)

Whether ... or not

Thus far we have examined sentences in which the adverbial subordinator indicates that the condition is unmarked, exclusive, emphatic, or negative:

> I will stay home *if* it rains. (unmarked)
> I will stay home *only if* it rains. (exclusive)
> I will stay home *even if* it rains. (emphatic)
> I will stay home *unless* it rains. (exclusive negative)

English has still another adverbial subordinator, *whether ... or not,* which indicates that the condition can be explicitly eliminated from playing any role in determining the outcome expressed in the result clause. Thus we can refer to such cases as irrelevant conditions:

> I will stay home *whether or not* it rains.

Our reason for indicating the potential separation of *whether* and *or not* in irrelevant conditions is that with short conditional clauses, the *or not* may also occur at the end of the clause separated from the *whether:*

> I will stay home *whether* it rains *or not.*

However, the longer the clause, the less felicitous such a separation becomes:

> ?I will stay home *whether* Professor Dickinson agrees to give the graduate students a lecture on plasma physics *or not.*

Conclusion

We are the first to admit that there is much more one could say about conditional sentences in English;[14] however, the above analysis has covered the essentials and has shown that these structures are used in a vast array of contexts ranging from scientific and mathematical writing to verbal insults in informal conversation. Hwang (1979) points out in fact that conditional sentences are even more frequent in speech (4.2 per 1,000 words) than in writing (2.7 per 1,000 words). This is true no doubt because the spoken language uses conditionals for

---

14. The most obvious deficiency in our description has been our focus on *if* and certain related forms. Some other words, phrases, and constructions that signal conditions are:

whatever	given that	The more, the merrier.
who(m)ever	assuming that	To know him is to love him.
wherever	no matter wh-	Put up your hands or I'll shoot.
however	as ⎫ long as	
whenever	so ⎭	
provided that		

A comprehensive study of conditionals would have to account for these examples—and others—and show precisely what relationshp they have to the conditional sentences discussed in this chapter.

Another deficiency is that we have not discussed certain social and pragmatic uses of conditionals.

sarcasm, exclamation, insults, and other emotive functions, as well as using them for the more straightforward inferential and hypothetical functions that predominate in the written language.

It should be obvious from our discussion that the conditional is too vast a topic for any ESL/EFL teacher to cover with one class. Thus if you are teaching conditionals, it is important that you teach your students those conditional sentences they are prepared to handle—both structurally and semantically. It is also important that you remember that students can learn the forms of certain conditional sentences such as counterfactuals and conditionals with negatives long before they are able to understand and interpret them. If you don't present too much at once, and if you always present and practice conditionals in realistic contexts, you will be able to avoid many of these problems.

TEACHING SUGGESTIONS

1   The factual generic conditional, which is often used to express physical laws, is important for students majoring in the sciences. If the condition is satisfied, the result is automatic. Note that the simple present tense is used in both clauses, i.e., no modals. For example:

If you lower the temperature of water to 0°C., it freezes.

If you raise the temperature of water to 100°C., it boils.

Given the following conditions and results, have groups of students first match the appropriate A and B items and then generate all the possible factual generic conditional sentence(s):

A	B
fly west/east	it curdles
mix milk with lemon juice	it floats
pour oil on water	you lose/gain time

Example: If you fly west, you gain time.

2   As well as expressing general truths, factual conditionals may also deal with inferences based on the speaker's prior knowledge. The frequent use of *should* and *must* in such result clauses reinforces their inferential nature, e.g.:

If it's 10 o'clock, then Grady (is/must be) taking a coffee break.

If it's Tuesday, then this must be Belgium.

Given part of Philip's daily schedule, make inferences about what he is doing based on the time:

6:30—get up
7:00—read the newspaper; have coffee
8:00—go to work; sell furniture
    ⋮
10:30—coffee break
    ⋮

1:00–2:00—lunch
    ⋮
5:00—go home
6:00—eat dinner
7:00—watch TV
    ⋮

Example: If it's 7 o'clock, Philip must be $\begin{Bmatrix} \text{reading the newspaper} \\ \text{having coffee} \end{Bmatrix}$.

This exercise can also be reversed so that the class can make inferences about the time based on what Philip is doing, e.g.:

> If Philip is reading the newspaper, it must be 7 o'clock.

3   The future or predictive conditional is often used to make plans for the future based on various contingencies. One good context for introducing this structure is a chart with information about pupils: their names, their grades. These pupils will either (a) pass, (b) fail, or (c) skip a grade at the end of the school year. The class can practice all the logical possibilities:

Pupil	Current Grade	Possibilities End of Year	Grade Next Year
Sam	5	• Pass (normal promotion)	?
Sally	4	• Fail "flunks" (no promotion)	
Kurt	3	• Fail "flunks" (no promotion)	
Edith	6	• Skip (double promotion)	

T: What will happen if Sam passes?
S1:   If Sam passes, he will be in grade 6 next year.
T: What if he flunks?
S2:   If Sam flunks, he will still be in grade 5 next year.
       Etc.

4   We use a past habitual conditional to talk about past habits or fixed past schedules which are no longer true. In this context *if* becomes similar to *when,* although it is never exactly the same as *when.*

Mr. Nelson, a retired high school history teacher, thinks about his experiences. He worked with many different types of students and had to handle many different situations:

a. a bright class ... make lessons challenging
b. a slow class ... present the basic facts carefully
c. an exceptionally intelligent student ... give special attention
d. a student with behavior problems ... contact the parents
e. a student with a physical disability ... treat as normal

Describe what Mr. Nelson did over the years, e.g.:

> If Mr. Nelson had a bright class, he made his lessons challenging.

5   The present counterfactual conditional (impossible, subjunctive) uses past tense and a special subjunctive form

$$\left(\begin{Bmatrix} \text{I} \\ \text{she} \\ \text{he} \end{Bmatrix} \dots \text{were} \right)$$

to express the imaginative present. This is a common and frequent construction and should be practiced in a variety of contexts:

a. Have pairs of students work at imagining that they are famous contemporary people and describing what they would or could do if they were these people. The teacher can provide cue cards with pictures of famous people, e.g.:

If I were the President, I would/could . . .

b. Have pairs of students imagine that they have something that they don't really have, or can do something that they really can't do. The teacher may provide cue cards with written or visual cues:

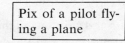

| $1,000,000.00 | Pix of a Rolls Royce | Pix of a pilot flying a plane | Pix of a driver racing in a Grand Prix event |

Example: If I had a million dollars, I would/could . . .

$$\text{If I } \left\{ \begin{array}{l} \text{could fly} \\ \text{flew} \end{array} \right\} \text{ planes, I would} \ldots$$

c. To make the situation emphatically counterfactual, completely imaginary, Barbara Hawkins suggests that teachers prepare cue cards with pictures of animals and objects—one for each student or, alternatively, five or six that the whole class can choose from. Then the student should imagine that he or she is the animal or object in question and write as many sentences as possible, which can then form the basis of a short composition.

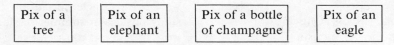

| Pix of a tree | Pix of an elephant | Pix of a bottle of champagne | Pix of an eagle |

Example: If I were an eagle, I would be able to fly very high in the sky.

6   Many popular songs and folk songs use the imaginative present. The ESL/EFL teacher can take advantage of this by teaching and singing one of these songs to introduce or reinforce the pattern, e.g.:

"If I had a hammer"   "If I were a carpenter"
"If I were a rich man"   Etc.

7   For practicing past counterfactuals, use the concept of "hindsight." Have your students imagine themselves to be a famous person (now deceased) and describe what they would have done or would not have done, e.g.:

If I had been Napoleon, I would not have fought the British at Waterloo.

8   Underlying each past counterfactual conditional sentence, there are indirect messages about what really happened or what was really the case. Ask your students to work in small groups to figure out the reality underlying counterfactual conditionals like these (note that negative markers have been added to several of them to make them more difficult), e.g.:

If Suzie hadn't been so lazy, she could have passed her history final.
(Suzie was lazy; Suzie didn't pass her history final.)

If I hadn't come early, I wouldn't have been able to help Joan.
(I came early; I helped Joan.)

If Bob had a million dollars, he wouldn't be poor.
(Bob doesn't have $1,000,000; he is poor.)

9 To contextualize past counterfactuals, have the class talk about Harry and everything that went wrong for him yesterday.

"Harry's Bad Day"
a. Harry did not get up on time. —→ He had to rush to get to work.
b. He was in a hurry. —→ He did not lock his door properly.
c. He did not catch his bus. —→ He was late for work.
d. Harry's boss was angry. —→ The boss fired Harry.
e. A burglar entered Harry's apartment. —→ All of Harry's belongings were stolen.

Have students work in pairs and write out all the things that might have happened/not have happened if Harry had not made any mistakes yesterday, e.g.:

If Harry had gotten up in time, he would not have had to rush to get to work.
If Harry had locked his door properly, the burglar would not have entered his apartment.

10 The following series of contextualized exercises for reviewing and relating various forms of the conditional to each other has been inspired by Edmonson (1975), who provides the ESL/EFL teacher with a number of interesting teaching contexts in his article.
   a. Familiarize the class with Gary's options for next summer:

Condition	Result
stay in Chicago	work for his father (shoe store)
go to San Francisco	work for his uncle (restaurant)
go to Urbana, Illinois (Univ. of Illinois)	study physics in summer session
go to Green Bay, Wisconsin	work as a camp counselor

Then have students practice the future conditional in small groups, e.g.:

If Gary stays in Chicago, he will work $\left\{\begin{array}{l}\text{for his father}\\\text{in his father's shoe store}\end{array}\right\}$.

   b. Using the same situation as in a, ask the students to switch to the present counterfactual (i.e., the subjunctive) by imagining that they are in Gary's shoes, e.g.:

If I were Gary, I would go to San Francisco and work for my uncle.

   c. Again refer back to the chart about Gary's summer, but now say that summer is over. Gary went to Wisconsin and worked as a camp counselor. Past counterfactual conditions can now be generated for everything else in the chart, e.g.:

If Gary had stayed in Chicago, he would have worked for his father.

After all the sentences have been generated, be sure to have the class interpret them too, e.g.:

Gary didn't stay in Chicago. Gary didn't work for his father.

11 The following exercises contain suggestions for teaching *unless* and *only if:*
   a. Make your students aware of the fact that *unless* is frequently used along with negative imperatives if the speaker is giving an ultimatum or a warning. The *unless* precedes the condition that is necessary for neutralizing the negation in the imperative, e.g.:

Don't run in a marathon unless you run long distances regularly.
(affirmative implication: If you run long distances regularly, you can run in a marathon.)

Have your students advise each other not to do the following things unless a necessary condition—which they are to specify—is met. Have them also indicate what the affirmative implication is in each case.

apply for admission to graduate school   go to a party the night before an exam
join the army   open up a restaurant
accept a job in Alaska   work for a low salary

Example: Don't apply for admission to graduate school unless you have at least a 3.25 GPA.
(affirmative implication: If you have at least a 3.25 GPA, you can apply for admission to graduate school.)

b. You can familiarize your students with the use of *only if* by referring to the same situations listed above. Emphasize that although the advice is overtly positive in this case, the implication is negative; i.e., if the necessary condition is not met, the advice in the result clause no longer applies. For example:

You (can/should) apply for admission to graduate school, only if you have at least a 3.25 undergraduate GPA.
(negative implication: If you don't have at least a 3.25 undergraduate GPA, don't apply for admission to graduate school.)

c. At some point your students also need to understand that an *unless* clause can be used with an affirmative result clause, too. This is particularly true if future plans are being discussed, e.g.:

We will vacation in Hawaii unless our schedule changes between now and May.
(implication: We expect to vacation in Hawaii but our schedule might change between now and May. If it does, we won't go.)

Have your students make up their own sentences using *unless* clauses with the plans below to express the idea that other things could intervene. Have them paraphrase their sentences to show the implication, too.

I'll see you next Sunday.   I will withdraw from my physics class.
Let's plan on going to the movies this   Sylvia is going to work part-time at a res-
weekend.   taurant.
Gary will travel to Europe in July.

Example: I'll see you next Sunday unless I have too much homework to do.
(implication: I'll see you next Sunday, though I may have too much homework to do, and if I do, I won't see you.)

EXERCISES

Test your understanding of what has been presented

1. Provide example sentences that illustrate the following terms. Underline the pertinent word(s) in your examples.

factual conditional
  generic
  implicit inference
future conditional
  weakened result clause
  weakened *if* clause
hypothetical conditional
counterfactual conditional

subjunctive use of *were*
adverbial fronting (of a conditional clause)
then insertion
if deletion with subject/auxiliary inversion
conditional clause pro-form
sarcastic use of a conditional

2. Give the tree diagrams and the derivations for the following sentences:

a. If I had the time, I would go to Europe.
b. If John had studied, then he would have received an A.
c. I will not stay at the meeting if he is there.
d. Don't go for an interview unless you want the job.

3. Why are the following sentences ungrammatical (or at best awkward)?

a. *If she had been there, she did the work.
b. *If John might be free, I'll invite him.
c. ?I'm a monkey's uncle if she's only 22 years old!
d. ?Then he'll keep his word if he made a promise.

Test your ability to apply what you know

4. If your students produce the following sentences, how will you make them aware of their errors, and what exercises and activities will you provide to correct the errors?

a. *If I were an American, I were speaking better English.
b. *What happens if I pushed this button?
c. *Why had some Americans said "Gesundheit" if someone sneezes?
d. *Only if you help me, I will study for the quiz.

5. One of your advanced students has heard native speakers say conditionals like these, and he or she wants to know whether they are correct or not. What will you say?

If I was Reagan, I'd do the same thing.
I would be less nervous if you would stop staring at me.

6. Select a passage or article and identify all the conditional sentences. Try to account for the sentences using the semantic taxonomy provided in this chapter. Are there any sentences that cannot be explained according to the taxonomy? If so, try to provide your own analysis or explanation of the sentence(s).

7. Use the semantic description of conditionals provided in this chapter and decide where a sentence such as the following one belongs:

If the gardener doesn't come tomorrow, Father will have to mow the lawn.

BIBLIOGRAPHY

References

Covitt, R. I. (1976). "Some Problematic Grammar Areas for ESL Teachers." Unpublished M.A. thesis in TESL, UCLA.

Edmonson, W. J. (1975). "Contrasts in Conditional Sentences," *The Art of TESOL,* Part I, in A. Newton (ed.), Selected Articles from the *English Teaching Forum.* Washington, D.C.: USIA.

George, H. V. (1968). "If," *English Language Teaching Journal* 22:113–119, 232–239.

Halliday, M., and R. Hasan (1976). *Cohesion in English.* London: Longman.

Harsh, W. (1968). *The Subjunctive in English.* University, Ala.: University of Alabama Press.

Hill, L. A. (1960). "The Sequence of Tenses with *If* Clauses," *Language Learning* 10:165–178.

Hwang, M. (1979). "A Semantic and Syntactic Analysis of 'If' Conditionals." Unpublished M.A. thesis in TESL, UCLA.

Quirk, R., and S. Greenbaum (1973). *A Concise Grammar of Contemporary English.* New York: Harcourt Brace Jovanovich.

Ronkin, L. (1976). "The Order of If-conditional Clauses in Sentences." Unpublished English 215 paper, UCLA, fall, 1976.

Schachter, J. (1971). "Presupposition and Counterfactual Conditional Sentences." Unpublished Ph.D. dissertation in Linguistics, UCLA.

Whitaker, S. F. (1970). "Unless," *English Language Teaching Journal* 24:154–160.

Suggestions for further reading

For useful information about conditional sentences in English, see:

Frank, M. (1972). *Modern English: A Practical Reference Guide.* Englewood Cliffs, N.J.: Prentice-Hall, pp. 253–266.

Jespersen, O. (1940). *A Modern English Grammar on Historical Principles* (vols. V, VII). Copenhagen: Einar Munksgaard.

Leech, G., and J. Svartvik (1975). *A Communicative Grammar of English.* London: Longman.

Schachter, J. (1971). See above references.

For excellent suggestions on how to present conditionals to ESL/EFL secondary school students, see Edmonson (1975).

For suggestions for teaching *hope* and *wish, even if* and *even though,* and conditional sentences, see:

Danielson, D., and R. Hayden (1973). *Using English: Your Second Language.* Englewood Cliffs, N.J.: Prentice-Hall.

For one of the few ESL texts that properly distinguishes hypothetical and counterfactual conditionals, see:

Rutherford, W. (1977). *Modern English* (2d ed., vol. II). New York: Harcourt Brace Jovanovich.

Other texts with good activities and exercises for teaching conditionals are:

Alter, J., et al. (1966). *Utterance-Response Drills: For Students of English as a Second Language.* Englewood Cliffs, N.J.: Prentice-Hall.

Brinton, D., and R. Neuman (1982). *Getting Along: English Grammar and Writing* (Book 2). Englewood Cliffs, N.J.: Prentice-Hall, pp. 115–116.

Hayden, R., et al. (1956). *Mastering American English.* Englewood Cliffs, N.J.: Prentice-Hall.

Ross, J., and G. Doty (1965). *Writing English: A Composition Text in English as a Foreign Language.* New York: Harper & Row.

Wohl, M. (1978). *Preparation for Writing: Grammar.* Rowley, Mass.: Newbury House, pp. 37–40.

Wright, A., et al. (1973). *Let's Learn English* (2d ed., Book 4). New York: Litton Educational Publishing.

26

Introduction to Relative Clauses

GRAMMATICAL DESCRIPTION

Introduction

There is a great deal you'll need to know about relative clauses as a teacher of ESL/EFL. In this chapter we will consider the form and function of restrictive relative clauses in English. The other major type of relative clause, the nonrestrictives, occur less frequently in the language. They will be dealt with in the next chapter along with some other relative clause constructions.

In this chapter we again encounter structures which derive from a basic structure consisting of more than one sentence. Actually, as early as Chapter 2 we learned that one basic structure sentence could be subordinated to another when preceded by an adverbial subordinator, e.g.:

> The baby learned to walk before she learned to crawl.
> S1 + Adv. Sub. + S2

This, of course, was also the type of subordinate structure we used to derive conditional sentences in the preceding chapter.

In Chapters 22 and 23 we analyzed sentences derived from two or more basic structure sentences which were conjoined, e.g.:

> The children dressed up for Halloween and they carved jack-o-lanterns out of pumpkins.
> S1 + conjunction + S2

The basic structure relationship among sentences that we consider in this chapter is different from that of subordination or conjunction. It is a relationship brought about by a process called *embedding*. In the case of restrictive relative clauses, the embedding consists of a sentence embedded within an NP. For example:

> The fans who were attending the rock concert had to wait in line for three hours.
> (NP(S))

We have the sense that the embedded sentence "who were attending the rock concert" is closely associated with the NP, "the fans." In fact, we find that the sentence has a modifying function much like an adjective; it tells us which "fans" had to wait in a long line. Perhaps now it is apparent why such clauses are called "restrictive" (or in some grammars "limiting"). They restrict or identify for us which noun(s)—of all nouns in the same set we are speaking about (i.e., anybody who could be called "a fan").

Before we go on to look more closely at the form of relative clauses in English, let us discuss some of the problems which may arise for nonnative speakers who are trying to master this structure.

Problems for ESL/EFL students

J. Schachter (1974:207–208), in discussing the work of Keenan and Comrie (1972), identifies three main dimensions along which relative clauses can differ. The first dimension has to do with the position of the relative clause with respect to the head noun. As should be clear from the example above, English relative clauses follow the head noun, i.e., here "the fans." This is also true of relative clauses in most European languages and in Persian and Arabic. Not all languages, however, adhere to this same syntactic pattern. Japanese, Chinese, and Korean, for instance, require that the relative clause occur before the head noun. Students who are native speakers of these languages will have to grasp this fundamental ordering difference.

The second dimension involves how relative clauses are marked. English uses a relative pronoun (in our example, "who") to mark that what follows is a relative clause. Persian, Arabic, and Chinese employ other kinds of markers between the head noun and the relative clause. For speakers of these languages, the concept of a relative pronoun should not cause undue hardship in learning English. Japanese, on the other hand, uses affixes in the relative clause itself to mark its restrictive function. Japanese students of ESL/EFL may require additional practice with English relative pronouns in order for them to become comfortable in using relative clauses.

The third dimension along which languages differ with respect to relative clause formation is the presence or absence of a pronominal reflex. In English the relative pronoun substitutes for the identical NP in the embedded sentence. For example, in the sentence:

> Shirley called out to the boy that she knew.

the "that" replaces "the boy" in the embedded sentence, "she knew the boy." In other languages, for instance, Arabic, Hebrew, and Persian, a relative clause marker is introduced but the object noun in the embedded sentence that is identical to the head noun is often retained in a pronominal form. Thus, speakers of these languages tend to commit errors in English such as the following:

> *Shirley called out to the boy that she knew him.

Chinese and Arabic also allow pronominal reflexes to occur as objects of prepositions; so speakers of these languages sometimes err in producing English sentences such as:

> *The man who you were talking to him is my uncle.

In addition to the variation that occurs along these three dimensions, there are also differences among languages with regard to the distribution of relative clauses which could conceivably cause problems for ESL/EFL students. P. Schachter (1972) points out, for instance, that, unlike English, Tagalog places restrictions on which NP can be relativized, i.e., be replaced with a relative pronoun. "Tagalog has no structure precisely paralleling the structure of English 'the table which the flowers are on' or 'the table on which the flowers are.' Tagalog can, of course, express the approximate *semantic* equivalent of these English structures," but it does not do so with a relative construction of any sort (1972:273).

Keenan and Comrie (1972; 1977) help us better understand the restrictions that obtain in any language on NPs that can be relativized. They posit the "noun phrase accessibility hierarchy," which lists the most "accessible" type of NP at the top and the least accessible type at the bottom:

> subject NP
> direct object NP
> indirect object NP
> oblique object NP (i.e., object of a preposition ≠ indirect object)
> genitive (i.e., possessive) NP
> object NP of a comparison

This hierarchy claims (among other things) that in universal grammar, subject NPs are easier to relativize than direct object NPs, which in turn are easier to relativize than indirect object NPs, etc. This means that all languages with relative clauses can relativize subjects, but it also implies there are some languages like Tagalog that can only relativize subjects. Furthermore, any language like Slovenian that can relativize object NPs of comparisons can also relativize all the other five types of NPs that are higher in the hierarchy.

English has a rich system of relativization with only a few restrictions on the kind of noun phrase that can be relativized, e.g.:

subject NP—The book *that* is on the coffee table was written by Wallace.
direct object NP—The authors *that* he mentioned are well known.
indirect object NP—The girl $\left\{ \begin{array}{l} \textit{(to) whom} \text{ we gave the message} \\ \textit{who} \text{ we gave the message } \textit{to} \end{array} \right\}$ is not here.
oblique object NP—The child $\left\{ \begin{array}{l} \text{from } \textit{whom} \text{ you took the candy} \\ \textit{who} \text{ you took the candy from} \end{array} \right\}$ is crying.
genitive NP—The man *whose name* you wanted to know is Cal North.
object NP of comparison— $\left\{ \begin{array}{l} \text{?The only person } \textit{that} \text{ I was shorter than was Fritz.} \\ \text{*The only person than } \textit{whom} \text{ I was shorter was Fritz.} \end{array} \right.$

Reviewing the NP accessibility hierarchy, we can see that the only marginal or unacceptable NP function for relativization in English is "object of a comparison." The other five functions are fully acceptable. This means that speakers of Tagalog and related languages that can only relativize subjects (e.g., Malay, Indonesian, Malagasy) will have some difficulty with the variety of NPs that can be relativized in English.

Being aware of these differences among languages will hopefully help you understand what background your students are bringing with them and allow you to be better prepared in presenting and practicing relative clause formation in English.

The relativization of the subject in the embedded sentence

There is a great diversity in English relative clause types. We will first treat those in which the subject of the embedded sentence becomes relativized. Consider the following sentence:

> The girl who speaks Basque is my cousin.

We understand that the "who" refers to the "girl." We understand this as speakers of English despite the fact that *who* can refer to persons of either sex in the singular or plural.

> The boy who speaks Basque is my cousin.
> The girls who speak Basque are my cousins.

Who is the relative pronoun in all these sentences. We know that it has the same referent as the head NP which directly precedes it. Thus, the basic structure for the first sentence above is:

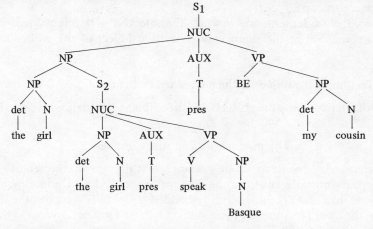

To account for sentences which are embedded within NPs, we have had to expand our phrase structure rule for rewriting the NP to include:

$$NP \longrightarrow NP + S$$

In order to become a relative clause, the embedded sentence must contain an NP which is identical in form and reference to the NP in the main clause. When this condition exists, a transformation called "relative pronoun substitution" replaces the NP in the embedded sentence with the appropriate relative pronoun. In order to derive the surface structure for our example sentence, then, the following transformations would be necessary:

Output of base: the girl (the girl pres speak Basque) pres BE my cousin
Relative pronoun substitution: the girl (who pres speak Basque) pres BE my cousin
Affix attachment (2✕): the girl (who speak + pres Basque) BE + pres my cousin
Subject-verb agreement and morphological rules: The girl who speaks Basque is my cousin.

The sentence we have just examined has an embedded sentence which modifies the subject NP of the main clause. It is also possible to have an embedded sentence modifying an NP which is the object of the main clause, e.g.:

I know the girl who speaks Basque.

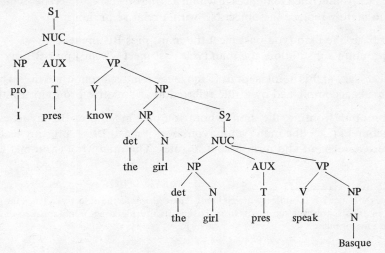

The transformations we applied to our first sentence would also apply here to give us the desired surface structure.

Next we will consider sentences in which the object NP of the embedded relative clause is identical to some NP in the main clause; i.e., the object of the embedded sentence is relativized.

The relativization of the object in the embedded sentence

In this type of relative clause the object NP of the embedded sentence is affected. Consider the following:

The man whom you met is my teacher.

What is the embedded sentence in this example? At first glance the relative clause in this sentence appears no different from the first two we looked at. Upon closer examination, however, we realize that the underlying embedded sentence is "you met the man" and that, therefore, in the basic structure the two identical NPs will not be adjacent as they were in the other sentences we have discussed.

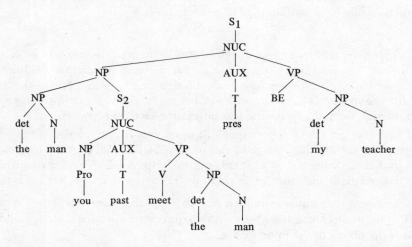

Notice that with embedded sentences in which it is the object NP that repeats the head noun, it won't do to merely replace the object NP with a relative pronoun.

Output of base: the man (you past meet the man) pres BE my teacher
Relative pronoun substitution: the man (you past meet whom[1]) pres BE my teacher

What is necessary at this point is for us to move the relative pronoun to initial position in the clause. This is accomplished by a rule referred to as "relative pronoun fronting."

Relative pronoun fronting: the man (whom you past meet) pres BE my teacher
Affix attachment (2X): the man (whom you meet + past) BE + pres my teacher
Subject-verb agreement and morphological rules: The man whom you met is my teacher.

---

1. Note that since it is the object which is being replaced, *whom,* the objective form of the relative pronoun *who,* is inserted. This, however, represents formal usage. In informal usage many speakers of English use *who,* even in this environment.

Earlier we saw that an embedded sentence with a relativized subject could modify the object as well as the subject of the main clause. This is also true of embedded sentences with relativized objects, e.g.:

I know the place that you mentioned.

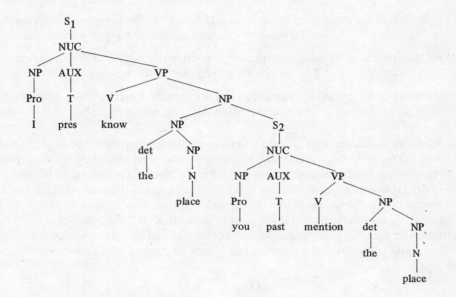

Output of base: I pres know the place (you past mention the place)
Relative pronoun substitution: I pres know the place (you past mention that)
Relative pronoun fronting: I pres know the place (that you past mention)
Affix attachment (2×): I know + pres the place (that you mention + past)
Morphological rules: I know the place that you mentioned.

Besides the need for relative pronoun fronting, another characteristic of embedded sentences with relativized objects is that the relative pronoun may be deleted without affecting the grammaticality of the sentence. To capture this fact, we can have a relative pronoun deletion transformation operate after relative pronoun fronting.

Relative pronoun fronting: I pres know the place (that you past mention)
Relative pronoun deletion: I pres know the place (you past mention)

After the affix attachment and morphological rules apply, we would get:

I know the place you mentioned.

If we had had the relative pronoun deletion rule apply to the other sentence with a relativized object that we discussed above, we would have produced:

The man you met is my teacher.

Relative pronoun deletion applies only to relativized objects; it does not apply to embedded sentences with relativized subjects:

*The girl speaks Basque is my cousin.   *I know the girl speaks Basque.

The order of difficulty of relative clauses

So far we have examined four basic types of relative clauses:

SS   Subject of the embedded sentence is identical to the subject of the main clause, e.g.:
      The girl who speaks Basque is my cousin.

OS   Subject of the embedded sentence is identical to the object of the main clause, e.g.:
      I know the girl who speaks Basque.

SO   Object of the embedded sentence is identical to the subject of the main clause, e.g.:
      The man who(m) you met is my teacher.

OO   Object of the embedded sentence is identical to the object of the main clause, e.g.:
      I know the place that you mentioned.

In 1974, Kuno hypothesized that OS and OO relative clause types would be easier to acquire than SS and SO types. He reasoned that when the embedded relative clauses interrupted the sentence by coming directly after the subject of the main clause,[2] they would be more difficult to process than those relative clauses that modified the object of the main sentence and thus came at the end of the sentence. Studies in the field of second language acquisition by Ioup and Kruse (1977) and Schumann (1978) tend to support Kuno's hypothesis.

Schumann, examining the production data of seven ESL learners, observed the following order. The numbers represent the percentage of times the seven subjects used relative clauses of each type.

OS	0.53
OO	0.35
SS	0.06
SO	0.04

(0.02 of the clauses could not be unambiguously assigned to any one of the four types.)

Stauble (1978) examined the frequency of these four relative clause types in samples of native speaker discourse drawn from three different registers: informal speech, spontaneous writing, and published writing. By calculating the number of instances and the frequency percentages for the four types of clauses, she obtained the following totals for the three combined discourse types:

	Instances	Percentage
OS	234	55
OO	108	25
SS	52	12
SO	30	7
Total	424	

Thus, there is an obvious correlation between the frequency of occurrence of the different types of relative clauses used by native speakers and the observed second language acquisition order. However, Stauble also points out that the transformational complexity and location of the various clause types may explain the order as well. The OS type may be the easiest simply because it requires only one major obligatory transformation, whereas SS sentences require one transformation plus center embedding, and OO sentences require two

---

2. This is called center embedding.

obligatory transformations. Finally, SO types require two transformations with the added difficulty of their being center embedded.

OS	+Rel Pro Substitution −Rel Pro Fronting −Center Embedding	OO	+Rel Pro Substitution +Rel Pro Fronting −Center Embedding
SS	+Rel Pro Substitution −Rel Pro Fronting +Center Embedding	SO	+Rel Pro Substitution +Rel Pro Fronting +Center Embedding

ESL/EFL teachers, of course, will have to be concerned with the teaching of all four types of relative clauses. It may be that ESL/EFL students will need extra practice in order to master relative clauses of the OO and SO types.

The diversity of relative clause types

So far we have dealt only with relative clauses modifying the subjects and direct objects of main clauses. Such a perspective belies the complexity which actually exists. The chart on page 368 illustrates the diversity of English relative clause structures.

The relativization of the object of the preposition in the embedded sentence

One of the relative clause types apparent in the chart which we have yet to examine is the one in which the object of the preposition in the embedded sentence is relativized. If we analyze an example sentence from the chart on page 368, e.g.:

I know the place which you spoke about.

we see that its basic structure is:

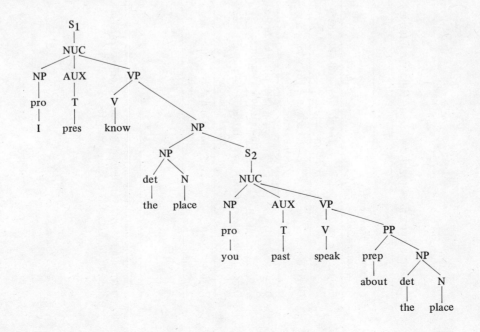

Example Sentences for the Various Relative Clause Structures in English[3]

Function of head noun in main clauses	Function of identical (i.e., relativized) noun in relative clauses			
	Subject	*Direct object*	*Indirect object*	*Object of a preposition*
Subject	The girl *who* speaks Basque is my cousin.	The man *who(m)* you met is my teacher.	The man *that* I gave the book to is over there.	The place *which* you spoke about is Denver.
Direct object	I know the girl *who* speaks Basque.	I know the place *that* you mentioned.	I gave the man *that* you mentioned the book.	I know the place *which* you spoke about.
Indirect object	We gave the boy *who* broke the window a warning.	I sent the boy *that* Mary saw a letter.	I told the boy *that* you gave the book to a story.	I gave the boy *that* you were talking about the book.
Object of the preposition	I talked with the girl *who* speaks Basque.	I work for the man *that* you met.	Mary knows about the boy *that* I gave the book to.	I know of the place *which* John spoke about.
Predicate noun	Mr. Thomas is a teacher *who* prepares his lessons.	Latin is the subject *that* Mr. Thomas teaches.	He's the boy *that* I gave the present to.	Denver is a place *which* you'll want to go to.

3. Note that in addition to the above structures the possessive determiner *whose* can relativize any noun functioning as a subject, direct object, indirect object, object of a preposition, or predicate noun, giving us in effect 40 distinct relative clause structures in English.

We have already seen how the rules of relative pronoun substitution and relative pronoun fronting operate on this sentence,

Output of base: I pres know the place (you past speak about the place)
Relative pronoun substitution: I pres know the place (you past speak about which)
Relative pronoun fronting: I pres know the place (which you past speak about)

and actually this is all that would be necessary to derive the desired surface structure. Another surface structure possibility, however, is to front the preposition along with its relativized object. If we were to do this we would get:

I know the place about which you spoke.

What results is a rather formal version of the sentence. Such a sentence is rarely appropriate in informal spoken discourse, but Stauble (1978) found that in both published writing and the quick first-draft writing of American graduate students the preposition is almost always fronted along with the relative pronoun. Thus, this appears to be a systematic difference between written exposition and informal spoken English.

One final point in keeping with this topic is that the relative pronoun *that* cannot be used to replace the relativized object of a preposition, if the preposition is fronted with the pronoun, i.e., *who(m)* and *which* are obligatory in this environment.

*The man with that you were talking is   *The chair on that you were sitting
    the principal.   broke.

The relative pronoun *that* can be used, however, if the preposition is not fronted along with the relative pronoun:

The man that you were talking with is the   The chair that you were sitting on broke.
    principal.

Finally, we have already learned that the relative pronoun which replaces an object can be deleted. This is the case even for relative pronouns which substitute for objects of prepositions; however, remember that deletion is possible only if the preposition has not been fronted, e.g.:

The place which you spoke about is Den-   The place about which you spoke is
    ver.   Denver.
The place you spoke about is Denver.   *The place about you spoke is Denver.

We should add a note of caution, however, in that Stauble found that preservation of the relative pronoun was preferred over deletion for all three language registers she sampled. In those cases where deletion of the relative pronoun was more frequent than preservation, the head noun was almost always nonhuman.

The relativization of the possessive determiner in the embedded sentence

A relative clause type not illustrated in the chart on page 368 is the relative clause which results when a noun marked for possession in the embedded sentence is the noun that repeats a noun in the main clause. The basic structure for an example sentence of this type follows:

The man whose wife you are admiring is a wrestler.

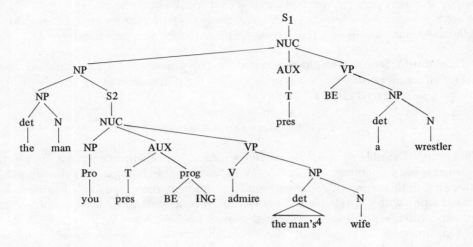

The derivation would proceed as usual but with the relative pronoun (*whose* in this case) being substituted for the possessive determiner, not an NP.

Output of base: the mean (you pres BE ING admire the man's wife) pres BE a wrestler
Relative determiner substitution: the man (you pres BE ING admire whose wife) pres BE a wrestler

At this point a difference emerges. Since the relative pronoun is replacing the possessive determiner, when the relative pronoun is fronted, the noun it modifies must also be fronted.[5]

Relative pronoun fronting: the man (whose wife you pres BE ING admire) pres BE a wrestler
Affix attachment (3×): the man (whose wife you BE + pres admire + ING) BE + pres a wrestler
Subject-verb agreement and morphological rules: The man whose wife you are admiring is a wrestler.

The choice of relative pronoun

So far we have been substituting relative pronouns for NPs without really being specific about the rules governing their use. Every relative pronoun is entered in the lexicon together with its features. The feature specifications allow us to select the appropriate relative pronoun depending upon the features of the NP it replaces and the discourse register in which it will be used. The following are the relative pronouns in English and some of their salient grammatical and discourse features:

---

4. Note that a noun phrase in the possessive form such as *a man's* fills the determiner slot just as a possessive adjective like *his* would.

5. If we were to omit this restriction, ungrammatical sentences such as the following would be possible:

*The man whose you are admiring wife is a wrestler.

who + subject case
  + human

whom + object case
  + human

Although it would always be prescriptively correct to use *whom* to replace a human NP in object position—or as the object of a preposition without a fronted preposition—native speakers do not always use it this way. Often they opt for the subject case form, *who,* instead:

I spoke with the student who(m) I loaned the book to.

On the other hand, if the *who(m)* is replacing the object of the preposition and the preposition is fronted with it, *whom* will almost always be used:

I know the student to $\left\{ \begin{array}{l} \text{whom} \\ \text{*who} \end{array} \right\}$ you loaned the book.

which − human
that ± human

In informal conversational discourse, *that* is preferred over either *which* or *who(m).* In written discourse, *which* and *who(m)* are preferred; when *that* is used, it usually indicates a nonhuman head noun (Stauble, 1978).[6]

whose ± human
  + possessive
    determiner

Whose generally refers to a human head noun, but sometimes sentences like the following occur where *whose* refers to an inanimate noun:

I found an old coin whose date has become worn and illegible.

Conclusion

In this chapter we have explored the form and function of restrictive relative clauses. We have noted the diversity of this construction in English. Without counting the relative clauses stemming from replacement of the possessive determiner by *whose,* we noted that there were 20 different constructions possible:

OS
(4 types)

Direct object/Subject: I saw the boy who kissed Mary.
Pred. noun/Subject: He is the boy who is running.
Obj. of prep./Subject: I thought about the boy who is absent.
Indirect obj./Subject: We gave the boy who broke the window a warning.

OO
(12 types)

Direct object/Direct object: I saw the boy Mary kissed.
Pred. noun/Direct object: He is the boy I saw.
Indirect object/Direct object: I sent the boy Mary saw a letter.
Obj. of prep./Direct object: I looked for the article Bill wrote.
Direct object/Indirect object: I saw the boy to whom Mary gave the present.
Pred. noun/Indirect object: He is the boy I gave the present to.
Indirect object/Indirect object: I told the boy you gave the book to a story.
Obj. of prep./Indirect object: Mary knows about the boy I gave the present to.
Direct object/Obj. of prep.: I bought the book that you were talking about.
Pred. noun/Obj. of prep.: *Moby Dick* must be the book that you were thinking about.
Indirect obj./Obj. of prep.: I gave the boy you were talking about the book.
Object of prep./Obj. of prep.: I know about the place Jim referred to.

---

6. There are other differences between these relative pronouns that we will call attention to in the next chapter.

SO
(3 types)

— Subject/Direct object: The girl who(m) I saw was sick.
— Subject/Indirect object: The girl to whom I gave the pencil was absent.
— Subject/Obj. of prep.: The girl that you were looking for is here now.

SS
(1 type)

——————— Subject/Subject: The girl who was sick went to the doctor's office.

ESL/EFL students will have to be given a great deal of practice in using relative clauses in English before they can be expected to produce all these relative clause types with facility. Also, as the frequency data we reported suggest, some of the clause types are more frequent than others and thus deserve priority.

TEACHING SUGGESTIONS

1   It has been our experience that presenting students with a transformational analysis of relative clauses can be very enlightening. Ordinarily we don't recommend introducing tree diagrams and transformational rules; however, for this particular construction, it has proved helpful for our ESL/EFL students to be able to see how relative clauses are formed in English. You may not wish to draw trees or to call the transformations by the names we have used here, but introducing the concept of an embedded sentence and showing how relative pronouns replace an NP in the embedded sentence seems to be a useful first step for many ESL/EFL students. For instance, give students handouts with sentences in parentheses embedded within a main clause, e.g.:

The students (the students arrived late) missed the announcement.

Show them how the *who* is substituted for the repeated NP. Have them do exercises of a similar nature on their own.

2   Once students have some idea of how to form relative clauses, they will need abundant practice to be able to do so with fluency. You may start by having students read a passage in class. Next have them divide into small groups. The group's task is to identify all the relative clauses in the passage. They are to underline all the relative pronouns they can find and determine to which head noun the relative pronoun refers. Finally, they should try to find all the relative clauses in which the relative pronoun has been deleted.

3   Begin oral production using fairly tightly controlled contexts and perhaps only concentrating on one relative pronoun at a time. For instance, use a class information sheet to practice producing relative clauses with *who*. The students can make sentences to identify one of their fellow students who has some unique attribute, e.g.:

The student who comes from Romania is _____ .
The student who speaks French is _____ .
The student who studies economics is _____ .

4   Cuisenaire rods can be used for giving students practice in both listening to and producing sentences containing relative clauses. Winn-Bell Olsen (1977) suggests that teachers give commands and ask questions such as the following, encouraging students to think up their own as soon as they are able to:

Give Dumduan the green rod which is beside the pink one.
Dumduan, which rod did Phetsamone just give you?
Put the yellow rod that is under the black rod in the box.
Sampong, which rod did Pheng just put in the box?

5   Pictures are useful tools when a teacher is attempting to elicit one type of relative clause using a variety of relative pronouns from the class. Ask students to make statements describing some aspect of a picture you show them. For instance, students may make statements with relativized subjects in embedded sentences like the following about a beach scene:

> It's like a beach that is near my house.
> The boy who is wearing a red bathing suit is the same age as my brother.
> I see three people who are swimming too far from the beach.
> I would like to ride in the boat which is near the dock.

6   Have students play a game in which they try to identify the name of a person or thing you or another student is thinking of. You may wish to use a "Twenty Questions" format with the modification that questions must contain a restrictive relative clause. Students ask questions like:

> Is this person someone who once was president of the United States?
> Is this thing something (that) I would use in the kitchen?
> Etc.

7   As another good practice exercise, have students write about some topics which would be likely to entail their using relative clauses. Including compositions of this sort would be important, since we have claimed in this chapter that there are differences in the use of relative clauses depending upon whether one is using them in informal speech or in writing. For example, ask your students to describe "The Most Interesting Character That I Have Ever Met." A topic such as this one would probably prompt them to use relative clauses.

EXERCISES

Test your understanding of what has been presented

1.   Provide an original sentence that illustrates each of the following terms. Underline the pertinent word(s) in your examples.

embedded sentence	relative pronoun substitution
restrictive relative clause	relative pronoun deletion
relative fronting	relativized possessive determiner
relativized object of a preposition	

2.   Give tree diagrams and derivations for the following sentences:

a. The boy who spoke with John is my brother.
b. The boat that he is building is large.
c. I know the student whose article was published.
d. Ann wrote the story you like.
e. The family with whom I am staying lives in town.

3.   Why are the following sentences ungrammatical?

a. *The river who is wide is the Mississippi.
b. *The woman with that you were working quit.
c. *I thought about the man whose we heard story.

Test your ability to apply what you know

4. If your students produce the following sentences, what errors have they made? How will you make them aware of the errors, and what exercises will you prepare to correct the errors?

    a. *The woman whom is walking towards us is my aunt.
    b. *The boy who John hit him is on the ground.
    c. *The student sits next to me is sick.
    d. *That she is wrapping the package is for Christmas.
    e. *I like people they are friendly.

5. An ESL/EFL student asks you to explain the difference between the two following sentences:

The person that called to you was a stranger.   The person that you called to was a stranger.

How would you answer?

6. Analyze some piece of published writing—a newspaper or magazine article, for instance. Identify all the restrictive relative clauses and their antecedents (i.e., the head noun or possessive determiner). Note in which contexts the relative pronoun is deleted. Do your observations confirm what Stauble found out about relative clause usage in published writing?

BIBLIOGRAPHY

References

Ioup, G., and A. Kruse (1977). "Interference versus Structural Complexity in Second Language Acquisition: Language Universals as a Basis for Natural Sequencing," in H. D. Brown, C. A. Yorio, and R. H. Crymes (eds.), *On TESOL 77: Teaching and Learning English as a Second Language: Trends in Research and Practice.* Washington, D.C.: TESOL.

Keenan, E., and B. Comrie (1972). "Noun Phrase Accessibility and Universal Grammar." Paper delivered at LSA Annual Meeting, Atlanta. (Published in *Linguistic Inquiry* 8:63–99, 1977.)

Kuno, S. (1974). "The Position of Relative Clauses and Conjunctions," *Linguistic Inquiry* V:1, 117–136.

Olsen, J. Winn-Bell (1977). *Communication-Starters and Other Activities for the ESL Classroom.* San Francisco: The Alemany Press.

Schachter, J. (1974). "An Error in Error Analysis," *Language Learning* 24:2, 205–214.

Schachter, P. (1972). "Transformational Grammar and Contrastive Analysis," in H. B. Allen and R. N. Campbell (eds.), *Teaching English as a Second Language.* New York: McGraw-Hill.

Schumann, J. (1980). "The Acquisition of English Relative Clauses by Second Language Learners," in R. C. Scarcella and S. D. Krashen (eds.), *Research in Second Language Acquisition.* Rowley, Mass.: Newbury House.

Stauble, A. (1978). "A Frequency Study of Restrictive Relative Clause Types and Relative Pronoun Usage in English." Unpublished English 215 paper, UCLA, fall, 1978.

Suggestions for further reading

For other second language acquisition studies which examine the effect of native language background on the acquisition of relative clauses by ESL learners, see:

Chiang, D. (1980). "Predictors of Relative Clause Production," in R. C. Scarcella and S. D. Krashen (eds.), *Research in Second Language Acquisition.* Rowley, Mass.: Newbury House.

Gass, S. (1980). "An Investigation of Syntactic Transfer in Adult Second Language Learners," in R. C. Scarcella and S. D. Krashen (eds.), *Research in Second Language Acquisition.* Rowley, Mass.: Newbury House.

For a more sophisticated analysis of relative clauses than the one we provide, see:

Stockwell, R., P. Schachter, and B. Partee (1973). *The Major Syntactic Structures of English.* New York: Holt, Rinehart and Winston, Chap. 7.

For information on relative clause formation for many different languages, consult:

Keenan, E., and B. Comrie (1979). "Data on the Noun Phrase Accessibility Hierarchy," *Language* 55:2, 333–351.
Maxwell, D. N. (1979). "Strategies of Relativization and NP Accessibility," *Language* 55:2, 352–371.

For texts with exercises designed to give ESL/EFL students practice in forming relative clauses, consult:

Danielson, D., and R. Hayden (1973). *Using English: Your Second Language.* Englewood Cliffs, N.J.: Prentice-Hall, Chap. 16.
Frank, M. (1972). *Modern English: Part II: Sentences and Complex Structures.* Englewood Cliffs, N.J.: Prentice-Hall, Chap. 3 (she calls them adjective clauses).
Rutherford, W. (1975). *Modern English* (2d ed., vol. 1). New York: Harcourt Brace Jovanovich, pp. 240–242, 246–247.
Wohl, M. (1978). *Preparation for Writing: Grammar.* Rowley, Mass.: Newbury House, pp. 116–122.

27

More on Relative Clauses

GRAMMATICAL DESCRIPTION

Introduction

In the previous chapter we described restrictive relative clauses. In this chapter we will consider nonrestrictive relative clauses. Then we will consider reductions in both types of relative clauses—restrictive and nonrestrictive. We have previously seen how a restrictive relative clause can be reduced by deleting the relative pronoun that replaces an object in the embedded sentence. In this chapter we will specify another way to reduce relative clauses which accounts for a variety of surface structures. Finally we will examine some additional English relative constructions which are formed by means other than pronominalizing a noun phrase or a possessive determiner.

Nonrestrictive relative clauses

Thus far the relative clauses we have been examining restrict the meaning of the noun phrases they are modifying. Not all relative clauses have this function, however. For instance, in the following sentence we could just as easily do without the relative clause yet remain sure of the identity of the head noun in the main clause.

> Mrs. Jensen, who lives next door, is a Girl Scout troop leader.

The relative clause in this sentence is called a nonrestrictive relative clause since it merely supplies additional information about Mrs. Jensen; it is not needed to tell us which woman is a Girl Scout troop leader in the same way that the restrictive relative clause is in the following sentence:

> The woman who lives next door is a Girl Scout troop leader.

Phonological features that mark nonrestrictive relative clauses are that they are accompanied by a drop in pitch and are preceded and followed by brief pauses. These phonological features are captured in writing by the use of commas, which set off nonrestrictive relative clauses from the rest of the sentence.

Perhaps another example would be useful at this point. Compare the two following sentences:

The climbers who reached the top were exhausted.	The climbers, who reached the top, were exhausted.

As you already know, the first sentence contains a restrictive relative clause. We interpret the head noun in this sentence as representing some portion of the group of climbers who began the ascent: those who were successful at reaching the summit. Since the nonrestrictive clause in the second sentence does not restrict the meaning of the head noun, we understand the head noun to refer to the entire group of climbers. In other words, they were all successful and they were all exhausted from their efforts.

Notice that we have just paraphrased the second sentence in the form of two underlying sentences. By hypothesizing that sentences containing nonrestrictive relative clauses are derived from two underlying sentences, we are able to capture the fact that their base structures are essentially different from those of restrictive relative clauses and that both the main clause and the nonrestrictive relative clause supply somewhat independent bits of information.[1] On the other hand, by positing two sentences in the base structure we would also be implying that the two clauses were of approximately equal status. Since this is misleading, we shall adopt the convention of labeling the main clause S1 and the nonrestrictive clause S2 at the base structure level, just as we did for sentences with restrictive relative clauses. Thus, two underlying sentences with nodes labeled S1 and S2 which meet certain conditions[2] and which are not joined by an explicit conjunction would motivate the application of the nonrestrictive embedding transformation. This transformation would embed the incidental, nonrestrictive information (i.e., the second clause) into the main clause. In other words, the nonrestrictive clause is a *derived* relative clause.

Let us now examine the underlying structure and the derivation of a sentence containing a nonrestrictive relative clause.

The climbers, who reached the top, were exhausted.

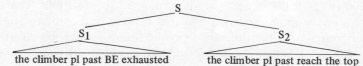

Output of base: the climber pl past BE exhausted (the climber pl past reach the top)
Nonrestrictive embedding: the climber pl (, the climber pl past reach the top,) past BE exhausted
(Note the use of commas in the derivation to distinguish relative clauses with a nonrestrictive source from those with a restrictive source.)

The rest of the derivation would be essentially the same as the one we followed for restrictive relative clauses:

Relative pronoun substitution: the climber pl (, who past reach the top,) past BE exhausted

---

1. The bits of information are, of course, related to one another, but the meaning of one clause is not dependent upon the other as is the case with sentences containing restrictive relative clauses.

2. There are two types of conditions corresponding to the two types of nonrestrictive clauses. One type requires an identical noun in the incidental clause—just as restrictive relative clauses do; the other type requires that the nonrestrictive clause be a comment on the fact or proposition expressed in the main clause.

Affix attachment (3×): the climber + pl (, who reach + past the top,) BE + past exhausted
Subject-verb agreement and morphological rules: The climbers, who reached the top, were
   exhausted.

The two nonrestrictive relative clauses that we have discussed so far have contained noun
phrases that are identical to noun phrases present in the main clause:

> Mrs. Jensen, who lives next door, is a Girl Scout leader.
> The climbers, who reached the top, were exhausted.

This type of nonrestrictive relative clause is sometimes called an appositive clause.

The other type of nonrestrictive relative clause has a relative pronoun (always *which*) that
refers to an entire clause instead of just a noun phrase. For instance, in the following sentence
the relative pronoun *which* refers to a fact (Jason's getting off work early) and the
nonrestrictive relative clause modifies the entire main clause; it is a comment on the fact
expressed in the main clause—occurring almost as an afterthought.

Jason got off work early, which was nice.

S

S_1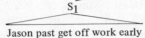

S_2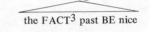

Output of base: Jason past get off work early (the FACT past BE nice)
Nonrestrictive embedding: Jason past get off work early (, the FACT past BE nice)

When the subject of the nonrestrictive relative clause refers to the fact expressed in the
preceding clause, we always use the relative pronoun *which*.

Relative pronoun substitution: Jason past get off work early (, which past BE nice)
Affix attachment (2×): Jason get + past off work early (, which BE + past nice)
Subject-verb agreement and morphological rules: Jason got off work early, which was nice.

In addition to those differences already mentioned, there are other characteristics which
distinguish restrictive and nonrestrictive relative clauses. Rather than go into great detail on
each, we will summarize the differences in the following lists based upon the analysis
provided in Stockwell, Schachter, and Partee (1973).

Summary of differences between restrictive and nonrestrictive relative clauses

Restrictive	*Nonrestrictive*
1. Provides information necessary for identifying a noun in the main clause.	1. Provides additional information but information unnecessary to determining the identity of a noun in the main clause.
2. Derived from an underlying embedded source.	2. Derived from two underlying sentences.
3. No pauses (no commas) or special intonation necessary to set off the relative clause from the main clause. (Certainly there is no separation from the head noun.)	3. Commas in writing and special pauses and intonation in speech set the relative clause off from the main clause.
4. May not modify an entire proposition.	4. May modify an entire proposition as a comment on a fact, e.g.: He decided to resign, which everyone thought was a good idea.

---

3. The entire proposition, i.e., "Jason's getting off early," is what is being modified. This is a bit difficult to
paraphrase as a single noun phrase; so the cover term "FACT" will have to do. Other nouns such as EVENT or
DEED might be more suitable cover terms to use in other sentences.

Restrictive	*Nonrestrictive*
5. *That* is freely used as a relative pronoun as well as *who(m), which,* etc., e.g.: The teacher { that / who } wears a fez is Professor Lees.	5. *That* cannot be used as a relative pronoun—only *who(m), which,* etc., e.g.: *Professor Lees, that wears a fez, is the teacher.
6. Does not usually modify proper nouns,[4] e.g.: *Professor Lees { who / that } wears a fez is the teacher.	6. May modify proper nouns as well as common nouns, e.g.: Professor Lees, who wears a fez, is the teacher.
7. May modify a head noun with generic determiners like *any* and *every,* e.g.: Any student { who / that } wears a fez becomes the teacher.	7. May not modify a head noun with a generic determiner like *any* or *every,* e.g.: *Any student, who wears a fez, becomes the teacher.

Reduction of relative clauses

Prepositional phrases

In the last chapter we saw that a relative pronoun which had replaced an object NP in the embedded sentence could be deleted after it had been fronted. For example,

> The curry which I cooked was too hot.

could be transformed to

> The curry I cooked was too hot.

by the relative pronoun deletion transformation.

We also noted that relative pronouns replacing the subject of the embedded clause could not be deleted:

The ice skater who is in the show looks familiar.	*The ice skater is in the show looks familiar.

While this is true enough, there is a way for relative clauses in such sentences to be reduced. This is accomplished when the subject NP in the embedded sentence is followed by a BE verb.[5] This BE verb may function as either a copula or an auxiliary (progressive or passive). When such a condition exists, the relative pronoun, the tense auxiliary, and BE may all be optionally deleted through the relative pronoun + BE deletion transformation. If we were to apply this transformation to the above sentence, we would get:

> The ice skater in the show looks familiar.

Not all prepositional phrases which appear in the surface structure have come from embedded relative clauses that have been reduced. We have already seen that many prepositional phrases are present in the base structure and function as adverbials. Recall sentences such as "Mary jogs through Central Park." Also, it is sometimes the case that a surface structure prepositional phrase may be ambiguous, as to whether its source is a

---

4. It is possible for a restrictive relative clause to modify a proper noun only if there is more than one person or thing which could be referred to by the same name, e.g.:

> I'm talking about the Marsha who was valedictorian of our class (not the one who has just moved here from Montreal).

In such cases the restrictive relative clause has the same function it normally does, i.e., to restrict the meaning of the head noun, which is functioning as a common noun rather than a true proper noun (see Chapter 14).

5. There are other verbs which may also be involved in this reduction but BE is far and away the most frequent, cf. the objection (which was *made*) to the proposal; the man (who *lives*) down the street.

restrictive relative clause or an adverbial already present in the base structure. For instance, in the following sentence,

Carla drew the picture in the den.

we may interpret the prepositional phrase "in the den" as telling us where Carla drew the picture, in which case the base structure would look like this:

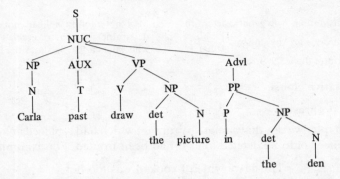

Alternatively, we may interpret the prepositional phrase as telling us which picture it was that Carla drew (i.e., the one in the den as opposed to the one in the dining room). This interpretation requires a base structure of a different sort, one in which the prepositional phrase is originally part of an embedded relative clause that restricts the meaning of the head noun.

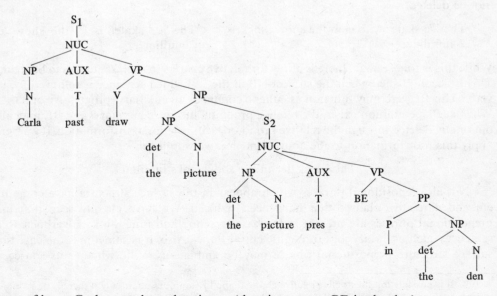

Output of base: Carla past draw the picture (the picture pres BE in the den)
Relative pronoun substitution: Carla past draw the picture (which pres BE in the den)
Relative pronoun + BE deletion:[6] Carla past draw the picture (in the den)
Affix attachment (1✕): Carla draw + past the picture (in the den)
Morphological rules: Carla drew the picture in the den.

---

6. As noted earlier, tense is also deleted with this transformation.

Appositives

Relative pronoun + BE deletion can also operate on some of the nonrestrictive relative clauses that contain a noun phrase identical to one in the main clause:

> Mr. Langstrom, who is our new neighbor, comes from Providence.
> Mr. Langstrom, our new neighbor, comes from Providence.
> Lansing, which is the capital of Michigan, has a population of 130,000.
> Lansing, the capital of Michigan, has a population of 130,000.

The resulting phrases are what traditional grammarians refer to as appositives, i.e., a group of words following an expression which further defines that expression.

Progressive or passive participial phrases

The relative pronoun + BE deletion transformation also provides us with a way of relating a number of sentences with progressive or passive participial phrases to synonymous sentences with full relative clauses. When this transformation is applied to a restrictive relative clause containing the progressive aspect, we are left with a progressive participial phrase modifying the head noun in the surface structure.

> How does the rodeo star who is riding the gray horse stay on? ⟶ How does the rodeo star riding the gray horse stay on?

Surface structures with embedded passive participial phrases can also be derived through the application of the relative pronoun + BE deletion transformation.

> Which cowboy was the one who was thrown by that horse? ⟶ Which cowboy was the one thrown by that horse?

Earlier we indicated that this transformation is optional. By now you will understand that when we use the term "optional," we mean that the sentence is grammatical with or without the application of the particular transformation. We do *not* mean that the transformation is arbitrarily applied. Presumably, there are discourse rules limiting the application of this transformation to appropriate contexts. While definite rules for when a relative clause may be reduced remain to be worked out, one can imagine that reduction might be favored in contexts where a number of relative clauses appear in sequence. Even within a single sentence, for instance, it is likely that reduction would occur in a relative clause when it is embedded within another relative clause, e.g.:

> I've forgotten the name of the contractor who submitted the bid which is now being considered by the Board. ⟶ I've forgotten the name of the contractor who submitted the bid now being considered by the Board.

On the other hand, the reduction of a relative clause might not be favored in those cases where an ambiguous surface structure would result (cf. Carla painted the picture in the den).

Adjectives

We said in the preceding chapter that restrictive relative clauses have an adjectival function in that they modify a head noun. The typical transformational analysis of adjectives captures this similarity of function by claiming that prenominal adjectives[7] are derived from restrictive relative clauses.[8] After undergoing relative clause reduction, the embedded

---

7. See the following chapter for a discussion of adjectives that cannot possibly be derived from restrictive relative clauses.

8. This is the usual transformational analysis of prenominal adjectives; however, we feel uncomfortable with this analysis for a variety of reasons. See the following chapter for an alternative analysis.

sentence is restructured so that what remains of the relative clause is moved to a prenominal position by the adjective preposing transformation. This transformation results in a radical restructuring of the underlying grammatical relationships in that only one sentence rather than two remains after adjective preposing has taken place.

To understand the usual transformational analysis of adjectives, consider the following sentence:

The controversial editorial appeared in the newspaper on Friday.

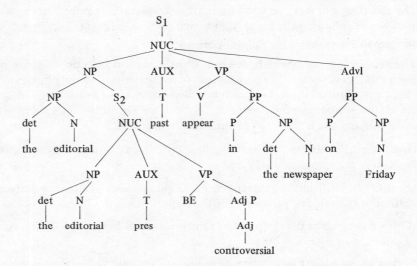

Output of base: the editorial (the editorial pres BE controversial) past appear in the newspaper on Friday

Relative pronoun substitution: the editorial (which pres BE controversial) past appear in the newspaper on Friday

Relative pronoun + BE deletion: the editorial (controversial) past appear in the newspaper on Friday

Adjective preposing: the controversial editorial past appear in the newspaper on Friday

Affix attachment (1×): the controversial editorial appear + past in the newspaper on Friday

Morphological rules: The controversial editorial appeared in the newspaper on Friday.

The usual transformational analysis also specifies that the adjective preposing rule may not apply when anything longer than a simple adjective phrase (i.e., intensifier + adjective) occurs in the reduced embedded sentence:

> The editorial favorable to the project appeared in yesterday's paper.
> *The favorable to the project editorial appeared in yesterday's paper.

As should be obvious by now, transformations which reduce relative clauses in English are very productive rules which can account for a variety of surface structures.

Before concluding this chapter, we will look at some additional relative constructions.

Relative adverbs

Another relative construction which we have yet to discuss is the relative clause which begins with a relative adverb. Consider the following:

Sam knows the place *where we're meeting* and the time *when we're meeting,* but he doesn't know the reason *why we're meeting.*

We will claim that each of the italicized clauses above are related to and therefore derived in a manner similar to restrictive relative clauses of the sort we have already analyzed. To support this position, let us examine the basic structure and derivation of one of these clauses.

Sam knows the place where we are meeting.

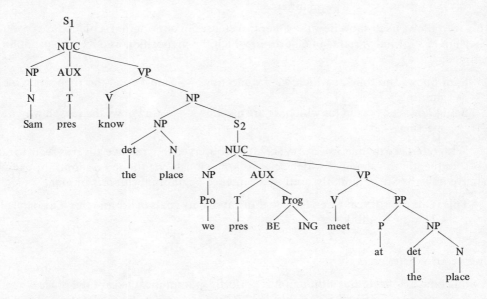

Output of base: Sam pres know the place (we pres BE ING meet at the place)
Relative pronoun substitution: Sam pres know the place (we pres BE ING meet at which)
Relative pronoun fronting: Sam pres know the place (at which we pres BE ING meet)

At this point, we could simply complete the derivation by applying the affix attachment, subject-verb agreement, and morphological rules and produce:

Sam knows the place at which we are meeting.

However, another possibility also exists. We could produce a less formal variant of this sentence by allowing a relative adverb substitution transformation to substitute the relative adverb *where* for the prepositional phrase containing the preposition *at* and the relative pronoun *which.*

Relative adverb substitution: Sam pres know the place (where we pres BE ING meet)
Affix attachment (3✕): Sam know + pres the place (where we BE + pres meet + ING)
Subject-verb agreement and morphological rules: Sam knows the place where we are meeting.

The function of the relative adverb substitution transformation, therefore, is to substitute the appropriate relative adverb for the corresponding preposition and relative pronoun combinations as follows:

$$\text{prep} + \text{which} \longrightarrow \text{where}$$
$$[+ \text{ place}]$$

$$\text{prep} + \text{which} \longrightarrow \text{when}$$
$$[+ \text{ time}]$$

$$\text{prep} + \text{which} \longrightarrow \text{why}$$
$$[+ \text{ reason}]$$

and for one other combination which we will examine shortly:

$$\text{prep} + \text{which} \longrightarrow \text{how}$$
$$[+ \text{ manner/way}]$$

This rule allows us to show how the other two clauses in our original sentence are produced. They are less formal variants of clauses in which the preposition and relative pronoun are retained:

Sam knows the time at which we are meeting. ⟶ Sam knows the time when we are meeting.

Sam knows the reason for which we are meeting. ⟶ Sam knows the reason why we are meeting.

With reference to their use, Snow (1978) has observed that relative adverbs seem to occur most frequently in sentences which refer to a previously mentioned notion. For example, relative adverbs are commonly used in a sentence beginning with *this* or *that:*

This is the time of year when I like to think about my goals in life and this is also the place where I can think best.

Free relative deletion

You may have noticed that although it is perfectly grammatical to say "the place where" in "Sam knows the place where we are meeting," it does seem redundant. A less formal variant of such a statement is:

Sam knows where we are meeting.

Here we apply an optional transformation called "free relative deletion" to delete the head noun where the use of both the head noun and the relative adverb together becomes redundant. It goes by this name since its application allows for a relative adverb to exist without a head noun in the surface structure, i.e., to exist freely. It could apply to the other sentences as well:

Sam knows the time when we are meeting. ⟶ Sam knows when we are meeting.

Sam knows the reason why we are meeting. ⟶ Sam knows why we are meeting.

Although deletion of the head noun is optional in these three instances, it becomes obligatory if the relative adverb is *how:*

*That is the way how he writes.

With the application of the free relative deletion transformation this sentence becomes grammatical:

That is how he writes.

It is interesting to note that the sequence "the way how" was acceptable in earlier versions of standard English and still is acceptable in some dialects—but not in current standard English. ESL/EFL students predictably have trouble with this exception and will have to learn to consistently delete the head noun in order to produce a grammatical sentence when this relative adverb is used.

Of course, while we say that the free relative deletion transformation is optional except for the relative adverb *how,* the head noun cannot be deleted without a concomitant loss of information when it is more specific than a general noun such as the *place* or the *time,* e.g.:

> She returned to (the town) where she was born.
> He can never remember (the date) when we were married.

Thus, for these cases the free relative deletion transformation seems to be syntactically optional, but the result is often a sentence which is less precise semantically.

Relative adverb deletion

Another way to make sentences of "the way how" type acceptable is to delete the relative adverb:

> That is the way he writes.

This transformation has also applied in the following sentences where relative adverbs have been deleted:

> (why) The reason I voted "no" was my opposition to the project.
> (when) I remember the time I tried to make a soufflé.

It is not clear, however, what the exact conditions on relative adverb deletion are. For instance, after certain prepositions or where the head noun is the object of a preposition, the relative adverb cannot always be easily deleted:

> ?/*Jersey City is the place I was born.

If the preposition is retained or if the free relative is deleted, full grammaticality is restored:

> Jersey City is the place I was born in.   or   Jersey City is where I was born.

Relative adverbs of place seem to be the most problematic ones with respect to deletion. More usage studies are needed to determine precisely when it is appropriate to delete the relative adverb as opposed to deleting the head noun.

Register differences

With the addition of the transformations we have discussed in this chapter we can now show that there could be as many as six surface variants[9] for a sentence in which a relative adverb could occur:

1. 1950 is the year which I was born in.

(after relative pronoun deletion)
2. 1950 is the year I was born in.

(if the preposition is fronted with the relative pronoun)
3. 1950 is the year in which I was born.

(after relative adverb substitution)
4. 1950 is the year when I was born.

---

9. We have already noted several times above that not all six variants are possible for all relative adverbs, e.g., a sentence like 4 would not be possible if the relative adverb was *how.*

(after free relative deletion)

5. 1950 is when I was born.

(after relative adverb deletion)

6. 1950 is the year I was born.

After conducting a discourse analysis in which she compared the frequencies of the latter three sentence types, Snow (1978) concluded that the full form (i.e., head noun + relative adverb exemplified in 4 above) occurred with the greatest frequency in written or formal contexts. Sentences with free relatives such as 5 occurred most frequently in spoken or informal contexts. Sentences with the head noun alone (6 above) were found by Snow to be the least frequent type in both written and spoken contexts with relative adverbs of time, place, and reason. Native speakers, however, showed a strong preference for use of the head noun alone (6) in both written and spoken usage when the relative adverb was *how*.

Thus, the distribution of these variants is in part discourse-dependent, and you may want to make your advanced ESL/EFL students aware of the preferences of native speakers.

Free relative substitution

In our discussion of the free relative deletion transformation, we indicated that its function was to delete a head noun when it was semantically redundant with the relative adverb. Next we will see that the free relative deletion transformation can also delete a lexically empty head noun occurring before a relative pronoun. Thus this process also occurs in the absence of any adverbial phrase or clause:

The new teacher is just the $\left\{ \begin{array}{c} \text{one} \\ \text{person} \end{array} \right\}$ who we're looking for. ⟶ The new teacher is just who we're looking for.

With certain combinations of head nouns and relative pronouns, simple deletion of the head noun cannot take place:

The new teacher is just the person that we're looking for. ⟶ *The new teacher is just that we're looking for.

In such cases, however, it is possible for the free relative substitution transformation to operate. It substitutes *who* for *the person* $\left\{ \begin{array}{c} \text{who} \\ \text{that} \end{array} \right\}$. It also works with relative pronouns which replace nonhuman NPs. It replaces *the thing* $\left\{ \begin{array}{c} \text{that} \\ \text{which} \end{array} \right\}$ with *what*.

Painting is the thing $\left\{ \begin{array}{c} \text{that} \\ \text{which} \end{array} \right\}$ he does best. ⟶ Painting is what he does best.

Free relative pronouns such as *who* and *what* can also occupy subject position.

The thing he does best is painting landscapes. ⟶ What he does best is painting landscapes.

The person that you are is in part determined by how you were raised. ⟶ Who you are is in part determined by how you were raised.

In summary, free relative clauses have no head noun in the main clause and are the result of either the free relative deletion rule or the free relative substitution transformation. As usual, much linguistic analysis remains to be done in this area of the language as well as in the others we have introduced in this chapter. We hope that you have at least gained some insight into the intricacies of the English relativization system.

TEACHING SUGGESTIONS

1   One way of presenting the difference between restrictive and nonrestrictive relative clauses was suggested by Walter Goodwin. There are three steps in all:

a. The teacher says, "If you do not speak Japanese, stand up." With the teacher's help and that of other students, one student writes a sentence on the blackboard about the students who speak Japanese, i.e.:

> The students who speak Japanese are seated.

The teacher asks the students to make observations about the form and function of the restrictive relative clause.

b. The teacher then says to the class, "If you speak some English, remain seated." One student with the help of the others writes the following on the blackboard:

> The students, who speak English, are seated.

The teacher draws out observations from the students about the form and function of a nonrestrictive relative clause.

c. The teacher now asks the students to make an explicit comparison between the two sentences. After doing this, students in small groups create examples of sentences containing each type of relative clause using information about the class or about class member(s).

2   To practice reduced forms of relative clauses, bring lots of "action" pictures to class—pictures of people doing things like skiing, surfing, hiking, and swimming.

First, elicit sentences with restrictive relative clauses reduced to prepositional phrases by asking students to make observations about where the people are performing the actions:

I can see the woman in the swimming pool.
I can see the man on the ski slope.

I can see the climber on top of the mountain.

Next, elicit sentences with restrictive relative clauses reduced to participial phrases by asking students to focus on the actions the people are performing:

I see the woman swimming in the pool.
I see the man skiing down the slope.

I see the woman climbing up the mountain.

Finally, have the students pair up and make statements to each other about who they would like to be and why, e.g.:

> I'd like to be the boy surfing in Hawaii because . . .
> I'd like to be one of the people hiking in the mountains because . . .
> I'd like to be the woman in the swimming pool because . . .

3   To practice reductions of nonrestrictive relative clauses, distribute small maps of the United States (or any other country/region) or display a large one which everyone can see. Have students make statements containing appositives, e.g.:

> Rhode Island, the smallest state, is located in the Northeast.
> Lake Superior, one of the Great Lakes, is the largest of the group.
> Florida, the southeasternmost state, is a popular vacation spot.
>   Etc.

4   Students can be given some fairly mechanical written drills asking them to replace prepositions and relative pronouns with the appropriate relative adverbs. Later on they could be given drills which require them to delete the head noun or the relative adverb.

Once students feel comfortable with manipulating the forms, they should be given some experience which will help them to become sensitive to register variation. Rutherford (1977:184) uses an exercise which could easily be adapted for practice of register with relative adverbs. He provides a series of sentences written in an informal register and asks the students to put them into a more formal register by moving the preposition to a position before the relative pronoun (e.g., This is the house that they live in. ──▶This is the house in which they live). Snow (1978) suggests that this same type of exercise could be used effectively to teach the degrees of formality of relative clauses containing relative adverbs (e.g., This is the park where I play tennis.──▶This is the park in which I play tennis).

5   Ultimately, of course, we would want our students to go beyond the manipulative stage inherent in some of these exercises and be able to use the various relative structures in natural discourse. One may start by having them identify and expand (if they have been reduced) all the relative constructions in a passage excerpted from a book. Later students should be asked to produce paragraphs or other sorts of extended writing in which they attempt to appropriately employ the various relative constructions to which they have been introduced. Topics involving classification can be useful in eliciting restrictive clauses; e.g., discuss the different kinds of students you see at this university:

> There are students who always study.
> There are students who never study.
> Etc.

EXERCISES

Test your understanding of what has been presented

1. Give an example sentence to illustrate each of the following terms. Underline the pertinent word(s) in your examples.

relative adverb substitution	appositive
free relative substitution	nonrestrictive relative clause
relative pronoun + BE deletion	nonrestrictive embedding
free relative deletion	relative adverb deletion

2. Give the tree diagrams and derivations for the following sentences:

a. Dr. Graber, who(m) you know, will lecture next week.
b. The place where he lived is unknown.
c. Marilyn lent me her car, which was very thoughtful.
d. The boys running in the marathon were very athletic.
e. That's the way he wants it.

3. Why are the following sentences ungrammatical?

a. *Christmas is the time at which when he's busiest.
b. *Any teacher, who is dedicated, must work hard.
c. *This is the office I work.

Test your ability to apply what you know

4. If your students produce the following sentences, what errors have they made? How will you make them aware of the errors, and what exercises will you prepare to correct the errors?

a. *I took that course with Mr. Hall, which is an excellent teacher.
b. *That is the way how he drives.
c. *Cooking is the thing what he enjoys.

5. One of your students asks you to explain the difference in meaning between the following two sentences. How will you respond?

My sister, who lives in Chicago, has three children.

My sister who lives in Chicago has three children.

6. Try to order the following sentences along a formality register continuum according to what has been discussed in this chapter as well as using your own intuitions. How could you make your students aware of the register differences among these sentence types?

Do you recall why he resigned?

Do you recall the reason he resigned?

Do you recall the reason for which he resigned?

Do you recall the reason why he resigned?

BIBLIOGRAPHY

References

Rutherford, W. E. (1977). *Modern English* (2d ed., vol. II). New York: Harcourt Brace Jovanovich.
Snow, M. A. (1978). "The Where, When, Why and How of Relative Clauses." Unpublished English 215K paper, UCLA, fall, 1978.
Stockwell, R. P., P. Schachter, and B. Partee (1973). *The Major Syntactic Structures of English*. New York: Holt, Rinehart and Winston.

Suggestions for further reading

For a good reference on the analysis of relative clauses that supplements Stockwell, Schachter, and Partee (1973), see:

Thompson, S. A. (1971). "The Deep Structure of Relative Clauses," in C. J. Fillmore and D. T. Langendoen (eds.), *Studies in Linguistic Semantics*. New York: Holt, Rinehart and Winston.

For an alternative analysis of relative clauses that accounts for the usual data as well as idioms like "the headway that John made . . . ," refer to:

Schachter, P. (1973). "Focus and Relativization," *Language* 49:1.

For suggestions regarding the teaching of nonrestrictive relative clauses, see:

Rutherford, W. E. (1975). *Modern English* (2d ed., vol. I). New York: Harcourt Brace Jovanovich, pp. 248–249.

For exercises contrasting restrictive and nonrestrictive relative clauses, see:

Wohl, M. (1978). *Preparation for Writing: Grammar*. Rowley, Mass.: Newbury House, pp. 122–127.

For useful ESL/EFL exercises using the relative adverbs, check:

Wishon, G. E., and J. M. Burks (1968). *Let's Write English*. New York: American Book Co., pp. 100–108.

28

Adjectives—Attributive vs. Predicate Position and Ordering Problems

GRAMMATICAL DESCRIPTION

Introduction

From the morphological point of view, adjectives in English are not as complicated as they are in many other languages. They are not inflected for gender, case, or number. Also, the form of the adjective does not change depending on whether it occurs in predicate position (i.e., after the copula BE) or in attributive position (i.e., preceding a noun). In fact, this surface simplicity regarding the form of English adjectives may well have contributed to the usual transformational account, which derives attributive adjectives from predicate adjectives that originate in restrictive relative clauses. For example (as was discussed in Chapter 27), an expression such as "the controversial editorial" can be derived from "the editorial that is controversial" if the usual transformational analysis is followed.[1]

In this chapter we want to summarize the deficiencies that Bolinger noticed in this type of transformational analysis. Based on Bolinger's work we will also look at potential semantic differences in attributive and postnominal use of the same adjective, and we will also posit a separate source for attributive adjectives. Finally, we will look at what is involved when we order two or more attributive adjectives before the same noun.

Why many attributive adjectives cannot derive from predicate adjectives

In 1967, Bolinger published a paper on adjectives in English in which he presented several arguments to show that not all attributive adjectives can be derived from predicate adjectives. First of all, he argued that many adjectives are always attributive, never predicative:

the *main* reason	*the reason is main
a *total* stranger	*the stranger is total
a *crack* salesman	*the salesman is crack
a case of *sheer* fraud	*the fraud is sheer

---

1. We are skeptical of the usual transformational analysis, since there seems to be a different relationship between the adjective when it directly precedes the noun and when it occurs in a relative clause—even when a reasonable paraphrase relationship exists. This is why we propose an alternative analysis for attributive adjectives in this chapter.

Second, Bolinger noted that there are also a few adjectives that are always predicative, never attributive:

The boy is asleep.   *the asleep boy
The boat is adrift.   *the adrift boat

He further pointed out that if all attributive adjectives *did* come from a predicate source, we would expect English to have more adjectives that are exclusively predicative than adjectives that are exclusively attributive. Since the facts of English show that the reverse is true (i.e., there are more adjectives that are exclusively attributive), the derivation of attributive adjectives from a predicate adjective source appears highly questionable.

Third, some adjectives permit special meanings to occur in attributive position that can't be paraphrased with a predicate use of the same adjective (even though the adjective may also occur in predicate position).

an angry storm   (but "I was angry" is OK)
*the storm was angry

Similarly, some adjectives take on distinctively different meanings when occurring in attributive and predicative position, e.g.:

The girl is sorry. (apologetic)   ≠   The sorry girl (like "a sorry sight")
The man is responsible. (to blame)   ≠   The responsible man (trustworthy)

Bolinger also suggests that sometimes an adverbial source is more reasonable for some attributive adjectives than is a predicate adjective, e.g.:

The daily newspaper ⟵ the newspaper appears daily

Finally, Bolinger points out that some sentences containing adjectives seem to be derived from two independent clauses rather than having a derivation where the adjective originates in a restrictive relative clause (i.e., the second sentence is like a nonrestrictive clause), e.g.:

John is a drowsy policeman.

*(John is a policeman ({ who / a policeman } is drowsy).)

That is:

John is a policeman.   John is drowsy.

We agree that adjectives that are nonrestrictive (i.e., nondefining descriptive additions) should not have embedded sources but should rather be derived from two independent sentences. Here is another example:

Old Farmer Cobb is harvesting his crops.
*Farmer Cobb that is old is harvesting his crops.
Farmer Cobb is harvesting his crops.
Farmer Cobb is old.

Only those adjectives that are truly restrictive could conceivably originate in a restrictive relative clause:

John bought a red house.
(John bought a house that's red.)
Mary made some amusing remarks.
(Mary made some remarks that were amusing.)

However, even in cases like these, we feel that there is a difference between the two versions of such pairs, the attributive adjective having a closer association with the noun than the restrictive relative clause. We are convinced that most discourse contexts would favor one form over the other. This is why we suggest an alternative analysis below.

Difference in meaning based on difference in position

Bolinger also noted that there is something semantically more permanent or characteristic about the adjectives that directly precede nouns than the adjectives that directly follow nouns,[2] which tend to reflect temporary states or specific events, e.g.:

1. a. The stolen jewels . . . (a characteristic of the jewels)
    b. The jewels stolen . . . (identified by a specific act—maybe they were recovered later)
2. a. The only navigable river . . . (usual fact about a given region)
    b. The only river navigable . . . (temporary state due to a drought or some such event)
3. a. The guilty people . . . (a characteristic, classifying modifier of the people)
    b. The people guilty . . . (the people are described in terms of one act or event)

The BE + adjective (or predicate adjective) construction, according to Bolinger, is potentially ambiguous, since if we say:

> The river is navigable.   These people are guilty.
> These jewels are stolen.

we cannot tell whether the adjective is being used to describe something that is permanent and characteristic of the subject noun or something that is temporary or occasional. Changing the adjective to either attributive position or immediate postnominal position can disambiguate in such cases. As Bolinger points out, attributive position tends to reject the temporary and the occasional, e.g.:

> The house was pink in the sunset.   ≠   The pink house . . .

It favors negatives that characterize, e.g.:

> the departed guests   *the arrived guests
> your absent friend   *your present friend

and compound attributive adjectives tend to reflect habitual or customary action as opposed to isolated events, e.g.:[3]

> Your friend writes plays.——→Your play-writing friend . . .
> The man broke a leg.——→ *The leg-breaking man . . .
> Carnivores are animals that eat meat.——→Carnivores are meat-eating animals.
> My brother bought a house.——→*My house-buying brother . . .

---

2. Note that in sentences with adjectives directly following nouns, the adjectives would be derived from restrictive relative clauses that have undergone the "relative pronoun plus BE deletion" transformation, e.g.:

> During the drought the only river that was navigable was the Merced.——→During the drought the only river navigable was the Merced.

3. We agree with Bolinger that customary action is one source of compound adjectives, but would also cite isolated events as another source provided that they have some historical significance or newsworthiness and are not mundane isolated events such as those in the starred sentences cited above:

> He batted in the run that won the game.——→ The game-winning run . . .
> Her time in the race broke the record.——→Her record-breaking time . . .

A separate source for attributive adjectives

Bolinger (1967) used the term "reference modification" to describe those adjectives that occur exclusively in attributive position. What kinds of adjectives are reference adjectives? Bolinger suggests several semantic subcategories; among them are:

1. Those adjectives that show the reference of the head noun has already been determined:

$$\text{the} \left\{ \begin{array}{l} \text{very} \\ \text{particular} \\ \text{precise} \\ \text{same} \\ \text{self-same} \\ \text{identical} \\ \text{exact} \end{array} \right\} \text{man I was seeking}$$

2. Those adjectives that show us the importance or rank of the head noun:

$$\text{their} \left\{ \begin{array}{l} \text{main} \\ \text{prime} \\ \text{principal} \\ \text{chief} \end{array} \right\} \text{faults}$$

3. Those adjectives that show the head noun is recognized by law or custom:

$$\text{the} \left\{ \begin{array}{l} \text{lawful} \\ \text{rightful} \\ \text{legal} \\ \text{true} \end{array} \right\} \text{heir}$$

4. Those adjectives which identify the reference of the noun itself, i.e., tell us (in part) what the noun means, and which may not occur after the copula BE:

a medical doctor	*a doctor (who) is medical
a regular policeman	*a policeman (who) is regular
a reserve officer	*an officer (who) is reserve

5. Those adjectives that qualify the time reference of the noun:

the future king	the $\left\{ \begin{array}{l} \text{present} \\ \text{former} \end{array} \right\}$ chairman
the late president	

6. Those adjectives that qualify the geographical reference of the noun:

a Southern gentleman	the urban crisis
a rural mailman	

Two other subcategories that are mentioned but not specifically defined by Bolinger are:

7. Those adjectives that intensify or emphasize the head noun:

a total stranger	a mere child
sheer fraud	utter nonsense

8. Those adjectives that show the uniqueness of the head noun:

the sole survivor	not a $\left\{ \begin{array}{l} \text{solitary} \\ \text{single} \end{array} \right\}$ individual
the only nominee	

There are probably some additional subcategories too.

Thus since there are so many "reference adjectives" which can only be generated in attributive position and since those adjectives that can occur in both attributive and predicate position often exhibit differences in meaning corresponding to position, we will not derive attributive adjectives from a predicate source. Instead we will revise our phrase structure rule for expanding noun phrases as follows:

$$NP \longrightarrow (det) \ (AP) \ N \ (pl)$$

There are, however, some important syntactic differences between attributive and predicate adjective phrases that we must point out at this time. Recall that our rule for expanding predicate adjective phrases is as follows:

$$AP \longrightarrow (intens)^n \ Adj \ (PP)$$
(pred.)

In attributive adjective phrases we often have more than one adjective, for example, "the *large white Mexican* rebozo." (The ordering of multiple attributive adjectives is discussed below.) Also, the optional prepositional phrase that follows predicate adjectives is no longer part of the attributive adjective rule, for reasons we give below. What these differences mean is that our rule for attributive adjective phrases must allow for more than one adjective as well as more than one optional intensifier.

$$AP \longrightarrow (intens)^n \ Adj^n$$
(attrib.)

We feel that these syntactic differences are an additional argument for a separate source for attributive adjectives.

In fact the only adjectives in attributive position that we would not derive from this new source are the nonrestrictive ones (cf. John is a *drowsy* policeman). As explained above, such sentences are the product of two underlying sentences that have been combined into one.

One consequence of having two sources for adjectives in our phrase structure rules is that every adjective must be marked in the lexicon for potential syntactic position, e.g.:

+*attributive* +*predicative*	+*attributive* −*predicative*	−*attributive* +*predicative*
red	main	asleep
big	total	awake
oval	mere	adrift
⋮	⋮	⋮

Also, homophonous adjectives having very different meanings depending on whether they were in attributive or predicate position (e.g., *sorry*) would have separate lexical entries for the two positions.

In addition to attributive and predicate adjective phrases, adjectivals can also take the form of a prepositional phrase immediately following a noun:

the city of New York   a man of honor

These seem very similar semantically to attributive adjectives:

New York City   an honorable man

as both are adjectival modifications of the head noun. It is also possible to have a double adjectival construction, with an attributive adjective preceding the noun and a prepositional phrase following it:

a true man of honor

In order to account for the prepositional phrase, we will have to modify our phrase structure rule for expanding noun phrases even further:

$$NP \longrightarrow (det)\ (AP)\ N\ (pl)\ (PP)$$

The function of the PP here in the NP is adjectival, unlike the PP in the VP, which is adverbial.

Complex adjective phrases are never attributive

When adjective phrases become more complex syntactically than "intens. + adj." (when they take prepositions or complements), they are generated in the verb phrase and are restricted to postnominal or predicative position; they may not occur in attributive position:

the man (who was) responsible for the accident
*the responsible for the accident man
the decision (that was) instrumental in the department's development . . .
*the instrumental in the department's development decision

The inability of such complex adjective phrases to function attributively is not surprising in that they almost always refer to specific actions, processes, or events—i.e., meanings that are incompatible with the attributive use of adjectives in English. The fact that such complex adjective phrases may occur prenominally in certain other languages (e.g., German and Japanese) suggests that these languages utilize syntactic and semantic principles different from those occurring in English with regard to the attributive use of adjectives.

The ordering of attributive adjectives

Our new phrase structure rule allows more than one adjective to be generated in attributive position:

$$AP \longrightarrow (intens)^n\ Adj^n$$
(attrib.)

The ordering of two or more attributive (i.e., prenominal) adjectives is a point of English grammar that is a minor source of error for nonnative speakers. This is partly so because not all languages follow a prenominal order the way English does. Many other languages such as Arabic place all attributive adjectives after the noun rather than before the noun. Also, there are languages like French which have a mixed order since some attributive adjectives referring to age, size, and evaluation precede the noun while other attributive adjectives referring to color or origin follow, e.g.:

une grande voiture jaune   une vieille femme   Italienne
(big)   (car)   (yellow)   (old)   (woman) (Italian)
"a big yellow car"   "an old Italian woman"

In certain cases two adjectives may precede a noun in French and one may follow:

une jolie petite voiture jaune
(pretty) (little) (car) (yellow)
"a pretty little yellow car"

French also seems to permit no more than two adjectives following a noun:

une voiture Japonaise jaune
(car)   (yellow)
"a yellow Japanese car"

Even this seems stylistically awkward to many French speakers, who would prefer to avoid such a construction altogether.

In Arabic, according to Svatko (1979), *all* attributive adjectives come after the noun and up to three adjectives are possible in this position; however, Svatko adds that the Arabic ordering system is less rigid than the English one; as a result of all these differences, Arabic speakers beginning their study of English make adjective ordering errors in their English speech and writing, e.g.:

*an American interesting movie   *a wooden big bowl

In her study Svatko found that more advanced Arabic speakers of English made fewer errors of this type since they were able to more closely approximate the English system.

Thus we can see that not all languages follow the same adjective ordering principles that English does and not all languages have as fixed an order as English. These differences can lead to errors when speakers of such languages—especially those who are beginning their study of English—try to use two or more adjectives to modify a noun.

Adjective ordering in English has been discussed by traditional and structural linguists, but it has been largely ignored by the transformationalists. Sledd (1959), for example, in his structurally based introduction to English grammar, gives the following order for elements in a noun phrase.[4]

1.   predeterminer (i.e., quantifier in this grammar)
2.   determiner (or possessive)
3.   limiting adjectival (i.e., quantifier in this grammar)
4.   adverbial of degree (i.e., intensifier in this grammar)
5.   descriptive adjectival
6.   noun adjunct
7.   nominal (i.e., noun or head noun in this grammar)

Some example sentences making use of this order are:

1	2	3	4	5	6	7
All (of)	the	dozen	very	tall	English	teachers
Both (of)	John's	two	extremely	fine	brick	walls

Kathleen Bailey (1975), in an empirical investigation of attributive adjective ordering in English, points out that Sledd's fifth category (i.e., descriptive adjectives) has several subcategories, some of which are:

a. *Coloration:* red, blue, green, pale, dark, etc.
b. *Measurement:* big, little, tiny, large, short, etc.
c. *Shape:* round, square, oblong, irregular, triangular, etc.

---

4. A similar though even less detailed structural ordering of prenominal modifiers is given in Halliday and Hasan (1976):

the	*two*	*high*	*stone*	*walls*
article	number	adjective	noun adjunct	Head noun

d. *Subjective evaluation:* poor, sweet, pretty, old, nice, etc. (may also be used to measure or describe with other more literal meanings)

Bailey's data, which included (1) analysis of both transcribed speech and written texts, (2) a card-sorting task, and (3) elicited speech samples, show that most of these subcategories have a relatively fixed ordering with respect to each other that is seldom violated. This ordering of elements in the noun phrase is as follows:

1. determiner
2. subjective or evaluative adjective
3. measurement adjective
4. coloration adjective
5. material adjective
6. head noun

Examples:

1	2	3	4	5	6
The	poor	little	pink	plastic	doll
An	ugly	old	black	wooden	statue

Svatko's (1979) study of adjective ordering in English starts with the description given in Praninskas (1975:262), which Svatko selects as the best one available. It is more detailed than Bailey's in that seven rather than four distinct semantic categories of adjectives are listed. (Note, however, that material adjectives are not distinguished from origin adjectives in this system.)

det	opinion	size	shape	condition	age	color	origin	noun
an	ugly	big	round	chipped	old	blue	French	vase

Both Praninskas and Svatko point out that sequences of more than three adjectives seldom occur in speech or writing and that two-adjective sequences are the most typical ones. We would like to add that adjective length also seems to be a factor in ordering; however, no study that we know of has taken this factor into consideration.

Svatko's study tested Praninskas' ordering rule by using a series of questionnaires with items such as the following, which presented two, three, or four adjectives that respondents were then asked to order with respect to each other in a given context:

This is a/an _____ , _____ , _____ car.
　　　large
　　　American
　　　red

This is a/an _____ , _____ test.
　　　short
　　　easy

Based on the responses of 30 native speakers of English, correlations were calculated to determine the strength of the relationship between the predicted position (i.e., Praninskas' order) and the observed position (i.e., the order emerging from the responses of the native speakers) for each semantic category of prenominal adjective. The results were as follows:

opinion	size	shape	condition	age	color	origin	noun
.80	.96	.66	.79	.85	.77	1.0	

For adjectives referring to origin, speaker performance matched order prediction 100 percent of the time; i.e., there was a perfect correlation. Adjectives of size exhibited a very strong correlation while adjectives of age, opinion, condition, and color also exhibited fairly strong correlations. Adjectives of shape exhibited the weakest correlation between the predicted and the observed order. These results indicate that while the established order is valid, it is not equally fixed for all types of adjectives.

Another point that we should mention about adjective ordering is that attributive adjectives are sometimes conjoined with *and* when there are two adjectives from the same category that both partially modify the same noun (i.e., using either of the two adjectives alone would be semantically misleading):

an orange and white marble   (but not: *a little and old man)
a wood(en) and metal implement

Also, two or more attributive adjectives are sometimes separated by commas in writing if there is repetition (i.e., intensification) or if the two adjectives are from the same class and are not incompatible (i.e., it would not be semantically misleading to use only one of them), e.g.:

a big, big airplane   a charming, attractive lady

Cases with variable order

The two kinds of adjectives that Bailey (1975) described as having a variable order depending on meaning are:

1. Proper adjectives[5] (and the way they order with material adjectives such as wooden, brick, and glass), e.g.:

$$\text{Three} \begin{Bmatrix} \text{wooden Japanese} \\ \text{Japanese wooden} \end{Bmatrix} \text{chests} \qquad \text{A large} \begin{Bmatrix} \text{porcelain Chinese} \\ \text{Chinese porcelain} \end{Bmatrix} \text{vase}$$

2. Adjectives denoting shape—i.e., words like round, oblong, wide, square, flat, etc., may, in combination with other adjectives, be rearranged according to the demands of the context, e.g.:

$$a \begin{Bmatrix} \text{large} \\ \text{yellow} \end{Bmatrix} \text{oblong box / an oblong} \begin{Bmatrix} \text{large} \\ \text{yellow} \end{Bmatrix} \text{box}$$

$$a \text{ round} \begin{Bmatrix} \text{blue} \\ \text{small} \end{Bmatrix} \text{table / a} \begin{Bmatrix} \text{blue} \\ \text{small} \end{Bmatrix} \text{round table}$$

Further study is needed to determine the semantic constraints and discourse contexts that will explain the variable order for these types of adjectives.

The primary stress rule

Another interesting finding of Bailey's study (1975) is that subjects produced strings such as the following one in two different contexts with two different stress patterns:

Context 1:   three large triangles—one blue, one red, one yellow, i.e., the large YELLOW triangle

Context 2:   three yellow triangles—two small, one large, i.e., the LARGE yellow triangle

---

5. Proper adjectives—"adjectives of origin" in the Praninskas system—refer to nationalities, religions, geographical regions, and directions (sometimes even cities—Venetian), months, seasons of the year, etc. They are often written with a capital letter.

That is to say, the ordering of measurement and color adjectives is more or less fixed, but English speakers assign primary stress to one adjective or the other depending on context— i.e., the adjective that most clearly limits and defines the noun with respect to the other nouns in the same context gets primary stress.

Special uses of adjectives having figurative meanings[6]

Finally, it might also be worthwhile for teachers to acquaint their students with some of the alternative meanings of adjectives. For example, it appears that in a noun phrase with two adjectives, one of which is *little,* the word *little* may denote more than size. For example, when we talk about "a cute little girl" or "a little old lady" or "a pretty little thing," there seems to be an implication of endearment as well as the size factor. This may be similar to the function of the suffix *-ito* (or *-ita*) in Spanish, which marks a diminutive form expressing familiarity or affection. Even more obvious is the evaluative meaning of the word *great,* which may function along with or instead of its semantic feature of measurement. These two words can even work together: "She was a great little gal" does not mean "She was a big small girl."

TEACHING SUGGESTIONS

1   In order to give intermediate to advanced ESL/EFL students a feeling for attributive versus postnominal position of those adjectives that can occur in both positions, exercises such as the following should be provided. The students should be asked to put the adjective specified in attributive position if a characteristic or permanent meaning is conveyed, and in postnominal position if a temporary or specific interpretation is called for.

a. *Available.* We didn't purchase any new equipment last month because there was so little (1) _____ money (2) _____ .

b. *Elected.* At the beginning of each Board meeting the chairman introduces the corporation's (1) _____ officers (2) _____ .

c. *Edible.* As part of their final exam, the botany majors were sent into the woods and asked to find and bring back ten (1) _____ plants (2) _____ .

d. *Assigned.* Jack has decided to take History 100 instead of History 121 next quarter because the professor teaching History 100 says there will be no (1) _____ term projects (2) _____ .

2   Tim Butterworth and Darlene Schultz suggest that a teacher who wants to have students practice adjective use and ordering should put on a desk a number of objects that two or more adjectives could describe. Then the teacher should tell his or her students to concentrate on the objects. After a few minutes the teacher covers the objects with a cloth. The students are then asked to remember and describe orally (or write down) as many objects as they can, e.g.:

> a small gold(en) cufflink
> a little blue stuffed animal
> Etc.

3   For a more advanced class the teacher might try a variation of "Mad-libs." To do this the teacher writes a passage leaving blanks where adjectives belong. Without showing the passage

---

6. These special connotations of adjectives such as *little, poor,* and *great* are much more typical of American than British English.

to the class, the teacher elicits an adjective of color, an adjective of shape, a proper adjective, etc. Then the students fill in the blanks in the passage using the adjectives that have been elicited. Usually, a humorous story results. Following this class exercise, the students could prepare their own similar passages (individually or in groups) and have other students supply them with adjectives to fill in the blanks.

The remaining suggestions come from Kathleen Bailey (1975), who suggested several teaching applications as part of her study of attributive adjective ordering in English.

4 The first step in teaching the order of English attributive adjectives would be to make the students aware of the general rules and formulas which seem to hold true under most circumstances. The teacher should also demonstrate the primary stress rule to the students, probably with a drill involving various choices. Using different colors and sizes of objects, the teacher could structure an activity in which the students had to place the primary stress correctly in order to get the object they were asking for. The activity could then be broadened to include student/student interaction in which student A must produce the correct stress pattern and student B must perceive it correctly before a sale or exchange of objects could be transacted.

5 Another activity involving adjectives and their ordering is a guessing game in which the teacher hides a sackful of objects behind the desk. The students are then called to the front of the class one at a time. The student facing the class is given one object which she or he can examine behind the podium, but which the rest of the class cannot see. The student must describe the object without naming it, until one of his or her classmates guesses what it is. For example:

Student 1: This is a long, yellow object.
Student 2: Is it a string?
Student 1: No, it's a long, yellow, wooden object.
Student 3: Is it a pencil?
Student 1: No, it's a long, flat, yellow wooden object.
Student 4: Is it a board?
Student 1: No, it's a twelve-inch long, flat, yellow wooden object.
Student 5: Is it a ruler?
Student 1: Right!

6 Another situation for practicing adjective ordering could be developed in a variation of a memory game. Each student must repeat what has been said by the previous student and add the indicated word in the appropriate slot:

Teacher: (possibly holding up a picture or an object or drawing a basic shape on the blackboard) What's this?
Student 1: That's a vase.
Teacher: Blue.
Student 2: That's a blue vase.
Teacher: Large.
Student 3: That's a large blue vase.
Teacher: Ceramic.
Student 4: That's a large blue ceramic vase.

Teachers might point out to their students during any discussion of adjective ordering that context may change the word order in cases involving an adjective of shape or in cases using both a material adjective and a proper adjective.

EXERCISES

Test your understanding of what has been presented

1. Provide example English sentences that illustrate the following terms. Underline the pertinent word(s) in your examples.

attributive adjective
predicate adjective
postnominal adjective
reference adjective

proper adjective
complex adjective phrase
restrictive adjective
nonrestrictive adjective

2. Provide tree diagrams and derivations for the following sentences:

a. The person involved in this scandal should be fired.

b. Paul Newman is a leading man.

c. I am looking for a gray sweater.

3. Why are the following sentences ungrammatical?

a. *The asleep children can have lunch later.

b. *This problem is chief.

c. *The fond of chocolates woman is Mrs. Holmes.

Test your ability to apply what you know

4. If your students produce any of the following errors, how will you make them aware of the errors, and what corrective exercises will you provide?

a. *She's a Mexican beautiful woman.

b. *I have black long hair and black eyes.

c. *He gave her a big nice bunch of roses.

5. Devise a drill for teaching the semantic principle governing the ordering of material adjectives and proper adjectives. Be sure to include sufficient context to allow for a sensible choice, e.g.:

a marble Italian statue vs. an Italian marble statue

6. Xerox a page from the descriptive part of a novel or short story. Underline all the noun phrases with two or more attributive adjectives. Do all the attributive adjective sequences follow the ordering rules given in this chapter? Have we presented a semantic category for each attributive adjective you found? Discuss any omissions and deviations.

BIBLIOGRAPHY

References

Bailey, K. M. (1975). "The Ordering of Attributive Adjectives in English: A Preliminary Study." Unpublished English 215 paper, UCLA.

Bolinger, D. (1967). "Adjectives in English: Attribution and Predication," *Lingua* 18, 1–34.

Halliday, M., and R. Hasan (1976). *Cohesion in English.* London: Longman.

Praninskas, J. (1975). *Rapid Review of English Grammar* (2d ed.). Englewood Cliffs, N.J.: Prentice-Hall.

Sledd, J. (1959). *A Short Introduction to English Grammar.* Chicago: Scott, Foresman and Co.

Svatko, K. (1979). "Descriptive Adjective Ordering in English and Arabic." Unpublished M.A. thesis in TESL, UCLA.

Suggestions for further reading

For discussions of the attributive vs. predicative functions of adjectives in English, see:

Bolinger, D. (1967). "Adjectives in English: Attribution and Predication," *Lingua* 18, 1–34.
Bolinger, D. (1972). *Degree Words*. The Hague: Mouton.

For discussions of the ordering of attributive adjectives, see:

Quirk, R., and S. Greenbaum (1973). *A Concise Grammar of Contemporary English*. New York: Harcourt
Brace Jovanovich, pp. 121–139.
Sledd, J. (1959). *A Short Introduction to English Grammar*. Chicago: Scott, Foresman and Co., pp. 115–117.

For suggested exercises on and explanations of attributive adjective ordering in English,
see:

Frank, M. (1972). *Modern English: Exercises for Non-native Speakers. Part I: Parts of Speech*. Englewood Cliffs,
N.J.: Prentice-Hall, pp. 118–122.
McIntosh, L., T. Ramos, and R. Goulet (1970). *Advancing in English*. New York and Manila: American Book
Co., pp. 142–146.
Praninskas, J. (1975). *Rapid Review of English Grammar* (2d ed.). Englewood Cliffs, N.J.: Prentice-Hall, pp.
262–263, 268–269.

For an exercise that introduces beginning-level ESL/EFL students to attributive and
predicative use of adjectives, see:

Brinton, D., and R. Neuman (1982). *Getting Along: English Grammar and Writing* (Book 1). Englewood Cliffs,
N.J.: Prentice-Hall, pp. 41–42.

29

Focus and Emphasis

GRAMMATICAL DESCRIPTION

Introduction

We have decided to treat grammatical focus and emphatic devices or expressions in the same chapter because they seem to be similar and to overlap in a number of respects; e.g., one of the meanings expressed by grammatical focus is emphasis, which is in turn the essence of any emphatic expression. The following sentences demonstrate that focus constructions, which are one type of grammatical focus, and emphatic words or expressions have certain semantic properties in common:

FOCUS CONSTRUCTION: It was *John* who cooked the dinner. ⎫
EMPHATIC WORD: John *himself* cooked the dinner. ⎬ (and no one else)

Types of grammatical focus

There are two different types of grammatical focus that we will discuss in this chapter. The first type of focus involves the reordering of constituents such that the constituent appearing in sentence-initial position—or sometimes sentence-final position—receives special emphasis in the discourse. The other type of grammatical focus entails the use of special constructions. For example, the focus construction used in the above example in the introduction puts greater emphasis on *John* than does the related nonemphatic or neutral sentence, which is not an explicit focus construction:

John cooked the dinner.[1]

---

1. Even a syntactically nonemphatic sentence such as this one may contain an emphatic constituent if the speaker assigns special stress or prominence to one of the constituents:

> JOHN cooked the dinner. (not someone else)
> John COOKED the dinner. (as opposed to doing something else)
> John cooked the DINner. (not something else)

This is a separate but related issue that we will be bringing up again later in the chapter.

Word-order focus

Word-order focus can be defined as the movement of a constituent into a position in the sentence where we would not ordinarily expect to find it (i.e., it would *not* be generated by the phrase structure rules in that position[2]). Sometimes other syntactic elements present in the sentence must be moved around to produce a grammatical sentence. The reasons for employing word-order focus that have most frequently been identified and described are: discourse constraints (e.g., the given-new information principle), the expression of counter-expectancy, contrast, or emphasis.

We will now discuss several different types of word-order focus.

Adverbial fronting

There are many types of adverbial fronting that occur in English; for example, we have already discussed this rule in Chapter 25 with regard to the fronting of *if* clauses in conditional sentences. Here we shall, first of all, discuss simple adverbial fronting, i.e., those types of adverbial fronting that do not involve subject/auxiliary inversion or subject/verb inversion.

Adverbials of time
　　He jogs in the morning.──➤In the morning he jogs.

Adverbials of manner
　　Garth proceeded to carve the roast $\left\{ \begin{array}{l} \text{with great skill} \\ \text{skillfully} \end{array} \right\}$. ──➤

　　$\left. \begin{array}{l} \text{Skillfully} \\ \text{With great skill} \end{array} \right\}$, Garth proceeded to carve the roast.

Adverbials of reason
　　I made some unfortunate remarks at the meeting because I was annoyed. ──➤Because I was annoyed, I made some unfortunate remarks at the meeting.

Adverbials of purpose/intent
　　We went to Boston in order to see Mr. Brown.──➤In order to see Mr. Brown, we went to Boston.

Adverbials of condition
　　We can have a picnic this weekend if it doesn't rain. ──➤ If it doesn't rain, we can have a picnic this weekend.

Adverbials of frequency (the postverbal ones like *everyday, once a week,* not the preverbal ones like *always, never*)
　　Jim drives 50 miles every day. ──➤Every day Jim drives 50 miles.

In each case, moving the adverbial to sentence-initial position gives it greater focus, and preliminary usage studies indicate that a sentence-initial position of the adverbial expresses either emphasis or contrast in the discourse.

There are, however, a few other instances of adverbial fronting which require that subject/auxiliary inversion also take place if a grammatical sentence is to be produced:

Adverbials of frequency (negative preverbal)
　　I have never seen such a mess!──➤Never have I seen such a mess!

Adverbials of extent or degree
　　His manner was so absurd that everyone laughed at him. ──➤ So absurd was his manner that everyone laughed at him.

---

2. Emonds (1976) has referred to a set of such operations as root transformations and has described their behavior in detail.

In such cases, the discourse function of the adverbial fronting appears to be that of reinforcing a sense of exclamation.

Two other instances of adverbial fronting occur that seem somewhere between the two above categories; i.e., they are grammatical whether or not the subject and main verb (not the auxiliary) are also inverted. Thus for the two following instances of adverbial fronting, two types of adverbial fronting are possible:

Adverbials of direction

John ran into the house. $\left\{\begin{array}{l}\text{(a)} \quad \text{Into the house John ran.} \\ \text{(b)} \quad \text{Into the house ran John.}\end{array}\right.$

Adverbials of position (for certain stative verbs)

An elm tree stands in the garden. $\left\{\begin{array}{l}\text{a)} \quad \text{In the garden an elm tree} \left\{\begin{array}{l}\text{stands} \\ \text{*is}^3\end{array}\right\}. \\ \text{(b)} \quad \text{In the garden} \left\{\begin{array}{l}\text{stands} \\ \text{is}\end{array}\right\} \text{an elm tree.}\end{array}\right.$

In both of these cases the (a) version seems to signal discourse emphasis or contrast of the initial adverbial element, whereas the (b) version of the two sentences[4] appears to give focus to the delayed subject of the sentence. There is an aura of suspense that has been introduced in the (b) versions and a feeling that perhaps the subject NP has been selected by the speaker or writer to go counter to the expectations of the listener or reader. A pilot study by Gary (1974) supports in part the counter-to-expectation interpretation with regard to the delayed subjects of the above (b) sentences.

For example, using texts such as the following ones, Gary claims that the counter-to-expectation function of the (b) version of the text-final sentence carries a special presupposition of counterexpectancy and that this contrasts with the neutral, noninverted (a) version, which has no special presuppositions.[5]

Keith Sebastian had given me detailed instructions on how to find his house; he was to meet me there with the money. I drove up the driveway and got out of my car. Just as the car door closed, I heard the main door to the house open.

a. $\left.\begin{array}{l}\text{Keith Sebastian} \\ \text{Dan Carlyle} \\ \text{The Sheriff}\end{array}\right\}$ stepped out of the house.

b. Out of the house stepped $\left\{\begin{array}{l}\text{\#Keith Sebastian} \\ \text{Dan Carlyle} \\ \text{the Sheriff}\end{array}\right\}.$

(Note: # = ungrammatical given the discourse context)

In the (b) version *Keith Sebastian* is not acceptable as the postposed subject because there is no counterexpectancy; i.e., the reader would normally expect *Keith Sebastian* to be the subject just as he is in the (a) version, but given the use of the (b) construction, which signals counterexpectancy, the reader expects someone else to be the postposed subject.

---

3. Note that in such cases the copula BE is not grammatical in final position because BE is not a full lexical verb and therefore subject/verb inversion or subject/auxiliary inversion must occur if adverbial fronting occurs.

4. The (b) versions of these sentences are, of course, examples of two of the many "root transformations" that Emonds (1976) discusses.

5. Gary convincingly demonstrates that concepts such as definiteness versus indefiniteness or new information versus old information do not explain this example—and all the other examples he cites—as effectively as does the notion of counterexpectancy.

Other examples of fronted constituents

Gary's study also points out that several constituents other than adverbials regularly get fronted in a similar manner:

Present participle fronting[6]
Our missing uncle was sitting at the kitchen table.⟶ Sitting at the kitchen table was our missing uncle.

Past participle fronting
Several barrels of wine were hidden in the cellar. ⟶Hidden in the cellar were several barrels of wine.

Comparative fronting
What he said was more important than what he did. ⟶More important than what he did was what he said.

Negated constituent fronting
(They will not leave the country under any circumstances.) ?They will leave the country under no circumstances.⟶Under no circumstances will they leave the country.

While Gary provides evidence that present and past participle fronting[7] also may signal counterexpectancy (just as the fronting of adverbials of direction and position did), he does not feel that fronting of comparative or negated constituents carries the same semantic information. We feel that comparative fronting puts focus or emphasis on the postposed constituent and that the fronting of negated constituents focuses on the negation expressed and gives it special emphasis; i.e., in both cases the effect of fronting is emphasis.

Focus constructions

As we mentioned earlier, a focus construction is a structure that frames (i.e., gives explicit grammatical focus to) the constituent appearing in the focus slot. The two most common focus constructions in English are cleft sentences and pseudo-cleft sentences.

Cleft sentences

A cleft sentence is a special marked construction that puts some constituent, typically an NP, into focus. The construction implies contrast. Note that contrastive stress alone without the cleft transformation could signal the same meaning as the cleft.

Neutral: John wants a car.
Cleft: It's a car that John wants (not a house).
Neutral: The manager mows the lawn.

Cleft: It's the manager $\left\{ \begin{array}{l} \text{who} \\ \text{that} \end{array} \right\}$ mows the lawn (not a gardener).

It is hard to formulate a transformational rule to account for cleft sentences since many different constituents such as subject NPs, object NPs, and even prepositional phrases can be put into the focus slot, e.g.:

It's the teacher who corrects the papers (not the aide).
It's power that the president wants (not money).
It's in the kitchen that I study (not in the den).

---

6. We use the term "fronting" while Gary (1974) and Emonds (1976) use the term "preposing" to describe these constructions.

7. The participle fronting examples used here also illustrate two more of Emonds' (1976) "root transformations."

In each case the negative presupposition can be moved forward, e.g.: "It's the teacher, not the aide, who corrects the papers." Note that a negative version of this construction yields sentences like the following (i.e., if the focus is negative, the affirmative presupposition is contrastive and is often expressed in a phrase marked by *but*):

It's not the gardener who mows the lawn (but the manager).

Again, the contrastive presupposition may be moved forward:

It's not the gardener, but the manager, who mows the lawn.

The following rule is, therefore, an approximation:

$$S \longrightarrow \text{It} + \text{AUX} + \text{BE} + (\text{NOT}) + \triangle + \begin{Bmatrix} \text{who} \\ \text{that} \end{Bmatrix} + S$$

focused   (minus focused
constituent   constituent)

In particular, our use of the "AUX" symbol in the cleft formula is a gross approximation. It has been suggested to us that only the "tense" constituent of the auxiliary be used in the *It BE* segment of the rule rather than the entire auxiliary. The logic behind this suggestion is that in Standard English the *It* + BE segment of a cleft can never take a periphrastic modal, a HAVE... EN (perfective), or a BE... ING (progressive):

It's in the kitchen that I am able to study.
*It is able to study that I am in the kitchen.

It's these books that Peter has written.
*It's have written these books that Peter has done.

It's the teacher who was correcting the papers.
*It's correcting the papers that the teacher was (doing).

It is, however, possible for the *It* + BE segment of a cleft to contain a modal auxiliary (logical use):

It might be Marty who stole the money.
It must be the butler who killed Mr. Smith.

Also, it has been claimed that the tense of the *It* + BE segment is merely a copy of the tense used in the main sentence. This claim is not always true because clefts such as the following occur, where different tenses are used in the *It* + BE segment and the main sentence:

So, it*'s* the butler who *killed* Mr. Smith (not his wife).
    pres   past

Thus, until all these complex factors have been resolved, we will continue to use the symbol "AUX" in this rule—with the added condition that the AUX may contain only a tense or a modal. Furthermore, if a modal and NOT are both present in the *It* + BE segment, the NOT will follow the modal and precede the BE:

It can't be Peter who wrote this book. (someone else did)

Note that *who* may come between the focused constituent and the S only if the former refers to a person. Otherwise, *that* is used to refer to objects and prepositional phrases as well as persons.

Except for the presence of contrastive stress in cleft sentences, they sometimes resemble relative clauses. For example, note the ambiguity of the following sentence, cited by Schachter

(1973) in his discussion of cleft sentences as focus constructions that sometimes resemble relative clauses:

It's the woman $\left\{ \begin{array}{l} \text{that} \\ \text{who} \end{array} \right\}$ cleans the house.

(answer to "Who's that?" = relative clause)
(answer to "Who cleans the house—the man or the woman?" = cleft)

Pseudo-cleft sentences

Another focus construction is the so-called pseudo-cleft. Consider the following examples:

> What he is, is a complete fool.
> Where we found the key was in the flowerpot.

Now compare these pseudo-clefts with their neutral counterparts, i.e.,

> He is a complete fool.   We found the key in the flowerpot.

The pseudo-cleft sentences give special emphasis to the constituent(s) following some form of the copula BE:

> *What he is* $\boxed{\text{IS}}$ a complete fool.
> presupposes—"he is something"   (element receiving focus, emphasis)

If there are two forms of BE present, the second form is the pivotal one in the structure.

This focus construction should not be confused with the less emphatic free relative clause construction (discussed in Chapter 27), which puts focus on the wh-word:

> What he said
> (= the thing that he said) $\Big\}$ doesn't concern me.
> Where he was born
> (= the place where he was born)

Note that in pseudo-clefts, the wh-word can only occur sentence-initially; however, in free relatives the wh-word occurs wherever a relative clause can occur, and thus free relatives occur as readily in final position as they do in initial position:

> I'm not interested in $\left\{ \begin{array}{l} \text{what he said} \\ \text{where he was born} \end{array} \right\}$.

Before closing this section of the chapter, we should point out that cleft and pseudo-cleft sentences both are more frequent in spoken than in written English, which may explain in part why they have often been ignored in ESL/EFL texts.

Emphasis

There are problems from the outset in trying to define emphasis in English because it overlaps with other topics such as exclamation and intensification. In addition, it must be recognized that emphasis is essentially a semantic notion and may be signaled in many ways including use of special stress and intonation patterns, choice of words, choice of grammatical patterns, etc. In this section we shall be discussing the content words and structural words that can function as emphatic forms in English. We make no claim to providing an exhaustive treatment of the topic.

Traditional and structural grammarians have long distinguished content words (i.e., nouns, lexical verbs, adjectives, and certain types of adverbs) from structural words (articles, prepositions, pronouns, auxiliary verbs, etc.). Content words are described as belonging to large, open lexical classes (i.e., new words are constantly added to these classes) and they typically carry most of the lexical meaning in a sentence. Structural words, on the other hand, belong to relatively small, closed form classes (i.e., new words are not easily added) and carry much less lexical meaning, but serve instead as the cement that holds together the content words in a sentence. The emphatic grammatical markers we discuss below are structural words.

Grammatical markers of emphasis

Emphatic DO

As Quirk and Greenbaum (1973) note, an entire sentence receives greater emphasis if the auxiliary is stressed. DO is introduced when no auxiliary verb is present to carry emphatic stress:

That *will* be nice![8]   It *does* taste nice!

DO occurs as a marker of emphasis in affirmative declarative sentences (like the above one) which have no BE copula or auxiliary verb. It also occurs in the two following constructions:

Emphatic affirmative imperatives (even those with the copula)

Do come in!   *Do* be civil this time.

Affirmative wh-questions that ask about the subject

What *did* happen?   Who *does* earn that kind of money?

Emphatic DO is used in several different discourse and syntactic contexts to express at least the following five meanings (categories are modified from those given in Frank (1972)):

1. Affirmative emphasis of a whole sentence (DO often occurs with an emphatic adverb like *certainly* or *really*):

I certainly *do* { hope they win the game / like that color on you }.

2. Emphasis of a verb used in conjunction with a preverbal adverb (e.g., *never, rarely, seldom, often, always*):

> (It *is* rather suspicious) The horse he bet on always *did* win.
> (To make a long story short) The guest we were waiting for never *did* arrive.

3. Emphasis of a positive result regarding something that had been unknown or in doubt:

> I'm relieved to know that he *does* like beef stroganoff.
> (because that's what we're having for dinner)

4. Affirmative contradiction of a negative statement:

> My teacher claims that I didn't turn in my term paper, but I *did* turn it in!

5. Strong concession bordering on contrast:

> Even though I dislike most nonclassical music, I *do* find myself fascinated by Dixieland jazz.

---

8. The accent marks used in these sentences and some of those which follow refer to primary sentence stress (´) and secondary sentence stress (ˋ).

Emphatic reflexives

In the above section we saw that DO was used to emphasize whole sentences or verb phrases. To emphasize nouns, on the other hand, reflexive pronouns are often used. Consider the following sentences:

1.   The owner himself built the house.
2.   The owner built the house himself.
3.   The victims themselves can't explain how the terrible accident occurred.
4.   I saw the president himself.

Examples 1, 3, and 4 demonstrate that an emphatic reflexive normally directly follows the noun that it modifies. Given the transformational framework, one might be tempted to say that 2 is a derived form of 1, i.e., that 1 and 2 share the same underlying structure.

There are, however, several problems with such an analysis. Sørland (1980), in a study of the frequency and usage of reflexive pronouns in English, demonstrates that sentences like 2 are almost twice as frequent as sentences like 1. Thus, 2 would seem to be a more likely candidate for being the underlying form than 1. (Sørland used a diversified corpus of more than 145,000 words.)

Furthermore, Sørland found that in most cases pattern 1 could not be replaced by pattern 2 without a change of meaning. In other words, 1 means that the owner emphatically took deliberate action; i.e., he built the house. On the other hand, 2 means that the owner performed the action of building the house to the exclusion of anyone else; i.e., he did it alone. Therefore, it would be semantically untenable to derive 2 from 1 or vice versa. Also, Sørland found that while pattern 1 can take both animate and inanimate subjects, pattern 2 strongly prefers animate subjects and inanimate subjects seem ungrammatical or at best awkward:

1.   a.   The owner himself built the house.
     b.   The house itself has little historical value.
2.   a.   The owner built the house himself.
     b.   ?The house has little historical value itself.

Thus we conclude that 1 and 2 are two separate patterns and that only 1, 3, and 4 represent genuine emphatic uses of the reflexives. Pattern 2 represents an adverbial function of the reflexives—a function perhaps closely related to the following:

> The owner built the house by himself.

Thus, only reflexives that directly follow the noun they are modifying can truly be considered emphatic uses of the reflexive pronouns.

Emphatic *own*

Possessive adjectives (and sometimes possessive nouns) that modify a head noun can be made emphatic by the addition of *own,* which in turn can be intensified by the addition of *very*:

> (After having accepted Chomsky's analysis of comparative sentences for several years), I later developed my own theory about such sentences.
> Is that Johnny's very own Ferrari? (I didn't know he had the money to buy such a car.)

In nonemphatic sentences the possessive (or genitive) case can be used to express an agent (e.g., Holbein's portrait of Henry VIII), a possessor (e.g., my house), an event (e.g., John's death), etc.; however, the use of emphatic *own* with a possessive adjective or noun usually signals the meaning of ownership or special interest rather than some other possible meaning of the genitive. Thus, if we take the above example for the possessive expressing an agent and add *own* (e.g., I prefer Holbein's own portrait of Henry VIII), English speakers who are naive about the historical names and facts involved will tend to understand that Holbein is the owner of—rather than the artist who produced—the portrait. The use of *own* to emphasize an agent is appropriate only when the person referred to in the possessive form is both the agent and the possessor of the head noun. There is a special construction in English for expressing this double relationship:

head noun + of + possessive + own + gerund
possession   form   agency

Example: That's a problem of his own making.
You will have an escort of your own choosing.

In volume 7 of his multivolume grammar of the English language, Jespersen (1961) notes that emphatic reflexives and emphatic *own* often function as paraphrases of each other:

He cooks his own meals.   He cooks his meals himself.

Jespersen goes so far as to suggest that *own* is the genitive form of *-self*.

Colloquial use of emphatic *here* and *there* with the demonstrative

The English language also has many colloquial and dialectal markers of emphasis such as the use of *here* and *there* to emphasize the demonstratives *this/these* and *that/those*, respectively:

1. This { a. here cow / b. cow here } has always given a lot of milk.

2. What do you think of that { a. there house? / b. house there?

All of the above sequences occur only in somewhat nonstandard colloquial usage; however, the b sentences represent a more acceptable variant than the a ones do.

Lexical markers of emphasis

Emphatic adjectives and adverbs

Quirk and Greenbaum (1973) point out that emphatic adjectives occur only in attributive position:

a pure fabrication   *that fabrication is pure
an outright lie   *this lie is outright

They distinguish these emphatic adjectives from amplifying adjectives, which may occur in both attributive and predicate position:

a complete victory   (the victory was complete)
their extreme condemnation etc.
his great folly

Quirk and Greenbaum (1973) also observe that certain emphatic adjectives and adverbs like *definite(ly)*, *certain(ly)*, *positive(ly)*, and *absolute(ly)* can be used freely in many environments, but that other emphatic adjectives and adverbs such as *frank(ly), honest(ly),* and *literal(ly)* are restricted and can be used only with a fairly small class of nouns and adjectives:

a frank discussion   literally true

Emphatic logical connectors

Halliday and Hasan (1976) suggest that some logical connectors are more emphatic than others. Thus, for expressing addition, *and* is a nonemphatic connector whereas *furthermore, moreover, in addition,* and some others are emphatic and thus not appropriate unless the discourse context merits special emphasis:

John went to the store, and he bought some bread.

?/*John went to the store; $\left\{\begin{array}{l}\text{furthermore}\\\text{moreover}\end{array}\right\}$, he bought some bread

John talked us into going out for dinner; furthermore, he insisted on paying the bill.

Obviously, this is an area in need of further research. Halliday and Hasan's observations and our examples are just a beginning.

TEACHING SUGGESTIONS

1   For teaching cleft sentences the teacher should give several examples showing how cleft sentences embody certain presuppositions and differ from their normal affirmative and negative statement counterparts, e.g.:

Sam studies physics.	John doesn't drive a Ford.
(Cue: He doesn't study chemistry.)	(Cue: He drives a Buick.)
It's physics that Sam studies, not chemistry.	It's not a Ford that John drives, but a Buick.

or   or

It's physics, not chemistry, that Sam studies.	It's not a Ford, but a Buick, that John drives.

In groups of three, students should be given one 3 × 5 card, each with a false affirmative or negative statement as a cue. The statements will be about their fellow students. They should write a mini-dialog that makes natural use of a cleft construction.

On cue card: Kim comes from Hong Kong. (It's a false statement.)[9]

Sample student-generated dialog:

A: Is anyone in this class from Hong Kong?
B: Yes, Kim comes from Hong Kong.
C: No, he doesn't. $\left\{\begin{array}{l}\text{It's Lee who comes from Hong Kong, not Kim.}\\\text{It's Korea that Kim comes from, not Hong Kong.}\end{array}\right.$

These dialogs can then be presented to the class as a whole for evaluation and correction.

---

9. This type of exercise is a version of Rutherford's (1974) false presupposition drill.

2   You might want to try the following sequence of activities for teaching emphatic reflexives.
a. Show the class sentences with emphatic reflexives:

Subject emphasis
1.   The owner himself built the house.   2.   Did you yourself have a good time?

Object emphasis (all objects)
3.   I met Joe Namath himself.
4.   We gave the President himself a copy of the proclamation.
5.   Susan did her term paper on Einstein himself.

b. Read these sentences and have the class repeat. Ask them to paraphrase the sentences and to describe the function of the reflexive pronoun.
c. Point out the position of the reflexive and ask them to explain what is emphasized in each sentence.
d. Show the class several picture cards with sentences and have students supply correct reflexive pronouns to emphasize the subjects, e.g.:

Cue: Mary made the dress.
S1:   Mary herself made the dress.

e. Then a student selects a card and someone else in the class asks a yes-no question based on the card. The student who selected the card should give a meaningful response, e.g.:

S1:   Did you yourself make that dress?
S2:   Yes, I did./No, I didn't. My mother did.

3   Emphatic DO might be introduced using the following context.
a. The teacher can give the class practice in using emphatic DO to contradict negative statements by giving some false negative statements as a cue and then putting an edited version of the dialog on the board, e.g.:

T: Ali, you didn't turn in your homework.
Ali: That's not true. I *did* turn in my homework. I gave it to you a few minutes ago.

b. The class should discuss the function of DO in such a dialog.
c. The students are divided into small groups and asked to write a dialog that incorporates use of emphatic DO to contradict a false negative statement.
d. The dialogs are performed in front of the class and evaluated and corrected.

4   Fronting adverbials of time. Have students talk about their daily schedules, giving focus to the time at which activities occur, e.g.:

This is what I do every day. At 7 a.m. I get up. By 8 o'clock I'm on my way to school. From 9 to 12 I have classes, etc.

Point out that it is appropriate to put focus on time adverbials and to produce them in initial position in such a discourse context.

5   Fronting directional adverbs. Read a short paragraph or anecdote to your class, e.g.:

Everyone but Harry had arrived on time for the meeting. We waited 15 minutes. There still was no sign of Harry. We had just decided to proceed without him, when into the conference room dashed Harry!

Ask them about the word order of the last sentence. Why does the adverbial come first? See if they can explain the fact that the others had decided Harry wouldn't come and when he did, they were surprised because their expectation that Harry would not come turned out to be false.

Divide the class into small groups giving each group a sentence involving some class member(s) with the directional adverb fronted (e.g., Out of the house came Maria and Rosa). Have each group write a paragraph that uses the inverted cue sentence as the last sentence. Groups will then switch paragraphs so that each group can judge the appropriateness and accuracy of another group's story.

6   Melinda Erickson suggests that pseudo-cleft sentences can be learned and practiced in the context of a small-town planning committee meeting. Each member of the committee is trying to present a different proposal.

Sample dialog

Chairman:	What our town needs is careful development. May I hear your proposals?
Head librarian:	What we see as important is a new library branch to supplement the main library.
High school principal:	What we need is better athletic facilities for the high school.
Businessman:	What we should have is a Chamber of Commerce like all the other towns in the area.
	Etc.

The class can be split into groups to practice and role-play the sample dialog. The follow-up activity could be for each group to make one or more suggestions/proposals concerning their ESL/EFL class, e.g.:

What we need is fewer exams.
What we would like is less homework.

What we would prefer is more conversation.
Etc.

EXERCISES

Test your understanding of what has been presented

1. Provide example sentences that illustrate the following terms. Underline the pertinent word(s) in your examples.

cleft sentence	emphatic DO
pseudo-cleft sentence	emphatic reflexive
adverbial fronting	emphatic possessive

2. Why are the following sentences ungrammatical (or at best awkward)?

a. *On his car a bumper sticker is: Have you hugged your kid today?
b. ?John mopped up the kitchen and wiped off the dirty walls yesterday himself.
c. ?On Tuesdays I have a class at 10:00; moreover, I have a class at 2:00.

3. Explain the ambiguity in the following sentences:

a. It's the graduate student who corrects the papers in our class.
b. Our Chairman criticized the Dean himself.

4. Do the following sentences illustrate pseudo-clefts or free relatives? Give reasons to support your choice.

a. I forgot what he said.

b. What he told is a big lie.

c. What he said is of little concern to us.

d. What he said is that you are a jerk.

Test your ability to apply what you know

5. If your students produce the following sentences, what errors have they made? How will you make them aware of the errors, and what exercises will you prepare to correct the errors?

a. *Never I have tasted such a delicious sandwich!

b. *Who you mean is that Oscar did it.

c. *After three months arrived all of my family.

6. Develop a mini-lesson for teaching appropriate use of sentence-initial negative constituents (e.g., Under no circumstances will we tolerate that!) to an advanced ESL/EFL class.

7. Describe the discourse or semantic differences, if any, in the following pairs of sentences:

a. (1) What he said is that he wasn't coming.
   (2) He said that he wasn't coming.
b. (1) The misbehaving child was standing in the corner.
   (2) Standing in the corner was the misbehaving child.
c. (1) Come back again.
   (2) Do come back again.
d. (1) Why doesn't Jim use his book?
   (2) Why doesn't Jim use his own book?

BIBLIOGRAPHY

References

Emonds, J. (1976). *A Transformational Approach to English Syntax: Root, Structure Preserving, and Local Transformations.* New York: Academic Press.

Frank, M. (1972). *Modern English: A Practical Reference Guide.* Englewood Cliffs, N.J.: Prentice-Hall.

Gary, N. (1974). "A Discourse Analysis of Certain Root Transformations in English." Unpublished paper. Department of Linguistics, UCLA. Reproduced and distributed by the Indiana University Linguistics Club.

Halliday, M., and R. Hasan (1976). *Cohesion in English.* London: Longman.

Jespersen, O. (1961). *A Modern English Grammar on Historical Principles,* Part VII (completed and edited by Niels Haislund). London: Allen and Unwin.

Quirk, R., and S. Greenbaum (1973). *A Concise Grammar of Contemporary English.* New York: Harcourt Brace Jovanovich.

Rutherford, W. (1974). "Pragmatic Syntax in the Classroom," *TESOL Quarterly* 8:2, 177–184.

Schachter, P. (1973). "Focus and Relativization," *Language* 49:1.

Sørland, K. (1980). "The Frequency and Usage of Reflexive Pronouns in English." Unpublished English 215 paper, UCLA.

Suggestions for further reading

For a discussion of cleft sentences, relative clauses, and their similarities and differences, see:

Schachter, P. (1973). "Focus and Relativization," *Language* 49:1.

The relationship between cleft and pseudo-cleft sentences is explored in the following articles:

Gundell, J. K. (1977). "Where Do Cleft Sentences Come from?" *Language* 53:3.
Prince, E. F. (1978). "A Comparison of Wh-clefts and *It* Clefts in Discourse," *Language* 54:5.

The discourse significance of several adverbial fronting and participle fronting rules is explored in the following source:

Gary, N. (1974). "A Discourse Analysis of Certain Root Transformations in English." Unpublished paper. Department of Linguistics, UCLA. Reproduced and distributed by the Indiana University Linguistics Club.

For a discussion of (1) emphatic DO, (2) emphatic adjectives and/or adverbs, and (3) emphatic use of reflexives, see the following sources:

Frank, M. (1972). *Modern English: A Practical Reference Guide.* Englewood Cliffs, N.J.: Prentice-Hall. (1) p. 95, (2) pp. 143–144, (3) p. 33.
Quirk, R., and S. Greenbaum (1973). *A Concise Grammar of Contemporary English.* New York: Harcourt Brace Jovanovich. (1) p. 427, (2) pp. 122, 132, 409–410, (3) pp. 425–426.

For a discussion of emphatic logical connectors, see:

Halliday, M., and R. Hasan (1976). *Cohesion in English.* London: Longman, pp. 246, 249.

For some useful information about focus and emphasis in general, see:

Leech, G., and J. Svartvik (1975). *A Communicative Grammar of English.* London: Longman, pp. 175–185.

Teaching materials for the topics covered in this chapter are rare. For some exercises for teaching emphatic reflexives, see:

Frank, M. (1972). *Modern English: Exercises for Non-native Speakers. Part I: Parts of Speech.* Englewood Cliffs, N.J.: Prentice-Hall, p. 25.

For a suggestion on teaching emphatic *own*, see:

Rutherford, W. (1977). *Modern English* (2d ed., vol. 2). New York: Harcourt Brace Jovanovich, p. 34.

For a suggestion on teaching pseudo-clefts—even though they refer to them as clefts, see:

Danielson, D., and R. Hayden (1973). *Using English.* Englewood Cliffs, N.J.: Prentice-Hall, p. 61.

For writing exercises that elicit pseudo-cleft sentences, see:

Wohl, M. (1978). *Preparation for Writing: Grammar.* Rowley, Mass.: Newbury House, pp. 111–115.

30

An Overview of English Complementation

GRAMMATICAL DESCRIPTION

Introduction

A complement is a construction consisting of a complementizer and an embedded sentence. It usually replaces a noun phrase in the base structure, e.g.:

NP surprised me.   Inez's coming early surprised me.

The additional phrase structure rules that we need to express this type of relationship are as follows:

$$NP \longrightarrow Comp \qquad Comp \longrightarrow C + S$$

These rules tell us that an NP can be rewritten as a complement, which in turn is expanded as a complementizer followed by a sentence. In branching-tree form this structure is represented as follows:

The three complementizers most frequently discussed in the transformational literature (e.g., Stockwell et al., 1973) are:

> *that* (i.e., introduces *that* clauses)
> *for* (i.e., introduces *for/to* infinitives)
> *possessive* (i.e., introduces gerunds taking possessive subjects)

These are not the only complementizers in English. We shall be discussing others such as *if* and *whether* in subsequent chapters.

Verb complements

Complements in subject position

The following sentences contain the verb *surprise* with the three types of complements introduced above functioning as the subjects, i.e.:

$$\text{NP} \left\{ \begin{array}{l} \text{surprised} \\ \text{would surprise} \end{array} \right\} \text{me.}$$

1. *That Inez came early* surprised me.
2. *For Inez to come early* would surprise me.
3. *Inez's coming early* surprised me.

You have probably already noticed that the first two sentences sound much better, i.e., seem more natural, if the subject complement is moved to the end of the sentence (we refer to this process as "extraposition"); however, once a complex subject is extraposed, we must then add a surface subject—i.e., *it*—because every English sentence that is neither imperative nor elliptical must have a surface subject. We refer to this process as "*it* insertion."

1a. *It* surprised me *that Inez came early.*
2a. *It* would surprise me *for Inez to come early.*

Note also that the third sentence above sounds better with the complement remaining in subject position, and it does not undergo extraposition as readily as the first two sentences:

3a. ?*It* surprised me *Inez's coming early.*[1]

Two transformational rules (i.e., "extraposition" and "*it* insertion") help us describe the movement of the complements and the appearance of the *it* subject in the two transformed sentences. The underlying structure for both sentence 1 and sentence 1a would be:

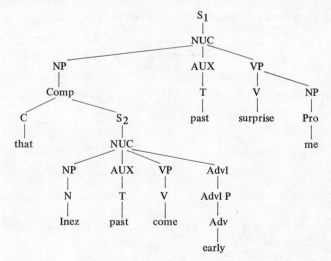

Following the principle of always deriving the lower (or embedded) sentence first, the derivation of sentence 1a would be as follows:

---

1. Whenever such a structure occurs, there is a pause between the main clause and the "complement," which suggests that the so-called complement is an elaboration or afterthought rather than an integral part of the sentence.

Output of base: (that (Inez past come early)) past surprise me[2]
Extraposition: past surprise me (that (Inez past come early))
It insertion: It past surprise me (that (Inez past come early))
Affix attachment ($2\times$): It surprise $+$ past me (that (Inez come $+$ past early))
Morphological rules: It surprised me that Inez came early.

Whenever *that* functions as the complementizer, the embedded sentence looks like a free unembedded sentence. This happens because the *that* protects the structure of the complement. Thus even though pronouns and pro-verbs may be substituted for longer noun phrases and verb phrases, no major constituent is completely deleted and the verb is inflected for tense just as it would be in an unembedded sentence.[3]

Contrast the above derivation with the one provided for sentences 2 and 2a below. Their underlying structure is:

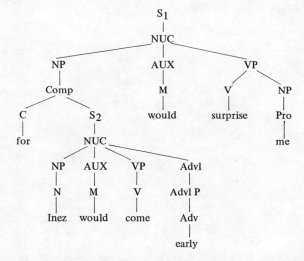

[The reconstruction of the auxiliary in the embedded sentence is a problem when one attempts to diagram the underlying structure of sentences with embedded infinitive or gerund complements. In some cases it suffices if you make the AUX in the embedded sentence identical to the AUX in the higher sentence. This is what we have done in the above tree as well as in the following one. However, we also diagram sentences later in this chapter (e.g., "John is very anxious for us to please you") where the AUX in the main clause is "present tense," yet the AUX in the embedded complement would seem to be a modal like "should." We suggest "should" in such a case because if we paraphrase the "*for* . . . infinitive" in this example with a *that* clause (i.e., "John is very anxious that we should please you"), the "should" emerges. One does not always have a grammatical *that* clause paraphrase to compare with an infinitive or gerund complement; however, even an ungrammatical *that* clause can often be a clue. In other words, a sentence such as "I want you to go" does not have a *that* clause equivalent, but we can ask ourselves what a *that* clause paraphrase would look like if there were one: *I want that you should go. Thus some very subtle semantic judgments are involved in reconstructing the underlying AUX for those complements that have no overt auxiliary element.]

---

2. Note that if at this point you were to apply the affix attachment rule twice and the morphological rules, sentence 1 rather than sentence 1a would be generated.

3. The only exceptions to this would be sentences such as "I insist that he go there," where the embedded verb is not inflected. These so-called "subjunctive" complements are discussed in Chapter 34.

Two special rules needed to derive these sentences are "object attraction"[4] and "infinitivalization." With the application of the first rule, *Inez*, the subject of S2, becomes the object of the complementizer *for*, which still retains a certain amount of prepositional force despite its complementizer function. Then the verb phrase of S2—having lost a subject to agree with—changes into an infinitive with simultaneous loss of the tense or any modal auxiliary that may be present—i.e., in this case the loss of "would."

The derivation of 2a is as follows:

Output of base: (for (Inez would come early)) would surprise me
Object attraction: (for Inez (would come early)) would surprise me
Infinitivalization: (for Inez (to come early)) would surprise me[5]
Extraposition: would surprise me (for Inez (to come early))
It insertion: It would surprise me (for Inez (to come early))
Output: It would surprise me for Inez to come early.

Consider now the underlying structure for sentence 3:

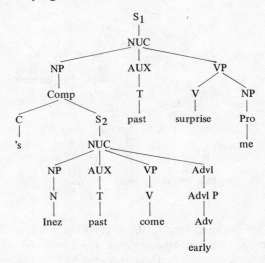

The two additional transformational rules needed to derive this sentence are "possessive attraction" (i.e., the *'s* complementizer attaches itself to the subject of S2, which then functions like a possessive determiner) and "gerundivization." Gerundivization occurs because the embedded verb phrase follows a possessive determiner or a noun phrase functioning like a possessive determiner; the embedded verb phrase becomes a gerund, since it must now function as a noun. Loss of the tense or modal auxiliary element occurs simultaneously with gerundivization just as it did with infinitivalization.

The derivation of 3 is as follows:

Output of base: ('s (Inez past come early)) past surprise me
Possessive attraction: (Inez's (past come early)) past surprise me
Gerundivization: (Inez's (coming early)) past surprise me

---

4. This rule is called "object attraction" because if the underlying subject of the embedded sentence is a pronoun, the pronoun must change from subject form to object form. Compare: *That she came early surprised me. For her to come early would surprise me.*

5. Note that if we ended the derivation at this point, sentence 2 would be generated.

Affix attachment (1✕): (Inez's coming early) surprise + past me
Morphological rules: Inez's coming early surprised me.

Note that the verb phrases of embedded sentences that have lost their subjects become either gerunds or infinitives and lose their tense or modal auxiliary. The auxiliary loss seems to occur because such embedded sentences do not need to have any inflection that expresses tense or mood.[6] Note also that in the context under discussion gerund complements semantically resemble *that* complements more closely than they do *for* complements.

Factual	*Possible, hypothetical*
That Inez came early surprised me.	For Inez to come early would surprise
Inez's coming early surprised me.	me.

This resemblance stems from the fact that the complementizer *that* is more neutral or flexible than either the *possessive* complementizer, which is typically factual, or the *for* complementizer, which is typically hypothetical. Thus the complementizer *that* can be used to paraphrase either of the other two:

Factual	*Hypothetical*
John's saying that was odd. = It was odd	For John to say that would surprise us. =
that John said that.	That John should say that would surprise us.

However, the *for* complementizer and the possessive complementizer usually cannot paraphrase each other. If we try to do this, one of the two sentences will seem awkward if not ungrammatical:

For John to say that would be odd.	John's saying that was odd.
?John's saying that would be odd.	?For John to say that was odd.

Complements in object position

Verbs do, of course, also take complements in object position:

$$\text{We} \begin{Bmatrix} \text{thought} \\ \text{planned} \\ \text{anticipated} \end{Bmatrix} \text{NP}$$

Example sentences involving derivations that would be similar to the ones provided above for subject complements are:

We thought *that he would be there.*	We anticipated *his being there.*
We planned *for him to be there.*	

There are even a few verbs that allow complements to occur in both subject and object position, although such sentences occur only rarely:

NP proves NP

Joe's solving the problem proves *that he is a genius.*
subject   object

---

6. Embedded infinitives and gerunds may, of course, use perfective aspect to express past time; i.e., not all auxiliary elements are incompatible with these complements—e.g., *I suspect him to have said that; We can remember his having said that.* We will discuss perfective forms in infinitives and gerunds again in the following chapter.

The tree diagram and derivation of this sentence is provided below to demonstrate that no new rules are required to account for such a sentence.

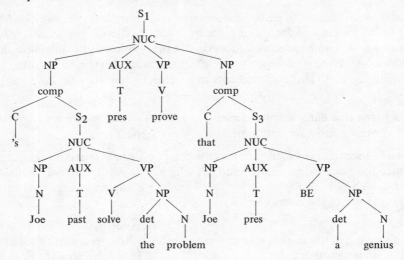

Output of base: ('s (Joe past solve the problem)) pres prove (that (Joe pres BE a genius))

Possessive attraction: (Joe's (past solve the problem)) pres prove (that (Joe pres BE a genius))

Gerundivization: (Joe's (solving the problem)) pres prove (that (Joe pres BE a genius))

Pro-noun phrase substitution: (Joe's (solving the problem)) pres prove (that (he pres BE a genius))

Affix attachment (2×): (Joe's (solving the problem)) prove + pres (that (he BE + pres a genius))

Subject-verb agreement and morphological rules: Joe's solving the problem proves that he is a genius.

Adjective complements

Complements in subject position

In English, adjectives may also take complements. These complements usually occur in subject position, e.g.:[7]

$$NP \left\{ \begin{array}{l} \text{is} \\ \text{would be} \\ \text{was} \end{array} \right\} \text{odd.}$$

Example sentences for this pattern are:

1. That Bob went to San Francisco is odd.
2. For Bob to go to San Francisco would be odd.
3. Bob's going to San Francisco was odd.

---

7. Note that predicate nouns, like adjective phrases, may also take complements in subject position, e.g., "Jack's telling that story was a real embarrassment." We do not treat this structure separately in this chapter but wish nonetheless to point it out. It can be derived using the rules we have provided.

Again, the *that* and *for* + *to* complements sound much better if they are extraposed:

    1a. It is odd that Bob went to San Francisco.
    2a. It would be odd for Bob to go to San Francisco.

and the "possessive . . . ing" complement is normally not extraposed:

    3a. ?It was odd Bob's going to San Francisco.

When structures such as 3a do occur, there is usually a pause between the adjective and the "complement," which indicates the so-called complement is an elaboration, or something added as an afterthought rather than an integral part of the structure.

    The derivation of the above three sentences would parallel those presented above for subject complements of verbs. Therefore, only sentence 2a will be diagrammed and derived to illustrate the similarity:

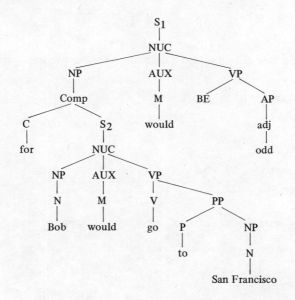

Output of base: (for (Bob would go to S.F.)) would be odd
Object attraction: (for Bob (would go to S.F.)) would be odd
Infinitivalization: (for Bob (to go to S.F.)) would be odd
Extraposition: would be odd (for Bob (to go to S.F.))
It insertion: It would be odd (for Bob (to go to S.F.))

Complements in predicate position

    In addition to the adjectives that take complements in subject position, there are also some transitive adjectives that take complements in predicate position, e.g.:

        Mr. Wilson is eager for Peter to run in the race.

We need to expand our phrase structure rule for adjective phrases to account for such possibilities:

$$\frac{AP}{(pred)} \longrightarrow (intens)\ adj\ (\ \left\{\begin{array}{c} PP \\ Comp \end{array}\right\}\ )$$

In branching-tree form, this possibility of having a complement in predicate position would be realized as follows:

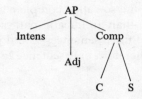

We shall now provide a tree diagram and a derivation for a sentence which exemplifies this structure:

John is very anxious for us to please you.

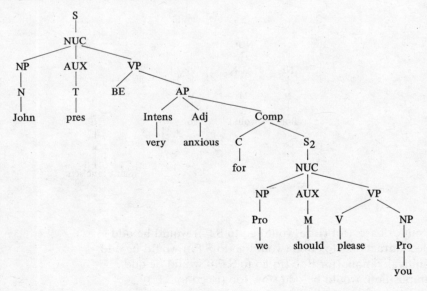

Output of base: John pres BE very anxious (for (we should please you))
Object attraction: John pres BE very anxious (for us (should please you))
Infinitivalization: John pres BE very anxious (for us (to please you))
Affix attachment (1✕): John BE + pres very anxious (for us (to please you))
Subject-verb agreement and morphological rules: John is very anxious for us to please you.

Equi-NP deletion

Complement sentences that are generated to the right of transitive verbs or transitive adjectives in the base structure, i.e., in object or predicate position, may, in some cases, have the same subject as the higher sentence; in other cases, they may have a different subject from the higher sentence. This causes no problem or change in derivation if the complementizer is *that:*

Same subject: *He* thought that *he* would be there.
Different subjects: *We* thought that *he* would be there.

However, in those cases where the embedded sentence surfaces as an infinitive or gerund, discernible structural differences emerge depending on whether the subject of the higher sentence is identical to or different from the subject of the complement. If the two subjects are identical, the second one is deleted:

Different subjects: We planned for him to be there.
Same subject: We planned to be there.

Different subjects: We anticipated his being there.
Same subject: We anticipated being there.

Different subjects: John is very anxious for us to please you.
Same subject: John is very anxious to please you.

Note that in the second example in each set, the embedded infinitive or gerund has no overt subject. The underlying subject is, however, the same as the subject of the higher (i.e., unembedded) sentence. The underlying structures for these three sentences are as follows:

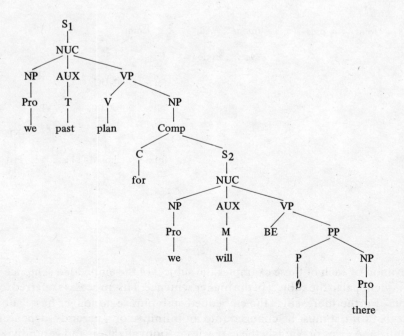

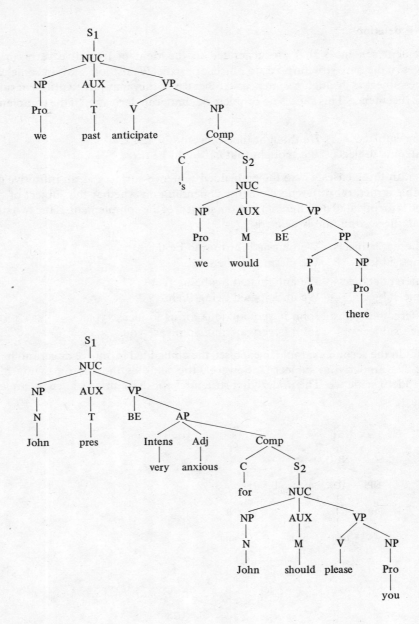

In the derivation of each of these examples the subject of the embedded sentence is deleted because it is identical to the subject of the higher sentence. This process is referred to as "equi-NP deletion." Furthermore, since the embedded verb phrase no longer has a subject noun phrase to agree with, it must be changed into an infinitive or a gerund—depending on the complementizer. As was previously the case with infinitivalization and gerundivization, the tense or modal elements of the embedded auxiliary are again lost. Finally, the complementizer (i.e., *for* or *'s*) is also deleted because there is no longer an overt subject noun phrase that the complementizer can attract. We refer to this process as "complementizer deletion."

The derivation of the first of the three sentences diagrammed above would be as follows:

Output of base: we past plan (for (we will BE there))
Equi-NP deletion: we past plan (for (will BE there))
Infinitivalization: we past plan (for (to BE there))
Complementizer deletion: we past plan (to BE there)
Affix attachment (1×): we plan + past (to BE there)
Morphological rules: We planned to be there.

Take a few minutes now and try to derive the other two sentences diagrammed above based on the example derivation.

Object complements without a *for* or *'s* complementizer

There are, of course, also a few object complements following certain transitive verbs that do not take a *for* complementizer preceding the subject of the infinitive or an *'s* complementizer preceding the subject of the gerund. For example:

$$We \left\{ \begin{array}{l} want \\ expect \end{array} \right\} John\ to\ be\ elected.$$

$$We \left\{ \begin{array}{l} appreciated \\ defended \end{array} \right\} Jay('s)\ being\ discreet.$$

In the first set, deletion of the *for* complementizer is obligatory even though the equi-NP condition has not been met. While Standard English does not have an overt *for* complementizer in such sentences, the growth and spread of the *for* complementizer in English can be documented both historically (cf. Visser, 1966) and with data from regional dialects in which sentences such as the following are fully acceptable:

I want for John to go.   Joe expects for you to be there.

Thus it does not seem unreasonable to derive all infinitives from *for* complements if one realizes that the *for* must be deleted under certain conditions, i.e., when the higher verb requires complementizer deletion.

The deletion of the *'s* complementizer, on the other hand, appears to be stylistic. There is, in fact, an ongoing debate in linguistic circles as to whether the subject of a gerund must occur in the possessive case or whether it may on occasion occur uninflected. Purists maintain that the subject of a gerund should take a possessive inflection in all cases; however, preliminary usage studies indicate that personal pronouns functioning as subjects of gerunds tend to take the possessive case, whereas other subject nouns are likely to appear in uninflected rather than possessive form—especially if they are long, e.g.:

We appreciate his being discreet.
We appreciate Professor Wesley Abernathy being discreet.

Informal usage, as well as several other factors, can also account for the absence of the possessive inflection. We shall have more to say about this issue in Chapter 34.

Noun complements

In addition to the verbs and adjectives that can take complements in English, there is also a small class of nouns that can take complements, e.g.:

> The fact that Bob went to San Francisco surprises me.

The phrase structure rule needed to derive such a construction is as follows:

$$NP \longrightarrow NP \ (Comp)$$

In branching-tree form this rule would be represented as:

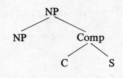

Examples of noun complements taking *that* and *for* complementizers follow:

The $\left\{ \begin{array}{l} \text{fact} \\ \text{suggestion} \\ \text{possibility} \\ \vdots \end{array} \right\}$ that Jolene is pregnant $\left\{ \begin{array}{l} \text{surprised} \\ \text{would surprise} \end{array} \right\}$ Jack.

I can't understand the $\left\{ \begin{array}{l} \text{need} \\ \text{request} \\ \vdots \end{array} \right\}$ for John to go there.

The underlying structure and derivation for "The fact that Jolene is pregnant surprised Jack," follow:

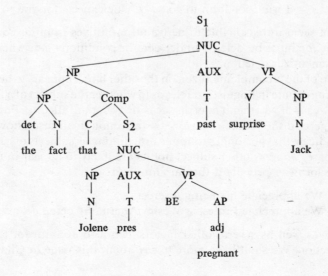

Output of base: the fact (that (Jolene pres BE pregnant)) past surprise Jack
Affix attachment (2×): the fact (that (Jolene BE + pres pregnant)) surprise + past Jack
Subject-verb agreement and morphological rules: The fact that Jolene is pregnant surprised
  Jack.

Noun complements vs. restrictive relative clauses

There are important differences between restrictive relative clauses beginning with the relative pronoun *that* and noun complements taking a *that* complementizer. Yet these constructions are often confused. This is understandable since the structures look superficially similar; however, the ESL/EFL teacher must be aware of the differences and should be careful not to confuse the two structures. To this end we exemplify and summarize some of the important semantic and syntactic differences below:

Restrictive relative clause
Example: The suggestion that John made is ridiculous.

1. Any common noun can serve as the head noun of a restrictive relative clause.

2. The relative pronoun *that* is part of the structure of the embedded relative clause (i.e., it functions as the subject or as an object).
3. The embedded clause limits or restricts the meaning of the head noun.
4. The embedded clause contains a repetition of the head noun.
5. The entire sentence cannot be paraphrased as another type of complement, e.g.:
   *To suggest that John made is ridiculous.

Noun complement
Example: The suggestion that John is a fool is ridiculous.

1. Only a limited set of nouns occur as the head noun in a noun complement: *fact, suggestion, idea, possibility, statement, proposal,* etc.
2. The complementizer *that* is *not* an integral part of the embedded sentence—it precedes the embedded sentence and sets it off.
3. The embedded sentence expands upon or makes more explicit what the head noun is referring to.
4. The embedded clause need not repeat the head noun (and it usually doesn't).
5. The entire sentence can often be paraphrased as another type of complement, e.g.:
   Suggesting that John is a fool is ridiculous.

Conclusion

This concludes our admittedly simplified introduction to the English complementation system. Elaborations and extensions of the material we have presented here will appear in the following four chapters of the book.

TEACHING SUGGESTIONS

1   Have your students combine two short sentences into one longer complement structure, e.g.:

> Max is a professor. It's a fact.——→ It's a fact that Max is a professor.
> We will go to Europe. It's possible.——→ It's possible that we will go to Europe.

2 Give your intermediate and advanced students a feeling for the "factual" meaning of *possessive-gerund* complements versus the more hypothetical nature of *for-infinitive* complements by having them match matrix sentences with the appropriate complement, e.g.:

1. John's arriving late . . .   (a) would be unusual.
2. For John to arrive late . . .   (b) was unusual.

Answer   (1) goes with (b)
          (2) goes with (a)

3 *That* complements following adjectives such as *possible* and *likely* are often used for making predictions. Give your students a set of adjectives such as the following: *likely, possible, unlikely, certain,* and *probable.* Have them rank the adjectives according to strength of prediction (i.e., *certain* = strongest prediction, *unlikely* = weakest prediction) and ask each one to make a prediction to share with the class. For example:

It's unlikely that we will make contact with people from another planet in the near future.
It's possible that new energy sources will be discovered in the next twenty years.

It might also be wise to point out to your students that modal auxiliaries can often be used to express these predictions without the use of a complement:

New energy sources may be discovered in the next twenty years.

4 Students can practice the contrast between complements that undergo equi-NP deletion and those that do not by drawing up lists such as the following and then producing the related complements:

Things that I want

myself to do	*my friend to do*
take Jenny to the movies	lend me $10
drive to San Diego	let me use his car
:	:

I want to take Jenny to the movies.
I want my friend to lend me $10.
I want to drive to San Diego.
I want my friend to let me use his car.

5 The meaning equivalence between noun complements beginning with *The fact that* and *possessive-gerund* subject complements can be brought out if students are asked to paraphrase such noun complements using the possessive-gerund construction:

T: The fact that Joe passed the exam is not surprising.
S: Joe's passing the exam is not surprising.

EXERCISES

Test your understanding of what has been presented

1. Provide original example sentences that illustrate the following terms. Underline the pertinent word(s) in your examples.

complement   possessive attraction
complementizer   extraposition
object attraction   equi-NP deletion
infinitivalization   complementizer deletion.
noun complement

2. Give tree diagrams and complete derivations for the following sentences:

a. John's lecturing on that topic was a surprise.
b. It is common for our secretary to have lunch before noon.
c. Mary thought that we would wait here.
d. We were eager to see the movie.
e. Sam wants you to write the letter.
f. We couldn't understand the need for everyone to be at the meeting.

3. Do the following sentences contain relative clauses or noun complements? Why?

a. The idea that John proposed is appealing.
b. We rejected the idea that John might be the chairman.
c. The committee considered the possibility that we had raised.
d. The possibility that it would rain put a damper on our plans.

Test your ability to apply what you know

4. If your students produce the following sentences, what errors or infelicities have they committed? How will you make them aware of the errors, and what exercises will you prepare to correct the errors?

a. *Is convenient that you live so close to school.
b. ?I want for you to stay here.
c. *I want that you should go there with us.

5. Five ways of distinguishing between relative clauses with *that* and noun complements with *that* were presented in this chapter. Can you think of another such "test" or any other distinction?

6. If an advanced ESL/EFL student asks you the following question, how will you answer it?

What difference in meaning is there, if any, between these sentences?
His missing class on Monday is typical.
For him to miss class on Monday would be typical.

BIBLIOGRAPHY

References

Stockwell, R. P., P. Schachter, and B. Partee (1973). *The Major Syntactic Structures of English.* New York: Holt, Rinehart and Winston.
Visser, F. Th. (1966). *An Historical Syntax of the English Language* (vol. 2). Leiden, Netherlands: E. J. Brill.

Suggestions for further reading

For a few of the most comprehensive linguistic descriptions of the English complement system, see:

Bresnan, J. (1970). "On Complementizers: Toward a Syntactic Theory of Complement Types," *Foundations of Language* 6:3, 297–321.
Lees, R. B. (1960). *The Grammar of English Nominalizations, IJAL* Publication 12, Indiana University, Bloomington, Ind., and The Hague: Mouton.
Rosenbaum, P. (1967). *The Grammar of English Predicate Complement Constructions.* Cambridge, Mass.: MIT Press.
Stockwell, R. P., P. Schachter, and B. Partee (1973). *The Major Syntactic Structures of English.* New York: Holt, Rinehart and Winston. (See Nominalization and Complementation chapter.)

For textbooks with suggestions on teaching complement structures in English, see:

Danielson, D., and R. Hayden (1973). *Using English: Your Second Language.* Englewood Cliffs, N.J.: Prentice-Hall. (See especially lesson 18—verb forms as complements.)
Rutherford, W. (1975). *Modern English* (2d ed., vol. I). New York: Harcourt Brace Jovanovich. (See especially units 13 and 14.)

31

Infinitives and Gerunds

GRAMMATICAL DESCRIPTION

Introduction

The use of infinitives and gerunds in English poses a problem for the majority of ESL/EFL students, since most languages (e.g., Spanish, French, Hebrew) have *that* clauses and infinitives but no gerunds. This is one of the reasons why students sometimes produce errors such as these:

*I avoided that I should talk to him.   *She enjoys to go to the movies.

Another explanation for such errors other than native language interference is that ESL students may learn earliest those complements that occur most frequently in native speaker speech. Butoyi (1977) examined over 8,000 words of spoken English from the *White House Transcripts* and established the following frequency order for complement types in English:

	Complement types (n = 185 complements)		Example
1.	*That* clause (with or without *that*)	(46%)	I know (that) he left.
2.	Infin. equi NP	(34%)	I want to leave.
3.	Infin. + object	(11%)	I want him to leave.
4.	Infin. with *to* deletion	(04%)	I let him leave.
5.	Gerund equi NP	(03%)	I enjoy swimming.
6.	Poss. + gerund	(02%)	I resent his leaving.

Thus we can see that *that* clauses and infinitives are much more frequent in spoken English than gerunds, which means that ESL learners would tend to hear few gerunds but many *that* clauses and infinitives when they interact with native speakers.

Anderson (1976) and Butoyi (1978) have studied the performance of several different groups of nonnative speakers with regard to their ability to use the various types of English complements. (They based their orders on the results of tests composed of multiple-choice items and translation items.)

Anderson (for native speakers of Spanish and Persian)
1. *That* clause   (Best performance)
2. Infin. equi NP
3. Infin. + object
4. Gerund equi NP
5. Infin. with *to* deletion
6. Poss. + gerund   (Worst performance)

Butoyi (for native speakers of . . .)

	Spanish and Japanese		Persian
1.	Infin. equi NP	1.	*That* clause
2.	Infin. + object	2.	Infin. equi NP
3.	Infin. with *to* deletion	3.	Infin. + object
4.	*That* clause	4.	gerund equi NP
5.	Gerund equi NP	5.	Infin. with *to* deletion
6.	Poss. + gerund	6.	Poss. + gerund

Even though there is some variation, these data indicate that all groups generally find *that* clauses and infinitives easier than gerunds. The data also agree in large part with the frequency order for complements in spoken English that we cited above. Thus it appears that both mother tongue interference and frequency of occurrence in English contribute to the problems that ESL/EFL learners have with English complements in general and infinitives and gerunds in particular.

The usual way of teaching infinitives and gerunds in the ESL/EFL classroom has been for the teacher or textbook to instruct students to memorize lists like the following:

Verbs that take infinitives	*Verbs that take gerunds*	*Verbs that take both forms*
want	enjoy	like
expect	avoid	begin
hope	risk	start
decide	admit	continue
refuse	finish	try
plan	deny	regret
ask (= request)	defend	remember
choose	:	forget
:	:	:

We shall be discussing alternatives to this approach in this chapter.

The Bolinger principle

Today ESL/EFL teachers have a better way to approach this teaching problem than encouraging rote memorization. Bolinger (1968) points out that there seems to be an underlying semantic principle: the infinitive very often expresses something "hypothetical, future, unfulfilled," whereas the gerund typically expresses something "real, vivid, fulfilled."

This principle explains why verbs like *want* and *hope* take only the infinitive (i.e., they represent future, unfulfilled events):

I want to go there.   John hopes to learn Russian.
*I want going there.   *John hopes learning Russian.

This also explains why verbs like *enjoy* and *avoid* take only the gerund (i.e., you can only *enjoy* things you've already directly experienced; to *avoid* something is a successful fulfillment of sorts):

Max enjoys swimming.	Judy avoided talking to Harry.
*Max enjoys to swim.	*Judy avoided to talk to Harry.

With those verbs taking both infinitives and gerunds, Bolinger's principle also helps to explain the frequent difference in meaning that exists between the infinitive complement and the gerund complement.

> I remember locking the door.
> (locking occurred before remembering)
> I remembered to lock the door.
> (remembering occurred before locking)

> I tried closing the window. } i.e., I closed the window.
> (but I still felt cold)
> I tried to close the window. } i.e., I didn't close the window.
> (but I couldn't; it was stuck)

So (1973) found the Bolinger principle appealing; he thus developed a questionnaire in an attempt to empirically verify the principle for those verbs that could take either the infinitive or the gerund. He used the judgments of 100 native speakers of English in his study. The items So developed were contextualized, and each item contained a blank where the native speakers had to choose either the infinitive or the gerund to complete the item. (Paired items such as the following were not adjacent in the questionnaire.) For example:

> I tried _____ the window, but that didn't help. I still felt cold.
> a. to close   b. closing

> I tried _____ the window, but I couldn't. It was stuck.
> a. to close   b. closing

For these two items, the native speakers preferred the gerund *closing* in the first context and the infinitive *to close* in the second, thus confirming Bolinger's hypothesis that the infinitive expresses unfulfilled action and the gerund fulfilled action. Using such a questionnaire, So was able to empirically validate Bolinger's principle for the following six verbs:

remember	regret[2]
forget	prefer
try[1]	sense[1]

Perhaps further research, for example, in discourse analysis, will help us to expand this list.

---

1. The verbs *try* and *sense* are less flexible than the other four in that *try* must take an equisubject (e.g., I tried to go. *I tried (for) John to go), while *sense* cannot take an equisubject, e.g.:

$$\text{I sensed} \left\{ \begin{array}{l} \text{him to be} \\ \text{his being} \end{array} \right\} \text{angry.} \qquad \text{*I sensed} \left\{ \begin{array}{l} \text{to be} \\ \text{being} \end{array} \right\} \text{angry.}$$

2. *Regret* is more limited regarding use with a following infinitive than are the other five verbs. It does take an infinitive with certain verbs as in: I regret *to inform* you, I regret *to announce* . . . , and a few others. However, it does not occur freely with other verbs: *I regret to go, *I regret to think, etc. This lexical limitation on the use of *regret* with infinitives should be noted.

Even though Bolinger and So did not treat the verb *stop,* special mention should be made of this verb. Many grammars list it as taking only gerunds:

John stopped smoking cigars.   We have stopped arguing with Gertrude.

These same grammars may point out that *stop* can also be followed by what appears to be an infinitive:

We stopped to have a cup of coffee.   Jack stopped to see Kate.

It is claimed that this *to* (paraphrasable with "in order to") is an infinitive of purpose,[3] not the same infinitive that occurs after verbs like *want, try,* and *like.*

Regardless of whether we observe this distinction or not, it is clear that Bolinger's principle can still help us explain the difference in meaning between pairs of sentences such as these:

I stopped to smoke. (I stopped doing something and then I smoked a cigarette.)
I stopped smoking. (I used to smoke but then I stopped.)

Nonnative speakers frequently say the first sentence when what they intend to say would be best expressed by the second one.

Bolinger also claims that some other verbs that take both infinitives and gerunds exhibit a rather subtle potential difference in meaning—one that So's study has demonstrated most native speakers do not readily perceive:

I like camping in the mountains. (It's so peaceful *here.*) } more immediate, more vivid
I like to camp in the mountains. (It's so peaceful *there.*) } more remote, more objective

Helen started doing her homework at 8 p.m. (and she finished at 11 p.m.) } suggests completion more strongly

Helen started to do her homework at 8 p.m. (but the phone rang and interrupted her work) } suggests completion less strongly

A few other aspectual verbs that seem to behave like *start* are *begin* and *continue,* whereas some other emotive verbs that behave the same as *like* are *hate* and *love.* The verbs in these two groups, for which any difference in meaning is very subtle, constitute a small number of items. For the other verbs discussed, however, it seems as if Bolinger's semantic guidelines help us understand why some verbs take only infinitives, why others take only gerunds, and why there is a significant difference in meaning with at least six of the verbs that take both infinitives and gerunds.

---

3. The infinitive of purpose is a reduced adverbial clause added to a structurally complete clause. It provides additional information that answers the question "Why?" or "For what purpose?" For example:

Jane has gone on a diet in order that she might lose weight. (full adv. *that* clause)
Jane has gone on a diet in order to lose weight. (infinitivalized adv. clause)
Jane has gone on a diet to lose weight. (infinitivalized adv. clause with adv. subordinator deleted)

In the preceding sentence the infinitive of purpose *to* can be paraphrased as "in order to" and "Jane has gone on a diet" is a complete sentence by itself.
A normal infinitive completes a clause by functioning as the subject or object, e.g.:

To err is human.   I want *to go there.*
(subject)   (object)

In such cases the infinitive is not signaling additional information since the sentences would be ungrammatical without the infinitive. Also, the infinitive marker "to" cannot be paraphrased as "in order to" in such cases.

Factive verbs and adjectives

Paul and Carol Kiparsky (1970) have also contributed to our understanding of infinitives and gerunds. They use semantic criteria to divide English predicates that take complements into two categories—factive and nonfactive—as follows (both subject complements and object complements are considered):

	Take subject complements	Take object complements
Factive predicates	be significant be odd make sense amuse ⋮	regret appreciate avoid make clear ⋮
Nonfactive predicates	be sure be likely turn out seem ⋮	suppose claim believe assert ⋮

Semantically, factive and nonfactive predicates can be distinguished by examining the presupposition associated with the complement. If this presupposition remains constant regardless of whether the predicate of the main clause affirms, negates, or questions the complement clause, then the predicate of the main clause is factive, e.g.:

John regrets
John doesn't regret } that he told you that lie { . / ? }
Does John regret

(i.e., The fact that John told you a lie is presupposed to be the case regardless of whether the main clause is affirmative, negative, or interrogative.)

On the other hand, the complements of nonfactive predicates undergo predictable changes in presupposition depending on whether the predicate of the main clause affirms, negates, or questions the complement, e.g.:

John claims
John doesn't claim } that he told you a lie { . / ? }
Does John claim

(i.e., "That John told you a lie" cannot be presupposed to be the case in any of the above sentences.)

The Kiparskys' semantic distinction ties in nicely with the use of infinitives and gerunds: in most cases, the complements of factive predicates must be reduced to gerunds or to possessive inflections plus gerunds (e.g., John 's do ing that annoyed me), while the complements of nonfactive predicates must be reduced to infinitives, e.g.:

Factive:

John regrets { that he told you that lie / telling you that lie } .

I appreciate $\left\{ \begin{array}{l} \text{(it) that you did that for me} \\ \text{your doing that for me} \end{array} \right\}$.

Nonfactive:

John claims $\left\{ \begin{array}{l} \text{that he told you a lie} \\ \text{to have told you a lie} \end{array} \right\}$.

$\left\{ \begin{array}{l} \text{It seems that we are arguing about nothing.} \\ \text{We seem to be arguing about nothing.} \end{array} \right.$

Thus the Kiparskys have isolated a semantic-syntactic parameter similar to, yet different from, Bolinger's. In many cases it can be used to explain the use of infinitives or gerunds with verbs that would seem to contradict Bolinger's principle. For example, consider the use of the gerund in the following sentence:

I would appreciate your doing this favor for me.

The gerund here cannot really be justified in terms of Bolinger's principle as being "real, vivid, and fulfilled" rather than "hypothetical, future, and unfulfilled." However, the gerund can be justified if we recognize that the verb *appreciate* is factive and remains factive even when used with the modal *would,* which signals an unfulfilled request here.

Implicative verbs

Another special class of verbs taking infinitives that has some members that would also seem to contradict Bolinger's principle are the implicative verbs. Positive and negative implicative verbs were first described by Kartunnen (1971); he noticed that there were certain English verbs taking infinitives that implied either the truth of their complements (positive implicative verbs) or the falsity of their complements (negative implicative verbs), e.g.:

Positive implicatives
John managed to get the loan.
  implies: John got the loan.
We got to see the movie.
  implies: We saw the movie.

Negative implicatives
Bert failed to sign the petition.
  implies: Bert didn't sign the petition.
I forgot to lock the gate.
  implies: I didn't lock the gate.

Note that if you negate a positive implicative verb you get a negative implication. (*I didn't manage to go* implies *I didn't go.*) Also, if you negate a negative implicative verb you get a positive implication. (*We didn't fail to finish the job* implies *We finished the job.*)

Some other positive implicatives are: *remember, hasten, bother, venture, condescend, happen,* etc. Some other negative implicatives are: *neglect* and *decline*; we should also mention that *avoid* and *refrain (from),* which take gerunds rather than infinitives, are negative implicative verbs too.

The majority of verbs taking infinitive complements are *not* implicative, e.g.:

I wanted to go to Europe.
  does *not* imply: I went to Europe.

Ben tried to lose weight.
  does *not* imply: Ben lost weight.

Two implicative verbs for which Bolinger would claim his principle works are *remember* and *forget.* Many implicative verbs, however, cannot be explained in light of the Bolinger principle. In fact, *manage* and *get* clearly contradict it:

I managed to go.   I got to see Mike.

(The infinitive is not future, hypothetical, or unfulfilled in these sentences.)

However, since the Bolinger principle does apply to so many cases, it would be wise to retain it for explanatory purposes and to consider those implicative verbs that contradict it as a special type of exception.

The use of perfect verb forms with infinitives and gerunds

Hofmann (1966) has pointed out that the use of perfect verb forms in infinitives and gerunds is somewhat parallel to their use with modal auxiliaries; i.e., they signal past time and replace the past tense morpheme which by definition cannot occur in nonfinite clauses. With gerunds this use of perfect forms is optional, with the result that the perfect and nonperfect form have virtually the same meaning:

$$I \text{ remember } \left\{ \begin{array}{l} \text{his doing that} \\ \text{his having done that} \end{array} \right\}.$$

With infinitives, however, the use of a perfect form signals a clear difference in meaning, and it is in these cases that their use must be explicitly taught to nonnative speakers:

$$\text{Mary believes Horace } \left\{ \begin{array}{l} \text{to be a thief} \\ \text{to have been a thief} \end{array} \right\}.$$

In such a case the plain infinitive expresses what Mary believes about Horace now, whereas the perfect infinitive expresses what Mary believes was true about Horace—but only at some time in the past.

We need a comprehensive usage study to show us the frequency and use of perfect forms occurring with infinitives and gerunds.

Sources for infinitives and gerunds

In the last chapter sources for infinitives and gerunds were mentioned. We shall review them briefly and add a new source for gerunds here.

The source for infinitives is the "*for-to*" complement structure, e.g.:

For John to do that was necessary.   It was necessary for John to do that.

Also, as we pointed out in the preceding chapter, infinitives occur in "infinitive-plus-object" constructions where no explicit *for* complementizer occurs, e.g.:

We want John to go.   John asked Roger to go.

Infinitives also occur in "*for-to*" complements in which the *for* complementizer and the identical subject have been deleted through application of the equi-NP deletion rule (i.e., the subject of the complement is identical to the subject of the higher sentence):

Michael is eager to visit the Orient.

One final manifestation of infinitives from this source are those cases where the *for* complementizer and the following subject are deleted because the subject of the infinitive is indefinite and nonspecific, e.g.:

For (someone/anyone) to err is human. ——▸To err is human.

Now we shall discuss the two principal sources for gerunds. First of all, the "possessive-gerund" construction is the major source, e.g.:

Sarah's leaving town surprised me.

As is the case with infinitives, another manifestation of gerunds from this source are those cases where the possessive complementizer and the subject noun phrase are deleted because the subject of the complement is identical to the subject of the higher sentence, e.g.:

I denied *having said that.*

And like the "*for-to*" construction the "possessive gerund" construction may take an indefinite, nonspecific subject that almost invariably is deleted, e.g.:

(Someone's/Anyone's) going to the movies is enjoyable.⟶ Going to the movies is enjoyable.

The other source of gerunds (not including the lexicalization of gerunds as nouns and compound nouns—e.g., *ice skating, rocking chair*) comes in sentences that are embedded following a preposition. That is, prepositions turn embedded complements into gerunds when they introduce such clauses, e.g.:

You can depend on it. (it = John does his work.)
You can depend on John doing his work.
I *plan to go* to Europe. / I *plan* ⟨ *on* ⟩ *going* to Europe.

Conclusion

There is much more we need to know about infinitives and gerunds in English. As attractive as Bolinger's hypothesis is, the work of the Kiparskys and the work of Kartunnen demonstrate that there are important exceptions. It would be nice to have a broader principle capable of reconciling and synthesizing the findings of all three studies. Also, any further study of infinitive and gerund complements should also include *that* complements so that a more comprehensive description will eventually emerge.

Finally, almost all of the descriptions of infinitives and gerunds (including ours) may have a serious flaw in that it can be argued that several of the verbs described in this chapter and elsewhere as taking gerunds (e.g., *begin, start, stop, continue*) actually take *-ing* participles instead. We have decided to follow the usual description of the verbs as taking gerunds to achieve a better match with those published sources that the ESL/EFL teacher is most likely to turn to.

TEACHING SUGGESTIONS

1 For verbs that take both infinitives and gerunds—but with a difference in meaning—Bill Gaskill has suggested that explicit time sequences be used to teach the difference between infinitives and gerunds with matrix verbs such as *remember, forget,* and *stop.* The teacher introduces these verbs along with a number of situations that can appropriately serve as complements:

call my parents   tell you the news
lock the door   smoke cigars

Then the notion of time sequence is introduced and an example is provided to show that if the action in the matrix clause *precedes* the action in the complement, the infinitive is used.

This happened earlier   *This happened later*
I remembered   I called my parents
(matrix)   (complement)
⟶ I remembered to call my parents.

The teacher must also show the reverse; i.e., if the action in the matrix clause *follows* the action in the complement, the gerund is used.

This happened earlier	*This happened later*
I called my parents	I remembered
(complement)	(matrix)

⟶ I remembered calling my parents.

Students can then manipulate the time sequence in other matrix clauses and complements and elicit the desired infinitive or gerund form from their peers. The use of movable sentence strips in a pocket chart or of plastic strips (for the overhead projector) is particularly effective.

2 Ilana Graff uses a technique that is very effective with younger students who have reached the intermediate or advanced level. She presents a set of "optimistic" verbs and a set of "pessimistic" verbs:

Optimistic verbs	*Pessimistic verbs*
hope	dislike
want	avoid
like	hate
love	deny

Then with a few example sentences from the students, she elicits the generalization that "optimistic" verbs take infinitives and "pessimistic" verbs take gerunds. Then the students proceed to talk about the things they *hope to do, want to do, like to do,* etc. After that they also talk about the things they *dislike doing, avoid doing, hate doing,* etc. Graff recognizes that two of the optimistic verbs also take gerunds and one of the pessimistic verbs also takes infinitives; however, she feels that since only grammatical sentences are generated by the students if they do this exercise and since the generalization is easy to grasp, the procedure is pedagogically justifiable; i.e., it works.

We suggest that a story or dialog that contextualizes Graff's "optimistic" and "pessimistic" verbs and uses them in the appropriate pattern would be a useful addition to this procedure.

3 For advanced ESL/EFL students who have at least a superficial knowledge of chess, Sandy Anderson and Margaret Blencowe suggest the following exercise. Students should work in pairs and fill in the blanks in the following dialog with the appropriate infinitive or gerund form of the following verbs: *play, move, take, do, use.* They are to use each verb at least once. After the answers have been verified, each pair should role-play the dialog a few times.

A Game of Chess

X: I advise you (1) _____ your pawn forward.

Y: You can't force me (2) _____ that!

X: Uh, uh! You should avoid (3) _____ your queen!

Y: (Sighs) Would you permit me (4) _____ my bishop?

X: Certainly—if you can justify (5) _____ it.

Y: I think I am able (6) _____ whatever I wish.

X: Why don't you postpone (7) _____ his pawn till he's moved his queen?

Y: I really don't anticipate his (8) _____ his queen.

X: Then I suggest (9) _____ your bishop.

Y: You want me (10) _____ my bishop?

X: My dear friend, I URGE you (11) _____ your bishop.

Y: (Knocking over chessmen and walking away) I don't enjoy (12) _____ chess at all.

X: That's strange! I love (13) _____ chess!

4   To encourage the use of gerunds functioning as subjects, show how sentences expressing activities that are followed by comments can be combined using a gerund, e.g.:

A graduate student named Sam talks about the things he does:
I wash dishes in the student cafeteria. It isn't much fun. ⟶ Washing dishes in the student cafeteria isn't much fun.

Tell your students to continue Sam's commentary on his daily activities by using the gerund subject construction and combining it with an appropriate comment.

Activity	*Comment*		
I study microbiology. I play handball with my roommate. I run experiments in the lab. I read reports of important research.	It { doesn't take / takes } a lot of { time / patience / skill }		
	It's (not) (very) { interesting / relaxing / rewarding / important }		

5   What follows is an outline of four lesson plans that could be used to introduce or review infinitives and gerunds. They are adapted from suggestions made by Rosensweig (1973).

Lesson 1: verbs taking only the infinitive
a. V1 to + V2: hope, decide, afford, tend, say, refuse, offer, fail, agree, claim, etc.
Teacher asks questions that elicit model sentences that can be put on the board:

What do you hope to do when you return home?
Where have you decided to go on vacation next year?

Teacher leads a drill where students generate sentences based on pairs of verbs, e.g.:

Teacher: refuse/accept
Student: I refuse to accept the decision.
Other such pairs: agree/help; manage/finish; decide/go; etc.

Student-to-student questioning (teacher provides a list of matrix verbs to be used in questions. All questions should be answered):

decide, endeavor, determine, offer, resolve, consent, proceed ...

b. V1 + N + to + V2: persuade, tell, motivate, train, teach, remind, trust, force, allow, etc.
Teacher asks questions to elicit pattern from students. Responses are written on the board:

Who persuaded you to come to the U.S.?
What motivates you to study?

A drill based on pairs of verbs:

> *Teacher:*   advise/study
> *Student:*   I advise Paul to study.

Other pairs: force/fight; order/bring; warn/pay attention; etc.

Student-to-student questioning using these verbs: cause, invite, urge, stimulate, warn, direct.

c. V1 + (NP) + to + V2: expect, want, ask, promise, etc.
    Teacher asks two questions with each such verb to bring out contrast (equi-NP as subject of the infinitive vs. some other NP as subject):

> What do you expect to get for your birthday?
> What does a teacher expect a good student to do?

Student-to-student questioning using the above list of verbs (two questions for each verb).

Lesson 2: verbs taking only the gerund

a. V1 + V2-ing: avoid, risk, finish, admit, etc.
    Teacher asks questions to elicit pattern:

> What does Bill avoid doing?   What do you do when you finish eating?

Students complete sentences:

> We will finish . . .   I admit . . .
> John doesn't risk . . .

b. V1 + (NP) + V2-ing: appreciate, mind, defend, detest, deny, adore, welcome, enjoy, etc., where the noun phrase is in either the possessive (formal) or objective (informal) case.
    Teacher contrasts usages:

> Do you mind my doing that?   Do you mind me doing that?

Verb/complement combining to create sentences using a noun phrase in either the possessive or objective case—as necessary or possible:

> mention/my father did it   (I mention my father('s) doing it.)

Other pairs: defend/Turkey invading Cyprus, detest/he came to see me, deny/they did it

Have students ask and answer questions matching verbs and complements as appropriate, e.g.:

favor	go to school
welcome	do that
enjoy	help me
mention	come to see me
:	:

Lesson 3: verbs taking both gerunds and infinitives

Begin with examples and a short explanation of Bolinger's principle. Practice the verbs that make a clear distinction: regret, try, forget, remember, prefer—elicit contrasts if necessary.

What do you remember doing yesterday?
What did you remember to do yesterday?

Given a context, students make the correct choice:

I saw you in London last year.

(I'll never forget $\left\{ \begin{array}{l} \text{to see} \\ \text{seeing} \end{array} \right\}$ you there.)

Don't worry about your valuables.

(I'll remember $\left\{ \begin{array}{l} \text{to lock} \\ \text{locking} \end{array} \right\}$ the door.)

Drills requiring combination:

Teacher: I came yesterday ... regret
Student: I regret coming yesterday.

Teacher: I will go there tomorrow ... plan
Student: I plan to go there tomorrow.

Lesson 4: encourage integration and transfer of rules learned in the preceding lessons
Test the ability of the students to discriminate all verbs and contrasts covered in the preceding lessons:

He avoided $\left\{ \begin{array}{l} \text{to eat} \\ \text{eating} \end{array} \right\}$ too much.   I advise you $\left\{ \begin{array}{l} \text{to go} \\ \text{going} \end{array} \right\}$ to see a doctor.

Oral role playing: Situation is a university student consulting his/her adviser: verbs used in the role playing should be selected from a list provided by the teacher:

advise, force, induce, motivate, permit, train, teach, urge, want, plan, expect, admit, postpone, anticipate, suggest, justify, etc.

Students will write short compositions based on the above situation.

EXERCISES

Test your understanding of what has been presented

1. Provide original example sentences that illustrate the following terms. Underline the pertinent word(s) in your examples.

the Bolinger principle	factive verb
implicative verb	perfect infinitive
positive	gerund with indefinite, nonspecific sub-
negative	ject
infinitive of purpose	infinitive with equisubject

2. Explain why the following sentences are ungrammatical:

a. *I want that I should go there.
b. *I stopped to take piano lessons (meaning "I no longer took them").
c. *He expects attending Harvard Law School.

Test your ability to apply what you know

3. If your students produce the following sentences, what errors have they made? How will you make them aware of the errors, and what exercises will you prepare to correct the errors?

a. *I enjoy to study English.
b. *I'll never forget to go to the party in Chinatown last week.
c. *I will go to Tehran for visiting my parents.

4. Can you see any reason(s) for distinguishing between regular infinitives and infinitives of purpose?

5. How would you teach ESL/EFL students to use infinitives and gerunds correctly with the verb *try*? Suggest a context and a teaching strategy.

6. One ESL teacher said he had his students memorize the verbs that take gerunds and told them to use infinitives everywhere else. Do you think this is a good teaching strategy? Why or why not?

BIBLIOGRAPHY

References

Anderson, J. I. (1976). "A Comparison of the Order of Difficulty of English Sentential Complements between Native Speakers of Spanish and Native Speakers of Persian." Paper presented at the Los Angeles Second Language Research Forum, UCLA, February 1976.

Bolinger, D. (1968). "Entailment and the Meaning of Structures," *Glossa* 2:2, 119–127.

Butoyi, C. (1977). "A Frequency and Usage Study of Gerunds, Infinitives, and *That* Clauses as Sentential Complements." Unpublished English 215 paper, UCLA, fall, 1977.

Butoyi, C. (1978). "The Accuracy Order of Sentential Complements by ESL Learners." Unpublished M.A. thesis in TESL, UCLA.

Hofmann, T. R. (1966). "Past Tense Replacement and the English Modal System." Harvard Computational Laboratory, NSF Report 17.

Kartunnen, L. (1971). "Implicative Verbs," *Language* 47:2, 340–358.

Kiparsky, P., and C. Kiparsky (1970). "Fact," in M. Bierwisch and K. Heidolph (eds.), *Progress in Linguistics*. The Hague: Mouton.

Rosensweig, F. (1973). "A Strategy for Teaching Gerunds and Infinitives to Advanced ESL Students." Unpublished English 215 paper, UCLA, fall, 1973.

So, Nguyen Van (1973). "The Semantic Interpretation of Infinitives and Gerunds as Sentential Complements." Unpublished M.A. thesis in TESL, UCLA.

Suggestions for further reading

For the theoretical background most relevant to this chapter, see the following sources:

Bolinger, D. (1968). "Entailment and the Meaning of Structures," *Glossa* 2:2, 119–127.

Kartunnen, L. (1971). "Implicative Verbs," *Language* 47:2, 340–358.

Kiparsky, P., and C. Kiparsky (1970). "Fact," in M. Bierwisch and K. Heidolph (eds.), *Progress in Linguistics*. The Hague: Mouton.

Stockwell, R., P. Schachter, and B. Partee (1973). *The Major Syntactic Structures of English*. New York: Holt, Rinehart and Winston. (See chapter on Nominalization and Complementation.)

For useful discussions of infinitives and gerunds in reference grammars, see:

Close, R. A. (1981). *English as a Foreign Language* (3d ed.). London: Allen and Unwin, Chap. 8.

Frank, M. (1972). *Modern English: A Practical Reference Guide*. Englewood Cliffs, N.J.: Prentice-Hall.

Jespersen, O. (1966). *Essentials of English Grammar*. University, Ala.: University of Alabama Press, Chaps. 31, 32.

For some additional suggestions for teaching infinitives and gerunds, see:

Brinton, D., and R. Neuman (1982). *Getting Along: English Grammar and Writing* (Book 2). Englewood Cliffs, N.J.: Prentice-Hall, pp. 200–202.

Martin, A. V., et al. (1977). *Guide to Language and Study Skills.* Englewood Cliffs, N.J.: Prentice-Hall, pp. 43–58.

Praninskas, J. (1975). *Rapid Review of English Grammar* (2d ed.). Englewood Cliffs, N.J.: Prentice-Hall, Chaps. 16, 17.

Wohl, M. (1978). *Preparation for Writing: Grammar.* Rowley, Mass.: Newbury House, pp. 63–68.

32

Participles

GRAMMATICAL DESCRIPTION

Introduction

Any discussion of participles must begin by distinguishing *-Ing* participles from gerunds, since so many reference grammars and ESL/EFL texts simply refer to both as "-ING forms."[1] We make this distinction below. We also distinguish *-Ing* and *-En* participles from verb forms and discuss the different forms that the two types of participles can take. Following that, we discuss some of the major functions of *-Ing* and *-En* participles that the ESL/EFL teacher should be familiar with. As we shall see, each construction discussed seems to have one or more functions associated with it.

Distinguishing *-Ing* participles from gerunds

Early in the history of English, *-Ing* participles and gerunds had different forms as well as different functions. At that time the *-Ing* participle inflection was *-end(e)* and the gerund inflection *-ing* or *-ung.* Modern German, a related language, still maintains a difference in form between gerunds and participles. In English, however, both forms merged into *-ing* over the years, and this merger has caused some confusion in many contemporary grammatical descriptions.

One of the best ways of distinguishing *-Ing* participles and gerunds is to remember that gerunds function as nouns whereas *-Ing* participles function as adjectives or adverbs. For example, the following list summarizes the major functions of gerunds:

1. *Nouns functioning as subjects, objects, or predicate nouns following BE:*

    Seeing is *believing.*   Jack hates *hunting.*

2. *Compound nouns (i.e., N + N):*

    a *sléeping bàg* (a bag used for sleeping)
    láughing gàs (a gas that makes people laugh)

---

1. Other misleading approaches refer to all "-ING forms" as either participles or gerunds and thus also ignore the distinction.

447

3. *Gerund clauses functioning as subjects, direct objects, or objects of prepositions:*

> *Having dinner in the garden* is possible when the weather is warm.
> I enjoy *taking a walk after dinner.*
> The injury kept Marcus from *playing football for two weeks.*

4. *Gerund clauses following a possessive determiner or possessive noun:*

> I dislike his *saying things like that.*   Peter's *having won the game* surprised us.

In contrast to the above, the major function of *-Ing* participles are summarized in the following list:

1. *Adjective + noun combinations (compare with (2) in the above list):*

> the *sleeping child* (the child who is sleeping)
> *laughing people* (people who are laughing)

2. *-Ing forms that resemble—but cannot possibly be derived from—reduced relative clauses (i.e., adjectival function):*

> The Johnsons have bought a house *resembling a barn.* (*The house is resembling a barn.*)
> The man in line in front of me purchased several items *totaling $205.*
>
> (*The items $\left\{ \begin{matrix} \text{are} \\ \text{were} \end{matrix} \right\}$ totaling $205.)

3. -Ing *adjectives in predicate or attributive position:*

> The movie was *interesting.*   Joe tells *exciting* stories.

4. -Ing *forms as complements of sensory perception verbs:*

> I saw Mark *running across the street.*
> Bruce heard Ann *walking down the stairs.*

5. -Ing *adverbial clauses:*

> *Approaching Ensenada,* we were stopped by two Mexican highway patrolmen.
> Men were climbing through the machinery, *repairing the long conveyor belt.*

Regarding the above list of *-Ing* participle functions, recall that function 1 was discussed in Chapters 27 and 28. Function 4 will be treated in Chapter 34. Thus in the remainder of this chapter, we will be discussing functions 2, 3, and 5, and we will be describing and contrasting the uses of *-Ing* participles with those of *-En* participles.

In fact, the existence of two different types of participles in English, i.e., *-Ing* participles and *-En* participles, is another major difference between participles and gerunds, since gerunds have only one form.

We close this comparison of gerunds and *-Ing* participles by pointing out that not all *-Ing* forms following prepositions are gerunds, although many grammar texts claim that they are:

Gerund: We discouraged John from *studying his history text the whole weekend.*
Participle: By *listening to some soft music,* I was able to relax.

In the first example the gerund is a structurally necessary part of the prepositional phrase—neither the preposition nor the gerund can be deleted without changing the meaning of the sentence. In the second example, deletion of the preposition *by* is possible with only a subtle change of meaning.[2] Also, the entire participle could be deleted (in addition to the preposition) without changing the meaning of the main clause. As adverbial or adjectival modifiers, participles generally have a looser connection with the structure of a sentence than do gerunds. Thus we feel that even following prepositions there is a distinction worth maintaining between gerunds and participles.

Distinguishing adjectival use of *-Ing* and *-En* participles from verb forms

The adjectival use of the *-Ing* and the *-En*[3] participles can be confused with progressive and passive verb phrases, respectively. This is not surprising because the forms involved are identical:

-Ing adjective:	The child is *interesting*.
Progressive verb:	The child is *interesting* me in tennis.
-En adjective:	The man was *exhausted*.
Passive verb:	My patience was *exhausted* by his behavior.

One way to differentiate these uses is to add an intensifier such as *very* before the italicized forms in the above sentences. When the participle is functioning as an adjective, the addition of the intensifier is acceptable, since adjective phrases may include intensifiers:

The child is very interesting.   The man was very exhausted.

This is not the case, however, when the participle is part of a verb construction; the addition of an intensifier directly before a true verb form makes these sentences ungrammatical:

*The child is very interesting me in tennis.   *My patience was very exhausted by his behavior.

---

2. Lorraine Kumpf (personal communication) has pointed out to us that the presence of the preposition *by* denotes a cause-effect relationship in:

By listening to some soft music, I was able to fall asleep.

Likewise, the presence of *while* denotes simultaneity in:

While listening to some soft music, I was able to fall asleep.

An unmarked-*Ing* participle, on the other hand, is somewhat ambiguous and denotes something more general than either cause-effect or simultaneity:

Listening to some soft music, I was able to fall asleep.

3. The *-En* participle is sometimes referred to as a "passive" participle. Such a label, however, can be misleading because the *-En* participle does not always imply a passive meaning. For example, "I am exhausted," where *exhausted* is a participle, does not necessarily mean "Someone/Something exhausted me." However, "I was paid" does mean "Someone paid me" because *paid* is a passive verb form. Note that *very* is O.K. before *exhausted* but not *paid* in the frame "I was _____ ." Note also that the presence of a "*by* phrase" will not always distinguish passive verbs from *-En* participles:

1. I was paid by the boss.   2. He was baffled by her behavior.

We cannot add *very* to the first example, the true passive verb, while we can add *very* to the second; i.e., it's an adjectival participle.

The surface similarities in these forms sometimes create potentially ambiguous sentences:

> John is entertaining.
> Adjective: He is an entertaining person.
> Verb: He is entertaining guests.

> We were relieved.
> Adjective: We felt a sense of relief.
> Verb: Other workers came to take our places.

In both examples, the meanings of the adjective and the verb are somewhat different despite the identity in form; thus when these sentences occur in context, it is highly unlikely that they will be perceived as ambiguous.

Forms and meanings of participles

The -*Ing* participle has three possible forms:

Basic form: *working* (signals a time overlapping with the time expressed in the main clause), e.g.:

> Working diligently on his paper, John began to type up the bibliography.

Perfective form: *having worked* (signals a time preceding the time expressed in the main clause), e.g.:

> Having worked on his paper since 4 p.m., John stopped at 8 to watch the DePaul basketball game.

Perfective-progressive form (rare): *having been working* (signals an action in progress at a time preceding the time expressed in the main clause), e.g.:

> Having been working on his paper for more than a week, John decided he would turn it in without further revision.

The -*En* participle also has three possible forms:

Basic form: *worn out* (signals a reason for the result expressed in the main clause), e.g.:

> Worn out from all the work, John decided to relax for a while.

Progressive form: *being worn out* (much like the basic form but with stronger emphasis on the fact that the participle gives a reason or cause for the result expressed in the main clause), e.g.:

> Being worn out from all the work, John decided to relax for the evening.

Perfective form: *having been worn out* (signals that the action in the participle is completed before—and is also the reason for—the result expressed in the main clause), e.g.:

> Having been worn out from three days' work on his paper, John decided to relax over the weekend.

The basic form is by far the most frequent one for both the -*Ing* and the -*En* participle. The other forms do occur, however, and grammar texts sometimes erroneously refer to the progressive and perfective forms of the -*En* participle as instances of the -*Ing* participle because of the initial -ING forms.

-*Ing* and -*En* adjective participles related to emotive verbs

A problem for many nonnative speakers of English is the adjectival use of -*Ing* and -*En* participles derived from "emotive" verbs. The term "emotive" is used to refer to verbs such as the following:

amuse	captivate	puzzle
annoy	interest	surprise
bewilder	intrigue	Etc.
bother	irritate	

A tendency that many nonnative speakers have is to overgeneralize the -*Ing* participle and produce sentences such as the following:

*I am interesting in sports.   (i.e., *interesting* for *interested*)

In such cases it must be made clear that if the adjective refers to the *experiencer,* i.e., the animate being or beings that are *feeling* the emotion, then the -*En* participle[4] should be used. If, on the other hand, the adjective refers to the *actor,* i.e., the thing or person that is *causing* the emotion, then the -*Ing* participle should be used. In all such cases, there is a semantically related sentence that contains the emotive verb without a participial form. Also, note that the participles can be used in either predicative or attributive position:

Emotive verb	-En *particle refers to the* experiencer *(the one* feeling *the emotion)*	-Ing *particle refers to the* actor *(the one/thing* causing *the emotion)*
Sports interest Max.	Max is interested in sports. He's a very interested basketball fan.	Sports are interesting (to Max). One very interesting sport is basketball.
Polish jokes don't amuse Kowalski.	Kowalski is not amused by Polish jokes. He is an unamused victim.	Polish jokes aren't amusing (to Kowalski). However, he does like other amusing ethnic jokes.
John's loud stereo annoys his neighbors.	John's neighbors are annoyed by his loud stereo. Several annoyed neighbors complained to the manager.	John's loud stereo is annoying (to his neighbors). They have had enough annoying noise for one weekend.

Since the participial forms (i.e., emotive adjectives) seem to be used more frequently than the simpler sentences with the emotive verbs, the ESL/EFL teacher must be alert to this semantic problem and show students how to use both adjective forms correctly. Furthermore, it may be useful to point out to students that both the -*Ing* and -*En* participles can function as adverbs if an -*ly* suffix is added:

---

4. Some grammar texts refer to the -*En* participle of emotive verbs as an -*Ed* form, perhaps for pedagogical reasons because all of the emotive verbs are regular in conjugation; i.e., the simple past and past participle are the same form. Such an analysis, however, is potentially misleading since these are past participles—not simple past verb forms taking -*Ed.*

John gazed contentedly at his new car. (John is contented.)
John's stereo is annoyingly loud most of the time. (The stereo is annoying.)

A problem related to use of the -*En* participle in this construction is one's choice of the preposition following the participle. Occasionally this preposition is idiosyncratic, e.g., *interested in.* The more usual prepositions are *by, with,* or *at.* Sometimes two—or even all three—of these prepositions can occur after the -*En* participle; however, there are subtle differences in meaning:

I'm surprised $\left\{ \begin{array}{c} \text{at} \\ \text{by} \end{array} \right\}$ Jack's behavior.   Ann is annoyed $\left\{ \begin{array}{c} \text{at} \\ \text{with} \end{array} \right\}$ Ralph.

We are not certain what these meaning differences are and thus would welcome discourse-based research that might shed some light on the semantic differences between *at, by,* and *with* when they follow these -*En* participles.

Participles functioning as adjectival clauses

When present participles function as adjective clauses, they are either restrictive or nonrestrictive—just as the adjectival relative clauses are that we discussed in Chapters 26 and 27. However, they are structurally different from reduced relative clauses, as we shall explain below.

Consider the following examples of restrictive and nonrestrictive participles.

> *Restrictive:*
> The Johnsons bought a house resembling a barn.
> A rug measuring 9 by 12 feet covered most of the floor.

> *Nonrestrictive:*
> Finally the Smiths arrived, resembling a couple out of the twenties.[5]
> William, not having heard the dinner gong, did not eat last night.

Note that none of these participles can be analyzed as reduced relative clauses with a progressive verb because they contain stative verbs which do not normally occur in the progressive (see p. 71); thus the underlying structure must have a nonprogressive source.

> *The Johnsons bought a house which is resembling a barn. (The Johnsons bought a house which resembles a barn.)
> *A rug which was measuring 9 by 12 feet covered most of the floor. (A rug which measured 9 by 12 feet covered most of the floor.)
> *Finally the Smiths arrived, who were resembling a couple out of the twenties. (Finally the Smiths, who resembled a couple out of the twenties, arrived.)
> *William, who had not been hearing the dinner gong, did not eat last night. (William, who had not heard the dinner gong, did not eat dinner last night.)

Despite the structural differences, we do not want to deny a functional and semantic similarity between such participial clauses and relative clauses. We tried to show this similarity by paraphrasing each of the above ungrammatical examples with a grammatical

---

5. This sentence is a stylistically preferred form of the following sentence, which more closely mirrors the underlying form but which is more awkward:

> Finally the Smiths, resembling a couple out of the twenties, arrived.

relative clause, i.e., the clauses in parentheses. Note that the relative clause paraphrases all have a simple (i.e., nonprogressive) verb form.

We will not go into detail in describing the derivation of the participial clauses here; we wish merely to point out that they are syntactically different from reduced relative clauses that have a progressive verb form in the underlying structure and would thus require a different derivation.

-En participles functioning as relative clauses do not pose a similar range of problems since they can always be derived from reduced relative clauses whenever the basic form of the participle occurs:

Restrictive
The house restored by the Johnsons is quite unusual. (The house which was restored by the Johnsons is quite unusual.)

Nonrestrictive
William, annoyed at having gone without dinner, refused to talk to anyone. (William, who was annoyed at having gone without dinner, refused to talk to anyone.)

Participles functioning as adverbial clauses

Sentence-initial adverbial participial clauses

The adverbial use of *-Ing* and *-En* participles in clause-initial position is a problem for native as well as nonnative speakers of English. Errors such as the following are traditionally referred to as "dangling modifiers" or "dangling participles," and they are the bane of many a high school English teacher's existence:

*Laughing hysterically and unable to answer Miss Fiddich, she sent poor Tom to the principal's office.

*Torn and bent beyond recognition, I received my mother's letter.

In such cases, the subject of the participle should also be the subject of the main clause. Whenever this is not the case—as in the two examples above—a dangling participle (i.e., an ungrammatical sentence) results.

Danielson and Hayden (1973) have pointed out that such participles can usefully be viewed as reduced forms of adverbial clauses; however, they caution that the reduction is grammatically acceptable only if both clauses have the same underlying subject. With this condition in mind, we can now correct the above sentences:

Because Tom was laughing hysterically and unable to answer Miss Fiddich, Tom was sent to the principal's office (by Miss Fiddich). ⟶ Laughing hysterically and unable to answer Miss Fiddich, Tom was sent to the principal's office.

After my mother's letter had been torn and bent beyond recognition, my mother's letter was delivered to me yesterday. ⟶ Torn and bent beyond recognition, my mother's letter was delivered to me yesterday.

Both native and nonnative users of English should be given ample opportunity to reduce sentence-initial adverbial clauses to participial clauses when the equisubject condition is met. Students should also be able to identify clauses which cannot be reduced to participles. Some teachers find it useful to point out to their students the unintended humor that occurs when a dangling participle is interpreted literally, e.g.:

*Following the recipe carefully, my cake was a great success. (= my cake followed the recipe carefully!)

*Flattened out of shape by Dmitri's serve, we could no longer play with the old volleyball. (= we were flattened out of shape by Dmitri's serve!)

The equisubject participles discussed above are the most common type of sentence-initial adverbial participle; however, it is also possible to have a sentence-initial adverbial participle with a subject that is different from the subject of the main clause:

The bus drivers being on strike, many people had to get to work using other means of transportation. (Since the bus drivers were on strike, ...)

When-*En* participles are used in this type of construction, only the progressive or perfect form occurs:

The house having been constructed poorly, the new owners had to cope with many unexpected repairs. (Since the house had been constructed poorly, ...)

Many grammarians refer to the two preceding sentences as absolute constructions, which they carefully distinguish from participial clauses. We see no need to do this, since the semantic function of the two clause types is parallel.[6] The only difference is whether the subjects of the two clauses are the same or not. The reasoning we used in Chapter 30 to show that sentences like the following have the same underlying structure:

I want to go.   I want John to go.

can be applied here equally well, i.e., an identical subject in the subordinate or embedded clause is deleted; and when the subjects are different, no deletion occurs. The problem with the dangling participles cited above, of course, was that the underlying subjects were different, but deletion occurred anyway.

Sentence-final adverbial participial clauses

A sentence-final participial clause is normally detached from the main clause by a comma in writing or by special features in speech such as a pause before and lowered pitch on the participial clause, e.g.:

Laura looked at him, consumed with contempt for what he represented.
An old woman shouts out a long apocalyptic interpretation of the Bible, prophesying the immediate arrival of the Messianic Kingdom.

While the use of a sentence-final participial clause seldom leads to ungrammatical sentences in the way that the use of the "dangling modifier" does, a potential for ambiguity exists in those cases where there is more than one noun in the main clause that could be the antecedent of the underlying subject in the participial clause:

?Meg met Tom in the corridor, laughing heartily about what had happened in class.

In the absence of additional context, either *Meg* or *Tom* could be the underlying subject of the participial clause in this sentence. Such ambiguity, however, rarely occurs. First of all, the main clause may have only one noun phrase:

Betty danced joyfully, never suspecting what was about to happen.

---

6. The semantic function of all these adverbial participial clauses is either temporal (i.e., *after x, y* or *during x, y*) or causal (i.e., *because of x, y* or *given x, y*).

Second, for many main clauses with two or more noun phrases, there is usually only one noun phrase that qualifies semantically as the subject of the participial clause:

> Sheila ignored the dog and the TV set, deeply engrossed in the new book-of-the-month that had come in the mail.

Even though the main clause in this example contains three noun phrases (i.e., *Sheila, the dog, the TV set*), only *Sheila* can serve as the underlying subject of the participial clause, i.e., someone who is deeply engrossed in reading a book.

Note that all the examples we have given above of sentence-final adverbial participles are of the equi-noun phrase variety; i.e., the subject of the participial clause is identical in reference to one of the noun phrases in the main clause. As shown before with sentence-initial clauses, not all sentence-final participial clauses conform to this pattern—some have an overt subject that is not identical in reference to any noun phrase in the main clause.

> They decided to wait for dawn, *each hiker taking his two-hour turn at watch.*
> She walked along hurriedly, *her purse clutched tightly in her arms.*

Again, we feel that there is no significant difference in structure or function between the examples involving identical noun phrases and nonidentical noun phrases. The identical noun phrases have simply been deleted.

The discourse function of adverbial *-Ing* participial clauses

In carrying out an extensive study of *-Ing* participial clauses, Thompson (1983) found that they occurred most frequently in descriptive prose and very rarely in factual, scientific writing. For example, she compared 10,000 words of text from two different sources—a historical narrative and a pharmacology text—and found that the former contained 74 *-Ing* participial clauses while the latter contained only 5. (We feel that a similar ratio would obtain for *-En* participial clauses if such a count were carried out.) Thompson feels that the differences in frequency can be explained by the discourse function of these participial clauses; namely, they evoke a visual image in the mind of the listener or reader. Thompson's term for this function is "depictive." She adds that the more formal the language, and the more descriptive the discourse, the higher the frequency of participial clauses. A corollary of this functional principle is that participial clauses do not occur frequently in speech, since conversation leaves little opportunity for the planning required to make one's language evoke images in the listener's or reader's mind, which is the function of this construction.

Conclusion

In this chapter we have shown that gerunds and *-Ing* participles are distinguishable. We have argued that it is useful for the ESL/EFL teacher to make such a distinction rather than indiscriminately grouping all -ING forms together. Once this distinction has been made, the contexts in which both *-Ing* and *-En* participles occur can be itemized and described. While even the teacher of beginners must deal with the emotive *-Ing* and *-En* participles discussed above, the teacher of advanced ESL/EFL students—who is concerned with composition and reading—is more likely to require assistance with the adjectival and adverbial participles discussed in this chapter. In fact, in these areas, the concerns of the ESL/EFL teacher and those of the teacher of native speakers overlap because of the formal, literary nature of these constructions.

TEACHING SUGGESTIONS

1   To help students practice the correct use of -*Ing* and -*En* emotive adjectives, the teacher can collect appropriate pictures which suggest that someone is interested in something, surprised at something, annoyed at something, etc. For example, the teacher can mount on a piece of cardboard a picture of a man intently watching a football game on TV. The verb *interest* is written in large block letters above or below the picture. After discussing what is going on in the picture, the students try to produce two appropriate sentences, e.g.:

> The man is interested in the TV game.   The TV game is interesting (to the man).

With 6 to 10 such pictures the two patterns can be practiced and, if necessary, the rule can be elicited (cause/actor ⟶ -ING; feeler/experiencer ⟶ -EN).[7]

2   Once the predicative use of the emotive adjectives has been established as suggested above, the same pictures can be used later—or with more advanced students—to elicit attributive use of emotive adjectives, e.g.:

> The man is watching an interesting game.
> An interested TV viewer doesn't like to be interrupted.

3   Helen Toy suggests that teachers prepare a cloze passage to practice the use of emotive adjectives. The recommended context has a critic reviewing a film. The students, working in groups, should pretend they are the critic and use appropriate -*Ing* and -*En* emotive adjectives to fill the blanks, e.g.:

> The film "E.T." was (1) a/an _____ experience for everyone in the audience—young and old. The children were both (2) _____ and (3) _____ by E.T. during the first half hour. Later they found E.T.'s relationship with Elliott, the young boy, particularly (4) _____ . Etc.

4   To introduce the form and function of sentence-initial adverbial participles, students can be given sentences with adverbial clauses and instructed to form a participial clause if the subjects in the adverbial clause and the main clause are identical, e.g.:

> As we looked down the road, we saw a herd of cattle. ⟶ Looking down the road, we saw a
>   herd of cattle.
> Since I was very tired, my mother did the dishes. (no participle possible)
> Since we were exhausted from the long hike, we decided not to go to the party. ⟶ Ex-
>   hausted from the long hike, we decided not to go to the party.
> Etc.

5   If students are producing dangling modifiers in their compositions, help them to distinguish acceptable adverbial participles from dangling modifiers by providing them with a worksheet containing both types of sentences. The students can work in pairs or groups to identify each example as either a good sentence or a dangling modifier:

> Swimming out in the lake, the water felt cold.
> Bitten by a strange dog, I went to see my doctor immediately.
> Flying over the Rockies, we saw that they were covered with snow.

---

7. Despite our word of caution in footnote 4, the ESL/EFL teacher may want to simplify this -EN to -ED, since all emotive verbs are regularly conjugated and thus use the -*ed* ending to form past participles.

Elected by his constituents, they immediately turned on Mr. Jason and tried to recall him. Etc.

6   To help advanced students become aware of the discourse function of participial clauses, the ESL/EFL teacher can select a text with a high frequency of this construction. After having read and discussed the text, the students can work in groups (a) to identify all the instances of *-Ing* and *-En* participial clauses and (b) to come up with a description of the function of such clauses.

Frank (1972:361), for example, cites the following passage from Mark Twain's *Life on the Mississippi* as an appropriate text:

> After all these years I can still picture that old time to myself now, just as it was then: the town drowsing in the sunshine on a summer's morning; the streets empty, or pretty nearly so; one or two clerks sitting in front of the Water Street stores with their splint-bottomed chairs tilted back against the walls, chins on breasts, hats slouched over their faces, asleep. . . .
> Etc.

EXERCISES

Test your understanding of what has been presented

1. Provide original example sentences to illustrate the following terms. Underline the pertinent word(s) in your examples.

perfective *-Ing* participle
progressive *-En* participle
-Ing participle used as an attributive
   adjective

-En participle in a sentence-initial adverbial clause
dangling participle
ambiguous participle

2. Do the following sentences contain gerunds or *-Ing* participles? In each case specify why you made your decision.

a. Rick has demonstrated an amazing attitude about that problem.
b. We were able to stop him from dropping the course.
c. His denouncing the present government surprised me.
d. Melvin walked away dejectedly, looking at the cracks in the sidewalk.

3. Are the following *-Ing* and *-En* participles grammatical or dangling (i.e., ungrammatical)? For each case, explain why.

a. Encouraged by his math professor, Harry took an advanced calculus course.
b. Correcting my original calculations, the problem was solved.
c. Seated around a large table, the banquet more than satisfied all of us.
d. Not knowing what to do, Jane asked her teacher for some advice.

Test your ability to apply what you know

4. If your students produce the following sentences, what errors have they made? How will you make them aware of the errors, and what exercises will you prepare to correct the errors?

a. *I am bothering by his bigoted remarks.
b. *Approaching our house, a package was left by the mailman on the doorstep.

5. The first example below can be changed into a participial construction, whereas the second one cannot. Why?

   a. As Mr. Black spoke to the students, he wrote a sentence on the blackboard.——►Speaking to the students, Mr. Black wrote a sentence on the blackboard.

   b. As we showed the students our pictures, they looked away.

6. Is either of the following participial clauses ambiguous? Why or why not?

   a. Roberta ate the ripe mango slowly, seduced by a vision of the tropical paradise that had produced such a fruit.

   b. The dog went after the cat, retreating soon thereafter because the fighting was fierce.

BIBLIOGRAPHY

References

Danielson, D., and R. Hayden (1973). *Using English: Your Second Language.* Englewood Cliffs, N.J.: Prentice-Hall.

Frank, M. (1972). *Modern English: A Practical Reference Guide.* Englewood Cliffs, N.J.: Prentice-Hall.

Thompson, S. (1983). "Grammar and Discourse: The English Detached Participial Clause," in F. Klein (ed.), *Discourse Perspectives on Syntax.* New York: Academic Press.

Suggestions for further reading

The single most useful source we have found on participles is:

Frank, M. (1972). *Modern English: A Practical Reference Guide.* Englewood Cliffs, N.J.: Prentice-Hall.

Some useful sources dealing with the gerund vs. *-Ing* participle distinction are:

Crowell, T. L. (1964). *Index to Modern English.* New York: McGraw-Hill.

Strang, B. M. H. (1963). *Modern English Structure.* New York: St. Martin's Press.

Zandvoort, R. W. (1957). *A Handbook of English Grammar.* London: Longmans, Green.

For a good account of *-Ing* participles used as adjectives that is geared to the ESL/EFL teacher, see:

Scovel, T. (1974). " 'I am interesting in English'," *English Language Teaching Journal* 28:4, 305–312.

For suggestions on teaching the adverbial sentence-initial use of participles, see:

Danielson, D., and R. Hayden (1973). *Using English: Your Second Language.* Englewood Cliffs, N.J.: Prentice-Hall, pp. 180–181.

For an exercise dealing with the adjectival use of emotive *-Ing* and *-En* participles, see:

Yorkey, R. (1970). *Study Skills for Students of ESL.* New York: McGraw-Hill, pp. 56–57.

The most extensive—albeit highly manipulative—set of exercises dealing with all the uses of participles is:

Frank, M. (1972). *Modern English: Exercises for Non-native Speakers. Part II.* Englewood Cliffs, N.J.: Prentice-Hall, pp. 81–96.

33

Indirect Speech

GRAMMATICAL DESCRIPTION

Introduction

When an English speaker wants to report what someone else has said, the speaker may choose to either directly quote the other person:

> Allen said, "I will buy this car tomorrow."

or to use indirect speech (also referred to as "reported speech"):

> Allen said that he would buy that car the following day.[1]

In addition to the punctuation differences between the two reports, we see there are quite a few structural differences as well. It is the purpose of this chapter to investigate what English speakers do to convert direct speech into indirect speech.

Since many non-European languages make less of a formal distinction than English does between the two reporting styles, ESL/EFL students often find indirect speech to be a problematic area of English grammar. What also complicates the area is that native speakers do not consistently abide by the grammar-book rules for producing indirect speech. The result of this is that students become confused when they encounter the many so-called "violations" of the "rules" they have learned.

From the example provided above, one is able to infer that to form indirect speech one must make use of the complementizer *that,* as well as possibly making changes in pronominal forms, in the verb tense, in demonstratives, and in adverbials of time and place. Each of these areas will be dealt with in turn. In addition, we will also be looking at word order differences between direct and indirect speech. Although word order differences are not evident in the example we have given, it is another area that is often affected when students attempt to convert direct speech into indirect speech.

---

1. *The following day* would be the appropriate time adverbial only if Allen's utterance was not reported the day it was spoken (in which case *tomorrow* would be retained) or the day after Allen made the statement (in which case *today* would be used).

The complementizer *that*

If we ignore punctuation differences, the first difference apparent between the two sentences above is the introduction of the complementizer *that* before the indirect speech clause. To illustrate this, let us draw the tree for the second sentence.

Allen said that he would buy that car the following day.

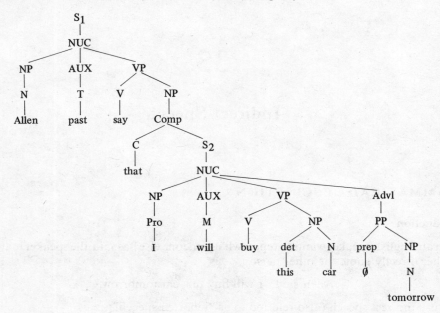

You can see from this basic structure that a reported sentence is embedded just as the other complements are that we looked at in Chapter 30. The difference between reported sentences and embedded sentences is that the former are a subcategory of the latter. Fewer verbs are used to report statements than to embed statements. (See Frank, 1972, p. 287).

It may also have already occurred to you that the complementizer *that* could be omitted without affecting the grammaticality of the sentence. In other words, with complementizer deletion (and affix attachment, morphological rules, and other rules that change direct to indirect speech) we could have produced:

>   Allen said he would buy that car the following day.

Although the *that* is optionally deletable in informal speech when the indirect statement is in object position, it would have to be deleted if the indirect statement appeared first in the sentence, although this type of inversion is admittedly rare:

>   *That he would buy that car the following day Allen said.
>   He would buy that car the following day, Allen said.

Shifts in pronouns

The next difference we observe between our two example sentences is that the *I* that Allen used in the direct report is transformed into *he* by the reporter. This is a typical shift, and the following is another example of it:

first person⟶ third person

Joanne: *I* have a fever and *my* throat hurts.
Joanne said that *she* had a fever and *her* throat hurt.

Another frequently occurring pattern is a shift from second to third person:

second person⟶ third person

Carl to David: *You* should come.
Carl to someone else: I told David that *he* should come.[2]
Carl to David: I like *your* new cowboy boots.
Carl to someone else: I told David that I liked *his* new cowboy boots.

If David were reporting these statements, there would, of course, be a shift from second person to first person:

Carl said that *I* should come.
Carl said that he liked *my* new cowboy boots.

Tense harmony

You will note that there was also a change in the tense of the verb in the indirect speech clause of our example sentence when compared with the tense of the direct speech clause. The change of tense in the indirect speech clause is accomplished by a process called tense harmony.[3]

The rules of tense harmony are often oversimplified in grammar books. While it is true that with a present tense reporting verb there is no change of tense in the indirect speech clause, there are problems when the reporting verb is in the past tense. (This is when tense harmony can apply to shift a tense in the reported clause.) Most reference grammars claim that when a past tense reporting verb is used, there must be a change of tense as follows:

Tense of direct quote clause
present (prog) ⟶
past (prog)
present perf (prog) }⟶
past perf (prog)

Tense of indirect speech clause
past (prog)

past perf (prog)

(no change)

Examples:
Meg: I have a new car.   (present ⟶ past)
Meg *said* that she *had* a new car.
Ralph: Joe saw "E.T." twice.   (past ⟶ past perfect)
Ralph said that Joe had seen "E.T." twice.

It is these rules regulating "tense harmony" which are particularly subject to "violations" by native speakers. Although no comprehensive study has been undertaken to account for all the

---

2. The usage of *come* and *go* in both direct and reported speech poses a number of problems in English. These verbs behave differently in some respects in English than in other languages. See Fillmore (1966) for a discussion of these verbs.

3. Tense harmony is sometimes called "backshifting" because the tense of the reported speech clause is often pushed back in time to agree with the tense of the reporting verb.

"violations" that occur, we can offer several exceptions to the rules based on our own observations and on the research of others:

1. Indirectly reported utterances expressing general truths (and often containing stative verbs) do not have to be shifted to the past even when the reporting verb is in the past:

$$\text{Columbus said that the earth} \begin{Bmatrix} \text{is} \\ \text{was} \end{Bmatrix} \text{round.}$$

2. Indirect speech which is an immediate repetition of what was just said seldom agrees in tense with the reporting verb (if there is in fact an explicit reporting verb; frequently there isn't one):

Joanne: I have a headache, too.   Joanne: (I said) I have a headache, too.
Martin: What did you say?

3. Many native speakers do not use tense harmony even for indirect remote past reports if the situation that is described in the reported clause still holds true or is assumed to still hold true by the speaker:

Shirley told me that she has a swimming pool.

4. When shifting from past to past perfect, a change of meaning might occur because of the addition of the perfective marker. In such cases, a shift is often avoided.

Pam: I wanted to go to Albany to visit friends last weekend.
Pam said that she wanted to go to Albany to visit friends last weekend. (i.e., It's possible to say that she wanted to go and that subsequently she did go.)
Pam said that she had wanted to go to Albany to visit friends last weekend. (i.e., With the past perfect tense in the report clause the implication is very strong that she did not go—i.e., she had wanted to go, but she didn't.)

Even if the meaning would be unaffected by the shift, often the shift does not take place in spoken English. This reflects informal usage (Thomson and Martinet, 1980).

5. This lack of tense harmony is sometimes true of written English as well. In a discourse analysis of the use of indirect speech in the writing of native speakers, Chang (1981), for example, found that when a present or future time adverbial occurred in the clause, tense harmony was not always adhered to:

Jeremiah said he hopes to begin his new exercise program by early next week.

6. Imaginative present and past conditional clauses when they are indirectly reported do not permit tense harmony because present conditionals would then be the same as past conditionals (Thomson and Martinet, 1980).

Ed: If I had the will, I would find a way.
Ed said that if he had the will, he would find a way.

Ed: If I had had the will, I would have found a way.
Ed said that if he had had the will, he would have found a way.

By itemizing all these exceptions we do not intend to undermine the value of the tense harmony rules. Indeed, tense harmony does frequently apply, especially in written and more formal spoken registers. In fact, sometimes tense harmony is obligatory, as Leech (1971) has shown us with the following example:

Socrates: I am blameless. (Socrates dies.)

Socrates said that he $\left\{ \begin{array}{l} \text{was} \\ \text{*is} \end{array} \right\}$ blameless.

Another circumstance in which Stein (1982) feels tense harmony may be obligatory is when the reporter is trying to appear detached or impartial—trying not to make a judgment as to the truth value of the reported statement. It is clear that Stein's hypothesis and others will have to be tested before we are able to account for all applications of and exceptions to the tense harmony rule.

A change in the modal auxiliary

In our discussion of the example sentence (i.e., Allen said that he would buy that car the following day), we observe that because of tense harmony the modal is shifted from *will* —→ *would*. This shift and others like it reflect the tenses the modals expressed in earlier periods of the English language (i.e., *will, can, may,* and *shall* were present tense forms while *would, could, might,* and *should* were the related past tense forms, respectively). In current English, if the context is formal and the modal being reported is historically a present tense form, the following shifts sometimes occur when the reporting verb is in the past tense:

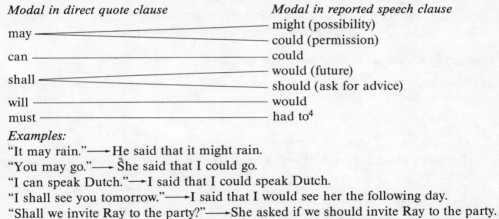

Modal in direct quote clause   *Modal in reported speech clause*

may ——————————————— might (possibility)
                                could (permission)
can ———————————————— could
                                would (future)
shall ———————————————— should (ask for advice)
will ———————————————— would
must ———————————————— had to[4]

Examples:
"It may rain."——→ He said that it might rain.
"You may go."——→ She said that I could go.
"I can speak Dutch."——→I said that I could speak Dutch.
"I shall see you tomorrow."——→I said that I would see her the following day.
"Shall we invite Ray to the party?"——→She asked if we should invite Ray to the party.
"The party will be held at Barbara's house."——→ He said that the party would be held at Barbara's house.
"I must finish the book."——→I said that I had to finish the book.

However, these shifts, like the other applications of the tense harmony rule, do not always take place. For example, if *will* is the modal in the reported utterance and it is being used to express future time, and if the situation described in the quote still holds true at the time of the indirect report, the *will* may not be changed to *would* even though the reporting verb is in the past tense:

Mr. Snyder said that the next big depression will be in 1998.

When the reference to time is more ambiguous, native speakers' usage is almost evenly divided between producing *will* and *would* (Shalit, 1979). Then, too, Chang (1981) found that when a modal involves inference or prediction, shifting is even more unlikely to occur

---

4. *Had to* is a periphrastic substitute. Historically, *must* was a past form that shifted to present time meaning in current English, which is why there is no historically-related past form of *must* (see p. 81, footnote 1).

because a change in modal would alter the meaning (i.e., the degree of probability) expressed by the original speaker. A shift changing *may* to *might,* for example, weakens the prediction of precipitation by the speaker of our example sentence, *He said that it might rain.* Another possible problem is that the listener(s) will reconstruct *might* instead of *may* as the modal used in the direct speech (i.e., He said, "It might rain"). Thus ambiguity can be introduced if a modal is shifted. More work in this area is obviously required before we can predict when and where native speakers will shift modals in indirect speech.

Shifts in demonstratives

The next change we note in our sentence above is the shift in demonstratives from proximate to remote—i.e., from *this* to *that* or *these* to *those.* The logic behind this shift is presumably the need to distance the listener from the referent when the referent is no longer present in the immediate physical environment. Thus, typically we get:

this ⟶ that
Ben: I don't like this fancy cooking.
Ben (to someone else later): I said I didn't like that fancy cooking.

these ⟶ those
Alice: These examinations are nerve-racking.
Alice said that those examinations were nerve-racking.

Changes in adverbials of time and place

The last change obvious in our original example sentence is a shift in the time adverbial from *tomorrow* to *the following day.* Other changes in time adverbials likely to take place are:

now ⟶ then, at that time

Ann: I'm leaving now.
(Reported by someone else later): (I was surprised because . . .) Ann said she was leaving then.

today ⟶ that day (yesterday, two days ago, etc., when appropriate)

tomorrow ⟶ $\begin{cases} \text{the following day} \\ \text{the next day} \\ \text{a day later} \end{cases}$

yesterday ⟶ $\begin{cases} \text{the previous day} \\ \text{the day before} \end{cases}$

next month/year ⟶ $\begin{cases} \text{the following month/year} \\ \text{the next month/year} \\ \text{a month/year later} \end{cases}$

last month/year ⟶ $\begin{cases} \text{the previous month/year} \\ \text{the preceding month/year} \\ \text{the month/year before} \end{cases}$

in two days/weeks ⟶ two days/weeks from then

two days/weeks ago ⟶ two days/weeks $\begin{cases} \text{before} \\ \text{earlier} \end{cases}$

In addition, there is one place adverbial which is likely to change:

here ⟶ there

Jim: I want to stay here.
(Reported by someone else later in another place): Jim said that he wanted to stay there.

Changes in word order and other considerations

We saw that there were no word order differences between the two sentences given earlier. As long as directly quoted statements are being compared with indirectly reported statements, word order does not seem to be a problem; however, when we consider other sentence types, various word order changes occur and thus potential problems arise for ESL/EFL students.

Exclamations

There are two basic ways we can indirectly report exclamations. The first is simply to paraphrase the exclamation in the form of an embedded statement. The use of a verb like *exclaim* reveals to the listener the reported clause was originally an exclamation.

> Marian: What a beautiful day (it is)!
> Marian exclaimed that it was a beautiful day.

Alternatively, a speaker could preserve the direct speech word order in the report; however, the speaker would have to report the full clause since direct exclamations often permit deletions that reported exclamations cannot have:

> Rachel: What a beautiful day!
> Rachel exclaimed what a beautiful day it was.
> *Rachel exclaimed what a beautiful day.

Imperatives

Directly quoted imperatives are usually transformed into infinitives in indirectly reported speech. There is greater variation in word order in the direct report than in the indirect report.

Teacher: { Johnny, stand up!   The teacher told Johnny to stand up.
{ Stand up, Johnny!

If the imperative is negative, then the sequence is NOT + the infinitive.

Teacher: Don't stand up, Johnny!   The teacher told Johnny not to stand up.

Although the imperative form can, of course, be used for functions other than commands, e.g., to invite, the change in form to an infinitive still applies if an imperative with such a function is reported:

> Sal: Stop by for some dessert and coffee tonight.
> Sal invited us to stop by for some dessert and coffee tonight.

Yes-no questions

The inversion of the auxiliary verb and the subject, which is so hard for some students to master in direct yes-no questions, must be suppressed when such questions are indirectly reported (or embedded):

Andy: Is Mason going?   *Andy asked if was Mason going.
Andy asked if Mason was going.

In addition to the word order difference, you have probably noted that *if*[5] was added. Another possibility would be to use *whether* as the complementizer in place of *if*:

Andy asked whether Mason was going.

Many traditional grammarians claim that the difference between *if* and *whether* is one of register, *whether* being used when a more formal register is desired. This observation, however, does not give us the whole picture.

Bolinger (1975) has suggested that there is a difference between these two complementizers in that *if* marks true yes-no questions, whereas *whether* implies the existence of alternatives. Although this distinction is subtle, it may be true that *whether* would be more frequently selected in situations where the listener is being asked to make a choice:

Margaret: Do you prefer Mexican or Greek food?
Margaret asked whether I preferred Mexican or Greek food.

Further support for Bolinger's hypothesis might be the fact that only *whether* can be immediately followed by *or not:*

$$\text{I wondered } \begin{Bmatrix} \text{whether} \\ \text{*if} \end{Bmatrix} \text{ or not Helen was coming.}$$

The subordinator *if,* however, may also be followed by *or not,* provided that there is a short clause intervening:

I wondered if Helen was coming or not.

A co-occurrence restriction that always distinguishes between *if* and *whether* is that only *whether* can occur after prepositions or participial *-Ing* forms functioning like prepositions:

$$\text{I inquired as to } \begin{Bmatrix} \text{whether} \\ \text{*if} \end{Bmatrix} \text{ there were any new developments.}$$

$$\text{We asked them regarding } \begin{Bmatrix} \text{whether} \\ \text{*if} \end{Bmatrix} \text{ there were any new developments.}$$

Wh-questions

Suppression of the inversion rule in indirectly reported yes-no questions does not seem to be a major problem; i.e., ESL/EFL students do not usually produce sentences like the following, perhaps because of the presence of *if* or *whether:*

*I asked if was Mason going.

However, with wh-questions problems emerge. There is no special complementizer to signal an indirectly reported or embedded wh-question—the main difference between direct and indirect speech for this structure is that subject/auxiliary inversion is suppressed when reporting a wh-question:

Eileen: What time is it?   Eileen asked what time it was.

---

5. Many students of English grammar confuse the adverbial subordinator *if* found in conditional sentences (see Chapter 25) with the indirect speech complementizer *if* discussed in this chapter. Only the latter alternates with *whether.* In fact even native speakers of English sometimes confuse these two *if*'s, with the result that they mistakenly produce hypercorrect subjunctive forms in embedded yes-no questions, e.g.:

*I asked if he were going.

Other languages often employ two completely different forms to express the two functions of English *if.* German, for example, uses *wenn* to mark conditional clauses and *ob* to signal indirect yes-no questions.

Many nonnative speakers of English as well as native speakers of certain dialects produce indirect questions like this instead of the standard English version:

$$\text{*Eileen asked what time } \begin{Bmatrix} \text{was} \\ \text{is} \end{Bmatrix} \text{ it.}$$

Indeed, as Cazden et al. (1975) found in their study of the acquisition of English interrogatives by native Spanish speakers, learning the proper form of an embedded wh-question was the last stage their subjects went through in acquiring English wh-questions. Long after ESL/EFL students have acquired and are using direct wh-questions, they continue to overgeneralize and to invert subjects and auxiliaries in embedded wh-questions, e.g.:

$$\text{*Do you know where is the shoestore?}$$

Conclusion

Despite the many differences between direct and indirect speech which we have detailed here, there are others which we have not even mentioned. What we have attempted to do is to touch upon the major differences between the two. Because of the complexity of all the potential form shifting, ESL/EFL students will need a great deal of practice before they will be able to effortlessly control all the changes necessary for indirectly reporting the speech of others.

TEACHING SUGGESTIONS

1   Initially students should be given a lot of input containing indirectly reported speech.A way of doing this might be for the teacher to turn statements that students make into indirect speech. After a while the teacher could do this with exclamations, imperatives, and questions that the students produce. Later on students could be asked to turn indirect speech into direct speech following the teacher's cues, e.g.:

Statements:
Teacher: Pierre, tell Esteban that you like his watch.
Pierre: I like your watch, Esteban.
Esteban: Thank you.

Imperatives:
Teacher: Li, tell Maria to close the door.
Li: Close the door, Maria.
Maria: O.K.

Yes-no questions:
Teacher: Claude, ask Liu if she is feeling better.
Claude: Are you feeling better, Liu?
Liu: Yes, I am. Thank you.

Wh-questions:
Teacher: Miriam, ask Theo where he's going after class.
Miriam: Where are you going after class?
Theo: To the library.

2   Adapting a procedure from the Community Language Learning approach, the teacher can invite students to have a conversation among themselves. Each line of the conversation is

tape-recorded. Directly after each student records his or her contribution to the conversation, the teacher tape-records the same statement, question, etc., in indirect speech form. Afterward, the conversation and the indirectly reported speech are transcribed. Students are invited to make observations about the differences between the direct and indirect speech.

3   By interacting with each other or the teacher, students can begin to practice producing indirect speech:

Statements: Direct quotes are written on slips of paper. Two students come up at a time. One pulls out a slip and reads; the second reports what the first one said to the class. With more advanced students, the teacher may want to give cues as to the tense and degree of formality involved.

Moto (reading from his slip): I'm ready to leave.

Present report

Formal: Moto says that he is ready to leave.

Informal: Moto says he's ready to leave.

Immediate past report

Formal: Moto said that he is ready to leave.

Informal: Moto said he's ready to leave.

Remote past report

Formal: Moto said that he was ready to leave.

Informal: Moto said he was ready to leave.

Exclamations: The first student selects a slip of paper which instructs the student to make an exclamation about something. The second student reports the exclamation of the first.

Paper: Make a comment about the cost of houses these days.
Gino: How expensive houses are these days!
Francesca: Gino exclaimed that houses are (were) expensive these days.
          or   Gino exclaimed how expensive houses are (were) these days.

Imperatives: Students come up in groups of three. The first student selects a slip of paper and reads a command to the third student, who does not "hear" it. The third student asks the second what the first one has said. The second paraphrases the command indirectly. Then the third student either carries out the command or gives an appropriate response (i.e., refusal, excuse, etc.).

Kim: Write your name on the blackboard.
Antonella (turning to Carlos):   What did she say?
Carlos: She said to write your name on the blackboard.
Antonella: Oh, O.K.

Yes-no questions (embedded): Each student asks the teacher a yes-no question. The teacher pretends not to hear and asks "What did you say?" or "Eh?" or "Pardon me?" The student then rephrases the response beginning with "I asked (you) if...".

Olga: Can I miss class tomorrow?
Teacher: What did you say?

Olga: I asked you if I $\begin{Bmatrix} \text{can} \\ \text{could} \end{Bmatrix}$ miss class tomorrow.

Teacher: What is your reason?

Wh-questions (embedded): Information questions are written on slips of paper. Students come up in pairs. The first student draws the slip and rephrases the wh-question as a polite request for information to which the second student responds. Then they switch roles and the second student draws the question and the first responds.

Written question: Where's the library?
Tomiko: Could you please tell me where the library is?
(The segment in italics remains the same throughout the exercise.)
Freda: Yes, it's on the other side of that building.

4   To provide more of a realistic context and an integrated review, have two students (who may have rehearsed in advance) come to the front of the class and have a conversation, which is tape-recorded and then transcribed on the board (or immediately transcribed if no tape recorder is available), e.g.:

Sam: Hi, Janet. How are you?
Janet: Fine thanks, and you?
Sam: Pretty good, but I'm worried about my chemistry exam.
Janet: Have you studied?
Sam: Of course. It's just that the class is very difficult.

Class members orally give an immediate report in the present tense. "What happens?"

Sam says "Hi" to Janet and asks her how she is.
Janet says that she is fine and returns the question.
Sam replies that he's pretty good but that he's worried about his chemistry exam. . . . Etc.

Then the students might also do a colloquial oral report in the immediate past. "What just happened?"

Sam said "Hi" to Janet and asked her how she is. . . .

Later (during the class hour) class members make another report in the past tense now more remote (and more formal—i.e., written).

Sam said "Hi" to Janet and asked her how she was. . . .

5   The teacher can give the class written dialogs to be paraphrased indirectly in either (a) the present, (b) the immediate past, or (c) the remote past. This can be done orally or in writing with colloquial or formal usage specified.

6   A teacher can get the class to practice appropriate changes in time, place, and person by manipulation of the situation, e.g.:

Direct quote by John: I'm leaving this house for good today.
Reports:
1.   by John—somewhere else—same day: I said I'm leaving that house for good today.
2.   by Susan—somewhere else—a later day: John said that he was leaving that house for good that day.
3.   by Joe—same place—a later day: John said that he was leaving this house for good that day.
4.   by John—same place—same day: I said I'm leaving this house for good today.
        Etc.

7   The teacher should find an anecdote or a fable that makes use of several direct quotes. The teacher can read it (or play a tape recording of a native speaker reading it) and follow these steps.

1st reading/playing: Students listen and answer a few general questions the teacher gave them ahead of time.

2nd reading/playing: Students listen and answer more detailed comprehension questions (e.g., who said what to whom).

3rd reading/playing (with pauses):   Students take notes.

4th reading/playing: Students retell orally, using indirect speech. And they may supplement their notes.

5th reading/playing: Students write the anecdote or fable in their own words using indirect speech.

EXERCISES

Test your understanding of what has been presented

1. Provide original sentences that illustrate each of the following terms. Underline the pertinent word(s) in your examples.

indirect statement	change in an adverbial of time
indirect exclamation	change in a demonstrative
indirect imperative	suppression of subject/auxiliary inversion
tense harmony applied to a main verb	
yes-no question complementizer	

2. Why are the following sentences ungrammatical?

a. *We questioned them concerning if they had seen Paul.
b. *The judge told the parolee don't to get in any more trouble.
c. *That it reached −25°F. in Milwaukee, the radio announcer said.
d. *I wonder if or not I should go there.

3. In what ways are the sentences or terms in each of the following pairs equivalent? How are they different or potentially different?

a. (1) reported question
   (2) embedded question
b. (1) Bob says that we can borrow his car.
   (2) Bob said that we could borrow his car.
c. (1) Joyce said, "The tickets were in my purse a minute ago."
   (2) Joyce said that the tickets had been in her purse a minute earlier.

Test your ability to apply what you know

4. If your students produce the following sentences, what errors have they made? How will you make them aware of the errors, and what exercises will you prepare to correct the errors?

a. *I asked Abdul what is the homework assignment.
b. John: I am happy to be here.
   John (elsewhere): *I said that I was happy to be here.
c. *My aunt told me that she has to go to Minneapolis last year.
d. Mr. Greenfield: I have to see Jamieson today.
   (Several days later): *Mr. Greenfield insisted that he had to see Jamieson today.
e. *Marjorie exclaimed what a fine new car.
f. *He asked am I going.
g. *Can you tell me where is the bus stop?

5. It has been suggested by Gasser (1975) and Agnello (1976) that direct quotation, which is rarer than indirectly reported speech, is used in the following situations:

a. (In speech) reporting *how* the speaker said the utterance, i.e., his or her emotional state (by imitation of speaker's intonation, etc.)
b. (In speech or writing) reporting of idioms, interjections, parenthetical expressions, etc.
c. Where it is important in reporting the speaker's exact words
d. Reporting a joke punch line that involves a piece of dialog

Find an example of a direct quote used in a larger piece of discourse. Does one of the above suggestions cover it? If not, how would you explain the use of a direct quote rather than use of indirectly reported speech for your example?

6. In Chapter 27 we encountered a transformation called free relative substitution which substituted the free relative pronoun *what* for *the thing that.* In this chapter we have seen that *what* can also occur sentence-internally in an indirectly reported question. Decide whether the following sentences are free relatives or embedded wh-questions. Give evidence to support your decisions.

a. The police discounted what he had said.   c. We asked him what he had seen.
b. What you don't know may hurt you!

7. Suppose you have been hired to carry out a survey to determine whether or not native speakers currently apply rules of tense harmony in contemporary English speech and writing. How would you proceed? Do some exploratory work and add one more rule to the tense harmony "violations" described in this chapter.

8. An ESL/EFL student asks you which complementizer he or she should use in the following sentence—*if* or *whether.* What would you say?

Peter came into the room and asked me _____ I knew what time it was.

BIBLIOGRAPHY

References

Agnello, F. (1976). "The Difference between Direct and Indirect Speech in Spoken and Written English." Unpublished English 215 paper, UCLA, fall, 1976.

Bolinger, D. (1975). "About Questions," a guest lecture presented at UCLA to a Linguistics Colloquium (Feb. 12, 1975).

Cazden, C., H. Cancino, E. Rosansky, and J. Schumann (1975). "Second Language Acquisition Sequences in Children, Adolescents and Adults." Final Report to U.S. Department of Health, Education and Welfare. Project 730744.

Chang, Yi-Wei (1981). "A Contextual Analysis of Tense Shifts in Reported Speech." Unpublished English 215 paper, UCLA, fall, 1981.

Fillmore, C. J. (1966). "Deictic Categories in the Semantics of 'Come'," *Foundations of Language* 2:219–227.

Frank, M. (1972). *Modern English: A Practical Reference Guide.* Englewood Cliffs, N.J.: Prentice-Hall.

Gasser, M. (1975). "Choice of Direct or Indirect Speech in Spoken English." Unpublished English 215 paper, UCLA, fall, 1975.

Leech, G. (1971). *Meaning and the English Verb.* London: Longman.

Shalit, M. (1979). "Tense Usage in American English Reported Speech." Unpublished M.A. thesis in TESL, UCLA.

Stein, A. (1982). "Speaker Attitudes in Reported Speech." Unpublished M.A. thesis in TESL, UCLA.

Thomson, A. J., and A. V. Martinet (1980). *A Practical English Grammar* (3d ed.). Oxford: Oxford University Press.

Suggestions for further reading

For useful traditional descriptions of indirect speech, consult the following sources:

Jespersen, Otto (1911). *A Modern English Grammar* (vol. IV). London: Allen and Unwin.

Quirk, R., and S. Greenbaum (1972). *A Grammar of Contemporary English.* New York: Harcourt Brace Jovanovich, pp. 785–789.

For a list of verbs typically used in indirect speech and for a discussion of the way English speakers may blend direct and indirect speech constructions, see:

Frank, M. (1972). *Modern English.* Englewood Cliffs, N.J.: Prentice-Hall, pp. 287, 300–301.

For a transformational account of the rules governing indirect speech in English and problem areas for native speakers of Persian, see:

Yarmohammadi, L. (1973). "Problems of Iranians in Learning English Reported Speech," *IRAL* 11:4.

For a discussion of direct quotation versus indirect speech in spoken English, see:

Zwicky, A. (1971). "On Reported Speech," in C. J. Fillmore and D. T. Langendoen (eds.), *Studies in Linguistic Semantics.* New York: Holt, Rinehart and Winston.

For further suggestions on teaching indirect speech, consult these texts:

Brinton, D., and R. Neuman (1982). *Getting Along: English Grammar and Writing* (Book 2). Englewood Cliffs, N.J.: Prentice-Hall, pp. 231–232.

Danielson, D., and R. Hayden (1973). *Using English: Your Second Language.* Englewood Cliffs, N.J.: Prentice-Hall, pp. 50–54, 203–214.

Rutherford, W. E. (1975). *Modern English* (2d ed., vol. I). New York: Harcourt Brace Jovanovich, pp. 181–194.

For a variety of exercises, including comparing situations in which original tense retention or tense harmony is more common, take a look at:

Sheeler, Willard D. (1978). *Grammar and Drillbook.* Washington, D.C.: English Language Services, Inc.

34

Other Aspects of Complementation

GRAMMATICAL DESCRIPTION

Introduction

In this chapter we will take up a number of topics that have not yet been covered in the preceding chapters and which can be thought of as being part of the English complementation system. Our focus is on areas that we feel are of importance to ESL/EFL teachers.

Infinitive versus object plus infinitive

English sentences such as the following two appear to have parallel surface structures:

>   We expected him to go there.   We told him to go there.

However, when we paraphrase the infinitives as *that* clauses, we realize that these sentences are structurally different:

>   We expected that he would go there.   We told him that he should go there.

In the sentence with *expect,* there is only one occurrence of *he,* i.e., as subject of the *that* clause. In the case of the verb *tell,* there are two occurrences of *he*: as subject of the *that* clause *and,* in its objective form, as an indirect object of the main clause.

   The generation of the first sentence, therefore, would be accomplished by object attraction, i.e., the *he* of the embedded sentence becomes the object of the complementizer *for* and gets changed to *him*; the rest of the embedded sentence then becomes an infinitive clause, and the *for* is deleted.

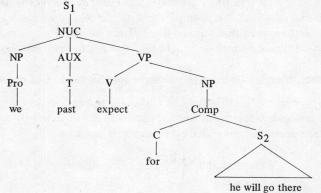

Output of base: we past expect (for (he will go there))
Object attraction: we past expect (for him (will go there))
Infinitivalization: we past expect (for him (to go there))
Complementizer deletion: we past expect (him (to go there))
Affix attachment (1✕): we expect + past (him (to go there))
Morphological rules: We expected him to go there.

The generation of the second sentence is a bit more complicated, since it includes an indirect object. Indirect object movement would take place first because the direct object is a clause and when the direct object is complex or "heavy," indirect object movement applies whenever possible (see Chapter 18). Since the indirect object *him* and the subject of the embedded sentence *he* refer to the same individual, the second pronoun, *he,* is deleted by an application of the transformation called equi-noun phrase deletion (see Chapter 30). The rest of the embedded sentence becomes an infinitive and the *for* complementizer is deleted.

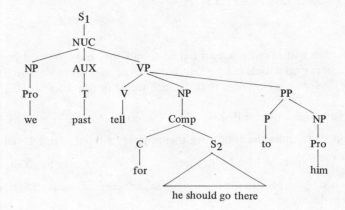

Output of base: we past tell (for (he should go there)) to him
Indirect object movement: we past tell him (for (he should go there))
Equi-noun phrase deletion: we past tell him (for (should go there))
Infinitivalization: we past tell him (for (to go there))
Complementizer deletion: we past tell him (to go there)
Affix attachment (1✕): we tell + past him to go there
Morphological rules: We told him to go there.

Other verbs which pattern like *expect* are: *want* and *desire.* Verbs like *arrange* and *plan* also fall into this category, although complementizer deletion does not take place in sentences with these verbs. Other verbs that pattern like *tell* are: *advise, urge, remind, teach,* and *warn.* Frank (1972:334–335) has a more complete list of verbs in each category.

Possessive versus objective or uninflected form for the subject of a gerund

Earlier, in Chapter 30, we mentioned the difficulty in pinpointing when the subject of a gerund is in the possessive form and when it occurs in the objective or uninflected form (i.e., objective form for pronouns, uninflected form for nouns):

We appreciate $\left\{ \begin{array}{c} \text{his} \\ \text{him} \end{array} \right\}$ being discreet.

$$\text{We appreciate} \left\{ \begin{array}{l} \text{Marion's} \\ \text{Marion} \end{array} \right\} \text{being discreet.}$$

Although this topic has engendered much discussion over the years, there is not as yet a rule or set of rules that is fully compatible with current usage.

Frank (1972) and Thomson and Martinet (1969) claim that the possessive and objective/uninflected forms are interchangeable in midsentence position and that the possessive reflects formal and the objective/uninflected informal usage. Frank adds that when the subject of the gerund is a personal pronoun rather than a noun, the possessive form is even more likely to occur.[1] When the subject of the gerund occurs sentence-initially, Frank points out that the possessive form is required:

$$\left. \begin{array}{l} \text{His} \\ \text{*Him} \end{array} \right\} \text{saying that surprised us.}[2]$$

Jespersen (1939) further refines the rule for us by pointing out that the possessive cannot be used in the following case:

1. For words functioning as nouns or pronouns that have no possessive form, e.g.:

Demonstratives: *that*—He will not hear of that being possible.
Numerals: *those three*—Those three telling such a story is odd.
Adjectives used as nouns: *young or old*—I'm not surprised at young or old falling in love with her.

and he adds that the possessive form is unlikely when:

2. The subject consists of conjoined noun phrases, one of which is a pronoun:

They remarked about my son and me being well qualified to keep each other company.

3. The subject of the gerund does not refer to a person:

$$\text{There is little chance of} \left\{ \begin{array}{l} \text{the money being found.} \\ \text{(compare with)} \\ \text{his being found.} \end{array} \right.$$

Marckwardt and Wolcott (1938) add another category to Jespersen's list of unlikely candidates for the possessive form:

4. When the subject of the gerund is a proper name—the longer the name, the less likely it is to be in possessive form:

We appreciated Professor Wesley Abernathy being discreet about the matter.

---

1. This claim was borne out in a study by Black (1977). He examined the *White House Transcripts* and analyzed 100 gerunds with subjects. Sixty-seven of the subjects were objective/uninflected in form and 33 were possessive. However, when Black considered only those cases with personal pronoun subjects, the possessive was used 63 percent of the time.

2. While this condition is generally adhered to, Black (1977) did find two instances in the *White House Transcripts* where the possessive form did not occur with gerund subjects in sentence-initial position:

Kleindienst revealing to Mitchell that he had contact with the Grand Jury is wrong.
Them coming down here to testify, say?

While the first sentence here reflects a variant frequently found when subjects of gerunds are proper names, the second example can only be characterized as highly informal, colloquial usage bordering on the nonstandard.

Black's 1977 study of gerunds in the *White House Transcripts* supports Marckwardt and Wolcott, since in those cases where proper nouns were used as subjects, the possessive form was used only 19 percent of the time.

Quirk et al. (1972) point out that verbs of sensory perception (*see, feel, hear, watch*) and verbs of interception (*discover, find, catch*) use only the objective form. (To us this is not surprising since we analyze complements of such verbs as participles, not gerunds.) For example:

$$\text{We watched } \left\{ \begin{array}{l} \text{John} \\ \text{*John's} \end{array} \right\} \text{ running across the field.}$$

However, they point out that there are other verbs—notably those of mental perception such as *remember, recall,* and *imagine*—that can take either possessive or objective forms:

$$\text{I remember } \left\{ \begin{array}{l} \text{his} \\ \text{him} \end{array} \right\} \text{ stealing the money.}$$

We believe that this multiplicity of forms can be explained by a number of factors. First of all, it is clear that informal register plays a role in simplifying the possessive subjects of gerunds to objective or uninflected forms and that the form of the subject (proper name vs. pronoun) is also a factor influencing whether or not the subject of a gerund will surface as an object or uninflected form rather than a possessive. However, we feel that another very important consideration is the fact that we have two distinct complement constructions that appear to be quite similar because participles and gerunds are both *-ing* forms:

> *object + participle:* We watched *John running across the field.*
> obj.   participle

(Here the focus is on the object NP *John,* who is in the act of running across the field; *John* cannot occur in the possessive form.)

> *possessive + gerund:* We appreciated *his   being discreet about the matter.*
> poss.   gerund

(Here the focus is on the whole embedded sentence, i.e., the fact that he was discreet about the matter. This is true even when *his* gets simplified to *him* in informal contexts.)

Some verbs like *remember, imagine,* and *recall* take both complement structures with corresponding differences in meaning. Thus we do not have only one construction (possessive + gerund) with two separate subject NP forms, we also have two distinct constructions that often appear to merge because when the possessive form of the possessive + gerund is simplified to an object or uninflected form, this gerund construction looks exactly like the object + participle construction.

Raising

Consider the relationship between the sentences in the following sets:

It (so) happens that Pauline likes movies.   It appears that Roger is absent.
Pauline happens to like movies.   Roger appears to be absent.

It seems that Nancy is sick.
Nancy seems to be sick.

In the first sentence in these three sets the *that*-clauses are embedded subject NPs that have been extraposed. Impersonal *it* has then been added in subject position to function as the surface subject. In the second version the subject noun phrase of the embedded clause has been raised to function as the subject of the higher sentence (i.e., as the surface subject of the higher verb). The remainder of the embedded clause becomes an infinitive and gets extraposed; then the complementizer is deleted. For example:

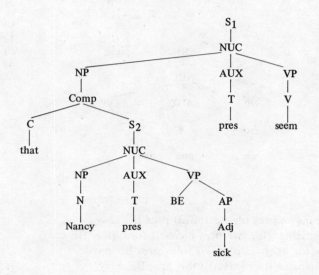

Output of base: (that (Nancy pres BE sick)) pres seem
Subject-to-subject raising: (that (pres BE sick)) Nancy pres seem
Infinitivalization: (that (to be sick)) Nancy pres seem
Complementizer deletion: (to be sick) Nancy pres seem
Extraposition: Nancy pres seem (to be sick)
Affix attachment (1×): Nancy seem + pres (to be sick)
Subject-verb agreement and morphological rules: Nancy seems to be sick.

A similar but slightly different raising rule operates in pairs of sentences such as these:

It is easy (for us) to please John.
John is easy (for us) to please.

It is difficult (for me) to do this work.
This work is difficult (for me) to do.

It was tough (for me) to finish that assignment.
That assignment was tough (for me) to finish.

In the first version of these cases the *for* complement is embedded in subject position (with object attraction and infinitivalization taking place) and then it is extraposed with subsequent addition of impersonal *it* to serve as the surface structure subject. In the second version, however, the object of the embedded complement is raised to function as the surface structure subject. The other rules take place as before (object attraction, infinitivalization, extraposition). For example:

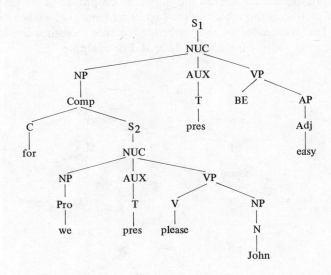

Output of base: (for (we pres please John)) pres BE easy
Object-to-subject raising: (for (we pres please)) John pres BE easy
Object attraction: (for us (pres please)) John pres BE easy
Infinitivalization: (for us (to please)) John pres BE easy
Extraposition: John pres BE easy (for us (to please))
Affix attachment (1×): John BE + pres easy (for us (to please))
Subject-verb agreement and morphological rules: John is easy for us to please.

While we have attempted to show that the first and second versions of these sentences are syntactically related, we will add our usual proviso by saying that depending upon the discourse context, one of these forms would presumably be preferred over the other. For instance, if we were listing John's personal qualities, the sentence we just derived would presumably be the more appropriate form, i.e., "John is helpful, cooperative, and easy to please."

We have discussed these two types of raising in English because while raising is fairly common in other languages, it is by no means universal. Also, different languages have different rules (or patterns) of raising. It has been our experience that ESL/EFL learners can better understand and produce the nonraised versions of sentences such as the above ones than they can the raised versions. This means that it is important for the teacher to provide exposure to and practice with common and frequent examples of raising in English.

Complex passives

Having discussed these complementation processes, we are now in a position to analyze the complex embedded passives mentioned briefly in Chapter 17. Note that for complex passives at least two surface sentences (and sometimes three) are possible.

It is believed that the President has accepted a compromise.
The President is believed to have accepted a compromise.

It is felt that Norma is well qualified.
Norma is felt to be well qualified.

It is rumored that Dick has been fired.
That Dick has been fired is rumored.
Dick is rumored to have been fired.

It has been mentioned that Dr. May is a candidate for Congress.
That Dr. May is a candidate for Congress has been mentioned.

Dr. May has been mentioned $\left\{ \begin{array}{l} \text{to be} \\ \text{as} \end{array} \right\}$ a candidate for Congress.

To demonstrate the syntactic relationship among sentences for a given set, we will derive the first two sentences from the same basic structure:

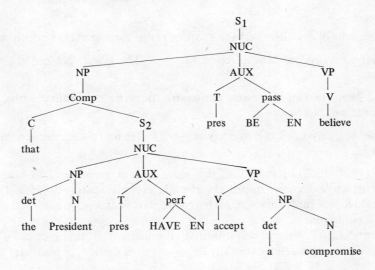

Output of base: (that (the President pres HAVE EN accept a compromise)) pres BE EN believe

Extraposition: pres BE EN believe (that (the President pres HAVE EN accept a compromise))

It insertion: it pres BE EN believe (that (the President pres HAVE EN accept a compromise))

Affix attachment (4×): it BE + pres believe + EN (that (the President HAVE + pres accept + EN a compromise))

Subject-verb agreement and morphological rules: It is believed that the President has accepted a compromise.

Output of base: (that (the President pres HAVE EN accept a compromise)) pres BE EN believe

Subject raising: (that (pres HAVE EN accept a compromise)) the President pres BE EN believe

Infinitivalization: (that (to HAVE EN accept a compromise)) the President pres BE EN believe

Complementizer deletion: (to HAVE EN accept a compromise) the President pres BE EN believe

Extraposition: the President pres BE EN believe (to HAVE EN accept a compromise)

Affix attachment (3X): the President BE + pres believe + EN (to HAVE accept + EN a compromise)

Subject-verb agreement and morphological rules: The President is believed to have accepted a compromise.

Once again we feel compelled to acknowledge that although these sentences are syntactically related, the discourse context would always tend to favor one over the other.

Causative constructions

There is a certain category of verbs whose function it is to signal that someone has caused someone/something to do something. The various features of these causative verbs will be treated in the following sections.

Syntax

The majority of causative verbs (e.g., *order, cause, force, get*) take infinitive complements.

The sergeant ordered him to report for duty.	The lawyer got her to admit her guilt.

Make and *have,* two of the more commonly occurring causative verbs, however, take complements without *to:*[3]

I made her stay until the mystery was solved.	He had the gardener trim the hedges last week.

Jespersen (1964) has observed that the more formal verbs tend to take full infinitive complements while the more informal verbs take complements without *to*. This observation seems to hold for the most part, with *get* being the glaring exception since it is informal and yet takes a full complement.

Make and *have* can have their infinitive complements further reduced when the verb in the complement is also deleted (usually BE or a verb of motion, as Martin (1981) points out):

He made her (be) his wife.	They had some friends (come) over.

The other causative verbs can also be found with elided complements when the *to* + verb has been dropped:[4]

She got him (to be) hired. He forced the door (to be) open.	The principal ordered him (to be) suspended.

One other observation we should make with regard to the syntax of causative verbs has to do with their interaction with the passive. Both *have* and *get* can act as passive auxiliaries and

---

3. While not in the causative verb category, two other commonly occurring verbs which also take infinitive complements without *to* are *let* and *help;* the latter may occur either with or without *to:*

I let her make a phone call.	I helped her (to) make a phone call.

4. Lorraine Kumpf (personal communication) has pointed out to us that the deletion of *to be* in such causatives is often lexically influenced. For example, in "He forced the door (to be) open," deletion is virtually obligatory; in "The principal ordered him (to be) suspended," deletion is truly optional; and in a sentence like "He forced the children (to be) quiet," deletion would be impossible.

In addition, note that the deletion of *to be* with a passive causative sometimes results in surface structures containing two consecutive passive participles.

The prisoner was ordered freed at once.

embed passivelike complements as easily as they do active ones.

I had someone cut my hair.	I got Brian to wash my car.
I had my hair cut.	I got my car washed.

This is not true of *make* and the other causative verbs, which require the BE auxiliary in the passive.

I made Jerry write the letter.	Jerry was made to write the letter.
*I made the letter written.	

You may have noticed the reversal with regard to the presence or absence of *to* in the infinitive complement. Unlike active *get,* passive *get* no longer takes the *to* when the complement is a passivelike construction. Conversely, active *make* takes no *to* in its infinitive complement, while passive *make* requires the *to*.

Semantics

There are some semantic differences among the causative verbs as well. Many of these differences can be explained by examining the relationship between the subject of the main clause and the subject of the embedded clause. We will treat only the three informal, most commonly occurring causative verbs here.

1. *Have* suggests that the embedded subject was routinely hired or selected to do a job by the subject of the main clause.

We had Ray mow the lawn.

2. *Get* conveys the sense that the subject of the main clause used persuasion or coercion to elicit the desired action from the embedded subject.

I got him to admit his mistake.

3. *Make* implies that the subject of the main clause has power or authority over the embedded subject.

The judge made him apologize for his wrongdoings.

The semantics of the passive variants of these three causative verbs seems, by and large, to be similar to that of the active forms. Passive *have* suggests that the action was routinely accomplished[5] and passive *get* implies that some effort was required to perform the action. The connection between active *make* and passive *make* is not quite as clear. Whether or not there is a difference in the authority between the higher subject and the embedded subject in the following is not obvious.

She was made to feel guilty.

Martin (1981), in a discourse analysis of causative verbs, generally supports these observations about the use of the causatives. For example, in one of the questionnaire items he devised, 20 out of 23 native speakers chose *get* when it was clear some difficulty was involved.

I had a lot of trouble finding someone to do it, but I finally
a. had the lawn mowed.   (3)   b. got the lawn mowed.   (20)

---

5. Note that the causative *have* is potentially ambiguous with the passive AUX *have,* as we indicated in Chapter 17. The interpretation depends upon the presence or absence of intention on the part of the subject:

I had my beard trimmed (by the barber).
I had my beard trimmed (when I got too close to the lawn mower).

On the other hand, he found native speakers also favoring *get* for some fairly routine activities. Seventeen out of 23 subjects chose *get* in the context of "cashing a check," for instance.

Another distinction between *get* and *have* that Martin's study verified is the degree of involvement of the subject of the main clause. *Get* may indicate that the subject of the main clause performed the action; *have* is more ambiguous. For instance, native speakers overwhelmingly chose *get* for the following item where it is clear that the subject of the main clause and the subject of the embedded clause are identical.

> Mary likes to cook, so she always
> a. gets the job done well.   (22)   b. has the job done well.   (1)

Frequency of occurrence

Although making no claim to generalizability, Martin (1981) analyzed the first 300 pages of the *White House Transcripts* and came up with the following form and frequency distributions:

active *have*	(to have someone do/doing something)	38 examples
passive *have*	(to have something done)	18 examples
active *get*	(to get someone to do/doing something)	17 examples
passive *get*	(to get something done)	32 examples
active *make*	(to make someone do something)	8 examples
passive *make*	(to be made to do something)	0 example

In addition, Martin noted there were 122 examples of synonyms (*cause, force,* etc.) which seemed "especially prevalent in formal settings: rehearsing for court testimony or press briefings, reporting on the speech of highly placed individuals who are not intimate friends, and in reporting on or speculating about journalistic reports."

Martin also reports that there were six examples of *have got someone to do/doing something,* although two of these examples were almost immediately followed by paraphrases using the simple causative verb *have.*

Verbs, adjectives, and nouns taking subjunctive complements

For a small class of English verbs that take *that*-clause object complements, the subjunctive form of the verb is used in the object complement. This is indicated by the lack of the *-s* inflection for third person singular verbs and by the use of one form (i.e., BE) for all persons when the BE copula is used:

We
$\begin{cases} \text{suggest} \\ \text{insist} \\ \text{recommend} \\ \text{urge} \\ \text{propose} \end{cases}$
that she leave the arrangements to us.

We
$\begin{cases} \text{suggest} \\ \text{insist} \\ \text{recommend} \\ \text{urge} \\ \text{propose} \end{cases}$
that Alex be the chairman.

Other verbs in this class are: *advise, ask, command, demand, forbid, move, order, request, require,* and *stipulate.* Some of these verbs permit an alternate way to express this same meaning, although the addition of *should* does seem to "soften" the speaker's request:

We suggest that Alex should be the chairman.

Also, a few of these verbs can be used with a *for* complementizer plus an infinitive and still retain a similar meaning.

We propose for Alex to be chairman.

The latter two constructions may be ways of avoiding the use of the subjunctive, which may seem overly formal and thus make some native speakers of English uncomfortable. The tree diagram for one of the above sentences with a subjunctive complement is as follows:

We suggest that Alex be the chairman.

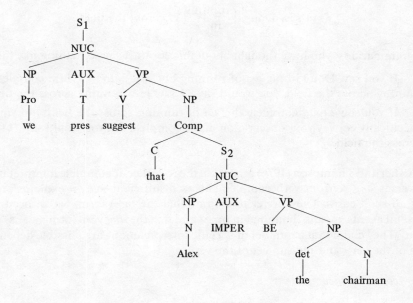

Use of the "IMPER" auxiliary simply ensures that the verb will not change from its base form, i.e., that subject-verb agreement will not be applied.

There are also a number of adjectives that take subjunctive complements:

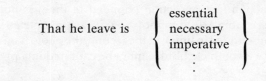

That he leave is $\left\{ \begin{array}{l} \text{essential} \\ \text{necessary} \\ \text{imperative} \\ \vdots \end{array} \right\}$

These are usually extraposed to yield:

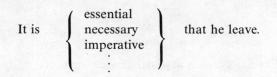

It is $\left\{ \begin{array}{l} \text{essential} \\ \text{necessary} \\ \text{imperative} \\ \vdots \end{array} \right\}$ that he leave.

In addition to the verbs and adjectives listed above as taking subjunctive complements, there are also some nouns derived from the verbs that can also take such a complement:

$$\text{The} \left\{ \begin{array}{l} \text{suggestion} \\ \text{recommendation} \\ \text{proposal} \\ \vdots \end{array} \right\} \text{that he be fired met with resistance.}$$

Sensory verb complements

Sensory verbs (e.g., *hear, feel, smell, taste, notice, observe, watch*) take two kinds of complements: the *-ing* participle and the base form.

$$\text{I saw Doug} \left\{ \begin{array}{l} \text{running} \\ \text{run} \end{array} \right\} \text{across the field.}$$

Most grammarians who have thought about this contrast say something like the following:

> If you saw Doug in the act of running but you didn't see him complete the act of running across the field, you would say, "I saw him running across the field."

> If you saw Doug complete the act of running across the field and you wanted to specifically convey your observation of the complete act, you would say, "I saw him run across the field."

Kirsner and Thompson (1976) argue that the complete-incomplete interpretation of base-form versus *-ing* sensory verb complements is insufficient—i.e., it explains some but not nearly all such cases. They prefer to assume that the base form, which occurs only with purposeful agents, means "bounded in time" and that the *-ing* verb form means "unbounded in time." They claim that a number of specific interpretations are possible depending on the nature of the verb and the subject of the verb:

1. *complete/incomplete:*

$$\text{I saw Bob} \left\{ \begin{array}{l} \text{*drown} \\ \text{drowning} \end{array} \right\} \text{, so I rescued him.}$$

$$\text{In this photo you can see Joan} \left\{ \begin{array}{l} \text{*blink} \\ \text{blinking} \end{array} \right\}.$$

Discussing a completed action (i.e., an action bounded in time) is not possible in these contexts because in the first example, Bob cannot drown (i.e., a completed action) and then be rescued (i.e., *drowning* is unbounded in time); in the second, the photo has frozen Joan's image in the act of blinking, since a complete blink cannot be captured in a photo (i.e., *blinking* is unbounded in time).

2. *single event/iterative:*

$$\text{I saw Laurie} \left\{ \begin{array}{l} \text{snap} \\ \text{snapping} \end{array} \right\} \text{her fingers.}$$

With punctual verbs like *snap, kick,* and *slap* the base form signals a single event (bounded in time) while the participial form signals repetition (unbounded in time).

3. *potential for independent action:*

$$\text{I saw the girl} \left\{ \begin{array}{l} \text{lie} \\ \text{lying} \end{array} \right\} \text{on the bed.}$$

$$\text{I saw the glasses} \left\{ \begin{array}{l} \text{*lie} \\ \text{lying} \end{array} \right\} \text{on the bed.}$$

With verbs of physical position like *lie, lean,* and *stand* agents can take both forms, but nonagents—which are incapable of independent action—can only take the *-ing* form, which is unbounded in time.

Complements of verbs of interception versus verbs of mental imagery

We extend Kirsner and Thompson's analysis of sensory perception verbs to verbs of interception (e.g., *find, catch, discover, come upon*) and verbs of mental imagery (e.g., *remember, imagine, recall, picture*). The verbs of interception take only the *-ing* participle form because the subject of the complement is discovered while in the act and thus the participle is always unbounded in time, i.e., never expresses completed action:

$$\text{We} \left\{ \begin{array}{l} \text{found} \\ \text{caught} \\ \text{discovered} \\ \text{came upon} \end{array} \right\} \begin{array}{l} \text{Billy} \\ \text{(him)} \end{array} \left\{ \begin{array}{l} \text{stealing} \\ \text{*steal} \end{array} \right\} \text{a cookie from the jar.}$$

Note that these verbs of interception can never take a complement with a possessive subject (e.g., *We found Billy's/his stealing a cookie from the jar...), which further proves that these *-ing* complements are participles, not gerunds.

The verbs of mental imagery also take the *-ing* participle to the exclusion of the base form because the speaker/writer has formed an image of an action in progress and is reporting the image:

$$\text{I can easily} \left\{ \begin{array}{l} \text{remember} \\ \text{imagine} \\ \text{recall} \\ \text{picture} \end{array} \right\} \begin{array}{l} \text{Billy} \\ \text{(him)} \end{array} \left\{ \begin{array}{l} \text{stealing} \\ \text{*steal} \end{array} \right\} \text{a cookie from the jar.}$$

We can paraphrase any of these sentences using "in the act of," e.g.:

I can easily picture Billy in the act of stealing a cookie from the jar.

However, some of these mental imagery verbs are ambiguous in that they can also be used to report facts:

$$\text{I} \left\{ \begin{array}{l} \text{remember} \\ \text{recall} \end{array} \right\} \text{(the fact) that Billy stole a cookie from the jar.}$$

The paraphrase for such a factual report would not be the above mental image construction with an object + participle but a possessive + gerund complement:[6]

$$\text{I} \left\{ \begin{array}{l} \text{remember} \\ \text{recall} \end{array} \right\} \begin{array}{l} \text{Billy's} \\ \text{(his)} \end{array} \text{stealing a cookie from the jar.}$$

---

6. Remember, however, that the possessive form in the possessive + gerund construction is often simplified to an object form. With some verbs this simplification creates ambiguity by making the mental imagery complement and the factual report complement homophonous.

In other words, *remember* and *recall* have two distinct functions taking correspondingly different types of complementation (see pages 474–476).

Conclusion

Much more could be said about the English complementation system. In this chapter we have limited ourselves to treating several topics that have traditionally caused problems for ESL/EFL students.

TEACHING SUGGESTIONS

1   Learning the rules of raising or those for forming complex passives both require students to become aware of a variety of syntactic forms operating in English which essentially share the same meaning. As we have been careful to underscore all along, however, a particular discourse context will favor the use of one form over the other.

In order to help ESL/EFL students become sensitive to the semantic synonymity and to the contextual differences, a teacher should present variations of a syntactic structure in different contexts, even if the context consists only of an immediately preceding or following utterance or clause, e.g.:

Raising:
It was enlightening for me to read the paper since I had never thought much about the
    topic before.
The paper was enlightening to read since it dealt with an area I had never thought much
    about before.

Complex passive:
A: Who did they offer the position to?
B: Norma. She was felt to be better qualified than the other applicants.
                    * * * *
C: Why did Norma get the offer?
D: It was felt that she was better qualified than the other applicants.

Once students develop some insight into the different uses based on such limited contexts, analysis of "authentic" language would be a useful activity for reinforcing the similarities and distinctions among the forms. The newspaper or news magazines, for instance, would be good sources of contexts containing complex passives. Divide your class into small groups and have each group of students locate the complex passives in a given article, describe their form, say why the particular form was used here, and suggest what would be necessary in the way of rewriting the article if a different form of the complex passive had been used instead.

2   The idea of using skits to give students practice with verbs and adjectives taking subjunctive complements was suggested by Shari Berman and Jayne Osgood. The teacher writes a skit which contains lots of examples of subjunctive complements. The students are assigned or volunteer for the various roles. The skit is then practiced and performed. Whether or not lines are memorized would be left up to the teacher to decide. After the skit is performed once, other students may be selected to take the roles for a second or third performance. Once the students are somewhat familiar with the skit, they may be given slips of paper with various lines from the skit and asked (in small groups) to put the lines of the skit into the order in which they occurred in the original. Ultimately, students may be asked to reconstruct the skit from memory by working together in small groups on the task.

Berman and Osgood have suggested that a meeting of the local school board would provide a setting for the skit in which subjunctive complements would naturally occur. The event might be the election of a new chairperson. Expressions such as, "I suggest that...," "I move that...," "It is essential that..." could be incorporated into the lines of the skit.

3   Sally Yates and Bill Heenan have developed a lesson for advanced learners in which they suggest using a role play to give students practice with expressions taking the subjunctive. The following steps are a slightly altered version of their lesson.

a. Introduction: I am from the World Bank. You are representatives of various countries seeking loans. You need to present arguments to get aid from the bank in various areas, e.g., education, agriculture, medicine, transportation, electric power. In formulating your arguments use such expressions as, "it's necessary that...," "it's important...," "it's essential...," "it's vital...," and verbs such as "demand," "recommend," "suggest," "request," and "ask."

b. Role play: Students engage in presenting their cases to the official from the World Bank. After each student has argued his or her case, the official makes recommendations as to how the funds are to be allotted. The official states his or her reasons for the recommendations. The entire role play is tape-recorded.

c. Analysis: The tape is replayed and the students make observations about the form of the verbs in the expression they were asked to use. If they haven't used the subjunctive themselves, the teacher will act as the official from the World Bank.

d. Practice: Students (on their own or in small groups) summarize in writing the recommendations of the official from the World Bank. The students will hopefully be using the subjunctive in their summaries, e.g., "S/he recommended that Ghana be given a million dollars and urged that they spend the money on health care."

e. Feedback: Students can read their summaries to each other or the teacher can collect them to determine if students have understood the structure.

4   Martin (1981) presents the causatives embedded within a dialog in which the students are prompted to give the correct answer for the presentation:

T:	Give me your pen, please.	S:	Here you are.
T:	I had X give me her pen.		
T:	Give me your pen, please.	S:	No.
T:	Come on, please give it to me. I need it.	S:	O.K. Here you are.
T:	I got X to give me his pen.		
T:	Give me your pen, please.	S:	No.
T (menacing gesture):	Give it to me.	S:	Here you are.
T:	I made X give me his pen.		

The teacher then elicits from the students the explanation for what they have seen.

The teacher can then ask a mixture of questions which require students to use causative constructions, e.g.:

If your son/daughter is disobedient, what do you do? (make him/her go to bed, go to his/her room, be quiet, etc.)

If your husband/wife doesn't want to go to the movies, but you really want to go, what do you do? (get him/her to go)

If the heel on your shoe is broken, what do you do? (go to a shoemaker and have him/her repair the shoe)

Etc.

5   A good situation for getting intermediate ESL/EFL students to practice the causative "have" is the barbershop/beauty parlor (suggested by Jill Rosenheim and Sue Weingarten). In an ESL context, students may be asked to visit a barbershop or beauty parlor and learn what the services are. There are a lot of things one can have done: have your hair cut, styled, blow-dried, permanented, colored; have your nails manicured, pedicured, etc. Students could write dialogs in groups in which these operations are included. The dialogs the different groups produced could be exchanged and practiced by other groups.

6   A teacher can make use of pictures to present the point that in certain sensory verb complements referring to physical position agentive subjects can take both plain and -*ing* verb forms whereas nonagentive subjects take only the -*ing* form. For instance, the teacher can show the class a picture of a building. The teacher can then place a picture of a man leaning against the building and say:

$$\text{I saw a man} \left\{ \begin{matrix} \text{leaning} \\ \text{lean} \end{matrix} \right\} \text{against the building.}$$

Next the teacher can place a picture of a ladder against the building and say:

$$\text{I saw a ladder} \left\{ \begin{matrix} \text{leaning} \\ \text{*lean} \end{matrix} \right\} \text{against the building.}$$

The teacher can provide a few more examples such as "a girl" vs. "a pair of glasses" "lying on a bed." Students can then be asked to figure out the rule. Once they are able to do so, they can be asked to make up their own examples and to illustrate them. These they can share with each other at a later time, after the teacher has had a chance to check to see if they have all understood the rule.

EXERCISES

Test your understanding of what has been presented

1. Provide an original example sentence for each of the following concepts. Underline the pertinent word(s) in your examples.

>   object plus infinitive
>   subject raising
>   object raising
>   complex passive
>   causative verb
>   sensory verb complement
>   verb ⎫
>   noun ⎬ taking a subjunctive clause
>   adjective ⎭

2. Give tree diagrams and complete derivations for the following:

a. We want him to stay here.

b. Marge is thought to have passed the test.

c. It is essential that you be on time.

d. The teacher told Tom to rewrite his composition.

3. Compare the sentences within each of the following pairs. In what ways are they similar? How are they different?

a. I advised him to leave soon.
   I advised that he leave soon.
b. It is relaxing to do deep-breathing exercises.
   Deep-breathing exercises are relaxing (to do).
c. It was reported that the hometown team had won the tournament.
   The hometown team was reported to have won the tournament.
d. I recall their making that point.
   I recall them making that point.

Test your ability to apply what you know

4. If your students produce the following sentences, what errors have they made? How will you make them aware of the errors, and what exercises will you prepare to correct the errors?

a. *I insist that you will apologize.
b. *John made Roger to steal the money.
c. *She saw the fishing-pole lean against the house.
d. *I told that he'd be sorry.
e. *It is imperative he does the job.

5. Jespersen (1964) notes that one difference between the causative *have* and the auxiliary *have* has to do with their pronunciation in colloquial speech and that this difference could disambiguate sentences like this one:

The car which he had polished sparkled in the sun.

Can you detect the difference? What is it?

6. We have seen how the subjunctive is used in this chapter with certain verbs, nouns, and adjectives; earlier we saw its use with conditionals. There is one other context in which we encounter the subjunctive in English, and that is in certain formulaic expressions such as:

Long live the King!

Can you think of other such expressions in which the subjunctive survives in the language?

7. In other languages, like Spanish, for instance, the subjunctive plays a much more important role than it does in English in that it indicates the attitude of the speaker toward what he or she is saying. For the sake of those students who speak languages where the subjunctive is more important than it is in English, can you briefly summarize the more limited use of the English subjunctive form?

BIBLIOGRAPHY

References

Black, A. (1977). "Accusative vs. Genitive as the Subject of the Gerund." Unpublished English 215 paper, UCLA, fall, 1977.

Frank, M. (1972). *Modern English: A Practical Reference Guide.* Englewood Cliffs, N.J.: Prentice-Hall.

Jespersen, O. (1939). *Essentials of English Grammar.* New York: Henry Holt and Co. Also (1964) by University, Ala.: University of Alabama Press.

Kirsner, R. S., and S. A. Thompson (1976). "The Role of Pragmatic Inference in Semantics: A Study of Sensory-Verb Complements in English," *Glossa* 10:2, 200–240.

Marckwardt, A., and F. Wolcott (1938). *Facts about Current English Usage.* New York: Appleton-Century-Crofts.

Martin, W. (1981). "Causative Verbs in English." Unpublished Independent Professional Project, School for International Training, Brattleboro, Vt.

Quirk, R., S. Greenbaum, G. Leech, and J. Svartvik (1972). *A Grammar of Contemporary English*. New York: Seminar Press.

Thomson, A. J., and A. Martinet (1969). *A Practical English Grammar*. London: Oxford University Press.

Suggestions for further reading

For accounts of raising, see:

Baker, C. L. (1978). *Introduction to Generative-Transformational Syntax*. Englewood Cliffs, N.J.: Prentice-Hall.

Postal, P. (1974). *On Raising*. Cambridge, Mass.: MIT Press.

Stockwell, R. P., P. Schachter, and B. H. Partee (1973). *The Major Syntactic Structures of English*. New York: Holt, Rinehart and Winston, Chap. 8.

For analyses of complex passives, see:

Lees, R. B. (1960). *The Grammar of English Nominalizations*. *IJAL* Publication 12, Indiana University, Bloomington, Ind.

Stockwell, R. P., P. Schachter, and B. H. Partee (1973). *The Major Syntactic Structures of English*. New York: Holt, Rinehart and Winston, Chap. 8.

For suggestions on how to teach complex passives, see:

Rutherford, W. E. (1975). *Modern English* (2d ed., vol. 1). New York: Harcourt Brace Jovanovich. See unit 15, especially p. 313.

For a discussion of the *forms* of causative constructions in English, consult:

Hudson, R. A. (1971). *English Complex Sentences: An Introduction to Systemic Grammar*. North Holland Linguistic Series. Amsterdam: North-Holland Publishing Co., pp. 188, 204–212.

To further study the historical development of the subjunctive in English, consult:

Harsh, W. (1968). *The Subjunctive in English*. University, Ala.: University of Alabama Press.

For a corpus-based frequency study of several different English complement structures, see:

Van Ek, J. A. (1966). *Four Complementary Structures of Predication in Contemporary British English*. Groningen: Wolters.

35

Degree—Comparatives and Equatives

GRAMMATICAL DESCRIPTION

Introduction

One of the most basic and powerful of human cognitive processes is the ability to comprehend and express the fact that there is some similarity or difference between two things. Usually such a similarity or difference is expressed in terms of degree, extent, quantity, etc. This chapter describes the two most important English constructions used to express similarities or differences, i.e., the equative and comparative constructions, respectively. We will also discuss the major ways in which the languages of the world express comparison.

From the outset, it is important that we distinguish the *absolute* use of adjectives or adverbs from the *relative* use of such words:

> ABSOLUTE: John is *tall.*
> John runs *fast.*
> RELATIVE: John is *tall*er than Bill.
> John runs *fast*er than Bill.

There are important semantic differences in these two underlying uses. For example, if we negate the assertion with the absolute form and conjoin the resulting negative statement with the affirmative statement, we produce a contradiction:

> *John is tall, but he isn't tall.

A contradiction does not result, however, when we conjoin the same negative absolute assertion with the sentence containing the affirmative relative usage:

> John is taller than Bill, but he (i.e., John) isn't tall.

The reason for this difference is that words such as *tall(er)* and *fast(er)* can be used in a relative sense without making any absolute assertion about the referent's height or speed.

In this chapter we will be discussing comparative and equative constructions, which involve the relative rather than the absolute use of such words.

491

Typological considerations

There seem to be at least four different ways in which languages of the world express comparison. We will use English words below to exemplify these different construction types.[1]

Comparison by juxtaposition[2]

Some languages express comparison by mere juxtaposition of clauses and have no explicit syntactic device or construction for expressing comparison, e.g.:

> My boat (is) big.   ("Your boat is bigger than mine.")
> Your boat (is) very big.

Limited scope comparison

Some languages such as Chinese and Japanese compare by limiting the scope of an adjective—or some other part of speech—so that it has a relative rather than an absolute meaning, e.g.:

> Compare(d) (to) } Mary John (is) tall.   ("John is taller than Mary.")
> From
> John compare(d) to Mary (is) tall.

"Surpass" comparatives

Still other languages such as many West African or Bantu languages express comparison using a verb that means "to pass" or "to surpass," e.g.:

> John { pass / surpass }   Mary (in) { tallness / height } .   ("John is taller than Mary.")

Many languages of this type cannot directly express the reverse of such a statement, i.e., Mary is shorter than John.[3]

Comparison using degree morphemes

Finally, there are languages like English (i.e., most Indo-European languages) which have developed verbs or adjectives or quantifiers, i.e., words like *more* and *less,* and which use these words or morphemes to directly express comparison, e.g.:

> John (is) tall MORE than Mary.   ("John is taller than Mary.")
> Mary (is) { short MORE / tall LESS }   than John.   ("Mary is shorter/less tall than John.")

---

1. For some examples of these constructions in other languages, see Celce-Murcia (1972:160–167).

2. We had been unaware of this typological pattern until R. Longacre (personal communication) informed us that several languages of New Guinea expressed comparison this way. Then later, Bonnie Glover (personal communication) confirmed that this mode of comparing also occurs in some American Indian languages.

3. Martin Mould (personal communication) has told us, for example, that Igbo and most Bantu languages cannot reverse such a "surpass" comparison to directly express the notion that "Mary is shorter than John"; i.e., the *pass* verb can only be used to compare in a positive direction. However, not all languages having a "surpass" comparative are quite so restricted. Dolly Meyers (personal communication) has informed us that in Yoruba it is possible to say "Mary surpasses John in shortness." At the moment we do not know whether Yoruba always had this flexibility or whether it acquired flexibility through internal change or through contact with other languages of the type discussed under "Comparison using degree morphemes."

In such languages, comparisons can always be reversed, but one form is usually preferred over the other in any given discourse context for semantic and/or pragmatic reasons. As we shall see below, the unmarked or positive form occurs most frequently.

Error types

In the preceding section we have seen that all languages have ways of expressing comparison but that the devices used can differ greatly from one language to another. Depending on the type(s) of comparison used in the native language of your students, different types of problems will occur, especially at the initial stage of learning. Then as students become more advanced, developmental errors occur that have nothing at all to do with first language interference.

Here are some of the common errors:

1. Omission of the comparative inflection—and perhaps also the copula:

    *John (is) tall than Mary.

2. Substitution of some other function word for *than* (a) or inappropriate use of *than* (b):

    a. *John is tall(er) from Mary.   b. *Paul is as tall than John.

3. Use of *more* where *-er* is required or vice versa:

    *John is $\left\{ \begin{array}{l} \text{tall more} \\ \text{more tall} \end{array} \right\}$ than Mary.   *Mary is beautifuller than Karen.

4. Use of a regular pattern where an irregular form is required:

    *His handwriting is badder than mine.

5. Double marking of the comparative:

    *Jim runs more faster than Paul.   *This car is more better than that one.

While the first three errors may be explained in terms of negative transfer or interference—it depends on the learner's native language—the last two are developmental errors that young English-speaking children also produce during first language acquisition.

What makes comparison in English difficult

Partly related to the developmental errors discussed above, there are a number of other factors the ESL/EFL teacher must be aware of in order to teach comparison effectively.

The range of construction types

Most reference grammars and ESL/EFL texts center their discussion of comparison in English around adjectives and adverbs. Actually, every major part of speech in English (i.e., nouns, verbs, adjectives, adverbs) permits comparison.

Recall that when we formulate a comparison, we presuppose a degree of *difference,* e.g.:

$$X \left\{ \begin{array}{l} \text{is} \\ \text{has} \\ \text{verb} \end{array} \right\} \left\{ \begin{array}{l} \text{MORE} \\ \text{LESS} \end{array} \right\} \text{A than Y}$$

(presupposes "X is different from Y with respect to A")

Each major part of speech in English can be used with some version of the above formula to make comparisons. (This must be made clear to ESL/EFL learners, since many languages do not have as large an inventory of comparative constructions as does English.)

Adjective: John is taller than Mary (is).
    Joe is less intelligent than Sam (is).

Adverb: Bill runs faster than Peter ($\left\{\begin{array}{l}\text{runs}\\\text{does}\end{array}\right\}$).

    Judy dances less gracefully than Sally ($\left\{\begin{array}{l}\text{dances}\\\text{does}\end{array}\right\}$).

Noun: Jack has more money than Harry ($\left\{\begin{array}{l}\text{has}\\\text{does}\end{array}\right\}$).

    Max has $\left\{\begin{array}{l}\text{fewer books}\\\text{less money}\end{array}\right\}$ than I ($\left\{\begin{array}{l}\text{have}\\\text{do}\end{array}\right\}$).

Verb: Paul weighs more than Alex (does).
    This book costs more than that one (does).

The ESL/EFL teacher must make sure that his or her students practice all of these patterns, and not just the adjective and adverb patterns illustrated in the first two sets of examples.

Collectively, these examples raise a number of problems and questions that we will discuss in the following subsection.

Morphological and syntactic variation

1. *Use of* more *vs.* -er

The decision of when to use *more* vs. *-er* with comparative adjectives and adverbs is a complicated process, since no one has carried out a study to fully determine current usage. In the absence of a more definitive, empirically based statement, we feel that some version of Frank's three-part formulation (1972:118–119) is the best set of rules available:

Part 1:   Use *-er* with one-syllable adjectives and adverbs and with those two-syllable adjectives ending in *-y*[4] or *-ple, -ble* and occasionally *-tle, -dle:*[5]

taller	happier	simpler
faster	noisier	humbler
harder	dirtier	subtler
		idler

Part 2:   Use either *-er* or *more* with two-syllable adjectives that take the following weakly stressed endings:[6]

-ly /liy/: friendlier, more friendly
-ow /ow/: mellower, more mellow
-er /ər/: cleverer, more clever
-some /səm/: handsomer, more handsome

    Note that there are also some two-syllable adjectives without any of the above suffixes which can take either *-er* or *more,* e.g., *stupid, quiet.*

Part 3:   Use *more* with other adjectives and adverbs of two or more syllables:[7]

    distant, exact, useful, wretched, etc.   arrogant, intelligent, beautiful, etc.

---

4. Note the change of spelling (*y* ⟶ *i*) when *-er* is added.

5. Note that one syllable is lost when the *-er* is added to the last four endings with the result that both the base form and the comparative form have two syllables.

6. Frank (1972:118) feels that the *-er* forms are less formal than their equivalents with periphrastic *more.*

7. Frank further points out (1972:118–119) that two-syllable adjectives ending in the following suffixes or consonant clusters usually take *more: -ous, -ish, -ful, -ing, -ed, -ct, -nt,* and *-st.*

Frank's rule notwithstanding, students should understand that the basic form of the comparative is *more* and that the *-er* forms are surface lexical manifestations of *more* + $\begin{Bmatrix} \text{Adj} \\ \text{Adv} \end{Bmatrix}$. Also, in our rules we should talk about "adjective stems" and not just "adjectives" since derived forms with three or more syllables also occur with *-er* (e.g., *unhappier*) if the stem form of the adjective fits the first or second part of the above rule.

As Frank's set of rules and our comments have suggested, there is a good deal of variability in the usage of comparative forms. Many two-syllable adjective stems must be listed in the lexicon according to whether they take *-er,* or *more,* or either, to express a comparison. For example, in Part 2 of the rule given above, we pointed out the variation that exists between comparative forms such as *cleverer* and *more clever.* Here the *-er* form is more informal and the periphrastic form with *more* would be preferred in formal speech and writing. Other adjectives that end in a weak *-er* syllable such as *tender* would follow the same tendencies. A good rule of thumb for nonnative speakers is the following: when the adjective has two or more syllables and you are in doubt, use *more;* the worst mistake you will make is a register error.

However, nonnative speakers should also be advised that the comparative affix *-er* is sometimes used by native speakers for effect (i.e., to get attention) in literature or other forms of creative writing. These are cases where the normal rules would not lead us to expect an *-er* comparative. The most famous example of this is perhaps when Lewis Carroll made Alice say "curiouser and curiouser!" in *Alice in Wonderland.* (We would normally use *more* not *-er* with an adjective that ends in *-ous,* such as *curious.*)

2. *Use of* less *vs.* fewer

A much less complicated rule describes the distribution of *less* and *fewer,* the negative counterparts of *more. More* may be used before both count and mass nouns, but in formal contexts *less* changes to *fewer* before count nouns, e.g.:

I have more $\begin{Bmatrix} \text{money} \\ \text{books} \end{Bmatrix}$ than Mr. Sims (does).

Mr. Sims has $\begin{Bmatrix} \text{less money} \\ \text{fewer books} \end{Bmatrix}$ than I (do).

In informal conversation, however, *less* often occurs before countable nouns rather than *fewer.*

3. *Clause reductions and case adjustments*

By now you may have noticed that the constituent following *than* sometimes resembles a reduced clause:

She has more books than I $\begin{Bmatrix} \text{have} \\ \text{do} \end{Bmatrix}$

and sometimes a noun phrase:

She has more books than John.

In the latter situation if a pronoun follows *than,* it tends to change from subject to object form (i.e., a subject form standing alone seems a bit awkward):

She has more books than $\begin{Bmatrix} \text{?I} \\ \text{me} \end{Bmatrix}$

In other words, if no verb or auxiliary follows the noun phrase, English speakers tend to analyze it as an object of a preposition because even though *than* is a complementizer, it also has prepositional force.

Irregular comparative forms

There are a number of irregular comparative adjective and adverb forms in English that cannot be explained with reference to the *-er* inflection or the periphrastic form *more:*

Base form	Irregular comparative form
much / many	more
little	less
good	better
bad	worse
far	farther (distance)
far	further (nonspatial progression)
old	elder (comparing ages of siblings)
	(*older* is the regular form used elsewhere)

In informal usage, *further* is often used instead of *farther* to compare distance, and in all contexts *older* is frequently used to refer to a sibling of greater age, i.e., *elder* is becoming somewhat archaic even in this function. The most common irregular comparative forms, *better* and *worse,* must be presented and practiced apart from the regular forms to help avoid errors such as these:

$$\text{*I'm speaking English} \begin{Bmatrix} \text{more better} \\ \text{gooder} \end{Bmatrix} \text{now.}$$

Substitute expressions used with comparatives

Another source of difficulty that we wish to discuss are the substitute expressions commonly used in comparative constructions. Since English comparative constructions often involve two clauses, the second of which has been greatly reduced, certain substitute expressions commonly occur as part of a comparison. The possessive pronouns are one such type of substitute expression:

> This car is bigger than *mine* (is). (= my car)

However, when a possessive pronoun is not appropriate, the substitute expressions *one* and *ones* are often used along with an appropriate determiner such as the definite article or a demonstrative:

> This car is bigger than that *one*.[8] (= car)
> The blue books are cheaper than the red *ones*. (= books)

The substitutes *one* and *ones* may also occur without a definite determiner to replace a modified noun with indefinite or generic reference:

> A wool garment is warmer than a cotton *one*.
> Wool garments are warmer than cotton *ones*.

---

8. In standard English the plural substitute *ones* does not follow a plural demonstrative:

These cars are bigger than those (*ones).

In more formal contexts the demonstrative substitutes *that* and *those* may be used in a comparison to introduce the second of two prepositional phrases; possessive constructions formed with *of the* are especially common in this type of construction:

The financial resources of the Republicans are greater than those of the Democrats.

A common error committed by both native and nonnative speakers is deletion of the demonstrative and *of the* in such a context:

*The financial resources of the Republicans are greater than the Democrats.

The substitutes *that* and *those* also introduce relative clauses that are part of a comparison:

Food which we cook at home is often better than that which we eat in a restaurant.

Again, there is a tendency on the part of both native and nonnative speakers to erroneously simplify such a construction. The result is an error such as the following:

*Food (which) we cook at home is often better than in a restaurant.

In both cases cited above, i.e., the possessive phrase and the relative clause, the speaker/writer must maintain parallel structure in the reduced clause following " $\left\{ \begin{matrix} more \\ -er \end{matrix} \right\}$ ... than" in order to produce a grammatical sentence. The demonstrative substitutes *that* and *those* help satisfy the parallelism condition in such contexts.

The possessive pronouns and the *one, ones* substitutes tend to occur in informal language, whereas the substitutes *that* and *those* are more typical of formal usage. Sometimes either substitute can be used, with the only difference being one of register:

INFORMAL: The stories she wrote 10 years ago are more interesting than the ones she is writing now.

FORMAL: The stories (which) she wrote 10 years ago are more interesting than those (which) she is writing now.

Other comparative constructions

In addition to the four major types of comparative constructions outlined above, there are a number of other types of comparatives that the ESL/EFL teacher should be aware of such as the following:

Type of comparison	Example
Comparison of two different properties of the same object rather than one property of two different objects.	The river is wider than it is deep.
Comparison involving two or more properties as well as two or more objects.	John enjoys movies more than I enjoy the theater.
Comparison with a measure phrase rather than another object used as the standard of comparison.	Mark is more than six feet tall. The book weighs more than two kilos.
Comparison with an absolute adjective used as the standard of comparison (used a lot in advertising).	Wilt is taller than tall. (i.e., he's gigantic!) This product is newer than new. (i.e., It's the very latest.)

Type of comparison	Example
Comparison with the comparative morpheme modifying a cardinal number.	Ben has $\begin{Bmatrix} \text{more} \\ \text{fewer} \end{Bmatrix}$ than three brothers.[9]
Comparison with a measure phrase modifying the comparative morpheme.	Mark is two inches taller than Phil. Danny is three years older than Alice.
Comparison expressing a progressive change of state.[10]	Arlene is getting prettier (and prettier). Your solution is becoming more (and more) attractive.
Comparison with *of* plus a predicate noun.	He's more of a fool than I thought.
Comparisons expressing a conditional relationship.	The greater the pressure, the higher the temperature. The more you learn, the less you know.
Comparison expressing preference (i.e., *more than* = *rather than*).[11]	Peter looks for danger more than adventure.

These 10 additional comparative constructions combine with the four basic types to yield 14 different semantic and syntactic combinations. Intermediate and advanced ESL/EFL students will ultimately have to become familiar with the 10 constructions listed above. Beginners should concentrate on the four basic patterns.

Before concluding this section, we should perhaps take note of a number of other English constructions which superficially appear to be comparatives but in fact function semantically as superlatives and thus will be discussed in the following chapter rather than this one:

Type of comparative	Example
Comparatives used as suppletive variants of superlatives when there are only two members in the set.	Clem is the taller of the two boys. Cf. Clem is the tallest of the $\begin{Bmatrix} \text{three} \\ \text{four} \\ \text{etc.} \end{Bmatrix}$ boys.
Comparatives with *(n)ever*, which express a superlative meaning.	That's more people than I've ever seen. (= That's the most people (that) I've ever seen.)
Comparatives with *any other*, which express a superlative meaning.	This play is better than any other play I've seen. (= This play is the best one (that) I've seen.)

Other devices used to express comparison in English

The English language also has a number of other syntactic and lexical means to express comparison. Some of these are reminiscent of the dominant comparative construction found in certain other languages (see above).

Type	Example
Some constructions limit the scope of an adjective or adverb, thereby making its meaning relative rather than absolute (see above).	Mary is tall for a girl. John is tall compared with Joey.

9. Note that in this example a determiner (not a noun, verb, adjective, or adverb) is being compared.

10. This is sometimes called a "free comparative," terminology which was first suggested by Browne (1964).

11. This type is not a comparative of degree or extent like the others. McCawley's term (1964) for this type of construction is "qualitative comparison."

Type	*Example*
Sometimes special verbs are used to express a superior degree or extent (see above).	John's height $\begin{Bmatrix} \text{exceeds} \\ \text{surpasses} \end{Bmatrix}$ Mary's height.
As an extension of the preceding type, some derived verbs using *out-*, *under-*, and *over-* as prefixes are also inherently comparative.	Bill *out*played his opponents. The professor $\begin{Bmatrix} \text{over} \\ \text{under} \end{Bmatrix}$ rated his own worth.
One of the meanings of prepositions such as *over* and *under* is inherently comparative (i.e., is equivalent to *more than* or *less than*).	The temperature rose to over 80°F. Bob's annual salary is under $20,000.

If the ESL/EFL teacher is using a semantically based syllabus rather than a structurally based one, these other devices should also be introduced under the topic of comparison in English.

Markedness and the use of comparative forms

Many adjectives and adverbs that are commonly used to express comparison in English form oppositions:

$$
\text{positive polarity } (+) \atop \text{(unmarked form)}
\left\{
\begin{array}{l}
\text{tall—short} \\
\text{big—small, little} \\
\text{old—young} \\
\text{broad, wide—narrow} \\
\text{heavy—light} \\
\text{fast—slow} \\
\text{pretty—ugly} \\
\text{Etc.}
\end{array}
\right\}
\text{negative polarity } (-) \atop \text{(marked form)}
$$

The existence of such paired positive and negative polarity forms gives us a way to avoid the use of *less* (which sounds awkward in many contexts) and to encourage the use of *more* or *-er* as often as possible in the expression of comparison, e.g.:

> John is taller than Mary.   Mary is shorter than John.
> (?Mary is less tall than John.)

Psycholinguists call *more* and the positive polarity forms listed above "unmarked" because they are used more frequently in any given language,[12] are learned first by children, and occur with greater frequency in the languages of the world. The unmarked forms also tend to be used in neutral contexts, e.g.:

> How old (?young) are you?   What more (?less) do you want?
> How tall (?short) is John?

Psycholinguists call *less* and the negative polarity forms listed above "marked" because they are used less frequently in any given language, learned later by children,[13] and used only in highly marked contexts.

---

12. See Celce-Murcia (1972) for empirical evidence that unmarked comparatives are produced far more frequently in English than are marked ones.

13. Donaldson and Balfour (1968), for example, have demonstrated that young English-speaking children cannot correctly distinguish *less* from *more* (i.e., they consistently interpret *less* as *more*) until they have reached a certain cognitive developmental stage that occurs somewhere around the age of 5.

In an attempt to determine when and why marked comparatives are used, Ssensalo (1976) examined the *White House Transcripts* and also a large number of advertisements. In both data bases the unmarked forms predominated significantly; however, Ssensalo found that two major principles explained many of the marked or negative comparatives in the *White House Transcripts*:

1. The marked form best expresses the speaker's message or point of view, e.g.:

They will have to redesign it as a *narrower* action. (*Narrower* cannot easily be changed to *wider* or *broader* in a paraphrase.)

2. The marked form was cued by the proximity of a related word or idea, e.g.:

In the *Post* article, we're so *low* now we can't go any *lower*. (*Lower* cannot easily be changed to *higher* in a paraphrase.)

In the advertisements Ssensalo found that marked comparatives were used only about 20 percent of the time. When they occurred, they were used to indicate either the poorer quality of a rival product (e.g., the same amount of the other detergent will do *fewer* dishes) or because the marked form signals something desirable to the potential buyer (e.g., Look *younger*! We have *lower* prices).

Equative constructions

Similarity to the comparative

In many respects (i.e., both semantically and syntactically) equative constructions are similar to comparatives. However, when we formulate an equative construction, we presuppose a degree of *similarity* or *identity* (as opposed to the degree of *difference* we presuppose when we formulate a comparison), e.g.:

$$X \begin{Bmatrix} \text{is} \\ \text{has} \\ \text{verb} \end{Bmatrix} \text{ as (MUCH) A as Y}$$

$$\left(\text{``X is } \begin{Bmatrix} \text{similar} \\ \text{identical} \end{Bmatrix} \text{ to Y with respect to A''}\right)$$

The equative construction—like the comparative—occurs with all four major parts of speech:

Adjective: Mel is as tall as George (is).

Adverb: Joe runs as fast as Bill ($\begin{Bmatrix} \text{runs} \\ \text{does} \end{Bmatrix}$).

Noun: Ed has as $\begin{Bmatrix} \text{much money} \\ \text{many books} \end{Bmatrix}$ as Jack ($\begin{Bmatrix} \text{has} \\ \text{does} \end{Bmatrix}$).

Verb: Roger weighs as much as Paul ($\begin{Bmatrix} \text{weighs} \\ \text{does} \end{Bmatrix}$).

Also, the complementizer *as*—like the complementizer *than*—can be followed by a reduced clause:

$$\text{She has as many books as I } \begin{Bmatrix} \text{have} \\ \text{do} \end{Bmatrix}.$$

or simply a noun phrase:

She has as many books as John.

In the latter context if a pronoun follows *as* instead of a lexical noun, it tends to change from subject to object form in informal conversation:

$$\text{She has as many books as } \left\{ \begin{array}{c} \text{me} \\ \text{?I} \end{array} \right\} .$$

In other words, if no verb or auxiliary follows the noun phrase, English speakers tend to treat that noun as the object of a preposition. Thus the complementizer *as*—like the complementizer *than*—appears to have some of the features of a preposition.

Surface variations

Notice that the underlying *much* in the formula "as (MUCH) . . . as" changes to *many* before plural count nouns and that the *much* must be deleted before adjectives and adverbs. The failure of some ESL/EFL students to observe these syntactically motivated alternations produces errors like these:

    *Sam has as much books as Harry.   *Jill types as much fast as Jack.

The negative equative

The equative construction has a negative form, which is equivalent semantically to a negative or marked comparative:

    Paul doesn't have as much money as Peter. = Paul has less money than Peter.

In many cases this type of equative is preferable to a negative comparative with *less* or *fewer* because it is perceived as being less direct or blunt. Negative equatives are also often preferred over comparatives with negative polarity adjectives because they seem to be less awkward stylistically or—as mentioned above—more tactful and polite, e.g.:

$$\text{Mary is not } \left\{ \begin{array}{c} \text{so} \\ \text{as} \end{array} \right\} \text{ tall as John (is).}$$

$$\text{(Mary is } \left\{ \begin{array}{c} \text{?less tall} \\ \text{shorter} \end{array} \right\} \text{ than John.)}$$

$$\text{Joe doesn't run as fast as Burt (} \left\{ \begin{array}{c} \text{runs} \\ \text{does} \end{array} \right\} \text{).}$$

$$\text{(Joe runs } \left\{ \begin{array}{c} \text{?less fast} \\ \text{slower} \end{array} \right\} \text{ than Burt (} \left\{ \begin{array}{c} \text{runs} \\ \text{does} \end{array} \right\} \text{).)}$$

A complete statement of when to use the negative equative rather than a *less/fewer* comparative or a marked comparative is not available (to our knowledge). However, the ESL/EFL teacher must be aware of the problem so that sentences such as those cited above as potentially questionable are not presented and practiced in class as normal, preferred usage. (We have observed such sentences being used as models or being elicited in drills—in inappropriate ways—in ESL/EFL classrooms and textbooks.)

The use of "so (MUCH) . . . as"

As one of the above examples indicates, *so* may replace the first *as* of the equative formula when it is immediately preceded by *not:*

$$\text{Mary is not } \left\{ \begin{array}{c} \text{so} \\ \text{as} \end{array} \right\} \text{ tall as John (is).}$$

Certain negative words other than *not* also account for some of the variation of *so* with *as*:

$$\textit{Nothing} \text{ is } \left\{ \begin{array}{c} \text{so} \\ \text{as} \end{array} \right\} \text{ exciting as this!}$$

$$\text{I've } \textit{never} \text{ seen } \textit{anyone} \left\{ \begin{array}{c} \text{so} \\ \text{as} \end{array} \right\} \text{ happy as Sue.}$$

Etc.

In addition to sentences like those above with overtly negative words such as *not, nothing,* and *never, so* may also occur instead of *as* in at least two other types of sentences that have the potential for negative (as well as positive) implication:

Wh-questions: What is $\left\{ \begin{array}{c} \text{so} \\ \text{as} \end{array} \right\}$ rare as a day in June?

("There is nothing $\left\{ \begin{array}{c} \text{so} \\ \text{as} \end{array} \right\}$ rare as a day in June.")

Conditionals: I'll be happy $\left\{ \begin{array}{c} \text{so} \\ \text{as} \end{array} \right\}$ long as I have you.

("If I don't have you, I won't be happy.")

A number of other factors must also be considered in accounting for *so/as* variation. First of all, the acceptability of *so* greatly diminishes when there are other lexical items intervening between the negative word and *so/as:*

$$\text{Joe does not speak} \left\{ \begin{array}{c} \text{as} \\ \text{?so} \end{array} \right\} \text{well as Mark.}$$

However, the probability of *so* occurring increases when an adverb with negative associations such as *nearly* (= not exactly) directly precedes the equative construction:

$$\text{Joe} \left\{ \begin{array}{c} \text{doesn't} \\ \text{does not} \end{array} \right\} \text{speak nearly} \left\{ \begin{array}{c} \text{so} \\ \text{as} \end{array} \right\} \text{well as Mark.}$$

Also, since *so* is perceived as somewhat formal—perhaps even literary—or slightly archaic, its use diminishes when *not* is contracted and there is no adverb like *nearly* present:

$$\text{Mary isn't} \left\{ \begin{array}{c} \text{as} \\ \text{?so} \end{array} \right\} \text{tall as John.}$$

The potential ambiguity of *as well as*

Because of the deletions that occur in degree constructions, sometimes these constructions are ambiguous. Consider, for example, a sentence such as the following:

Jane can type as well as Sarah.

In one interpretation "Jane is as good a typist as Sarah" and *as well as* expresses the similarity in their degrees of proficiency as typists. The other meaning for this sentence is "In addition to Sarah, Jane can also type" and *as well as* is functioning as a prepositional logical connector; i.e., no element of degree is being expressed.

Conclusion

This chapter has in no way exhausted all that could be said about comparative and equative constructions in English. We have not provided a syntactic analysis (i.e., tree diagrams and derivations) because the available transformational descriptions were either inadequate or too complicated to incorporate here. Furthermore, it is obvious that a number of important questions of usage (e.g., *-er* vs. *more*) deserve careful future study.

TEACHING SUGGESTIONS

1 A good way to introduce comparison of adjectives (the simplest pattern) is to give your students information about people and ask them to make comparisons:

	Age	Height	GPA	Number of pounds he can press
Hamid	22	5'8"	3.7	150
Mario	19	5'10"	3.1	200

Examples: Mario is taller than Hamid.
Hamid is older than Mario.
Etc.

2 To introduce comparison of noun quantities, have your students compare the amount of coins and money that two people have in their wallets:

	Pennies	Nickels	Dimes	Quarters	Dollars	Total money
Greta	3	2	4	2	5	$6.03
Christine	2	4	1	3	4	$5.07

Example: Greta has more pennies than Christine.
(*or* Greta has one more penny than Christine.)
Etc.

3 One of the best ways to integrate different patterns of comparison is to give a variety of data concerning two people such that the data naturally elicit a variety of comparative structures:

	Age	Height	Weight	Year in college	Number of classes this term	Can run the mile in:
Pablo	20	6'	170 lb	Junior	4	4½ minutes
Marc	21	6'2"	180 lb	Senior	3	5 minutes

Examples: Marc weighs more than Pablo.
Pablo runs (the mile) faster than Marc.
Etc.

4 A realistic environment for eliciting negative polarity (or marked) comparatives is to show students objects—or present them with situations where both things are smaller, shorter, less, etc., than normal. In such a case, it makes sense to use a negative polarity form, e.g.:

a. Two pencils—both short but one more so than the other: "The blue pencil is shorter than the yellow one."

b. Two cars—both new but one newer than the other (Last year George bought his car March 1st and Alice bought her car April 15th): "Alice's car is newer than George's (car)."

c. Stick figures of Stan and Bill (Stan is short. Bill is very short): "Bill is shorter than Stan."

    Etc.

5   To introduce equatives use the concept of identical twins so that equatives can be practiced naturally.

	Age	Height	Weight	Number of brothers and sisters	Year in college
Sandra	18	5'5"	115 lb.	3	freshman
Sheila	18	5'5"	115 lb.	3	freshman

Examples: Sandra is as $\begin{Bmatrix} \text{old} \\ \text{tall} \end{Bmatrix}$ as Sheila.

               Sheila weighs as much as Sandra.
               etc.

6   Negative equatives can be presented as a tactful alternative to negative polarity comparatives. Use information like that in the chart in 1 above. Then introduce two people: Marta, who is direct and often rude, and Theo, who is polite and tactful. Show how they would report the same facts differently:

Marta: Hamid is shorter than Mario.
Theo: Hamid is not as tall as Mario.

Marta: Mario is dumber than Hamid.
Theo: Mario is not as intelligent as Hamid.
          Etc.

7   Comparatives and equatives can often be combined if information about cities, states, or countries can be assembled for purposes of comparison:

	Area	Population	Year of statehood	State bird	Highest point
Kentucky	about 40,000 sq. miles	3,500,000	1792	Cardinal	4,150 ft.
Virginia	about 40,000 sq. miles	5,000,000	1788	Cardinal	5,730 ft.

Example: Kentucky is the same size as Virginia.
          Virginia has a larger population than Kentucky.
          Etc.

8   One way of teaching free comparatives is to present information about an individual over a period of time:

Sally	Age	5	7	9	11
	Height	3'	3'9"	4'5"	5'2"

Example: Sally $\left\{\begin{array}{l}\text{is}\\\text{has been}\end{array}\right\}$ getting taller and taller.

Harvey

Age	10	13	16	19	21
GPA	2.5	2.9	3.3	3.6	3.8

Example: Harvey $\left\{\begin{array}{l}\text{is}\\\text{has been}\end{array}\right\}$ getting smarter and smarter.

(or)   Harvey $\left\{\begin{array}{l}\text{is}\\\text{has been}\end{array}\right\}$ studying harder and harder.

9 You can present the use of *-er* vs. *more* to your students by contrasting short, informal adjectives with longer, more formal adjectives in a context where both types of adjectives are being used to make similar comparisons.

Situation:
Mrs. Harrison owns a public relations firm. She is creating a new position and asks her manager if she should promote Ms. Franklin or Ms. Thomas.

Manager (on the phone with Mrs. Harrison):
Oh, I'd hire Ms. Thomas. She's *smarter, works harder,* and is much *friendlier.*

Manager (in a written memo to Mrs. Harrison):
I recommend Ms. Thomas for the promotion because she is *more intelligent* and *more industrious* than the other person being considered. Also, Ms. Thomas is *more personable,* which will also be an important asset to bring to the new position.

EXERCISES

Test your understanding of what has been presented

1. Provide an original example sentence for each of the following terms. Underline the pertinent word(s) in your examples.

the comparative construction	relative use of adverbs
the equative construction	free comparative
irregular comparative adverb	unmarked adjective
absolute use of adjectives	

2. Describe the ambiguity in the following sentences:

a. Phyllis likes Carol more than Sue.   b. Mark teaches Sam as well as Ralph.

3. What part of speech is being compared in the following sentences?

a. Harry throws the ball farther than Ned does.
b. John has more than two cars.
c. I bought more oranges than we can eat.
d. This book costs more than I want to pay.
e. This movie is more interesting than the one we saw last week.

4. Why are the following sentences awkward or questionable?

a. ?Joan sings less well than Sally.   b. ?Mary is less tall than Alice.

Test your ability to apply what you know

5. If your students produce the following sentences, what errors have they made? How will you make them aware of their errors? What exercises will you prepare to correct them?

a. *To make the story more short, I'll just tell you the ending.
b. *I like this book more better than that one.
c. *I was lucky than my little brother.
d. *John is as tall that Joe.
e. *The newspapers in Los Angeles have better international coverage than in San Diego.

6. Many languages express the free comparative with its meaning of progressive change in a way that more clearly parallels more formal English constructions like these:

He grew ever taller.   It became progressively more overcast.

To learners who are only familiar with such a construction, how would you present the more frequent and more colloquial English construction? For example:

He grew taller and taller.   It became more and more overcast.

7. Consider the following sentences:

a. I've seen monkeys more intelligent than Herbert.   b. I've seen more intelligent monkeys than Herbert.

What's the difference in meaning?

8. A student brings you a magazine article that contains the following:

Benjamin Franklin was both smarter and loyaler than . . . .

He asks you why the writer used *loyaler* instead of *more loyal.* He thinks *loyaler* may be a mistake and wants your opinion. What would you say to the student?

BIBLIOGRAPHY

References

Browne, W. (1964). "On Adjectival Comparisons and Reduplication in English." Unpublished paper, MIT Department of Linguistics.
Celce-Murcia, M. (1972). "A Syntactic and Psycholinguistic Study of Comparison in English." Unpublished Ph.D. dissertation in Linguistics, UCLA.
Donaldson, M., and G. Balfour (1968). "Less Is More: A Study of Language Comprehension in Children," *British Journal of Psychology* 59:461–472.
Frank, M. (1972). *Modern English: A Practical Reference Guide.* Englewood Cliffs, N.J.: Prentice-Hall.
McCawley, J. D. (1964). "Quantitative and Qualitative Comparison in English." Paper presented at the annual LSA winter meeting, New York, Dec. 29, 1964.
Ssensalo, D. A. (1976). "Markedness and the Usage of Comparatives." Unpublished M.A. thesis in TESL, UCLA.

Suggestions for further reading

For reference grammars with useful accounts of the English comparative, see:

Frank, M. (1972). See citation in above references.

Jespersen, O. (1964). *Essentials of English Grammar.* University, Ala.: University of Alabama Press.
Quirk, R., and S. Greenbaum (1973). *A Concise Grammar of Contemporary English.* New York: Harcourt Brace Jovanovich.

For a transformational analysis of the comparative and the equative construction in English, see Celce-Murcia (1972) in the above references, pp. 35–84.

For ESL/EFL texts with good ideas for teaching the comparative, see:

Azar, B. S. (1981). *Understanding and Using English Grammar.* Englewood Cliffs, N.J.: Prentice-Hall, Chap. 13.
Brinton, D., and R. Neuman (1982). *Getting Along: English Grammar and Writing* (Book 1). Englewood Cliffs, N.J.: Prentice-Hall, Chap. 14.
Danielson, D., and R. Hayden (1973). *Using English: Your Second Language.* Englewood Cliffs, N.J.: Prentice-Hall, Chap. 14.
Fingado, G., et al. (1981). *The English Connection.* Cambridge, Mass.: Winthrop Publishing, Chap. 10.
Praninskas, J. (1975). *Rapid Review of English Grammar,* Lesson 18. Englewood Cliffs, N.J.: Prentice-Hall.

36

Degree—Complements and Superlatives

GRAMMATICAL DESCRIPTION

Introduction

In this chapter we continue the discussion of degree constructions that we began in the preceding chapter, which covered comparatives and equatives. First of all, we discuss several degree complements expressing notions such as "excess" (*too much/too many*), "insufficiency" (*too little/too few*), "sufficiency" (*enough*), and "causality" (*so much/so many; so little/so few* and *such*). Then we briefly examine the absolute use of *too* and *so* with attention to contexts where they function as emphatic counterparts of the intensifier *very*.

The final degree construction that we consider is the English superlative (*-est, most, least*). We comment on the highly marked nature of this form since many languages of the world do not have a superlative degree that is morphologically distinct from their comparative degree. We also contrast the superlative with the comparative degree because this contrast is the crux of many of the teaching-learning problems encountered when superlatives are presented in the ESL/EFL classroom.

Degree complements

There are several degree complements that resemble comparatives and equatives in that they make relative (rather than absolute) use of the four major parts of speech.

1. Too (much/little) *plus infinitive*

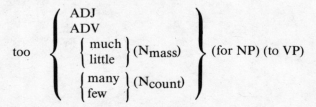

Examples: He's *too old* to join the Army.
　　　　　　She left *too quickly* for me to thank her.

Burt has *too* $\left\{ \begin{array}{l} \textit{much money} \\ \textit{many investments} \end{array} \right\}$ to understand what it's like to be poor.

I have *too little time* to watch TV.

There were *too few examples* in his paper to support his hypothesis.

Martha *weighs too much* to work as a flight attendant.

Semantically, this construction indicates either an "excess" or an "insufficiency" of some quality or of something measurable. When *much* or *many* occurs, the meaning of excess is explicit. Likewise, when *little* or *few* occurs, the meaning of insufficiency is overtly expressed. None of these quantifiers, however, occurs before an adjective or an adverb. In such cases, an adjective or adverb with positive polarity would express excess (e.g., *too tall*), whereas an adjective or an adverb with negative polarity would express insufficiency (e.g., *too small*). Note that *much* and *little* precede mass nouns and follow verbs while *many* and *few* are the related forms that precede count nouns.

2. So (much/little) *plus* that *clause*

$$\text{so} \left\{ \begin{array}{l} \text{ADJ} \\ \text{ADV} \\ \left\{ \begin{array}{l} \text{much} \\ \text{little} \end{array} \right\} (\text{N}_{\text{mass}}) \\ \left\{ \begin{array}{l} \text{many} \\ \text{few} \end{array} \right\} (\text{N}_{\text{count}}) \end{array} \right\} \quad \text{(to VP)} \; that + \text{S}$$

Examples: They're *so noisy* that we can't sleep.

He ran *so fast* that no one could catch him.

I have *so* $\left\{ \begin{array}{l} \textit{much work} \\ \textit{many errands} \end{array} \right\}$ to do that I'll never finish.

Bess has *so* $\left\{ \begin{array}{l} \textit{little ability} \\ \textit{few skills} \end{array} \right\}$ that she won't find a good job.

He runs *so little* that it won't help him get in shape.

When *so (much/little)* is used in this construction, the notion of "causality" is conveyed, i.e., the degree, extent, or amount—positive or negative—expressed in the main clause is sufficient to bring about the result expressed in the *that* clause. Just as in the previous construction, *much* and *little* occur before mass nouns and after verbs while *many* and *few* occur before countable nouns. Also, none of these quantifiers precedes an adjective or an adverb; the *so* occurs alone in such environments.

3. Such (a/an) *(adj) NOUN plus* that *clause*

$$\text{such} \left\{ \begin{array}{l} \left\{ \begin{array}{l} \text{a} \\ \text{an} \end{array} \right\} (\text{adj}) \; \text{N}_{\text{count}} \\ \emptyset \left\{ \begin{array}{l} (\text{adj}) \; \text{N}_{\text{plural}} \\ (\text{adj}) \; \text{N}_{\text{mass}} \end{array} \right. \end{array} \right\} \quad that + \text{S}$$

Examples: Bobby was *such a nuisance* that he was sent to his room.

They are *such racists* that they would rather close down their schools than integrate.

The victim was in *such agony* that she was taken to the hospital.

This construction closely parallels 2 above in meaning and structure. In both constructions causality is expressed in the clause containing *so* or *such* and a result is expressed in the *that* clause. Unlike *so,* however, *such* modifies only nouns or noun phrases. *Such* is used instead of *so (much/little),* etc., when the degree or extent of a noun is being conveyed rather than its quantity or amount. When *such* modifies a countable noun, the indefinite article *a/an* must follow *such.* In other environments *such* may directly precede the noun it modifies. Note, however, that an adjective frequently occurs between *such (a/an)* and the noun:

> such an unusual incident...   such easy questions...

There is often a near paraphrase relationship between *so* and *such* in those cases where an adjective occurs, e.g.:

> Jane is such an athlete that all the boys want her to play on the varsity team.
> Jane is so athletic that all the boys want her to play on the varsity team.
>
> The test had such easy questions that I finished it early.
> The questions were so easy that I finished the test early.

4. Enough *plus infinitive*

$$\left\{ \begin{array}{l} \text{ADJ} \\ \text{ADV} \\ \text{verb} \\ <\text{noun}_x>^1 \end{array} \right\} \quad \text{enough} <\text{noun}_x>^1 \text{ (for NP) (to VP)}$$

Examples: She's *qualified enough* for them to hire her.
He ran *fast enough* to win the race.
He *weighs enough* to compete as a heavyweight.

I have $\left\{ \begin{array}{l} \textit{enough money} \\ \textit{money enough} \end{array} \right\}$ to get by for a while.

Enough, unlike the two previous degree complements we have discussed, follows adjectives and adverbs as well as verbs. It expresses "sufficiency" and it usually precedes nouns; however, there is a less frequent variant of the *enough* + NOUN construction where *enough* may follow the noun instead. (See the last example above.) Another difference is that *enough* doesn't occur with the quantifiers *much/many/little[2]/few.*

Semantically, of course, *not* + *enough* is similar to *too little/few* since in both cases the meaning of "insufficiency" is conveyed, e.g.:

> He doesn't have enough time to watch   He has too little time to watch TV.
>   TV.

There are some important differences we should mention with regard to infinitives and *that* clauses in degree complements. When *not* + *enough* is used to paraphrase *so little/few,* any *not* occurring in the *that* clause which follows the *so* must be deleted in the corresponding infinitive following *not enough,* e.g.:

> He exercises so little that he is not in good shape.
>
> He doesn't exercise enough $\left\{ \begin{array}{l} \text{to be in good shape} \\ \text{*not to be in good shape} \end{array} \right\}$.

---

1. This notation (i.e., <   >) indicates that a given noun (i.e., noun$_x$) may occur either before or after *enough* but not in both positions at the same time.

2. There is one fixed expression where we find *enough* modified by *little:* e.g., "I have little enough time as it is, and now they tell me to do more!" In this usage, *little enough* means something like *too little.*

The same thing happens when *too (much/little) (for NP) (to VP)* is used to paraphrase *so (much/little) that* or *such (a/an) (adj) N that.* In other words, any overt negative in the *that* clause following *so* or *such* must be deleted in the parallel infinitive following *too (much/little),* e.g.:

He is so weak that he can't speak coherently.

He is too weak $\left\{ \begin{array}{l} \text{to speak coherently} \\ \text{*not to speak coherently} \end{array} \right\}$.

Thus, the ESL/EFL teacher must make it clear that the infinitive complements following *not enough* or *too (much/little)* are implicitly negative since this fact is not always obvious to ESL/EFL learners.

A note on *so, too,* and *very*

Quirk et al. (1972) have pointed out that *so* is sometimes used absolutely as an emphatic form of *very:*

I'm *so* tired!   The party was *so* delightful!

They add that this usage is more typical of women's speech than men's. To these observations we add that in environments where *so* does not precede an adjective or adverb, *so much/many* may also be used absolutely as emphatic forms of *very much/many:*

I enjoyed this book *so much!*   They have *so many* friends!

Quirk et al. also mention that *too* is sometimes used absolutely as a colloquial emphatic counterpart of *very:*

He isn't *too* bright.   I don't feel *too* good.

They add that this use is more typical of informal American English than of British. Note, however, that this informal use of *too* as an intensifier is acceptable only in semantically negative contexts. When ESL/EFL learners overgeneralize this absolute use of *too* to affirmative contexts, errors result:

*This food is too good.

What they want to say, of course, is "This food is very good."

In all dialects of English *too much* and *too little* can be used "absolutely," but again only in contexts where a negative meaning is implied:[3]

He smokes too much.   They study too little.

Some ESL/EFL learners incorrectly extend this pattern to affirmative contexts and produce errors such as this:

*We like you too much.

when what they mean to say is "We like you very much."

---

3. We use the term "absolutely" in a very guarded sense here because these *too*'s are not like *very* in that there is always an infinitive complement implied, and this implied complement always expresses a negative implication:

He smokes too much $\left\{ \begin{array}{l} \text{to have good health} \\ \text{for his own good} \end{array} \right\}$. (He is not in good health).

They study too little to succeed academically. (They are not succeeding.)

The superlative construction

How the languages of the world express the superlative degree

ESL/EFL teachers should be aware of the fact that most languages do not have morphologically distinct comparative and superlative forms; however, English and other related languages (i.e., other Germanic languages such as German, Dutch, and Danish) are somewhat idiosyncratic, in having distinct superlative forms. Languages without a true superlative form express a superlative meaning by using either a definite article or some other defining word with a comparative morpheme, e.g.:

> (literally) Ben is the more intelligent student in the class.
> (meaning) "Ben is the most intelligent student in the class."

or by using a construction that excludes all other members of the set to which the subject belongs, e.g.:

> (literally) The VW is more economical than any other car.
> (meaning) "The VW is the most economical car."

Using examples like our two VW sentences above, Jespersen (1924) points out that the superlative does not necessarily indicate a higher degree than the comparative but rather that it expresses degree from a different point of view. For this reason, Jespersen feels that many languages are able to make do without distinct superlative forms. Furthermore, some languages, such as those in the Romance family (e.g., French, Italian, Spanish) which formerly possessed a true superlative, have since discarded their superlative form and have simply extended the semantic domain of their comparative. In other words, many languages have no distinct superlative form either because they have never developed one or because they had one but discarded it over time, i.e., found it unnecessary.

In addition, in his work on language universals, Greenberg (1966) has pointed out that superlatives are more "marked" than comparatives. That is to say, comparatives occur more frequently in any language that has both forms as well as among languages of the world. He also noted that if a language has a superlative form, it must also have a comparative form; however, the reverse is not necessarily true.

All this evidence suggests that the English superlative may be harder for most ESL/EFL students to learn than the comparative, or that the two forms will frequently be confused. Neuman (1977) did, in fact, find errors in compositions written by intermediate-level ESL students, verifying our hypothesis that these forms will be confused. Furthermore, her work revealed that this confusion extends beyond the beginning level:

> *I am the younger in my family.
> *That food is worst than the food for the pig.
> (examples from Neuman (1977:131))

Similarities and differences between comparatives and superlatives

In terms of distribution, the -*est* and *most* forms of the superlative behave exactly like the -*er* and *more* of the comparative. The following is a brief, simplified restatement of the morphological rule that was given in greater detail for the comparative in the preceding chapter:

1. Use -*est* with one-syllable adjectives and adverbs and with those two-syllable adjectives ending in -*y*:

tallest	happiest
fastest	noisiest
hardest	dirtiest

2. Use either *-est* or *most* with two-syllable adjectives that take the following weakly stressed endings:

-ly: friendliest, most friendly   *-er:* cleverest, most clever
-ow: mellowest, most mellow   *-some:* handsomest, most handsome

3. Use *most* with other adjectives and adverbs of two or more syllables:

$$\text{most} \begin{Bmatrix} \text{distant} \\ \text{exact} \\ \text{useful(ly)} \\ \text{wretched} \end{Bmatrix} \qquad \text{most} \begin{Bmatrix} \text{arrogant} \\ \text{intelligent} \\ \text{beautiful(ly)} \end{Bmatrix}$$

Also, the same adjectives and adverbs that were morphologically irregular in the comparative (see the preceding chapter) are also irregular in the superlative (e.g., *good—better—best*). These morphological similarities are probably the major reason why so many people erroneously believe that comparative and superlative constructions are essentially the same, with the only difference being the number of persons or objects compared; i.e., they believe that when two things are being compared, one should use the comparative; when three or more things are being compared, one should use the superlative. This, in fact, is the rule given in most ESL/EFL texts as well as in most reference grammars. If we do nothing else in this chapter, we hope to dispel this misleading oversimplification.

Comparatives are often used quite appropriately when three or more persons, objects, or properties are involved, e.g.:

Jack is taller than John $\begin{Bmatrix} \text{and} \\ \text{or} \end{Bmatrix}^4$ Bill.

Jill and Ann have more A's than B's $\begin{Bmatrix} \text{and} \\ \text{or} \end{Bmatrix}^4$ C's.

Likewise, many speakers of English feel comfortable about using superlatives informally when only two objects or properties are being compared, even though use of the comparative form is considered to be formally more accurate in such cases, e.g.:

Bill is 6 feet tall and Joe is 6 feet 2 inches tall.
Who's the tallest?

In fact, if we say "Who's the taller (of the two)?" which would be the prescriptively correct form here, we are merely using a comparative form in a superlative sense. This is because the semantic function of the superlative is to select one or more members out of a set because they rank first or last (with respect to other members of the set) on a scale that measures a particular attribute (e.g., height, size, weight, age, intelligence, speed). This is why superlatives, like ordinals, tend to co-occur with a definite determiner and to be followed by *of* phrases or *that*

---

4. Note that in most such cases it doesn't seem to make much difference whether *and* or *or* is used as the conjunction following *than,* although a difference in meaning is possible and additional modifiers are sometimes used to suggest an additive rather than an alternative meaning, e.g.:

Jill and Ann have more A's than B's and C's put together.

clauses which express the whole set out of which the subject of the superlative has been selected. (The subject may be singular or plural.) For example:

$$\left. \begin{array}{l} \text{Clem is} \\ \text{Clem and Bob are} \end{array} \right\} \text{ the tallest } \left\{ \begin{array}{l} \text{(one(s)) of the four boys} \\ \text{boy(s) in my class} \end{array} \right\} .$$

The superlative thus concerns itself with the extremes of a given scale with regard to a specific set, whereas the comparative ignores the extreme and looks at two points anywhere on the scale with regard to two or more individuals, objects, etc. The number of persons or objects involved in a comparison is therefore not the most important thing to consider when deciding whether to use a comparative or a superlative form.

This distinction gets muddied, however, since it's a fact that English comparative forms are sometimes used to express a superlative meaning. One example of this was given above (i.e., "Who's the taller of the two boys?"), and at least two other situations exist where comparative forms are used to express a superlative meaning:

1. Comparatives with *(n)ever*

I've never seen more people.
or
That's more people than I've ever seen.   ("That's the most people I've ever seen.")

2. Comparatives with *any (other)*

This play is better than any other play   ("This is the best play (that) I've ever
   I've seen.   seen.")

As a rule, if a sentence containing a comparative form can be paraphrased using a sentence with a superlative form, then we can say that the comparative form is being used to express a superlative meaning. In fact, all superlative sentences in English can be paraphrased using a comparative. Superlative forms, on the other hand, are never used to paraphrase a comparative meaning.

Other uses of superlative forms

Note that the word *most* is often used absolutely as an intensifier, with a meaning similar to *very,* to express a strong degree, e.g.:

He was a most gracious host.   That was most thoughtful of you.

The use of the indefinite article in the first of the two preceding examples demonstrates that *most* is not being used to express a superlative meaning[5] since a true superlative always selects the definite article (if it occurs with an article).

A colloquial use of the superlative involves using it without explicitly specifying any set. In such cases, a superlative meaning is intended nonetheless, e.g.:

You're the most!   Ali still thinks he's the greatest!

Another type of abbreviated superlative that occurs in colloquial usage are sentences like the following, which end in *ever:*

That book was his best ever. (i.e., "That was the best book that he ever wrote.")

---

5. Another meaning of *most* that is not superlative is the meaning "majority," e.g., "Most (of the) voters were in favor of the measure."

The play was the most resounding flop ever. (i.e., "The play was the most resounding flop of any play ever performed.")

The presence of *ever* makes such sentences sound more emphatic.

Co-occurrence of superlatives with the definite article

Superlatives usually co-occur with the definite article or some other definite determiner or defining word; however, the underlying *the* can be omitted if *-est, most,* or *least* is not followed by a noun or a noun substitute[6] in the surface structure—i.e., if the underlying noun has been deleted.[7] For example:

the obligatory:	*the* optional:
Which is the highest mountain?	Which mountain is (the) highest?
Which mountain is the highest?	Who climbed (the) highest?

Marked and unmarked superlatives

In the preceding chapter, we stated that there were semantically related adjectives and adverbs that had positive and negative polarity and that the positive forms were unmarked while the negative forms were marked:

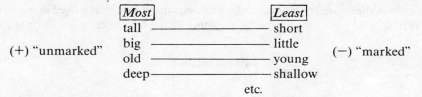

(+) "unmarked"

Most		Least
tall	———————	short
big	———————	little
old	———————	young
deep	———————	shallow

(−) "marked"

etc.

These oppositions are as valid for superlatives as they are for comparatives, with the added caveat that superlatives are inherently more marked than comparatives,[8] as Jespersen (1924) and Greenberg (1966) have suggested.

The superlative form *least* is the most highly marked of all these forms. In other words, we tend not to say phrases such as "the least tall":

?Bob is the least tall of all the boys.

but prefer to use *most*—or its morphological variant *-est*—when we have a negative polarity word such as *short,* which we can combine with *most* or *-est*:

Bob is the shortest of all the boys.

---

6. The forms *one* and *ones* are the noun substitutes that occur most frequently with superlatives, e.g.:

the best one(s)

7. The only case where it is difficult to reconstruct an underlying noun is with adverbial use of the superlative, e.g.:

Roger behaves the most politely (of all the boys).

Ultimately, one might perhaps argue that such a sentence is related to one with a noun paraphrase and that this relationship accounts for the presence of *the:*

Roger exhibits the most polite behavior (of all the boys).

However, exploring such an analysis in detail is beyond the scope of this textbook.

8. This means that superlatives occur less frequently than comparatives (in any given language or across the languages of the world).

Thus, whenever there are negative and positive polarity adjectives and adverbs available for English speakers to combine with *most* or *-est*, the form *least* tends not to occur.

So when does the form *least* occur? It is used frequently as the opposite of *most* whenever the ranking or scaling of items is involved, e.g.:

the most/least $\left\{ \begin{array}{l} \text{likely} \\ \text{expensive} \\ \text{important} \\ \vdots \end{array} \right\}$ [9]

The other environment in which *least* occurs is a negative one, where the use of *least* indicates the least negative (i.e., most nearly positive) member(s) of a set that is viewed as being completely negative, e.g.:

the least $\left\{ \begin{array}{l} \text{objectionable} \\ \text{sinister} \\ \text{reprehensible} \\ \vdots \end{array} \right\}$

There is, of course, the related comparative form *lesser,* which also can be used in negative contexts with this special type of superlative meaning if the set described has only two members, e.g.:

the lesser $\left\{ \begin{array}{l} \text{of two evils} \\ \text{evil} \end{array} \right\}$

Lesser, however, has more semantic flexibility than *least,* since it can also be used in a comparative sense that has no superlative counterpart, e.g.:

a lesser punishment   (= "a less severe punishment")

We should also briefly mention *fewest,* the suppletive variant of *least* that occurs before countable nouns in formal or prescriptively correct usage. (In informal usage *least* often occurs in this environment instead of *fewest.*) Semantically, *fewest* is like *least* in that it occurs as the opposite of *most* when items are being ranked or scaled, e.g.:

Of all the children in the class, Barbara seems to have the most friends and Jennifer the fewest (friends).

Fewest also occurs in predominantly negative contexts to indicate the least negative (or most nearly positive) member of a set that is viewed as having only negative members, e.g.:

Paul has reservations about all the proposals; however, he has the fewest reservations about the third one.

---

9. Adverbs or adjectives that use *un-* or some other negative prefix to derive their negative polarity form are different from adjectives and adverbs that have preexisting polar opposites that are lexically distinct (e.g., *big—little*). Whenever such overt negative prefixes are needed, the tendency is to avoid the derived negative and to use *least* with the stem form (e.g., *least important*) rather than *most* with the derived negative (e.g., *most unimportant*); however, the latter pattern does occasionally occur:

Lester always seems to dwell on the most $\left\{ \begin{array}{l} \text{unimportant} \\ \text{uninteresting} \end{array} \right\}$ details.

Arguments for presenting comparatives and superlatives separately

Part of the general confusion between comparatives and superlatives no doubt stems from the fact that most ESL/EFL textbooks present them in the same lesson or chapter. From a semantic point of view, it would seem more sensible to present comparatives and equatives along with verbs, adjectives, nominals, and prepositions such as the following, which all express similarity or difference:

Verbs	Adjectives	Nominals	Prepositions
to differ from NP	to be different from (than[10]) NP	to be the same as NP	(to be) like NP
sound / feel / look / taste / seem — to ___ like NP	to be similar to NP to be equal/equivalent to NP to be identical to NP to be alike		(to be) unlike NP
to behave like NP			

Examples: John is different from Bill.   John is taller than Bill (is).

In other words, comparatives can usefully be considered a complex type of transitive adjective.

Superlatives, on the other hand, should be presented in the context of ordinals and ordinal-like prenominal modifiers:

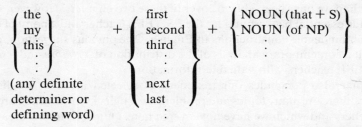

$$\left\{ \begin{matrix} \text{the} \\ \text{my} \\ \text{this} \\ \vdots \end{matrix} \right\} + \left\{ \begin{matrix} \text{first} \\ \text{second} \\ \text{third} \\ \vdots \\ \text{next} \\ \text{last} \\ \vdots \end{matrix} \right\} + \left\{ \begin{matrix} \text{NOUN (that + S)} \\ \text{NOUN (of NP)} \\ \vdots \end{matrix} \right\}$$

(any definite determiner or defining word)

Examples: This is my first Shakespeare course./This is the best Shakespeare course (that) I have taken.

This exercise is your next assignment./This exercise is the hardest assignment (that) you'll have to do.

In other words, it may be useful to classify superlatives as a type of prenominal, postdeterminer adjective. The modified phrase structure rule that we adapted from Bolinger (1967) in Chapter 28 to account for attributive adjectives is also applicable here:

$$NP \longrightarrow (det) (AP) N (pl)$$

The node "AP," which is used to generate all attributive adjectives, would also be used to generate ordinals and superlatives. However, with superlatives, a prepositional phrase or a *that* clause would normally follow the head noun. The presence of these prepositional phrases or *that* clauses adds further complexities to our grammar—complexities which we will not be able to explore further at this time.

---

10. The phrase "different than" is acceptable in colloquial American English. In formal situations "different from" is preferred. Many speakers of British English do not find "different than" grammatically acceptable.

Therefore, given all these differences—syntactic and semantic—we feel that it is important for the ESL/EFL student to practice first the comparative and then, at some later time, the superlative, each in different contexts and in conjunction with the syntactically related patterns given above. Once the two forms have been fairly well established, the teacher can combine them in contexts where the students must learn to properly distinguish the use of the comparative and the superlative.

One noteworthy exception to this suggestion has been brought to our attention by Werner Kruse (personal communication). Kruse points out that when ESL/EFL students are speakers of German or some other Germanic language, they are already familiar with comparative and superlative forms similar to the English ones and use them in their own language in much the same way that they are used in English. For such students the main learning problem is a morphological one, i.e., they need to learn when to use -er versus more and when to use -est versus most. We agree with Kruse that for such students our reasons for strict segregation of the two constructions at the initial stage of instruction no longer apply. The teacher of such students should concentrate on presenting and practicing, in communicative contexts, the distributional differences between the inflectional forms (-er, -est) and the corresponding periphrastic ones (more, most).

Conclusion

This chapter concludes our discussion of degree constructions in English. Certainly there is much more to say about comparatives, equatives, superlatives, and the other degree complements than we have been able to cover in these two chapters. However, we do feel the chapters provide essential background for the ESL/EFL teacher and a point of departure for further research on degree constructions in English. One obvious suggestion for additional research is that a contemporary analysis of the distribution of -er/more and -est/most would provide ESL/EFL teachers with valuable information.

This chapter also concludes our treatment of selected areas in English grammar. Needless to say, there are many topics and problems in English syntax which are of interest to ESL/EFL teachers and which we have not covered here. Our work in this area will not end; however, our textbook must.

The following and final chapter is a brief closing statement which summarizes what we have done and attempts to put our work into the larger context of current issues in language learning and language teaching.

TEACHING SUGGESTIONS

1   To elicit superlatives you can provide your students with data on several people, for example, four brothers (you may want to use similar data representing four of your students):

	Jack	Bill	Tom	Henry
Height	6'	5'9"	6'2"	5'10"
Weight	200 lb	150 lb	180 lb	170 lb
Age	25	23	21	19

The students' task is to generate all the possible superlative sentences:

Jack is the oldest.   Tom is the tallest.   Jack weighs the most.
Henry is the youngest.   Bill is the shortest.   Bill weighs the least.

2   Comparing statistics about places such as states can also elicit authentic use of superlatives:

	Alaska	*California*	*Texas*	*Vermont*
Area (square miles)	586,412	158,693	267,338	9,609
Population	407,000	21,896,000	12,830,000	483,000
Highest point	Mt. McKinley 20,320 feet	Mt. Whitney 14,494 feet	Guadalupe Peak 8,751 feet	Mt. Mansfield 4,393 feet
Year of statehood	1959	1850	1845	1791

Examples: Alaska is the largest of the four states.
Vermont is the oldest/smallest of the four states.
Etc.

3   For presenting a variety of superlative forms in context Paul Le Vasseur suggests that ESL/EFL teachers give their students a handout consisting of several advertisements extracted from newspapers and magazines. In groups, students are instructed first to identify all the superlative forms and meanings and then to ask each other questions (and to answer them) about the content of the ads, e.g.:

a. "The Gillette TRAC II Shaving System. The closest thing to a perfect shave."
b. "Everyone agrees the only rums worth coming back to are the Rums of Puerto Rico. The best-tasting, best-selling rums made."
c. "New York Life's Best-Seller Policy. It's not our least expensive policy. But, then again, no other life insurance can do quite as many things for you."
Etc.

4   To introduce *so (much) . . . that* degree constructions the ESL/EFL teacher can present contexts like this one to students:

Salwa is having a bad day at school.
She's sleepy. She can't pay attention to the lecture.
She's hungry. She can't concentrate on the quiz.
It's hot (i.e., the weather). She can't study.
Later in the day Salwa goes home and tells her roommate about her bad day:
"I was so sleepy (that) I couldn't pay attention to the lecture."
Etc.

5   Students can practice "*too (much) . . . to*" and "*enough . . . to*" degree constructions if the teacher gives each pair (or small group of students) a situation like this written on a card:

You have to be 18 years old to vote in   Harry is 17 years old.
  California.   Ned is 20 years old.

The students must then write down at least one sentence with *too,* one with *enough,* and one with *not enough:*

Harry is too young to vote.   Harry isn't old enough to vote.
Ned is old enough to vote.

6 To learn differences in the meaning and distribution of *so, too,* and *very,* students should work with two types of modified "cloze" exercises—(a) informal conversation and (b) expository writing.

    a. *X:* I'm not hungry today. It's (1) _____ hot.
       Y: Why don't you try the salad? It's (2) _____ good.
       X: I have (3) _____ much work to do. I'll just skip lunch.
       Y: Don't rush off (4) _____ fast. You could get sick if you skip (5) _____
       many meals.

    b.   The results of yesterday's election are (1) _____ ambiguous at this point that we don't know who won. Both candidates are still making (2) _____ optimistic statements, and even the experts feel that the race is (3) _____ close to call.

7 Ultimately, the ESL/EFL teacher will need to focus on exercises that will help students discriminate between comparative and superlative forms. Here are some suggestions:

    a. Modified "cloze" exercises in dialog or story form where the correct degree must be supplied for each word indicated.

    X: Are you _____, or am I?
               (1) tall
    Y: I don't know. Let's ask Lars. He's _____ than either of us.
                                 (2) tall
    X: Yeah. He's the _____ one in the class.
                 (3) tall

Note that irregular forms can be practiced this way too.

       Mr. Jenkins was asked to judge the apple pies at the fair. So he started and each new

       one tasted _____ than the previous one. He had a very hard time picking
                (1) good

       the _____ one.
          (2) good

    b. Three-term problems can be used to test comprehension of comparative and superlative forms. The teacher can provide the problems orally or in writing and the students can give a name (orally or in writing) to indicate their answer, e.g.:

    (1) If Bob is taller than Joe and Joe is taller than Mike, who's the tallest?
    (2) If Mary is younger than Nancy and Nancy is older than Judy, who's the oldest?
        Etc.

    c. To bring out the similarity of content but difference of form and focus between comparatives and superlatives, the teacher can use data such as were presented in the first and second teaching suggestions above. The students would be asked to generate either comparative or superlative sentences using the data and then to paraphrase using the other form (if possible), e.g.:

    S1: Tom is taller than his three brothers.
    S2: Tom is the tallest of the four brothers.
    S1: Alaska is the largest state (largest of the 50 states).
    S2: Alaska is larger than the other 49 states.

It should be emphasized that while all superlatives can be paraphrased with a comparative form, not all comparatives (e.g., Ann runs faster than Harry) can be paraphrased with a superlative.

EXERCISES

Test your understanding of what has been presented

1. Provide original sentences that illustrate the following terms. Underline the pertinent word(s) in your examples.

a comparative used in a superlative sense	a marked superlative
the negative import of *too (much/little)*	absolute use of *too*
intensifying, nonsuperlative use of *most*	comparative and superlative uses of *lesser*

2. Why are the following sentences ungrammatical?

a. *She's the $\left\{\begin{array}{l}\text{boringest}\\\text{boredest}\end{array}\right\}$ person I know.

b. *John $\left\{\begin{array}{l}\text{lives the fartherest away}\\\text{is the elderest}\end{array}\right\}$ of all.

3. In each of the following cases decide whether the sentence should be completed with a comparative or a superlative form or could be completed with either, and explain why. If both forms are possible, is there a difference in meaning?

a. Alex has financial problems, but Joe and Robert don't because they have

_____ money.
      (more, the most)

b. Of the five candidates for president, I voted for Sheila because I definitely think she's

_____ .
   (the best, better)

c. After examining several books I finally bought this novel because I felt that it was

_____ .
   (the most interesting one, more interesting than the others)

Test your ability to apply what you know

4. If your students produce the following sentences, what errors have they made? How will you make them aware of the errors, and what exercises will you prepare to help your students avoid these errors?

a. *Joe is the older child in a big family.
b. *February is the most coldest month in my country.
c. *The first and important thing of all is studying English.
d. *I was worst than my roommate at making friends.

5. If you are using an ESL/EFL textbook that presents comparatives and superlatives in the same lesson, what will you do?

6. You are using an ESL/EFL textbook that tells your students to use the comparative for two persons or objects and the superlative for three or more persons or objects. One of your students asks you if this rule always works. What will you say?

7. In a newspaper article entitled "The 'Usefulest' Adjectives" William Safire (1980) quotes two famous authors:

> Thomas Carlyle—"Surely of all the 'rights of man' this right of the ignorant to be guided by the wiser... is the indisputablest."
>
> Mark Twain—"...the confoundedest, brazenest, ingeniousest piece of fraud."

What point do you think Safire was trying to make in this article?

BIBLIOGRAPHY

References

Bolinger, D. (1967). "Adjectives in English: Attribution and Predication," *Lingua* 18: 1–34.
Greenberg, J. H. (1966). *Language Universals*. The Hague: Mouton.
Jespersen, O. (1924). *The Philosophy of Grammar*. London: Allen and Unwin.
Neuman, R. A. (1977). "An Attempt to Define through Error Analysis the Intermediate ESL Level at UCLA." Unpublished M.A. thesis in TESL, UCLA.
Quirk, R., S. Greenbaum, G. Leech, and J. Svartvik (1972). *A Grammar of Contemporary English*. New York: Seminar Press.
Safire, W. (1980). "The 'Usefulest' Adjectives," *New York Times,* Sec. 6, p. 10, June 22.

Suggestions for further reading

For useful descriptive information about the English superlative, see:

Bolinger, D. (1972). *Degree Words*. The Hague: Mouton.
Jespersen, O. (1964). *Essentials of English Grammar*. University, Ala.: University of Alabama Press, Chap. 22.

For a transformational analysis of most of the degree complements discussed in this chapter, see:

Celce-Murcia, M. (1972). "A Syntactic and Psycholinguistic Study of Comparison in English." Unpublished Ph.D. dissertation in Linguistics, UCLA.

For a good discussion of the degree complements formed with *so, such, too,* and *enough,* see:

Gary, E. N. (1979). "Extent in English: A Unified Account of Degree and Quantity." Unpublished Ph.D. dissertation in Linguistics, UCLA, pp. 129–178.

For ESL/EFL textbooks that offer good suggestions for practicing superlatives, see:

Azar, B. S. (1981). *Understanding and Using English Grammar*. Englewood Cliffs, N.J.: Prentice-Hall, pp. 330–333.
Brinton, D., and R. Neuman (1982). *Getting Along: English Grammar and Writing* (Book 1). Englewood Cliffs, N.J.: Prentice-Hall, pp. 206–209, 213–214.
Danielson, D., and R. Hayden (1973). *Using English: Your Second Language*. Englewood Cliffs, N.J.: Prentice-Hall, pp. 189–191.
Praninskas, J. (1975). *Rapid Review of English Grammar* (2d ed.). Englewood Cliffs, N.J.: Prentice-Hall, pp. 320–321.

For exercises integrating the use of the comparative and superlative, see:

Fingado, G., L. J. Freeman, M. R. Jerome, and C. V. Summers (1981). *The English Connection*. Cambridge, Mass.: Winthrop, pp. 175–178.

Four of the above references also have good exercises for practicing *so . . . that* and *such . . . that:* Azar (pp. 284–287); Danielson and Hayden (pp. 174–176); Fingado et al. (pp. 236–256), and Praninskas (pp. 343–344, 350).

For exercises dealing with *too* and *enough,* see:

Brinton, D., and R. Neuman (1982). *Getting Along: English Grammar and Writing* (Book 1). Englewood Cliffs, N.J.: Prentice-Hall, pp. 91–93, 100–102.

37

Conclusion

Nowadays it has become quite commonplace to acknowledge that learning a language involves much more than learning how to form grammatical structures correctly; it involves learning how to use them appropriately in a variety of social contexts as well. Indeed, it has recently been argued that a syllabus based on the uses or functions of language would prove to be superior to one based on grammatical structures. Wilkins (1976), for example, has urged that instead of employing a grammatical or structural syllabus, teachers adopt a notional-functional syllabus in which the individual units are made up of the functions of English (i.e., the speech acts that speakers perform when using language). Such a syllabus would have units on denying, persuading, (dis)agreeing, inviting, etc. It is not our purpose here to argue the merits of one syllabus type over another, but we note that Wilkins himself was the first to point out that even if one finds a notional-functional syllabus attractive, there is no denying that a teacher is also responsible for teaching linguistic structures:

> It is taken here to be almost axiomatic that the acquisition of the grammatical system of a language remains a most important element in language learning. The grammar is the means through which linguistic creativity is ultimately achieved and an inadequate knowledge of the grammar would lead to a serious limitation on the capacity for communication. A notional syllabus, no less than a grammatical syllabus, must seek to ensure that the grammatical system is properly assimilated by the learner. We do not express language functions in isolation. (Wilkins, 1976:66)

Teaching functions and the linguistic forms which express them, however, is still not enough. There is a broad spectrum of other factors that ESL/EFL teachers must consider if they desire to help their students achieve communicative competence in English. Larsen-Freeman (1981), for example, in reviewing the literature on communicative competence, identifies three categories in which second language acquisition research has been conducted in addition to the linguistic structures and speech acts (functions) we have already mentioned. The three other categories are: propositional content (the content of the message the speaker wishes to express), interactional patterns (turn-taking and pacing), and strategic competence[1] (strategies which are responsible for controlling or restoring the smooth flow of communication).[2] Included in the discussion of the five categories, but worthy of special mention here, are

---

1. A term borrowed from Canale and Swain (1980).
2. For a fuller description of each category and an account of the research being conducted in the five categories, see Larsen-Freeman (1981).

some additional aspects of communication which one must be aware of: the register appropriate for the medium or occasion, pragmatic competence (using the appropriate form depending upon the situation and one's relation with one's interlocutor), discourse constraints (achieving coherence and cohesion at the suprasentential level),[3] and sensitivity to context (choosing the appropriate form from competing forms which have similar functions).

With all these factors in mind, we have chosen to adhere to a format which gives prominence to linguistic structure. We have gone far beyond merely describing the form of linguistic structures, however. Acknowledging that many ESL/EFL teachers have the goal of helping their students attain communicative competence in both speech and writing, we have included information pertaining to the functions[4] of the linguistic structures. Recall, for example, our discussion of imperatives. We made the point that the main function of imperatives was to get someone else to comply with the speaker's wish when the cooperation of the other person could be taken for granted by the speaker. We have also attempted to portray the register differences that exist within the language with regard to forms which would be acceptable in the spoken medium versus forms that would be acceptable in the written medium. An example of this was when we observed that although native speakers frequently use nonreferential *there* with a contracted singular form of BE in informal speech (i.e., *there's*), even with a plural subject, we also noted that this would be unacceptable in writing to most speakers in all but the most informal contexts. Regarding pragmatic competence, we advised you to teach your students to select different forms in the language according to who their listeners were. We dealt with this competence, for example, when we discussed modals of social interaction: knowing when one should use *should* or *could* in giving advice depends, among other things, upon one's relation with one's interlocutor. Such considerations are important in maintaining smooth social relations with others.

As for discourse constraints, we were careful to point out that the linguistic context often determines the sequence of constituents within a sentence or even the forms within the sentence itself. For example, the order of adverbials that should be used within a sentence might depend upon a question that had just been asked. Whether the form of an article in a sentence is definite or indefinite might depend upon some earlier linguistic reference to the noun the article occurs with. Furthermore, because we believe that there are extralinguistic factors, which have not yet been fully specified, but which operate to favor one linguistic form over another in a given context, we have included information concerning the frequency of usage by native speakers of certain linguistic forms or the preferences of native speakers for certain forms where competing forms are available in the language to serve the same basic function. For instance, we reported the frequency of occurrence of short answers to yes-no questions versus other possible responses; we also reported when native speakers prefer a certain possessive form for inanimate versus animate nouns.

Finally, where possible, we have included information about language typology and findings from second language acquisition research. It is our hope that such information will help teachers to better understand what linguistic background learners are bringing with them to their classes and what the nature of the learners' linguistic experience will be as they strive to master English.

---

3. Coherence has to do with semantic contiguity in discourse; cohesion has to do with syntactic contiguity in discourse. See Widdowson (1978) for an elaboration of this distinction.

4. The term *functions* here refers to what purposes linguistic structure serves, which is different from the meaning of *functions* in the speech act sense.

In order to accomplish some of our objectives we have relied chiefly, although certainly not exclusively, on transformational grammar. We have used it for its effectiveness in parsing and because we believe its dynamic nature can be exploited pedagogically.[5] Where transformational grammar has not been enlightening (e.g., in dealing with functional and discoursal aspects of language) we have called attention to insights from other linguistic schools or insights based upon our own research or that of others. Since it is the nature of any science to change, doubtless the findings and analyses that we have offered here will be challenged and/or expanded by additional research. This may well come from adherents of other schools of linguistics (e.g., stratificational grammar, tagmemics, systemic grammar) or by followers of other perspectives that have emerged subsequent to transformational grammar (e.g., generative semantics, daughter-dependency grammar, case grammar, Montague grammar, discourse analysis).[6] Such challenges, however, each with its own value, are welcome since we certainly do not claim to have provided the last word on the English language. Indeed, as we have indicated many times in this text, there is much yet to be discovered, and we welcome the contributions of researchers working within all of these various perspectives.

Since it was our objective to provide you with some training in linguistic analysis, we decided to select a particular model for describing English. Now that you have completed our course, it is our hope that you have gained some experience in analyzing linguistic structures which will enable you on your own to analyze other structures that we have not treated in this book. If we had merely supplied you with a compendium of facts about the English language, we would have reneged on our promise to aid you in discovering those facts about the English language that you will need to know when you can find no explanations in textbooks or reference grammars or when you find that only inadequate or inaccurate accounts exist. Moreover, we also hope that you have developed the skill of being able to apply what you have learned about English to error detection, analysis, and remediation, and to being able to answer your students' questions with satisfying explanations. Perhaps more importantly, through your adaptations of the teaching suggestions we have made and through your own creative endeavors, we hope you feel prepared to present the structures of the English language in meaningful contexts to your ESL/EFL students, given your own teaching approach and the situation(s) in which you are teaching.

It was also our intention to share with you our feeling that linguistics is an exciting, vital discipline—not the dry subject that it is sometimes made out to be. Perhaps we have been able to inspire some of you to conduct original research using contextual analysis,[7] one type of methodology we have employed in much of the research reported here. It is certainly true that a great deal of work remains to be done in helping us to understand all the various facets of the English language: form, function, register, pragmatics, discourse, and the effect of context. It is also true that if we work together our collective efforts will be invaluable in helping ESL/EFL teachers and students come to a better understanding of English syntax. It is our sincere wish that you will join us in this worthwhile task.

---

5. We suggested that a good way of presenting the form of yes-no questions, for example, would be to make students aware of how they are "transformed" from statements.

6. Many insights emerging subsequent to transformational grammar have, of course, been incorporated in this text since we have not adhered to a strict transformational model. Furthermore, some of these—discourse analysis, for instance—are not a challenge in the truest sense since there will presumably always be a need for a sentence-level grammar such as the one we provide.

7. See Celce-Murcia (1980) for a detailed statement on the procedures involved in conducting contextual analysis.

References

Canale, M., and M. Swain (1980). "Theoretical Bases of Communicative Approaches to Second Language Teaching and Testing," *Applied Linguistics* 1, 1:1–47.

Celce-Murcia, M. (1980). "Contextual Analysis of English: Application to TESL," in D. Larsen-Freeman (ed.), *Discourse Analysis in Second Language Research.* Rowley, Mass.: Newbury House.

Larsen-Freeman, D. (1981). "The WHAT of Second Language Acquisition," in M. Hines and W. Rutherford (eds.), *On TESOL '81.* Washington, D.C.: TESOL.

Widdowson, H. (1978). *Teaching Language as Communication.* London: Oxford University Press.

Wilkins, D. A. (1976). *Notional Syllabuses.* London: Oxford University Press.

Appendix

Suggested Answers to the Chapter Exercises

The following answers to the exercise questions are included in the hope that they will provide a useful *guide* to instructors and students of our course. We make no claim that these are the only possible answers to the questions. Indeed, with many of the more "open-ended" questions, there is no *one* correct answer. Answers to questions which ask, "How would you make learners aware of these problems?" or "How would you explain this to an ESL/EFL student?" for example, clearly would vary depending upon the teacher, the students, the approach being used, and the situation. When questions like the former occur with regard to error correction, we simply state what the error is and point out any additional information which we feel will be helpful. It is up to you to answer the rest of the question in a pedagogically sound manner. Many solutions are possible.

Furthermore, it is important to note that in the exercises which ask you to identify the source of ESL/EFL students' errors, we are only providing answers which point to a linguistic misunderstanding on the part of the student. Certainly ESL/EFL students commit numerous errors which are attributable to sources other than their not knowing a particular linguistic rule. Our purpose in this course, however, is to help you to understand the linguistic facts of English; for this reason we have answered these questions from a linguistic perspective.

Thus, we leave a great deal of the presenting, analyzing, explaining, and troubleshooting to the creativity of you, the ESL/EFL teacher-to-be. This is how it must be. We feel we cannot be prescriptive in this area, for after all, this is your challenge and you will make your own contribution to the art of successful teaching.

CHAPTER 2: Word Order and Phrase Structure Rules—Part I
Pages 9–20

1. adverbial of reason—Annie hated her hometown *because it was so small.*
   adverbial of frequency—The children go to camp *every summer.*
   adverbial of manner—Ray paced the floor *impatiently.*
   adverbial of direction—I am going *to town* after class.
   adverbial of position—The teacher is standing *near her desk.*
   sentence modifier—*Perhaps* it is too late to call her tonight.
   adverbial clause of time—We can all go together *after Pat arrives.*

intensifier—He spoke *very* highly of your work with the children.
deletable preposition—I've waited *four months* for that letter. (i.e., for four months)

2. a. The girls talked after the teachers left.

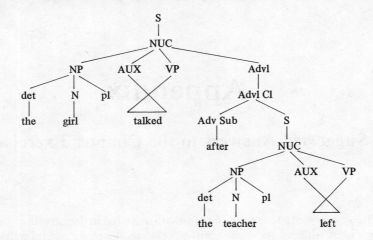

b. Surely John exercises on Sunday.

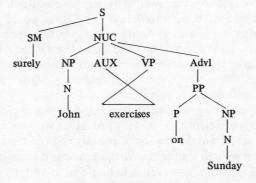

c. The baby cried because she was hungry.

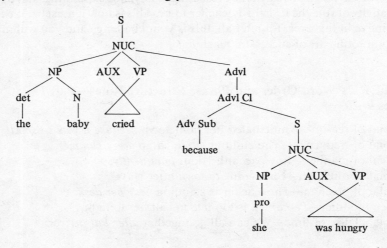

d. Fortunately his brothers work very quietly.

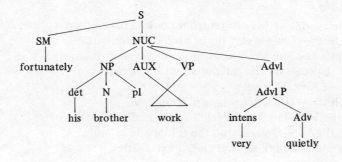

e. Perhaps Mary has been studying in the library.

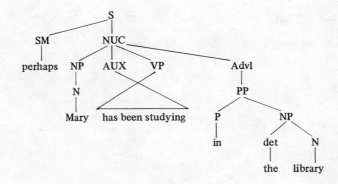

3. a. Incorrect ordering of adverbials. An adverbial of direction usually precedes an adverbial of time.
   b. Lack of agreement between the determiner and noun. The verb form further indicates that the noun must be made plural. Note the irregular plural.
   c. Incorrect formation of adverbial clause of reason. The clause lacks a subject NP. The subject *it* should be inserted after the adverbial subordinator *because*.
4. All three sentences contain time adverbials. All three time adverbials are derived from prepositional phrases. The difference is the presence or absence of the preposition. In the first sentence, the preposition is necessary; in the second sentence, it is optionally present; in the third sentence, it is obligatorily not present. We discuss the reasons for these differences in Chapter 19.
5. The locative noun *home* is not preceded by a preposition when it follows a verb of motion or direction.

*Joanne raced to home.

It may, however, take a preceding preposition when the verb describes a state.

Joanne stayed (at) home.

CHAPTER 3: Phrase Structure Rules—Part II
Pages 21–32

1. periphrastic modal—I *have to* return a book to the library.
   modal auxiliary—I *might* stay home and study tonight.
   perfective aspect—Sue *has* work*ed* here for seven years.
   progressive aspect—We *are* talk*ing* about the accident.
   imperative—*Leave* it alone!
   adjective phrase—His letter was *very thoughtful*.
   PP inside the VP—Jan put the letter *in the mailbox*.
   PP outside the VP—Doug found the folder *on the table*.
2. a. Ian is going to be taking that class next quarter.

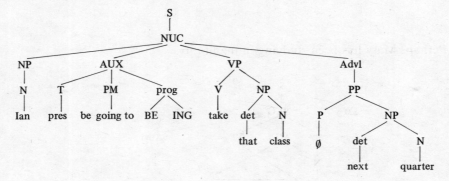

   b. He has been jogging since noon.

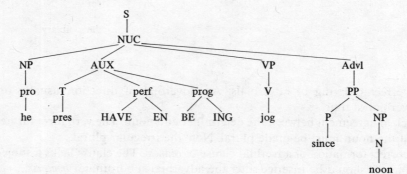

   c. Anne could have done her homework.

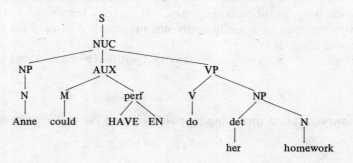

d. Jim might come tomorrow.

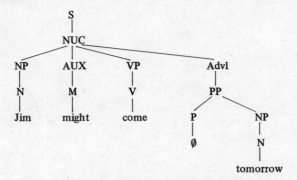

e. She has been very helpful.

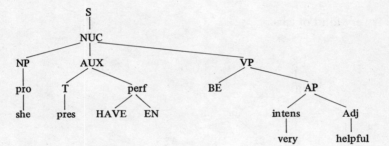

f. We left the chairs in the hallway.

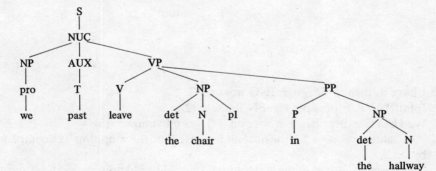

g. Maybe they are newcomers.

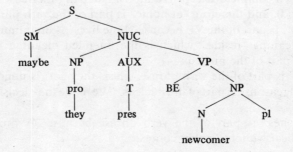

h. The meeting has to be at noon.

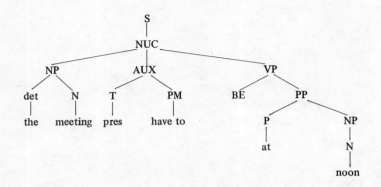

i. Sara is very fond of cats.

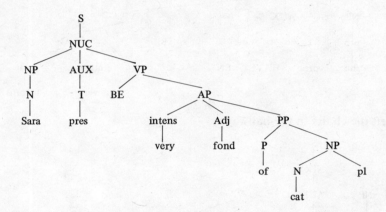

3. a. I have + pres to BE go + ING now. (2×)
   b. John HAVE + pres pass + EN the test. (2×)
   c. We HAVE + pres BE + EN swim + ING all summer. (3×)
4. a. "On Saturdays" is part of the nucleus because "I do the shopping" is a complete sentence by itself.
   b. "Off the curb" is part of the verb phrase, since "The old man stepped" is ungrammatical by itself.
   c. "Bob isn't" is incomplete (except as a short answer, in which case the rest of the sentence is understood), and therefore "at home" is part of the verb phrase.
   d. "In Phoenix" is part of the VP because "Jane lives" is ungrammatical if you interpret "live" as meaning "reside," which is the intended meaning here. "Because of the weather" is part of the nucleus.
   e. "In trouble" is part of the verb phrase, since "they got" is ungrammatical.
   f. "For several reasons" is part of the nucleus. "We made that decision" is grammatical by itself.
   g. "In the bushes" is part of the verb phrase because "A prowler was lurking" is ungrammatical without further context.

5. a. Verbs in sentences with modal auxiliaries are tenseless.
   b. Progressive aspect consists of two components: a form of BE and the suffix ING, which in this sentence should be attached to the main verb *jump* to form *jumping*.
   c. Use the "to-less" infinitive form after a modal.
   d. Perfective aspect consists of two components: a form of HAVE + the past participle. The HAVE auxiliary is missing from this sentence.
6. Emphasize that the progressive has two parts: BE + ING. The required form of BE precedes the verb and the ING is attached to the next verb in the sentence. Thus, it is incomplete to use *run* without ING in "*She is run now" or to use *running* without BE in "*She running now."
7. English can, of course, be used to express future time, but English has no "future tense" in the structural sense since verbs are not inflected in English for future. English speakers use auxiliary verbs (e.g., *will*) or future time adverbials (e.g., *tomorrow*) with present tense verbs to express future time.

CHAPTER 4: The Copula and Subject-Verb Agreement
Pages 33–48

1. the copula function of BE—Hawaii *is* a beautiful state.
   an auxiliary function of BE—We *were* thinking of vacationing there.

   collective noun subject—The *clergy* $\begin{Bmatrix} \text{has} \\ \text{have} \end{Bmatrix}$ taken a stand on the issue.

   mass noun subject—*Beer* is in the fridge.
   third-person singular present inflection—June *rides* her bike to school every day.
   the proximity principle—Either the steering mechanism or the *brakes were* the cause of the accident.
   the nonintervention principle—*One* of the reasons he went away to college *was* to get away from home.
   the clause principle—*Where our friends work* is unimportant.
2. a. I am very tired.

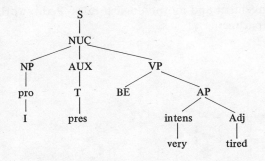

   Output of base: I pres BE very tired
   Affix attachment: I BE + pres very tired
   Subject-verb agreement and morphological rules: I am very tired.

b. Jacques is from France.

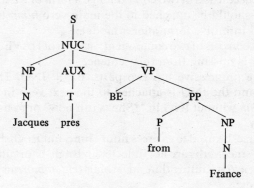

Output of base: Jacques pres BE from France
Affix attachment: Jacques BE + pres from France
Subject-verb agreement and morphological rules: Jacques is from France.

c. Pedro works for the mayor.

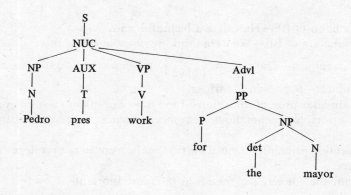

Output of base: Pedro pres work for the mayor
Affix attachment: Pedro work + pres for the mayor
Subject-verb agreement and morphological rules: Pedro works for the mayor.

d. We live in an apartment.

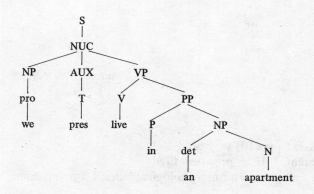

Output of base: we pres live in an apartment
Affix attachment: we live + pres in an apartment
Morphological rules: We live in an apartment.

e. My parents were teachers.

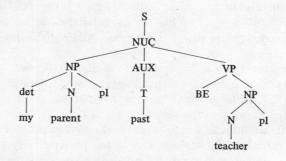

Output of base: my parent pl past BE teacher pl
Affix attachment: my parent + pl BE + past teacher + pl
Subject-verb agreement and morphological rules: My parents were teachers.

f. Barbara was working in Rome last year.

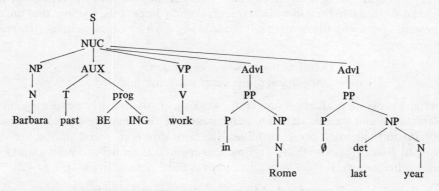

Output of base: Barbara past BE ING work in Rome last year
Affix attachment: Barbara BE + past work + ING in Rome last year
Subject-verb agreement and morphological rules: Barbara was working in Rome last year.

3. Subject-verb agreement is applied for all third person singular present tense verbs and for all forms of the verb BE. In other cases, the basic structure is the same as the surface structure, making application of this transformation unnecessary. Subject-verb agreement is not applied if the AUX contains an IMPER or a modal. Subject-verb agreement is also not applied in the past tense to verbs other than BE, and in the present tense it is not applied for all persons other than third person singular.

4. The traditional subject-verb agreement rule is often not maintained in sentences with both *neither ... nor* and personal pronouns, e.g.:

> Neither you nor she have (rather than *has*) made appointments yet.

The traditional rule is also often not maintained in informal sentences beginning with *there,* e.g.:

> There's (rather than *there are*) a lot of people here.

5. a. A plural verb *are* is used for both singular and plural second person pronouns in English. The present tense forms of BE are difficult because they are irregular. Remind the student of these patterns: *I am . . . , Am I . . . ?; He/She/It is . . . , Is he/she/it . . . ?; You/We/They are . . . , Are you/we/they . . . ?* and give them practice contrasting each.
   b. Third person singular present tense verbs take an *-s* at the end. Here, of course, the *-s* is realized phonetically as /z/ and has the irregular spelling of "es."
   c. Copula BE is needed before an adjective phrase. All English sentences contain a verb or a copula.
   d. Subject-verb agreement is never applied to modal auxiliaries.
   e. Only the third person singular present tense verbs agree in number and person with the subject. Some ESL/EFL students tend to reanalyze the *-s* ending, thinking that it marks the verb for the plurality of the subject.
6. The proximity rule would lead you to expect that native speakers use the verb *is* to agree with the closest noun phrase subject. This is the prescriptively correct rule; however, sometimes native speakers will break this rule, especially when they are speaking. Not all native speakers abide by the prescriptive rules of the language. You will not be wrong in following this rule, however. Perhaps this is an area of the language that is changing.
7. After having established that mass noun subjects take singular verbs, plural subjects take plural verbs, and collective noun subjects take either singular or plural verbs depending on the meaning, you can then introduce fractions and percentages. Explain that the number of the verb agrees with the noun that is modified by the fraction/percentage (if there is such a noun), e.g.:

> Half of the *tomatoes are* rotten.
> 90 percent of the *water was* contaminated.

Almanacs are good sources of contexts for working in this area. Recipes are a good context for fractions and census data for percentages. If students are taking other courses, problems in their math books or tables/diagrams/charts in social studies texts may be consulted. Remember also that if arithmetical operations are being done without a specific noun in the context, subject-verb agreement is third person singular, e.g.:

> Ten percent of 50 is 5.   Two-thirds of 9 is 6.

CHAPTER 5: The Lexicon
Pages 49–60

1. verb requiring an adverb of position—The dog *lay* in front of the fire.
   determiner requiring a mass noun—I don't have *much* money.
   incorporated noun—I already *salted* the vegetables.
   change-of-state verb—The stores *close* early on Saturday.
   noun compound—The *postman* left a huge package.
   inflectional affix—Lou work*s* very hard.
   derivational affix—Bonnie could use some excit*ement.*
   transitive adjective—My family is *fond* of Szechuan food.
   transitive verb—We *enjoy* spicy food.
   common noun—A *wok* is very useful.
   irregular noun—Some *men* are coming to help us move today.
   proper noun—*Joyce Chen* is the author of a well-known Chinese cookbook.

2. a. syntactic problem—*Lurk* requires an adverbial of position.
   b. semantic problem—*Fascinate* requires an animate object, a higher-order animal.
   c. syntactic problem—*Fall asleep* is intransitive.
   d. syntactic problem—The determiner *these* modifies only plural, not singular, nouns (i.e., Did the student intend to say *this book* or *these books?*).
3. a. *Information* is a mass (noncount) noun in English and therefore does not take the plural *-s* or the determiner *many.*
   b. *Discriminating,* not *discriminatory.* The latter has a negative meaning, implying prejudice. *Discriminating* has a positive connotation regarding the person's ability to evaluate the quality of something.
   c. *From my point of view* is the usual idiom. However, we also have *in my opinion* as a near paraphrase.
   d. *Tact* is a noun. The adjective form is *tactful.*
   e. *Many books* is the correct form, since *books* is a plural count noun. *Much* is used only with noncountable nouns.
   f. *Broke* is the correct past tense form of the irregular verb *break.*
   g. *Firecrackers* is the correct word, since "pyrotechnics" are referred to here. Although *crackerfires* follows the rules of compounding, it is not a word in English. If there were such a word, it might refer to fires made by people burning crackers.
   h. The student may have been trying to generate a verb from the noun *passion.* The correct verb form is *impassioned.* Another problem is word choice, since *impassion* is emotionally very strong. Perhaps *fascinated* would be a better choice (which may, in fact, be what the student was trying to produce).
   i. The correct preposition following *aware* is *of,* not *to.*
   j. In this word, the prefix that means *not* is *un-,* not *in-,* making *unpleasant* the correct form.
4. They are collective nouns. Grammatically, they can be singular or plural. When they are used as singular forms, reference is made to the group. When they are used with a plural verb, reference is made to the individuals which comprise the group.

CHAPTER 6: The Tense-Aspect System: Forms and Meanings
Pages 61–79

1. simple future—Sally *will live* in Boston until she graduates.
   present perfect—Catherine *has* just *been* offered a job.
   past time axis—Margie *had worked* on her thesis for two years before she finally *finished* it. Then, she *got* a good job almost immediately.
   progressive aspect—Sherry *is living* in New York while she *is attending* NYU.
   habitual past—Mike *used to* dream about going to Paris.
   verb of state (stative meaning)—Agnes could *smell* the dinner cooking in the next room.
   durative action verb—He's *making* the bed.
2. The speaker of the sentence no longer plays tennis. The use of *used to* implies a past habit that no longer obtains.
3. In both sentences the ordering is the same because *before* makes explicit the ordering such that the past perfect is not obligatory; i.e., the simple past with *before* suffices to indicate the sequence of events and the past perfect becomes a form of emphasis—or double marking of the sequence.

4. *Since* does not usually occur with the simple past because it signifies something that began at a definite time in the past and has continued until now. This is the meaning compatible with the present perfect, not the simple past.

5. a. Since the progressive aspect of a punctual verb indicates repetition, and since John is only one person, it would be impossible for him to arrive repeatedly. The second sentence, however, contains a plural subject, *they,* which allows for repeated arrivals by different people.

   b. The first question must refer to a specific past time. We can imagine it being asked of someone who was speaking about the time when he or she lived in New York. The second question asks whether at any past time, up to the present, the action has occurred.

   c. The first sentence implies that the action has been completed. The second sentence implies the action still has not been completed.

6. a. *Has bought* (present perfect) refers the action to the present (see Bull's time axis) and is therefore incompatible with the specific past time adverbial, *last Saturday,* which refers to the action in the past (time axis).

   b. The use of the progressive aspect here is wrong because the stative verb *cost* cannot take the progressive aspect. Just as with the other verbs of state, however, *cost* can take the progressive aspect when it is used in an active sense. It seems to take the ING, for instance, any time someone is being assessed the cost of something, e.g.:

   Your education is costing me a fortune.

   c. The student has not stayed within one time axis. The tense of the verb in the subordinate clause should be the present perfect so that it is in the same axis as the verb in the main clause.

7. Besides representing events occurring now, the "present progressive tense" can be used to refer to a planned future event. In this usage, it is usually accompanied by a future time adverbial.

8. *Just, yet,* and *already* are some of the signals which often occur with the present perfect tense. *Just* indicates recent completion in the past; *yet* indicates current noncompletion; *already* indicates a result that turned out earlier than anticipated. Other signals are *since* and *only.*

9. This statement does refer to present time; it also refers to adjacent past and presumably adjacent future time. One of the major uses of the simple present tense is to indicate that a particular action is habitual. This is its function in this sentence. This use of the simple present is sometimes referred to as an extended present.

10. In the first sentence *now* is the time when he habitually goes to the store. In the second sentence the present perfect entails a resultant state: "you" did something which has relevance now.

11. For some speakers of American English these sentences are synonymous; however, other speakers feel that the first sentence reflects the speaker's point of view (i.e., the speaker just heard the news and wants to know if his listener just heard it, too). On the other hand, the second sentence is more likely spoken with the listener's perspective in mind (i.e., the listener looks surprised or shocked, so the speaker tries to show empathy and asks if the listener has just heard the news). A discourse analysis would have to be conducted to determine whether this is supported and if there are other differences.

CHAPTER 7: Modal Auxiliaries and Periphrastic Modals
Pages 80–94

1. periphrastic modal—I *have to* go to the bank.
   social interactional use of a modal—*Would* you close the window?
   logical probability use of a modal—He *could* be in the shower.
   function of a perfect-form modal—He *must* not *have waited* long. (i.e., the perfect modal signals a deduction about the past)
   a sequence with more than one modal or periphrastic modal—Adrian *should be able to* find something else to do.
   polite form of a request—*Could* you drop me off at my apartment?
2. The sentence is ambiguous since *may* could mean that his mother was uncertain about the possibility of his going *or* that she has given her permission for him to go.
3. a. *Must be* makes a present inference; *must have been* makes a past inference.
   b. *Would you* is a softer, more polite form of the request than *will you*.
   c. The first sentence implies that the action took place; the second implies that it did not.
   d. *May* expresses possibility. *Must* expresses strong inference—the speaker is sure of the conclusion if he or she uses *must*.
   e. *Should* implies advisability. *Had better* is more insistent, almost a threat.
4. They imply that we weren't warned; i.e., the action was unfulfilled.
5. a. Subject-verb agreement is never applied to a modal auxiliary.
   b. A modal verb followed by a modal verb is not a grammatical sequence in English (although we acknowledge that certain regional dialects in the United States do allow some modal + modal combinations).
   c. A modal precedes a lexical verb directly without an intervening infinitive *to*.
   d. *May* is used to ask for permission, whereas *can* asks about the possibility of performing the action and *will* asks about the willingness of the person being asked to perform the action. Note that if the pronoun were changed from *you* to *I*, the sentence is grammatical because the speaker is seeking permission to do something.
   e. The perfect form, *should have studied,* is needed here because the past time adverbial *last term* indicates the advice is "hindsight" referring to past time.
6. In both requests the speaker is seeking information, but in a the speaker asks the addressee the possibility of his or her giving the directions, while in b the speaker assumes the addressee is able to comply and is querying his or her willingness to do so.
7. As we said in the text, *need* and *dare* are really archaic modals that now often function like regular verbs; nevertheless, they have retained some of their modal qualities. We see this happening in example b where *needn't* functions like other negative modals, e.g., *can't, won't,* and unlike lexical verbs or those periphrastic modals which require a DO verb in the negative, e.g., "You don't have to worry." In d again we see *need* functioning as a modal verb; cf. "Can I bring anything?" which does not require a DO in question formation the way lexical verbs and some periphrastic modals do, e.g., "Do I have to bring anything?" In c we see there is a DO verb in the question, but notice that *dare* has retained the characteristic of other modals in that there is no *to*-infinitive between *dare* and the main verb, *think*. In example a it could be argued that *need* functions as a lexical verb, e.g., "I want to see him," or like a periphrastic modal, e.g., "I have to see him." In example e *dare* seems to function like an ordinary lexical verb. Thus, the answer to the question really is that *need* and *dare* are shifting in their functions and presently represent a mixture of forms.

8. The first example is ambiguous. The principal could be saying that Joe had permission to go or that it was possible that Joe would go. The second example is unambiguous. The principal says it is possible that Joe went.

9. *Could* is not used to refer to ability or possibility with a human agent performing a specific punctual action with a specific recent past time adverbial, e.g., *last night*. It is possible, however, to use it if the subject is a perceiver or experiencer:

$$I \begin{Bmatrix} \text{could} \\ \text{was able to} \end{Bmatrix} \text{see many stars in the sky last night.}$$

Moreover, it is possible to use *could* with both specific and general time adverbials in the remote past:

I could read when I was three years old.   I could read at an early age.

In the negative, these distribution problems are not as complicated. In all the contexts, *couldn't* and *wasn't able to* are possible paraphrases. We can say "I couldn't pick up the tickets last night" because the specific, punctual action referred to was not accomplished.

CHAPTER 8: Negation
Pages 95–106

1. NOT contraction—Julia is*n't* studying very hard.
   DO support—She *does*n't do the homework.
   some ⟶ *any* suppletion—She didn't buy *any* of the required books.
   sentence-level negation—She *doesn't* see the need for school.
   word-level negation—Julia is *un*motivated.
   multiple negation
        grammatical—She is*n't un*intelligent.
        ungrammatical—*She wo*n't* get *no* degree.
2. a. We might not be having that class today.

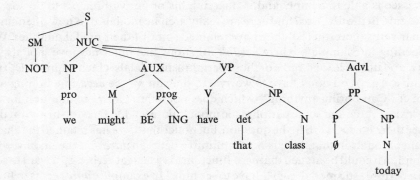

Output of base: NOT we might BE ING have that class today
NOT placement: we might NOT BE ING have that class today
Affix attachment (1✕): we might NOT BE have + ING that class today
Morphological rules: We might not be having that class today.

b. *Alice doesn't know any jokes.*

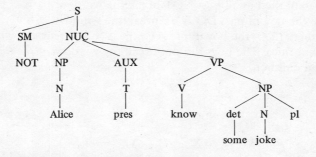

    Output of base: NOT Alice pres know some joke pl
    NOT placement: Alice pres NOT know some joke pl
    DO support: Alice pres DO NOT know some joke pl
    NOT contraction: Alice pres DO + N'T know some joke pl
    some ⟶ *any* suppletion: Alice pres DO + N'T know any joke pl
    Affix attachment (2✕): Alice DO + N'T + pres know any joke + pl
    Subject-verb agreement and morphological rules: Alice doesn't know any jokes.

c. *You haven't been around this neighborhood.*

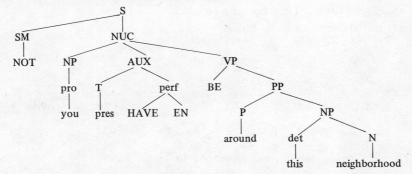

    Output of base: NOT you pres HAVE EN BE around this neighborhood
    NOT placement: you pres HAVE NOT EN BE around this neighborhood
    NOT contraction: you pres HAVE + N'T EN BE around this neighborhood
    Affix attachment (2✕): you HAVE + N'T + pres BE + EN around this neighborhood
    Morphological rules: You haven't been around this neighborhood.

d. *The boys did not break the window.*

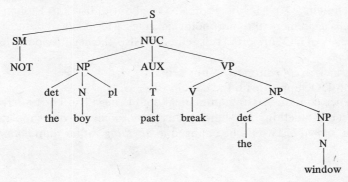

Output of base: NOT the boy pl past break the window
NOT placement: the boy pl past NOT break the window
DO support: the boy pl past DO NOT break the window
Affix attachment (2✕): the boy + pl DO + past NOT break the window
Morphological rules: The boys did not break the window.

e. They have no children.

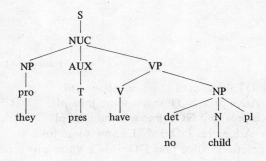

Output of base: they pres have no child pl
Affix attachment (2✕): they have + pres no child + pl
Morphological rules: They have no children.

f. Meg is not about to listen to Philip.

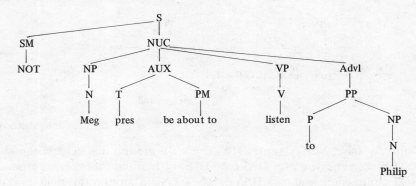

Output of base: NOT Meg pres be about to listen to Philip
NOT placement: Meg pres be NOT about to listen to Philip
Affix attachment (1✕): Meg be + pres NOT about to listen to Philip
Subject-verb agreement and morphological rules: Meg is not about to listen to Philip.

3. a. There is a lack of DO support in this sentence. Also, the negative particle should be *not* instead of *no*.
   b. There is a lack of DO support in this sentence.
   c. There is no DO support with the copula BE.
   d. This sentence contains an ungrammatical double negative. The underlying output is: NOT I past do something. With the application of *some* ⟶ *any* suppletion after NOT placement, *something* would be changed to *anything* rather than *nothing*.

4. *Regular (disyllabic)*

is + n't = isn't
are + n't = aren't
was + n't = wasn't
were + n't = weren't
does + n't = doesn't
did + n't = didn't
have + n't = haven't
has + n't = hasn't
had + n't = hadn't
must + n't = mustn't
may + n't = mayn't (very rare)
might + n't = mightn't (rare)
could + n't = couldn't
should + n't = shouldn't
would + n't = wouldn't
ought + n't = oughtn't (rare)
need + n't = needn't
dare + n't = daren't (rare)
used + n't = usedn't (British English only)

Irregular (monosyllabic)

can + n't = can't
do + n't = don't
shall + n't = shan't (rare)
will + n't = won't
am + n't = ain't (nonstandard)

No matter which way you choose to teach the irregular forms, remember that since both orthographic and phonological irregularity exist, both oral and written exercises should be provided. Another thing you should be aware of is that ESL/EFL students sometimes have trouble distinguishing *can* from *can't* in their pronunciation since the final /t/ in the latter is unreleased. Pointing out to these students that in usual nonemphatic American speech *can* has a reduced vowel (schwa), whereas the vowel in *can't* /æ/ is not reduced, may help them overcome this difficulty.

5. I am ⟶ I'm
you are ⟶ you're
he / she / it } is ⟶ he / she / it } 's

we are ⟶ we're
they are ⟶ they're

I / you / he / she / it / we / they } had ⟶ I / you / he / she / it / we / they } 'd

I / you / we / they } have ⟶ I / you / we / they } 've

he / she / it } has ⟶ he / she / it } 's

I / you / he / she / it / we / they } will ⟶ I / you / he / she / it / we / they } 'll

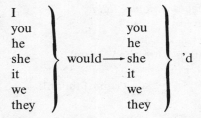

You'd can be the contraction of *you had* or *you would. It's* can be the contraction of *it is* or *it has.*

Contractions occur in normal speech for reasons of economy in the production of sound. *NOT contraction* and *AUX contraction* do not apply to the same constituent in a negated sentence because the deletion of so many vowels would result in sequences of unpronounceable English consonants.

6. Perhaps making your students aware of the frequency with which native English speakers use contractions would encourage them to use them in informal speech and writing. In an ESL context, students might be given an assignment to canvas native speakers with a list of questions that would be likely to elicit negative responses. They could be instructed to listen not only to the content of the answers but also to the frequency of contracted forms versus uncontracted forms. For demonstration of the use of contracted forms in written informal language, the teacher could bring in a letter from a friend and have the students look for the contracted forms. Students could also be assigned to look for the contractions in a page of comic strips.

7. This sentence contains an unacceptable double negative. The student could express what he wants to say in one of the two grammatical ways:

> I have not studied *any* other foreign language besides English.

or, a more emphatic variant:

> I have studied no other foreign language besides English.

CHAPTER 9: Yes-No Questions
Pages 107–121

1. negative yes-no question
   with contraction (informal)—Aren't we going to the movies tonight?
   without contraction (formal)—Are you not a graduate student?
   yes-no question with DO support—Do you like bagels?
   yes-no question without DO support—Should we send them a thank-you note?
   yes-no question with a periphrastic modal
   requiring DO support—Do you have to go to class now?
   not requiring DO support—Is she going to go to France?
   short-form answers—Is he from Vermont? *Yes, he is.* Does he like to ski? *Yes, he does.*
   elliptical yes-no question—Something bothering you?
   the semantics of responses to negative yes-no questions:
   Don't you understand DO support?
   No. (= *I don't understand it.*)
   Yes. (= *I do understand it.*)
   (An English speaker responds to a negative yes-no question as if it were an affirmative one with a different presupposition.)

2. a. Did he write the letter?

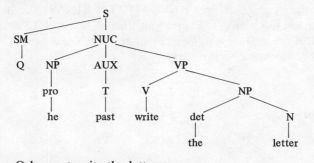

Output of base: Q he past write the letter
Subject/auxiliary inversion: past he write the letter
DO support: past do he write the letter
Affix attachment (1✕): do + past he write the letter
Morphological rules: Did he write the letter?

b. Wasn't she in San Francisco yesterday?

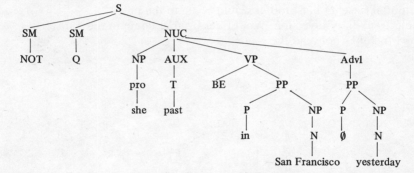

Output of base: Q NOT she past BE in San Francisco yesterday
NOT placement: Q she past BE NOT in San Francisco yesterday
NOT contraction: Q she past BE + N'T in San Francisco yesterday
Subject/auxiliary inversion: past BE + N'T she in San Francisco yesterday
Affix attachment (1✕): BE + N'T + past she in San Francisco yesterday
Subject-verb agreement and morphological rules: Wasn't she in San Francisco yesterday?

c. Have you been living in New York?

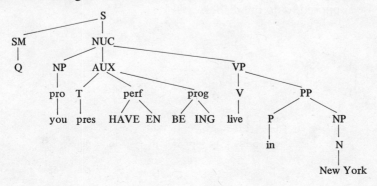

Output of base: Q you pres HAVE EN BE ING live in New York
Subject/auxiliary inversion: pres HAVE YOU EN BE ING live in New York
Affix attachment (3✕): HAVE + pres you BE + EN live + ING in New York
Morphological rules: Have you been living in New York?

d. Would her brother come to the party?

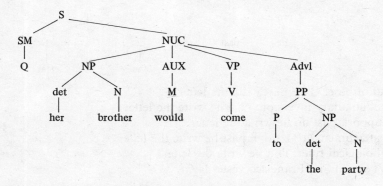

Output of base: Q her brother would come to the party
Subject/auxiliary inversion: Would her brother come to the party?

e. Has Mr. Jones not read the report?

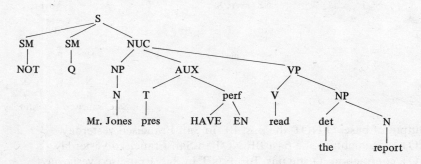

Output of base: Q NOT Mr. Jones pres HAVE EN read the report
NOT placement: Q Mr. Jones pres HAVE NOT EN read the report
Subject/auxiliary inversion: pres HAVE Mr. Jones NOT EN read the report
Affix attachment (2✕): HAVE + pres Mr. Jones NOT read + EN the report
Subject-verb agreement and morphological rules: Has Mr. Jones not read the report?

f. Aren't we supposed to do the dishes?

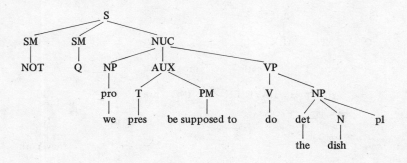

Output of base: NOT Q we pres be supposed to do the dish pl
NOT placement: Q we pres be NOT supposed to do the dish pl
NOT contraction: Q we pres be + N'T supposed to do the dish pl
Subject/auxiliary inversion: pres be + N'T we supposed to do the dish pl
Affix attachment (2✕): be + N'T + pres we supposed to do the dish + pl
Subject-verb agreement and morphological rules: Aren't we supposed to do the dishes?

3. a. Part of the subject/auxiliary inversion rule was violated. The past tense in the auxiliary was not inverted with the subject and was therefore mistakenly attached to the main verb.
   b. The subject/auxiliary inversion rule was violated. Only the first auxiliary verb and tense (if present) should be inverted with the subject.
   c. The DO support rule was not applied.

4. The first auxiliary verb or copula BE verb—and the tense constituent if there is one—is involved in both of them. They are either followed by NOT with the NOT placement transformation or inverted with the subject/auxiliary inversion transformation. If there is neither an auxiliary verb nor a BE verb in the sentence, both require DO support following their application.

5. a. The main verb (other than BE) is not inverted with the subject in English question formation. Only the past tense would be inverted in this sentence, and then DO support would be applied.
   b. Tense should only be marked once. In sentences with a DO verb, the DO acts as the tense carrier and the main verb has the base form.
   c. NOT should be contracted with the verb if it appears before the subject in the sentence (Isn't she intelligent?) or should be uncontracted if it appears after the subject (Is she not intelligent?).
   d. If there is no auxiliary verb or copula BE in the sentence, then the DO verb is used in short answers to yes-no questions.

   Do you like ice cream? Yes, I do.

   Alternatively, since *like* is a transitive verb, if a full form answer were given, *like* must be followed by an NP.

   Do you like ice cream? Yes, I like $\begin{Bmatrix} \text{it} \\ \text{ice cream} \end{Bmatrix}$.

6. Do you have any homework?   Don't you have any homework?
   Explain that the presupposition of the native speaker asking either of the two questions above differs depending on which form he chooses (see footnote 4). However, the listener should respond to either question in the same way. If he has homework, he should respond affirmatively; if not, he should respond negatively.

7. He is correct, of course. Native speakers do produce uninverted yes-no questions. You should point out, however, that native speakers do so only when they have certain expectations about the answer they will receive (see footnote 6). Since inverting yes-no questions is definitely the norm, often this student's uninverted questions will seem inappropriate (i.e., aggressive, presumptuous, and rude).

CHAPTER 10: Pronouns and Possessives
Pages 122–134

1. subject pronoun—*They* have been living together for a year.
   object pronoun—I went to visit *them* recently.
   possessive pronoun—I thought the car outside the apartment was *theirs.*
   possessive determiner—*Their* apartment was small and cluttered.
   reflexive pronoun—I bought *myself* a new dress.
   indefinite pronoun—*Anybody* without a ticket should stand in the other line.
   demonstrative pronoun—The last exercises were harder than *these.*
   's possessive—*Erin's* voice was the loudest in the room.
   of possessive—The title *of the story* was "The Lottery."

2. a. The *of* possessive is preferred here as *the room* is inanimate and does not perform an action.
   b. *Him* is an object pronoun being used where the subject pronoun *he* should be used.
   c. *Mines* is the incorrect form of this possessive pronoun. It should be *mine.* This is perhaps an overgeneralization error since the other possessive pronouns end in *s.*
   d. The last pronoun in the sentence should be the object pronoun *me* since it is the object of the preposition *besides.*

3. a. *My friend's house* is the correct form of an animate possessor, especially here where the possessor is not a long or complex NP.
   b. The third person singular masculine reflexive pronoun is *himself.* This is perhaps an overgeneralization error, since other reflexive pronouns are formed with the possessive determiner followed by *self* or *selves,* e.g., *myself, ourselves.*
   c. The student neglected to use the *'s* possessive form to mark *Mary* as the possessor.
   d. The subject *Everybody,* like all the other compound indefinite pronouns, requires a singular verb.

4. Since the *'s* morpheme and the plural morpheme are both suffixed to NPs and both pattern the same way phonetically, their similarity may cause some confusion. Also, *'s* is unstressed and may not therefore be perceived by students. (In other words, *'s* has low perceptual saliency.) On the other hand, some students may perceive *'s* but not be able to produce it because their native language has few or no consonant clusters.

5. Spanish speakers may use the *of* possessive incorrectly in place of the *'s* possessive:

   *the garden of Milly

   They may also omit the *'s* possessive altogether by analogy with noun adjuncts:

   *Milly garden

6. Other pronouns in English that can also mean "everyone in general" are:

   you—You gotta study hard to get good grades.
   we—We should study hard if we want to get good grades.
   everyone (body)—Everyone should learn a foreign language.

7. Two ways of avoiding the usage of *he, his,* and *him* when these forms are used in a general sense are:
   a. to use plurals

   A student should plan his schedule wisely.——►Students should plan their schedules wisely.

b. to use *one*

> A person should not reveal his deepest thoughts to total strangers.⟶ One should not reveal one's deepest thoughts to total strangers.

Of course, both these ways have drawbacks. Sometimes using the plural will not work, when you simply want to discuss an individual's doing something. And the use of *one* can easily be overdone, resulting in stilted (or overly formal) language.
8. Native speakers sometimes do violate the prescriptive rules of pronoun usage and use subject pronouns where object pronouns are called for, e.g., *The book is by she and Professor Hansen. Native speakers also sometimes use object pronouns where the prescriptive rule says subject pronouns are necessary, e.g., *Me and Mark are going to the store.

> You can explain to your ESL/EFL students that they won't be wrong in following the prescriptive rules, even though not all native speakers abide by them all the time.

CHAPTER 11: A Closer Look at Transformations—Imperatives and Reflexives
Pages 135–146

1. synonymous sentences—I gave the book to him. I gave him the book.
   ambiguous sentence—Mother said that she could go. (Mother could go or some other
        female could go, e.g., Mother gave her daughter permission to go.)
   imperative
        affirmative—Go ahead and leave!
        negative—Don't do that!
   reflexive verb—We *enjoyed* ourselves at the party. (*Enjoy* is optionally reflexive.)
   deletable reflexive pronoun—We prepared (*ourselves*) for the onslaught.
   inclusive imperative—*Let's* reflect on that for a while.
   diffuse imperative—Someone open the window, please.
2. a. Be quiet.

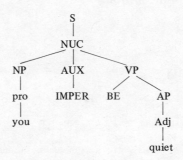

> Output of base: you IMPER BE quiet
> *You* deletion: IMPER BE quiet
> Affix attachment (1✕): BE + IMPER quiet
> Morphological rules: Be quiet.

b. He dressed himself every morning.

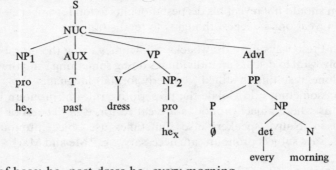

Output of base: he$_x$ past dress he$_x$ every morning
Reflexive: he past dress himself every morning
Affix attachment (1×): he dress + past himself every morning
Morphological rules: He dressed himself every morning.

c. Come here.

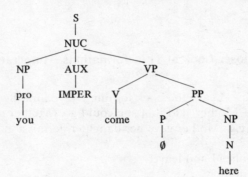

Output of base: you IMPER come here
You deletion: IMPER come here
Affix attachment (1×): come + IMPER here
Morphological rules: Come here.

d. Mary looked at herself in the mirror.

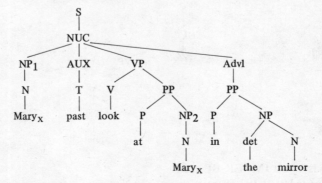

Output of base: Mary$_x$ past look at Mary$_x$ in the mirror
Reflexive: Mary past look at herself in the mirror
Affix attachment (1×): Mary look + past at herself in the mirror
Morphological rules: Mary looked at herself in the mirror.

e. Don't you forget her birthday.

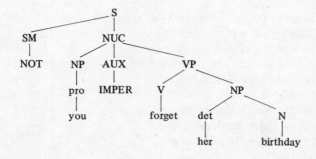

Output of base: NOT you IMPER forget her birthday
NOT placement: you IMPER NOT forget her birthday
DO support: you IMPER DO NOT forget her birthday
NOT contraction: you IMPER DO + N'T forget her birthday
Subject/auxiliary inversion: IMPER DO + N'T you forget her birthday
Affix attachment (1X): DO + N'T + IMPER you forget her birthday
Morphological rules: Don't you forget her birthday.

3. a. The two NPs in the basic structure sentence must be identical in form and reference in order for the rightmost NP to be transformed into a reflexive pronoun. This condition has not been met in the basic structure of this sentence.
    b. Only second person pronouns, i.e., *you,* are subjects of imperatives.
    c. Imperatives are formed with "bare" infinitives. They do not contain tense in the auxiliary and subject-verb agreement is not applied; i.e., imperatives never take an inflection.
    d. There are two possible causes of the error in this sentence. If the reflexive pronoun is supposed to refer to Mary, then it should be, of course, *herself.* If the reflexive pronoun is supposed to refer to the subject *he,* then the reflexive transformation was misapplied. The condition that both NPs must be within the *same* basic structure sentence has been ignored. *He* is the subject of the sentence; *himself* is the object of the sentence which has Mary as its subject. Thus for this second interpretation, the reflexive pronoun *himself* should be changed to the object pronoun *him.*

4. a. The correct form of the third person plural reflexive pronoun is *themselves,* formed with the object pronoun *them + selves.* The student has incorrectly combined the possessive pronoun *their + selves,* perhaps overgeneralizing from *my/her/your/our + self/selves.*
    b. If there are two NPs which are identical in form and reference within the same basic structure sentence, the rightmost NP must be changed to a reflexive pronoun. Here *me* should be made *myself.*
    c. The student neglected to add *do.* The IMPER auxiliary must combine with DO to form a negative imperative.

5. This is one of those instances where it is difficult to be prescriptive. What a teacher might want to do is to concentrate on giving students practice producing contracted negative imperatives, e.g., Don't be late! rather than uncontracted forms, Do not be late! The reasoning is that contracted forms occur more frequently in the language and whether or not the *you* is left in or deleted, a grammatical sentence will result:

> Don't be late!   *Do not you be late!
> Don't you be late!

CHAPTER 12: Wh-Questions
Pages 147–159

1. wh-question focusing on the subject—Who speaks Swahili?
    wh-question focusing on a preposition object
        formal—To whom did you send the card?
        informal—Who did you send the card to?
    wh-question focusing on a determiner
        possessive—Whose money is this?
        demonstrative—Which flavor do you prefer?
        quantity—How many students arrived?
    uninverted wh-question—He left when?
    negative wh-question
        contracted—Why didn't you stay?
        uncontracted—Why did you not stay?
    wh-question with ellipsis of the auxiliary—Where ya goin'?
2. a. How is your father today?

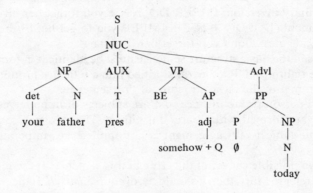

    Output of base: your father pres BE somehow + Q today
    Wh-replacement: your father pres BE how today
    Wh-fronting: how your father pres BE today
    Subject/auxiliary inversion: how pres BE your father today
    Affix attachment (1×): how BE + pres your father today
    Subject-verb agreement and morphological rules: How is your father today?
   b. Who should we invite to the party?

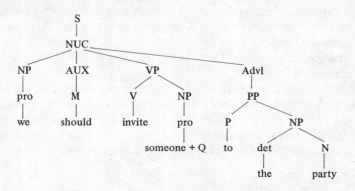

Output of base: we should invite someone + Q to the party
Wh-replacement: we should invite who to the party
Wh-fronting: who we should invite to the party
Subject/auxiliary inversion: Who should we invite to the party?

c. Whose book is on the table?

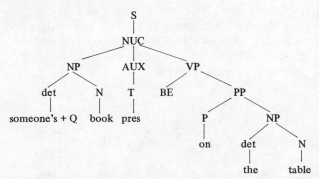

Output of base: someone's + Q book pres BE on the table
Wh-replacement: whose book pres BE on the table
Affix attachment (1×): whose book BE + pres on the table
Subject-verb agreement and morphological rules: Whose book is on the table?

d. How long is the table?

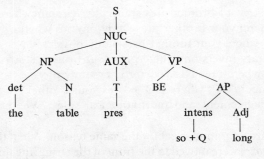

Output of base: the table pres BE so + Q long
Wh-replacement: the table pres BE how long
Wh-fronting: how long the table pres BE
Subject/auxiliary inversion: how long pres BE the table
Affix attachment (1×): how long BE + pres the table
Subject-verb agreement and morphological rules: How long is the table?

e. What didn't you understand?

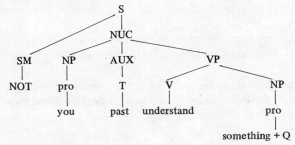

Output of base: NOT you past understand something + Q
NOT placement: you past NOT understand something + Q
DO support: you past DO NOT understand something + Q
NOT contraction: you past DO + N'T understand something + Q
Wh-replacement: you past DO + N'T understand what
Wh-fronting: what you past DO + N'T understand
Subject/auxiliary inversion: what past DO + N'T you understand
Affix attachment (1✕): what DO + N'T + past you understand
Morphological rules: What didn't you understand?

f. Where does your brother study physics?

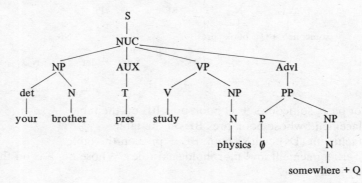

Output of base: your brother pres study physics somewhere + Q
Wh-replacement: your brother pres study physics where
Wh-fronting: where your brother pres study physics
Subject/auxiliary inversion: where pres your brother study physics
DO support: where pres DO your brother study physics
Affix attachment (1✕): where DO + pres your brother study physics
Subject-verb agreement and morphological rules: Where does your brother study physics?

3. Both questions are ungrammatical for the same reason. When the determiners marked + Q (*which* and *whose*) were moved to the front of the string, the nouns they modify (*car* and *handbag*) should have been moved as well.

4. a. When the wh-question focuses on something in the predicate, subject/auxiliary inversion must take place. It has not been applied to this question.

b. This question lacks a DO auxiliary. If a question has no auxiliary verb or copula and it focuses on something in the predicate, DO support is necessary.

c. The preposition *to* should either be fronted with the wh-question word to produce "To whom did he say that?" or it should remain behind when the wh-question word is fronted to produce "Who did he say that to?" It should not appear twice as it does in this question.

d. English sentences require a verb. In this case, it is most likely the BE verb which has been omitted. The question should be "Where is Benny?" or "Where's Benny?"

5. Structure:
With *why* the normal rules for wh-question formation apply.
With *what . . . for* the normal rules for wh-question formation apply, except that *for* cannot be fronted with the *what*:

*For what did he say that?

With *how come,* the word order is the same as for an affirmative statement; i.e., there is no subject/auxiliary inversion.

Meaning:

All three can be used to ask for a reason; however, unless questions with *why* are given a particular intonation pattern, they appear to be more neutral than do *what . . . for* and *how come.* One can imagine the latter two being used as challenges, e.g.:

What did you do that for? (Surely, there was a better alternative.)

Another difference may be that *why* and *how come* can be used to ask about the cause of something, whereas *what . . . for* seems to ask about purpose.

Why is the sky blue?
How come the sky is blue? $\Big\}$ (cause)   What is the sky blue for? (purpose)

Register:

Why questions appear to be the most formal, with *how come* and *what . . . for* being used informally. *How come* is probably the least formal of the three.

In addition to these differences, another instance where they cannot be used to paraphrase each other is in the formation of negative questions. *What . . . for* cannot be used as a negative paraphrase of the other two:

Why didn't he say that?   *What didn't he say that for?
How come he didn't say that?

6. In the questions with *did*—i.e., a, b, and e—the question is focusing on information contained in the predicate. In these questions the subject and auxiliary must be inverted, and the DO auxiliary has been added to carry the tense. In the questions without *did*—i.e., c and d—the question is focusing on information contained in the subject. No inversion and therefore no DO auxiliary is required.

CHAPTER 13: Other Question Types
Pages 160–170

1. tag question:

idiosyncratic—Let's talk about that money I lent you, shall we?
marked—So you're going to pay me back next week, are you?
unmarked—You thought I forgot about it, didn't you?

a yes-no question that looks like an alternative question:

Do you want to go to a movie tonight or the ⁄concert?

No, let's stay home.

alternative question:

Do you want to go to a movie tonight or the ⁄concert?

Let's go to the concert.

rhetorical question:

Instructor to class: Are you here to worry about grades or to learn something?

2. a. Jerry isn't president, is he?

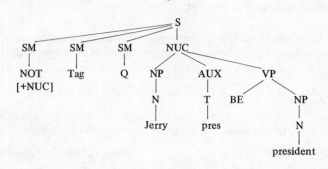

Output of base: NOT [+NUC] tag Q Jerry pres BE president
Tag: NOT [+NUC] Jerry pres BE president Q he pres BE
NOT placement: Jerry pres BE NOT president Q he pres BE
NOT contraction: Jerry pres BE + N'T president Q he pres BE
Subject/auxiliary inversion: Jerry pres BE + N'T president pres BE he
Affix attachment (2X): Jerry BE + N'T pres president BE + pres he
Subject-verb agreement (2X) and morphological rules: Jerry isn't president, is he?

b. The Smiths go to every concert, don't they?

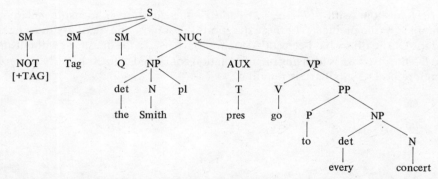

Output of base: NOT [+TAG] tag Q the Smith pl pres go to every concert
Tag: NOT [+TAG] the Smith pl pres go to every concert Q they pres
DO support: NOT [+TAG] the Smith pl pres go to every concert Q they pres DO
NOT placement: the Smith pl pres go to every concert Q they pres DO NOT
NOT contraction: the Smith pl pres go to every concert Q they pres DO + N'T
Subject/auxiliary inversion: the Smith pl pres go to every concert pres DO + N'T they
Affix attachment (3X): the Smith + pl go + pres to every concert DO + N'T + pres they
Morphological rules: The Smiths go to every concert, don't they?

3. a. The tense should be the same in both the NUC and the tag. The tense of the tag should be present (i.e., doesn't he) since the tag question transformation copies the tense of the main verb.

b. Alternative questions and yes-no questions with conjuncts should join two similar interrogative structures. This is not the case here where a yes-no question is joined with a wh-question.

c. Just as with negative yes-no questions and negative wh-questions, the NOT in a negative tag question must be contracted if it is to precede the subject in the tag (i.e., didn't he).

d. Although the nucleus doesn't contain a NOT sentence modifier, it does contain a negative lexical item, *never,* which expresses syntactic negation. As such, the tag should be affirmative following one of the usual unmarked tag question patterns, i.e., a syntactically negative nucleus followed by an affirmative tag.

4. a. Is Janet blue-eyed or is she not blue-eyed?

   b. You're looking forward to vacation, aren't you?

   c. Was it Bill who wrote the letter or was it Bob who wrote the letter?

5. a. If there is an auxiliary verb in the main sentence, the tag question is formed using the same auxiliary verb. The subject in the main sentence and the tag must be the same as well, although the latter is pronominalized if necessary. Thus the tag must be *aren't we* rather than *isn't it.*

   b. *Yes* is never an appropriate tag question in English, although native speakers will sometimes use *no* as a tag with a rising intonation in informal situations.

   c. This is the intonation pattern of an alternative question; the listener is being asked to make a choice between two alternatives. Since it is not a yes-no question, the response *yes* is ungrammatical. *No* would also be an ungrammatical response here.

6. a. These two utterances differ with regard to the presupposition of the speaker. 2 would be uttered by the speaker if he or she did not expect it to rain, whereas 1 signals that rain is expected by the speaker.

   b. A discourse analysis will have to be carried out before we can be sure of the difference between 1 and 2. It may be that 2 is more formal than 1 or more emphatic; e.g., one can imagine 2 being uttered by a speaker who is losing patience with his or her listener.

   c. In sentence 1, the speaker expects that the listener will have carried out the action. In sentence 2—depending on stress and intonation—the speaker may be expressing disbelief that the action was performed or the speaker may be trying to ascertain whether or not the action was performed. The second option for 2 is more characteristic of British than American usage.

CHAPTER 14: The Article System
Pages 171–188

1. proper noun

   proper name—*Washoe, Lucy,* and *Lana* are chimpanzees who have learned sign language.

   geographical name—*Honolulu* is on the island of *Oahu.*

   mass noun—*Water* is composed of oxygen and hydrogen.

   abstract noun—*Beauty* is in the eyes of the beholder.

   indefinite noun

   specific—I'm looking for *a pen* that I misplaced.

   nonspecific—If I don't find it, I'll have to buy *a new pen.*

   predicate noun—John Locke was *a philosopher.*

   generic usage with

   definite article—*The heart* is often described as the body's pump.

   indefinite article—Few people have ever seen *a California condor.*

   parti-generic—What he wants most to do in life is to make *money.*

2. a. *Coffee* is a mass noun here and does not take an article. *A coffee* means a serving/cup of coffee. If the coffee were spilled, it would no longer be contained within a cup and therefore could not be referred to with the indefinite article.

   b. *Water* is a mass noun here. Mass nouns are uncountable and do not take a plural ending.
   c. A specific, indefinite countable noun (here the examination the speaker is introducing to the listener) takes the indefinite article.
3. a. Singular predicate nominals that classify the subject noun are preceded by an indefinite article.
   b. *European* does not have an initial vowel sound, although it looks as if it does. It begins with a /y/ sound, and therefore should take *a*—rather than *an*. Alternatively, if *European* is being used as an adjective, no article is necessary.
   c. Here *poetry* is a mass noun used generically. No article is necessary.
4. An indefinite article used in object position may be ambiguous with regard to whether it modifies a specific or nonspecific noun in the speaker's mind. *A car* could be nonspecific, i.e., any car, or it could be specific, i.e., a particular car that John has in mind.
5. All three are used generically. *The German* seems the most formal and seems to be used to talk about the group as an abstract unit. What differentiates *the Germans* and *Germans* is sometimes difficult to detect; the former views the members of the group collectively whereas the latter generalizes via pluralization and is more informal than *the German*.

   Nationalities that have names ending in a sibilant sound (i.e., -s, -z, -š, -ž, -tš, -dž) occur without any overt plural form (e.g., Japanese, Chinese, Polish) and thus cannot be referred to with all three patterns, since the first is ungrammatical with such nationalities if the reference is generic.

> *The Chinese is hard-working.   Chinese are hard-working.
> The Chinese are hard-working.

CHAPTER 15: Measure Words, Collective Nouns, and Quantifiers
Pages 189–202

1. measure word
     general—a *sack* of flour
     specific—a *cup* of sugar
     idiomatic—a *sprig* of parsley
   numberlike quantifier—Claude has *a great deal* of talent.
   quantifier for count nouns only—There are *many* questions one could ask.
   quantifier for mass nouns only—I'll have to give this one *a little* thought.
   quantifier for count and mass nouns—We have *a lot of* chores to do. We have *a lot of* fun in store for you.
   negative connotation quantifier—They had *little* success in solving the problem.
   collective noun
     singular reference—*The jury* brought in *its* decision.
     plural reference—*The jury* brought in *their* decision.
2. a. *Chalk* is a mass noun. In order to talk about individual items, you use the quantifier *(a) piece(s) of* (e.g., a piece of chalk, three pieces of chalk).
   b. *A lot of* and *lots of* always take the *of* unless they are functioning as nouns or pronouns.
   c. *Few* is a quantifier with a negative connotation. Since *although* signals a contrast, you would expect a quantifier with a positive connotation to be used. Here the correct quantifier is *a few;* alternatively, the logical connector *because* should replace *although* if *few* is truly intended to convey a negative connotation.

3. a. *Many* is followed by *of* only when the noun it quantifies is definite. In 2 *people* is not definite as it is in 1.

   b. *Class* is a collective noun. In 1 *class* refers to a collective whole, while in 2 it refers to the individuals that make up the collective whole.

   c. *Not . . . a lot of* implies "some, but not much," according to Neuman (1975). *Not . . . much,* on the other hand, implies "very little."

   d. *Lots* seems more informal than *a lot.* It also seems to signify a greater amount, perhaps because it can be reduplicated (i.e., lots and lots and lots) whereas *a lot* cannot.

4. a. *Problem* is a count noun and must have the *-s* ending for plural. *Much* is used before mass nouns, not plural count nouns. *Many* is the correct form; i.e., the correct NP is *many problems.*

   b. The student is overgeneralizing the pattern for making mass nouns countable. When you have a specific noun-based numerical word like *million* with an indefinite plural head noun like *people,* the use of *of* is ungrammatical. Also noun-based numerical words remain in the singular even when modified by a number greater than one. This phrase should be *eight million people.*

   c. *A lot of* is preferred over *much* with positive assertions, especially in informal language.

   d. *Bread* is a mass noun, not a countable one. *Bread* may be made countable by using preceding measure words such as *three slices of* or *three pieces of.*

   e. There is no plural on a specific measure-phrase construction when it is used as a prenominal modifier without *of.* This should be *two-word verbs.*

5. Nouns like *the meek* and *the rich* do not exhibit duality of number like collective nouns when referred back to. That is, for collective nouns you may say either

$$\text{The mob was restless;} \left\{\begin{array}{l}\text{they were}\\\text{it was}\end{array}\right\}\text{ready for action.}$$

whereas you may only refer to adjectivally derived nouns with a plural referent.

$$\text{The aged are not privileged in America;} \left\{\begin{array}{l}\text{they often suffer}\\\text{*it often suffers}\end{array}\right\}\text{social and economic}$$
hardships.

They, therefore, are always plural since they can only refer to an indefinite number of individuals.

6. The rule you have learned holds only for *specific* measure phrases in prenominal position. Thus you could not say

$$\text{*Greece: a Five-centuries-old Framework . . .}$$

but it is grammatical to use the plural when the measure phrase is used with a general rather than specific number reference. Recall that this is also why we can say "millions of stars" in a general sense but must say "four million dollars" (i.e., no "s" on *million*) when the numerical reference is specific.

CHAPTER 16: Preverbal Adverbs of Frequency
Pages 203–220

1. specific or general adverbial of frequency
   specific—Lorraine jogs five miles *every week.*
   general—Lorraine jogs *on occasion.*

preverbal adverb of frequency
  positive—I *often* see her brother on campus.
  negative—He *rarely* comes to visit.
phrasal preverbal adverb of frequency
  positive—Beth is *almost always* on time.
  negative—She is *not usually* late.
negative constituent fronting (with preverbal adverb)—*Never* have I seen such a glorious day!

2. a. Mr. Nelson rarely waters his lawn.

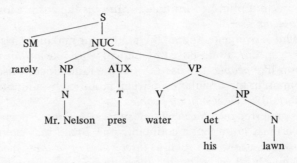

Output of base: rarely Mr. Nelson pres water his lawn
Preverbal adverb placement: Mr. Nelson rarely pres water his lawn
Affix attachment (1×): Mr. Nelson rarely water + pres his lawn
Subject-verb agreement and morphological rules: Mr. Nelson rarely waters his lawn.

   b. I have often overslept.

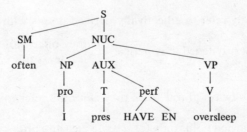

Output of base: often I pres HAVE EN oversleep
Preverbal adverb placement: I pres HAVE often EN oversleep
Affix attachment (2×): I HAVE + pres often oversleep + EN
Morphological rules: I have often overslept.

   c. Jim is not always correct.

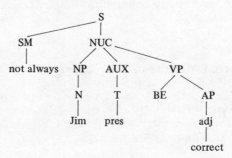

Output of base: not always Jim pres BE correct
Negative preverbal phrasal adverb placement: Jim pres BE not always correct
Affix attachment (1×): Jim BE + pres not always correct
Subject-verb agreement and morphological rules: Jim is not always correct.

   d. Have you ever tasted papaya?

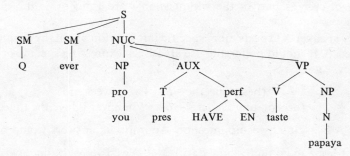

Output of base: Q ever you pres HAVE EN taste papaya
Ever placement: Q you pres HAVE ever EN taste papaya
Subject/auxiliary inversion: pres HAVE you ever EN taste papaya
Affix attachment (2×): HAVE + pres you ever taste + EN papaya
Morphological rules: Have you ever tasted papaya?

3. a. It should be *Isn't he ever . . .* or *Is he not ever. . . . Not ever* placement patterns like NOT placement, and the *not* and the *ever* stay together as a unit.

   b. The preverbal adverb of frequency can only separate an auxiliary verb that occurs in the nucleus or the BE copula from NOT. Since in this case neither of these underlying forms is present, only two orders are possible:

     Marvin does not often dance.   Marvin often does not dance.

   c. The answer is not given in a full sentence; rather, it occurs in a reduced clause. In such cases, preverbal adverbs of frequency cannot be the final constituent. The order should be *I never am.* Alternatively, the response could be even further reduced to "No, never" or simply "No" or "Never" without the subject pronoun and copula being present.

4. a. If the nucleus contains an unstressed auxiliary verb, place the preverbal adverb of frequency after it. Thus, this sentence should be:

     José can sometimes play handball after work.

   b. If a negative preverbal adverb of frequency has been fronted, subject/auxiliary inversion must take place:

     Rarely can we eat outside in the garden!

Alternatively, the preverbal adverb of frequency could be placed after the first auxiliary verb in the nucleus:

     We can rarely eat outside in the garden.

This second form should be used if emphasis (i.e., exclamation) is not intended.

   c. If *not* is retained, *never* should be changed to *ever.* A negative preverbal adverb such as *never* does not co-occur with sentence modifier NOT. Thus one must say either

    "I $\begin{Bmatrix} \text{have not} \\ \text{haven't} \end{Bmatrix}$ ever told a lie."   or "I have never told a lie."

5. a. The second sentence emphasizes the absolute frequency with which Alice uses dental floss, although both sentences indicate her use of dental floss is habitual.
   b. It isn't completely clear what the difference between these two is, but perhaps the sentence with *never* is more emphatic. Further study of such forms as they occur in context would be useful.
   c. The use of *ever* as part of the wh-question word transforms the question into an exclamation.
6. a. Probably speaker A expects more specific information about the frequency of B's trips to the beach. B should preferably use an adverb expressing specific or at least general frequency, e.g.:

   (best) Specific—*B:*   Every weekend.
   (acceptable) General—*B:*   Whenever I have the time.

   b. Speaker A is asking a yes-no question. Appropriate answers would be:

   No, but I hope to go there some day.   Yes, I've been there twice.

7. In sentence *b,* the preverbal adverb of frequency precedes the auxiliary verb, which means that the auxiliary carries emphatic or contrastive stress. In sentence *a* the auxiliary verb has reduced stress and the sentence is in the unmarked form; i.e., it is not emphatic.

CHAPTER 17: The Passive Voice
Pages 221–235

1. active voice—Two million people *watch* the program every week.
   a passive with agent—"The Road Not Taken" *was written* by *Robert Frost.*
   a verb that is never passive—Water *consists* of hydrogen and oxygen.
   a verb that is always passive—Jonathan *was born* in Japan.
   the agentless change-of-state verb construction—School enrollment *increased* this year.
   the agentless passive—Work has not yet *been completed* on the underground transit system.
   the GET passive—The dog *got hit* on its way home.
   the stative passive—The window *is broken.*
2. a. The report is being studied by the committee.

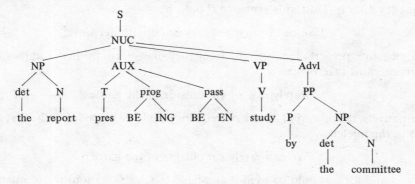

   Output of base: the report pres BE ING BE EN study by the committee
   Affix attachment (3×): the report BE + pres BE + ING study + EN by the committee
   Subject-verb agreement and morphological rules: The report is being studied by the committee.

b. John was arrested yesterday.

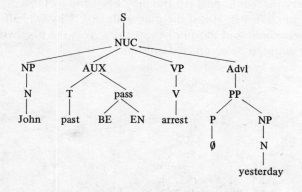

Output of base: John past BE EN arrest yesterday
Affix attachment (2×): John BE + past arrest + EN yesterday
Subject-verb agreement and morphological rules: John was arrested yesterday.

c. The parcel should not have been delivered to the hospital.

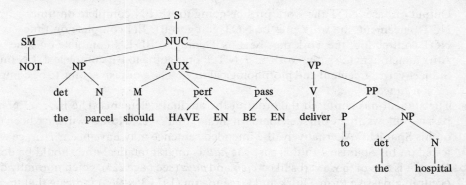

Output of base: NOT the parcel should HAVE EN BE EN deliver to the hospital
NOT placement: the parcel should NOT HAVE EN BE EN deliver to the hospital
Affix attachment (2×): the parcel should NOT HAVE BE + EN deliver + EN to the hospital
Morphological rules: The parcel should not have been delivered to the hospital.

d. Was the play written by O'Neill?

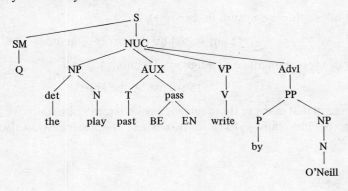

Output of base: Q the play past BE EN write by O'Neill
Subject/auxiliary inversion: past BE the play EN write by O'Neill
Affix attachment (2×): BE + past the play write + EN by O'Neill
Subject-verb agreement and morphological rules: Was the play written by O'Neill?

e. The work isn't going to be completed on time.

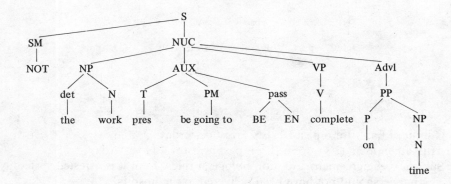

Output of base: NOT the work pres be going to BE EN complete on time
NOT placement: the work pres be NOT going to BE EN complete on time
NOT contraction: the work pres be + N'T going to BE EN complete on time
Affix attachment (2×): the work be + N'T + pres going to BE complete + EN on time
Subject-verb agreement and morphological rules: The work isn't going to be completed on time.

3. a. The student has confused the order of the auxiliary elements. The BE ... EN of the passive follows all the other elements of the auxiliary, i.e., "Horace will have been tested on his Spanish." Alternatively, the intended sentence may have been "Horace will be tested on his Spanish." In this case the *had* is ungrammatical and should be deleted.

b. *Contain* is one of those verbs like *weigh* and *have* (see page 224) which normally do not occur in a passive form. Quirk and Greenbaum (1973:359–360) indicate that there are four such categories of verbs:

1. "Reciprocal" verbs (e.g., resemble, look like, equal, agree with)

*Her sister is resembled by Nancy.

2. Verbs of "containing" (e.g., contain, hold, comprise, lack)

*Confidence is lacked by him.

3. Verbs of "suiting" (e.g., suit, fit, become)

*I am suited by this arrangement.

4. Verbs of measurement (e.g., weigh, cost, contain)

*$15 is cost by the shirt.

You will recall that many of these categories overlap with the stative verbs we discussed in Chapter 6. Thus many verbs which do not take progressive aspect also do not occur in the passive.

4. a. It is a normal passive with the agent deleted. An active voice counterpart is possible with an agent:

> Professor Cohan edited the book prior to publication.

Alternatively, the agent could easily be added to the passive form:

> The book was edited by Professor Cohan prior to publication.

   b. It is a stative passive. There is no active counterpart, and one cannot add a *by*-phrase with agent to the so-called passive.

   c. This is ambiguous. It is probably a stative passive, in the sense of "is located," to which one would not add a *by*-phrase. An active reading is also possible but more likely in the past tense: Mr. Burke was seated at the end of the first row by the usher.
               (active): The usher seated Mr. Burke at the end of the first row.)

   d. It is a normal passive with the agent deleted. An active counterpart is possible:

> The inhabitants of East Africa speak Swahili.

Alternatively a *by*-phrase with an agent can be added to the passive:

> Swahili is spoken by 15 million people in East Africa.

5. a. *To be born* is passive. The student has forgotten the obligatory BE auxiliary.

   b. The student has used *sang*, the simple past tense of the verb *sing*, instead of the correct form of the passive participle, i.e., *sung*.

   c. *Die* is intransitive and therefore can never occur in the passive.

   d. Since *Korea* is the agent and active word order is used, the active verb form should also be used:

> Korea has cut down its birthrate from 3 to 2 percent.

6. The chapter points out that verbs of state which can take the BE passive do not take the GET passive; however, there are also some verbs which are not verbs of state that cannot take the GET passive but which can take the BE passive:

> It was said . . .   It was performed . . .
> *It got said . . .   *It got performed . . .

7. Although the differences are not glaring, English speakers tend to use the BE passive when the agent, at least, is understood:

> Sheila and Steven were married on August 28 (by the rabbi).

The GET passive tends to be used informally when there is no expressed or understood agent:

> Sheila and Steven got married on August 28.

In addition, the BE passive is used whenever the speaker or writer wants to express a stative passive:

> Sheila and Steven are married (i.e., they are not single).

The GET passive can never be used in this meaning.

CHAPTER 18: Sentences with Indirect Objects
   Pages 236–249

1. direct object—He gave her *a diamond ring*.
   eliciting indirect object—Debbie requested a favor *of Penny*.
   benefactive indirect object—She bought a valentine *for her boyfriend*.
   directional indirect object—Anthony mailed an invitation *to Marie*.
   passive with indirect object as subject—*The expectant parents* were given a shower.
   dominance—Wait! You're giving the money to the wrong person. Give that money *to me!*
   indirect object movement—The kindergarten teacher read the story to his class.——▸ The
      kindergarten teacher read his class the story.
   benefactive *for*—She planned a surprise party *for* him.
   proxy-*for*—Then she became ill so her sister was hostess *for her*.
   object complement—Everyone considered the party *a big success*.
2. a. I handed Sue the note.

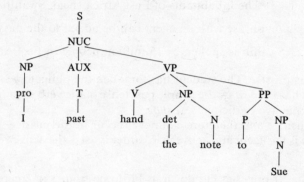

   Output of base: I past hand the note to Sue
   Indirect object movement: I past hand Sue the note
   Affix attachment (1✕): I hand + past Sue the note
   Morphological rules: I handed Sue the note.
   b. He was offered a job by the supervisor.

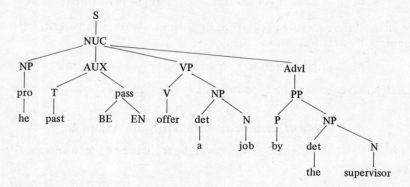

   Output of base: he past BE EN offer a job by the supervisor
   Affix attachment (2✕): he BE + past offer + EN a job by the supervisor
   Subject-verb agreement and morphological rules: He was offered a job by the
      supervisor.

c. The information was given to him yesterday.

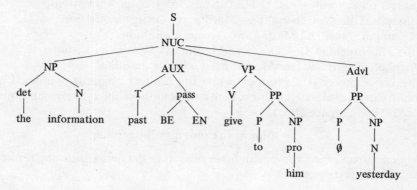

Output of base: the information past BE EN give to him yesterday
Affix attachment (2×): the information BE + past give + EN to him yesterday
Subject-verb agreement and morphological rules: The information was given to him
yesterday.

d. We bought Horace a watch.

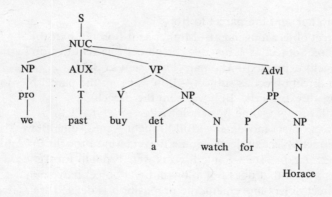

Output of base: we past buy a watch for Horace
Indirect object movement: we past buy Horace a watch
Affix attachment (1×): we buy + past Horace a watch
Morphological rules: We bought Horace a watch.

e. Did Martha ask George a question?

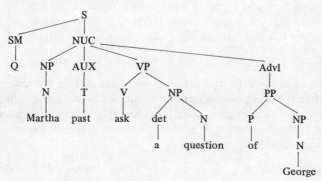

Output of base: Q Martha past ask a question of George
Indirect object movement: Q Martha past ask George a question
Subject/auxiliary inversion: past Martha ask George a question
DO support: past DO Martha ask George a question
Affix attachment (1X): DO + past Martha ask George a question
Morphological rules: Did Martha ask George a question?

3. a. The direct object is a pronoun while the indirect object is a noun. Under these conditions, the rules of dominance tell us that indirect object movement shouldn't take place. This sentence should be:

   John hasn't sent it to his brother.

   b. When indirect object movement takes place (i.e., the dative meaning is intended), the preposition is deleted:

   Mary bought me the book.

   Alternatively, if the proxy meaning is intended, the prepositional phrase would not move forward since the direct object is not long and complex enough to merit movement of the PP.

   c. With eliciting verbs, the preposition *of* precedes the indirect object, not the preposition *to*.

4. a. *active*—Mother sent the parcel to Bob.
   with indirect object movement—Mother sent Bob the parcel.
   passive (direct object as subject)—The parcel was sent to Bob by mother.
   with no agent expressed—The parcel was sent to Bob.
   passive (indirect object as subject)—Bob was sent the parcel by mother.
   with no agent expressed—Bob was sent the parcel.

   b. *active*—Bill brought some flowers for Agnes.
   with indirect object movement—Bill brought Agnes some flowers.
   passive (direct object subject)—Some flowers were brought for Agnes by Bill.
   with no agent expressed—Some flowers were brought for Agnes.

5. a. *Explain* is a verb that does not allow indirect object movement.
   b. With indirect object movement, the preposition is deleted (i.e., Give me an answer).
   c. *Open* is a verb that does not allow indirect object movement.
   d. Since *ask* is an eliciting verb, the underlying preposition in this sentence is *of*:

   We asked something of Harry.

   But even if the student were to have used *of*, he or she would have been incorrect here since no preposition can be used if the direct object is deleted.

   e. *Excuse* does not take an indirect object. Either *me* or *my poor English* may function as the direct object but one cannot use both.

   Please excuse me.   or   Please excuse my poor English.

6. With the exception of the verb *say*, Fraser is correct in stating that one-syllable verbs that take indirect objects may optionally undergo indirect object movement. They can do this whether their indirect objects are marked by *to, for,* or *of*. Although Fraser did not explicitly mention this, it is also important to note that no verb of three or more syllables may take indirect object movement:

*Educate us these children.   *Evaluate NSF this proposal.
*Communicate your father this message.   Etc.

The real problem arises with two-syllable verbs. Except for the two-syllable eliciting verbs, which never take indirect object movement, it appears that neither the stress pattern nor the co-occurring preposition is a good predictor of indirect-object movement:

	to "dative"	*for* "benefactive"	*of* "eliciting"
stress on first syllable	*mention offer	*open scramble (i.e., eggs)	
stress on second syllable	*explain award	*perform reserve	the two-syllable eliciting verbs do not take indirect object movement: *demand *request

We hope that future research will reveal some system in what now appears to be rather arbitrary behavior.

7. In conversation, *giving* is usually reduced to *givin'*, making the present and passive participles hard to distinguish. You would therefore want to have your students concentrate on listening for the differences in the prepositional phrases. The *by* phrase always marks the agent and the whole phrase is often deleted. On the other hand, the *to* phrase is obligatorily present with many directional or dative verbs.

8. *Beg* can only take an indirect object when it is an eliciting verb:

> I beg this favor of you.

When it is used in this way, it cannot undergo indirect object movement:

> *I beg you this favor.

For other uses, *beg* does not take an indirect object. It does, however, take a direct object which could be phrasal (e.g., I beg *your pardon*) containing within itself an indirect object. As a different example, in the following sentence, all that follows *beg* is the direct object:

> D.O.
> I beg *you to stop.*

If the direct object is a phrase, it might have an indirect object embedded within it:

> D.O.
> I beg *you to do something for me.*

But here, the benefactive indirect object phrase belongs to the verb *do,* not *beg.*

CHAPTER 19: Prepositions
Pages 250–264

1. instrumental case—Ren ate her rice *with chopsticks.*
   "means" case—The president left the airport *by helicopter.*
   ablative case—Snoopy stole the blanket *from Linus.*
   double preposition—When we got *out of* the meeting, it was after dark.
   deletable preposition
   > optional—*On* Thursday, softball practice began late.
   > obligatory—Most of us just wanted to go Ø home.

preposition co-occurring with an adjective—Elaine is *interested in* linguistics.
preposition variation (i.e., synonyms)—We went fishing *along/by* the shore of the lake.
co-occurring nonadjacent prepositions—*Out of* the frying pan, *into* the fire.

2. a. The verb *rely* must always be followed by the preposition *on*.
   b. A measured amount of time (as in this sentence) is indicated by the preposition *in*. A future termination point is signaled by *by*.
   c. *Interested* co-occurs with *in*, not *by*.

3. a. Use *on* for the street alone (*on* Main Street); use *at* for the number and street together because they indicate a specific point.
   b. *Since* refers to the beginning of a span of time. *For* refers to the duration of the span of time. In this sentence, *for* is the appropriate preposition.
   c. *Discuss* requires no preposition (unlike *talk about, argue about*). One might say that the meaning of *about* is already part of the meaning of *discuss*.
   d. We say *problems with our English* or *problems in English* but not **problems in our English*.

4. After verbs of motion like *go, come,* and *drive,* no preposition is required before *home.* Think of *home* as meaning "to someone's house." Many languages have single verbs which mean *to go home* (e.g., *pulong* in Indonesian). *Approach,* in the second example, means "to go to" or "to go near to," so no preposition is required, i.e., the meaning of *to* is already part of the meaning of *approach.*

5. Although both forms (with and without the preposition) are correct, the preposition *for* is not needed with an expression of time that signals duration. *On* can be deleted when it precedes days of the week. These sentences sound more informal and colloquial to native speakers without the prepositions. The ESL/EFL student could be given many examples of dialogs between native English speakers with the prepositions deleted so that she or he could begin to appreciate the frequency of such deletion in informal speech.

6. We describe five such prepositions below:

Preposition	Space	Time	Degree	Other
after	My house is after the big barn as you are heading south.	after 9:00 a.m. after ten minutes	—	after all
beside	beside the still waters	—	—	beside himself
forward	Forward of aft is the bow.	Let's move the clocks forward an hour.	—	He was rather forward.
into	She crawled into the cave.	As we came into the 20th century . . .	divide 21 into 207	He's really into TM.
within	You should reach the rest stop within two miles.	. . . within an hour	. . . within 5° of boiling	within reason

CHAPTER 20: Phrasal Verbs
   Pages 265–279

1. verb plus preposition—Alice *fell down* the hole.
   separable phrasal verb—We *put* our coats *on.*
   inseparable phrasal verb—I'll *go over* those problems in class tomorrow.
   intransitive phrasal verb—Last night I just *fooled around.*
   transitive phrasal verb—Lois is always *making up* stories.
   phrasal verb plus preposition—I am really *put off by* a pushy salesperson.
   literal phrasal verb—Please *pick up* your clothes.
   completive phrasal verb—Did Dad *eat* the cake *up?*
   figurative phrasal verb—The dog finally *turned up* at the neighbor's place.
   particle movement
       in the active voice—Randy *handed* the note *back* to Elaine.
       in the passive voice with an indirect object as subject—Elaine was *handed* the note
           back (by Randy).

2. a. John warmed the soup up.

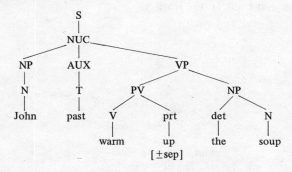

    Output of base: John past warm up the soup
    Particle movement: John past warm the soup up
    Affix attachment (1✕): John warm + past the soup up
    Morphological rules: John warmed the soup up.

  b. The man walked up the street.

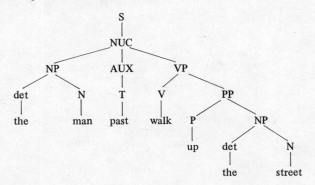

    Output of base: the man past walk up the street
    Affix attachment (1✕): the man walk + past up the street
    Morphological rules: The man walked up the street.

c. The child ate it up.

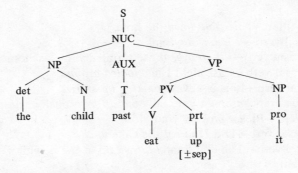

Output of base: the child past eat up it
Particle movement: the child past eat it up (obligatory because of pronoun object)
Affix attachment (1✕): the child eat + past it up
Morphological rules: The child ate it up.

d. I came across that book in the library.

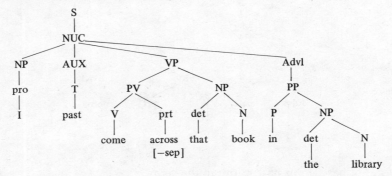

Output of base: I past come across that book in the library
Affix attachment (1✕): I come + past across that book in the library
Morphological rules: I came across that book in the library.

e. Anne puts up with murder.

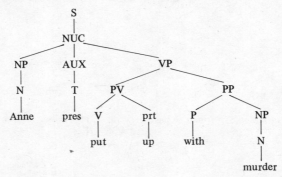

Output of base: Anne pres put up with murder
Affix attachment (1✕): Anne put + pres up with murder
Subject-verb agreement and morphological rules: Anne puts up with murder.

3. a. *Call on* meaning "to pay an informal visit" is an inseparable phrasal verb. Alternatively, the wrong form of the particle may have been used. For example, if the meaning of "to telephone" was intended, *up* should have been used.

   b. Even though the particle *over* can be separated from its verb *look,* the direct object is long and complex; so the particle should follow the verb directly.

   c. *Run into* in the sense of "meet by accident" is an inseparable phrasal verb. Alternatively, this sentence could be interpreted as containing a verb + preposition sequence, in which case, what is missing is the object of the preposition:

   > The lawyer ran his client into a ditch.

   d. Indirect object movement has already been applied to this sentence. At this point, particle movement must take place since the object following the particle is a pronoun:

   > I gave him back the money.

   Depending on how dominant the direct object is, the particle may be moved to the right of the direct object as well:

   > I gave him the money back.

   In both sentences the direct object is more dominant than the indirect object. We know this because indirect object movement has taken place to move the direct object into the more dominant position and because the indirect object is a pronoun, while the direct object is a noun. In the second sentence, however, the direct object is not as dominant as it is in the first, where it occupies sentence-final position.

4. a. If the phrasal verb is separable and the object is a pronoun, the object must be placed between the verb and its particle.

   b. Here the problem is the verb preceding the particle. The student probably means to say *put on.* Other possibilities are *turn on, switch on,* and even *flick on,* depending upon the register and the type of light fixture involved.

   c. Here the problem is the particle. We *turn off* (or *put off, switch off, flick off*) lights, but a candle *burns out* or is *put out* or is *blown out.* A candle can also *burn down.*

5. It would probably be very difficult for students to remember all the different meanings of the different particles that can go with a particular head verb. In general we suggest choosing a theme and presenting a small group of phrasal verbs that regularly occur within the theme (cf. teaching suggestions 1 and 2) without regard to whether they share a common head verb or not. This will provide students with a meaningful context with which to associate certain phrasal verbs. Alternatively, we recommend using the same particle with the same meaning and varying the verb rather than vice versa (cf. teaching suggestion 6).

6. They are similar, since both are made up of two constituents co-occurring together. In other ways, they are structurally different, however. The particle can be moved to the other side of the object in the case of separable phrasal verbs; the preposition following a verb cannot. On the other hand, the preposition can be fronted in wh-questions and relative clauses; the particle cannot. There is often a semantic distinction as well: phrasal verbs function as lexical units with meanings that are often different from the sum of their individual parts. The meanings of verb-plus-preposition sequences are usually literal.

   Thus, the differences between phrasal verbs and verb-plus-preposition sequences seem significant enough for us to recommend that the two not be taught together.

CHAPTER 21: Simple Sentences with Nonreferential *it* or *there* Subjects
Pages 280–294

1. filler *it*—How far is *it* to the beach?
   referential *it*—Have you seen my house key? I can't find *it*.
   referential *there*—Let's go to the mountains. It's so peaceful *there*.
   nonreferential *there*
   > locative—*There* is a bottle of wine in the refrigerator.
   > existential—*There* are several issues we need to discuss.
   there introducing a list—*There's* still the lawn to be mowed, the hedges to be trimmed, and
   the weeds to be pulled.
2. *reside*—verb of existence or position

   In the village there resided a woman who claimed she could read fortunes.

   stir—verb of motion or direction

   In the evening there stirred a faint breeze, a welcome relief from a blistering hot day.

   grow—event verb

   Where there once had been nothing, there now grew bushes of lilacs.

   So far we have not found any fully grammatical examples with verbs that do not fit our
   categories; however, it is possible that you will discover such a set of verbs.
3. a. The existence of Santa Claus is being asserted. Singular proper nouns, which normally
      take no article, take an indefinite article when co-occurring with nonreferential *there*,
      since the meaning of the construction is

      > "There exists a(n) $\left\{ \begin{array}{l} \text{person} \\ \text{entity} \end{array} \right\}$ $\left\{ \begin{array}{l} \text{named} \\ \text{referred to as} \end{array} \right\}$ Santa Claus."

   b. The sentence is ungrammatical because filler *it* is always followed by a singular verb
      regardless of whether a singular or plural noun follows the verb (i.e., It's 4 o'clock).
   c. A list may consist of only one member. When *there* is being used to assert the existence
      of a list, pronouns which follow must be in their object form. However, the hypercorrect
      usage of some native speakers may include utterances like this: "Well, there's Joe, Helen,
      and I" where *me* would be the grammatically correct form.
4. a. The correct sentence should be:

      > $\left. \begin{array}{l} \text{It's} \\ \text{It is} \end{array} \right\}$ sunny today.

      When describing general weather conditions, nonreferential *it* should be used.
   b. The student has incorrectly omitted the nonreferential *it* as the subject of this sentence.
      Every nonimperative English sentence requires a surface subject.
5. This is an area where the language seems to be changing. Many native speakers will accept
   and even produce *there is* in contracted form (i.e., *there's*) regardless of whether the logical
   subject of the sentence is singular or plural. This is particularly true if the register is
   informal speech.
6. a. The difference here is one of discourse context: the first sentence could be one piece of
      information in a longer description where the writer is setting the reader up to expect
      something to happen. The second sentence may simply be a description without any
      accompanying expectation being aroused in the reader.

In addition, there is a tendency on the part of speakers to place given information at the beginning of a sentence and new information toward the end of the sentence. This would explain why NPs in predicate position are usually indefinite: new information is indefinite at the first mention.

b. The first sentence is more formal than the second and might be expected to be said by a radio announcer. The second sentence, especially in its contracted form, occurs far more frequently and represents the typical usage. (Contraction of *It is* would add the notion of informality.)

CHAPTER 22: An Introduction to Conjunction
Pages 295–307

1. pro-form—Jeffrey is very athletic. *He* loves to ski and *does so* often.
   coordinating conjunction—Kristin likes to cook *but* she doesn't like to clean up.
   obligatory *too* addition—Abby exercises every day and Andrew does *too*.
   optional *too* addition—Every day Kevin runs five miles and swims a mile (*too*).
   parallel structure—Helene teaches English and she writes poetry.
2. NOT incorporation
   (without NOT incorporation): Gene doesn't like the smell of strong perfume and Paula *doesn't either.*
   (with NOT incorporation): Gene doesn't like the smell of strong perfume and *neither does* Paula.
   NOT absorption
   Dennis is not complaining *nor is Joanne whining.*
   restructuring—Rosemary studies hard and Lynn studies hard.—(with restructuring): Rosemary and Lynn study hard.
   pro-verb phrase substitution—Jeanne likes to eat popcorn at movies, and I *do too.*
3. a. Jim got the job, and he likes it.

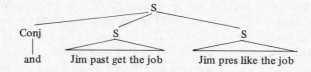

   Output of base: and Jim past get the job Jim pres like the job
   Conjunction movement: Jim past get the job and Jim pres like the job
   Pro-noun phrase substitution: Jim past get the job and he pres like it
   Affix attachment (2×): Jim get + past the job and he like + pres it
   Subject-verb agreement and morphological rules: Jim got the job and he likes it.
   b. Jill has a car and Jack does too.

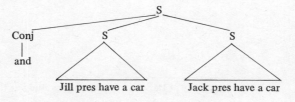

   Output of base: and Jill pres have a car Jack pres have a car
   Conjunction movement: Jill pres have a car and Jack pres have a car

Pro-verb phrase substitution: Jill pres have a car and Jack pres DO
Too addition: Jill pres have a car and Jack pres DO too
Affix attachment (2✕): Jill have + pres a car and Jack DO + pres too
Subject-verb agreement and morphological rules: Jill has a car and Jack does too.

c. I have read Tolstoy and Pushkin.

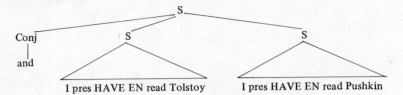

Output of base: and I pres HAVE EN read Tolstoy I pres HAVE EN read Pushkin
Conjunction movement: I pres HAVE EN read Tolstoy and I pres HAVE EN read
    Pushkin
Identical constituent deletion: I pres HAVE EN read Tolstoy and ∅∅∅∅∅ Pushkin
Restructuring: I pres HAVE EN read Tolstoy and Pushkin
Affix attachment (2✕): I HAVE + pres read + EN Tolstoy and Pushkin
Morphological rules: I have read Tolstoy and Pushkin.

d. Alice doesn't swim, and Judy doesn't either.

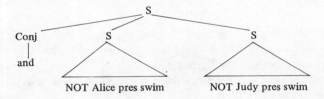

Output of base: and NOT Alice pres swim NOT Judy pres swim
NOT placement: and Alice pres NOT swim Judy pres NOT swim
DO support: and Alice pres DO NOT swim Judy pres DO NOT swim
NOT contraction: and Alice pres DO + N'T swim Judy pres DO + N'T swim
Conjunction movement: Alice pres DO + N'T swim and Judy pres DO + N'T swim
Pro-verb phrase substitution: Alice pres DO + N'T swim and Judy pres DO + N'T
Either addition: Alice pres DO + N'T swim and Judy pres DO + N'T either
Affix attachment (2✕): Alice DO + N'T + pres swim and Judy DO + N'T + pres either
Subject-verb agreement and morphological rules: Alice doesn't swim and Judy doesn't
    either.

e. Fuad and Sven study at Harvard.

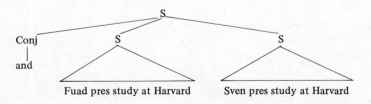

Output of base: and Fuad pres study at Harvard Sven pres study at Harvard
Conjunction movement: Fuad pres study at Harvard and Sven pres study at Harvard

Identical constituent deletion: Fuad pres study at Harvard and Sven Ø Ø Ø Ø
Restructuring: Fuad and Sven pres study at Harvard
Affix attachment (1×): Fuad and Sven study + pres at Harvard
Morphological rules: Fuad and Sven study at Harvard.

4. a. *But* is used when sentences contrast; *and* is the correct coordinating conjunction. *But* could be retained if one of the two conjoined sentences was made negative.
   b. The NOT in the second sentence is absorbed by the *nor*. The second sentence should therefore contain no NOT: "... nor does Lee."
   c. After *so* fronting, subject/auxiliary inversion must take place: "... so does Kathi."

5. a. Student has used *too* instead of *either*. *Either* signals some common element in the second of two negative verb phrases, whereas *too* signals a repetition of some element in affirmative verb phrases.
   b. When the two verb phrases of the conjoined sentences are identical, but the subjects are not, *too* must be added to the end of the second sentence.
   c. The answer requires a pro-verb: I do too!
      or if the student wanted to use a shortened, elliptical form, the object form of the pronoun should be used:

      Me too!

      or if the student wanted to retain the *I too,* a predicate must be added after *too* (but this is somewhat formal and not appropriate for informal conversation):

      I too like to play (baseball).

6. The forms "he does too" and "he doesn't either" should probably be taught first, since they are uninverted unlike the other two and therefore are presumably easier to learn. The uninverted forms also occur more frequently and are more versatile.

7. Some other pro-adverbs and what they might replace are:

   now—"at this time"
   here—"at this place"
   that way—"to the $\left\{ \begin{array}{c} \text{left} \\ \text{right} \end{array} \right\}$," "in the manner specified"
   that fast—"60 miles per hour," etc.
   that often—"twice a day," etc.
   that long—"for twenty years," etc.

CHAPTER 23: More on Conjoined Sentences
Pages 308–322

1. correlative conjunction—*Neither* Amy *nor* I have seen the movie.
   phrasal conjunction—*Sonny and Cher* were quite a pair.
   sentential conjunction—Agatha Christie and Graham Greene have written many books.
      (i.e., Agatha Christie has written many books, and Graham Greene has written many books.)
   reciprocal pronoun—David and Peggy help *each other* with their homework.
   correlative movement—Cheryl and I *both* are looking for jobs.
   respectively addition—Evelyn and Maurice teach Spanish and French, *respectively*.
   reciprocal pronoun deletion—Ali and Frazier fought for the title (i.e., fought each other).

multiple restructuring—Karl and Ray studied linguistics and chemistry, respectively (i.e., derived from "Karl studied linguistics and Ray studied chemistry").

2. a. Robin and Batman are a duo.

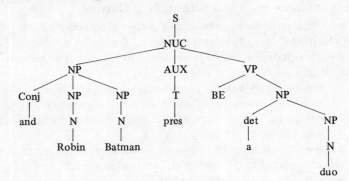

Output of base: and Robin Batman pres BE a duo
Conjunction movement: Robin and Batman pres BE a duo
Affix attachment (1X): Robin and Batman BE + pres a duo
Subject-verb agreement and morphological rules: Robin and Batman are a duo.

b. John and Bill kissed Ann and Alice, respectively.

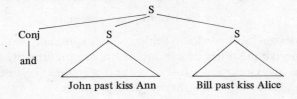

Output of base: and John past kiss Ann Bill past kiss Alice
Conjunction movement: John past kiss Ann and Bill past kiss Alice
Identical constituent deletion: John past kiss Ann and Bill Ø Ø Alice
Multiple restructuring: John and Bill past kiss Ann and Alice
Respectively addition: John and Bill past kiss Ann and Alice respectively
Affix attachment (1X): John and Bill kiss + past Ann and Alice respectively
Morphological rules: John and Bill kissed Ann and Alice, respectively.

c. Ken and Doug hate each other.

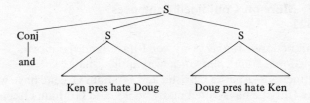

Output of base: and Ken pres hate Doug Doug pres hate Ken
Conjunction movement: Ken pres hate Doug and Doug pres hate Ken
Identical constituent deletion: Ken pres hate Doug and Doug Ø Ø Ken
Multiple restructuring: Ken and Doug pres hate Doug and Ken
Reciprocal pronoun substitution: Ken and Doug pres hate each other

Affix attachment (1✕): Ken and Doug hate + pres each other
Morphological rules: Ken and Doug hate each other.
d. Either Morris or Hansen could give the lecture.

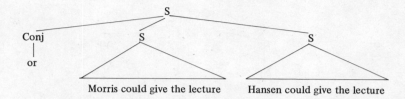

Output of base: or Morris could give the lecture Hansen could give the lecture
Conjunction movement: Morris could give the lecture or Hansen could give the lecture
Identical constituent deletion: Morris could give the lecture or Hansen ∅∅∅∅
Restructuring: Morris or Hansen could give the lecture
Correlative addition: Either Morris or Hansen could give the lecture.
e. John and Bill both speak Italian.

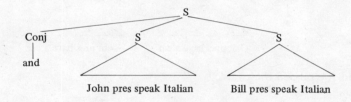

Output of base: and John pres speak Italian Bill pres speak Italian
Conjunction movement: John pres speak Italian and Bill pres speak Italian
Identical constituent deletion: John pres speak Italian and Bill ∅∅∅
Restructuring: John and Bill pres speak Italian
Correlative addition: both John and Bill pres speak Italian
Correlative movement: John and Bill both pres speak Italian
Affix attachment (1✕): John and Bill both speak + pres Italian
Morphological rules: John and Bill both speak Italian.
f. Neither you nor I should do that job.

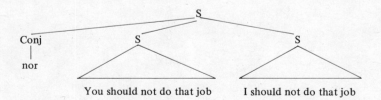

(Assume NOT placement has taken place in the constituent sentences.)
Output of base: nor you should not do that job I should not do that job
Conjunction movement: you should not do that job nor I should not do that job
Identical constituent deletion: you should not do that job nor I ∅∅∅∅∅
Restructuring: you nor I should not do that job
NOT absorption: you nor I should do that job
Correlative addition (obligatory): Neither you nor I should do that job.

3. a. Gail and Tom have a car.
   Phrasal:

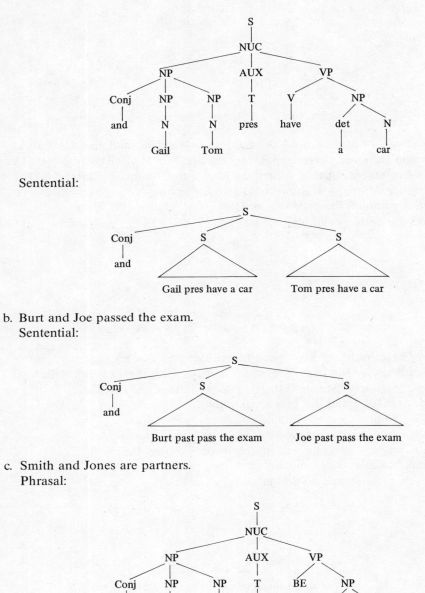

   Sentential:

   b. Burt and Joe passed the exam.
      Sentential:

   c. Smith and Jones are partners.
      Phrasal:

4. a. Since a duet is performed by two people, one expects Joe and Harry to be a team. If this is
   the case, phrasal conjunction would be necessary, i.e., Joe and Harry sang a duet, not
   sentential conjunction as it is here. A less likely interpretation is that they sang
   independently, in which case you would expect the second affirmative verb phrase to be
   replaced by *did too*.

b. Conjoined sentences that are mirror images of each other, can be combined: Mary and Linda hit Linda and Mary, and a reciprocal pronoun can be substituted for the second conjoined pair: Mary and Linda hit each other. The sentence with the reciprocal pronoun gives the sense that the actions were simultaneous (and perhaps repeated); the sentence with *respectively* seems to imply that each woman hit the other only once and that the actions were nonsimultaneous.

c. The reciprocal pronoun in this sentence is redundant. The word *parallel* implies a reciprocal relationship.

d. The rule of correlative addition stipulates that the correlative conjunction be inserted before the conjoined constituents. This sentence should thus be:

> I speak both English and Spanish.

5. a. *Respectively* is added only if there are at least two parallel pairs of constituents conjoined through restructuring. In this case the subject noun phrases are parallel but the object noun phrases of the conjoined sentences are identical, not parallel.

b. *Respectively* addition is not correct, since the conjoined subject noun phrases are identical, not parallel.

c. In English the correlative and related conjunction are all lexically distinct. In this case the correct pair is *neither . . . nor.*

d. According to prescriptive rules, one should use the proximity principle when two subjects are joined by *either . . . or* or *neither . . . nor.* In this case, therefore, the verb should be singular (i.e., *is*) to agree with *Judy.*

6. It would be important to distinguish between the different meanings conveyed by the two types of pronouns. A reflexive pronoun indicates the action of the verb is carried out by the subject on the subject:

He looked at himself in the mirror.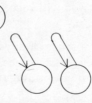

They looked at themselves in the mirror.

A reciprocal pronoun indicates the action was carried out by one subject on the other subject and vice versa:

They looked at each other in the mirror.

7. *Respectively* is an adverb which links one member of a pair of parallel conjoined constituents with a member of another pair of parallel conjoined constituents.

> Charlie and Pete went to Denver and Detroit respectively.

Respective is an adjective which precedes a plural object noun phrase and links one member of the object noun phrase with one of the subject noun phrases. *Respective* does not show the connection as precisely as *respectively,* since it modifies a plural noun phrase, not a conjoined pair of noun phrases, e.g.:

> Charlie and Pete went their respective ways.

8. *Neither . . . or* may be used informally by some native speakers of English; however, *neither . . . nor* is always correct and would be more appropriate in formal speech and in writing.

CHAPTER 24: Logical Connectors
Pages 323–339

1. negative logical connector—There was no money left for groceries, *let alone* the mortgage.
   formal register of a logical connector—The forecast calls for rain. *As a consequence,* it is not likely that the game will be played as scheduled.
   referential word—I know nothing regarding *that* (matter).
   concession—Logical connectors can be categorized according to their meanings. *In spite of this,* the variation within each category causes problems.
   clause-initial position—Jacob has just begun studying Russian. *Nonetheless,* he has learned a great deal.
   clause-medial position—Jacob has just begun studying Russian. He has, *nonetheless,* learned a great deal.
   clause-final position—Jacob has just begun studying Russian. He has learned a great deal, *nonetheless.*
   clause order variations—Because there was a traffic jam downtown, Cindy was late to work. Cindy was late to work because there was a traffic jam downtown.
2. a. *While* cannot introduce an independent clause. The second sentence, therefore, is a fragment. The two clauses should be joined into one sentence.
   b. Unless irony is intended, there seems to be a semantic problem here. A sequential logical connector was used where a combination of concessive and adversative connectors would seem more appropriate, e.g.:

   If you try hard, you will succeed. However, in spite of following this advice, Bill failed the test.

   c. The error is in the absence of a referential word or a noun phrase after *in spite of.*
   d. *Although* always precedes a dependent clause. In this particular sentence the *although* could be moved to the beginning of either clause:

   Although the general surrendered at last, he never gave up in spirit.
   The general surrendered at last, although he never gave up in spirit.

3. a. There is an incorrect overuse of logical connectors of concession. Choose either *although* or *but,* not both of them.
   b. A logical connector of contrast such as *but* would probably be more appropriate here. Even if this logical connector of concession were acceptable, it would need to be followed by an independent clause, e.g.: Even so, Mohammed does not. As it is here, this sentence is an unacceptable fragment.
   c. *Because of* must be followed by a referential word. For this sentence, the logical connector *because* without the *of* would convey the intended meaning in a grammatical way.
   d. In this sentence the student would need to add *such* before the *as* or use another logical connector of exemplification, e.g., *like. As* by itself can be used for exemplification, but only in certain contexts; e.g., dictionaries often use *as* in order to give an example of how a particular word is used (e.g., *Dan* (archaic), master; sir; a title: As Dan Cupid).
4. a. The difference is in what caused what. In 1, we say she caught a cold and that this is

because she hasn't taken good care of herself. In 2, we deduce that she hasn't taken care of herself from the fact that she has caught a cold.

b. *Even though* is followed by a full clause. *In spite of* is followed by a reduced clause. In this case there may also be a difference in register, with the second sentence being more formal than the first one.

c. There is a difference in register: sentence 2 is more formal than sentence 1. Also the logical connector in sentence 1 is followed by a full clause. The logical connector in 2 is followed by a reduced clause.

5. a. All three connectors express summation.

    b. All three connectors express addition.

CHAPTER 25: Conditional Sentences
Pages 340–359

1. factual conditional

    generic—Water freezes if the temperature gets to 0°C.

    implicit inference—If it's 9 o'clock, the library is closed.

future conditional

    weakened result clause—If the snow keeps melting so fast, *there may be a flood.*

    weakened *if* clause—*If it happens to be nice on Friday,* we can always go sailing.

hypothetical conditional—If I felt more energetic, I would weed the garden.

counterfactual conditional—If there had been less snow cover, the bulbs would have suffered greater damage.

subjunctive use of *were*—If that dog *were* here now, you would know it.

adverbial fronting—*If this hadn't been a long weekend,* I don't know what I would have done.

then insertion—If you don't think that's funny, *then* you missed the point.

if deletion with subject/auxiliary inversion—*Had we* only known, we would have been there.

conditional clause pro-form—Do you have a reservation? *If so,* go right in.

sarcastic use of a conditional—If you had any brains, you'd be dangerous.

2. a. If I had the time, I would go to Europe.

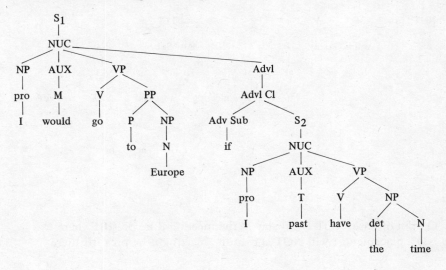

Output of base: I would go to Europe if I past have the time
Adverbial fronting: if I past have the time I would go to Europe
Affix attachment (1✕): if I have + past the time I would go to Europe
Morphological rules: If I had the time, I would go to Europe.

b. If John had studied, then he would have received an A.

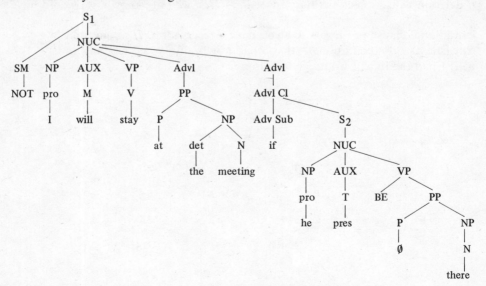

Output of base: John would HAVE EN receive an A if John past HAVE EN study
Adverbial fronting: if John past HAVE EN study John would HAVE EN receive an A
Pro-noun phrase substitution: if John past HAVE EN study he would HAVE EN receive an A
Then insertion: if John past HAVE EN study then he would HAVE EN receive an A
Affix attachment (3✕): if John HAVE + past study + EN then he would HAVE receive + EN an A
Morphological rules: If John had studied, then he would have received an A.

c. I will not stay at the meeting if he is there.

Output of base: NOT I will stay at the meeting if he pres BE there
NOT placement: I will NOT stay at the meeting if he pres BE there

Affix attachment (1✕): I will **NOT** stay at the meeting if he **BE** + pres there
Subject-verb agreement and morphological rules: I will not stay at the meeting if he is
there.

d. Don't go for an interview unless you want the job.

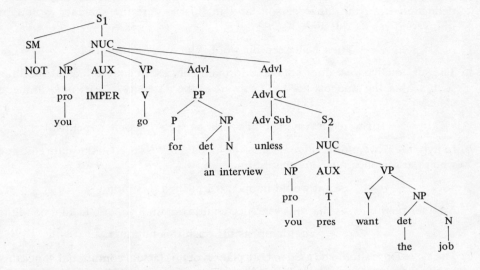

Output of base: NOT you IMPER go for an interview unless you pres want the job
NOT placement: you IMPER NOT go for an interview unless you pres want the job
DO support: you IMPER DO NOT go for an interview unless you pres want the job
NOT contraction: you IMPER DO + N'T go for an interview unless you pres want the
job
You deletion: IMPER DO + N'T go for an interview unless you pres want the job
Affix attachment (2✕): DO + N'T + IMPER go for an interview unless you want + pres
the job
Morphological rules: Don't go for an interview unless you want the job.

3. a. Implicit inferential factual conditionals should have the same tense and aspect or
modal in both clauses. This should be:

> If she was there, she did the work.

Alternatively, this sentence may be a counterfactual conditional referring to past time,
in which case it should be:

> If she had been there, she would have done the work.

where the main clause should contain *would* + the present perfect tense.

b. The normal pattern for future conditionals is to have a present tense in the *if* clause.
Thus, this sentence should read:

> If John is free, I'll invite him.

Alternatively, the conditional clause could be weakened by using *should,* not *might:*

> If John should be free, I'll invite him.

c. The *if* clause almost always precedes the result clause in sarcastic speech.

d. This *if* clause really does not mean "on the condition" so much as "on the assumption." In such cases of "strong deductions," the *if* clause precedes the *then* clause. Even if the *if* clause is not fronted, *then* does not typically begin a conditional sentence; i.e., the *then* insertion rule should not have been applied. The only circumstance in which this sentence might be acceptable is a conversation in which the speaker is trying to elicit a deduction from the other person, and in this context the sentence would be an uninverted yes-no question:

> Then he'll keep his word if he made a promise?

4. a. The subjunctive *were* does not occur in main clauses. In counterfactual conditionals such as this, the students need to be aware of the necessity to use *would* in the result clause:

> If I were an American, I would be speaking better English.

b. In hypothetical conditional sentences, the modal *would* is used in the main clause, even when the sentence refers to present time:

> What would happen if I pushed this button?

Another possibility is that this sentence could contain a generic factual conditional:

> What happens if I push this button?

c. The same tense should be used in both clauses of this factual conditional. Since this is a habitual factual, and the "habit" still obtains, present tense should be used:

> Why do some Americans say "Gesundheit" if someone sneezes?

d. There are three possible ways to correct this sentence:
   (1) Since the *only if* adverbial clause has been fronted, subject/auxiliary inversion is necessary in the main clause:

> Only if you help me, will I study for the quiz.

   (2) Do not front the *only if* adverbial clause:

> I will study for the quiz, only if you help me.

   (3) Weaken the condition by dropping *only:*

> If you help me, I will study for the quiz.

5. Both of these sentences are colloquial variants which are not consistent with what traditional grammar prescribes. Prescriptive usage would call for subjunctive *were* to be used in the *if* clause in the first sentence, since it is a present counterfactual conditional clause.

The second sentence is a hypothetical conditional. Prescriptive usage would lead one to expect a simple past tense in the *if* clause, rather than the modal *would,* which results in a "double *would* construction."

Thus, your answer to your student's question depends upon a definition of correctness. The sentences your student reports are not prescriptively correct, i.e., they do not adhere to the rules in a grammar book, but they are produced by, and acceptable to, native speakers in informal conversation.

We have encountered this discrepancy between grammar book rules and native speaker usage many times. Which rules you teach and whether you present or allow any variation from these will presumably depend upon how *you* use the language and who your students are and why they are studying English. For example, if you are uncomfortable with the colloquial variants, which we claim many native speakers use, and if you are teaching in an EFL context where your students are concerned with obtaining a high score on a standardized language proficiency examination, then perhaps only the prescriptive rules should be presented and practiced. On the other hand, if your students are adult immigrants in an ESL situation, perhaps you would choose to teach both the prescriptive rules and colloquial variants.

6. To be done on your own.

7. This is a future conditional. It is more complicated than those described in this chapter since the main clause contains both the *will* modal to signal future time and the *have to* periphrastic modal to signal necessity. Periphrastic modals may be used in the main clause of a conditional to express additional meaning—in this case, the periphrastic modal expresses the necessity of father's mowing the lawn.

CHAPTER 26: Introduction to Relative Clauses
Pages 360–375

1. embedded sentence—The woman *who is just entering the room* is my teacher.
   restrictive relative clause—She's the one *who has the books in her arms.*
   relative fronting—The course (she is teaching *that*) is very popular. ⟶ The course (*that* she is teaching) is very popular.
   relativized object of a preposition—Isn't she the one about *whom* you asked?
   relative pronoun substitution—The package (*the package* arrived yesterday) is for Christmas. ⟶ The package (*which* arrived yesterday) is for Christmas.
   relative pronoun deletion—Sally raved about the sale *that* they are having downtown. ⟶ Sally raved about the sale *Ø* they are having downtown.
   relativized possessive determiner—Julie is the student *whose* birthday we'll be celebrating next week.

2. a. The boy who spoke with John is my brother.

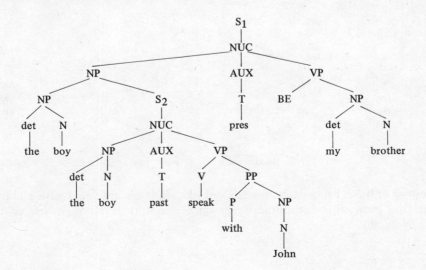

Output of base: the boy (the boy past speak with John) pres BE my brother
Relative pronoun substitution: the boy (who past speak with John) pres BE my brother
Affix attachment (2×): The boy (who speak + past with John) BE + pres my brother
Subject-verb agreement and morphological rules: The boy who spoke with John is my
    brother.
  b. The boat that he is building is large.

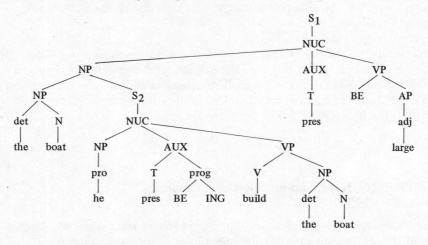

Output of base: the boat (he pres BE ING build the boat) pres BE large
Relative pronoun substitution: the boat (he pres BE ING build that) pres BE large
Relative pronoun fronting: the boat (that he pres BE ING build) pres BE large
Affix attachment (3×): the boat (that he BE + pres build + ING) BE + pres large
Subject-verb agreement and morphological rules: The boat that he is building is large.
  c. I know the student whose article was published.

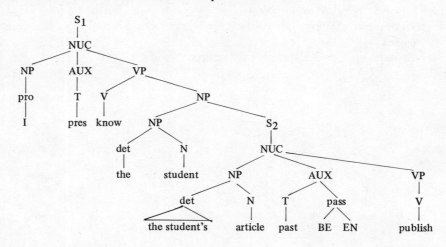

Output of base: I pres know the student (the student's article past BE EN publish)
Relative pronoun substitution: I pres know the student (whose article past BE EN
    publish)

Affix attachment (3×): I know + pres the student (whose article BE + past publish + EN)

Subject-verb agreement and morphological rules: I know the student whose article was published.

d. Ann wrote the story you like.

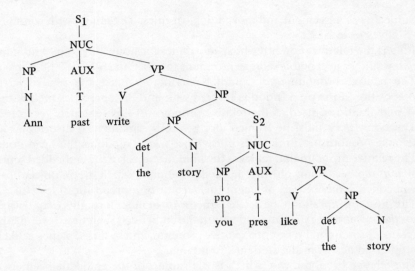

Output of base: Ann past write the story (you pres like the story)

Relative pronoun substitution: Ann past write the story (you pres like that)

Relative pronoun fronting: Ann past write the story (that you pres like)

Relative pronoun deletion: Ann past write the story (you pres like)

Affix attachment (2×): Ann write + past the story (you like + pres)

Morphological rules: Ann wrote the story you like.

e. The family with whom I am staying lives in town.

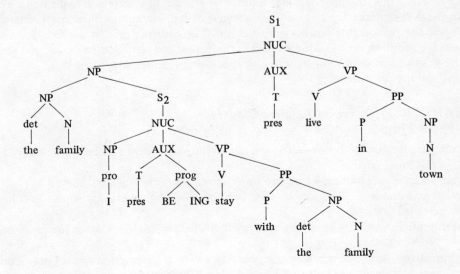

Output of base: the family (I pres BE ING stay with the family) pres live in town

Relative pronoun substitution: the family (I pres BE ING stay with whom) pres live in town

Relative pronoun fronting: the family (with whom I pres BE ING stay) pres live in town

Affix attachment (3×): the family (with whom I BE + pres stay + ING) live + pres in town

Subject-verb agreement and morphological rules: The family with whom I am staying lives in town.

3. a. *Who* is the relative pronoun which substitutes for nouns marked (+human). *Which* or *that* would be acceptable relative pronouns to substitute for the (−human) subject *river*.

   b. The relative pronoun *that* cannot be used to replace the relativized object of a preposition if the preposition is fronted with and thus precedes the relative pronoun. *Whom* should be used as the relative pronoun in this sentence.

   c. The noun *story* must be fronted along with the relativized determiner *whose* when relative pronoun fronting takes place since *whose* modifies the head noun *story*.

4. a. The relative pronoun that replaces the human subject of the embedded sentence is *who*. *Whom* replaces noun phrases marked (+human) which are in object position in the embedded sentence (i.e., object of the verb or of a preposition).

   b. The pronoun *him* should be deleted since *who* (or more formally, *whom*) was substituted for *the boy* and was then fronted within the embedded sentence. Several languages can retain a pronominal reflex of a relative pronoun, and so this sentence is likely the result of interference from the student's first language.

   c. The relative pronoun *who,* which is the subject of the embedded sentence, has been deleted. Subject relative pronouns are not deletable by themselves; however, relativized objects are.

   d. The embedded sentence *that she is wrapping* must be placed after the noun that it is modifying (i.e., *the package*). Not all languages have the relative clause following the noun it modifies as does English.

   e. *They are friendly* could be an embedded sentence or a conjoined sentence; if it is an embedded sentence, its subject is coreferential with the object of the main sentence, *people.* Thus, the pronoun *they* should be replaced by the relative pronoun *who*.

5. In the first sentence the person (the stranger) called you and in the second sentence you called the person (the stranger). Structurally, this means that in the first sentence the relative pronoun replaced the subject of the embedded sentence; in the second sentence, the relative pronoun replaced the object of the embedded sentence.

6. To be done on your own.

CHAPTER 27: More on Relative Clauses
Pages 376–389

1. relative adverb substitution—If we only knew the place *where* we were going to stay, I would rest more easily.

   free relative substitution—I had to think about *what* she had told me.

   relative pronoun + BE deletion—The boy doing handsprings is my son. (*who is* has been deleted after *boy*)

   free relative deletion—I'm trying to remember where we met each other. (*the place* has been deleted before *where*)

   appositive—Amherst, *a center of higher education*, is a home for several major colleges.

   nonrestrictive relative clause—Chris, *who is a Beethoven fan*, appreciates classical music.

nonrestrictive embedding—Andy has a great deal of energy. *Andy is my nephew.* ⟶

Andy, $\left\{\begin{array}{c} Andy \\ \downarrow \\ who \end{array}\right\}$ *is my nephew,* has a great deal of energy.

relative adverb deletion—By the time (*when*) I arrived, the excitement was over.

2. a. Dr. Graber, who(m) you know, will lecture next week.

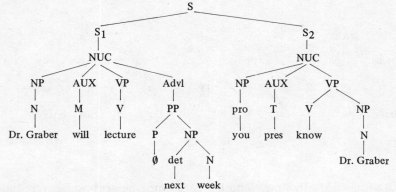

Output of base: Dr. Graber will lecture next week (you pres know Dr. Graber)

Nonrestrictive embedding: Dr. Graber (, you pres know Dr. Graber,) will lecture next week

Relative pronoun substitution: Dr. Graber (, you pres know who(m),) will lecture next week

Relative pronoun fronting: Dr. Graber (, who(m) you pres know,) will lecture next week

Affix attachment (1×): Dr. Graber (, who(m) you know + pres,) will lecture next week

Morphological rules: Dr. Graber, who(m) you know, will lecture next week.

b. The place where he lived is unknown.

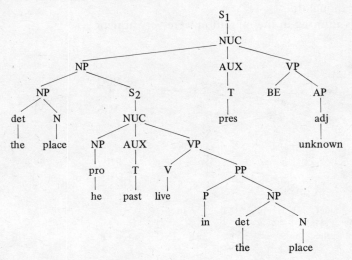

Output of base: the place (he past live in the place) pres BE unknown

Relative pronoun substitution: the place (he past live in which) pres BE unknown

Relative pronoun fronting: the place (in which he past live) pres BE unknown

Relative adverb substitution: the place (where he past live) pres BE unknown
Affix attachment (2✕): the place (where he live + past) BE + pres unknown
Subject-verb agreement and morphological rules: The place where he lived is unknown.
c. Marilyn lent me her car, which was very thoughtful.

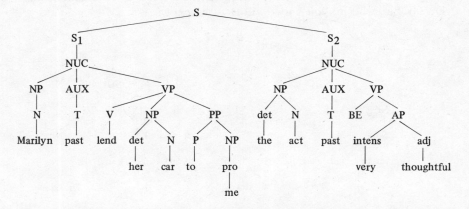

Output of base: Marilyn past lend her car to me (the act past BE very thoughtful)
Nonrestrictive embedding: Marilyn past lend her car to me (, the act past BE very
    thoughtful)
Relative pronoun substitution: Marilyn past lend her car to me (, which past BE very
    thoughtful)
Indirect object movement: Marilyn past lend me her car (, which past BE very
    thoughtful)
Affix attachment (2✕): Marilyn lend + past me her car (, which BE + past very
    thoughtful)
Subject-verb agreement and morphological rules: Marilyn lent me her car, which was
    very thoughtful.
d. The boys running in the marathon were very athletic.

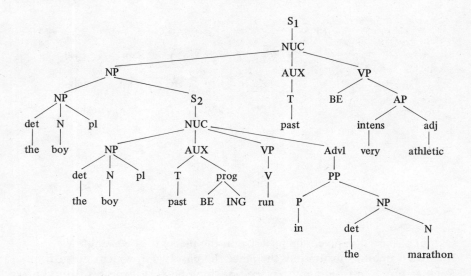

Output of base: the boy pl (the boy pl past BE ING run in the marathon) past BE very
athletic

Relative pronoun substitution: the boy pl (who past BE ING run in the marathon) past
BE very athletic

Relative pronoun + BE deletion: the boy pl (ING run in the marathon) past BE very
athletic

Affix attachment (3✕): the boy + pl (run + ING in the marathon) BE + past very
athletic

Subject-verb agreement and morphological rules: The boys running in the marathon
were very athletic.

e. That's the way he wants it.

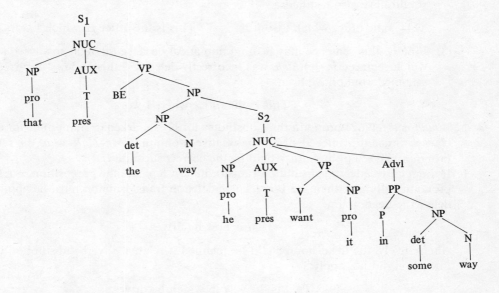

Output of base: that pres BE the way (he pres want it in some way)
Relative pronoun substitution: that pres BE the way (he pres want it in which)
Relative pronoun fronting: that pres BE the way (in which he pres want it)
Relative adverb substitution: that pres BE the way (how he pres want it)
Relative adverb deletion: that pres BE the way (he pres want it)
AUX contraction: that + 's pres the way (he pres want it)
Affix attachment (2✕): that + 's + pres the way (he want + pres it)
Subject-verb agreement and morphological rules: That's the way he wants it.

3. a. The relative adverb *when* is supposed to substitute for the preposition + relative
pronoun. When relative adverb substitution is properly applied, the following sentence
results:

Christmas is the time when he's busiest.

If relative adverb substitution does not occur, the preposition + relative pronoun would
be retained:

Christmas is the time at which he's busiest.

One could have a sentence without either form (i.e., Christmas is the time he's busiest) but not one with both!

b. A nonrestrictive relative clause may not modify a head noun preceded by the generic determiner *any*.

c. There are three possible reasons for the ungrammaticality:

(1) Relative pronoun deletion took place and the preposition was incorrectly deleted along with the relative pronoun. If the preposition had not also been deleted, the following would have been produced:

This is the office I work in.

(2) Of course, if relative pronoun deletion had not occurred, a grammatical sentence would have also resulted:

This is the office which I work in.   This is the office in which I work.

(3) Finally, this sentence may be ungrammatical because the relative adverb *where,* which replaced *in + which,* was incorrectly deleted. If this had not occurred, the sentence would have been:

This is the office where I work.

4. a. *Which* is a relative pronoun that substitutes for NPs marked (−human) or for entire clauses. Since the antecedent for the relative pronoun is *Mr. Hall, who,* the relative pronoun marked (+human), would be the correct substitution.

b. If the relative adverb substitution transformation replaces the preposition + relative pronoun with *how,* then the free relative deletion transformaion must be applied to delete the head noun:

That is how he drives.

Alternatively, the head noun could be retained if relative adverb substitution transformation did not apply:

That is the way in which he drives.

Or, the preposition and the relative pronoun could be deleted to produce:

That is the way he drives.

c. The free relative substitution transformation replaces *the thing* $\left\{ \begin{array}{l} that \\ which \end{array} \right\}$ with *what.*

The student would have been correct if he or she had retained the head noun *the thing* with *that* or *which* as the relative pronoun:

Cooking is the thing that he enjoys.

Another correct sentence would have resulted if the relative pronoun had been deleted:

Cooking is the thing he enjoys.

Finally, the sentence would have been correct if the student had used the free relative without the head noun:

Cooking is what he enjoys.

5. The first sentence implies that the speaker has only one sister (or at least only one sister relevant to the discourse); the fact that she lives in Chicago is incidental information. The

second sentence implies that the speaker has more than one sister relevant to the discourse, one of whom lives in Chicago. The second sentence tells us which of the speaker's sisters has three children.

6. The second sentence, "Do you recall the reason for which he resigned?" appears to be the most formal. The next most formal is probably "Do you recall the reason why he resigned?" The other two seem the least formal, with the first (i.e., "Do you recall why he resigned?") occurring more frequently than "Do you recall the reason he resigned?"

CHAPTER 28: Adjectives—Attributive vs. Predicate Position and Ordering Problems Pages 390–402

1. attributive adjective—What a *beautiful* day it is!
   predicate adjective—The sky is clear *blue*.
   postnominal adjective—Jack accepted the only job *available*.
   reference adjective—They were in *total* accord.
   proper adjective—What is your *Roman* costume going to look like?
   complex adjective phrase—The only position *agreeable to all concerned* was to continue the strike.
   restrictive adjective—Stuart wrote a very *newsy* letter.
   nonrestrictive adjective—Amy is our *studious* neighbor.

2. a. The person involved in this scandal should be fired.

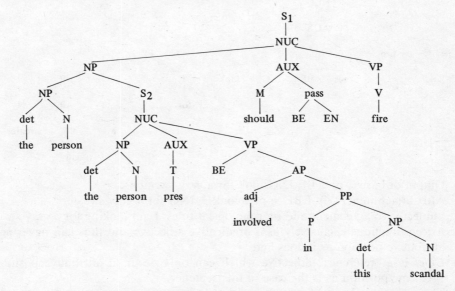

Output of base: the person (the person pres BE involved in this scandal) should BE EN fire

Relative pronoun substitution: the person (who pres BE involved in this scandal) should BE EN fire

Relative pronoun + BE deletion: the person (involved in this scandal) should BE EN fire

Affix attachment (1✕): the person (involved in this scandal) should BE fire + EN

Morphological rules: The person involved in this scandal should be fired.

b. Paul Newman is a leading man.

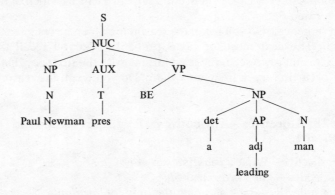

Output of base: Paul Newman pres BE a leading man
Affix attachment (1×): Paul Newman BE + pres a leading man
Subject-verb agreement and morphological rules: Paul Newman is a leading man.

c. I am looking for a gray sweater.

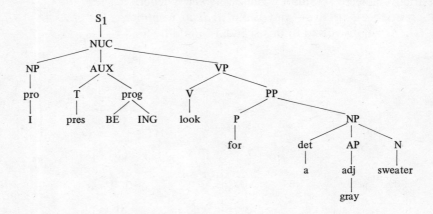

Output of base: I pres BE ING look for a gray sweater
Affix attachment (2×): I BE + pres look + ING for a gray sweater
Subject-verb agreement and morphological rules: I am looking for a gray sweater.

3. a. *Asleep* functions exclusively as a predicative adjective and thus can never occur in attributive position as it does here.

b. *Chief* is a "reference" adjective which can only occur in attributive position, not predicate position as is the case in this sentence.

c. The adjective phrase "fond of chocolates" is complex and is therefore restricted to postnominal or predicative position. Complex adjective phrases cannot occur prenominally as is the case in this sentence.

4. a. Adjective ordering rules indicate that origin adjectives are placed directly preceding the noun phrase they modify. Thus, an adjective of opinion such as *beautiful* should precede *Mexican,* the adjective of origin in this sentence.

b. Size adjectives normally precede color adjectives. This sentence should read:

I have long black hair and black eyes.

c. Opinion adjectives normally come before size adjectives. *Nice* should therefore precede *big* in this sentence.

5. This could be accomplished in many different ways; however, one effective way would be to establish two different sets of objects: one set contains marble statues of different origins; the other set contains Italian statues of different materials:

Marble statues		Italian statues	
x	(It)	x	(marble)
y	(Fr)	y	(silver)
z	(Gk)	z	(bronze)

The set of marble statues

x: The Italian marble statue   z: The Greek marble statue
y: The French marble statue

The set of Italian statues

x: The marble Italian statue   z: The bronze Italian statue
y: The silver Italian statue

The students could then be asked to identify the objects (x, y, z) in each set.

6. To be done on your own.

CHAPTER 29: Focus and Emphasis
Pages 403–416

1. cleft sentence—It's the coach that calls the plays.
   pseudo-cleft sentence—What we discovered was the theft.
   adverbial fronting—*Carefully,* Detective Woodburn assessed the evidence.
   emphatic DO—The Thanksgiving turkey *did* look wonderful.
   emphatic reflexive—The author *himself* did not expect the acclaim his book received.
   emphatic possessive—She used up some of her *own* assets in her unsuccessful bid for state office.

2. a. The adverbial of position *on his car* has been fronted in this sentence, but the copula BE is ungrammatical in sentence-final position. Thus subject/auxiliary inversion must take place to produce:

   On his car is a bumper sticker...

   b. If this sentence means that John took deliberate action, i.e., if the use of the reflexive is supposed to be emphatic, then the reflexive pronoun *himself* should follow John directly. If, instead, the use of the reflexive pronoun signals that John did the chores alone, perhaps the preposition *by* should precede the reflexive pronoun *himself,* and the optional adverbial of time *yesterday* would sound better if it came last in the sentence.

   c. *Moreover* is an emphatic logical connector; the limited context provided in this sentence would not seem to warrant emphasis. Perhaps a nonemphatic connector like *and* would be more appropriate.

3. a. This could be either a cleft sentence or a sentence with a relative clause. If it is a cleft sentence, we understand that the speaker is underscoring the fact that the graduate student corrects the papers; the professor doesn't. If it is a sentence with a relative clause,

we understand that we are singling out the graduate student who corrects the papers in our class from all other graduate students.

b. The ambiguity involves the antecedent of *himself.* Does *himself* emphasize our chairman (acting on his own) or the dean (someone presumably above reproach)?

4. a. This is a sentence with a free relative. In pseudo-clefts, the wh-word can only occur sentence-initially. Free relatives can occur in any NP position.

 b. This is a pseudo-cleft. The emphasis is on the NP that follows the copula BE. Notice that this is an emphatic counterpart to the neutral sentence:

He told a big lie.

 c. This is a sentence with a free relative. What follows the BE does not identify "what he said" but merely comments on it. Furthermore, this could not come from the neutral sentence:

*He said of little concern to us.

 d. This is a pseudo-cleft. What follows the copula BE is emphasized. We can easily reconstruct an equivalent neutral sentence:

He said that you are a jerk.

5. a. When a negative preverbal adverb of frequency is fronted, subject/auxiliary inversion must take place. This sentence should be:

Never have I tasted such a delicious sandwich!

 b. This is an incorrect form of a pseudo-cleft. The emphatic constituent following the BE copula is not a person; therefore the wh-word should not be *who.* The wh-word should be *what* instead:

What you mean is that Oscar did it.

 c. There should be no subject/auxiliary inversion when adverbials of time are fronted. To be grammatical, this should be:

After three months, all of my family arrived.

6. To be done on your own.

7. a. Sentence 1 is the emphatic or pseudo-cleft equivalent of sentence 2. One could imagine 1 being said after the speaker had already said 2, and the listener then asked for a repetition.

 b. In sentence 2 the adverbial has been fronted as compared with sentence 1. In sentence 2 the delayed subject receives more focus than the normal subject does in sentence 1. Gary (1974) suggests that a sentence like 2 would be more apt to be chosen when the speaker or writer has made the listener or reader expect that someone else other than the missing child would be standing in the corner.

 c. Sentence 1 is a normal affirmative imperative; sentence 2 is an imperative with emphatic DO. The DO receives strong stress and gives affirmative emphasis to the invitation.

 d. Sentence 2 contains emphatic *own* before the object NP; sentence 1 is unmarked in this respect. One could imagine sentence 2 being uttered in a context in which the speaker was annoyed that Jim was always borrowing the speaker's (or someone else's) book.

CHAPTER 30: An Overview of English Complementation
    Pages 417–432

1. complement—We were sorry *that she decided to leave him.*
   complementizer—Pam*'s* coming home for the holidays was a surprise.
   object attraction—For *him* to admit his guilt took a lot of courage.
   infinitivalization—For Donald *to come early* would be quite a feat.
   noun complement—The company's fear *that Karen would leave* resulted in her being given
       a raise.
   possessive attraction—We all thought *Donna's* winning the prize was a thrill.
   extraposition—(It) was assumed *that they would agree to the proposal.*
   equi-NP deletion—She plans (*for her* ⟶ *∅*) to live in Pittsburgh for a few years.
   complementizer deletion—It's true (*that*) we were foolish in our youth.

2. a. John's lecturing on that topic was a surprise.

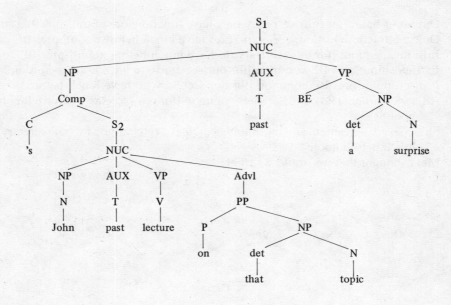

Output of base: ['s (John past lecture on that topic)] past BE a surprise
Possessive attraction: [John's (past lecture on that topic)] past BE a surprise
Gerundivization: [John's (lecturing on that topic)] past BE a surprise
Affix attachment (1×): [John's (lecturing on that topic)] BE + past a surprise
Subject-verb agreement and morphological rules: John's lecturing on that topic was a
    surprise.

b. It is common for our secretary to have lunch before noon.

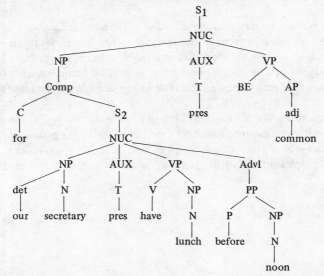

Output of base: [for (our secretary pres have lunch before noon)] pres BE common

Object attraction: [for our secretary (pres have lunch before noon)] pres BE common

Infinitivalization: [for our secretary (to have lunch before noon)] pres BE common

Extraposition: pres BE common [for our secretary (to have lunch before noon)]

It insertion: it pres BE common [for our secretary (to have lunch before noon)]

Affix attachment (1✕): it BE + pres common [for our secretary (to have lunch before noon)]

Subject-verb agreement and morphological rules: It is common for our secretary to have lunch before noon.

c. Mary thought that we would wait here.

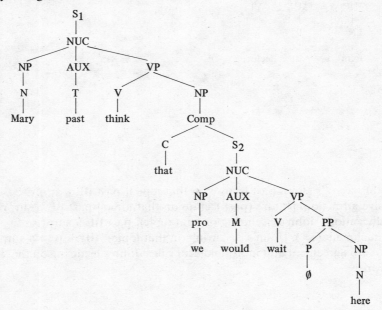

Output of base: Mary past think [that (we would wait here)]
Affix attachment (1×): Mary think + past [that (we would wait here)]
Morphological rules: Mary thought that we would wait here.

d. We were eager to see the movie.

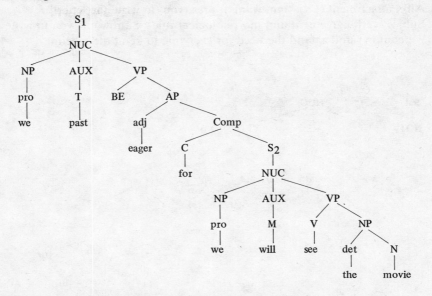

Output of base: we past BE eager [for (we will see the movie)]
Equi-NP deletion: we past BE eager [for (will see the movie)]
Infinitivalization: we past BE eager [for (to see the movie)]
Complementizer deletion: we past BE eager (to see the movie)
Affix attachment (1×): we BE + past eager (to see the movie)
Subject-verb agreement and morphological rules: We were eager to see the movie.

e. Sam wants you to write the letter.

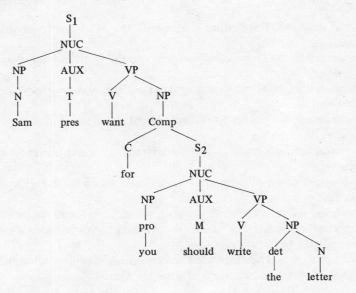

Output of base: Sam pres want [for (you should write the letter)]
Object attraction: Sam pres want [for you (should write the letter)]
Infinitivalization: Sam pres want [for you (to write the letter)]
Complementizer deletion: Sam pres want [you (to write the letter)]
Affix attachment (1×): Sam want + pres [you (to write the letter)]
Subject-verb agreement and morphological rules: Sam wants you to write the letter.

f. We couldn't understand the need for everyone to be at the meeting.

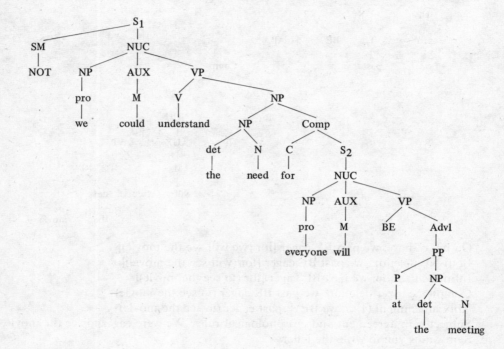

Output of base: NOT we could understand the need [for (everyone will BE at the meeting)]

Object attraction: NOT we could understand the need [for everyone (will BE at the meeting)]

Infinitivalization: NOT we could understand the need [for everyone (to BE at the meeting)]

NOT placement: we could NOT understand the need [for everyone (to BE at the meeting)]

NOT contraction: we could + N'T understand the need [for everyone (to BE at the meeting)]

Morphological rules: We couldn't understand the need for everyone to be at the meeting.

3. a. relative clause—*That* is a relative pronoun substituting for *the idea* which is the object of the embedded sentence. The *idea* is not restated but rather identified as the one that John proposed.

   b. noun complement—The embedded sentence makes explicit what the head noun, *the idea,* is referring to; i.e., we are told what *the idea* is.

c. relative clause—The embedded sentence does not expand the head noun but rather restricts it. The speaker/writer is referring to one particular possibility: the one we had raised.

d. noun complement—The complementizer *that* is not part of the embedded sentence. It just serves to set the embedded sentence off from the rest of the sentence. The embedded sentence tells us *what* the possibility is (i.e., that it would rain), not *which* possibility is being referred to.

4. a. English sentences require subjects. *It* should be used as the subject of this sentence since extraposition has moved the complement from subject to object position.

b. An infinitive complement in object position following the verb *want* does not take the complementizer *for* in Standard American English. Several dialects, however, do permit *for* in such a sentence in informal speech.

c. The verb *want* never takes a *that*-clause complement in English. This may have to do with the fact that the subject of *want* is expressing an *unfulfilled* desire—something that would be much more naturally conveyed by an infinitive (see Chapter 31).

5. Deletion patterns differ: the *that* complementizer appears to be optionally deletable except when the *that* complement occurs initially in subject position or when it is serving to make a noun complement. *That* as a relative pronoun can be deleted when it replaces the object of the embedded sentence or the object of a preposition in the embedded sentence.

6. In the first sentence the speaker is reporting a fact: the one referred to as "he" missed class on Monday. In the second sentence the speaker is speculating about a future event, i.e., that he is apt not to attend class on Monday.

CHAPTER 31: Infinitives and Gerunds
Pages 433–446

1. the Bolinger principle
   I prefer to go on Wednesday. (The infinitive refers to a future, unfulfilled event.)
   I forgot having that nightmare. (The gerund indicates that the nightmare occurred.)
   implicative verb
   positive—Stu *hastened* to agree with the plan. (implies that he agreed)
   negative—Shirley *declined* to defend her position. (implies that she did not defend herself)
   infinitive of purpose—Marsha has moved to the city (*in order*) *to be closer to where she works.*
   factive verb—I *recall* that he sent you that letter.
   perfect infinitive—Paula hoped *to have been chosen* as director.
   gerund with indefinite, nonspecific subject—*Waiting for something to happen* is nerve-racking.
   infinitive with equi-NP—Larry is afraid *to volunteer.*

2. a. *Want* does not take a *that*-clause complement. The only complement it takes is an infinitive:

   I want to go there.

   b. The gerund *taking* is required in place of the infinitive *to take* if the meaning is that the speaker no longer takes piano lessons. We understand the infinitive here to be an infinitive of purpose (i.e., I stopped taking voice lessons in order to take piano lessons).

c. *Expects* is a verb which takes infinitives. This can be explained by the Bolinger principle.

3. a. *Enjoy* requires a gerund. The Bolinger principle will help your students understand why it does.

   b. A gerund (*going*) or perfect gerund (*having gone*) is necessary here, since the speaker already attended the party.

   c. An infinitive of purpose is needed here.

   > I will go to Tehran (in order) to visit my parents.

4. Regular infinitives follow a certain set of verbs and complete a clause. Infinitives of purpose provide additional information to an already-completed clause. They are not restricted from occurring in sentences with only certain verbs.

5. Use the Bolinger principle to distinguish between *try* with an infinitive complement and *try* with a gerund complement. A context may be that you are sick and you try to do various things to get better:

   > I tried to call the doctor, but the line was busy.
   > I tried calling the doctor, but he was of no help.
   > I tried to take some aspirin, but I couldn't get the cap off the bottle.
   > I tried taking some aspirin, but they didn't do any good.
   >   Etc.

   We'll leave it to you to work these suggestions into a teaching strategy.

6. It is not a good teaching strategy. First of all, not all verbs take complements. Second, certain verbs take both infinitives and gerunds. A certain amount of memorization may be necessary since we don't have a principle which will work in all cases to predict which verbs will take gerunds, which will take infinitives, and which will take both. The Bolinger principle will help eliminate some of the need for memorization, however.

CHAPTER 32: Participles
Pages 447–458

1. perfective *-Ing* participle—*Having nodded off and on* for half an hour, Harold finally fell into a deep sleep.

   progressive *-En* participle—*Being thwarted* at every turn, Meredith finally gave up.

   -Ing participle used as an attributive adjective—The *irritating* thing about it was that I never did find out what really happened.

   -En participle in a sentence-initial adverbial clause—*Excited* at opening our presents, we flung the wrappings far and wide.

   dangling participle—*Driving much too fast,* the policeman stopped the speeding motorist.

   ambiguous participle—We were *moved*.

   > adjective: We felt some emotion.
   >   verb: The moving company moved our possessions from one location to another.

2. a. This sentence contains a participle: *amazing*. We know that it is a participle because it is functioning as an adjective.

   b. *Dropping* is a gerund. It is a structurally necessary object of the preposition *from*.

   c. *Denouncing* is a gerund. It is functioning as the subject of a poss... ING gerund complement: *his denouncing*.

d. *Looking* is a participle. The clause in which it appears has an adverbial function.

3. a. grammatical—*Henry* is the subject of both the participle and the main clause.

   b. ungrammatical—*I* is the subject of the participle; *the problem* is the subject of the main clause.

   c. ungrammatical—*We* is the subject of the participle; *the banquet* is the subject of the main clause.

   d. grammatical—*Jane* is the subject of both the participle and the main clause.

4. a. The experiencer of a feeling or emotion should be modified by an adjective formed with the -*En* participle:

> I am *bothered* by his bigoted remarks.

   b. The participle is dangling. The subject of the participle (*the mailman*) and the subject of the main clause (*the package*) are different. This sentence could be corrected if both subjects were the same:

> Approaching our house, the mailman left a package on the doorstep.

5. In sentence *a*, both clauses have the same subject; in sentence *b*, the subjects are *we* and *they* and are therefore not identical. Only when the two clauses share a subject can one of them be changed into a participial construction.

6. a. The clause in this sentence is not ambiguous. *Roberta* is the only possible antecedent of the underlying subject in the participial clause.

   b. The clause in this sentence is potentially ambiguous, since either *the dog* or *the cat* could be the antecedent of the underlying subject in the participial clause. Since *the dog* is the subject of the main clause, however, we are much more likely to assume that *the dog* is also the subject of the participial clause.

CHAPTER 33: Indirect Speech
Pages 459–472

1. indirect statement—Joe: I am going to leave on Friday.⟶ *Joe said that he was going to leave on Friday.*

   indirect exclamation—Marge: What a wonderful party! ⟶ *Marge exclaimed what a wonderful party it was.*

   indirect imperative—Passenger to taxicab driver: Follow that car! ⟶ *The passenger told the taxicab driver to follow that car.*

   tense harmony applied to a main verb—Grace: I love anchovies on my pizza.⟶ Grace said that she *loved* anchovies on her pizza.

   yes-no question complementizer—I asked *if* she had been to Europe before.

   change in an adverbial of time—Grant: I won the lottery yesterday!⟶ (Two days later) Grant called to say that he had won the lottery *three days ago.*

   change in a demonstrative

     Mike to Annie: Where did you get all these coupons?

     Mike to Pat later: I asked Annie where she got all *those* coupons.

   suppression of subject/auxiliary inversion

     Jan: Is the term over yet?

     Jan asked if the term $\left\{ \begin{array}{l} \text{is} \\ \text{was} \end{array} \right\}$ over yet.

2. a. *Whether* must be the yes-no question complementizer following a participle -*ing* form functioning as a preposition.

> We questioned them concerning whether they had seen Paul.

   b. A negative imperative is reported as NOT + the infinitive.

> The judge told the parolee not to get in any more trouble.

   c. If the indirect statement appears first in a sentence, the *that* complementizer has to be deleted:

> It reached −25°F. in Milwaukee, the radio announcer said.

   d. *If* cannot be followed directly by *or not* as can *whether.*

> I wonder whether or not I should go there.

   If can be followed by *or not* if there is an intervening short clause:

> I wonder if I should go there or not.

3. a. Reported questions are a subcategory of embedded questions. Reported questions follow a more limited set of verbs than do other embedded questions. For example, the following embedded question need not have been produced as a report of what Jackie said to someone else:

> Jackie doubted if she would be able to do the job.

   b. Both sentences are indirect statements. Sentence 1, however, contains a present tense reporting verb. As such, there is no change of tense in the indirect speech clause. In sentence 2 the reporting verb is in the past tense. As a result, there was a change in the modal auxiliary from the historically present tense form *can* to the historically past tense form *could.* Sentence 2 can be interpreted as being more tentative than sentence 1; i.e., Bob's willingness to lend his car seems stronger in report 2.

   c. Both speakers are telling listeners what Joyce said. Sentence 1 contains a direct quote; sentence 2 uses indirect speech. Presumably there is a difference in discourse function and style between the two which would make native speakers prefer one over the other for a particular context. One could continue sentence 1 with "so they should still be there." Sentence 2, however, introduces the counterfactual aspect of the past perfect and thus conveys more strongly the possibility that the tickets are no longer in Joyce's purse. See question 5 as well for some suggestions about situations that would favor the use of direct quotations over indirect speech.

4. a. Indirect wh-questions do not undergo subject/auxiliary inversion. This sentence should be:

> I asked Abdul what the homework assignment is.

   b. When the place in which the original speech was made has changed, the place adverbial *here* shifts to *there:*

> I said I was happy to be there.

   c. Since the reporting verb is in the past tense and there is a past tense time adverbial in the reported statement (*last year*), we would expect the rules of tense harmony to apply:

> My aunt told me that she had to go to Minneapolis last year.

d. We would expect the time adverbial *today* to change since Mr. Greenfield's statement was reported several days earlier and the reference for *today* is not the same now as it was then:

> Mr. Greenfield insisted that he had to see Jamieson several days ago.

e. If the speaker wishes to preserve the same word order as in the direct speech, the full clause would have to be reported following the reporting verb:

> Marjorie exclaimed what a fine new car it was.

f. Presuming that this is a report of the question, "Am I going?" there are three problems with this sentence. First of all, subject/auxiliary inversion needs to be suppressed in the indirect question. Second, a complementizer needs to be added preceding the question. Third, unless the indirect question was an immediate repetition of what he had just said, the rule of tense harmony should be applied:

> He asked if I was going.

g. *Where is the bus stop?* is an indirect wh-question. Indirect wh-questions suppress subject/auxiliary inversion. This question should be:

> Can you tell me where the bus stop is?

5. To be done on your own.
6. a. free relative—*Discount* is not the type of verb that reports an indirect question. *What did he say?* is not a direct quote paraphrase of what the police said.
   b. free relative—Free relatives can occur sentence-initially; reported questions cannot.
   c. embedded question—The question is paraphrasable as a direct quote:

> You and I asked him: What did you see?

Ask is a typical reporting verb which embeds indirect questions.
7. To be done on your own.
8. *If* would seem to be the preferred complementizer for this sentence since what is being asked is probably a true yes-no question, not a question which implies the existence of alternatives. The use of *whether* would thus imply some emotion as sarcasm on Peter's part (i.e., I should know the time because Peter and I had an important date in ten minutes!).

CHAPTER 34: Other Aspects of Complementation
   ### Pages 473–490

1. object plus infinitive—The priest urged *them to marry in the church.*
   subject raising—*Roy* seems to be learning Spanish.
   object raising—*Dennis* is fun to work with.
   complex passive—It had been thought that Kennedy had presidential ambition.
   causative verb—The teacher *ordered* the unruly student to stay after class.
   sensory verb complement—I watched Denise $\left\{ \begin{array}{l} slide \\ sliding \end{array} \right\}$ *down the banister.*
   verb taking a subjunctive clause—I *requested* that he wait.
   noun taking a subjunctive clause—The *stipulation* that he resign was challenged.
   adjective taking a subjunctive clause—It is *forbidden* that anyone enter.

2. a. We want him to stay here.

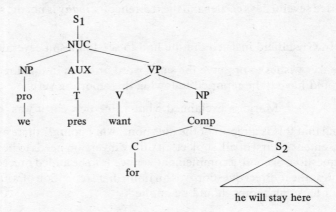

> Output of base: we pres want [for (he will stay here)]
> Object attraction: we pres want [for him (will stay here)]
> Infinitivalization: we pres want [for him (to stay here)]
> Complementizer deletion: we pres want [him (to stay here)]
> Affix attachment (1✕): we want + pres [him (to stay here)]
> Morphological rules: We want him to stay here.

b. Marge is thought to have passed the test.

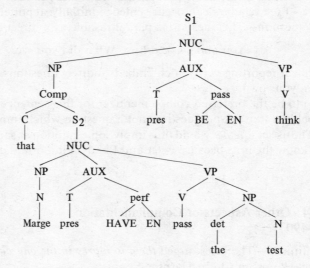

> Output of base: [that (Marge pres HAVE EN pass the test)] pres BE EN think
> Subject raising: [that (pres HAVE EN pass the test)] Marge pres BE EN think
> Infinitivalization: [that (to HAVE EN pass the test)] Marge pres BE EN think
> Complementizer deletion: (to HAVE EN pass the test) Marge pres BE EN think
> Extraposition: Marge pres BE EN think (to HAVE EN pass the test)
> Affix attachment (3✕): Marge BE + pres think + EN (to HAVE pass + EN the test)
> Subject-verb agreement and morphological rules: Marge is thought to have passed the
>   test.

c. It is essential that you be on time.

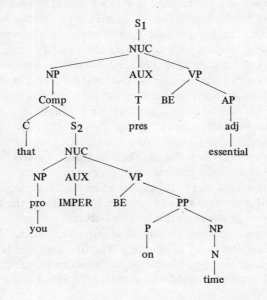

Output of base: [that (you IMPER BE on time)] pres BE essential
Extraposition: pres BE essential [that (you IMPER BE on time)]
It insertion: it pres BE essential [that (you IMPER BE on time)]
Affix attachment (2✕): it BE + pres essential [that (you BE + IMPER on time)]
Subject-verb agreement and morphological rules: It is essential that you be on time.

d. The teacher told Tom to rewrite his composition.

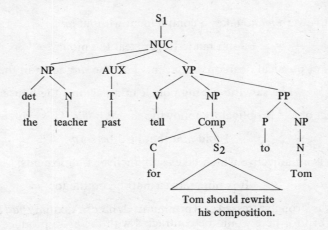

Tom should rewrite
his composition.

Output of base: the teacher past tell [for (Tom should rewrite his composition)] to Tom
Indirect object movement: the teacher past tell Tom [for (Tom should rewrite his composition)]
Equi-noun phrase deletion: the teacher past tell Tom [for (should rewrite his composition)]

> Infinitivalization: the teacher past tell Tom [for (to rewrite his composition)]
> Complementizer deletion: the teacher past tell Tom (to rewrite his composition)
> Affix attachment (1×): the teacher tell + past Tom (to rewrite his composition)
> Morphological rules: The teacher told Tom to rewrite his composition.

3. a. They are similar semantically, although there are some differences. For example, the first sentence seems to imply that the speaker delivered the advice to *him* directly; in the second, this is not necessarily the case. The second difference is in their structure. The first sentence contains an infinitive complement in object position; the second sentence contains a *that*-clause object complement with a subjunctive.

   b. The sentences mean basically the same thing. They would, however, presumably occur in different discourse contexts—the first perhaps in a context where deep-breathing exercises have not yet been introduced. Their mention, then, is new information, and thus the exercises occur in the new information position at the end of the sentence. In contrast, the second sentence implies the exercises are already the topic of the conversation and thus occur in subject position. Syntactically, the sentences are related, with the second coming about as the result of object raising.

   c. They are both complex passives which would most likely occur in different discourse contexts, despite their similarity in meaning. The first sentence is more impersonal or neutral. The second sentence was derived from the same basic structure as the first but subject raising was applied. This second sentence implies that the hometown team is a topic of interest.

   d. The sentences have a similar meaning. The difference is whether the speaker recalls the mental image of them "in the act of" making that point (the object + -*Ing* participle of the second sentence) or recalls the fact that they made that point (the possessive + gerund of the first sentence).

4. a. The problem with this sentence is the presence of the modal *will*. This sentence would be grammatical without the *will*, since *insist* takes a subjunctive form of the verb in the object complement. Another possibility is to substitute the subjunctive modal *should* for *will*.

   b. The causative verb *make* takes a complement without *to:*

      John made Roger steal the money.

   c. With verbs of physical position, nonagents take the -*ing* form in their complements:

      She saw the fishing pole leaning against the house.

   d. The indirect object is obligatory following the verb *tell*. This sentence should be:

      I told *him* that he'd be sorry.

   e. *Imperative* is an adjective which takes subjunctive complements:

      It is imperative (that) he do the job.

5. Causative *had* is strongly stressed and pronounced /hæd/. Auxiliary *had* is unstressed and pronounced /həd/ or here would be contracted with the *he* to produce *he'd*.

6. God *bless* you.   *Be* that as it may . . .   *Come* what may . . .   So *be* it.

7. The English subjunctive is used
   a. in the *if*-clause of imaginative conditionals and in complements following the verb *wish*.
   b. in *that*-clause complements of a certain limited number of verbs, adjectives, and nouns.
   c. in certain formulaic expressions.

CHAPTER 35: Degree—Comparatives and Equatives
  Pages 491–507

1. the comparative construction—Sam has *more clothes than* Evelyn.
   the equative construction—He has *as many clothes as* Ben.
   irregular comparative adverb—Margaret sings *better* than her brother.
   absolute use of adjectives—That's a *beautiful* painting.
   relative use of adverbs—The "bullet" train travels *faster* than any other train in Japan.
   free comparative—The pumpkins are growing *bigger (and bigger)* every day.
   unmarked adjective—How *old* is your daughter?

2. a. The ambiguity comes from the fact that there is a reduced clause following the complementizer *than*. The full clause could be either:

   Phyllis likes Carol more than Sue likes   or   Phyllis likes Carol more than Phyllis
     Carol.   likes Sue.

   b. The ambiguity derives from the two possible meanings of the phrase *as well as*. It could be expressing the degree of similarity in their teaching ability; i.e., they both teach Sam equally well. *As well as* could also mean *in addition*, which in turn has two possible readings:

   Mark teaches Sam. In addition, Ralph teaches Sam.
   Mark teaches Sam. In addition, Mark teaches Ralph.

3. a. adverb—*far*   d. verb—*costs*
   b. determiner—*two*   e. adjective—*interesting*
   c. noun—*oranges*

4. a. *Less* is a marked form which often sounds rather awkward. The usual way to avoid it is to use the negative polarity form with the comparative when such a form is available, i.e., the adverb *worse* in this case:

   Joan sings worse than Sally.

   Another possibility is to make *Sally* the subject of the sentence and to use a positive polarity adverb:

   Sally sings better than Joan.

   b. Here one can avoid the awkwardness by using the negative polarity adjective, *short:*

   Mary is shorter than Alice.

   Using a negative equative is another possibility that is more tactful:

   Mary is not as tall as Alice.

   Alternatively, if *Mary* is not necessarily the topic of the conversation, one could make *Alice* the subject of the sentence and use a positive polarity adjective:

   Alice is taller than Mary.

5. a. Since *short* is a one-syllable adjective, the *-er* suffix should be used when making comparisons:

   To make the story shorter, I'll just tell you the ending.

   b. *Better* is the irregular comparative form of the adjective *good.* There is no need for *more,* since it unnecessarily and incorrectly marks the comparative a second time.

c. This comparative construction is incomplete. It contains neither *-er* nor *more*. Two-syllable adjectives ending in *-y*, like *lucky*, take the *-er* suffix in the comparative:

> I was luckier than my little brother.

d. The equative construction is *"as x as,"* not *"as x *that."* This sentence should be:

> John is as tall as Joe.

e. The structure of the reduced clause must be parallel to that of the main clause. Adding the demonstrative *those* and the preposition *in* to the reduced clause will bring about the necessary parallelism and thus achieve grammaticality:

> The newspapers in Los Angeles have better international coverage than *those in* San Diego.

6. To be done on your own.
7. From this first sentence, where the comparative construction has been derived from a restrictive relative clause, we understand that Herbert's intelligence is being compared with that of certain monkeys. However, *a* does not imply that Herbert himself is a monkey.

    One interpretation of the second sentence is that the speaker has seen other monkeys that are more intelligent than the monkey known as Herbert. The other interpretation of *b* is that both the speaker and Herbert have seen monkeys but that the speaker has seen more intelligent monkeys than Herbert has seen. In fact, even the phrase "more intelligent monkeys" is ambiguous in *b*. It could refer to the number of intelligent monkeys or the degree of intelligence of the monkeys being referred to.
8. The decision to use *more* vs. *-er* is very complicated. The rules outlined by Frank (1972) would lead one to expect that *loyal* should be made comparative with a preceding *more*. However, it is possible that in the interests of parallelism with *smart,* the author chose to use the affix *-er* with *loyal*. Since there are many two-syllable adjectives which can take either *-er* or *more* there is considerable variation—and some aesthetic license—involved in such decisions.

CHAPTER 36: Degree—Complements and Superlatives
Pages 508–523

1. a comparative used in a superlative sense—This is *a longer* Indian summer than any other on record.

    the negative import of *too (much/little)*—It was such an old bridge that it couldn't support vehicles. ⟶The bridge was too old to support vehicles.

    intensifying, nonsuperlative use of *most*—The fireworks made for a *most* dazzling spectacle.

    a marked superlative—This is the *shallowest* part of the river.

    absolute use of *too*—I can't say that I care *too* much for their attitude.

comparative and superlative uses of *lesser:*

comparative—A *lesser* mind could not have accomplished what Einstein did.

superlative—The *lesser* traveled road is the one of which Robert Frost writes.

2. a. If we wish to say that she is the cause of the boredom, we would say:

She's the most boring person I know.

Boring is a two-syllable adjective that takes *most* to form the superlative construction.

If, on the other hand, we wish to say that she is the experiencer of the boredom, we would say:

She is the most bored person I know.

Most adjectives ending in derivational suffixes use *most* in the superlative construction.

b. The speaker has added the superlative suffix -*est* to an adverb/adjective that is already in its comparative form with an -*er* ending. The -*est* should be added to the *base* form. Here this would give us:

John $\begin{cases} \text{lives the farthest away} \\ \text{is the eldest} \end{cases}$ of all.

Then, too, *furthest* and *oldest* would probably be used more frequently these days.

3. a. *More* should be used here. Even though there are three people involved, Alex is being compared with the other two together; i.e., *he* has financial problems but *they* don't, since they both have more money.

b. *The best* would probably be used here. Sheila is at the "end of the scale" of candidates for the speaker. Notice, however, the comparative form would be appropriate if Sheila was being compared with the other candidates as a group:

Of the five candidates for president, I voted for Sheila because I definitely think she's better than $\begin{cases} \text{the others} \\ \text{the rest} \end{cases}$

c. Either form could be used here. The difference would be whether the speaker found his or her choice superior to the other books along an interest scale (in which case the superlative form would be appropriate) or the speaker was comparing his or her choice with all the other books as a group for the quality of "interesting." If the latter was the case, the comparative form would be correct.

4. a. The error is in the use of the comparative form *older* where the superlative form *oldest* is more appropriate. The use of the superlative form *oldest* follows the definite article and indicates that Joe is at the extreme of the scale for age of children in his family.

b. The superlative is formed by adding -*est* to an adjective or adverb or preceding either with *most.* Here the student has used both forms and has produced an incorrect double marking. Since *cold* is a single-syllable adjective, the correct way to form the superlative construction would be to use the -*est* suffix.

c. The syntactic context (a preceding *the*) and the semantic context (an indication that something is first on a scale of importance) necessitate the use of a superlative form:

The first and *most* important thing . . .

d. The student has used the incorrect form of this irregular adjective. The comparative form *worse* is to be used here.

5. If you agree with us that comparatives and superlatives are quite different semantically, you may choose to teach the comparative form at one time and then come back to the superlative form at a later time. This problem is greatest if your students speak languages without distinctive comparative and superlative forms.

6. As we have tried to indicate, this is an oversimplification of the difference between comparatives and superlatives. Whether a speaker chooses to use a comparative or superlative to a large extent depends upon the speaker's perspective, not upon the number of things/people being compared.

7. Perhaps that the rules of superlative formation are complicated, variable, and not universally adhered to and therefore can be violated when an author is striving to achieve a certain effect.

Index of Names

Index of Languages and Language Groups

Index of Words and Phrases[*]

a, an (*see* Topic Index)
ability 509
about 257, 260
above 257, 260
absent 392
absolute(ly) 411
acceleration 182
accordingly 327
ache 71 n., 181 n.
achievement 182
actually 325
in addition (to THIS) 324, 329 n., 330, 331, 412
additionally 324, 330
admit 434
admittedly 326
adrift 391, 394
advise 474, 482
be afraid of 253
after 251, 256, 454 n.
after THIS 328
afternoon 259
afterwards 328
against 253, 257
two days/weeks ago 464
agony 509
agree 165, 166
ain't 113
air(s) 174
albeit 326
alike 517
all 39, 40, 179, 192, 193, 194, 204, 251, 396
(all) in all 328
all the time 215 n.
almost 203 n., 216
alone 410
along 260
along with 42
already 73
also 324, 330, 331

alternatively 325
although 302, 326, 333, 334, 351
altogether 328
always 17, 63, 72, 203, 204, 205, 206, 208, 209, 211, 214, 215, 216, 217, 404, 409
am 22, 42, 113, 313
American 396, 397
amuse, amusing 391, 437, 451
an (*see* A, an *in the* Topic Index)
and 42, 289, 295, 296, 298 ff., 308 ff., 313 ff., 324, 347, 360, 398, 513
anger 226
angry 391
annoy 55, 56, 437, 451, 452, 453
annoyingly 452
anoint 256
another 130, 184
to put it another way 326
anticipate 421, 425, 426
anxious 419, 424, 425, 426
any 100, 101, 102, 115, 129, 178, 379
anybody 102, 128, 129, 142
anyhow 328
anymore 73
anyone 102, 128, 502
anything 102, 128
anyway 328
anywhere 102
any other 498, 512, 514
appear 35, 288, 476
appreciate 427, 437, 438, 474, 475, 476
approach (ing) 288, 448
are 22, 42, 113, 165, 313
arise 265, 288
(the) aristocracy 192
around 257, 260
arrange 474
arrogant 494, 513
as 325, 327, 500 ff.

---

[*]Note: The phrases in this index are not listed in strict alphabetical order. Instead, the key word in each phrase is used as the basis for alphabetizing. Thus "two days ago" is listed under "ago"; "to put it another way" is alphabetized under "another"; and "as a matter of fact" goes with "fact," etc. However, in those cases where there is no one single key word (e.g., "by the way") or where there are competing key words (e.g., "each and every"), the expression is alphabetized according to the first word.

Index of Topics

ISBN 0-8384-2850-9

90000>

9 780838 428504

THE GRAMMAR BOOK